AN ECONOMIC AND DEMOGRAPHIC HISTORY OF SÃO PAULO, 1850–1950

SOCIAL SCIENCE HISTORY

Edited by

Stephen Haber and David W. Brady

AN ECONOMIC AND DEMOGRAPHIC HISTORY OF SÃO PAULO, 1850–1950

FRANCISCO VIDAL LUNA

AND HERBERT S. KLEIN

STANFORD UNIVERSITY PRESS

Stanford, California

Stanford University Press
Stanford, California

Printed in the United States of America on acid-free, archival-quality paper

Library of Congress Cataloging-in-Publication Data

Names: Luna, Francisco Vidal, author. | Klein, Herbert S., author.
Title: An economic and demographic history of São Paulo, 1850–1950 / Francisco Vidal Luna and Herbert S. Klein.
Other titles: Social science history.
Description: Stanford, California : Stanford University Press, 2018. | Series: Social science history | Includes bibliographical references and index.
Identifiers: LCCN 2017009856 | ISBN 9781503602007 (cloth : alk. paper) | ISBN 9781503604124 (epub : alk. paper)
Subjects: LCSH: São Paulo (Brazil : State)—Economic conditions—19th century. | São Paulo (Brazil : State)—Economic conditions—20th century.
Classification: LCC HC188.S3 L855 2018 | DDC 330.981/61—dc23 LC record available at https://lccn.loc.gov/2017009856

Typeset by Newgen in 10.5/13 Bembo

To
Nicolás Sánchez-Albornoz
and
Iraci del Nero da Costa

CONTENTS

TABLES AND ILLUSTRATIONS

Tables

Figures

Maps

PREFACE

This volume is the continuation of our earlier study of colonial and imperial São Paulo and brings our analysis of the state up to the middle of the twentieth century. Together, the two volumes provide the first full-scale survey of the economy and society of the state of São Paulo in this two-century period.[1] Although studies of the economy and society of Brazil have included particular themes on the evolution of the state of São Paulo and there have been specific studies—from the history of particular crops to the study of immigration, industrialization, and urbanization—there are few extensive studies of the economy and society of São Paulo over this long period. Moreover, even the studies that do exist often deal with only one region or one city and rarely with the whole state.[2]

Today São Paulo is by far the most populated state of Brazil, being double the size of the second-largest state. It is also the richest and most industrialized one and is still Brazil's primary agricultural producer as well as its primary industrial exporter. It is the world leader in the production of sugarcane and orange juice and houses one of the world's major airplane manufacturers. It generated a gross domestic product (GDP) of 450 billion dollars in 2010, which would have ranked it, if it were a country, as the thirty-sixth-largest economy in the world, almost double the size of Portugal or Finland and close to the size of the entire economy of Colombia or Venezuela.[3] Among Brazil's states, its GDP is three times the size of the state of Rio de Janeiro, its nearest competitor.[4] If it were a country, its population of 41.2 million persons in the census of 2010 would make it the thirty-first-largest nation in the world, just behind Colombia and ahead of Argentina, and the third-largest in Latin America.[5] The metropolitan region of the capital city of the state held an estimated 20.8 million inhabitants in 2014, making it the fourth-largest metropolitan area in the world, behind Tokyo (37.8 million), Delhi, and Shanghai and equal to Mexico City and Mumbai.[6] It is also home to the largest overseas immigrant communities of Lebanese and Japanese in the world.

Although this extraordinary dynamism was not apparent in 1850, by 1950 it was clear that São Paulo was the dominant economic and population center of the country. By the middle of the twentieth century, the state had settled its frontier and was effectively farming its entire territory. It had the most complex network of railroads and paved roads of any state in the federal republic, and its capital had become the second-largest city in the nation and would soon overtake Rio de Janeiro. Its principal port of Santos had become the second-most-important port of the nation in international commerce. Seen from a long-term perspective, as we adopt in this volume, the evolution of São Paulo from 1850 to 1950 is a story of extraordinary change comparable with only a few other areas of recent settlement in the world.

Our decision to end this study in 1950 has to do with our perception of the changes that occurred in this state in the late twentieth century. In 1950 coffee still dominated the economy of the state, and the massive urbanization and industrialization were still in their early stages. The emergence of São Paulo as a world leader in sugar production, oranges, and other commercial agricultural exports was still a decade or two in the future. While urban growth of the capital city had been spectacular, the rest of the state's urban centers were still quite small. Similarly, a large and complex industrial structure had been created, but it was primarily made up of light industry directed at the national consumer market. The age of heavy industry (producing durable and capital goods) that would transform São Paulo into an industrial powerhouse was just beginning. The state's banking and financial institutions were still in their early stages and just beginning to challenge the leadership of Rio de Janeiro, but their growth would be extraordinary after 1950 and would result in São Paulo becoming the dominant banking and financial center of Brazil. Yet, as we show, the groundwork for these next major transitions had already been achieved by the 1950s.

The settlement of São Paulo's last frontier by the 1940s meant that virgin soils were no longer available to the state's farmers. This led to the declining efficiency of local coffee plantations compared to Paraná and other virgin land zones, but it also led to the first attempts at alternative commercial crops. It was Paulista farmers who led the nation in mechanization and the use of insecticides and fertilizers. The state now also became a world player in the export of sugar and oranges and was even a major producer of the new crop of soybeans. Thus, despite the opening up of frontier lands in the Brazilian regions of the Central-West and the North of Brazil in the past fifty years, São Paulo still maintains its leadership in agricultural production, far surpassing Mato Grosso, the premier state of the post-1960 frontier.

São Paulo by 1950 was also a national leader in health and education and even in basic road, rail, and port infrastructure. The Paulista population by mid-century was among the best-educated and healthiest of Brazil. By 1950 the majority of the state's population, both male and female, was literate, well ahead of all but one other state. Its levels of mortality and fertility were now well below the national average, and it had a labor force of over half a million well-educated industrial workers. In short, infrastructure was in place for the state to enter a new era of growth and diversification. The flow of internal migrants into São Paulo was initially modest compared to that of foreign-born immigrants but grew after the 1920s, and in the last three decades of the twentieth century a massive influx of over two million northeastern migrants arrived in São Paulo and significantly altered the social dynamics of the state in the post-1950 period.

None of this explosive growth was apparent a century earlier. In 1850 the province that would become the state of São Paulo had just half a million people, and its capital, São Paulo, had less than 25,000 residents. It had few roads and no railroads, and its principal port of Santos was a coastal trading port with little international trade.[7] The province occupied only a marginal position in Brazil, being lightly settled over a vast territory and of little importance in the international context. In fact, most of the state was under the control of numerous Indian tribes that had not been integrated into the Brazilian Empire. The province of São Paulo in 1850 contained just 6 percent of the total Brazilian population and had only a few urban settlements, most of which were half the size of the capital city.[8] This contrasted to other provinces, whose capital cities were quite significant. Rio de Janeiro possessed 166,000 inhabitants, Recife (in Pernambuco) and Mariana (in Minas Gerais) around 70,000, and Salvador (in Bahia) close to 60,000.

In the previous century (1750–1850) the province had experienced significant economic growth. It supplied food to the mines and slowly shifted from Indian labor to African slave workers. It even developed a modest sugar industry that was concentrated in the counties (municípios) of Campinas, Itu, and Piracicaba. But while important locally, even this sugar industry was a minor producer within the Brazilian Empire. In 1854 São Paulo produced less than 10 percent of the sugar exported from Brazil. Moreover, in 1850 the population occupied only about a quarter of the area that it did in the state of São Paulo in 1950. Its population was overwhelmingly rural, and virtually all its economic occupation was limited to a band extending from north to south not more than two hundred kilometers inland from the coast. In the absence of significant roads, most goods were moved on the backs of mules. It was a rural-dominated society, and its agriculture was quite rudimentary, mostly dedicated to food crops produced for local or regional markets. About a quarter of the population were slaves, the white population had a heavy admixture of Amerindian origin, and there were few European immigrants. In short, this frontier region showed few signs that it would become a significant region within the Brazilian Empire.

All this changed in the following century. The basic reason for this extraordinary change was the introduction of coffee production throughout the state, which turned São Paulo into the leading coffee-producing region in the nation and the world and Brazil's largest and most valued exporter. In the 1850s coffee farming entered the state in a significant fashion. Coffee farms first appeared along the coast and penetrated into the Paulista part of the Paraíba Valley from Rio de Janeiro, which was the leading coffee-producing province at that time. By 1854 São Paulo was producing 51,000 metric tons of coffee, the major part of which was exported through the port of Rio de Janeiro.[9]

The opening up of the coffee frontier in the state occurred just as the international slave trade was finally stopped in 1850. But the movement of slaves from other regions and the transfer of slaves from other activities allowed coffee farming to continue its expansion into the Paulista part of the Paraíba Valley and to slowly penetrate the western part of the state. The high productivity of the new coffee farms permitted the provincial coffee farmers to import Africans from other regions. The tightness of the local slave labor market would eventually stimulate the use of immigrant labor in the coffee plantations. But efforts to combine slave and free workers or to use immigrants in the same type of gang work regimes as slaves were unsuccessful. Only with the end of slavery in Brazil and the creation of a new work scheme based on family labor did mass European immigration to the country begin.

Given the dynamism of the coffee economy in the state, São Paulo led the nation in shifting from slave to immigrant labor after emancipation occurred in 1888. After 1870 it would also become the leader in establishing an extensive rail network, which was completed by the first decade of the twentieth century and opened up the entire state to settlement. With the labor and transport problems resolved and the high-quality virgin lands brought constantly into production as the center of coffee shifted ever westward, the state increased its leadership of coffee production by the early twentieth century. Overall, while Brazilian coffee production grew at an impressive 3.85 percent per annum after 1889 and total output reached

27.2 million bags (average for 1929–1933), the state's coffee production in the same period rose from 1.9 million bags, which represented 38 percent of the national total, to 17.0 million bags in the late 1920s—for an annual growth of 5.1 percent. This spectacular growth meant that São Paulo now accounted for 63 percent of national production.

Our aim in this second volume of the history of the state of São Paulo is to explain how São Paulo changed from being a frontier province of little importance to being one of the most important agricultural and industrial regions of the world. Although it is unusual to produce a two-century history of a particular region, rather than a city or a country, the size of the state of São Paulo and the importance of its historical evolution justify a comprehensive study equal to that of a nation-state. In our view, the case of São Paulo, a region that itself has dimensions comparable to mid-size nations, can be compared to other successful cases of the occupation, growth, and development of a major unsettled frontier. Thus, the period 1850–1950 was a pivotal one in terms of São Paulo's economic and social transformation and can be compared to other frontier settlement successes of the same period, such as regions of Canada, Argentina, or Australia, which are usually presented as examples of unusually rapid land occupation and were accompanied by economic and social transformation that enabled societies with high productivity to fully insert themselves in the global economy and create a high living standard for their populations.

The primary causes for this extraordinary growth are well known and have been much discussed by numerous authors: fertile lands close to the coast, a dynamic frontier population, a massive European immigration of nonslave labor, and an explosive coffee economy were the driving forces.[10] There is little debate among social scientists in Brazil about why São Paulo became a dominant world player in everything from agriculture to industry. But as yet there is no detailed analysis of the stages of this growth and how the various factors that explain this growth were integrated. This is what we do in this volume for the first time.

In undertaking this review of the history of São Paulo, we should note that while slavery was the fundamental labor institution from 1850 to 1888, we deal with it in only a cursory manner in this volume. We examine it in detail in our first volume and further elaborate on it in *Slavery in Brazil*, published in 2009. Here we summarize our findings. Though given a more extensive discussion, our analysis of European and Asian migration is also essentially a summary of the extensive work that Klein has published on the Spanish, Portuguese, and Italian migrants in several articles and in *A imigração espanhola no Brasil*. Also, our earlier volume explains why coffee entered

São Paulo and how it slowly evolved in the half of the Paraíba Valley that was within the confines of the province and how it replaced sugar as the dominant economic crop. Here we examine coffee's spread throughout the great plains of the high plateau region, promoted by a railroad revolution and the opening up of extraordinarily productive virgin soils in regions extremely well adapted for coffee production and limited to well-defined ecological zones. We also examine how this explosive growth led to a long-term crisis of overproduction for much of the twentieth century.

Finally, we only marginally discuss political developments in this period, since this has been covered by others,[11] as has been the labor movement and urban and rural working-class conditions.[12] But we do explore in great detail the extraordinary structural development that occurred as the province transformed into a semi-independent state. To understand the evolution of the state of São Paulo, one must understand its administrative and fiscal framework, which was fundamental in allowing the state to undertake key infrastructure projects, particularly railways, and to subsidize immigration, which profoundly altered the demographic landscape of São Paulo. Moreover, in our discussion of social change we are concerned primarily with large-scale transformations in terms of education, health, urbanization, and demographic change. Thus, our aim is not a definitive history of São Paulo in this period but rather an examination of the basic institutions that were created and how they changed over time. Other scholars may use our basic framework to refine and deepen knowledge about this very important region in the world.

For this and the previous volume we use historic definitions of regions for the São Paulo province and state that were developed by previous scholars and based on the influence of the railroads. Today's standard divisions used by the state and federal governments divide the state primarily by metropolitan area. In our first study of São Paulo, 1750–1850, we divided the province (the captaincy) into five regions: Paraíba Valley, Capital, West Paulista, Southern Road, and Coast, in agreement with the pioneering work of Maria Luiza Marcílio.[13] In this volume we adopt the ten regional divisions used by most commentators until the middle of the twentieth century and simplify some of the names: Capital, Vale do Paraíba (instead of Paraíba Valley and North Coast), Central, Mogiana, Baixa Paulista, Araraquarense (instead of Araraquarense, Douradense, and Paulista), Noroeste (instead of Noroeste and Alta Paulista), Alta Sorocabana, Baixa Sorocabana, and Santos (instead of Santos and Litoral Sul) (see Map P.1).[14] The regions of Central, Mogiana, and Paulista, located in the interior of the state of São Paulo, already were settled and productive by the middle of the

Map P.1 Ten Regional Divisions of the State of São Paulo

nineteenth century, together with the traditional regions of the Vale do Paraíba, Capital, and Coast. Other regions occupied after 1850 are Araraquarense, Northwest, and Alta Sorocabana. Finally, the districts known as municípios are the equivalent of North American counties, since they include large rural areas as well as small towns. Thus we use *county* and *município* interchangeably in this text.

We convert all traditional Brazilian units of measure into metric units for most of the factors of production. Until the full adoption of the metric system in Brazil in the 1860s and 1870s,[15] most quantitative information was given in traditional Brazilian or Portuguese weights and measures: *arrobas* for weight and *alqueires* for land measures.[16] Finally, we use standard Brazilian currency, the mil réis, where appropriate in the tables. The mil réis was established in 1833 and remained in circulation until 1942, when it was replaced by the cruzeiro. In the conversion, 1 mil réis became 1 cruzeiro, eliminating the mil réis's three zeros and creating a one-to-one ratio between the two currencies. The mil réis is written as 1$000, and the next-largest denomination is the conto, written as 1,000$ (or 1,000 mil réis). The smaller unit is the réis, which is written after the symbol $, but in this volume we round all réis to the nearest mil réis. Most of our tables are in this unit, while the data presented after 1942 are in cruzeiros. For most of the nineteenth century, an English pound was worth around 8 mil réis. At the end of the empire this fell to an average of 11 mil réis in the 1880s. The crisis of coffee overproduction of the early republic temporarily doubled the value of the pound to 23 mil réis, but it dropped to an average of 18 mil réis in 1900–1909 and to 16 mil réis in 1910–1920. In 1922 the mil réis lost half its value in relation to the English pound, but by the 1930s it was up to 57 mil réis to the pound. For the early decades of the twentieth century and later, we convert Brazilian currency to US dollars for international comparison. In the 1880s the exchange was 2 mil réis per US dollar, falling in the next two decades to around 4 mil réis from 1890 to the 1920s. It fell again to 8 mil réis to the dollar in the 1920s and fell further, to 15 mil réis to the dollar, in the 1930s. With the introduction of the cruzeiro in 1942, the rate was 20 cruzeiros (or 20 old mil réis) to the dollar.[17]

We organize the chapters both chronologically and structurally. Chapters 1 and 2 describe the evolution of the agricultural economy and the construction of the provincial government under the empire. Chapters 3 and 4 deal with the same themes under the republic. Chapter 5 treats the crisis of coffee overproduction and how the state responded and discusses the Vargas revolution and the government that the Paulista elite had created. In Chapter 6 we examine the progressive integration of the state and its principal port of Santos into the world economy. Chapter 7 examines the growth of an industrial complex within the state, and the state's evolving infrastructure and urbanization is discussed in Chapter 8. The changing population is described in Chapter 9.

In writing this book we received support from several persons, including Carlos Eduardo de Oliveira Silva, Bruno Teodoro Oliva, Matiko Kume Vidal, Nelson Nozoe, Laurindo Boyo Inoue, Marta Dora Grostein, Silvia Anette Kneip, and William Summerhill. Rodolfo Dirso discussed environmental issues with us, and Sonia Rocha enlightened us on the complex development of Brazil's social welfare system. Eric Wakin, associate director of the Hoover Institution and director of the Hoover Archives, has been a major supporter of this project from the beginning. We are grateful for his generous aid. We thank Carlos Bacellar for providing us with the digital shape files for our maps and David Medeiros of the Stanford University Geospatial Center for the creation of the county (*município*) maps based on these files. Several other maps using these files were made for us by Renato Augusto Rosa Vidal. We are in debt to the extraordinary work on the foreign born in São Paulo carried out by the research group Núcleo de

Estudos de População, Campinas, and to the census reconstructions of 1872 undertaken by the Centro Brasileiro de Análise e Planejamento (CEBRAP) group under the leadership of Felipe Alencastro. Our work would have been impossible without the digitization carried out by numerous organizations, beginning with the scanning of the complete library of the Fundação SEADE by the Brazilian government, as well as the extraordinary websites maintained by the Finance Ministry (Memória Estatística do Brasil, Projeto Nemesis), by the state legislative assembly for all nineteenth- and twentieth-century laws, by the Foundation IBGE, by the Instituto de Pesquisa Econômica Aplicada, and by the Center for Research Libraries for its collection of Brazilian government documents, including the provincial presidential reports from 1830 to 1930.

AN ECONOMIC AND DEMOGRAPHIC HISTORY OF SÃO PAULO, 1850–1950

Chapter 1

São Paulo Agriculture in the Nineteenth Century

There is little question that the single most important change in the province of São Paulo in the second half of the nineteenth century was the introduction of coffee into the mix of sugar and food products. By mid-century, sugar and cotton were important local crops, but neither of these crops could replace coffee. The expansion of coffee is the single most important factor in explaining the extraordinary growth of São Paulo in this period. Understanding the dynamics of the coffee industry, its culture, the functioning of its market, and the relative position of São Paulo in the international coffee market is essential to understanding the history of the province in the second half of the nineteenth century.

Coffee had been cultivated in Brazil since the mid-eighteenth century. It arrived in the province of Rio de Janeiro in the last quarter of that century, and in the first decade of the nineteenth century a modest amount was exported to Lisbon. From Rio de Janeiro, coffee farms slowly expanded north and west into the province of Minas Gerais and south and southwest into São Paulo. In the province of São Paulo, coffee entered the northern portion of Vale do Paraíba, which the province shared with the neighboring province of Rio de Janeiro. This Paulista zone had the same natural resources as the surrounding region, which was then the largest producer of coffee in Brazil. At the same time, coffee production spread along the coast of Rio de Janeiro and reached the coastal towns of São Sebastião and Ubatuba on the northern coast of São Paulo. From there, production crossed over the Serra do Mar coastal range, entering other parts of the Vale do Paraíba. From its dominant position in Vale do Paraíba in the 1820s and 1830s, coffee then spread to the rest of the province and reached the interior plains in the final years of the nineteenth century. In turn this new zone became the main coffee-growing region of Brazil in the twentieth century.

To study the evolution of this rural economy from early in the nineteenth century, we examined censuses taken in each *município*, or county, of São Paulo from the late eighteenth century with some consistency until well into the nineteenth century.[1] By 1829 there are enough of these censuses to form a rather complete picture of agricultural production in the province.[2] These county censuses report that the province in 1829 had 40,000 households, of which 24,000 were dedicated to agricultural activities. Of these agricultural households, 7,000 possessed slaves. The remaining rural households relied on family labor, since in this period there were few wage workers in agriculture. Some 1,725 of these rural households produced coffee, and 61 percent of these coffee fazendas owned slaves (with just under 10,000 slaves working the coffee fields). The average coffee fazenda had fewer than 10 slaves, and only 60 coffee farmers owned more than 30 (two farmers had more than 100). Coffee fazendas were concentrated in Vale do Paraíba, especially in the município of Areias and on the province's northern coast. In this same year there were 585 farms producing sugar in the province, and they owned 18,000 slaves, for an average of 31 slaves per sugar mill (*engenho*). Another 316 farms produced *aguardente* (cane alcohol) from sugarcane. Of these 316 farms, 84 percent owned slaves, for an average of a dozen slaves per estate. These sugar and alcohol producers were concentrated in the Central region of the province, especially in the municípios of Porto Feliz and Campinas.[3] Of the 24,000 farms listed in the province in that year, 8 of 10 also produced food crops.[4]

By 1836 there existed the fairly complete census compiled by Daniel Müller, which provides data on both population and farm production.[5] Although coffee production was expanding rapidly by this date, corn still represented half the value of provincial agricultural output. In fact, products grown for the domestic market (corn, rice, beans, and aguardente) represented close to two-thirds of the value of total agricultural production. Coffee accounted for only 20 percent and sugar for 14 percent of the total. There was even some production of tobacco and cotton in the province. Clearly, Vale do Paraíba and the Central region were the most important growing areas, accounting for 81 percent of the value of all crops produced in that year. In these two areas resided 72 percent of the free persons and 79 percent of the slaves. As in 1829, coffee production was still concentrated in Vale do Paraíba region (87 percent) and sugar in the Central region (91 percent).

Almost two decades later, an 1854 census prepared by José Antonio de Saraiva showed that coffee production had attained much greater importance in the province.[6] In that year the coffee crop was 3.4 million arrobas, the equivalent of 50,827 metric tons, or 847,000 sacks of coffee at 60 kilograms per sack. This was seven times greater than the crop harvested in 1836. Sugar also increased in the same period, by 50 percent, but coffee now represented six times the value of sugar production. In 1829 coffee estates had 10,000 slaves, and by 1854 they contained 50,000 slaves. Coffee also now had 2,000 *colonos*, or free immigrant workers, helping produce the crop. As Nabuco D'Araujo, the president of the province, noted in 1852, coffee was prospering and promised a great future. He declared that "changing the cultivation of sugar for coffee and tea is a natural trend for our farmers," not only because coffee was easier to produce and paid higher returns but also because it was easier to transport over the very poor roads of the province.[7] The poor quality of roads was a fundamental restriction on the São Paulo economy. Few wagons could navigate them, which meant that the primary form of transport of persons and goods was mule train. Aside from the usual difficulties these poor roads created for movement within the province, an additional difficulty was accessing the main port of Santos. The main Paulista agricultural region then in production was at an elevation of 700 meters, with a complex and difficult path leading down to the port of Santos, which was about 140 kilometers from the county of Campinas, a major agricultural production area in the nineteenth century. Thus, creating a comprehensive transport system in the second half of the nineteenth century was crucial for the provincial government.

Despite the major growth of coffee production in two decades, little changed in the regional concentration of coffee fazendas: Vale do Paraíba contained two-thirds of them, and the Central region was second in importance. Sugar was still concentrated in the Central and Mogiana regions, but unlike with coffee, there were no colonos on the sugar plantations, and the average number of slaves per producer was less than in 1829.[8] Because mules were the primary transport for moving all crops to port, coffee fazendas had 22,000 mules and sugar estates had another 13,000 (Table 1.1).

In 1854, Bananal, Taubaté, Pindamonhangaba, and Campinas were the most important coffee-producing areas (see Map 1.1) and accounted for half the production of the province.[9] Bananal, with an average fazenda output of 116 metric tons, was the largest producer, compared to an average of 19 metric tons in the province as a whole.[10]

TABLE 1.1

Coffee and Sugar in São Paulo in 1854: Workers, Quantity Produced, and Value of Production

		WORKERS				PRODUCTION		
Region	Farms	Agregados	Colonos	Slaves	Total	Quantity (t)	Value (mil réis)	Transport animals
Coffee								
Capital	2	17		60	77	48	3,560	24
Vale do Paraíba	1,830	2,951	90	36,949	39,990	38,473	6,852,062	15,353
Central	556	666	844	12,489	13,999	7,716	1,582,391	4,550
Mogiana	72	174	38	1,382	1,594	1,201	327,000	1,589
Baixa Paulista	134	353	1,173	3,234	4,760	3,282	611,290	842
Araraquarense								
Noroeste								
Alta Sorocabana								
Baixa Sorocabana	6	32		161	193			60
Santos	12	30	14	206	250	107	29,200	
Total	2,612	4,223	2,159	54,481	60,863	50,827	9,405,503	22,418
Sugar								
Capital								
Vale do Paraíba	29	40		276	316	51	28,380	62
Central	473	356	1	12,239	12,596	8,542	997,970	8,241
Mogiana	83	40	9	2,203	2,252	3,506	480,700	3,734
Baixa Paulista	55	130		689	819	624	126,700	700
Araraquarense								
Noroeste								
Alta Sorocabana								
Baixa Sorocabana	3	5		47	52			8
Santos	22	49		117	166	2	11,000	
Total	665	620	10	15,571	16,201	12,725	1,644,750	12,745

SOURCE: Saraiva, "Quadro estatístico de alguns estabelecimentos rurais da Província de São Paulo (1855)."
NOTE: The original production quantity data were given in arrobas and have been converted to metric tons.

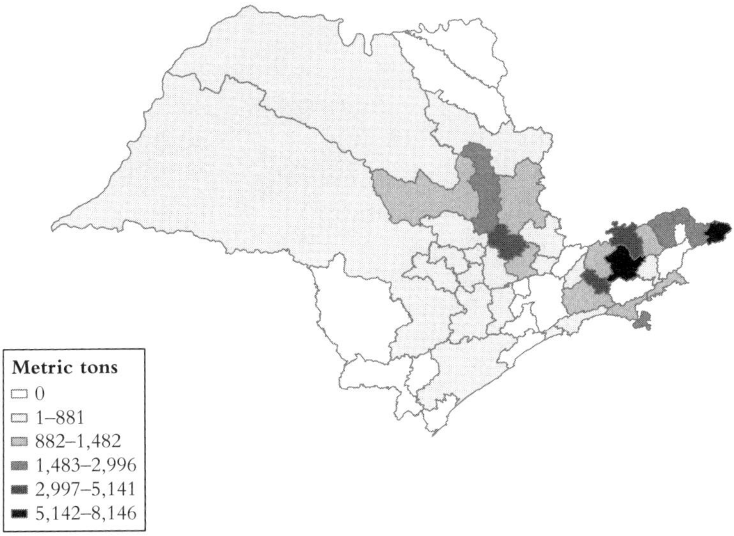

Map 1.1 Coffee Production by Município in São Paulo, 1854

Sugar was less distributed throughout the province. The ten counties producing the most sugar accounted for 96 percent of the crop, whereas the ten counties producing the most coffee accounted for only 73 percent of total production. The four counties of Mogi Mirim, Itu, Piracicaba, and Capivari produced almost three-quarters of the sugar. Itu had more fazendas (164 out of a total of 665) than any other município. Mogi Mirim generated the largest output per fazenda: 3,334 metric tons of sugarcane, or 58 metric tons of sugar, compared to an average of 19 metric tons per fazenda for the province. Campinas had the highest average (45) of slaves per fazenda (see Table 1.2).

Unfortunately, the 1854 census does not provide data on other crops, but it does give information on ranching. The province had 532 ranches, which is probably an undercount. These cattle ranches had 4,342 slaves and 1,767 *agregados* (free wage workers) who raised 24,000 head of cattle in that year. Population, as could be expected, was concentrated in the same zones as the major agricultural crops and farms. The Central and Vale do Paraíba regions accounted for almost two-thirds of the provincial population (see Map 1.2).

By mid-century coffee and sugar were thus firmly established in the province. But despite the existence of large virgin territories propitious for cof-

TABLE 1.2

Coffee and Sugar Production in the Ten Leading Municípios, 1854

		WORKERS			CROP PRODUCED			AVERAGE			
Município	Fazendas	Agregados	Colonos	Slaves	Quantity (t)	Value (mil réis)	Fazenda average (t)	Slaves	Colonos	Agregados	Kilos per worker
Coffee											
Bananal	70	330	10	7,622	8,146	1,227,750	116	108.9	0.14	4.71	1,023
Taubaté	240	272		4,345	5,210	1,221,235	22	18.1	0.00	1.13	1,128
Pindamonhangaba	112	316		2,800	5,141	700,000	46	25.0	0.00	2.82	1,650
Campinas	177	28	198	6,000	4,929	1,006,650	28	33.9	1.12	0.16	792
Jacarei	96	176		2,435	2,996	742,999	31	25.4	0.00	1.83	1,148
Queluz	76	800		2,300	2,938	600,000	39	30.3	0.00	10.53	948
Areias	341	338	1	4,069	2,733	379,628	8	11.9	0.00	0.99	620
Lorena	57	43		1,621	1,836	250,000	32	28.4	0.00	0.75	1,103
Limeira	65	40	942	1,747	1,789	365,400	28	26.9	14.49	0.62	656
Vila Bela	225	75		1,725	1,652	337,000	7	7.7	0.00	0.33	918
Subtotal	1,459	2,418	1,151	34,664	37,370	6,830,662	26	23.8	0.79	1.66	977
Total province	2,612	4,223	2,159	54,481	50,827	9,405,503	19	20.9	0.83	1.62	835
Sugar											
Mogi Mirim	57		9	1524	3,334	452,000	58	26.7	0.16	0.00	2,175
Itu	164	40		3408	2,336	254,512	14	20.8	0.00	0.24	678
Constituição (Piracicaba)	51			1889	1,924	262,000	38	37.0	0.00	0.00	1,019
Capivari	70			1500	1,469	140,000	21	21.4	0.00	0.00	979
Campinas	44			1967	915	99,694	21	44.7	0.00	0.00	465
Porto Feliz	38			942	636	61,950	17	24.8	0.00	0.00	675
Pirapora	47	10	1	962	632	81,950	13	20.5	0.02	0.21	649
Rio Claro	30	108		501	499	53,600	17	16.7	0.00	3.60	820
Jundiai	19	60		720	323	50,000	17	37.9	0.00	3.16	414
Sorocaba	10	3		409	181	19,720	18	40.9	0.00	0.30	439
Subtotal	530	221	10	13,822	12,249	1,475,426	23	26.1	0.02	0.42	872
Total province	665	620	10	15,571	12,725	1,644,750	19	23.4	0.02	0.93	785

SOURCE: Saraiva, "Quadro estatístico de alguns estabelecimentos rurais da Província de São Paulo (1855)."

NOTE: Original data were given in arrobas and have been converted to kilos and metric tons.

Map 1.2 Distribution of Population by Region in São Paulo, 1857

SOURCE: *Almanak Administrativo, Mercantil e Industrial da Província de São Paulo para o ano de 1857.*

fee production, expansion of coffee was limited by two key factors, shortage of labor and a very precarious system of transport, which made farming at any distance from the coast far too costly to be commercially profitable.

The end of the Atlantic slave trade in 1850 created a serious labor constraint on expanding coffee plantation agriculture. Although the province already had a large slave population by this time, and there would be internal transfers of slaves from less developed centers within Brazil, the end of the trade put into question the future of slave labor. This explains the first attempts to import free immigrant labor to coffee estates as early as the decade of the 1850s. But these two forms of labor were incompatible, and efforts to exploit the free wage laborers more systematically led to intense conflict.[11] The new plantings in the interior plains were the most affected by the scarcity of labor, and it was in that region that the first attempts were made to use free wage immigrant laborers. These early efforts failed, and planters continued to make systematic attempts to find a solution to the labor question.

The gradual transfer of slaves from other activities and other regions temporarily solved the demand for labor, but this supply was insufficient to meet the growing demand from the expanding coffee fazendas. Moreover, the transfer of slaves from the Northeastern provinces to the south was the subject of intense debates because of the economic and political consequences of this migration. On the one hand, it weakened the sugar economies of the Northeast because of the loss of labor, and on the other hand, it reduced Northeast support for slavery. The leadership of the Northeastern provinces was opposed to the interprovincial slave trade and demanded that the parliament prohibit it. But the initial debate led nowhere, and the trade continued. It was not until 1871, with the enactment of the Law of Free Birth, that the issue was again raised. The law declared that all children born after the enactment of the law would be free but remain under the control of their former masters until they reached age eight. Despite the massive loss of slaves to the south in this decade, the conservative leadership of the Northeast did not oppose the Law of Free Birth, which showed how the institution of slavery had lost its importance there. As the historian Evaldo Cabral de Mello has noted, the interprovincial slave trade represented for the Northeast "abolition with indemnity."[12] This change in attitude by the other provinces caused serious concern for the southern coffee elite such that in the 1880s, when the parliament still refused to prohibit the trade, the principal slave-importing provinces imposed heavy taxes on imported slaves and prohibited new transfers of slaves from other provinces.[13]

Besides the individual initiatives to experiment with free wage laborers, such as the early experiments of Senator Nicolau Pereira de Campos Vergueiro,[14] the government and the Paulista elite also sought a solution to the labor shortage. After passage of the Law of Free Birth, the provincial parliament approved a law that authorized the issuing of bonds to support the financing of farmers who wished to bring in free immigrant laborers.[15] In this same year a group of Paulista entrepreneurs formed the Association to Aid Colonization and Immigration (Associação Auxiliadora de Colonização e Imigração), whose aim was to bring in immigrants to work the coffee fields.[16] But despite all the public and private initiatives, the results were modest throughout the 1870s.[17] The creation in 1881 of the province-supported labor exchange and residence called the Hospedaria dos Imigrantes was a major advance in the effort to foment immigration.[18] The law that established this residence stipulated that immigrants would have their railroad fares paid from Santos to the capital and would also be paid the difference in cost between passage from Europe to Brazil and passage from Europe to the United States.[19]

In the 1880s the slave regime began to fall apart, and the problem of labor for the coffee planters became acute. In 1884, under pressure from the coffee growers, the government of the province of São Paulo passed a law that required the province to assume the entire cost of passage of European male immigrants who came to work in Paulista agriculture. This financial aid was paid directly to the immigrant as long as he was married or accompanied by children.[20] With this law, the province established the basis for a massive migration of Europeans to São Paulo.

The last obstacle to this European migration was resolved by the abolition of slavery in 1888. Between 1827 and 1884, only 37,000 foreign immigrants had arrived; in the ten years following the 1884 law, 509,000 European immigrants arrived (see Figure 1.1). Of the 2.3 million immigrants who came to São Paulo between 1887 and 1928, half had their passage subsidized by the province (now a state). Although other states of the nation received immigrants in this period, the majority came to São Paulo.[21] Thus, despite the progressive destruction of slavery during the 1880s, coffee production did not collapse, as immigrants replaced slaves.

The end of slave labor and the successful establishment of wage labor signified consolidation of the interior plains and other frontier regions of the province as the hegemonic areas of Paulista agriculture. The dominance of the western Paulista area began in the 1870s, as soil exhaustion brought the dominance of Vale do Paraíba to an end. The expansion of the coffee

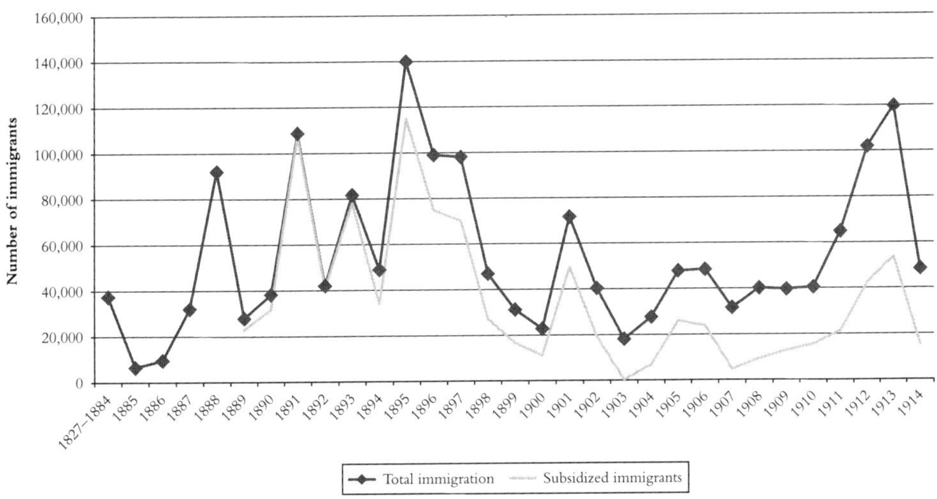

Figure 1.1 Entrance of Immigrants into São Paulo, 1827–1914

SOURCE: *A immigração e as condicões do trabalho em São Paulo*, 8–9.

fazendas to these new regions was due to their virgin soil and a climate extremely favorable for coffee cultivation. Although Vale do Paraíba still produced coffee on a significant scale until the end of slavery, costs there were too high and productivity too low to compete with the frontier regions for wage labor.

To take full advantage of their labor, planters usually consigned immigrant workers to coffee production rather than other tasks, such as clearing land or planting trees. Land clearance and tree plantings were contracted out to so-called *empreiteiros* (contractors). Part of the payment for this work usually came in the form of the right to plant other crops among the coffee trees before the trees began producing coffee beans.[22] This right also was granted to the colonos when they in turn came to care for the maturing trees; they were authorized to plant subsistence crops among the coffee trees or in areas of the fazenda not occupied by coffee. In the newer and more productive zones, colonos also received a fixed income for the care of a given number of coffee trees and based in part on the amount of coffee their trees produced. The majority of colonos desired this wage-and-benefit system, and it predominated in the new frontier zones and western Paulista area. In the less advanced and poorer coffee zones of Vale do Paraíba, planters arranged for sharecropping, with the coffee planters and the colonos both assuming the risks associated with the production and sale of coffee. This option required less capital and diluted the risks of production.

But labor was not the only obstacle blocking the expansion of coffee production in the state. By the middle of the nineteenth century it became evident that an efficient system of rail transport was necessary to move the growing coffee crop.[23] The traditional Brazilian system of mule transport[24] was sufficient for the initial phase of coffee cultivation but eventually limited its expansion.[25] The early coffee plantations in Vale do Paraíba and in Rio de Janeiro and Minas Gerais used the same rough roads and trails that had been used to move gold to the coast in the eighteenth century, which directed most Paulista output to the port of Rio de Janeiro.[26] The coffee produced in the interior plains traveled to the port of Santos by roads far more difficult and costly to use.[27] It was even suggested at the time that the poor roads and slow transport of sugar from the Central region to the port of Santos affected the sugar's quality.

The first attempts to establish a railroad in Brazil started as far back as 1835. But despite the government's offer of exclusive rights to land along the route of the railroads, the necessary capital was not forthcoming. The solution came in 1852 with a law that guaranteed interest on investments made in the railroad. The government guaranteed 7 percent interest on all capital invested, of which Rio de Janeiro paid 2 percentage points.[28] The Estrada de Ferro D. Pedro II, a railway connecting the port of Rio de Janeiro to Cachoeira in São Paulo, was the first railroad to be successfully established in Brazil.[29] The branch of the railroad to Vassouras opened in 1858, but not until 1875 did the railroad reach Paulista territory, when the station at Cachoeira was opened.[30] This railroad permitted the movement of coffee directly from Vale do Paraíba coffee producers to the port of Rio de Janeiro.[31] For the port of Santos and its hinterland, the solution came in 1867 with the inauguration of the São Paulo Railway Company, linking the port of Santos to the city of Jundiaí, which was the traditional entrance to the interior plains. The company, which operated only 167 kilometers of railway, was created with English capital and had the same guarantee of a 7 percent return on investment, of which 2 percentage points was paid by the province of São Paulo.[32]

The second half of the century was a period of rapid expansion of railroads throughout Brazil, with most construction occurring in São Paulo.[33] Much railway construction was financed by the coffee planter elite with some participation of foreign capital, and it resulted in a complex railroad network that eventually covered all areas of the state.[34] Although the impetus for building railroads was transporting coffee, railroads also moved people and noncoffee products throughout the state and across state borders and thus were crucial in expanding domestic and export markets.

The development of an extensive rail network also was an important stimulant to local manufacturing, since the railroads required maintenance and repair facilities, but the railroads were often deficit operations. The government had to either take them over or, if they were still independent, guarantee interest on investments in them. At the same time, the government was caught between the railroads and the planters over freight charges, which became a crucial issue when world prices declined. As the president of the province of São Paulo noted in 1883, the cost of building railways through non-coffee-producing areas to reach coffee-producing zones, in addition to interest payments for railroads that were not always profitable, meant that the government could not accept the reduction of freight charges, since that would leave it "incapable of granting equal guarantees to new companies that would develop the areas that absolutely needed them."[35]

There were also other problems. Though the rail system in São Paulo was quite extensive, it was not well integrated. The system used various track gauges and often could not directly move wagons and engines between lines.[36] As Caio Prado Jr. notes, the railroads were independent entities and not coherently linked. They were also designed for exporting coffee or other valuable commercial crops and thus did not always satisfy the needs of the internal market.[37] But whatever their deficiencies, these railroads promoted the growth of the port of Santos, which became the residence of the major coffee merchants, the headquarters of leading import houses, and a center for banking agencies.[38] The port itself was also modernized to accommodate the large volume of merchandise exported from and imported to the state. The expansion of Santos was directly related to the shifting production of coffee within the province. It is important to stress the fundamental difference between the production of Vale do Paraíba and that of the western plains—that is, between the old and the new zones. For these newer fazendas, the natural port of exit was through Santos via the São Paulo Railway, while for counties of Vale do Paraíba it was through the port of Rio de Janeiro. All the new coffee-producing zones were better located for exporting through Santos, and this further promoted development of the province's capital city and linkage of its interior to Santos. Thus, the capital city had four different railroad lines entering it, and this furthered its role as the principal financial and commercial center of the state. But the capital was not a port city, and Santos carried out the typical functions of a major port city, including the marketing, financing, storage, transportation, and shipments of the main products imported or exported from the state.

Resolution of the labor and transport issues opened up the frontier lands to exploitation in the second half of the century. The soil of these areas was of exceptional quality, permitting Paulista coffee growers to easily meet growing international demand for coffee. Especially after the abolition of slavery, the state of São Paulo finally assumed a hegemonic role in the world production of coffee as it replaced Rio de Janeiro as the leading producer in Brazil. This was accomplished through the gradual penetration of western São Paulo, with its high-quality virgin soils. Between 1854 and 1900, Paulista coffee production grew by a factor of ten, yielding 9 million sacks of coffee by 1900, which was two-thirds of national production and 62 percent of the coffee consumed in the world in that year.[39] The frontier regions also allowed the average size of coffee fazendas to increase significantly.

Unfortunately, little systematic information is available on Paulista agriculture for the second half of the nineteenth century. Only after the proclamation of the republic in 1889 did the state begin gathering statistical information on local agriculture, population, commerce, and industry. The only systematic information we have for this period relates to exports to national and international markets. From the information we do possess, it is evident that the patterns established earlier in the century continued to evolve. Not only did coffee and sugar production increase and their quality improve, but food crop production, mostly on the same estates that grew commercial export crops, also steadily expanded.

Some of these developments can be seen in the São Paulo almanac for 1873. It contains general information with respect to each county, including its major economic activities. In the case of agriculture, the almanac lists 4,872 farmers by type of production, without specifying quantities produced. In some counties the information is precise, specifying each farm's major product.[40] In other cases the information is less precise, and a farm's crops cannot be precisely determined. For example, it lists fazendas that produced both coffee and sugarcane without specifying which was the predominant crop. In other cases it uses generic terms such as *fazendeiros* (plantation owners) or *lavradores* (farmers). For the cases in which only one activity or product was clearly specified, we find 934 producers of coffee, 379 of sugarcane, 316 of cotton, and 110 of tobacco. Little information is available on cereals produced. The coffee producers were in Vale do Paraíba, Central, Mogiana, and Baixa Paulista regions. Sugarcane was in the Central region's municípios of the so-called sugar quadrangle (*quadrilátero do açúcar*: Sorocaba, Piracicaba, Mogi Guaçú, and Jundiaí)[41] and in the Mogiana region and Vale do Paraíba. Cotton was concentrated in the Central region. The Vale do Paraíba region, which also produced tobacco, saw minor production of cotton, as did the Baixa Paulista region.

All the available data, including producers with multiple products or activities, show this same regional specialization, though with the Mogiana region increasing its importance in cotton and the Vale do Paraíba region in tobacco plantings. What is worth noting is the continued importance of Vale do Paraíba in coffee production, as well as in cotton and tobacco. There is also an evident increase in agricultural activity in the part of western São Paulo composed of municípios in the Central region and several in the Mogiana and Baixa Paulista regions, such as Mogi Mirim, Mogi Guaçú, Rio Claro, and Pirassununga, not far from the Central region (Table 1.3).

The next major survey we have is for 1886.[42] In the annual report of the province submitted to its president is a partial census of population by município, as well as data on crop production, with the most complete information given for coffee. Unfortunately, a few localities are missing, including the município of Bananal, a traditional producer of coffee. For the province as a whole, the document lists an annual production of 157,209 metric tons of coffee. Vale do Paraíba, Central, Mogiana, and Baixa Paulista

TABLE 1.3

Farmers by Region and by Product, São Paulo, 1873

	FARMERS PRODUCING ONE CLEARLY IDENTIFIED PRODUCT								FARMERS PRODUCING MORE THAN ONE PRODUCT						
Region	Coffee	Sugar[b]	Sugar[c]	Cotton	Tobacco	Tea	Cattle	Pigs	Coffee	Sugar[b]	Sugar[c]	Cotton	Tobacco	Animals	Farmers[a]
Capital	0	2	0	0	0	0	4	0	0	0	0	0	0	4	10
Vale do Paraíba	173	76	0	45	55	0	17	0	509	82	0	90	226	22	567
Central	169	105	5	201	6	16	19	0	165	57	35	187	0	23	454
Mogiana	306	63	11	3	5	0	84	15	295	6	7	270	12	132	91
Baixa Paulista	247	42	10	38	34	0	29	5	87	0	87	87	0	34	14
Araraquarense	0	0	6	0	0	0	9	0	0	0	0	0	0	9	139
Noroeste															
Alta Sorocabana	39	47	0	27	0	0	0	0	34	34	0	0	0	34	6
Baixa Sorocabana	0	11	1	2	10	0	31	0	10	26	7	9	4	31	58
Santos	0	0	0	0	0	0	0	0	0	0	0	0	0	0	50
Total	934	346	33	316	110	16	193	20	1,100	205	136	643	242	289	1,389

SOURCE: Luné and Fonseca, *Almanak da província de São Paulo para 1873*, 97–566.

[a] Farmers listed without any specific crops.

[b] Includes sugarcane farmers who also produce aguardente.

[c] Includes producers of sugar who also produce aguardente.

each accounted for 20 percent of the output. Given the lack of data from Bananal (which accounted for 21 percent of Vale do Paraíba production in 1854), the importance of Vale do Paraíba is probably underestimated. Nevertheless, the production numbers show the slow decline of the valley and the rise of new producing zones as major participants in the coffee economy. As for sugar, it remained concentrated in the Central and Mogiana regions with the counties of Itapetininga and Tatuí being significant sugar producers (see Table 1.4).

Using the more systematic export data that we have for the second half of the nineteenth century shows how coffee had come to completely dominate the local economy. Already in the harvest year of 1856/1857 coffee made up 96 percent of the value of exports from São Paulo and averaged 90 percent after 1870. Cotton, whose production increased greatly in the 1860s during the Civil War in the United States, had little importance as an export afterward (see Figure 1.2). Sugar, which had been a leader in the province's exports up until 1830, was supplanted by coffee, and production severely declined in later decades.

In 1877–1887, after the railroads opened up the port of Santos to the new western coffee regions, a significant share of Paulista exports moved through the port.[43] Along with coffee and sugar, cotton and hides were now mostly shipped through Santos. Santos also developed a significant coastal trade (cabotage) to other provinces, which involved the export of finished cotton textiles, bacon, and shoe leather, all destined for the national market. Only Paulista tobacco still went via coastal shipping to Rio de Janeiro for international export. In general, though, the coastal trade was only around 200 metric tons, compared to the 20,000 metric tons sent to the international trade. Coffee exports alone now represented 95 percent of the value of all exports shipped from Santos from 1877 to 1887.[44]

The increasing importance of new coffee zones can be seen in their role in Brazilian exports. In the 1880s the "Rio zone" of coffee production, which referred to the provinces of Rio de Janeiro, Minas Gerais, and Espírito Santo and the Paulista part of Vale do Paraíba, shipped coffee through the port of Rio de Janeiro. In 1870 the zone accounted for 85 percent of Brazilian coffee exports, but by 1890 that was down to 51 percent and continued to decline throughout the twentieth century (see Table A1.1). Production from the Paulista part of the Rio zone remained stable between 1870 and 1890. In contrast, the production from the so-called Santos zone of producers, those shipping out of the port of Santos, increased by a factor of five in this same period. This result reflects both the rise of the western zones and the movement of some of the crop of the Paulista part of Vale do

TABLE 1.4

Agricultural Production by Product and Region, São Paulo, 1886

Region	Number of municípios	Population	Coffee (kg)	Sugar (kg)	Corn (L)	Aguardente (L)	Tobacco (kg)	Brown sugar (kg)	Beans (L)	Cotton (kg)	Rice (L)	Manioc flour (L)	Wine (L)
Capital	5	74,893			720,000		130,000		72,000			72,000	
Vale do Paraíba	3	325,216	31,487,000	484,000	72,540	2,556,000	465,242		47,270	450,000		41,400	160
Central	29	299,210	44,532,760	3,127,552	2,600,000	476,000	551,138		750,000	5,170,104	100,000		106,600
Mogiana	20	170,296	33,360,000	3,090,000	10,000,000	41,000	190,000		400,000	207,000	800,000		600
Baixa Paulista	12	133,607	36,932,000	470,000		42,000	113,000			115,000			
Araraquarense	5	47,516	7,929,000	315,000			82,500						
Noroeste													
Alta Sorocabana	10	71,903	2,430,000	540,000		300,000	52,500				16		
Baixa Sorocabana	5	27,004	538,440	147,816	52,240,000	2,562,000	164,688	1,050,000	6,000,000		630,000		
Santos	5	42,434									3,000,000		
Total	124	1,192,079	157,209,200	8,174,368	65,632,540	5,977,000	1,749,068	1,050,000	7,269,270	5,942,104	4,530,016	113,400	107,360

SOURCE: *Relatório apresentado ao Exmo. Sr. Presidente da Província de São Paulo*, 24–26, app. 4.

NOTE: Except for coffee, products are not always presented with their total numbers, indicating just that these products are planted.

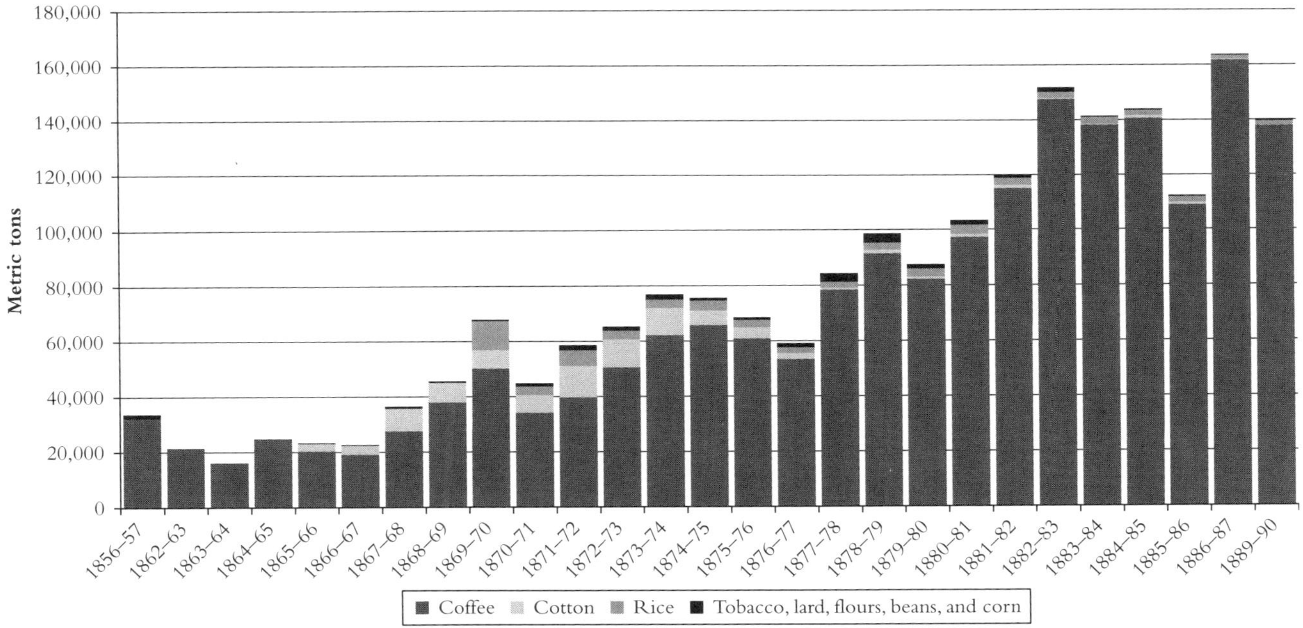

Figure 1.2 Exportation of Coffee, Cotton, Rice, Tobacco, Lard, Flours, Beans, and Corn, 1856–1890

SOURCE: Assembleia Legislativa do Estado de São Paulo, leis orçamentárias, various years, http://www.al.sp.gov.br/leis.

Paraíba to the port of Santos after rail connected the northeastern region and Santos.

For 1881 and 1883, we can use the excellent work of C. F. Van Delden Laerne, who divided coffee production into zones according to whether it was shipped from the port of Santos or Rio de Janeiro.[45] He examined records of fazendas that obtained mortgages from the Banco do Brasil. These fazendas represent some of the biggest plantations and are thus atypical, but they give a reasonable view of the largest producers and are the best available data we have on coffee slave plantations at the height of their coffee boom. The data from 1881 for the Santos zone are a sample of 146 coffee fazendas. These fazendas produced only coffee, while another 61 fazendas grew coffee, sugar, tobacco, and cotton. The coffee group had an average of 36 slaves per fazenda, though with significant variations by region. For example, the 49 coffee fazendas of Campinas had an average of 53 slaves per farm. The average size of the 146 coffee fazendas was 633 hectares, and they cultivated on average 88,384 coffee trees. The fazendas producing coffee, sugar, tobacco, and cotton were on average larger—some 829 hectares, with an average of 42 slaves per farm. For the entire Santos group, Van Delden Laerne estimated that slaves represented approximately 40 percent of the value of the fazendas.

The sample of fazendas in the Rio zone that had Banco do Brasil mortgages in 1883 tended to be larger than those in the Santos zone, containing 727 hectares, and their average slave holdings were also larger, at 47 slaves per fazenda. The fazendas that produced only coffee in Rio de Janeiro in the Rio zone were on average 628 hectares but had more slaves, 56, per farm than the Santos zone. The 53 Paulista fazendas of Vale do Paraíba had an average of 37 slaves per farm. Slaves represented 46 percent of the total value of the Rio zone fazendas (see Table 1.5).

Although Brazil lost its dominant position in the world sugar market to the new Caribbean producers in the eighteenth century, it still produced a significant amount of sugar and exported to the world market when international conditions were favorable. Thus, when the Haitian Revolution at the end of the eighteenth century eliminated the world's leading producer of cane sugar, the Brazilian industry took note. The resulting rise in world sugar prices initially stimulated local production, and with the introduction of new cane varieties and some improvement in local milling, Brazil began again exporting refined sugar.[46] But Cuba and other centers of production introduced innovations more quickly, and when prices once again fell Brazil found itself less able to compete on the international market. Later, the local industry faced two other problems that delayed its modernization.

The first was the end of the slave trade toward the end of the nineteenth century and the increase in the cost of labor, and the second was the expansion of the beet sugar industry in Europe. By 1853 beet sugar accounted for 14 percent of the world's sugar market, rising to 25 percent by 1860 and accounting for over half of world consumption of sugar by the 1880s.[47] This considerably reduced world demand for cane sugar and lowered prices on the world market (see Figure 1.3).

Cane sugar's high production costs and low profits discouraged local planters from investing in new technology, making Brazilian sugar less competitive on the world market.[48] In the mid-1870s, when world sugar production reached 2.5 million metric tons, Brazil accounted for only 5 percent of world sugar production and 8 percent of cane sugar output.[49] Although in long-term crisis, the Brazilian sugar industry represents the main economic activity of the northern provinces. Both private and government income for Pernambuco and the neighboring provinces came from sugar production.

Other crops of the northeast could be expanded—cotton, for example—but none were more appropriate to the soil and climate in the region than sugarcane. Sugar production in the northeast played the same role as coffee in the provinces of Rio de Janeiro and São Paulo, with its multiplier effect for other activities and the government tax base.[50] But given the difficulties faced by northeastern producers in the international market, the majority of their sugar was sent to the national market. In 1904, for example, 72 percent of northeastern production was internally consumed. The Federal District (then Rio de Janeiro) was the primary consumer, and the state of São Paulo was the second.[51] Thus, while coffee primarily went to the international market, sugar became the major agricultural product in interprovincial and interstate trade. Although São Paulo itself remained a major producer, it could not satisfy local demand and remained dependent on imports from the northeastern states.

While other producers in the Americas installed modern steam-driven mills, only a few such mills were installed in Brazil. Not until the late adoption of modern massive central mills did Brazil's sugar finally reach a quantity and quality sufficient for world trade. In some countries cane-growing operations separated from sugar milling because of the size and expense of these new steam-driven central mills (*engenhos centrais*). They often could grind much more cane than one farm could produce, and thus farmers sought the cane of other farmers. In the 1870s these mills were much discussed in Brazil, and the imperial government launched a program to stimulate their creation. It offered the right to expropriate lands, removed

TABLE 1.5

Sample of Coffee Plantations in the Santos Zone (1881) and Rio Zone (1883)

Districts	Number of fazendas	Size of fazendas (ha)	Number of coffee trees (thousands)	Number of slaves	Value of slaves (contos)	Value of fazendas (contos)	Total value (contos)	Percentage of total value due to slaves	Slaves per fazenda	Coffee trees per slave	Average value of slave (mil réis)
Santos zone, 1881											
GROWING ONLY COFFEE											
Campinas	49	26,189	5,023	2,613	3,662	4,912	8,574	42.7%	53	2	1
Amparo	19	4,102	1,153	397	575	915	1,490	38.6%	21	3	1
Belém do Descalvado	14	15,215	1,397	486	695	1,439	2,134	32.6%	35	3	1
Casa Branca	12	7,193	1,252	461	631	1,074	1,705	37.0%	38	3	1
S. João de Rio-Claro	11	15,634	1,140	332	447	956	1,403	31.8%	30	3	1
Jundiahy (Jundiaí)	9	4,895	514	260	336	555	890	37.7%	29	2	1
Itatiba	5	840	335	108	168	246	414	40.6%	22	3	2
Pirassununga	5	3,848	365	133	202	314	516	39.1%	27	3	2
S. Carlos do Pinhal	5	4,026	288	88	124	252	376	32.9%	18	3	1
Brotas	2	2,954	172	42	59	202	261	22.7%	21	4	1
Botucatú	2	1,315	190	32	50	201	251	19.8%	16	6	2
Capivary	2	984	143	73	99	144	243	40.8%	37	2	1
Jahú	2	769	242	72	117	186	303	38.7%	36	3	2
Penha do Rio do Peixe	2	790	141	26	36	130	166	21.6%	13	5	1
S. Simão	2	1,591	260	31	44	198	241	18.1%	16	8	1
Araras	1	329	80	18	21	60	81	26.4%	18	4	1
Mogy-Guassú	1	329	44	14	22	40	62	35.0%	14	3	2
Serra Negra	1	194	52	11	16	42	58	27.9%	11	5	1
S. João de Boâ Vista	1	621	68	35	43	81	125	34.6%	35	2	1
Tieté	1	624	46	34	44	34	78	56.1%	34	1	1
Subtotal	146	92,442	12,904	5,266	7,392	11,981	19,373	38.2%	36	2,450	1,404
GROWING COFFEE, SUGAR, TOBACCO, AND COTTON	61	50,553	4,967	2,565	3,286	5,058	8,344	39.4%	42	1,936	1,281
Total Santos zone	207	142,995	17,871	7,831	10,678	17,039	27,717	39%	38	2,282	1,363

Rio zone (including parts of four provinces), 1883											
RIO DE JANEIRO											
Only coffee	191	119,945	37,639	10,712	12,531	14,120	26,651	47%	56	3,514	1,170
Coffee and sugar	160	130,876	14,269	8,170	9,114	9,549	18,663	49%	51	1,747	1,116
Subtotal, Rio de Janeiro	351	250,821	51,908	18,882	21,645	23,669	45,314	48%	54	2,749	1,146
MINAS GERAIS	153	90,453	20,633	5,568	6,660	8,463	15,122	44%	36	3,706	1,196
ESPÍRITO SANTO	12	24,794	791	569	551	506	1,057	52%	47	1,390	968
SÃO PAULO											
Pindamonhangaba	14	7,495	1,925	444	566	732	1,298	44%	32	4,336	1,275
Bananal	12	5,706	1,877	688	794	613	1,406	56%	57	2,728	1,153
Taubaté	11	14,927	1,484	370	465	710	1,175	40%	34	4,011	1,258
Guaratinguetá	5	9,393	794	176	243	402	645	38%	35	4,511	1,381
Jacarehy	3	3,230	405	111	125	345	470	27%	37	3,649	1,128
Lorena	3	3,277	791	30	40	387	427	9%	10	26,367	1,340
Caçapava	2	895	205	51	79	81	160	49%	26	4,020	1,553
Mogy das Cruzes	1	968	104	42	63	103	165	38%	42	2,476	1,490
Queluz	1	1,089	170	42	34	107	142	24%	42	4,048	817
S. José dos Campos	1	444	126	33	53	55	108	49%	33	3,818	1,606
Subtotal, São Paulo Province	53	47,424	7,881	1,987	2,462	3,534	5,997	41%	37	3,966	1,239
Total Rio zone	569	413,492	81,213	27,006	31,317	36,172	67,489	46%	47	3,007	1,160

SOURCE: Laerne, *Brazil and Java*, 222–223.
NOTE: Fazendas listed here are those with mortgages from the Banco de Brazil as of June 30, 1881.

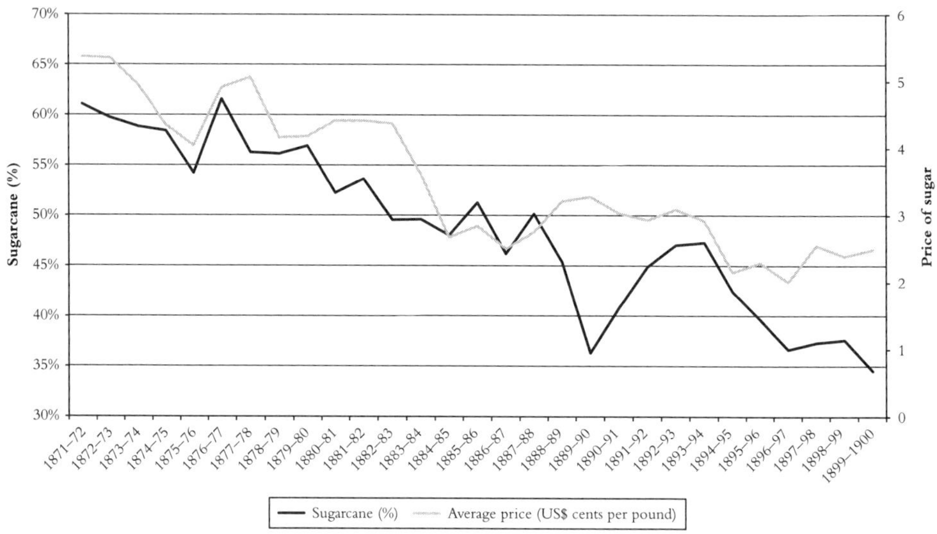

Figure 1.3 Price of Sugar and Importance of Sugarcane in Total World Sugar Exports, 1871–1900

SOURCE: U.S. Bureau of Statistics, *The World's Sugar Production and Consumption*, 2589.

restrictions on importing machinery, and guaranteed a 5 percent return for twenty years on mill investment.[52]

The hope was that these mills would not only make Brazilian sugar competitive on the world market but also reduce the slave labor required in the sugar-processing industry. Given the international market conditions, the survival of Brazil's sugar industry depended on cost reduction, better sugar processing, and better management.[53] The government also made the condition that central mills would be operated exclusively by wage workers. In 1882, the minister of agriculture expected the mills to make Brazil competitive on the world market and help modernize national agriculture.[54] Although numerous permits were offered, few central mills were established in this period.[55] In 1890 the minister of agriculture reported that of the eighty-seven projects approved by the government program of the 1870s, only twelve were active, of which three were in the state of São Paulo.[56] Several reasons were offered for this failure: A lot of financial speculation occurred with some of these permits, and mills that were built experienced technical problems and never achieved the quality of the advanced Caribbean producers. Some of the mills were simple upgrades of older mills and used old and inadequate machinery.[57] And there was no systematic increase in the quality of the cane milled. For all these reasons Brazil could not create a modern sugar-refining industry and produced low-quality sugar for national and international markets until the end of the century.

Even when a modern mill was built, it suffered from an insufficiency of raw material. Given the conditions of the market, most producers were content to mill low-quality sugar or produce alcohol, continuing to use their old mills and not systematically sending cane to the central mills, and thus the mills lacked regular large supplies of cane. The poor quality of roads was another impediment. In addition, these mills never reached international standards and thus could not pay the high prices for cane that might have attracted producers.[58] Not until the beginning of the twentieth century were central mills established, but unlike other world regions, in Brazil they mostly processed their own cane. With this transformation, the Brazilian sugar industry, especially in São Paulo, went from being one of the more backward producers to being the most modern of world producers by the second half of the twentieth century.[59]

The São Paulo experience with central mills promoted by the provincial and national governments differed little from the rest of Brazil. In 1883, the president of the province, Francisco de Carvalho Soares Brandão, expressed great hope for the sugar industry and the benefits from the new central mills.[60] He noted that São Paulo had obtained five permits to build central mills, but only three mills were functioning. The three were established in 1881, and eventually all were capitalized at 500 contos each. These mills were in Porto Feliz, Piracicaba, and Lorena. Unfortunately, these central mills never reached the output expected of them for technical reasons, such as poorly trained workers and the quality and volume of cane they processed.[61] The government even established the agricultural colonies of Rodrigo Silva (in 1887) and Canas (in 1888) to encourage cane production. In the face of these difficulties, the three central mills established in the province, aside from having little effect on local sugar output, lived in permanent financial crisis, and eventually all of them ended up in the hands of French capitalists.[62]

In 1886, a permit was granted for the Engenho Central de Capivari. Along with the usual subsidies, the imperial government authorized the company to buy lands and promote immigration. This was the solution needed, for the mills could now produce and grind all their own cane rather than relying on third parties. In effect, this marked the end of the central mills and presaged mills that used another model of sugar organization, called the *usinas* (central mills). Although for some time to come they would still be called engenhos centrais, their role had completely changed.

The other major crop that had a significant development in the second half of the nineteenth century was cotton. Planted in São Paulo from the province's beginning, cotton was locally consumed to produce crude cotton textiles. Although other regions of the colony exported cotton to the international market, São Paulo always restricted its production to local consumption. In the 1836 census it was estimated that local production reached 132 metric tons, compared to the total of 7,344 metric tons for coffee and sugar.

The US Civil War in the middle of the nineteenth century profoundly altered the international cotton market. The United States, principal supplier to the world cotton market, practically withdrew from that market after 1861, provoking a profound crisis in the great producers of cotton textiles, particularly England, then the world's leading manufacturer.[63] US cotton exports went from more than 4.9 million bales of cotton (at 500 pounds per bale, the total was 101,854 metric tons) in 1859 to just 300,000 bales by 1864.[64] Although Brazil, Egypt, Turkey, and India and other Asian producers significantly increased their exports in the 1860s, global exports fell to half pre–Civil War volumes, because other producers were unable to replace the total supplied by the United States.

Paulista cotton production expanded to fill some of the gap in cotton supply. In the 1850s Brazil exported on average 14,000 metric tons per annum, with an average price of £45 per metric ton. The Northeast was traditionally the great producer of cotton. In the 1860s Brazil doubled its average exports to 29,000 metric tons, and the value of these cotton exports increased by a factor of four. In this period cotton replaced sugar as the second-most-important export of the country. Thus, Brazil, which in 1860 accounted for less than 1 percent of the world market, increased its share to 5 percent of the world market in the 1870s. Although cotton prices fell after the end of the Civil War, the increasing internal demand for cotton and the beginnings of a major national textile industry generated a steady demand for raw cotton at both the national and the provincial levels.[65]

England encouraged Brazil to produce cotton during the crisis.[66] In the case of Paulista production, the English brought the latest technology and seeds to the province. English technicians introduced a variety of cotton with an annual cycle and suited to São Paulo's soil and climate. It became the primary type of locally grown cotton and, much later, the principal type produced in all of Brazil.[67] Because of the lack of government support, such as through agricultural agents and experimental farms, individuals[68] and private organizations like the Sociedade Auxiliadora da Indústria Nacional[69] distributed the seed and published information about it.[70] Despite

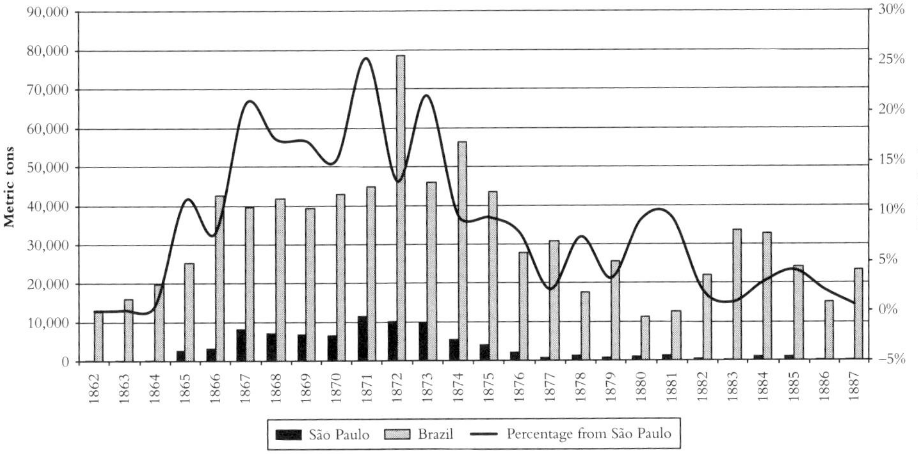

Figure 1.4 Exports of Cotton from Brazil and São Paulo, 1862–1887

SOURCE: Canabrava, *O algodão em São Paulo, 1861–1875*, app. 2; Instituto Brasileiro de Geografia e Estatística, *Séries estatísticas retrospectivas*, 3:308.

these difficulties, the increase in local production was exceptional. Cotton was grown in the Central, Mogiana, and Baixa Paulista regions and was especially important in the municípios of Cunha, Itu, Jundiaí, São Roque, Piedade, Bragança, Atibaia, Santa Barbara, Capivari, Amparo, and Rio Claro. São Paulo cotton exports, practically nonexistent until 1865, grew rapidly, reaching 11,364 metric tons in 1871, or a quarter of all Brazilian cotton exports (see Figure 1.4).

But for all the increase in sugar and cotton, they could not replace coffee, which remained the primary engine of expansion for the entire Paulista economy. Although coffee never turned Paulista agriculture into a monoculture economy, it did significantly reduce the relative importance of these other crops in the export market.

The explosive growth of coffee, along with increasing sugar and cotton production, allowed the provincial government to establish a significant tax base, which funded provincial government services and development. This development included everything from establishing a significant tax bureaucracy and provincial judicial and legislative systems to paying for crucial infrastructure needed to export coffee. Taxes on agriculture were the key factors that allowed the province to lay out roads and railroads, install infrastructure for potable water distribution and public illumination in cities, build schools, and provide health services and public safety for the province as a whole.

Chapter 2

Government and Public Finance in the Empire, 1850–1889

The fazendeiros alone, no matter how wealthy, could not resolve the issues facing the Paulista coffee economy. Roads were poor, mule transport was slow and expensive, railroads were too costly for private investment alone, and the port of Santos was incapable of handling the growing volume of exports. Slave labor was increasingly viewed as doomed to extinction, and the planters could not afford the wages and transport costs to make Brazil attractive to European immigrants. The province was also being constantly struck by cholera plagues and virulent local outbreaks of yellow fever. Thus, the planters needed a state capable of resolving the issues of labor, transport, and health, as well as providing security through a provincial police force. It was thus in their interest to create as powerful a provincial government as possible under the empire, which was a highly centralized government, both politically and administratively.

The construction of a provincial government in São Paulo took several decades. In the highly centralized monarchy that Brazil inherited upon independence, there was little room for local government. But the crisis in imperial leadership that led to a long and complex regency period allowed the provinces some modest autonomy in creating their own legislatures and their own tax systems. Unfortunately, there exist few studies on how these governments were established.[1] In this chapter we survey the evolution of the provincial government of São Paulo, with special emphasis on the development of a provincial tax system and its evolution over time.

To finance the construction of roads, bridges, ports and public services, the provincial government initially had a limited range of taxes at its disposal and was constrained by the imperial government in what it could do. Thus, provincial officials under the empire constantly tried to expand local taxes and to convince the central government to support the special needs of the province, especially with the approaching emancipation of the slaves. The provincial government, with the aid of the central government, would initiate a major railroad era in the last quarter of the century. It would also create a limited public education system and embark on major road, bridge, and port construction. It began to promote alternatives to slave labor and to deal with serious public health issues. But the lack of local autonomy and resources limited the efforts of the local elite to resolve many of these issues under the empire. The tax base was limited not only by the modest local economy but also by the precarious nature of the provincial government and the limited fiscal instruments available to it.

In analyzing this theme in this and later chapters we rely on two sets of data: projected expenditure and income of annual budgets,[2] and the actual funds collected and spent during the given fiscal year.[3] These totals are available for all years of the nineteenth and twentieth centuries. We also have detailed budget items of income and expenditure proposed annually by the legislature for all years, but we have the corresponding actual income and expenditure items for only a few select years under the empire and for the republic from 1900 to 1939. After 1939 we have itemized actual income for all years to 1950, but we do not have itemized expenditures made by the state treasury for 1940 to 1950.

For income and expenditure by major category during the empire we use occasional data provided in various annual reports of the presidents of the province of São Paulo.[4] An important study by João Maurício Wanderley, Baron Cotegipe, provides a detailed analysis of actual income and expenditure for various provinces from 1876/1877 to 1885/1886.[5] For the republican period, the contemporary study of Eugênio Lefevre, who for decades was the director general of the Secretariat of Agriculture, contains excellent information.[6] Lefevre made detailed analyses of the public finances of the state of São Paulo in the period of the Old Republic from which we gathered information on the principal sources of income and expenditure for 1892 to 1929. This is supplemented with detailed studies from the state's treasury.[7] For 1930 to 1950, along with the budget laws, we also use annual publications of the Secretariat of Finance and the treasury of the state of São Paulo,[8] which we supplemented with aggregated actual income and expenditure in the *Anuário estatístico de São Paulo*.[9]

In contrast to contemporary budgeting, the annual budgets proposed by the provincial legislature in the imperial period were most often unbalanced, with expenditure exceeding income. In only five of the fifty years for which we have information were the budgets balanced, in eleven of those years the legislature proposed that income would exceed expenditure, and in all the rest it projected expenditures to exceed income (Figure 2.1). Differences in actual income and expenditure throughout the year resulted in an unbalanced bottom line in most years. Although actual revenue usually exceeded the estimated revenue in the budget, it was also quite common for actual expenditures to exceed those proposed in the original budget. Thus, the final balance was often negative (see Figure 2.2).

The organization of provincial governments began in 1822 with the creation of a constitutional monarchy under Emperor Dom Pedro I. The territory of this new empire was divided into provinces but had an extremely centralized regime. In 1823 the position of province president was created, appointed by the emperor. Initially, the provincial government was administered by the president of the province and an elected council composed of six wealthy individuals.[10] In the first Brazilian constitution, in 1824, the elected council expanded to twenty-three elected members, but its powers remained limited to consultation.[11] Although substantial changes in the system of provincial administration were made throughout the nineteenth century, the provincial executive was always appointed by the imperial government. Moreover, the president of the province was usually a non-

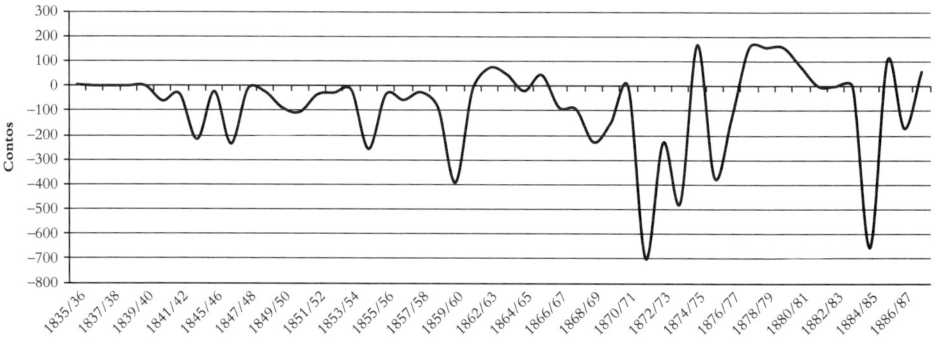

Figure 2.1 Annual Budgeted Balance of Provincial Accounts, 1835–1888

SOURCE: Assembléia Legislativa do Estado de São Paulo, leis orçamentárias, various years, http://www.al.sp.gov.br/leis; Departamento de Estatística do Estado, *Anuário estatístico de São Paulo, 1908*, 2:140.

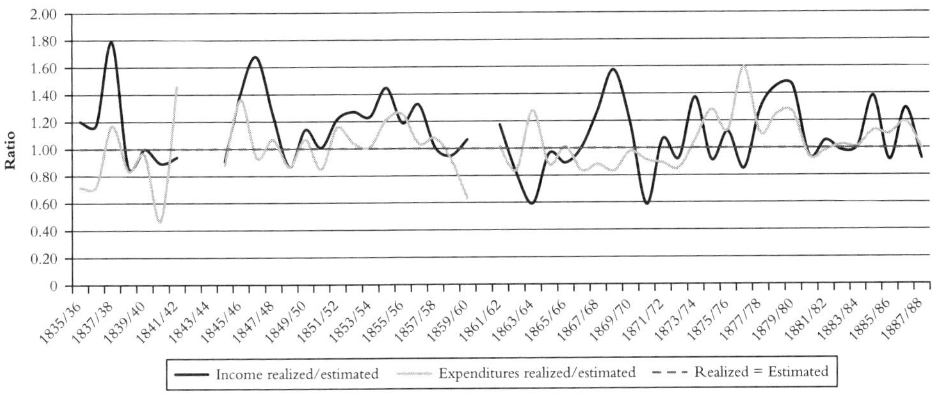

Figure 2.2 Relation Between Actual and Estimated Income and Expenditure for the Provincial Budget of São Paulo, 1835–1888

SOURCE: Assembléia Legislativa do Estado de São Paulo, leis orçamentárias, various years, http://www.al.sp.gov.br/leis.

resident of the province and held the position for a very short time, on average just a little more than a year. This in many ways guaranteed that the local elite would have only modest influence on the presidents, since their tenures were so short and many served in several different provinces.[12] It has been argued that the provincial presidents were really political agents of the imperial government, rarely aware of the special needs and interests of their provinces and seeking to advance to higher posts in the imperial court in Rio de Janeiro. Named under the aegis of a particular political party, the prime aim of the presidents was to guarantee that their party would win the local elections for the imperial legislature.[13]

In 1831 Dom Pedro I abdicated in favor of his five-year-old son, Dom Pedro II. The resulting regency period was one of conflict over the question of the centralization or decentralization of political power, a constant theme until the end of the empire in 1889.[14] Although the 1824 constitution was clearly absolutist and centralizing, the regency marked a period of relative decentralization.[15] The Penal Code of November 1832 temporarily allowed for autonomous provincial judges,[16] and then came the far more important decree called the Additional Act (Ato Adicional) of August 1834.[17] The Additional Act temporarily suspended the emperor's moderating power during the regency, but more importantly it permanently established more autonomous governments for the provinces.[18] It replaced the general councils with provincial assemblies that had responsibility for establishing a budget for annual income and expenditure, including determining provincial and municipal expenditures and imposing taxes. But this taxing power was limited, and provinces were explicitly prohibited from taxing imports, which were the tax base of the central government. In addition to the usual political conflicts, the fiscal divisions between empire and province were fertile ground for clashes between centralism and federalism, between the court and the provinces.[19]

The imperial fiscal structure was developed by the fiscal laws of 1832 and 1833. The Imperial Budget Law of August 24, 1832, separated and defined expenses, organized bookkeeping procedures, and decreed that the tax income of the imperial and provincial governments be held separately. It also established how the central government would support provincial governments in meeting their costs. The final legal piece establishing the provincial fiscal structure was law 99 of October 31, 1835, which clearly distinguished the central government and provincial spheres of influence over taxation and expenditures. These several acts supported the decentralization process under the regency and created relative autonomy for the budgets and finances of the provinces.[20]

The administrative structure of public finance was defined by a law of 1831 that created the National Treasury Court (Tribunal do Tesouro Nacional). This institution was given ultimate direction and supervision of national income and expenditure, with the Treasury minister serving as its president.[21] The General Treasury (the Tesouraria Geral of the Tribunal do Tesouro) under this court served as its operational agent. The law also established provincial treasuries, subordinate to the National Treasury Court, that collected taxes and carried out expenditures at the provincial level.[22] The law also created an operational structure with the necessary employees to deal with the provincial finances.[23] Public revenues, which until then had been collected by the national treasury, now were divided into general revenue (central government collections) and provincial revenue. The provincial revenue consisted of all taxes not included in the general revenue.[24] Initially, the law stipulated that provincial revenues and expenditures would be fixed by the general councils, from budget proposals submitted by the presidents of the provinces. These budgets would then be approved by the imperial general assembly. When provincial revenues were not enough to cover expenses, the general councils could impose taxes if they did not create a "greater burden on the people." But once provincial assemblies were created by the Additional Act of 1834, the local governments no longer had to send their budget for approval by the imperial court.[25]

The 1833/1834 imperial budget classified expenditures as belonging to either the central government or the provinces.[26] Provinces were responsible for the costs of local government, police, and maintenance of local public institutions like schools, hospitals, prisons, asylums, libraries, and parks. Education and public health were considered a local concern, as was urban street lighting. Roads, bridges, and other public infrastructure and maintenance of local churches and related buildings were under the purview of the provincial government.[27]

A São Paulo provincial law of 1838 created its provincial treasury (the Contadoria Provincial), whose powers and duties included the collection, accounting, monitoring, storage, and distribution of provincial revenues.[28] But creation of an autonomous provincial system took time, and despite the imperial decision to segregate the imperial and provincial tax collections, this did not occur formally until 1848. Even then there was still some overlap of imperial and provincial fiscal administrations until mid-century.[29]

The tithes (*dízimos*) that later became the export tax (*direitos de saída*) represented one of the most important taxes collected by the province of São Paulo. Tithes were due on all types of goods of Paulista production exported beyond the limits of the province. Sugar, cotton, coffee, rice, wheat, and tobacco were the main exports and "would be subject to the payment of tithes only at the time of shipment."[30] These tithes were charged mostly on agricultural goods that left the state.[31] The law of 1835 established that tithes would be due on goods exported beyond the province, but goods exported out of the empire were initially exempt. An 1840 law called this tax on provincial exports the *direitos de saída*, although the tax also retained the name of tithes (*dízimos*). In 1855 the law was modified so that exports to foreign countries would pay the same tithe as those paid on exports to the ports of the empire.[32]

Another important tax was that on animals entering the province. This tax had its origin in a colonial tax and custom house known as the Contribution of Guarapuava, created in 1809 to finance the construction of a road connecting São Paulo to the southern province of Rio Grande do Sul. The tax was supposed to be temporary but remained in existence throughout the first half of the nineteenth century. The most important of these animal import taxes until the mid-1850s was the one charged at the Registro de Passagem do Rio Negro (Rio Negro Registry), an internal, or dry port, customs house. This tax was on animals raised in the southern provinces and brought to the São Paulo market for sale.[33] In 1851, the Contribution of Guarapuava and Registro de Passagem do Rio Negro taxes were replaced by a single tax.[34] In 1853 these two custom houses became part of the independent province of Paraná. After that, the customs post at Sorocaba, which remained within the province of São Paulo, became the key post to tax mules and other animals entering the province.[35]

Next in importance were road taxes, or right-of-way charges, the so-called *barreiras* (barriers) taxes. By the 1840s there were some fifteen of these dry-port customs houses on all the major roads in and out of the province.[36] All goods moving along these roads were taxed to pay for expansion, renovation, and maintenance of roads and bridges.[37] Until the arrival of the railroads, barreiras taxes were a principal source of revenue for the province.[38] Unlike other taxes, these were earmarked for a specific end, that of maintaining and expanding the road system in the areas of influence of each of the barriers.[39]

The barrier taxes and the animal import taxes remained important parts of provincial budgets until the arrival of the railroads. In response to this major change in the transport system, the provincial government in 1872 abolished the barrier taxes and created instead the transit tax (*imposto de transito*) on the movement of persons and goods by the railroads. This tax was paid by passengers and by the railroads for goods shipped. Imported farm machinery was exempt from the tax.[40]

From the colonial period and through the empire several types of taxes based on slave ownership were imposed, from the purchase and sale of slaves to their movement across territories.[41] Important to provincial revenues was the tax on the sale of slaves (called *meia sisa*, or half sales tax).[42] An 1809 law established a 5 percent sales tax on ladino, or Brazilian-born, slaves. Purchases of newly imported African-born slaves were exempted from this tax on their first sale in America. The law stated that this tax would be collected by private individuals,[43] and it became part of the provincial revenue in the separation of imperial from provincial rents in the general budget law of 1831.[44] The law exempted from this tax slaves purchasing their own freedom.[45] Given that the tax was based on the declared sale price, the government established stringent provisions to prevent fraud. If the collector of the sales tax saw that the slaves sold were worth more than 25 percent above the declared price, the seller would be required to sell the slaves to the collector or pay the tax on the value stipulated by the tax collector.[46] Over the course of the century several new taxes were charged on slaves owned.[47] The two most important were the taxes on slaves employed in agricultural and nonagricultural activities, which were created in 1884 to cover the costs of subsidizing European farm labor immigration. Then in 1881 the Special Registry of Slaves (Matrícula Especial de Escravos) was created to tax interprovincial trade of slaves.[48] The prohibitive character of this tax meant that it generated little revenue but virtually paralyzed the internal slave trade, which was the intent of the law.[49]

There were other taxes charged on property that involved bequests, inheritance, and usufruct. The tax on bequests and inheritances (*décima de legados e heranças*) was created in 1809,[50] and it passed to São Paulo's treasury in 1835. The procrastination in doing inventories, however, apparently limited its potential.[51] Again, slaves either purchasing their freedom or receiving bequests to enable them to purchase their freedom were not taxed.[52] The urban building tax (*décima urbana*), created in 1808, charged 10 percent on net income on all occupied urban buildings.[53] It became a provincial tax in 1835, and then in 1842 it was given over to the município governments.[54] In 1881 the urban building and the urban convent taxes were combined into a building tax (*imposto predial*), with the building owner being charged 6 percent of the estimated annual rental value. For buildings belonging to convents and other mortmain corporations, the tax was 10 percent. Exempt were the buildings belonging to the central government, provinces, municipalities, and hospitals and other charities.[55]

There were also a number of taxes imposed on consumption, trade, and economic activities in general. Of these, taxes on slaughtered cattle and consumption, both existing since the first provincial budget of 1835, brought in the most revenue. In the 1850s and 1860s these two taxes went at first to the municipalities but eventually were returned to the control of the province. The provincial income also included rents based on bureaucratic activities and others of a more general character. In 1877 there was added an important Additional Tax (Imposto Adicional), establishing that all objects that were not previously taxed by other means would pay 20 percent. An 1881 law made the Additional Tax permanent and specified that coffee exports be taxed at 10 percent.[56]

Attempts at taxing personal income proved difficult to collect and had little impact. But taxes on business were more feasible. One of these, the so-called capitalist tax (*imposto sobre capitalistas*), created by the province in 1872, taxed each "capitalist" (moneylender) at one hundred mil réis. In the following year it was stipulated that individuals or companies that carried out a foreign exchange or a bank or brokerage operation be taxed.[57]

There were also nontributary fees for using government services such as the Government Printing Office (Tipografia Oficial), using stamped paper, and so on, and even on income from work in prisons. Furthermore, for several years revenue was collected on outstanding debts, on fines paid, and on income from interest earned on imperial bonds purchased by the provincial treasury or from interest earned from this account. In some years there were extraordinary dividends paid on the shares of the state-owned Ituana Railroad Company. Finally, in the 1880s the national government contributed funds for provincial security forces, replacing the failed personal taxes.

Thus, a tax base was being created in the nineteenth century for maintenance of the province of São Paulo. In general, this base was comprehensive, looking to tax economic activities, personal wealth, and the movement of goods, provided that such taxes did not conflict with the tax base of the empire itself. But, as the provincial presidents constantly complained, the limited government tax administration meant that it was confined to taxing easily controlled areas such as the movement of goods in ports and along roads. Attempts to create broader taxes led to high levels of evasion, and direct taxes on salaries and income would not be enacted until the twentieth century. As noted by most of the presidents, this limited fiscal base did not provide adequate funds for provincial investments in security, health, and education. Although the expansion of coffee created a major source of tax revenues, the volatile nature of the coffee market affected the stability of government revenues. The real problem was not so much fluctuating receipts, but overspending beyond the estimated fixed costs of the government. It seems that the provincial government could not withstand pressures for spending that materialized during the fiscal year. In fact, the government budget was not balanced in most years. This was especially the case when railroad subventions and subsidies were involved or, in the 1880s, when European immigration was being subsidized.

Table 2.1 shows the province's estimated and actual expenditure and income and the final results.[58] In the planned budget, except for 1835/1836 to 1839/1840, when the legislature expected a surplus, it expected that expenditures would be greater than income. Actual funds spent and received shows the amount spent or taken in by the province and the resulting balance. In half the periods a modest surplus was produced. Surprisingly, in all the decades, taxes and rents taken in by the state always exceeded what the legislature expected. In contrast, the province spent more than it expected to in half the periods, including two consecutive periods after 1870. The conclusion from this analysis is that the legislature was unduly pessimistic about how high its income would be and unduly optimistic about how low expenditures would be.

The overspending can be explained by unusual developments. In the decade 1870/1871 to 1879/1880, for example, the province estimated a deficit of 1.3 million contos, but the actual expenditure was 2.3 million contos.

TABLE 2.1

Explained Components of the Annual Fiscal Balance, Budgeted and Realized, Roughly by Decade, 1835/1836–1887/1888 (mil réis)

	1835/36–1839/40	1840/41–1849/50	1850/51–1859/60	1861/62–1869/70	1870/71–1879/1880	1880/81–1887/88
Planned budget						
(1) Budget estimated receipts	1,573,051,814	3,436,267,000	7,483,775,242	11,745,459,940	23,242,341,951	30,893,878,797
(2) Budget authorized expenditures	1,568,688,814	4,131,062,207	8,524,920,469	12,171,347,318	24,510,499,431	31,476,801,773
Anticipated balance = (1) − (2)	4,363,000	*-694,795,207*	*-1,041,145,227*	*-425,887,378*	*-1,268,157,480*	*-582,922,976*
Actual funds spent and received						
(3) Total income obtained	1,813,666,621	3,882,223,191	8,567,987,406	12,177,077,300	25,706,861,764	32,672,540,005
(4) Total expenses	1,383,797,045	4,149,043,677	8,415,000,250	11,639,496,521	27,976,447,571	33,101,572,145
Actual effective balance = (3) − (4)	429,869,576	*-266,820,486*	152,987,156	537,580,779	*-2,269,585,807*	*-429,032,140*
Differences between budgeted and actual funds						
Income = (1) − (3)	240,614,807	445,956,191	1,084,212,164	431,617,360	2,464,519,813	1,778,661,208
Expenditure = (2) − (4)	184,891,769	*-17,981,470*	109,920,219	531,850,797	*-3,465,948,140*	*-1,624,770,372*

SOURCE: Departamento de Estatística do Estado, *Anuário estatistico de São Paulo, 1908*, 2:140; Ministério da Agricultura, Indústria e Commercio, *Finanças*, 144–145.

In fact, the province had a surplus in four of the six years of this decade due largely to income coming in at much higher rates than expected. But in 1876/1877 not only was income below expectations, but expenditures were 1.5 million contos more than expected. The report of the president of the province for 1878 explained that this deficit was due to the interest paid on the provincial debt and by the guaranteed interest that was paid to investors in the Paulista railroad companies in that year.[59] The same situation was repeated with a certain frequency throughout the rest of the decade and for most of the next decade because of payment of the guaranteed interest to railroad investors and, at the end of the 1880s, because of the costs of subsidizing European immigration. Servicing provincial debt became an ever-increasing burden on its finances.

How taxes generated income for the state over the course of the century and how they were expended tell us a great deal about the role of the provincial government in the economy of São Paulo. However, detailed item-level information for annual accounts is scarce. So we used annual budget laws approved by the provincial government, which give the estimated income and expenditure information by year. As we have already noted, the actual provincial expenditure often exceeded what was budgeted by the province. This also occurred with income items, but we based our estimates on the average actual income of the previous three years.[60]

Over the course of the nineteenth century the relative share of taxes and rents estimated in the annual budgets varied over time.[61] The export tax (the *direitos de saída*) and the barrier tax dominated income for most of the century, along with the tax on animals, which was significant until mid-century. The export tax remained important in the second half of the century, but the other two lost their significance and were replaced by the railroad transit and inheritance taxes by the 1880s (see Figure 2.3 later in the chapter). The 10 percent tax on goods shipped outside the province represented a growing source of planned revenues, going from 20 percent to 40 percent from 1835 to 1865 and reaching 50 to 60 percent in the last years of the empire. The 1872 railroad transit tax represented more than 20 percent of estimated provincial income in the last years of the empire. In practice it replaced the barrier tax, whose potential income was dramatically reduced by the arrival of the railroads and the tax on animals, mostly mules used in transport until the arrival of the railroads. By 1885–1889 more than 70 percent of provincial estimated income was budgeted to come from just the export tax and the railroad transit tax.[62] The tax on legacies, inheritances, and usufruct and the various forms of property taxes in the period was supposed to account for between 5 and 10 percent of the total budgeted income. The various forms of taxation on the ownership, handling, buying, and selling of slaves were estimated to represent 5 percent of provincial revenues by 1885, but those revenues declined dramatically thereafter until emancipation eliminated them in 1888. Taken together, the taxes on auctions and fashion, vehicles, equestrian companies, and lotteries, liquor, and slaughtered meat remained around 10 percent until mid-century. They declined significantly in the budgeted items in the second half of the nineteenth century because of the end of the taxes levied on brandy and slaughtered cattle. Most of the budgets included an item for outstanding debt collection, usually estimated at below 3 percent of the total expected income. The Additional Tax generally increased its importance from its inception in 1877 and in the last quinquennium was estimated to produce 7 percent of state income (see Table A2.1).

Over time, the province also obtained income derived from the interest on securities it had purchased with surplus funds from previous years[63] and from the dividends on investments in railroads. These incomes were irregular and never represented a significant part of revenues except in the period 1841–1845, when they accounted for 4 percent of proposed income. One suggestion was to use these funds to create a provincial bank, but no bank was ever established, and these funds were used to buy central government bonds. Because of legal considerations, the collection of outstanding debt never represented a significant percentage of revenue.[64]

How accurate are these estimated figures for major sources of income? Did the relative importance of realized income differ from what the province budgeted for that category? This question can be answered for a few select years in which we have both actual receipts by category and the budget estimates of what the government expected to receive. Baron Cotegipe, president of the council of ministers, in 1886 carried out a detailed analysis of provinces' income and expenditures—both estimated and actual—for 1876/1877 to 1885/1886. In our analysis of these figures, we consider just the five years for which we have the approved estimated income budgeted by category and actual income received by category, which permits a comparison between the two.[65] For these five years the estimated and actual values are in reasonable agreement. Export, or exit, taxes represent about half the total collection, and the sums of estimated and actual amounts are very close; considered together, actual income from the railroad transit tax and barrier tax was 19 percent above the estimated amount. In contrast, inheritance taxes came in on average at 82 percent of the budgeted amount (see Table 2.2).

To get an idea of what the major expenses were in the province, we can again use the projected budgets for 1835–1889. Police, education, pub-

TABLE 2.2

Income and Expenditure, Budgeted and Actual, in Province of São Paulo, Selected Years, 1876/1877–1885/1886 (mil réis)

	1876/1877		1877/1878		1880/1881		1884/1885		1885/1886	
	Budgeted	Actual	Budgeted	Actual	Budgeted	Actual	Budgeted	Actual	Budgeted	Actual
Income										
Exit tax and tithes (direitos de saida; dizimos)	1,434,848	1,027,854	1,465,368	1,590,792	1,700,000	1,641,100	1,665,000	2,197,717	1,850,000	1,656,864
Transit and barrier taxes[a]	423,781	442,290	429,744	815,272	898,609	853,783	648,000	1,036,236	993,100	879,403
New tax on animals at Sorocaba	10,184	7,042	8,782	5,124	5,671	73,065	13,500	2,894	17,600	12,037
Port and embarkation fees in Santos	52,118	44,642	55,185	64,193	73,078	76,728	93,000	142,263	130,900	115,550
Meia sisa and other taxes on slaves	166,934	189,232	191,021	194,636	200,000	165,331	100,000	283,590	213,400	155,735
Inheritance taxes	200,765	234,491	279,956	147,930	236,082	212,841	209,800	201,874	205,800	130,728
Tithe on usufruct					47,216	7,228	8,000	21,492	7,050	6,402
Urban property taxes	30,764	36,499	31,843	41,808	43,248	47,344	150,000	194,088	330,000	229,264
Tax on auction houses, etc.	3,692	6,942	6,363	7,487	12,328	5,276	14,100	14,450	15,660	21,570
Additional Tax				293,280	350,000	327,400	80,000	125,536	146,000	135,504
Tax on capitalists	7,485	9,289	11,321	10,143	12,000	7,750	15,600	6,572	17,700	5,200
Fees and stamp paper duty	10,153	9,598	9,666	12,728	20,000	31,617	49,000	40,081	12,000	15,956
New taxes on various products							14,500	12,044	15,200	22,646
Rents from provincial establishments, including penitentiary	21,653	14,773	19,104	13,949	13,611	8,454	9,000	11,661	10,800	10,847

Eventual dividends from Ituana and fines		15,795		93,275		9,721	50,000	65,388	62,000	211,599
Income from indemnifications and fines	12,953		22,341		65,161		5,000	708	80,000	130,573
Eventual income	6,025		5,059		5,365					
Collection of the active provincial debt	21,697	2,269	21,533	2,821	20,000	22,948	30,000	33,172	30,000	32,712
Aid from the central government for public safety	30,000	30,000	30,000	30,000	30,000	30,000	29,500	7,375	29,500	29,500
Total	2,433,052	2,070,716	2,587,286	3,323,438	3,732,369	3,520,586	3,184,000	4,397,141	4,166,710	3,802,090
Percentage of actual total to budgeted total		*85%*		*128%*		*94%*		*138%*		*91%*
Expenditures										
Provincial assembly	47,632	43,821	48,558	46,064	48,558	51,079	62,512	65,074	65,188	72,220
Secretariat of the government	51,249	47,459	49,849	46,208	49,849	51,659	54,904	54,446	52,504	64,044
Costs of taxation and collection of rents	250,985	239,071	245,474	247,006	264,294	324,742	400,522	428,219	344,321	355,058
Public cult, church expenses	73,198	10,524	71,198	12,276	62,514	11,975	15,164	13,653	15,164	14,276
Public security forces	547,231	617,982	547,231	692,311	1,076,089	901,398	980,000	968,939	982,235	1,010,574
Public garden, theater in the capital, monument of Ipiranga	12,100	12,910	12,030	12,399	13,325	13,182	10,605	10,652	10,605	10,953
Hospitals, Santas Casas, leprosy and other asylums and hygiene	46,260	28,054	43,400	28,182	60,000	43,201	50,000	56,284	55,300	64,118
Penitentiary, local jails, etc.	146,486	80,477	135,886	80,282	114,753	90,550	94,825	106,335	93,565	120,526

(continued)

Table 2.2 (continued)

	1876/1877		1877/1878		1880/1881		1884/1885		1885/1886	
	Budgeted	Actual	Budgeted	Actual	Budgeted	Actual	Budgeted	Actual	Budgeted	Actual
Public works	444,000	304,333	444,000	232,534	350,000	333,658	480,000	424,752	551,784	355,724
Tax engineer (roads and railways) and Public Works Division	46,640		65,744		61,044		60,000		54,200	
Public lighting	143,720	149,026	143,000	149,081	169,000	164,270	193,000	176,014	194,200	189,926
State employees, police retirement fund	67,732	67,490	67,732	74,947	93,700	90,492	93,232	94,836	100,081	107,040
Public instruction	510,746	419,479	504,382	424,962	597,096	500,021	630,000	730,010	643,940	809,570
Subsidized immigration and agricultural colonies		1,200					52,680	372,842	213,610	332,529
Catechism of the Indians					1,000	92				
Restitutions, indemnifications, etc.							55,000	17,092	2,000	31,032
Miscellaneous	14,000	8,320	2,000	16	20,500	12,681	20,000	18,273	12,000	14,782
Subtotal (1)	*2,401,979*	*2,030,146*	*2,380,484*	*2,046,268*	*2,981,722*	*2,589,000*	*3,252,444*	*3,537,421*	*3,390,697*	*3,552,372*
Subventions (navigation, etc.)	25,367		25,367		20,000		20,000		21,600	
Passive debt, immigration debt, interest paid and depreciation	100,000				130,000		102,000		123,000	

Administration costs (publications, archive, printing office, etc.)	18,000		25,000		22,000		12,000		8,000	
Guarantee of railroad interest					500,000		440,000		400,000	
Companhia Cantareira de Esgotos									120,000	
Contracts and subventions		49,161		34,863		44,709		31,850		112,744
Various interest payments and differences in exchange rates						669,777		351,772		407,658
Subtotal (2)	*143,367*	*49,161*	*50,367*	*34,863*	*672,000*	*714,486*	*574,000*	*383,622*	*672,600*	*520,402*
Total [(1) + (2)]	2,545,346	2,079,307	2,430,851	2,081,131	3,653,722	3,303,486	3,826,444	3,921,043	4,063,297	4,072,774
Actual expenditure as percentage of budgeted expenditure		*82%*		*86%*		*90%*		*102%*		*100%*
Granting of special credits		29,672		14,824		125,169		405,243		407,946
Expenditures of the legislature		1,967,034		605,322						
General total	2,545,346	4,076,014	2,430,851	2,701,278	3,653,722	3,428,656	3,826,444	4,326,287	4,063,297	4,480,721

SOURCE: Assembleia Legislativa do Estado de São Paulo, leis orçamentárias, various years, http://www.al.sp.gov.br/leis; Cotegipe, *Breve notícia do estado financeiro das províncias*.

[a] We put together the two distinct taxes because there was some confusion of which went to which in the budgets and final income.

lic works, and the maintenance of the tax collection structure were the principal categories. The government institutions (provincial assembly, secretariat of the government, and administrative costs) accounted for some 5 percent of expenditure budgeted. The cost of tax collection included a 7–10 percent charge paid to the private agents collecting these taxes (see Table 2.3).[66]

Public security was one of the largest expenditures of the province, with costs exceeding 15 percent before 1870 and exceeding 25 percent in the last period. Prisons added between 2 and 8 percent to proposed public security expenses. Health and social assistance consisted of sporadic aid to hospitals, including the Leper Hospital, the Santas Casas de Misericórdia, insane asylums, and homes for the indigent, as well as support for campaigns against yellow fever and to promote public hygiene.[67] In 1850 there was an outbreak of yellow fever, and resources were allocated to combating the epidemic.[68] Despite the comprehensiveness of these items, they were usually around 2 percent of expenditures. Education, however, was a significant and growing expenditure. Consisting of old (e.g., public schools, the Normal School, and the School of Painting and Drawing) and new institutions (e.g., the Lyceum of Arts and Crafts), education represented approximately 10 percent of budgeted expenditure at the beginning of the period and approximately 20 percent in the 1880s.[69]

Pensions for government employees show a clear upward trend, reaching just under 3 percent at the end of empire. The so-called Public Worship expenditures—for the maintenance of the Roman Catholic Church in the province—exceeded those for security in the first decade but dropped significantly thereafter, becoming almost negligible in the 1880s. In addition to these expenses, the province provided significant sums for the upkeep of church buildings. There were also other related items of public management budgeted by the province, such as hiring engineers to supervise public works and the railways and the cost of the bureau in charge of public works. These were relatively unimportant, but of increasing importance were provisions for street illumination, which reached 5 percent of expenditures by the 1870s. Expenditures for road and bridge construction varied and were highly correlated with the estimated income from the barrier tax. This meant that the greater the proportion of barrier tax in total revenue, the larger the share of public works investments in total budgeted expenditure.[70]

Once the rail transit tax replaced the road tax, maintaining long-distance dirt roads and bridges connecting to the ports was no longer a priority of the province because they no longer served as the primary means of coffee and human transportation. The priority now was funding railroads, and the expenditure on guaranteed interest payments to the railroads represented a significant and growing category of proposed expenditures from the 1870s, reaching over 10 percent in the five-year period 1881–1885 and dropping to just over half of that in 1886–1889. A new area of budgeted public investment was payment of guaranteed interest to the sewerage construction firm the Companhia Cantareira de Esgotos, which appeared at the end of the empire.[71]

The interest paid on the ongoing passive debt, which reflected the provincial debt service liabilities, remained modest until the mid-1860s, ranging between 3 and 7 percent. In the 1880s the expenditure forecasts were repeated annually and referred to 6 percent interest on the funded debt, interest on current accounts and letters, and the difference in foreign exchange that required payment in gold. In the budget approved in 1888 a high value appeared on the interest for bonds issued to consolidate the provincial debt and for immigration subsidies, which explains the significant increase in debt service in the total value of expenditures.

A major new expense in the 1880s was subsidization of foreign immigration. In February 1888 the province passed a law that authorized the president of the province to hire the Society for the Promotion of Immigration to recruit a hundred thousand immigrants from Europe, the Azores, and the Canary Islands. The government agreed to pay for the tickets of immigrants and their families. The law also provided for payment to aid immigrants who were not recruited. Those who were admitted through the program of the central government would be entitled to the difference between what was paid by the central government and what was paid by the province. The law also authorized the society to administer the special immigrant housing for arriving immigrants. According to the president of the province, none of the services provided by the government in 1888 inspired more interest in the province than the subsidization of immigration.[72]

How effective was the provincial government in estimating these expenses? We use budgets from the same years in the 1870s and 1880s to determine the relationship between estimated expenditures and actual expenditures by type of budget item. If we adopt the same procedure we used with income—that is, summing five years of expenditures—we see that expenditures in government services, education, public safety, and public lighting were close to what was budgeted; on the other hand, health services and the cost of "workhouses, prisons and livelihoods of poor prisoners" were underbudgeted by about 20 percent below actual expenditures. In the

TABLE 2.3

Percentage of Fixed Budget Expenditures by Type of Expenditure in the Province of São Paulo by Quinquennium, 1835–1889

	1835/1840	1841/1845	1846/1850	1851/1855	1856/1860	1861/1865	1866/1870	1871/1875	1876/1880	1881/1885	1886/1889
Government administration											
Provincial assembly	2.97	2.18	2.25	3.16	2.75	3.42	2.23	1.81	1.68	1.62	1.85
Secretariat of the government	1.62	1.46	1.18	1.01	1.82	2.00	2.20	1.75	1.75	1.36	1.40
Collection of taxes	6.47	7.43	8.57	8.72	8.79	9.19	7.86	8.45	8.82	9.44	7.96
Administrative costs (publications, archive tipografia, etc.)	0.76		0.45	0.68	0.15	0.08	0.01	0.73	0.75	0.25	0.05
Administration of justice	7.39	1.65									
Retired employees and retired police	0.58	1.00	0.76	0.78	1.14	1.98	2.13	2.35	2.66	2.45	2.61
Aid to municipal governments		0.13	0.76	0.69	0.50	0.37	0.23				
Government expenses subtotal	*19.79*	*13.85*	*13.97*	*15.03*	*15.14*	*17.04*	*14.66*	*15.08*	*15.65*	*15.12*	*13.88*
Public works, street lighting		0.26	1.76	1.68	1.92	2.43	2.24	5.04	5.28	4.91	3.96
Public works, roads, bridges, canals and custom houses	32.42	48.75	43.96	44.07	45.43	29.54	31.60	27.77	14.35	13.08	11.46
Inspectors (engineers) and repair of public works	0.00	0.10	0.85	1.22	0.86	1.03	0.99	1.82	2.01	1.45	1.33
Companhia Cantareira de Esgotos										1.52	2.99
Interest guarantees for railroads								1.07	5.79	10.65	6.14
Subventions for navigation and other activities						0.95	0.74	0.34	0.82	0.53	0.47
Infrastructure subtotal	*32.42*	*49.11*	*46.56*	*46.97*	*48.21*	*33.95*	*35.57*	*36.03*	*28.25*	*32.13*	*26.35*
Security (Força Policial, barrier police)	15.40	12.30	12.73	14.34	15.45	15.98	19.19	20.21	25.15	24.87	26.14
Casa de Correção, Penitênciaria, prisons and sustenance of poor prisoners	1.30		1.70	2.73	5.49	7.87	8.13	4.97	4.60	2.39	2.22
Public safety subtotal	*16.70*	*12.30*	*14.43*	*17.06*	*20.93*	*23.85*	*27.32*	*25.19*	*29.75*	*27.26*	*28.36*

Church (Culto Público; Matrizes, Catedral, churches)	16.69	13.67	7.57	1.60	1.00	2.63	4.77	3.67	2.40	0.38	0.35
Catechism of Indians	0.70	0.83	0.49	0.41	0.18	0.14	0.03	0.00	0.01		0.06
Church subtotal	*17.39*	*14.51*	*8.06*	*2.01*	*1.18*	*2.77*	*4.79*	*3.67*	*2.41*	*0.38*	*0.41*
Public education	10.48	8.49	13.30	13.81	11.37	13.26	12.44	15.97	18.68	16.15	19.49
Hospitals, santas casas, leprosarium, orphanages, hygiene	0.33	0.39	1.05	0.57	1.14	0.91	1.78	2.83	1.73	1.33	1.67
Education and health subtotal	*10.81*	*8.88*	*14.35*	*14.38*	*12.51*	*14.18*	*14.22*	*18.80*	*20.42*	*17.48*	*21.16*
Passive debt; debt for immigration services, interest and debt payment	1.11	0.47	1.45	0.76	0.44	7.54	2.56	0.00	2.67	2.85	6.74
Miscellaneous	1.08	0.58	0.54	0.46	0.43	0.47	0.73	0.98	0.42	0.41	0.13
Repatriated funds, indemnities, and previous years' accounts								0.03		0.72	0.02
Public debt subtotal	*2.19*	*1.04*	*1.99*	*1.22*	*0.86*	*8.01*	*3.29*	*1.01*	*3.09*	*3.98*	*6.89*
Immigration support for arriving colonos				1.63	0.69					3.38	2.72
Public garden, theater in capital, monument of Ipiranga	0.69	0.30	0.65	1.68	0.47	0.20	0.15	0.22	0.43	0.27	0.23
Total	100.00	100.00	100.00	100.00	100.00	100.00	100.00	100.00	100.00	100.00	100.00
Total expenditure (mil réis)	2,089,733	1,563,508	2,761,076	3,494,542	4,463,188	5,128,181	6,865,752	12,270,986	8,629,919	7,889,741	18,715,646

SOURCE: Assembleia Legislativa do Estado de São Paulo, leis orçamentárias, 1835–1889, http://www.al.sp.gov.br/leis.

case of public works, the actual expenditures were on average 27 percent above the budgeted estimates. Also, the subsidy costs of European immigration were at least two and a half times greater than what the government expected them to be.[73]

Finally, in Baron Cotegipe's figures on expenditure are items called "allocation of special credits" and "expenses at the disposition of the legislature," which were not defined in detail but accounted for some 10 percent of actual expenditures over this five-year period. These two categories, surprisingly, were not included in the estimated budget for 1876/1877. In this same year these undefined extraordinary expenditures reached 49 percent of total actual expenditures, which resulted in actual expenditures being 1.6 times as large as what had been budgeted for that year.[74] The increase in both estimated and actual expenditures in this five-year period, which resulted in increasing public debt, was due to the rising costs of the railroad subsidies and real expenditures for which no taxes or rents had been supplied (see Table 2.2).[75]

In addition to detailed annual data on budgeted expenditures and the size of the provincial government workforce, we also have the excellent presentation made in 1884 by the provincial treasury accountant of São Paulo (Contador do Tesouro Provincial de São Paulo), which provides a more in-depth analysis of the fiscal organization of the state in terms of actual income and expenditure (see Tables 2.5 and 2.6 later in the chapter). In previous fiscal years (1880/1881 to 1882/1883), the major income came from the exit tax, which was 44 percent of the average effective tax collection, 25 percent came from the railroad transit tax, 6 percent from the 10 percent tax on benefits and inheritances, and 5 percent from the Additional Tax, which as we have noted was an extra 2 percent charge added to all other taxes. The barrier tax, which previously represented one of the most important taxes, lost its importance, being replaced by the transit tax, charged on all goods and people using the railways. The 1884/1885 budget's revenue was 13 percent lower than the average revenue of the previous three years because of the reduction of the revenue forecast for the railroad transit tax, which was explained in the report, and of the Additional Tax. There was also a fall in the meia sisa slave sales tax, which had been progressively declining in the previous years.

When examining in detail the estimated and actual expenditures for the fiscal year 1882/1883 the treasurer's report showed that the legislature both overestimated and underestimated collections on individual taxes. But despite these mistaken estimates all these changes seemed to balance each other out, and the difference between provincial estimated income and actual income collected in that year was only 2 percent. Finally, it is worth noting that in this year coffee exports accounted for 97 percent of the export tax on agriculture (the *direito de saida*, or tithe).

The treasurer also found that actual expenditures in 1882/1883 were lower than expected from the estimates. The most important expenditures were for police (24 percent),[76] public education (15 percent), administration and collection of taxes (10 percent), and the interest for bonds (7 percent). Public works represented 15 percent of the total expenditures carried out by the province. Among the major expenditures, a difference between what was planned and what was spent occurred with the overspending on the administration and collection of taxes (+36 percent) and on interest payments (+53 percent).

We can get a picture of the structure of the public debt of the province from the detailed information provided by the treasurer for this same year. The public debt of the province was 6,573 contos, of which 1,200 contos was funded debt and the remaining floating debt. The funded debt was composed of 1,200 debt bonds, each 1,000 mil réis at 6 percent interest. The floating debt (5,373 contos) was composed of several items, the most important being the interest paid by the national treasury to the railroad Companhia São Paulo e Rio de Janeiro, which on June 30, 1883, reached 4,304 contos.[77] This last item represented a liability of São Paulo to the national treasury that honored a bond given for the railroad company that guaranteed interest payments.[78] In 1883 the guaranteed interest paid by São Paulo to railroad investors amounted to 9,557 contos, or about three times the revenue of the province that year (see Table 2.4).

From 1850 to 1888, there was significant real growth in the province's budgeted revenues and expenditures, on the order of 3.7 percent per annum. But the periods 1850–1869 and 1870–1888 have major differences. The first period had an annual revenue growth rate of 3 percent and the second period 5 percent. Also, the ability to balance the budget was beginning to change toward the end of the imperial period. As the provincial president Rodrigues Alves declared in his annual report of 1888, the treasury could have balanced its budget were it not for immigration costs, which were now exceptional and could be met only with special bonds or credit operations.[79]

Another important consideration is whether revenue kept up with the increase in population to find whether the provincial government was able to keep up with the expansion of its tax base over time. In our comparison we also include the changing price of coffee, the primary São Paulo export (see Figure 2.3). In the case of tax income per capita, there is clear evidence

TABLE 2.4

Capital Guaranteed to the Railroads of the Province of São Paulo (contos)

Company	Capital guaranteed	Capital realized	Capital paid to November 30, 1883	Capital amortized as of June 30, 1883	Total state debt to railroads
Bragantina	1,400	1,400	229		229
Ituana	2,500	2,043	1,312		1,312
Mogyana (Mogiana)	5,500	4,777	430	165	265
Paulista	5,000	4,250	401	401	
Sorocabana	5,500	5,500	3,265		3,265
São Paulo e Rio de Janeiro	10,655	10,655	183		183
Total	30,555	28,625	5,820	566	
Interest paid by the national treasury to São Paulo e Rio de Janeiro					4,304
Total	30,555	28,625	5,820	566	9,557

SOURCE: *Fala dirigida à Assemblea Legislativa Provincial de S.Paulo na abertura da 1a. Sessão da 25ª. legislatura, em 16 de janeiro de 1884*, 25.

NOTE: Decree 5.607, April 24, 1874, conceded finances to guarantee the interest paid by the province to São Paulo e Rio de Janeiro.

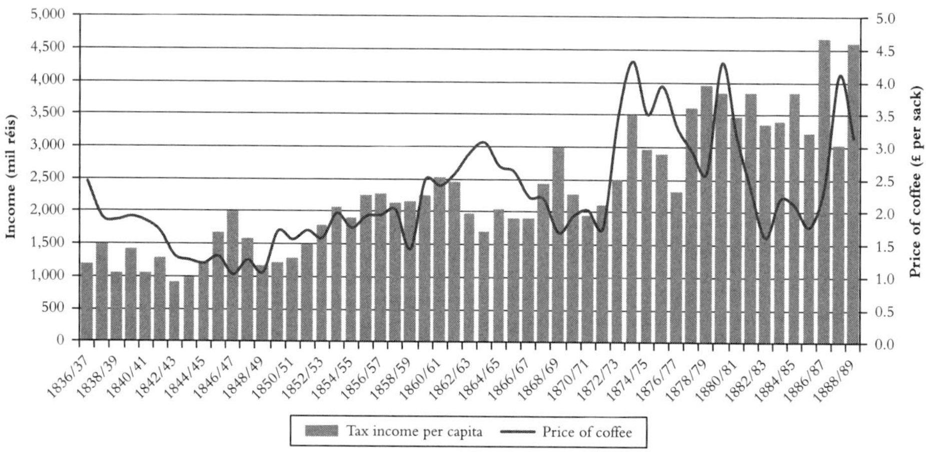

Figure 2.3 Provincial Tax Income per Inhabitant and Price of Coffee, 1836–1889

SOURCE: Instituto Brasileiro de Geografia e Estatística, *Séries estatísticas retrospectivas*, 3:312, table 6.43.

of growth, from an average of 1,306 mil réis between 1836 and 1850 to 2,092 mil réis between 1851 and 1870, finally reaching an average of 3,321 mil réis between 1871 and 1888. The annual variation around these averages was probably due to the strong fluctuation in the price of coffee.

The availability of selected budgets from the neighboring provinces of Minas Gerais and Rio de Janeiro allows us to put São Paulo's provincial budgets into comparative perspective. For Minas Gerais also we have data on estimated income.[80] Table 2.5 shows the estimated income for 1867–1885 in São Paulo and Minas Gerais to be of similar magnitude. In all cases the difference between the two provinces was only between 10 and 15 percent. In both provinces the largest estimated income was expected to come from exports; in the case of São Paulo basically it was the *direitos de saída* (or tax on locally produced agricultural goods leaving the province), and for Minas Gerais, export taxes encompassed manufactured goods, coffee, and other goods created and produced in the province. Imports for Minas Gerais were animals that entered the province (*bestas novas*). In São Paulo, import taxes had been very important in previous years, but after Paraná Province separated, this tax declined for São Paulo. In both cases the various taxes on slaves represented around 10 percent of income, and those on administrative activities accounted for roughly another 10 percent. In neither province was the collection of outstanding debt of any significance.

We have data on Rio de Janeiro expenditures for selected years in the nineteenth century (see Table 2.6). While the proposed expenditures in Rio de Janeiro were two to three times as large as São Paulo's, both provinces spent approximately the same proportion for general administration: on average 6 percent in Rio de Janeiro and 7 percent in São Paulo. The same is true for the costs of collecting taxes—8 percent and 9 percent of budgeted expenditures, respectively. Differences appear in education, with São Paulo spending 3 percent more than Rio de Janeiro. Surprisingly, given that Rio de Janeiro contained the imperial capital, São Paulo spent more on average for police (29 percent of its expenditures) than did Rio de Janeiro (only 20 percent). Public works was more nearly the same in both—a fifth to a quarter of all proposed spending. Public health and social assistance was negligible in Rio de Janeiro but was 2 percent of proposed expenditure in the more southern province. The much larger budgeted payments on loans and for guaranteed interest in Rio de Janeiro is significant, with the lesser costs of São Paulo having to do with timing issues. For São Paulo the big loans came only in the 1870s, for subsidizing interest for railroads. Moreover, big payments would come in the 1890s and 1900s for São Paulo's

TABLE 2.5

Budgeted Income of the Provinces of São Paulo, Minas Gerais, and Rio de Janeiro, 1867–1885 (mil réis)

	1867/1868 value	1867/1868 %	1868/1869 value	1868/1869 %	1874/1875 value	1874/1875 %	1884/1885 value	1884/1885 %
São Paulo								
Export taxes	671,000	54%	722,000	56%	1,934,586	71%	2,438,000	77%
Import taxes	10,000	1%	10,000	1%	12,480	0%	13,500	0%
Production and internal commerce	2,500	0%	2,400	0%	2,395	0%	28,600	1%
Possession and sale of slaves	135,300	11%	133,500	10%	106,325	4%	100,000	3%
Internal circulation	250,900	20%	265,200	21%	384,541	14%	48,000	2%
Administration income	139,200	11%	121,000	9%	232,013	9%	441,400	14%
Active debt and other collections	42,000	3%	33,000	3%	34,102	1%	85,000	3%
Subtotal	1,250,900	100%	1,287,100	100%	2,706,442	100%	3,154,500	100%
Aid from the central government and bond sales							29,500	
Total	1,250,900		1,287,100		2,706,442		3,184,000	
Minas Gerais								
Export taxes	590,508	43%	671,106	45%	928,756	41%	1,889,989	53%
Import taxes	324,715	23%	251,211	17%	332,622	15%	752,417	21%
Production and internal commerce	118,759	9%	109,792	7%	167,580	7%	261,482	7%
Possession and sale of slaves	158,739	11%	165,935	11%	411,520	18%	116,640	3%
Internal circulation	24,639	2%	26,529	2%	2,622	0%	53,372	1%
Administration income	131,448	9%	184,304	12%	375,633	17%	361,026	10%
Active debt and other collections	35,055	3%	93,804	6%	39,416	2%	128,913	4%
Total	1,383,863	100%	1,502,681	100%	2,258,149	100%	3,563,839	100%

Rio de Janeiro								
Export taxes	1,436,929	53%	1,534,177	55%	2,080,000	37%	2,482,296	40%
Production and internal commerce	136,514	5%	130,900	5%	133,260	2%	242,120	4%
Possession and sale of slaves	289,304	11%	266,826	10%	168,673	3%	324,000	5%
Internal circulation	79,911	3%	66,973	2%	68,295	1%	100,510	2%
Administration income	504,602	19%	496,323	18%	540,424	10%	773,230	12%
Active debt and other collections	240,005	9%	313,418	11%	2,594,127	46%	2,307,029	37%
Subtotal	2,687,265	100%	2,808,617	100%	5,584,779	100%	6,229,185	100%
Aid from the central government and bond sales		0%		0%		0%	30,000	0%
Total	2,687,265	100%	2,808,617	100%	5,584,779	100%	6,259,185	100%

SOURCE: For São Paulo data, see Assembleia Legislativa do Estado de São Paulo, leis orçamentárias, 1867–1885, http://www.al.sp.gov.br/leis/; for Minas Gerais data, see Mendes and Godoy, "Finanças públicas da província de Minas Gerais"; for Rio de Janeiro data, see Laemmert, *Almanak administrativo, mercantil e industrial.*

Table 2.6

Budgeted Expenditure of the Provinces of Rio de Janeiro and São Paulo, 1848–1882 (contos)

	1848/1849	1853/1854	1854/1855	1868/1869	1869/1870	1873/1874	1877/1878	1882/1883
Rio de Janeiro								
General administration	68	47	98	206	245	470	469	370
Costs of collecting taxes	141	112	180	275	272	330	437	406
Maintenance of the church	44	12	13	12	24	24	24	24
Education	94	147	150	275	319	837	852	926
Public works	250	400	392	1,176	738	1,567	472	598
Police forces	125	195	243	376	366	625	591	710
Payment on loans and interest	322	373	373	495	445	1,884	617	914
Purchase of Estrada de Ferro Cantagalo								1,393
Public health and social assistance	27	42	42	1	1	1	1	1
Public lighting				33	33	72	120	110
Subtotal	1,070	1,328	1,490	2,849	2,444	5,810	3,585	5,451
Miscellaneous	80	76	63	560	664	595	727	807
Total	1,150	1,404	1,553	3,409	3,108	6,405	4,312	6,258
São Paulo								
General administration	31	41	57	89	99	159	201	195
Costs of collecting taxes	59	75	59	105	188	222	245	264
Maintenance of the church	61	20	10	33	40	157	71	63
Education	76	93	94	198	211	411	504	597
Public works	235	317	374	496	480	659	444	350
Police forces	79	123	150	429	447	708	751	1,285
Payment on loans and interest	7	9	11	70	24			630
Public health and social assistance	5	5	4	25	30	63	43	60
Public lighting	8	11	11	37	34	138	143	169
Subtotal	560	692	769	1,482	1,552	2,518	2,403	3,612
Miscellaneous	5	6	40	23	28	18	27	42
Total	564	699	809	1,505	1,580	2,536	2,431	3,654

SOURCE: Gouvêa, *O império das províncias*, table 4; Assembleia Legislativa do Estado de São Paulo, leis orçamentárias, various years, http://www.al.sp.gov.br/leis.

subsidization of immigration and the early twentieth-century government program to control coffee prices. In contrast to São Paulo, Rio de Janeiro was far more dependent in this period on loans to meet expenses.

Finally, we return to the question of how important Paulista provincial income and expenditure were for the central government treasury compared to other provinces of the empire.[81] The economic evolution of São Paulo and its importance in the empire can be evaluated by the significance of its income in the total of all provincial incomes and expenditures collected and spent by the central government. São Paulo's share of all provincial incomes stood at just 2 percent between 1830 and 1860 but increased significantly in the next thirty years, reaching a high of 8.4 percent in the last decade of the empire. Interestingly, the province was a net source of funds for the empire from 1830 to 1889, accounting for 5.3 percent of imperial revenue but only 1.8 percent of imperial expenditures (see Table 2.7). The provinces of Paraná, Bahia, Pernambuco, Rio de Janeiro, and Maranhão contributed about the same amount, but São Paulo was the largest donor in terms of what it generated for the central government and what the central treasury spent locally, receiving from the imperial capital only 35.8 percent of the amount collected there between 1830 and 1880. In absolute amounts, the net transfer of Pernambuco and Bahia each surpassed the net transfer of São Paulo. The net income of the court itself was more than the sum of the payment of central government taxes made by São Paulo, Bahia, and Pernambuco. The court over the course of the nineteenth century absorbed two-thirds of the total funds raised by the empire. Because of the power imbalance, the southern region, which included the court, was a net receiver of tax resources and the north and northeast were net donors of fiscal resources.[82]

Another way to highlight the importance of São Paulo in the national context is through the general and provincial revenue obtained in its territory. In São Paulo in fiscal year 1886/1887, the total of both national and provincial taxes was 14,895 contos, or 17 percent of total national and provincial revenues, the highest collected that year in all the provinces. Some 65 percent of this 14,895 contos was national taxes. If we consider only the provincial revenue, São Paulo accounted for 15 percent of total provincial tax revenues of the various provinces and was surpassed only by Rio de Janeiro, with 17 percent of the total (see Table 2.8).

The budgets at the end of the imperial period finally provide detailed information on the costs and size of the provincial government. São Paulo had the most employees in tax collection, public safety, and education. In the 1888/1889 budget, the provincial treasury had a total of thirty-six

TABLE 2.7

Actual Income and Expenditure for the Empire in São Paulo, 1830–1889

	Imperial income or expenditure	Income from or expenditure in São Paulo	Percentage from or in São Paulo
Imperial income (contos)			
1830–1839	125,938	2,441	1.9%
1840–1849	220,843	4,711	2.1%
1850–1859	402,478	8,662	2.2%
1860–1869	639,571	21,667	3.4%
1870–1879	1,057,409	53,110	5.0%
1880–1889	1,300,299	109,224	8.4%
Imperial income and expenditure (pounds sterling)			
Total income	355,268	18,947	5.3%
Total expenditure	367,832	6,781	1.8%

SOURCE: Diniz, "Centralização política e concentração de riqueza."

TABLE 2.8

Actual Imperial and Provincial Receipts, 1886/1887 (contos)

Province	Period	Imperial	Provincial	Total	Province %
São Paulo	1886/1887	9,659	5,237	14,895	17%
Bahia	1886/1887	10,885	3,047	13,932	16%
Pará	1887	9,029	3,961	12,989	15%
Pernambuco	1886/1887	10,126	2,715	12,841	14%
Rio Grande do Sul	1886/1887	7,379	2,807	10,186	11%
Rio de Janeiro	1887	1,284	6,017	7,302	8%
Minas Gerais	1886/1887	1,660	3,410	5,071	6%
Maranhão	1886/1887	2,237	716	2,953	3%
Amazonas	1886/1887	961	1,939	2,900	3%
Ceará	1887	1,173	977	2,149	2%
Alagoas	1886/1887	928	742	1,670	2%
Paraná	1887	548	969	1,517	2%
Sergipe	1886/1887	383	800	1,183	1%
Santa Catarina	1886/1887	783	374	1,157	1%
Paraíba	1887	395	523	918	1%
Espirito Santo	1887	306	439	745	1%
Mato Grosso	1887	395	228	623	1%
Rio Grande do Norte	1886/1887	178	391	569	1%
Piauí	1886/1887	271	273	544	1%
Goiás	1886/1887	61	240	301	0%
Total		53,643	35,804	89,446	100%

SOURCE: Cotegipe, *Breve notícia do estado financeiro das províncias*, table 3.
NOTE: There is no data for the Court itself, which generated the majority of the income.

functionaries, who cost an estimated 89 contos, of which 90 percent represented salaries and commissions. The tax office of the provincial treasury had seven functionaries, and the other tax offices (*mesas de rendas*) in Ubatuba, Sorocaba, and Itararé had another six among them. The largest group of Treasury employees were the forty-six soldiers deployed at barrier posts; they cost 32 contos. A large budgeted expenditure item was the percentage on receipts given to tax collection agents. In the case of the tax office of the provincial capital, the budget estimated payment of 7 percent on an estimated 250 contos to be collected, which amounted to 17.5 contos. In addition, the budget added an expenditure of 208 contos for collection of revenues at railway stations. The budget contained a total expenditure of 391 contos for collecting taxes in all areas, which represented 8 percent of the total budgeted expenditure for 1888/1889.[83]

Public security was another major part of the government.[84] For 1877/1878 the province had 680 men in its police force, including officers. The so-called urban companies had another 120, of both police and firefighters. Ten years later the police force had increased to 1,493 men. The urban companies had been split into urban police companies, with 242 men, and the capital fire section, with 42 men. The budget allocated 1,016 contos for annual salaries for the provincial police force, 171 contos for the urban police companies, and 23 contos for the firefighters. Other expenses included 138 contos for uniforms and 5 contos for armaments and equipment (see Table 2.9).

The third major expected expenditure at the end of the empire was for public education. Throughout the nineteenth century major changes were made as to which institutions belonged to this area of expenditures. We put into this category public instruction schools, the lyceums, the Normal School, the Vocational School for Apprentices (Seminário de Educandos/as, which housed male and female orphans and poor youth), and the School of Drawing and Painting. In the 1886/1887 budget total educational expenditures were estimated at 830 contos, of which 9 contos were for the staff and relevant expenses of the office of the Inspector General of Education; 27 contos for the personnel and other expenses of the Normal School; 459 contos for the 518 male public school teachers, and 315 contos for the 359 female primary public school teachers. There was a provision for 20 contos for school furniture, books, and supplies. The Seminário da Gloria was to receive 31 contos, of which 24 contos were for food and clothing for a hundred apprentices; 12 contos were for the Lyceum of Arts and Crafts and 4 contos for the Seminário Episcopal.[85]

TABLE 2.9
Structure of the Police Force of the Province of São Paulo, 1877/1878 and 1888/1889

BUDGET YEAR 1877/1878		BUDGET YEAR 1888/1889		SALARY (MIL RÉIS)	
Position	Number of personnel	Position	Number of personnel	Monthly	Daily
Police corps					
ESTADO MAIOR					
Comandante, tenente coronel	1	Coronel Comandante	1	300	
Capitão-mandante	1	Major fiscal	1	200	
Tenente-cirurgião	1	Capitão cirurgião	1	220	
Alferes ajudante	1	Tenente ajudante	1	116	
Alferes quartel-mestre	1	Tenente quartel-mestre	1	116	
Alferes secretário	1	Tenente-secretario	1	116	
ESTADO MENOR					
Sargento ajudante	1	Sargento ajudante	1		2.20
Sargento quartel-mestre	1	Sargento quartel-mestre	1		2.20
Mestre de Música	1	Mestre de Música	1	18	2.20
Corneta-mor	1	Corneta-mor	1		2.20
Musicos	18	Musicos	24		1.60–1.80
COMPANIES					
Tenente comandante	14	Capitão Comandante	7	155	
Alferes	12	Alferes	7	96	
1os. Sargentos	4	1os. Sargentos	7		2.10
2os. Sargentos	8	2os. Sargentos	14		2.00
Forrieis	4	Forriel	7		1.90
Cabos	24	Cabos	42		1.85
Cornetas	4	Cornetas	14		1.80
Soldados	582	Soldados	1,361		1.80
Total police force	680	Total police force	1,493		
Urban companies					
Comandante, capitão	1	Comandante, capitão	1		
Alferes	1	Alferes	1		
1os. Sargentos	4	1os. Sargentos	5		
2os. Sargentos	4	2os. Sargentos	5		
Guardas	110	Soldados	230		
Total urban companies	120	Total urban companies	242		

SOURCE: Law 61, May 12, 1877; law 27, March 10, 1888.

NOTE: Urban companies include city police and firemen. In 1888/1889 the firefighters composed a separate section, with 1 comandante, 1 alferes, 5 first sargentos, 5 second sargentos, and 30 firemen.

Added to the data on the number and salaries of provincial government employees that appear in some nineteenth-century documents, the 1888/1889 budget gives more complete information on the total of state employees. The annual remuneration of provincial government employees was primarily by salary and a bonus corresponding to 50 percent of the annual value of their salaries. The salary of the highest-paid functionaries, heads of departments, was above 5,000 mil réis. The professors of the Normal School were to be paid between 2,400 and 3,600 mil réis; the total remuneration of the professors of the public schools varied between 900 and 2,200 mil réis, depending on their position, courses taught, and level of the school. Some civil servants who were directly related to tax collection received an annual salary plus a percentage of the funds collected, but it is unclear how this commission was divided among them.

Despite the increasing expenditures on education, Rodrigues Alves, president of the province and future president of the republic, stated in his 1888 report that the development of public education had not kept pace with the growth of the province. He noted that there were 1,030 schools, of which 805 were provided with teachers, with 26,939 students enrolled and 20,596 attending classes. He said that compared to previous years these figures showed that there was little progress made in this important branch of the public service and that without massive effort of public and private institutions this lamentable situation would not change.[86]

A subset of the fiscal history of the province is the special budgets for the capital city of São Paulo. Although the local municipal councils had administrative autonomy, municipal budgets depended on the approval of the provincial legislature. Municipal budgets, even for the capital, were quite small compared to the provincial budgets. In 1851/1852, for example, the city's revenues were estimated at around 6 contos, compared to an estimated revenue of over 400 contos for the province; in 1885/1886, the difference declined but was still a very significant one-fourteenth: 290 contos against 4,167 contos for the province. A detailed analysis of the 1885/1886 budget of the capital reveals that the majority of its receipts came from taxing local businesses and activities. This included business taxes on grocery stores, textile and notions stores, the sale and consumption of products (fresh meat, liquor and alcoholic beverages, etc.), the possession and handling of vehicles (such as carts, vehicles with movable axles), the exercise of activities in general (permits for practicing an occupation or opening a business), municipal ordinances (putting up walls, placing signs on houses, etc.), rents of public services (use of the municipal cemetery, measurement of weights and measures), and rental of municipal-owned buildings. In

1885/1886 approximately 250 different sources of municipal income were budgeted, with most being insignificant and sixteen accounting for over two-thirds of the proposed revenue. In that year, the largest source of income was expected to come from taxing wholesale and retail stores, fresh meat, the circulation of goods, and the ownership of wagons in general. Alone, these four items accounted for a third of municipal revenue. The urban property tax, which subsequently represented an important part of municipal revenues, still belonged at that time to the provincial treasury. In the fiscal year 1885/1886, the main expenses planned for the city of São Paulo were public works (34 percent), debt repayment (14 percent), street cleaning and transportation of waste (7 percent), and eminent domain land purchases (7 percent).[87] These four items consumed 61 percent of the estimated income to be collected by the municipality.[88]

It is evident from these data that over the course of the nineteenth century an autonomous government with an independent fiscal structure slowly emerged in the provinces. But these local provincial governments developed within a highly centralized political and administrative system. The conflict of the taxing powers was permanent because of the division of the imperial and provincial taxes and their similar tax base. The national government had under its control all the standard older taxes and did not allow taxation of trade between provinces. It reserved for itself all taxes levied on imports and exports. Despite this prohibition, provincial taxes were created in São Paulo (such as the charges put in place on the road barriers, which taxed the movement of goods, including goods moving between provinces), even a tax on exportable agricultural products (*direitos de saída*), levied in the form of tithing. With this budgetary autonomy and the creation of the provincial assemblies, the provinces were gradually creating autonomous administrative structures.

The detailed analysis of provincial finances that we provide shows that the tax base of the province changed over time. Initially, the province could collect only taxes that were focused on fixed points, such as the barriers in the roads, the tithes (*direitos de saida*) on agricultural production leaving the farms, and rights of way. These taxes maintained a steady share of the total income budgeted of around 75 percent of the collection. In the 1870s and onward the barrier taxes would be replaced by a railway tax on goods and passengers that would in turn become the primary source of provincial revenues. Other taxes on property; on transactions such as slave sales; on economic activities or consumption, such as the taxes on brandy and slaughtered beef; and on auction houses and clothing stores were a fourth or less of all funds collected.

In the case of budgeted expenditures, the concentration occurred in well-defined areas. Education and public safety showed increasing expenditures, explaining 30–50 percent of total expenses in the second half of the century. Provincial administration, considering only the provincial assembly, the government departments, and the tax collection administration, represented approximately 10 percent of the budget. Public works expenditures, which remained very important until the 1850s, systematically declined because of the increasing loss of road-barrier income, which had been both the main source of its income and the biggest source of its expenditures. Nevertheless, until the arrival of the railroads these roads, especially those linking production areas to ports of embarkation, were extremely important for the provincial economy. On the other hand, revenues related to exports and the railroad transit tax that replaced the barrier tax as a source of revenue grew dramatically as a result of all this government investment in railroads. The taxes on rail movement of goods and persons provided strong stimulus to railroad construction, which revolutionized the communications of São Paulo in the late nineteenth century. The guaranteed-interest payments from the government on capital investments in the railroads proved fundamental in developing this transport infrastructure. As a result, in the second half of the century the servicing of the provincial debt and the guaranteed minimum interest granted to the water and sanitation utilities and railroad companies gained importance and explained 15 percent of spending by the 1880s.

Despite its limited capacities, the province of São Paulo under the empire was able to support the deployment of an extensive rail network; construct roads, bridges, and ports; initiate potable water and urban sanitation projects; and start the European immigration process to replace slaves. Still within the framework of the empire, São Paulo would create the conditions that permitted the subsequent state government in the first decades of the twentieth century to lead the economic process of the country. Nor did the province have to rely on only its own resources, as the empire showed itself willing to intervene in the provincial economy when necessary to preserve its economic activity and its main sources of income.[89] We can see from these fiscal data that the São Paulo economy was growing quite rapidly, especially in the last decades of the empire, and its taxes, both imperial and provincial, were becoming the single most important source of revenue for the central government.

This experience with the provincial government of São Paulo convinced the Paulista elite of the need to create an even more powerful and autonomous state government once the republic was proclaimed. Under the regime established in 1889, they were able to create a state government in total control of its own executive. This government was rapidly equipped with professional administrators who in turn would develop a modern state structure in everything from education and public health to its own military force. This state government quickly emerged as the most powerful and modern in republican Brazil.

Chapter 3

Government and Public Finance in the Old Republic, 1889–1930

The Brazilian monarchical regime was a unitary state, with a high degree of political centralization along with some local administrative autonomy. The republican regime that followed it reversed that centralization and opted for a far more decentralized state. The first republican constitution created the most complete federal system that ever existed in Brazil, with a high degree of autonomy given to the states. No subsequent republican constitution in Brazil proposed such a decentralization of political and economic power as this one. Given São Paulo's leadership in the coffee economy, it defended this extreme decentralization, because it could act with autonomy and create a powerful and quasi-independent state government, which then defended the state's multiple economic interests at the local and national levels.

Much of this Paulista demand for local autonomy had to do with what the local elite thought was a lack of support from the imperial government during the period of massive expansion of the state's economy in the second half of the nineteenth century. They felt that the imperial government was more concerned with the Northeast planter class and with the growing economy of the Federal District and the state of Rio de Janeiro than it was with the needs of São Paulo. For this reason the coffee barons felt that local control would allow the state to play a greater role in defending and expanding the coffee economy.

These São Paulo coffee barons and their allies formed an elite that was made up of a surprisingly high ratio of university graduates—92 percent had a tertiary education, with almost two-thirds having a degree from the São Paulo law school. Some 43 percent of its members were related through family ties, and more than a third shared a single complex network of kinship and business ties. Though almost all were born Catholic, they were primarily secularized Catholics. One powerful leader, twice governor of the state, was even an avowed atheist. In short, by the standards of the day in Brazil, this elite was a very coherent, highly educated, and secular group with a great deal of business and farming experience and, more than most Brazilian elites in other states, with significant international experience. Two-thirds of them resided in the capital city of São Paulo, and the rest were scattered throughout the state. In fact, 51 percent of the fazendeiros in this class resided in the capital, but in the rural areas many resided in municípios other than the one they were born in, reflecting the constant expansion of the coffee economy ever westward. This elite had multiple occupations, including administrative and commercial ones as well as the usual political ones, and were deeply involved in the local economy. This cohesion, education, secular worldview, and intense involvement in the coffee economy explain the extraordinary dynamism of the Paulista elite.[1] Moreover, the control the elite exercised over the state Republican Party and a complex set of município bosses guaranteed a tight relation between the state government, the elite, and the regional political base, creating a coherent and powerful governing structure.[2]

The state structure that was created by this local elite and how it was financed is the basic theme of this chapter. In later chapters we show how these government institutions developed policies that affected the welfare of its citizens and how and why the state of São Paulo emerged as a national leader in many areas, providing modern electricity and a major industrial base and creating the most advanced education and health policies and institutions in the nation. Here we show the formal structure of the powerful and semiautonomous state government that the elite created and how the state generated the taxes and fees to pay for these developments. Finally, the educational institutions that the state now promoted and the creation of a large and complex state bureaucracy that it established led to the rise of a new middle class with the skills to create a modern state apparatus.[3]

The republican revolution of 1889 ushered in a completely new era of provincial government and state finances for São Paulo. For the first time, the state gained major control over its taxes and was allowed to establish its own apparatus with a great deal of autonomy. Its ability to tax its international exports gave it a massive infusion of income, which the coffee elite of the state used to establish a modern state government along the lines of European and North American models. An independent state treasury was established, statistics were gathered by all the major state agencies, and courts and police and state education institutions were developed, and they all survived until the 1930 revolution. All this was in response to the tremendous growth of the state economy at the end of the empire and the beginning of the republic. Coffee now dominated São Paulo and the new republic. Moreover, the shift to a free labor market economy created an industrial sector and a modern metropolis within the state. Also, the elite now had to deal with anarchist, socialist, and syndicalist ideologies arriving with these immigrants. The so-called social question would become of major importance as strikes and social conflict now became the norm within this formerly rural slave-based economy and society.[4] Building roads and providing primary education alone were insufficient to meet the needs of these wage workers. Investments in secondary education, health, and social assistance also became major concerns if the state was to prosper and prevent anarchy. It also invested heavily in public safety forces, creating a well-armed and powerful state police force.

The overthrow of the monarchy was supported by the Paulista elite. Despite the increasing importance of the province in the national economy, the imperial government did not have the finances to fully accommodate the needs of the complex coffee economy. The Paulista coffee barons were thus increasingly hostile to a centralizing imperial government in which they had only limited representation and their interests were not fully supported. Although the republican movement already existed among professionals in cities before the 1870s, after the 1870s it gained momentum when it began to include the participation of conservative groups. This was the case of the Paulista Republican Party, created in 1873, which soon incorporated the coffee bourgeoisie of São Paulo.[5] Although the movement's primary interest was creating a republic, the Paulista elite was also committed to creating a federalist system.[6] The São Paulo coffee bourgeoisie wanted autonomy and strong control over the provincial government so as to access its power and resources to promote local economic growth. Although they supported slavery, they were the slave-holding class most willing to consider alternative labor and were willing to abandon the empire in the name of greater power for themselves. Although the army initially led the republican government, internal conflicts in the officer class soon opened the way for the civilian oligarchies to come to power, and they maintained that power virtually uncontested until 1930.[7]

The first republican constitution enshrined the liberal federalist ideas proposed by the Paulista elite by granting broad autonomy to the states.[8] The provinces were transformed into states, and to the states were granted the mines and vacant lands situated within their respective territories. States could conclude agreements and nonpolitical adjustments between themselves and had the powers and rights that were not explicitly denied them by the federal constitution. The central government held the exclusive power to tax imports and maintain custom houses (*alfândegas*); it also controlled shipping and the mails and had the right to create banks with powers to print currency. The constitution prohibited states from enacting taxes on interstate commerce or movement of people. However, the states had exclusive jurisdiction over taxes on export of goods from state production, on urban and rural properties, and on industries and professions and the right to charge the stamp tax for acts emanating from their governments and state resident businesses. In addition, the states could create other income, provided they did not contradict the rights and powers of the central government.[9] The states were barred from establishing, subsidizing, or restraining the exercise of religious cults, and Brazil declared itself a secular nation. The constitution defined further that states would be organized in a way that secured the autonomy of its municípios "in all matters concerning their peculiar interest."[10] On the economic front, the constitution gave the states not only broad powers to tax exports but also the right to take loans and act as an entrepreneur or promoter of policies appropriate to their economic development.

In São Paulo, the constitution created the conditions for strengthening the power of the coffee bourgeoisie, who took control of the politics and administration of the state.[11] In addition, the coffee bourgeoisie soon established powerful control over the federal government. This was especially the case from the time of the Manuel Ferraz de Campos Sales presidency (1898–1902) onward. He represented the arrival of civilians to political power after the political and economic turmoil the country experienced in the first years of the republic, which included the economic bubble of the Encilhamento. Campos Sales established economic stability and carried out a successful economic stabilization program, implemented by his Treasury minister Joaquim Murtinho. He also created the "policy of the governors," which gave direct power to the regional elites, above all to those of São Paulo and Minas Gerais, to name the president of the republic.[12] The policy of the governors reserved political power to local oligarchies. In São Paulo this consisted of the coffee bourgeoisie, whose interests were not limited to coffee production but also embraced railroad transport;

commercial activities, particularly in foreign trade; public services; banks; and industrial production.[13] Their multiple interests, along with the increasing complexity of São Paulo society with the entry of immigrants and the expansion of its major urban centers, were reflected in state policies and state finances and would find support in the federal government now under their control.

In the Old Republic, the coffee interests predominated in São Paulo because they represented the economic base of the state and provided its main source of revenue. They sought to structure a powerful state government to support their economic and social interests. The period of the Old Republic thus marked the creation of a large and complex state bureaucratic organization, which would leave lasting marks on São Paulo society.[14] If before the provincial government had supported the establishment of railroads and tried to promote immigration, the republican state government now counted on greater legal and financial autonomy to engage in many other actions in these and other key areas that would eventually give São Paulo the economic leadership of the country.

The new state governments established an autonomous tax structure, a powerful judiciary, an independent police force, and an important and complex system of institutions for education, health, and even basic scientific research. This powerful state government became the basis for a complex institution that could accompany the major changes in the economy and society of São Paulo. The early years of the Old Republic saw a major effort go into organizing the state structure. Although the revolution of 1930 and the 1964 military coup shifted the balance of power back to the central government, the states maintained strong fiscal and administrative powers that were even amplified in the democratic constitution of 1988.

From the beginning of the republic, great attention in São Paulo was given to the elaboration of the new tax structure of the state and particularly the organization of the state Secretariat of Finance, which would collect taxes and manage public resources but also was charged with administering key economic programs in the state. The treasury oversaw the coffee valorization policy.[15] The organization of the treasury was established by decree in 1892. It specified that the administration of the state finances would be exercised by the state president, through the intermediary of the state's Secretariat of Finance, which had under its direct control the state treasury and tax collection agencies. The decree established a civil service with examinations for functionaries of these fiscal institutions and required its staff to be professionally trained. A decree of 1896 consolidated the structure of the state treasury and that of the court of the state treasury, establishing a strong hierarchical bureaucracy. The decree reinforced the importance of technical training for candidates for all treasury positions and established the job hierarchy and pay.[16] The deepening of the bureaucratization process and technical competence occurred with another law of 1900, which required establishing procedures and competitive tests and demanded that tax attorneys be law graduates. These in turn were preferred over those who simply practiced law. Graduates of the Escola Politécnica de São Paulo could be appointed without examination.

The state treasury for all its newly developed organization faced difficulties in collecting taxes. The director general of the treasury often reported that the structure of tax collection was inadequate and that collection centers needed to be expanded to increase revenues. Initially, there was also the difficulty in finding qualified personnel to man the collection centers.[17] Another problem was tax evasion. As coffee represented the fundamental income of the Paulista treasury, coffee tax evasion was a major concern. But slowly these issues were resolved, and the volume of income generated by the state would increase over time.

In addition to the typical functions of collection and efficient management of public resources, the Secretariat of Finance, as we note, also played a key role in the administration of coffee policy, thus holding a position of great political importance, just below that of the provincial president.[18] The coffee valuation policy under his control gradually strengthened the power of the Secretariat of Finance, to whom were subordinated the institutions that would be created to manage this process.[19] This connection of the Secretariat of Finance to state coffee policy was in large part driven by fiscal concerns. State tax income came primarily from the taxes on coffee exports, whose value fluctuated, depending on annual unpredictable crop production, international prices, and a floating exchange rate. It was in the interest of the Paulista government to create greater stability in the value of coffee exports so as to maintain greater stability in its tax revenue and, therefore, provide greater predictability in government spending. As the state's president, Jorge Tibiriçá, declared in 1905, "As long as . . . the crisis in our large farming sector exists, it will affect the major source of our budget revenue . . . duties on exports of coffee."[20]

Later, when needed, several entities were created to support the management of coffee policy, particularly in the 1920s. The Paulista Institute for the Permanent Defense of Coffee and the State Bank of São Paulo were two institutions established with the object of controlling state coffee production.[21] The bank would finance coffee defense operations. The institute, run by a board chaired by the treasury minister, controlled the arrival and shipment of coffee at the port of Santos. The same 1924 law that created the institute established the tax on transport, which included coffee transiting state territory, which would serve as collateral for a loan to stockpile coffee as part of the permanent defense of coffee.

Besides the structuring of the tax collection system, various organs and institutions were created or reformed in the early years of the Old Republic to meet the needs of running a state with administrative autonomy. According to the federal constitution of 1891, the local judiciary became a state responsibility, and the federal judiciary considered only cases in which the central government was involved or constitutional issues were a concern. The former Courts of Appeal of the Provinces were replaced by the Courts of the States (Tribunais de Justiça dos Estados), representing the highest state court of common justice.[22] The 1891 constitution did not address directly the state judiciary but allowed each state to be governed by its own constitution and laws subject to the constitutional principles of the union, and it stated that the judiciary would be made up of local judges and juries.[23] The state created a justice tribunal composed of judges who were appointed by the president and nominated from among the most senior magistrates of the state. By 1893 the judicial establishment was in place, and state civil and criminal codes had been established. Local court judges and prosecutors were installed in the ninety municípios of the state, and an attorney general and public prosecutors were appointed.

The local police authority also fundamentally changed under the republic. Whereas the provincial police (*força pública*) had been under imperial control and often subsidized by the central state, in the republic the police in São Paulo became a totally state-controlled entity.[24] In the Old Republic oligarchic conflicts were often solved by federal intervention. Even powerful states like São Paulo could suffer such interventions, which explains the state's effort to maintain a strong police force, not only to maintain internal security but also to protect against threats from the central government or other states.[25] The state government contracted a French military group in 1906 to provide military training to the state police force. Officers of state police, from 1910 onward, were paid salaries at or above the salaries of officers in the federal army.[26] In 1896 the São Paulo police force was reorganized into a police brigade, a civil guard for the interior, and a civil guard for the capital. All three were subordinated to the president of the state. The brigade maintained order and security in the capital, Santos, and Campinas and was composed of three infantry battalions, a cavalry regiment, and a fire department. The civil guard of the interior policed the entire state, except for the three major cities.[27] The Civil Guard (Guardia

Civil), or civil police, was in turn created under the empire in 1841, reorganized in 1897, and strengthened in 1905 under the republic with the establishment of formal career structure. It acted as a local police force for local crimes and public order primarily in the capital and the other major cities of the state. The three highest officials of this civilian police were required to have a bachelor's degree. The police were thus professionalized and modernized, in line with the general process of modernization of society and state economy.[28]

Education, health, and sanitation were also concerns of the Paulista elite and the object of the organization of new institutions or reorganization of existing structures. State public education was quite backward until late in the imperial period. The Central Statistical Commission in its report of 1887 declared that public education did not reach the standards of the other branches of the public service. Qualified personnel were lacking, school buildings were poor, and regional distribution of schools was insufficient.[29] As the Secretariat of the Interior noted in 1893, the education system was deficient in schools, teachers, and pupil attendance levels.[30]

The federal constitution of 1891 left it up to Congress to create institutions of higher and secondary education in the respective states, with the proviso that nonreligious education would be provided in public facilities. The wording of the act suggested that primary education would be the competence of the states and that secondary and higher education would not be the exclusive competence of the federal government.[31] The state constitution of 1891 defined the principles of free and compulsory primary education, but it also determined that the state congress should legislate not only primary education but also secondary, higher, and vocational schools, whether under control of individuals or associations, subsidized or not by the state. In fact, it would appear that the federal constitution by default left to the states the task of organizing public education at all levels.[32] The result was not a simple division of labor or responsibilities between the states and the central government but one of overlapping jurisdictions, and both the federal government and the state secretary of education would deal with vocational, secondary, and higher education in the next several decades.[33]

Two decrees in 1892 established the basic outlines of the state educational system: Public education would be free and divided into primary, secondary, and higher education. Primary education was compulsory for both sexes up to the age of twelve and started at age seven. The state also created four normal schools for training primary education teachers and three for training secondary education ones. It also added a higher education course for the normal school in the capital. The law stipulated that any community in the state that had twenty to forty primary-school-age children would be provided free schooling. Everywhere that there were at least thirty potential students, a free night school was to be established, offering the same subjects as the daytime primary school. The law stipulated that no appointment would be made without competition, except graduates of normal schools.

Education came directly under the purview of the president of the state, and its daily function was under the control of the Superior Council of Inspection and the individual inspectors of local districts. The state was divided into thirty districts. The law stipulated the salaries of teachers, with the director general and the director of the normal schools receiving 10 contos per annum; directors of normal primary schools, directors of gymnasiums, and directors of the Superior Council of Inspection received 6 contos. Teachers were to be paid between 2.4 and 4.8 contos, depending on their position and school. The state educational reform of 1893 was concerned mainly with primary education and the preparation of primary school teachers through a renewed normal school system. This educational reform was quite extensive, which explains why it lasted, with later modifications, more than other reforms in education and influenced educational reform in other Brazilian states.[34]

Public health was even more of a concern for the Paulista elite than education. The public health problems of São Paulo increased with the massive influx of immigrants, who settled in germ-infested, unsanitary areas without the necessary infrastructure and training to ensure satisfactory living conditions. The maintenance of a healthy work force in coffee required that the epidemics that traditionally affected the state had to be dealt with quickly and efficiently.[35] For this reason it was necessary to adopt a health policy that could prevent epidemics, and the state's health priority in the early years of the republic was to control epidemics, especially yellow fever, which destabilized the entire political and administrative life and threatened both urban populations and coffee farm workers. Even before the end of the empire, the imperial government in 1886 sent sanitary inspectors to all the provinces. In São Paulo the first sanitary inspector greatly stimulated provincial interest in public health issues and gained the support of Paulista leaders. These inspectors and their supporters argued that São Paulo relied almost exclusively on coffee production and that the region had to be healthy to attract settlers and had to keep them healthy to support production. To do this they had to adopt the latest developments in health measures from Europe and North America. As several scholars have noted, this intense interest led to São Paulo developing institutions and practices in public health well ahead of the other states of the republic and even well ahead of most countries of Latin America.[36]

As the republican constitution of 1891 left public health within the purview of the states, São Paulo was soon taking steps to create a formal structure to act in this essential field. In 1891 the State Sanitation Service was created. Health officers were aided by the newly created Vaccine Institute and recently established chemical and bacteriological pharmaceutical laboratories. Among the many activities of the State Sanitation Service was its regulation and inspection of tenement houses and other collective housing, operation of hospitals, control of communicable diseases, inspection of stables, and inspection of food and medicines. Already by 1894 the state had published the first rudimentary sanitary code.

In addition to direct action in the health area, law 35 of 1892 authorized the president of the state to guarantee loans obtained by local governments for potable water and sewage works, requiring municípios to provide a portion of their revenues to guarantee repayment of loans. In the capital São Paulo and Santos these services were undertaken directly by the state government because of the key economic importance of these two cities.[37] Thus, a major platform of the contemporary sanitation movement, the provision of drinking water and the proper handling of human waste, would become a major state-funded obligation under the republic.

The successive changes that occurred in the first thirty years of the state in public health and sanitation reflected new situations and also conflicts regarding the responsibility of the state sector.[38] The changes in the management structure of public health were accompanied by the creation or consolidation of numerous organs that would gain an essential role in health and health services of the state. The local Faculty of Medicine began its activities in 1913.[39] In response to the outbreak of bubonic plague in the port of Santos in 1899 the Instituto Serumtherápico was established, which later became the Instituto Butantan. The institute's mission was to develop serum and vaccines and carry out investigations.[40] The Instituto Bacteriológico of São Paulo and the Instituto Bromatológico, both created in 1892, joined to become the research center Instituto Adolfo Lutz.[41]

The state also became concerned with scientific knowledge and agriculture. The fundamental characteristics and the type of development of the state economy during the Old Republic explain the priority given to agriculture.[42] In 1886 a provincial law created the Geography and Geology Commission of São Paulo, charged with providing thematic maps of the state.[43] That same year the empire founded an agronomy station in the province of São Paulo, the Agronomic Institute of Campinas, "a pioneering entity at the time, and for many decades [it] would remain as the most important in Brazil in this type of agricultural research."[44] In 1892 the state government established the College of Agriculture and the College of Engineering. In 1901 the first students entered the Superior School of Agriculture Luiz de Queiróz, in Piracicaba, which would soon become the main agronomy school in the country.[45] The state Biological Institute of Agricultural and Animal Defense, created in 1927, represented another fundamental science center supporting agriculture. Its creation was motivated by the emergence of a coffee plague in 1924, which demonstrated the need to establish a scientific research center and defensive measures to preserve plants and animals from disease.

The government also promoted engineering. In 1892 the Polytechnic Institute of São Paulo was created as a college of math and science applied to the arts and industries.[46] Initially, the institute would contain a preparatory school and offer special courses in civil engineering, mechanical engineering, architecture, applied chemistry, mathematics, and the natural sciences. The Polytechnic Institute was also established to engage in basic research. It soon became a major center of scientific production in the country.[47] In 1934 the Materials Testing Laboratory of the Polytechnic Institute was transformed into the Institute of Technological Research (IPT), which would have a key role in helping develop industry in São Paulo.[48]

The republican government, despite the chronic budget problems it faced, managed to fund these major structural initiatives in public safety, health, education, and science thanks to the economic growth of the state. The local economy provided a tax base that allowed the state to obtain loans that would be required to fund key services and develop infrastructure that in turn supported the expansion of the coffee economy. It also provided the state with funding to help resolve the periodic crises of overproduction experienced by the coffee producers themselves. Moreover, despite running deficits over the course of this period, the state had little difficulty in selling its government bonds to make up income shortfalls.

Along with promoting the railroads, the most important fiscal activity of the state in support of the local economy was the subvention of European and Asian immigrant labor to replace slaves. The republic was proclaimed one year after the end of slavery, which forced profound changes in the production structure of the coffee economy because of the need to replace slaves with paid labor. That labor consisted mainly of foreign immigrants whose arrival had to be subsidized by the state. Without state subsidization, Brazil could not compete against Argentina, Canada, and above all the United States for European immigrants. The remuneration offered in the coffee fazendas was below that offered by these other importing nations, and Brazil could be made attractive to Europeans only by paying transportation costs, which in turn would provide the incentive to attract such workers. In turn, not all regions of Brazil could compete for such workers. Only the richest coffee zones of São Paulo could initially provide the wages that would attract workers. The fertile areas of the state that were served by its extensive rail network would be most able to substitute slave for free labor.

All this institution building required a well-funded and powerful state government able to intervene in the economy, to provide public services and mobilize resources for infrastructure investments, directly or by ensuring profits for private investors. The division of tax authority between the federal and state governments in the republic led the state to broaden its tax base, increasing its revenues and hence its ability to invest. Although this structure remained the basic one inherited from the empire, there was a gradual change over the course of the Old Republic. In the last budget approved in the empire, for 1889/1890, the export taxes on production accounted for 45 percent of revenue, followed by the railroad transit tax at 26 percent, the building tax (7 percent), and numerous other taxes that added another 22 percent. In the first budget approved in the republican regime (1892), the types of taxes and fees remained the same, but revenue predicted from the export tax significantly increased, reaching 71 percent. According to the constitution of 1891 the states now had exclusive right to tax the export of their production, a right that had been far more limited under the empire. The transit tax, tax on property sales, and inheritance tax also became important sources of expected revenue (see Table 3.1).

Even after ten years of republican government, the 1900 budget showed essentially the same taxes as being the important ones. The tax on coffee exports now accounted for 64 percent of proposed income, taxes on property sales and inheritances were 16 percent, transportation and transit tax 5 percent, and the Additional Tax just 2 percent. The state also collected fees on services, which varied from 5 percent to 15 percent annually of state income and from 1889/1890 to 1938 averaged 10 percent of all receipts, and from time to time obtained sums from credit operations.[49] Province president Francisco de Paula Rodrigues Alves recognized in 1901 that the tax structure had not undergone major changes and that the taxes included in the budget revenue were the same that existed in the old regime.[50]

Nor had most of the expenditure categories changed since the end of the empire. Expenditure on public administration and education in the three years considered (1889/1890, 1892, and 1900) also changed little, going

TABLE 3.1

Budgeted Income for the State of São Paulo, 1889/1890, 1892, and 1900

1889/1890

	Contos	Percentage of income
Ordinary income	*4,890*	*96.6%*
Export tax (*direitos de saida*)	2,300	45.4%
Port fees	112	2.2%
Inheritance tax	216	4.3%
Usufruct inheritance tax	15	0.3%
Animal tax (Itarare and Sorocaba)	31	0.6%
Barrier tax (*taxa de barreiras*)	16	0.3%
Railroad transit tax	1,300	25.7%
Tax on auctions	3	0.1%
Tax on clothing stores	2	0.0%
Tax on wagons	5	0.1%
Tax on capitalists	15	0.3%
Tax on lottery tickets	5	0.1%
Property tax (*imposto predial*)	350	6.9%
Tax on equestrian companies	6	0.1%
Fees for services	16	0.3%
Miscellaneous	19	0.4%
Payment from outstanding debts	70	1.4%
Additional Tax	400	7.9%
Extraordinary income	*171*	*3.4%*
Indemnities	58	1.1%
Income from fines, etc.	101	2.0%
Rental of state properties	11	0.2%
Total	5,061	100.0%

1892

	Contos	Percentage of income
Ordinary income	*13,886*	*99.1%*
Taxes on state good exports	10,000	71.5%
Tax on Santos exports	100	0.7%
Fees for leaving port	16	0.1%
Tax on property sales and transfers	2,000	14.3%
Inheritance tax	300	2.1%
Railroad transit tax	350	2.5%
Sale of state stamps	300	2.1%
Income from state printer	30	0.2%
Property tax on buildings in the capital	350	2.5%
Sale of public lands	20	0.1%
Additional Tax	320	2.3%
Payment from outstanding debts	80	0.6%
Extraordinary income	*120*	*0.9%*
Indemnities	20	0.1%
Occasional income	80	0.6%
Rental of state buildings	20	0.1%
Total	13,986	100.0%

1900

	Contos	Percentage of income
Ordinary income	*36,966*	*96.5%*
Taxes on state good exports	24,600	64.2%
Tax on Santos exports	160	0.4%
Tax on property sales and transfers	5,000	13.1%
Inheritance tax	1,000	2.6%
Sale of state stamps	500	1.3%
Railroad transit tax	2,000	5.2%
Property tax on buildings in the capital	75	2.0%
Sanitation fees	1,000	2.6%
Fees for water usage in capital	1,000	2.6%
Fees for matriculation	20	0.1%
Sale of public lands	36	0.1%
Payment from outstanding debts	100	0.3%
Additional Tax	800	2.1%
Extraordinary income	*1,330*	*3.5%*
Indemnities	1,000	2.6%
Occasional income	180	0.5%
Rental of state buildings	150	0.4%
Total	38,296	100.0%

SOURCE: Law 107, April 9, 1889; law 15, November 11, 1891; law 688, September 16, 1899.

from 23 percent to 26 percent. Public safety expenses increased in 1892 but returned in 1900 to the level corresponding to that of 1889/1890, in the range of 27–29 percent. The set of activities that were part of the Secretariats of Agriculture, Commerce, and Public Works fell slightly but remained in the range of 20 percent. The largest percentage changes occurred in the functions that would be performed by the Secretariat of Finance, and these were influenced by changing costs of foreign exchange and foreign debt servicing (see Table 3.2).

For the state finances, as for the provincial ones, we have complete data on budgeted expenditures and income.[51] In contrast to what occurred with the budgets of the provincial legislature during the empire—which for the most part were approved with a deficit—under the republic all approved budgets were balanced. Of course, in the actual expenditure and income a deficit frequently occurred, due to overspending or income generated being less than budgeted. Fairly typical of this pattern was the budget year 1893, when actual income exceeded planned income by 12,409 contos but planned expenditures were also underestimated, which left the state with an actual deficit of 8,779 contos. In 1892–1938, both revenue and expenses were usually underestimated in the budget. Of those forty-seven years, in only eleven did budgeted revenues exceed actual revenues and always in proportions of less than 20 percent. In the other twenty-seven years, the realized revenue was more than the estimated budgeted amount and usually missed by a large amount.

The counterpart occurred in spending, which usually greatly exceeded the estimated fixed expense. The final budget usually generated a deficit, which in some cases reached extremely high proportions. In more than half the years, the deficit exceeded more than 20 percent of budgeted revenues; in five years it exceeded 50 percent of revenue. In terms of average prices of 1892–1894, revenue between 1898 and 1930 grew from 39,386 to 99,939 contos (or an average increase of 3 percent per year); expenses in the same period grew from 35,163 to 153,876 contos (an average of 4.7 percent per year). This result shows that the unbalanced budget occurred primarily because of excessive spending and not lack of revenue (Table 3.3 and Tables A3.1 and A3.2).

Although actual expenditure and income often led to a final unbalanced budget throughout the period, the deficit from 1905 onward undeniably increased (see Figure 3.1). The state government's commitments increased greatly as it expanded public services and instituted policies designed to support the economy, such as the intervention in the coffee market, support for immigration, and the upgrading and expansion of the transport system. The chronic deficits were covered by loans, obtained mostly in the

TABLE 3.2

Budgeted Expenditures for the State of São Paulo, 1889/1890, 1892, and 1900

1889/1890	Contos	Percentage of expenditures
Administration and Public Education	*1,227*	*23.9%*
Provincial assembly	95	1.8%
Secretary of government	81	1.6%
Religion	14	0.3%
Gloria Seminary	33	0.6%
Insane asylum	60	1.2%
Hygiene office	25	0.5%
Public education	918	17.9%
Justice and Public Security	*1,497*	*29.2%*
Police	1,386	27.0%
Penitentiary	27	0.5%
Poor prisoners	80	1.6%
Police medical service in the capital	4	0.1%
Secretariat of Agriculture, Commerce and Public Works	*1,111*	*21.6%*
Roads	11	0.2%
Repair of public works	65	1.3%
Public lighting (capital)	130	2.5%
Public lighting (Campinas)	33	0.6%
Public works	640	12.5%
Immigration subsidization	25	0.5%
Contracts and subventions	207	4.0%

1892	Contos	Percentage of expenditures
Secretariat of Interior and Public Education	*3,578*	*26.3%*
President of the state	66	0.5%
State legislature	349	2.6%
Secretary and cabinet	50	0.4%
Directorate of public education	33	0.2%
Normal schools	87	0.6%
Teacher salaries for primary schools	2,090	15.4%
Teacher salaries for night primary schools	9	0.1%
Seminary of Educandas	47	0.3%
Insane asylum	63	0.5%
Hygiene office	50	0.4%
Chemical and pharmaceutical labs	36	0.3%
Social assistance and sanitation	50	0.4%
		0.3%
Office of statistics	35	
Diário Oficial and state printing office	62	0.5%
Charity hospitals	24	0.2%
Lyceum of Arts and Crafts and Coração de Jesus	22	0.2%

1900	Contos	Percentage of expenditures
Secretariat of Interior and Public Education	*8,838*	*23.2%*
President of the state	76	0.2%
Senate	214	0.6%
Chamber of deputies	385	1.0%
Secretariat administration	221	0.6%
Public library	25	0.1%
General inspector of education	110	0.3%
Normal schools	343	0.9%
Escola complementar de Piracicaba	120	0.3%
Model school	57	0.1%
Model schools (Prud. Moraes and José Maria)	302	0.8%
Primary education	4,058	10.6%
High schools (capital and Campinas)	296	0.8%
Polytechnic Institute	545	1.4%
Seminary of Educandas	92	0.2%
Insane asylum	368	1.0%
Office of statistics	124	0.3%
Diário Oficial	194	0.5%
State museum	46	0.1%

(continued)

TABLE 3.2 (CONTINUED)

1889/1890

	Contos	Percentage of expenditures
Administration and Collection of Taxes	*1,296*	*25.3%*
Collection and	391	7.6%
administration of taxes		2.5%
Employee pensions	129	
Sporadic expenses	6	0.1%
Interest and exchange costs	769	15.0%
Devolutions	1	0.0%
Total	5,130	100.0%

1892

	Contos	Percentage of expenditures
Aid to municipalities	500	3.7%
Sporadic expenses	5	0.0%
Secretariat of Justice and Public Security	*5,700*	*41.9%*
Administration	146	1.1%
Judges	949	7.0%
Administration of courts	32	0.2%
Police office	176	1.3%
Penitentiary administration	55	0.4%
State police (*Força Pública*)	4,315	31.7%
Police stations	27	0.2%
Secretariat of Agriculture,	*2,514*	*18.5%*
Commerce and Public Works	30	0.2%
Secretary and cabinet	278	2.0%
Personnel	1,200	8.8%
Public works	60	0.4%
Geography commission	450	3.3%
Office of lands and colonization	200	1.5%
Public lighting	200	1.5%
Water and sanitation service		
Navigation service at Iguape, etc.	36	0.3%
Junta Comercial	30	0.2%
Public roads and sidewalks	18	0.1%
State museum	7	0.0%
Sporadic expenses	5	0.0%

1900

	Contos	Percentage of expenditures
Sanitary service	865	2.3%
Public assistance	400	1.0%
Subventions	20	0.1%
Occasional expenses	25	0.1%
Department of Justice and Public Security	*10,322*	*27.1%*
Secretariat	137	0.4%
Tribunal of justice	249	0.7%
Procuradoria Geral do Estado	26	0.1%
Justiça de la Instancia	1,251	3.3%
Junta Comercial	39	0.1%
Police office	591	1.5%
State prisons	799	2.1%
State police (Força Pública)	7,134	18.7%
Almoxarifado da Força Pública	71	0.2%
Despesas Eventuais	25	0.1%
Secretariat of Agriculture	*6,828*	*17.9%*
Secretariat administration	144	0.4%
Superintendent of public works	330	0.9%
Inspector of railroads, canals, etc.	137	0.4%
Colonies and immigration	1,600	4.2%
service		0.4%
Agricultural Institute	146	
Geography and geology commission	285	0.7%

Treasury Secretariat	*1,816*	*13.3%*
Secretary	30	0.2%
State treasury	180	1.3%
Tax offices	625	4.6%
Exercícios findos	50	0.4%
Reposições e restituições	4	0.0%
Interest and payment of funded debt	500	3.7%
Interest on short-term floating debt	25	0.2%
Guaranteed interest payment	150	1.1%
on railways	60	0.4%
Difference in exchange rate		
Employee pensions	187	1.4%
Miscellaneous	5	0.0%
Total	13,608	100.0%

Agricultural school of Piracicaba	89	0.2%
Public works (bridges, roads, etc.)	1,300	3.4%
Contracts and subventions	738	1.9%
Water and sanitation service (capital and Santos)	2,000	5.2%
Office of Immigration	10	0.0%
Sporadic expenses	50	0.1%
Treasury Secretariat	*12,155*	*31.9%*
Secretariat	53	0.1%
State treasury	399	1.0%
Tax collections	1,614	4.2%
Exercicios findos	1,700	4.5%
Reposições e restituições	50	0.1%
Interest and payment on foreign debt	1,544	4.0%
Interest and payment on internal funded debt	328	0.9%
Interest on floating debt	539	1.4%
Difference in exchange rate	4,320	11.3%
Employee pensions	379	1.0%
Special worker pensions	113	0.3%
Subventions	960	2.5%
Pension for children of Carlos Gomes	6	0.0%
Miscellaneous	150	0.4%
Total	38,142	100.0%

SOURCE: Law 107, April 9, 1889; law 15, November 11, 1891; law 688, September 16, 1899.

TABLE 3.3

Approved Budget and Actual Income and Expenditures for the State of São Paulo, 1892–1938 (contos)

	APPROVED BUDGET (ESTIMATED)		ACTUAL BUDGET			
Fiscal year	Income	Expenditure	Income	Expenditure	Balance/deficit	Balance as % of income
1892	13,986	13,986	38,105	34,020	4,086	11%
1893	22,125	22,125	34,534	43,313	-8,779	-25%
1894	25,480	25,480	37,282	42,368	-5,086	-14%
1895	34,482	34,482	50,172	49,690	483	1%
1896	36,308	36,308	50,808	51,568	-760	-1%
1897	47,270	47,270	48,571	58,712	-10,141	-21%
1898	41,962	41,962	42,280	54,787	-12,508	-30%
1899	39,650	39,650	42,874	36,749	6,124	14%
1900	38,296	38,296	42,651	36,298	6,353	15%
1901	41,728	41,728	45,685	45,692	-7	0%
1902	40,325	40,325	37,649	40,913	-3,264	-9%
1903	39,744	39,744	34,127	40,743	-6,616	-19%
1904	34,893	34,893	37,582	35,873	1,709	5%
1905	36,775	36,775	51,009	111,861	-60,852	-119%
1906	47,359	47,359	52,860	61,615	-8,755	-17%
1907	54,171	54,171	52,178	68,570	-16,392	-31%
1908	48,724	48,724	42,693	67,989	-25,295	-59%
1909	49,167	49,167	56,597	67,758	-11,161	-20%
1910	52,171	52,171	43,281	65,852	-22,571	-52%
1911	58,341	58,341	63,946	83,860	-19,914	-31%
1912	69,760	69,760	75,641	96,643	-21,003	-28%
1913	81,915	81,915	76,008	107,738	-31,730	-42%
1914	79,195	79,195	65,711	100,160	-34,448	-52%
1915	74,485	74,485	79,316	93,697	-14,381	-18%
1916	80,618	80,618	79,248	87,444	-8,196	-10%
1917	85,788	85,788	82,556	97,794	-15,238	-18%
1918	91,194	91,194	77,642	103,747	-26,104	-34%
1919	95,370	95,370	94,235	110,902	-16,667	-18%
1920	107,447	107,447	111,211	223,359	-112,148	-101%
1921	137,484	137,484	160,580	197,995	-37,415	-23%
1922	152,391	152,391	157,019	204,888	-47,868	-30%
1923	189,181	189,181	202,722	233,135	-30,412	-15%
1924	201,511	201,511	227,020	278,656	-51,636	-23%
1925	288,981	288,981	353,271	406,687	-53,416	-15%
1926	324,700	324,700	352,584	511,230	-158,645	-45%
1927	342,710	342,710	404,044	549,333	-145,289	-36%
1928	378,237	378,237	408,424	436,915	-28,490	-7%
1929	453,607	453,607	438,460	599,104	-160,644	-37%
1930	495,772	495,772	400,204	616,197	-215,993	-54%
1931	444,390	444,390	429,571	662,906	-233,334	-54%
1932	400,920	400,920	382,424	676,871	-294,447	-77%

TABLE 3.3 (CONTINUED)

Fiscal year	APPROVED BUDGET (ESTIMATED)		ACTUAL BUDGET			
	Income	Expenditure	Income	Expenditure	Balance/deficit	Balance as % of income
1933	447,760	447,760	432,283	600,799	-168,516	-39%
1934	492,600	492,600	475,919	656,967	-181,048	-38%
1935	671,971	671,971	657,142	745,583	-88,440	-13%
1936	718,371	718,371	703,590	747,458	-43,868	-6%
1937	749,910	749,910	665,239	837,684	-172,445	-26%
1938	761,402	761,402	696,033	787,906	-91,873	-13%

SOURCE: Assembleia Legislativa do Estado de São Paulo, lei orçamentárias, various years, http://www.al.sp.gov.br/leis; Departamento de Estatística do Estado, *Anuário estatístico de São Paulo*, various years; Secretaria da Fazenda do Estado de São Paulo, *Contas do exercício de 1938*, 421–445.

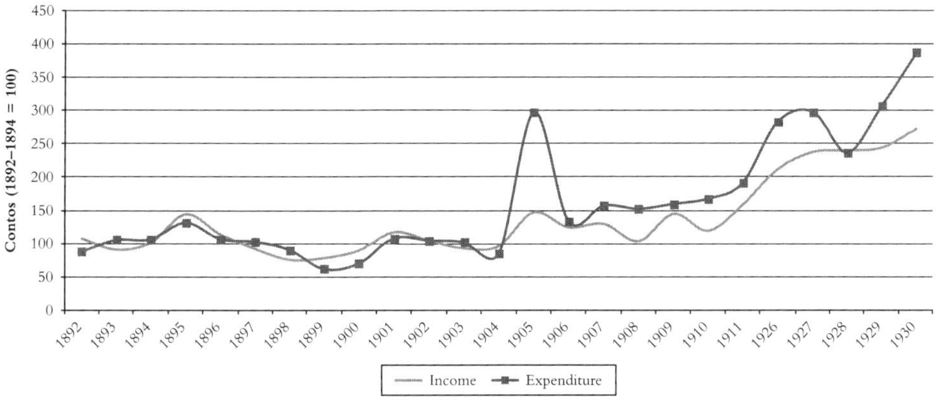

Figure 3.1 Actual Income and Expenditure of the State of São Paulo, 1892–1930

NOTE: The base for the calculation of constant prices is the three-year average of 1892–1894.

SOURCE: Assembléia Legislativa do Estado de São Paulo, leis orçamentárias, various years, http://www.al.sp.gov.br/leis; Secretaria da Fazenda do Estado de São Paulo, *Contas do exercício*, various years; Departamento de Estatística do Estado, *Anuário estatístico de São Paulo*, various years.

international market. The ability of the state to constantly turn to international markets to finance its debt shows the high quality of the state's credit in those markets.

Beginning in 1892 the preponderance of state income directly or indirectly came from the tax on exports. This tax would be fundamental for the state until 1930, when the international crisis in the coffee market deeply affected both the state and national economies. Income from the export tax remained stable until 1909, exceeding 60 percent. A period of instability occurred during World War I and the crisis in 1920, but its contribution returned to 40 percent in the second half of the 1920s (see Figure 3.2 and Table A3.1).

As taxes on coffee exports began to decline, the state in the 1920s and 1930s began to diversify its tax structure and sought new sources of income. The tax on property transfers between living persons, also levied in the imperial period, now accounted for between 10 and 20 percent of income. The transit and traffic tax was also an inherited imperial tax, representing between 5 and 10 percent of total revenues. Property tax also usually accounted for less than 5 percent of collections. The stamp duty, inheritance taxes, liquor consumption taxes, and the tax on lotteries were also maintained from earlier periods but had little impact on state income. Republican-era taxes were created, such as the territorial (or land) tax, the tax on commerce, an industry tax, and a tax on vehicles, but they were of little importance up to 1930. The most important of these miscellaneous taxes were the fees charged for water and sewer services. Together, they accounted for approximately 10 percent of total revenue from 1910. The earlier provincial Additional Tax charged throughout the state now resulted in around 5 percent of revenue under the republic. Numerous other charges were maintained or created, such as an expedient tax for government services used, a judicial fee, an enrollment fee, and taxes on slaughterhouses. None of these had great importance in state income (see Tables A3.1 and A3.2).

Overall, there was significant instability in state income in 1892–1930 because of the state's dependency on export duties of coffee; both coffee production and the international market fluctuated dramatically from year to year. The situation became even more complex because some important public commitments were fixed in foreign currency, which was affected by the floating exchange rate.[52]

Considering actual expenditure over the period analyzed, important changes occurred in the composition of major expense items. In the early period of the republic, health and sanitation represented around 30 percent

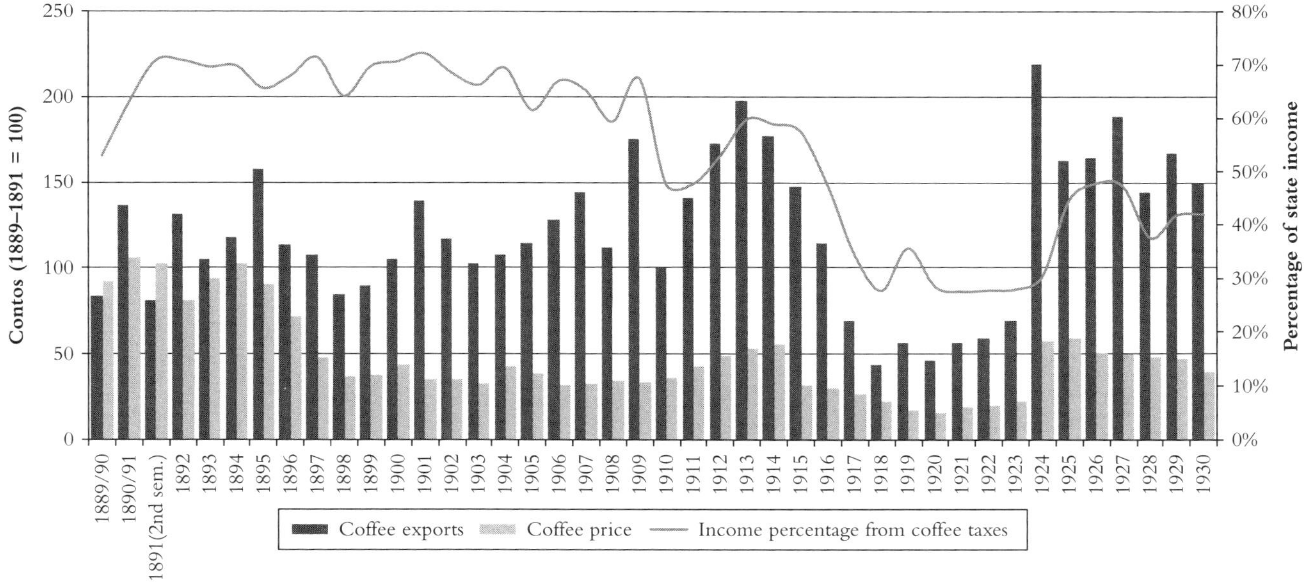

Figure 3.2 Participation of Coffee in Ordinary Income, Prices, and Export of Coffee, 1889–1930

NOTE: The base for the calculation of constant prices is the three-year average of 1889–1891.

SOURCE: Nozoe, *São Paulo: Economia cafeeira e urbanização*, 19.

of state expenditure, gradually declining to around 15 percent (Figure 3.3 and Table 3.4). This variation of spikes in spending in these areas and then declines was repeated in the 1910s and 1920s. A major expense was the port of Santos. Sanitation in Santos was essential because the port was the gateway to the state, especially for European and Asian immigrants, and was the most vulnerable place in terms of epidemics. Although supposedly of municipal concern, costs for the sanitation of Santos were entrusted to the state, given the scale of the problem it was facing.[53] Thus, water and sanitation bonds for the capital and the port of Santos began to appear regularly in budgets approved by the assembly, representing a significant amount. Fees for water and sewage services throughout the state were an important item of revenue for the state government.

In addition, several regional health offices were created in Santos and the interior of the state. There were also significant appropriations in the budget for the subsidy of the Santas Casas, the charity hospital, and for social assistance. The Santa Casa de Miseracórdia of São Paulo, especially, was usually provided with significant appropriations.[54] In 1929, the appropriations for the health service included funds for the usual inspectorates and hospitals but also funds for the collection of demographic and health statistics, sanitary engineering, an organization to promote health education, and an organization for early child protection. Separately, funding was provided for the Hygiene Institute of São Paulo,[55] and funding for health issues was in the budget under "auxílios e subvenções" (aids and subventions). Dozens of entities were related to health (such as the Paulista Association of Popular Sanatoriums and the Maternity Hospital), some entities were for social assistance related to the protection of infants and children, and some added buildings and personnel to the state government. As we see when examining the demographic change in the state, the effectiveness of these investments resulted in a population far healthier than was the average in Brazil.

The state also invested heavily in sanitation works, which also had a direct effect on population health. The state invested in the water and sewerage service for the capital and in sanitation services for Santos, Campinas, and the interior. The state's Bureau of Water and Sewers (Repartição de Águas e Esgotos) was created later, as was a special such entity for Santos (Repartição de Saneamento de Santos). In general, most of the appropriations authorized in the annual budget were for the bureaus of sanitation of the capital and Santos, with specific allocations to other locations in public works and in grants supporting local construction for potable water and sanitation. In 1929 the expenditures for sanitation became part of the new

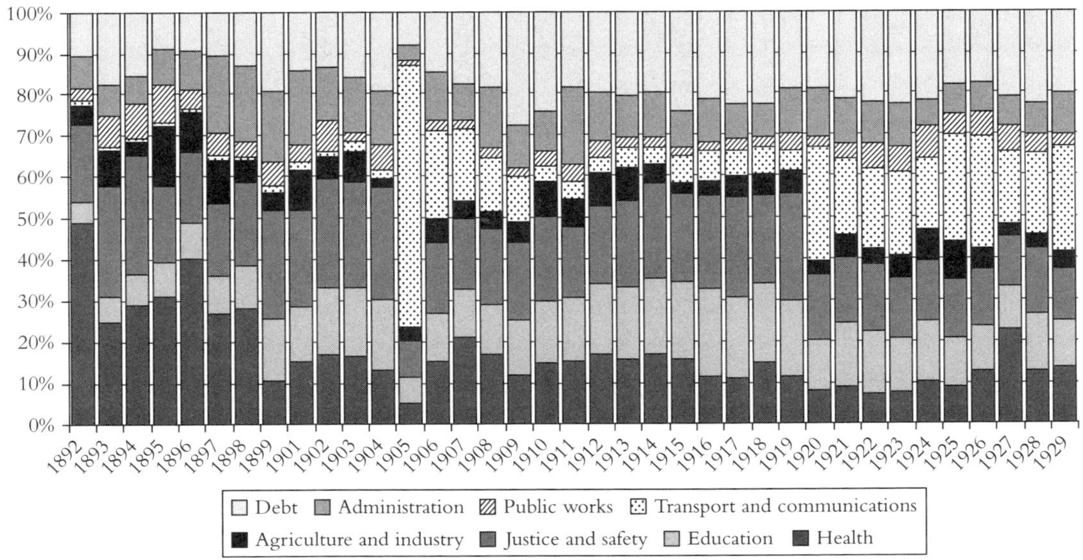

Figure 3.3 Relative Importance of Major Actual Expenditures, 1892–1929

SOURCE: Lefevre, *A administração do estado de São Paulo na República Velha.*

TABLE 3.4

National and International Public Debt of the State of São Paulo, by Operations Realized to 1929

Year	Purpose	Extinction year	Original value of contract	Unit	Balance Dec. 1930 (mil réis)	Bank
1904	Water and sewage service in capital	1935	1,000,000	Libra	11,186,282	Bank of London and South America
1904	Purchase of EF Sorocabana	1943	3,800,000	Libra	109,071,038	Dresden Bank
1907	Redemption of external debt of state	1957	2,000,000	Libra	81,229,626	Société Générale and others
1921	Redemption of fluctuating internal debt	1951	2,000,000	Libra	89,933,548	Baring Brothers & Co. and others
1926	Water and sewage service in capital	1956	2,500,000	Libra	119,362,707	Baring Brothers & Co. and others
1928	Railroad purchases and capital sewage	1968	3,500,000	Libra	172,077,024	Baring Brothers & Co. and others
Subtotal			*14,800,000*		*582,860,225*	
1921	Redemption of fluctuating internal debt	1936	10,000,000	Dollar (US)	51,039,450	Speyer & Co.
1925	Maintenance of EF Sorocabana	1950	15,000,000	Dollar (US)	154,665,000	Speyer & Co.
1926	Water and sewage service in capital	1956	7,500,000	Dollar (US)	73,775,000	Speyer & Co.
1928	Railroad purchases and capital sewage	1968	15,000,000	Dollar (US)	153,185,871	Speyer & Co. and others
Subtotal			*47,500,000*		*432,665,321*	
1921	Redemption of fluctuating internal debt	1936	18,000,000	Florin	36,917,442	Lippmann, Rosenthal & Co. and others
Total balance of external debt (mil réis)					1,052,442,988	

Year	Purpose	Deadline (years)	Value realized up to 1929	Unit	Balance (mil réis)	Type of operation
1905	Extension of EF Sorocabana	50	5,000,000	Mil réis	4,124,000	3rd tranche
1905	Extension of EF Sorocabana	50	4,000,000	Mil réis	3,349,500	4th tranche
1905	Extension of EF Sorocabana	50	4,000,000	Mil réis	3,349,500	5th tranche
1907/1908	Extension of EF Sorocabana	50	8,000,000	Mil réis	6,986,000	6th tranche
1907/1910	Public buildings construction	30	10,000,000	Mil réis	6,432,500	7th tranche
1909/1910	Consolidation of fluctuating debt	50	10,000,000	Mil réis	8,730,500	8th tranche
1910	Acquisition of schools	50	10,500,000	Mil réis	9,957,000	9th tranche
1913/1914	Consolidation of fluctuating debt	20	25,000,000	Mil réis	12,168,000	10th tranche

1917/1918	Liquidation of judicial sentence	40	2,500,000	Mil réis	2,295,000	11th tranche
1918/1919	Lease termination of EF Sorocabana	40	48,694,000	Mil réis	44,545,000	12th tranche
1919/1920	Commemoration of Independence	40	18,000,000	Mil réis	16,465,000	13th tranche
1920	Liquidation of judicial sentence	50	5,000,000	Mil réis	4,833,000	14th tranche
1927/1929	Purchase of EF Santos a Juquiá	30	31,348,000	Mil réis	30,515,000	15th tranche
1906	Support for Banco Crédito Rural	10	950,000	Mil réis	29,000	Agricultural support
1916/1917	Support for Banco Crédito Popular	40	150,000	Mil réis		Popular credit
1920/1921	Redemption and consolidation of internal debt	25	150,000,000	Mil réis	150,000,000	Obligation
1920/1927	Redemption and consolidation of internal debt	30	19,638,000	Mil réis	75,085,000	Obligation
1926	Loans to stock market of Mercadorias São Paulo	30	5,740,000	Mil réis	5,545,000	Obligation
1926/1927	Prophylaxis for leprosy	30	9,056,500	Mil réis	8,964,500	Obligation
1921/1923	Aid to neighboring railroads	30	581,000	Mil réis	545,500	Obligation
1921/1926	Aid to neighboring railroads	30	6,361,000	Mil réis	5,986,500	Obligation
1921/1928	Aid to neighboring railroads	30	2,416,000	Mil réis	2,416,000	Obligation
Total internal funded debt (mil réis)			376,934,500		402,321,500	

SOURCE: Secretaria da Fazenda do Estado de São Paulo, *Contas do Exercício de* 1930, 88–94.

Ministry of Transportation and Public Works. Also in this department were allocations for sanitation works in numerous other municípios besides the principal ones. That year, the total spending on sanitation accounted for 3.4 percent of the approved budget, and the Bureau of Water and Sewer for the capital received the most support.[56]

Education came to represent another significant expenditure of the state government under the republic. Major investments and persistent increases in expenditure in the sector demonstrate the commitment of the state government to this important area. Basic education, the primary schools, was the priority. The period from 1892 to 1929 can be divided into two distinct periods of investment in education. In the first period, 1892–1917, there was an accelerated growth in state spending on education, and this was probably the phase of installing the basic structure within the state (see Figure 3.4). In this period education went from 5 percent to almost 20 percent of actual state expenditures. After that period, although expenditures continued to increase, they did not accompany the rate of growth of total expenditures, and thus their percentage of actual state expenses declined. Other items such as transport and communication now gained relative importance in total expenditure. Although over the period new educational institutions emerged at all levels, such as normal schools, professional schools, the Lyceum of Arts and Crafts, the Polytechnic Institute, and the Faculty

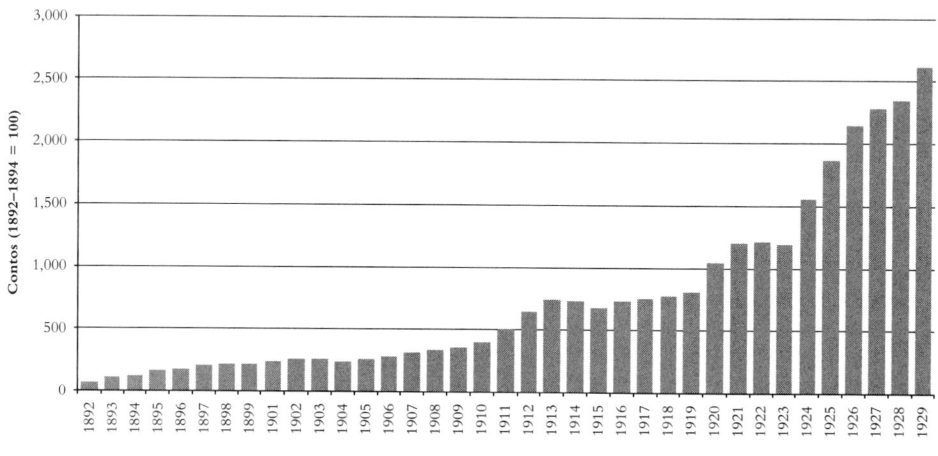

Figure 3.4 Total Education Expenditure, 1892–1929

NOTE: The base for the calculation of constant prices is the three-year average of 1892–1894.

SOURCE: Lefevre, *A administração do estado de São Paulo na República Velha.*

of Medicine, the priority was on primary education, which throughout the period represented more than 70 percent of budgeted annual sums spent for education. Secondary education increased its role modestly in this period and went from 10 percent to 15 percent of total expenditures in education; vocational education was of little significance in terms of the budget; and higher education, limited to the Polytechnic Institute and the Faculty of Medicine, represented between 6 and 10 percent of educational costs.

The data also permit us to calculate what was spent versus budgeted for education. After a slow start in the first two decades in which the state failed to spend between 10 and 20 percent of what it had planned to spend, by the 1910s it was spending at or above what it had budgeted in this area (see Figure 3.5).[57]

As to the effective educational expenditures per capita, Figure 3.5 shows that growth in educational expenditure in nominal terms had significant and constant growth throughout the entire period. By the end of the period, expenditure in mil réis of the day—that is, in nominal terms—was six times what it had been at the beginning, with only a short pause during and right after World War I. In real, or constant, terms, expenditures

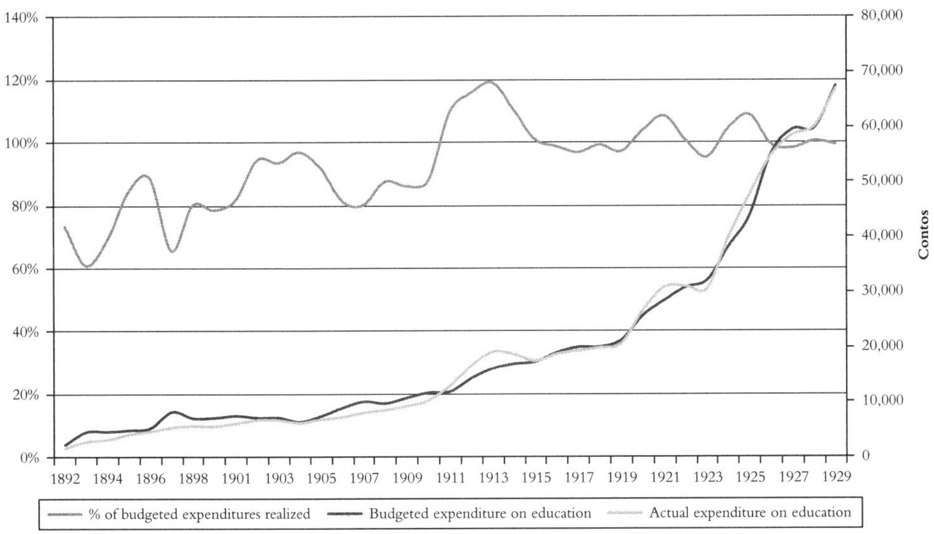

Figure 3.5 Expenditures on Education Budgeted and Actually Spent, 1892–1929

SOURCE: Assembléia Legislativa do Estado de São Paulo, leis orçamentárias, various years, http://www.al.sp.gov.br/leis; Lefevre, *A administração do estado de São Paulo na República Velha.*

per capita dropped dramatically after reaching a peak in 1913, though the amount ended at almost three times as high as the amount in 1929 than the amount spent per capita in 1892. Clearly, for all their enthusiasm, state legislators were not keeping up with population growth in terms of public educational investments.

Justice and public safety represented another important budget item from 1892 to 1929. In real terms, there was an average annual growth of 2.1 percent in budgetary spending on justice and security, whose expenditures represented approximately 25 percent of total expenditure in the budget until 1915 and gradually declined in subsequent years to around 20 percent in the 1920s. Of these expenditures the police absorbed approximately 85 percent, with the remaining 15 percent spent on the judicial system. In public safety, there was significant growth in the civil police, represented by the expenditures of the Bureau of Police (Repartição Policial). The penitentiary administration also showed strong growth for the period. The security forces over time slowly reduced their share of such police and justice expenditures to about 50 percent in the late 1920s.

Throughout the period, the legislature annually approved a law that fixed the security forces of the state for the following year. In 1929 a state law specified that the public force would have a contingent of 8,493 men, under a general command, divided into seven infantry battalions, two regiments of cavalry, a battalion of firefighters, an air squadron, a medical corps, and a division for materials. The law had a provision for civilian auxiliaries and funding for a course of military instruction.[58] The number of Civil Guard members was also fixed annually by the legislature. A 1930 law, for example, provided for 1,571 men for surveillance and policing of the capital, inspection and supervision of traffic on state roads, and policing public events. The policing of the capital needed 69 inspectors and 925 subinspectors and guards.

The Secretariat of Finance was another major area of state expenditures, and while budgeted expenditures for this institution increased over time, the share of these expenditures going to administration declined from about 6 percent to 4 percent of the total budget. In contrast, the proposed debt service expenditures increased not only in total volume but also as an increasing share of total expenditure over time. Debt servicing, which had remained around 5 percent in the late nineteenth century, was up to 18 percent in 1900, remaining at around 20 percent of total expenditures until 1929, when it reached 24 percent (see Figure 3.6). Borrowing reached 1,454,764 contos at the end of 1930, with foreign loans accounting for 72 percent. This debt represented about three times the revenue expected

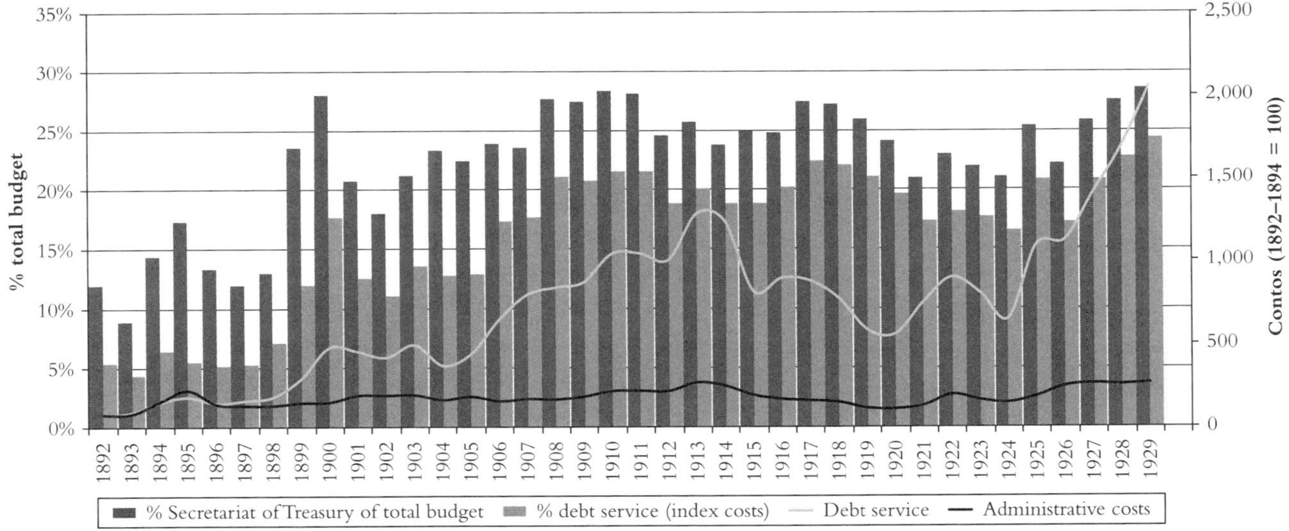

Figure 3.6 Department of Treasury Debt Service and Expenditure

NOTE: The base for the calculation of constant prices is the three-year average of 1892–1894.

SOURCE: Assembléia Legislativa do Estado de São Paulo, leis orçamentárias, various years, http://www.al.sp.gov.br/leis; Affonseca, "Inflação, custo de vida, alimentação, ponderação."

for 1930 (495,772 contos). The main cause for this liability was the state absorption of the Sorocabana railroad, which had been leased to private interests but now returned to state administration, along with additional investments in the railroad, investments in sanitation, and debt consolidation (Table 3.4).

The item presented by Lefevre as composed of agriculture, industry, and immigration initially reflected the weight of immigration in the closing years of the nineteenth century, when the financial outlay for immigration was most important. During this period the state paid approximately 10 percent of annual effective expenditure on subsidizing the European immigrants. In the same period, however, the legislature estimated costs identified as "Immigration and Settlement" at just 8 percent of total budgeted expenditures, which meant that they were consistently underestimating its costs, although over time these ratios declined (see Table A3.3). Thomas H. Holloway addressed this by comparing the costs of subsidizing immigrants and the taxes received on coffee and concluded that the state received in coffee taxes about ten times the amount spent on immigration.[59]

Thanks to the wealth generated by coffee, the state succeeded in expanding its income and expenditures while creating an ever more complex administration and intervening ever more deeply as a significant player in the coffee market. Health, sanitation, education, and public safety were also important state concerns as the coffee elite tried to anticipate the modernization and control of the economy and society through state spending and an active interventionist state. The coffee elite pushed the state to ever-greater intervention in the state economy. However conservative and neoliberal the elite in its political ideology, in the end it was as committed to state action to control the market as later Keynesian economists would be. Moreover, this confirms the thesis of scholars who have stressed that the so-called liberal regimes of the Old Republic were in fact quite active interventionists and created numerous institutions and programs that were distinctly nonliberal in their approach to the market.[60] The government at the federal and local levels, especially in the case of São Paulo, was defensive of coffee, even when it led to a direct intervention in the economic domain. The state's coffee policy, subvention of immigration and railways, and policies for the education and health of its workforce are a clear demonstration of direct public action in the market, which was quite different from the liberal tradition.

Chapter 4

Paulista Agriculture, 1899–1950

The growth of the powerful Paulista government to 1930 would be crucial to the survival of the state's agriculture into the twentieth century. The secular growth of the coffee economy up to the end of the nineteenth century was spectacular. But the constant incorporation of ever more virgin lands into the coffee economy was beginning to create problems of overproduction. São Paulo coffee planters by the early twentieth century were producing more coffee than the world market could consume. Yet despite the increasing limitations of that market, Paulista planters had difficulty responding to these market signals and in the end would require significant assistance from the state government to control crop output. Direct intervention of the state and federal governments in the coffee economy defines Paulista agriculture in the twentieth century.

By the first years of the twentieth century the production of São Paulo coffee planters alone was approaching world consumption levels. That meant that the international coffee market was unstable, with wide fluctuations in prices, and local producers were unable to adequately respond to these changes, leading to numerous crises of local overproduction. Although demand steadily grew for coffee in the international market, prices tended to fluctuate because of both periodic economic crises in consuming countries and overproduction in the producing countries. Planters had few restrictions on production and little ability to anticipate demand. Planting of new trees was determined by current prices, but new trees began to produce only after four years and often could be productive for twenty or thirty years more. If the market changed during this postplanting period, producers were unable to curtail production. This was aside from weather conditions, which could lead to overproduction in one year and severe shortage in the next.[1] Finally, even price signals were often muted for producers. The price in the international market was in English pounds, but the referential price for the producer was in local currency, the mil réis.[2] The price producers received depended on the international price and the rate of conversion between English pounds and the mil réis—that is, it depended on fluctuations in the exchange rate.

There were three long price cycles in coffee during the second half of the nineteenth century, according to the economist Antonio Delfim Netto. All these cycles were initiated by international economic crises.[3] Depending on the intensity of the crisis and expectations about future developments, foreign coffee merchants could replenish their stocks while taking advantage of the fall in prices. Given the importance of coffee in exports, crises in the international coffee market usually provoked a devaluation of the mil réis. Its depreciation in turn cushioned some of the impact of the fall in international prices. The devaluation also made imports more costly, thus leading to equilibrium in the balance of payments. This process functioned relatively well until the end of the 1880s. But in the next decade, there were severe shocks due to the fall of the empire and the bursting of a financial bubble, the Encilhamento, and the crisis that followed. This period of crisis only ended in 1898 with the stabilization policies enacted by President Manuel Ferraz de Campos Sales.

In the previous cycles, the fall in international prices, despite the devaluation of the local currency, led to a fall in incomes and suppression of new coffee tree plantings. Though total output kept increasing from established trees, demand increased to ultimately meet existing supply, and without new tree plantings supply and demand stabilized. But in the 1890s this dynamic was altered. In 1892 the price of coffee in the international market began a long-term secular decline, but the very severe devaluation that then occurred cushioned the shock for producers, maintained their profitability, and even stimulated new plantings. This led to a structural excess in supply and put pressure on world prices, which fell by 60 percent between 1891 and 1898.

Faced with a severe internal financial crisis, Campos Sales in 1898 carried out a strict stabilization program, which succeeded in raising the value of the mil réis. A low price for coffee and a recuperation in the national currency were factors that reduced the remuneration of producers and led to a decline in new plantings. But coffee production continued to grow because of earlier plantings, which led to serious overproduction for the international market.

In 1900, for example, Brazil produced 13.8 million sacks of coffee (at 60 kilograms per sack), of which 8.9 million sacks came from São Paulo. In that same year 5.8 million sacks of coffee were held off the market, of which 3.6 million were of Brazilian origin. At the same time the world was consuming 14.3 million sacks per annum. In 1906, the most critical year, Brazil produced 20.6 million sacks, of which 15.4 million were from São Paulo. Unsold stocks then reached 9.6 million sacks (7.5 million of which was Brazilian coffee), while world consumption reached just 17.5 million sacks. Clearly, coffee planters in Brazil were producing more than the world market could consume.

This seeming long-term structural crisis gave rise to demands that the government intervene in the coffee market, which before this had been functioning as a traditional market free of government regulation. Despite the general consensus that there was a severe crisis in the coffee economy,[4] there was no consensus about its causes and how to resolve it. Some thought it could be resolved by increasing demand, and others firmly believed that the market would self-correct without government intervention.[5] Thus, at first both the state and federal governments took a position of nonintervention. This was evident in the words of Joaquim Murtinho, the Treasury Minister responsible for carrying out the stabilization program, who declared that he was "convinced that government intervention would only make matters worse. The government should let coffee production be reduced by natural forces."[6] In 1902 Francisco de Paula Rodrigues Alves, who was governor of the state, became president, but he still opposed government intervention in the market.

Nevertheless, in the same year, as a preventive measure, the state finally prohibited coffee tree plantings for five years.[7] At the same time production remained relatively stable from 1904 to 1906, thus reducing the demand for state intervention, though prices continued low and consumption remained below world output. But the crisis once again became acute in the second semester of 1906 because new plantings began producing. Stocks of unsold coffee were still large, and it looked as if the crop of 1906/1907 would be one of the biggest ever.[8] In that crop year, Brazil alone produced more than the world consumed (Figures 4.1 and 4.2).

In 1905 a law authorized the president of the state to enter into agreements with the federal government and other coffee-producing state governments to adopt measures that would ensure the recovery of prices. The

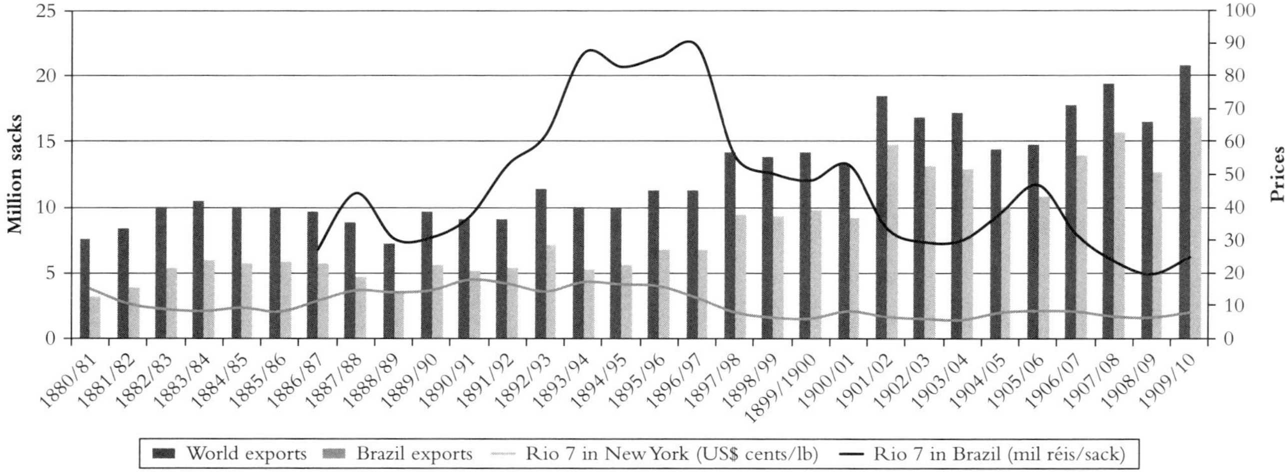

Figure 4.1 World and Brazilian Exports of Coffee and Export Prices of Coffee, 1880–1910

SOURCE: Bacha and Greenhill, *150 anos de café*, apendice estatístico, tables 1.6 and 1.8.

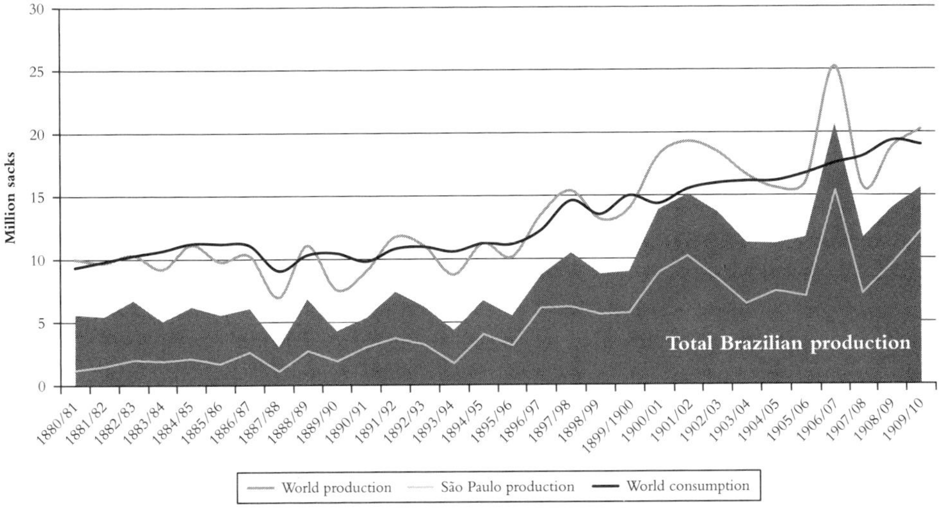

Figure 4.2 World Production and Consumption of Coffee and São Paulo and Brazilian Production, 1880–1910

SOURCE: Bacha and Greenhill, *150 anos de café*, apendice estatístico, tables 1.6 and 1.8.

law allowed the state government to make any contract, including guaranteeing interest and ensuring premiums, with the approval of the state legislature.[9] The budget approved for 1906 allowed for the creation of a tax of three gold francs on each coffee sack exported by the state. The revenue from the tax would be used exclusively for a price support scheme and for service of loans obtained for such purpose. The collection of this tax began when the price support program went into effect.[10]

With the authorization of the legislature, the president of the state in 1906 signed the Taubaté Agreement with the states of Minas Gerais and Rio de Janeiro. This agreement offered price support for coffee producers, with the state governments regulating the coffee trade by purchasing and selling stocks of coffee and by promoting increased consumption of coffee. The Convênio de Taubaté stipulated that all three states would charge the three gold francs tax on coffee bags exported. This would be used to pay the loan of up to £15 million arranged by the state of São Paulo to carry out this valorization (price support) program. The agreement also provided that the loan would be used as collateral for gold and cash conversion by the Currency Board (Caixa de Conversão) that would be created by the Brazilian Congress for fixing the value of the currency.[11]

The Currency Board, whose formation the presidents of the three states suggested, depended on support from the federal government. The board purchased foreign currencies at a fixed rate to guarantee that, even if coffee prices appreciated and resulted in greater flows of foreign currency, there would be no impact on the domestic currency. But there was a risk to this system. If there was a shortage of foreign exchange, which would have the effect of devaluing the mil réis, the maintenance of a fixed conversion rate by the Currency Board would result in a selling pressure because the Currency Board would be paying more for the national currency than could be obtained in the free market. This could result in the bankruptcy of the Currency Board, which actually occurred just before World War I.[12]

Although the federal government was reluctant to implement the Taubaté Agreement, the state government began to take steps to carry out its terms. In 1906 São Paulo obtained two loans totaling £3 million and started buying coffee. In 1907 and 1908 the federal government took out foreign loans in its own name and passed the proceeds to the state of São Paulo to support the plan. By late 1908 the state government had purchased and removed from the market 8.4 million bags of coffee. The extraordinary harvest of 1906–1907 forced the state government of São Paulo to anticipate the execution of the recovery plan agreed on in the Taubaté Convênio.[13] The state government took out another ten-year loan of £15 million guaranteed by the three-franc tax, the state-owned coffee stocks, and the federal government, which now effectively endorsed the operation, giving a clear signal to the market of the viability of the operation.[14] From that point on the market believed in the operation, and prices began an upward movement. With the loan obtained there was now organized a management committee in Europe charged with selling the coffee stocks of the state.[15] Favorable market conditions permitted the committee to sell part of the stocks in 1911.[16]

According to Joseph Love, overproduction crises and stabilization policy increased the role of foreign exporters in the coffee economy. They now began to play an important role in the provision of short-term credit to the coffee producers, gradually filling the role previously carried out by the coffee brokers (*comissàrios*). They also increased their holdings of coffee estates as they acquired the lands of coffee producers who had difficulty surviving the crises.[17]

From the beginnings of the republic, the state government carried out more exact surveys of the rural economy, such as appeared in the 1900 issue of the *Anuário estatístico de São Paulo*, which provides a good picture of Paulista agriculture in this moment of crisis for the coffee economy. Of the

172 municípios that then existed in São Paulo, the census contained information on 101. There were 68,061 farms in the state, with the greatest concentration of them in the Central region, followed by the Mogiana and Araraquarense regions. Coffee of course was the dominant crop in value, accounting for 72 percent of the state's agricultural production, followed by corn at 13 percent, beans at 5 percent, and aguardente at 3 percent. Other products, like rice, sugar, cotton, and wine, accounted for less than 2 percent. Regionally, Mogiana was the richest agricultural zone, with a quarter of the value of output, followed by the Araraquarense and Vale do Paraíba.[18]

The largest coffee region was now the Alta Sorocabana region, which accounted for 36 percent of the coffee production, followed by the Mogiana region, which accounted for 21 percent. The other regions produced amounts on the order of 10 percent, and this included Vale do Paraíba.[19] The municípios listed in the survey produced 488,775 metric tons of coffee in that crop year valued at 114,175 contos (approximately US$17.3 million). Only 337,547 metric tons of coffee were exported from the port of Santos in this same year, and thus a significant portion of the crop was stockpiled, since the international market could no longer absorb the full output of the state. Between 1896 and 1906, coffee stocks increased by a factor of ten, going from 1.3 million to 10.1 million bags of coffee beans.

In 1900 the government estimated that a total of 251 million trees were in production and 90 million were recently planted and not yet producing coffee. But this proportion between new and producing trees rapidly changed. Between 1898 and 1904 the proportion of new plantings to producing trees went from 46 percent to just 16 percent. As could be expected there was a great disparity in where the new trees were planted. The new coffee-producing regions of Araraquarense and Alta Sorocabana had the highest ratio of new plantings, while the older coffee regions like the Vale do Paraíba, Central, and Mogiana regions had the lowest. The Mogiana region had the most producing trees, followed by the Araraquarense and Vale do Paraíba regions (see Table 4.1). This concentration also occurred even in regions where only a few select municípios produced most of the coffee.

The 1900 survey also shows the growing importance of other crops in the state. Local farmers produced 7,326 metric tons of sugar, 7,003 metric tons of cotton, 9,283 metric tons of tobacco, and 112,384 casks of aguardente in this same year. There was also a significant output of food crops, with 329,000 metric tons of corn, 39,000 metric tons of beans, 18,000 metric tons of rice, and 1,197 casks of wine produced. The production of sugar was concentrated in the Central region, an area relatively similar to

TABLE 4.1

Number of Coffee Trees in Production and New Coffee Trees, São Paulo, 1898–1904

	1900			NEW TREES TO PRODUCING TREES (%)					
Region	Producing trees	New trees	Total	1898	1900	1901	1902	1903	1904
Capital	1,003,000		1,003,000						
Vale do Paraíba	53,110,210	10,473,259	63,583,469	22%	20%	26%	21%	13%	8%
Central	22,337,900	9,327,780	31,665,680	32%	42%	26%	27%	25%	12%
Mogiana	69,083,940	24,405,200	93,489,140	46%	35%	29%	15%	23%	18%
Baixa Paulista	30,648,000	5,998,400	36,646,400	50%	20%	25%	16%	16%	14%
Araraquarense	55,922,850	29,245,200	85,168,050	100%	52%	68%	56%	31%	17%
Noroeste	1,050,000	2,500,000	3,550,000						
Alta Sorocabana	14,231,540	5,764,500	19,996,040	60%	41%	32%	32%	29%	25%
Baixa Sorocabana	3,218,000	2,405,300	5,623,300	60%	75%	20%	59%	0%	0%
Santos	935,860	100,000	1,035,860						
Total	251,541,300	90,219,639	341,760,939	46%	36%	36%	26%	25%	16%

SOURCE: Departamento de Estatística do Estado, *Anuário estatístico de São Paulo*, 1898–1904.

NOTE: The data are not complete, but we have corrected them wherever possible, and the results are consistent with the 1900 production data. New trees are recently planted ones not yet producing coffee.

the old sugar quadrangle region, as was cotton production. Mogiana produced the most corn, beans, and rice, while tobacco was exclusively produced in Vale do Paraíba, which was also a major producer of aguardente for local consumption.

The agricultural labor force in 1900 consisted of 388,000 workers, of whom 55 percent were foreign born. The Araraquarense region had 98,000 workers and Mogiana 91,000, and together they accounted for half the agricultural laborers. The foreign workers were dominant in areas of recent settlement such as the Mogiana, Alta Sorocabana, Baixa Paulista, and Araraquarense regions. Two-thirds, or 388,000, of the agricultural workers in these zones were foreign born. These workers represented less than 20 percent of the state's population, and a third of them were fifteen to sixty years old.

By comparing the 1900 results with the partial survey of 1894/1895 and using as well the first complete agricultural census made in the state in 1905 we can obtain a good idea of the general structure and evolution of Paulista agriculture in this early republican period. As of 1900/1901 an area of 1.2 million hectares was under cultivation, of which 63 percent was dedicated to growing coffee. Cereals occupied 31 percent of these cultivated lands, with corn alone accounting for a fifth of the land. Sugarcane, cotton, and tobacco used only 2 percent each of the cultivated hectares. Moreover, all crops except tobacco consistently expanded at impressive rates. Also, total cultivated lands doubled between the first two surveys and increased by another 30 percent by the crop year of 1904/1905.

Although existing agricultural statistics relating to the nineteenth century are limited, we do have the well-known and complete survey conducted by Daniel P. Müller in 1836.[20] Coffee production expanded significantly from less than 9,000 metric tons in 1836 to 50,000 metric tons in 1854, reaching more than 500,000 metric tons in 1905, representing about 9 million bags.[21] In other words, from 1854, when the state produced just over 100 kilograms per inhabitant, to 1905, output nearly doubled. Data from 1902 for the port of Santos suggest that state production of sugar was able to cover only a third of the local consumption, and São Paulo needed to rely on imports for two-thirds of its needs. In contrast, cotton production, which was a significant input into Paulista industry, did grow substantially in this period, though it could not completely satisfy local demand, which still relied on imports from the northeastern states. Some 685,000 metric tons of corn was produced in 1905. But São Paulo was already self-sufficient in corn, importing none from outside the state in 1902.[22] Similarly, rice and beans were not imported in 1902 from other states, which shows that São Paulo remained self-sufficient in these two other basic staples.[23]

Ranching was a minor part of the state's agricultural economy. In 1900, ranches produced only 32,099 contos' worth of products, or approximately 20 percent of the value of agricultural production.[24] There were 10,000 farms with animals employing 20,000 workers, of whom a quarter were foreign-born immigrants. These farms had 85,000 horses and mules, 43,000 sheep, 450,000 pigs, and 224,000 cattle. Most of the value of animal production was in pigs and cattle, at 40 percent each, with horses and mules accounting for most of the rest. There was also a significant production of honey (39,000 liters) and animal fat (26,000 liters), though this latter product, important in the imperial period, was no longer an economically significant product. Vale do Paraíba accounted for 26 percent of these animals and their products, followed by the Mogiana (23 percent), Araraquarense, and Central regions.

The most basic change in this period, of course, was the total abandonment of slavery and the shift to a wage-labor system of free persons. The last eleven years of the nineteenth century and the early years of the next required a massive shift in the origin, cost, and organization of rural labor in São Paulo. Between 1827 and 1887, only 85,000 European immigrants entered São Paulo, but in the next ten years 823,000 Europeans came to the state. Of these immigrants, almost two-thirds were Italian, with Spaniards and Portuguese each contributing 10 percent.[25] These immigrants primarily moved to the new western areas of coffee production, which were the most profitable in the state. Given the lack of indemnity for planters with the loss of slaves, many planters in the older coffee regions found it difficult to make the transition, and some tried offering sharecropping as an alternative. But by far the most common payment for the immigrants was a combination of piecework, wages for harvesting coffee, access to land for planting food crops that immigrant families harvested, and free housing.[26]

The integration of these immigrants into the labor market followed a similar pattern. Upon arrival at Santos they were taken by rail to the capital and there temporarily housed in the state-run labor exchange and residence known as the Hospedaria dos Imigrantes. From there they were sent to the regions with the greatest demand for labor. This movement greatly increased in the 1890s and the first decade of the twentieth century. According to the census of 1890, the state had only 75,000 foreign born in a population of 1.4 million persons. By 1900 there were 214,000 immigrant workers just in Paulista agriculture, 60 percent of whom resided in just two regions, Mogiana and Araraquarense.

Although cotton and sugar continued to be produced in the state, their export fell as the local market expanded. The local textile industry absorbed almost all locally produced cotton and still needed to import even more from the Northeast. By the turn of the century the state had to import sugar from Pernambuco and other northeastern states. These two products were exported until the first years of the 1890s, but from 1883 to 1905 they no longer were significant in the export mix. The same occurred with flour, beans, corn, bacon, and wine. These were still being produced, but the local market was absorbing all local production and little was exported.

In 1905 the state government decided to undertake a full analysis of the rural situation. The result, one of the first agricultural censuses in Latin America, was unprecedented in its size and scope, reaching all the São Paulo municípios then in existence.[27] This census, carried out in a crisis period of overproduction, provides the most complete picture we have of this dominant world center of coffee production at the height of its development and one of the most complete surveys that exists of a fully developed plantation economy.[28]

The census of 1905 contains data on 49,184 farms and their owners in 165 municipalities. The farm proprietors were predominantly male (94 percent)[29] and of Brazilian birth (91 percent). Among the foreign-born owners the leaders were Italians and Portuguese (3 percent each), with a small number of Germans and Spaniards. Many of these foreigners were of immigrant-labor origin according to the analysis of this census by Thomas H. Holloway.[30] The majority of properties were owned by individuals, but corporations and partnerships representing heirs and enterprises were also owners. Some 1,607 proprietors owned more than one property and accounted for 3,695 farms. The census does not clarify the property rights of the land surveyed or the means by which the properties were acquired. But the spread of state population, made by clearing unexplored regions, may suggest the incidence of a high proportion of virgin lands obtained by the aggressive action of squatters.[31]

Coffee was cultivated by 21,152 planters, who harvested 534,000 metric tons of coffee, or 8.9 million sacks of coffee at 60 kilograms each. Nevertheless, the primary agricultural product of the state was corn, with 80 percent of the farms harvesting it. Next in importance was beans, also produced by a large number of farmers but whose total output was only 13 percent of corn production. Rice production was similar to beans, but was obtained on a smaller number of farms (see Table 4.2). As the statistical yearbook of the state stressed in its 1906 edition, there had been "great progress in the expansion of cereal cultivation compared with those of previous eras."[32] If

TABLE 4.2
Number of Farms, Area, Quantity, and Value of Production in São Paulo, 1905

Number of farms	49,184
Total area of farms (ha)	11,378,912
Total area cultivated (ha)	1,413,804
Average size of farms (ha)	237
Average cultivated area (ha)	32
Number of farms producing coffee	21,152
Number of farms producing corn	37,995
Number of farms producing beans	31,372
Number of farms producing rice	17,251
Total area planted in coffee (ha)	842,624
Total area planted in corn (ha)	389,707
Total area planted in beans (ha)	151,632
Total area planted in rice (ha)	59,640
Production of coffee (t)	534,181
Production of corn (L)	823,203,950
Production of beans (L)	113,345,688
Production of rice (L)	105,383,047
Total value of production (mil réis)	261,514,091
Proportion of coffee	64%
Proportion of corn	16%
Proportion of beans	7%
Proportion of rice	4%
Proportion of other products	9%

SOURCE: Instituto de Economia Agricola, *Censo agrícola de São Paulo, 1905.*

we compare the average from 1898–1901 with 1904–1906, we find the following rates of growth: rice grew by 112 percent, beans by 43 percent, and corn by 77 percent.[33]

The census mentions the existence of 413,341 agricultural laborers, of whom 55 percent were foreign born. What is surprising is the large number of native-born workers even on the coffee plantations, a group hitherto not recognized as an important part of the post-1900 workforce. Almost all studies of the coffee plantations have stressed the complete transition from Afro-Brazilian slave labor to European and later Asian immigrant labor and virtually ignored the existence of a native labor force in Paulista agriculture. Although these native-born workers were a minority of the rural labor force, they were present in twice as many farms as were the foreign-born workers. Foreigners obviously resided in the largest of the farms, which explains the average of seventeen foreign workers per fazenda, compared to only five native-born workers per farm. The existence of so many native-born workers is surprising, since it shows their continued importance in Paulista agriculture despite the intense foreign immigration that occurred in the last decade of the nineteenth and the beginning of the twentieth century. Nor were these native-born farmworkers just in domestic food production; they were also present in two-thirds of the farms that produced coffee and represented a third of coffee workers.[34] But it was the penetration of foreign-born immigrants into the state's interior that would bring about crucial changes in the evolution of the economy and society of the state in the first half of the twentieth century.

Despite the size and international importance attained by the coffee economy in São Paulo, the census shows the very low technology used by the state's farmers. Three-quarters of the municípios used no plows or harvesting equipment. In only six municípios was there relatively ample use of plows. The same is true of fertilizers. In just six municípios was any type of fertilizer usage by a farmer noted, and then it was principally manure and straw.[35] Although a few larger coffee farms had started agricultural mechanization at the beginning of the twentieth century,[36] these farms did not use such innovations in all parts of the crop production. When such machinery was used, it was usually confined to the processing of coffee beans and not used in planting and cultivation of crops.[37]

A large number of municípios, especially those with greater cultivation of coffee, were served by the railroad. The breadth of that system in São Paulo is seen in the fact that of the 165 municípios analyzed, 87 had a station, another 58 had rail service available at a distance of thirty miles or less, and 9 municípios were between thirty and sixty miles from a railhead. Only 11 municípios were more than a hundred miles from a station. Local transport to the railhead of course was still carried out by mule trains, horse-drawn wagons, or ox carts. But final shipment out of the município was now almost exclusively by rail.

Property size was not uniform across the state. Newly settled and frontier lands tended to be above average size. The largest farm owner declared that he possessed a fazenda of 242,000 hectares, and the twenty largest landowners had on average 48,400 hectares. These very large properties in general cultivated a smaller proportion of their land than smaller-sized farms[38] and were situated in municípios of recent settlement, like Bauru, Campos Novos Paulista, and São José do Rio Preto.[39] But there did seem to be an optimal size for efficient production. The top 20 percent of farms in size, those of 242 hectares and above, controlled 80 percent of the land, planted two-thirds of the area in crops, and accounted for three-quarters of coffee produced and two-thirds of the corn grown.[40] The smaller farms, 80 percent, possessed only 17 percent of São Paulo's total land, cultivated a third of the soils, and produced a fourth of the coffee and a third of the corn. This group of small farmers absorbed over a third of the farm laborers, equal to their share of cultivated lands.

The unequal distribution of farms is reflected in São Paulo's high Gini index, which indicates income inequality: 0.794 for properties and 0.801 for the owners. The index being higher for owners is due to the existence of multiple-farm owners in the census. If we compare these results to the indices of Gini for land distribution in São Paulo in 1817 (0.860)[41] and in 2003 (0.816),[42] it is evident that the high concentration of land ownership in São Paulo has historical roots going back more than two centuries. This pattern of unequal ownership was and is the norm throughout Latin America.[43]

That the coffee fazenda was not a monoculture farm can be seen in the fact that coffee-producing fazendas accounted for three-quarters of bean production; two-thirds of corn; around half of sugar, aguardente, and rice; and a third of tobacco in 1905. Given all these other products grown or produced by the coffee planters, the weight of the coffee fazendas in the total value of production was higher than just the value of the coffee crop. They accounted for 86 percent of the total agricultural production of São Paulo, even though coffee alone explained only two-thirds of this value, and a fourth of the value of the production of the coffee fazendas came from other crops. These results demonstrate the importance of the coffee fazenda within Paulista agriculture, as much for the value of its coffee production as for its production of multiple other crops for the internal market. It is evident that besides the small farmers who produced foodstuffs for themselves and for sale in the market, there was also an intense production of food products intercropped with coffee. We know that it was usual to plant other seasonal crops between the coffee trees, especially in the newer fazendas. The practice of allowing colonos to cultivate food crops among the coffee trees or in areas less suited for coffee production was also a common part of worker contracts. Contractors who planted coffee trees on a fazenda also often had this stipulated in their contracts.[44] Unfortunately, it is not possible to identify the proportion of these food crops that pertained to the owners, colonos, or contractors. All we know is that noncoffee production was carried out on the coffee plantations.[45]

To work the coffee estates, the fazendeiros employed on average half a dozen workers, compared to just three workers on average for noncoffee farms. This explains why, overall, coffee fazendas employed 80 percent of all farm workers and 94 percent of foreign-born workers. Because these workers were employed simultaneously in the production of coffee and other crops, it is impossible to identify the employment of the coffee fazenda labor force on each farm.

The average coffee fazenda produced annually 25,254 kilograms of coffee (the equivalent of 421 sacks of coffee), though with wide variation in terms of both farms and regions (see Table 4.3). The average output per coffee tree was 788 grams, the average production per hectare of coffee cultivated was 642 kilograms (or 11 sacks), and each farmworker produced on average 1,616 kilograms of coffee (or 27 sacks), though the latter number could be influenced by the existence of other crops in coffee farms and the age of the producing trees. Since part of this production of other crops pertained to the colonos' own crops, it was done in their leisure time and did not affect coffee output.

The Mogiana region had the most coffee fazendas and was the largest producer in the state, accounting for a third of production (see Map 4.1). But the Baixa Paulista region had the highest coffee production per fazenda in the state, which reflected its having the largest average area planted in coffee and the largest number of workers per fazenda, demonstrating its greater scale of production. Among the five highest regional producers of coffee,[46] the Araraquarense and Alta Sorocabana regions showed the best indicators of productivity, such as coffee output per hectare, and production per coffee tree and per farm laborer. Moreover, as can be seen in Map 4.2, only selected municípios within each region produced significant quantities of coffee. At the other end, the traditional Vale do Paraíba region made up only 5 percent of the output.[47] These results confirm the general view of the decay of the Vale do Paraíba region, whose decline began in the mid-nineteenth century and intensified with the emancipation of the slaves.

Also beginning to show indications of decline was the Central region, which in the second half of the nineteenth century had been a premier coffee zone. It too produced coffee in terms of area, tree, and worker well below more recently settled regions, such as the Mogiana, Baixa Paulista, Araraquarense, and Alta Sorocabana. Average output was half that of these new regions, in part because of lesser scale of production but also because of lower productivity.[48] These results suggest these areas had a virgin agricultural frontier that allowed high average yields, which boosted the state's coffee productivity. Railroad lines pushing into the frontier fortified the role of the state of São Paulo in the world coffee market. As long as there were virgin lands, available labor, and efficient transport, the Paulista coffee economy could continue to increase production. Only international market factors could limit its expansion, which in fact did occur in the first decade of the twentieth century with the crisis of overproduction.

TABLE 4.3

Production Indicators for Coffee in São Paulo, 1905

Indicator averages	Capital	Vale do Paraíba	Central	Mogiana	Baixa Paulista	Araraquarense	Noroeste	Alta Sorocabana	Baixa Sorocabana	Santos	Total state
Area of fazenda (ha)	75	166	214	259	342	251	1,498	429	661	461	270
Area in coffee (ha)	3.1	21.5	28.8	49.7	68.2	42.8	39.5	35.8	6.1	4.2	39.5
Trees per fazenda	1,842	19,701	23,794	38,872	55,671	34,706	31,070	28,689	4,879	1,245	32,062
Workers per fazenda	3.1	6.7	14.0	19.2	27.2	16.0	17.2	14.9	8.3	2.0	15.7
Output per tree (kg)	1.310	0.375	0.718	0.826	0.778	0.925	0.622	1.173	0.974	1.332	0.788
Output per worker (kg)	785	1,102	1,225	1,678	1,598	2,006	1,272	2,346	591	825	1,616
Output per hectare (kg)	789	344	597	647	635	750	489	941	780	429	642
Output per fazenda (kg)	2,414	7,396	17,079	32,099	43,297	32,105	19,340	33,656	4,750	1,658	25,254
Trees per worker	599	2,935	1,705	2,032	2,053	2,169	2,044	2,000	607	620	2,051
Value of coffee to total value (%)	45%	63%	64%	80%	76%	79%	74%	82%	30%	62%	75%
Foreign-born to all workers (%)	1%	5%	56%	73%	76%	77%	59%	65%	4%	2%	65%
Fazendas with foreign-born workers (%)	4%	6%	37%	61%	76%	71%	41%	46%	8%	4%	46%

SOURCE: Instituto de Economia Agricola, *Censo agrícola de São Paulo, 1905*.

Map 4.1 Principal Regions of Coffee Production in São Paulo, 1905

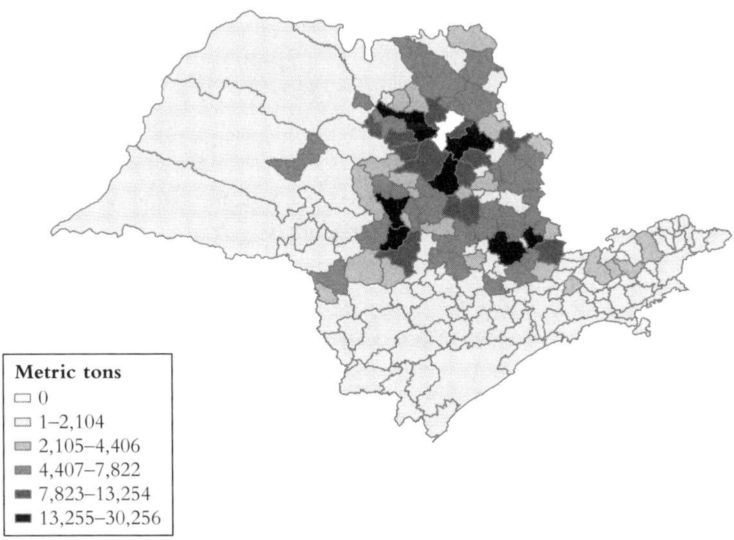

Map 4.2 Coffee Production by Município in São Paulo, 1905

Further displaying this concentration is that the 34 largest fazendeiros in terms of land owned 149 coffee fazendas, which accounted for just 2 percent of the area surveyed by the census but was a tenth of the area planted in coffee. They showed a similar ratio for trees owned and production. They also accounted for a tenth of the state's production of sugar and beans and 3 percent of its rice, corn, and aguardente. As a result, they generated 8 percent of the total value of agricultural production in the state and used 6 percent of farm laborers, almost all of whom were foreign immigrants.

Corn, because of the ease of its cultivation and the great internal demand, was the most widespread crop grown in the state and attracted a great number of small producers. Half the farms produced up to 10,000 liters per year, or 8 metric tons (or 133 sacks), and accounted for just 14 percent of the state's output. The same distribution occurred with the area planted in corn: more than two-thirds of the producers planted up to 3 hectares of corn, but contributed less than a quarter of total production. At the other end, the farmers with the largest croplands dedicated to corn—just 8 percent of the producers—generated half the corn harvest. Noncoffee producers averaged 15,000 liters of corn per farm, while the coffee estates averaged almost double that, with each coffee fazenda on average producing 29,000 liters of corn. Despite these results, corn production was less concentrated than coffee production, as demonstrated by the Gini indices of inequality: 0.663 for corn and 0.774 for coffee.

The agricultural census of 1905 thus presents a complex picture of a dominant and highly concentrated coffee economy but without the usual monoproduction consequences associated with other plantation societies in the Americas. These large fazendas, with millions of coffee trees, not only produced millions of tons of coffee for the international market and employed thousands of agricultural workers but also were major producers for the internal market of basic agricultural products of crucial importance to the local economy. These large estates also coexisted with small farms, which were the majority of farm units. Thus, at the beginning of the twentieth century, agriculture was still open to small and medium-sized farmers. We have already noted the tendency of coffee fazendas in the first half of the nineteenth century to produce alternative food crops. What is revealed by this 1905 census is that even in its period of maturity the coffee fazendas of São Paulo still produced cereal on a grand scale. Corn, rice, beans, sugar, and aguardente were all primarily produced on these great estates. Moreover, corn remained the essential second crop in São Paulo even at the height of the state's coffee boom.

Despite no significant technological adoption or increased productivity, Paulista agriculture changed in the first half of the twentieth century. Coffee dominated the rural world until well past mid-century, but there was also growth in the area cultivated in other crops and in the quantities of commercial and food products produced. There was also an increasing integration between agriculture and industry. Agriculture, in the form of coffee exports, not only generated the foreign currency needed to pay for machinery imports but also provided food for industrial workers and, most crucially, the raw inputs for industry. The key industries developing in the state were textiles and food and drink processing, and local agriculture supplied the bulk of the cotton, silk, animals, and other raw materials for them. Also, machinery was slowly beginning to liberate rural workers for participation in the industrial workforce, especially as significant foreign immigration ended after 1920.

During the first forty years of the century, the coffee frontier continued to evolve, with the traditional regions rapidly declining in production as coffee moved toward the west and northwest of the state. By the end of the 1930s new coffee-producing centers, such as Pirajuí, Lins, Marília, Cafelandia, and Araçatuba, outperformed the traditional coffee municípios of Campinas, Jaú, Ribeirão Preto, São Manoel, and São Simão. Pirajuí, in the Northwest region, grew rapidly in the twentieth century with the extension of the Noroeste do Brasil railway. By the harvest of 1935/1936, it was producing 50,000 metric tons of coffee (845,000 sacks) from 45 million coffee trees. The same occurred with the município of Lins, also along the Noroeste do Brasil railroad, which in the crop year 1935/1936 produced 41,000 metric tons (690,000 sacks) from 37 million trees. In contrast, Ribeirão Preto output dropped by more than half, going from 36,000 metric tons in 1909/1910 to 15,000 in 1935/1936, and the município of Jaú, which had produced 39,000 metric tons of coffee in the harvest of 1909/1910, produced half that in the harvest of 1935/1936.

If in 1900 the Central region accounted for almost a quarter of production, followed by Mogiana and Alta Sorocabana, by 1905/1906 Mogiana was the leading producer, at 30 percent, followed by Baixa Paulista. In 1929/1930, when the total harvest reached 1.14 million metric tons (or 19 million sacks), Araraquarense became the leader with 26 percent. Mogiana now accounted for 23 percent. In 1935/1936, when the harvest reached 930,000 metric tons (or 16 million sacks), the Northwest region accounted for 30 percent, followed by the Araraquarense region with 26 percent (see Table 4.4). Production thus shifted to the west of the state of São Paulo in this thirty-year period. As new areas entered the market, overproduction

TABLE 4.4
Production of Coffee by Region, 1900–1936 (metric tons)

Year	Vale do Paraíba	Central	Mogiana	Baixa Paulista	Araraquarense	Noroeste	Alta Sorocabana	Total
1900	55,237	115,346	101,621	57,356	52,760	2,208	101,756	488,775
1904	13,210	47,809	77,696	38,947	39,041		37,736	255,070
1906	24,685	92,570	216,798	163,730	148,789	5,288	70,679	725,867
1909/1910	22,201	79,363	275,744	144,794	126,470	4,563	64,577	720,338
1910/1911	20,987	65,268	177,729	100,162	91,035	1,169	44,467	502,537
1911/1912	19,815	65,740	235,912	125,418	109,660	3,601	57,205	619,599
1912/1913	19,065	58,572	220,977	112,453	92,216	3,066	29,200	537,114
1913/1914	21,783	73,502	244,980	115,415	122,638	6,136	62,859	649,909
1914/1915	23,440	70,218	216,421	109,309	84,809	2,479	47,510	556,389
1915/1916	21,992	80,782	239,276	125,846	140,592	6,548	68,726	686,083
1916/1917	22,935	72,113	201,620	120,267	107,874	6,830	51,824	585,401
1917/1918	17,839	75,827	255,938	140,047	142,741	9,635	74,831	718,646
1918/1919	12,837	47,077	151,341	83,390	87,590	6,624	33,846	424,217
1919/1920	10,572	32,394	86,900	46,420	41,639	3,408	20,756	243,167
1921/1922	14,929	54,100	150,449	87,717	99,967	16,774	48,896	473,469
1922/1923	12,093	51,778	123,012	74,733	88,113	17,523	44,926	412,811
1923/1924	15,538	64,991	187,588	103,784	154,635	22,910	54,460	604,655
1924/1925	13,457	57,565	156,545	105,034	126,743	25,337	52,818	538,350
1925/1926	13,407	59,260	157,241	110,521	131,408	33,471	73,701	579,799
1926/1927	12,392	49,989	168,971	99,380	169,153	38,353	51,357	590,198
1927/1928	15,560	91,895	232,029	173,107	263,209	140,849	132,493	1,049,966
1928/1929	16,786	45,813	126,798	93,347	135,369	43,682	58,196	520,333
1929/1930	18,223	90,883	261,696	182,572	294,627	133,778	158,478	1,140,821
1930/1931	16,592	56,044	161,357	119,446	199,043	108,742	97,131	759,831
1931/1932	16,725	80,301	203,111	152,190	285,654	195,418	125,700	1,061,309
1932/1933	17,125	55,977	153,213	115,916	262,800	181,851	88,112	877,352
1934/1935	13,140	53,889	132,654	93,741	208,893	193,887	103,745	802,009
1935/1936	11,471	45,394	142,385	86,210	238,074	276,469	128,910	930,805

SOURCE: Camargo, *Crescimento da população no Estado de São Paulo e seus aspectos econômicos*; *Boletim da Diretoria de Indústria e Comércio*, various issues.
NOTE: The Baixa Sorocabana, Capital, and Santos regions produced less than 1 percent in these years.

became a constant issue, which finally led in the 1930s to the government destroying stocks of coffee as the only long-term solution.

Despite this continued expansion into virgin lands, overall average state productivity was declining as productivity in the older areas went into ever-deeper decline. Whereas productivity was relatively stable until 1910, it was badly affected by the severe frost of 1918. Aside from reducing that year's harvest, the frost damaged many coffee trees and reduced their productivity for many years afterward. Not until the 1920s did average productivity rise again, but then came the world economic crisis of 1929. Not only were poorer-producing trees abandoned, but the care and cultivation of producing trees was reduced, which affected productivity.

The case of Ribeirão Preto, one of the most important coffee centers, shows the effects of the 1918 freeze and the 1929 crisis. Until 1916/1917 it was producing 35,000 metric tons of coffee, with productivity greater than 1 kilogram per tree. Because of the 1918 freeze, production declined to 8,000 metric tons in the harvest of 1919/1920, and productivity dropped to 0.3 kilograms per tree. In the 1920s productivity rose to between 0.6 and 0.8 kilograms per tree, but this was inferior to what had been achieved a decade earlier. By 1920 Ribeirão Preto was no longer the principal producer of coffee in the state, having been replaced by the new western zones. Other crops now became important in Ribeirão Preto, such as cotton and sugarcane, and its economy began to develop industrial and service activities related to its developing urban center.[49]

This agricultural diversification was happening throughout the state but especially after the world economic crisis of the 1930s. Diversification can be seen already in 1920, when the first national agricultural census was produced. The census lists the existence of 21,341 coffee-producing farms in the state, with some 882 million coffee trees planted on a million hectares. More than 70 percent of the coffee was now concentrated in the Mogiana, Baixa Paulista, and Araraquarense regions. The state averages in terms of coffee productivity were 324 kilograms of coffee beans per hectare, 405 kilograms per thousand trees, and 801 trees planted per hectare. But in the case of coffee, so dependent on both new and old plantings and on soil quality, there were wide regional variations around these averages. The principal coffee-producing municípios in the crop year of 1919/1920 were Campinas, which produced almost 12,000 metric tons; Ribeirão Preto, at 11,000 metric tons; São Carlos and Amparo, at 10,000 metric tons each; São José do Rio Pardo, at 9,800 metric tons; and Jaú, at 9,000 tons (see Table 4.5).

According to the 1920 census there were 80,921 farms in São Paulo, of which 59,000 were 100 hectares or less. These 59,000 smaller farms accounted for 12 percent of Brazil's farms and contained 13 percent of the total national cultivated lands. The average size of all farms in the state was 172 hectares, in comparison to 270 hectares for the national average. This lower average size of Paulista farms was influenced by the smaller size of the largest estates. For farms in the state with 101 hectares or more, the average size was 552 hectares, similar to the averages found in Bahia and Minas Gerais, but far less than the national average of 865 hectares. The

TABLE 4.5

Number, Size, and Production of Coffee Fazendas in São Paulo, 1920

Region	Number of producers	Production (t)	Area (ha)	Coffee trees	Output per hectare (kg)	Output per 1,000 trees (kg)	Trees per hectare	Output per fazenda (kg)	Average area per fazenda (ha)	Trees per fazenda
Vale do Paraíba	2,276	11,489	51,359	103,502,705	224	111	2,015	5,048	23	45,476
Central	3,645	41,690	123,678	98,943,092	337	421	800	11,437	34	27,145
Mogiana	5,720	118,780	302,519	242,015,910	393	491	800	20,766	53	42,310
Baixa Paulista	3,184	64,732	203,208	160,527,894	319	403	790	0,330	64	50,417
Araraquarense	4,148	61,049	223,398	178,167,113	273	343	798	14,718	54	42,953
Noroeste	348	10,857	34,954	27,964,108	311	388	800	31,199	100	80,357
Alta Sorocabana	1,394	25,881	87,779	70,220,938	295	369	800	18,566	63	50,374
Baixa Sorocabana	161	401	1,351	1,081,960	297	371	801	2,491	8	6,720
Santos	451	193	418	335,102	462	577	801	429	1	743
Subtotal	*21,327*	*335,073*	*1,028,665*	*882,758,822*	*326*	*380*	*858*	*15,711*	*48*	*41,392*
Total	21,341	333,769	1,028,673	823,942,616	324	405	801	15,640	48	38,608

SOURCE: Diretoria Geral de Estatística, *Recenseamento do Brazil realizado em 1 de setembro de 1920*, vol. 3, part 2a, pp. 110–337.

NOTE: We exclude the Capital region because of its minimal output. Also, several regional totals are incomplete, since they were obtained by adding up only the municípios whose data was complete. The totals we use are the totals given in the census for São Paulo.

larger national average was influenced by the existence of large unproductive landholdings in many states. In turn, the average value of both these larger and smaller farms in São Paulo was far higher than the average value of such farms in the nation, indicating the greater economic profitability of rural properties in São Paulo. But São Paulo in 1920 still had a highly skewed distribution of land ownership. About half the rural establishments of less than 101 hectares controlled only 15 percent of the land, and those between 101 and 1,000 hectares accounted for 23 percent of all farms and controlled 40 percent of the agricultural area of the state. The large fazendas, those with 2,000 or more hectares, controlled 45 percent of the total rural property but were only 2.5 percent of the farms.[50] This unequal distribution is confirmed by the Gini index for land ownership, which was 0.748.

Of the 545,000 farm owners in Brazil, some 79,000 were foreign born, and they were concentrated in Rio Grande do Sul and São Paulo, which together accounted for two-thirds of foreign-born farm owners. These foreign-born farmers in Brazil controlled only 6 percent of the land, but in the two states the figures were double or more—12 percent in Rio Grande do Sul and 16 percent in São Paulo. In São Paulo, as in Rio Grande do Sul, the average area of the foreign-born-owned farms was a little more than half the average size of the native-born-owned farms. In São Paulo Italian farm owners were the dominant group among the foreign born, with some 11,800 of them; Portuguese farmers were second (3,900), and then came the Spaniards (3,500) and the Japanese (1,100). In terms of average area, the Portuguese had the largest farms, probably because of their longer history as migrants to Brazil. It is no surprise that the average Japanese farm was smaller than all the others. The Japanese did not begin to arrive in Brazil until after 1908, when the United States closed its doors to Japanese migration.

Almost a quarter of the cultivated land of Brazil (some 6.6 million hectares) was in the state of São Paulo. Of these 2 million hectares in the state, a million were in arable lands, where the principal cereals, potatoes, cotton, tobacco, and sugarcane were grown, and another million hectares were dedicated to coffee growing. The state had 46 percent of the national lands planted with coffee trees (see Table 4.6). Its 21,000 fazendas contained 824 million trees. This resulted in a harvest in the 1919/1920 season of 5.6 million sacks of coffee, which corresponded to 42 percent of national production. Minas Gerais was now the second-largest producer, with 4.2 million bags of coffee, followed by Rio de Janeiro, with 1.3 million, and Espírito Santo, with 1 million. Paraná was still just a minor producer.

TABLE 4.6

Producers, Area Planted, and Principal Agricultural Products by State, 1920

Product	São Paulo	São Paulo (% of total)	Bahia	Minas Gerais	Paraná	Pernambuco	Rio de Janeiro	Rio Grande do Sul	Total Brazil
Coffee									
Number of producers	21,341	17%	17,415	41,393	1,215	5,347	10,766	25	128,424
Area planted (ha)	1,028,673	46%	71,144	650,706	23,815	45,104	194,490	47	2,215,658
Number of trees	823,942,616	48%	49,799,853	480,036,200	14,287,666	29,316,825	155,594,703	25,191	1,708,418,893
Quantity (60 kg sacks)	5,562,820	42%	422,143	4,212,505	84,770	254,430	1,360,697	107	13,141,468
Value of production	434,445,960	42%	32,927,180	328,575,390	6,612,060	19,845,540	106,134,340	8,320	1,025,034,530
Kilos per hectare	324		356	388	214	338	420	137	356
Kilos per 1,000 trees	405		509	527	356	521	525	255	462
Corn									
Number of producers	69,871	14%	31,651	101,248	27,875	14,330	16,999	108,537	491,370
Area planted (ha)	571,600	23%	84,550	620,441	178,094	63,685	58,826	535,106	2,451,382
Quantity (60 kg sacks)	19,870,842	24%	2,408,628	21,194,265	6,107,682	1,778,373	2,984,654	19,143,902	83,328,295
Value of production	238,450,100	24%	28,903,540	254,331,180	73,292,180	21,340,480	35,815,840	229,726,820	999,939,540
Kilos per hectare	2086		1709	2050	2058	1675	3044	2147	2040
Cotton									
Number of producers	19,764	22%	3,886	11,690	482	10,406	45	422	91,785
Area planted (ha)	109,788	29%	18,508	10,429	2,165	70,013	501	1,222	378,599
Quantity (60 kg sacks)	1,045,842	31%	159,099	86,666	17,816	619,776	3,018	6,097	3,323,382
Value of production	209,168,400	31%	31,819,800	1,333,200	3,563,200	13,955,200	603,300	1,219,400	664,676,400
Kilos per hectare	560		505	488	483	520	354	293	516

Beans									
Number of producers	9,053	14%	658	5,260	8,566	177	1,986	32,408	66,790
Area planted (ha)	188,692	28%	38,880	156,998	30,799	17,798	17,115	102,615	672,912
Quantity (60 kg sacks)	3,558,450	29%	762,825	2,580,936	401,502	294,145	466,217	2,018,565	12,084,490
Value of production	74,727,450	29%	16,019,325	54,199,670	8,431,535	6,177,045	9,790,550	42,389,900	253,774,290
Kilos per hectare	1132		1177	986	782	992	1634	1180	1078
Tobacco									
Number of producers	4,615	6%	17,916	9,563	6,515	3,679	300	12,998	74,004
Area planted (ha)	6,102	6%	29,391	22,798	1,033	4,851	618	20,939	106,145
Quantity (60 kg sacks)	3,668	5%	28,758	11,473	666	2,278	251	14,480	73,647
Value of production	5,503,050	5%	43,137,600	17,209,500	999,750	3,417,600	377,250	21,720,900	110,470,800
Kilos per hectare	36		59	30	39	28	24	41	42
Rice									
Number of producers	52,864	22%	9,050	75,433	4,955	909	6,702	28,237	242,979
Area planted (ha)	218,522	41%	10,433	116,404	5,666	948	8,029	51,590	532,384
Quantity (60 kg sacks)	5,800,330	42%	212,452	2,885,375	176,398	16,313	315,062	1,878,790	13,858,252
Value of production	174,009,900	42%	6,373,550	86,561,250	5,291,950	489,400	9,451,850	56,363,700	415,747,550
Kilos per hectare	1,593		1,222	1,487	1,868	1,032	2,354	2,185	1,562
Total value of production	1,136,304,860	33%	159,180,995	742,210,190	98,190,675	65,225,265	162,173,130	351,429,040	3,469,643,110

SOURCE: Diretoria Geral de Estatística, *Recenseamento do Brazil realizado em 1 de setembro de 1920*, vol. 3, part 2a, p. xxi.

NOTE: Quintais were converted to kilograms at 58.7464 kg per quintal. Value of production is given in mil réis.

The average productivity of the São Paulo coffee planters was 324 kilograms of beans per hectare, 405 kilograms per thousand trees, and 15.6 metric tons per worker. The productivity per hectare and per thousand trees was similar to the national average, but the output per worker was much greater than the national average, indicating a greater scale of production in São Paulo. Even so, this same 1919/1920 harvest was not a typical year, since São Paulo coffee producers were still suffering damage from the frost of 1918. In this crop year Paulista output reached more than a million sacks of coffee, representing a third of national production and accounting for a little less than a third of the national area planted in coffee.

The frost also affected other agricultural products produced in the state in that year.[51] It is difficult to estimate the loss in the 1919/1920 harvest given the lack of data for food products for many of the previous years. In that harvest year, the state's farmers produced 20 million sacks of corn (or 1.2 million metric tons), which represented 24 percent of national production. But the productivity in the state, 2,086 kilograms per hectare, was little different from the national average. In the country as a whole, half a million corn farmers used 2.4 million hectares—more than that dedicated to coffee—and generated a value of production practically identical to coffee. But the importance of coffee came not from its land absorption, use of manpower, or value of production; it came from its representation in Brazilian exports. Unlike most other agricultural products, which were destined for the domestic market, coffee was the crucial international export of Brazil. Within São Paulo, however, the area planted in corn was half that used for coffee, and its value was half that of the coffee crop.

The state also accounted for 42 percent of the national rice production and 29 percent of beans grown in the 1919/1920 harvest. The total size of the area sown with these three cereal and pulse crops (corn, rice, and beans) was similar to that producing coffee. But the value of all Paulista cereal and pulse production was now greater than the value of coffee grown in the state. São Paulo produced significant quantities of cotton, mostly to supply the local textile industry. While production was initially insufficient to meet local demand, by the early decades of the new century cotton production was increasing greatly. Thus, in 1911 some 53 percent of the 14,000 metric tons of cotton consumed in the state was imported from other states. By 1919 only 7 percent of the 24 million metric tons of cotton consumed in the state was imported. But the local cotton plants suffered from a plague, and production dropped by half in the harvest of 1919/1920, leading to a greater importation of cotton in 1920.[52] In that year Paulista production reached a million bags of cotton, which represented a third of national production, with just under a third of the national area planted in cotton.

Paulista sugar growing was less successful in this period. The state generated in the 1919/1920 harvest some 56,000 metric tons of sugar, which accounted for just 8 percent of national production. Of this amount, according to statistics gathered by São Paulo, only 12 percent was produced using traditional mills (*engenhocas*), and 88 percent came from the sixteen modern mills (*usinas*) then operating in the state.[53] This production was not sufficient to meet local demand. Local consumption in the 1910s was some 90,000 metric tons, and thus at least 60,000 metric tons of sugar was annually imported into Santos from other states.[54] Average output per hectare varied considerably, going from 40 metric tons per hectare in Lorena, Piracicaba, Porto Feliz, and Jaboticabal to 45 metric tons in Capivari, 50 in Franca, and 59 in Campinas.[55]

All regions grew cereals regardless of their specialization in a given crop. Corn, rice, and beans were planted everywhere. They were vital for both human and animal consumption. The Capital region and the southern municípios by this time were insignificant farming areas with only two exceptions. Considerable rice was grown in the southern coastal município of Iguape, and English potatoes were grown in Cotia in the Capital region. Araraquarense, Mogiana, and the Central region were major producers of corn, rice, and beans, with the Araraquarense and Northwest regions having a high average production of rice, while corn was more concentrated in the Mogiana and Alta Sorocabana regions. Beans were more dispersed than other crops, though there was major production in the Baixa Paulista, Mogiana, and Northwest regions (see Table 4.7).

Over the next twenty years the state maintained its leadership position in Brazilian agricultural production. By the census of 1940, São Paulo had some 1.7 million hectares in permanent plant production and 2.6 million in annual temporary cultivation, corresponding to 28 percent and 21 percent, respectively, of the total country. The state employed 1.8 million persons in agriculture, or 16 percent of the national total. Those farms without animals accounted for 31 percent of the value of national food and commercial crop production, against only 14 percent for Minas Gerais, the next-most-important state.

Although we cannot generate good productivity data from the 1940 census, it is clear that if São Paulo accounted for just 9 percent of the cultivated area of the nation, employed 16 percent of agricultural workers, and generated 25 percent of the value of all rural production—farms, mixed farms (those raising animals and growing crops), and ranches—its indices

TABLE 4.7

Production of Principal Agricultural Crops in São Paulo by Region, 1920

	RICE			CORN			BEANS			POTATOES			COTTON			TOBACCO		
Regions	Farms	Production (t)	Area (ha)	Farms	Production (t)	Area (ha)	Farms	Production (t)	Area (ha)	Farms	Production (t)	Area (ha)	Farms	Production (t)	Area (ha)	Farms	Production (t)	Area (ha)
Capital	180	94	51	1,915	11,232	5,405	1,827	3,038	2,532	1,697	7,916	1,319	11	38	39	21	4	6
Vale do Paraíba	5,779	33,207	24,900	9,023	66,132	29,244	8,436	14,177	13,215	1,665	5,124	883	194	2,194	2,630	1,274	1,286	2,159
Central	9,854	24,740	14,545	15,199	191,475	89,918	13,707	28,208	24,642	2,264	10,327	1,668	5,438	21,559	29,753	470	297	828
Mogiana	8,416	53,268	30,297	9,553	229,559	105,264	9,004	47,022	40,591	786	5,506	879	1,446	11,272	11,599	562	513	858
Baixa Paulista	6,269	49,314	30,984	6,702	144,408	65,816	5,886	35,088	31,326	413	3,635	606	1,501	9,117	10,379	140	120	210
Araraquarense	11,524	116,808	66,826	12,172	226,360	108,064	11,040	46,617	40,149	185	196	44	2,565	14,057	16,006	517	339	577
Noroeste	3,513	42,421	31,415	3,896	66,910	38,141	3,638	18,474	18,593	577	4,982	745	1,366	5,637	6,629	182	129	225
Alta Sorocabana	4,536	11,742	6,850	6,662	159,950	75,559	6,016	16,154	13,759	133	140	25	2,919	21,569	23,208	351	172	284
Baixa Sorocabana	2,103	2,382	1,902	3,359	75,629	32,507	2,847	3,795	3,162	179	530	88	1,840	9,479	10,469	457	571	952
Santos	2,883	11,230	10,751	1,492	4,815	3,582	944	725	723	80	89	15				1	2	3
Total	55,057	345,206	218,522	69,973	1,176,468	553,500	63,345	213,297	188,692	7,979	38,446	6,273	17,280	94,922	110,712	3,975	3,432	6,102

Region	RICE			CORN			BEANS			POTATOES			COTTON			TOBACCO		
	Kilos per farm	Output per hectare	% of cultivated area	Kilos per farm	Output per hectare	% of cultivated area	Kilos per farm	Output per hectare	% of cultivated area	Kilos per farm	Output per hectare	% of cultivated area	Kilos per farm	Output per hectare	% of cultivated area	Kilos per farm	Output per hectare	% of cultivated area
Capital	523	1,833	0%	5,865	2,078	1%	1,663	1,200	1%	4,665	6,001	21%	3,491	997	0%	167	583	0%
Vale do Paraíba	5,746	1,334	11%	7,329	2,261	5%	1,681	1,073	7%	3,077	5,801	14%	11,309	834	2%	1,009	596	35%
Central	2,511	1,701	7%	12,598	2,129	16%	2,058	1,145	13%	4,561	6,191	27%	3,964	725	27%	631	358	14%
Mogiana	6,329	1,758	14%	24,030	2,181	19%	5,222	1,158	22%	7,005	6,261	14%	7,795	972	10%	914	598	14%
Baixa Paulista	7,866	1,592	14%	21,547	2,194	12%	5,961	1,120	17%	8,802	5,997	10%	6,074	878	9%	854	570	3%
Araraquarense	10,136	1,748	31%	18,597	2,095	20%	4,223	1,161	21%	1,062	4,477	1%	5,480	878	14%	656	589	9%
Noroeste	12,075	1,350	14%	17,174	1,754	7%	5,078	994	10%	8,634	6,683	12%	4,127	850	6%	706	571	4%
Alta Sorocabana	2,589	1,714	3%	24,009	2,117	14%	2,685	1,174	7%	1,055	5,612	0%	7,389	929	21%	490	605	5%
Baixa Sorocabana	1,133	1,252	1%	22,515	2,327	6%	1,333	1,200	2%	2,961	6,030	1%	5,152	905	9%	1,250	600	16%
Santos	3,896	1,045	5%	3,227	1,344	1%	768	1,002	0%	1,118	5,948	0%			0%	1,900	571	0%
Total	6,270	1,580	100%	16,813	2,126	100%	4,764	1,130	100%	4,818	6,129	100%	5,493	857	100%	863	563	100%

SOURCE: Diretoria Geral de Estatística, *Recenseamento do Brazil realizado em 1 de setembro de 1920*, vol. 3, part 2a, pp. xxi–lv.
NOTE: Quintais were converted at 58.7464 kg per quintal.

of productivity per hectare and per worker were superior to the rest of the country. The state had 86,000 farms that produced just food and commercial crops, and these farms employed 476,000 permanent workers, or 20 percent of all persons permanently employed in Brazilian agriculture. Thus, the state employed on average 5.5 workers in food and commercial production farms, 8.8 workers in mixed farms, and 11 workers per cattle ranch. In the nation as a whole, the figures were 4.4, 5.9, and 10 workers, respectively.

The predominance of São Paulo agriculture into the 1940s can be explained by several factors. Although São Paulo had lost relative share in coffee production from the shift of production to other regions of Brazil, the state remained Brazil's primary coffee producer, accounting for approximately two-thirds of production. In addition, other agricultural products gained in importance within the state because São Paulo had the best transportation infrastructure and port facilities in the nation and its soils remained highly productive. To the present day São Paulo is the national leader in the production of grains, sugarcane, fruits—particularly oranges—and legumes. Moreover, Paulista agriculture was sustained by the needs of a major local market. In the period when interstate transport was still precarious, this state market was a major stimulus to local production. Paulista industry, particularly the food and fabrics sector, received most of its inputs from state farms. In addition, the state of São Paulo was not only the most populous state but also the most urbanized and the most influenced by the varied demand generated by immigration. Moreover, it was the richest state, having a higher per capita income and higher education levels than the rest of Brazil (see Table 4.8), and thus represented a relatively sophisticated local market for Paulista agriculture. In general, most of the local production, except coffee, served domestic demand, primarily supplying the local state market. The few Paulista agricultural products that were exported beyond the state included cotton, rice, frozen meat, fruit, and castor oil (*mamona*). But none of these exports approached the role played by coffee, still the main product in Brazilian exports. Between satisfying the growing local market and the export of these other products, São Paulo agriculture was strengthened, and the fact that the state imported only wheat and sugar showed how local production was able to supply all the needs of the rapidly growing state population.

The continued flow of foreign-born immigrants into São Paulo as agricultural workers over the course of some fifty or more years resulted in there being an even greater presence of foreign-born farm owners in the state by 1940. They now owned 64,000 rural establishments in the state,

TABLE 4.8

Principal Economic and Social Characteristics of São Paulo and Other Major States in Brazil

	Total no. for Brazil	São Paulo (no.)	São Paulo (%)	Minas Gerais (%)	Rio de Janeiro and Federal District (%)	Rio Grande do Sul (%)	Bahia (%)
Population	*41,236,315*	*7,184,316*	*17%*	*16%*	*9%*	*8%*	*10%*
Whites	26,171,778	6,100,862	23%	16%	9%	11%	4%
Foreign born and naturalized	1,406,568	814,102	23%	3%	19%	8%	1%
Literate (over 5 years old)	13,292,605	3,196,556	24%	14%	9%	11%	6%
Persons with more than 10 years in agriculture	9,453,512	1,529,055	16%	17%	4%	8%	11%
Persons with more than 10 years in industry	1,400,056	428,478	31%	10%	7%	1%	3%
Persons 5 to 39 being educated	3,405,765	731,832	21%	13%	16%	11%	6%
Persons 5 to 39 studying for a postsecondary degree	40,294	10,746	27%	10%	36%	7%	4%
Persons with a postsecondary degree	96,943	29,583	31%	13%	34%	9%	5%
Value of agricultural production in 1940	8,192,838	3,248,610	40%	15%	5%	8%	5%
Hospital beds	90,597	22,814	25%				
Estimate of industrial production in 1938	12,000,000	5,000,000	42%				
Residents in noncapital cities with more than 10,000 persons	2,582,560	1,003,337	39%				
Number of noncapital cities with more than 10,000 persons	121	39	32%				

SOURCE: Instituto Brasileiro de Geografia e Estatística, *Recenseamento geral do Brasil, 1940*; Instituto Brasileiro de Geografia e Estatística, *Anuário estatístico do Brasil, 1941*.

far more than in any other state: more than half the national farms owned by the foreign born were in São Paulo. Within the state itself they had 32 percent of all rural establishments, against just 8 percent in the rest of the country. Even many of the major rural farm-related industries were now owned by foreigners, from the usinas to the modern packing houses.

By 1940 the foreign born had increased their ownership of individually owned farms (of which there were 201,000) to 32 percent and now controlled 27 percent of all farmland. In 1920 the average farm size of the native born was 181 hectares and of foreigner born just 87 hectares. In 1940 the average farm size of both groups declined, to 64 hectares for native born and 53 hectares for foreign born.[56] Among the foreign born, Italians still owned the most farms (34 percent) but were now followed in importance by Japanese (25 percent), Spaniards (18 percent), and Portuguese (13 percent).

More than half the rural properties in the state were 20 hectares or less, those with 100 hectares or less controlled 28 percent of farmland, and those with more than 100 hectares (13 percent of the properties) controlled 72 percent of the land. Despite this rural concentration of landholding in São Paulo, land in this state was still much more equally distributed than in the country as a whole. The Gini index for São Paulo was 0.76 and for Brazil as a whole it was 0.82.

It would only be in the 1970s, with the integration of industry and agriculture, that a massive mechanization of Brazilian agriculture would occur. But even in 1940 there was significant proliferation of plow use, which had hardly existed in the census of 1905. In 1940 São Paulo had 250,000 farms using 168,000 plows and 32,000 harrows, and these were well distributed throughout the state. São Paulo had a third of the nation's plows and together with Rio Grande do Sul had 78 percent of all plows listed in the census. But even more impressive was the existence of a significant number of trucks. The 6,000 trucks listed in the state represented more than half of the trucks in Brazil.[57]

By 1940 coffee was in decline in São Paulo. While there were 65,457 fazendas producing coffee in the state, output was just 12 million sacks of coffee. This now represented 60 percent of the 1939/1940 Brazilian harvest. Minas Gerais was the second-largest producer and Espírito Santo the third, and Paraná was now fourth in importance of coffee output. On average São Paulo coffee farmers were producing 183 bags of coffee per farm, an amount greater than the other producing states because it still had a billion coffee trees. But only 2 percent (or 20 million) of Paulista coffee trees were newly planted (and not yet in production), and the state had only 11 percent of the newly planted trees in the nation, indicating the long-term decline in expected state production. In contrast, in Paraná and Espírito Santo the ratio of new to old trees was much higher, at 37 percent and 21 percent, respectively. In output per thousand trees, São Paulo produced 672 kilograms compared to a national average of 566 kilograms. And as had occurred throughout the late nineteenth and early twentieth centuries in 1940, the newer regions predominated in coffee production, especially the Northwest and Araraquarense regions, both of recent settlement and with virgin soils. This can be seen in their higher productivity (see Table 4.9).

Cotton remained an important crop in Brazil as of 1940, though with two distinct varieties being planted. In the states of the Northeast region was grown long-strand arboreal cotton, which was called *mocó*. In the other states, including São Paulo, the principal cotton produced was short-strand herbaceous cotton, which was of annual production. The state of São Paulo had 100,000 producers of cotton and generated a harvest of 840,000 metric tons. The Paulista volume represented 72 percent of short-strand cotton in the country. Almost all of this Paulista-grown cotton was consumed locally by the expanding textile industries. Despite this significant production, the state still had to import raw cotton from the growers in the Northeast to satisfy its textile industry.

São Paulo in 1940 continued to be a significant producer of food and other agricultural products. Rice, for example, was grown by 132,000 farmers, producing 270,000 metric tons. Beans were grown on 148,000 farms that produced 115,000 metric tons. Corn was grown on 188,000 rural

TABLE 4.9

Coffee Fazendas, Production, Trees, and Productivity by Region in São Paulo, 1940

	COFFEE FAZENDAS			COFFEE TREES			
Region	Fazendas with information on production	Production (t)	% of total	Fazendas with information on trees	In production	New	Output (kg/1,000 trees)
Capital	163	1,324	0.2%	212	2,167,206	20,036	
Vale do Paraíba	2,852	3,195	0.4%	4,222	15,415,734	700,890	
Central	7,170	28,296	3.9%	7,618	56,476,556	798,738	501
Mogiana	9,940	103,303	14.4%	10,090	185,283,716	2,405,273	558
Baixa Paulista	5,151	52,873	7.3%	5,890	113,853,296	1,081,690	464
Araraquarense	15,098	165,122	22.9%	17,208	294,803,425	1,522,717	560
Noroeste	12,798	232,988	32.4%	13,395	246,083,370	10,171,039	947
Alta Sorocabana	10,263	130,121	18.1%	11,059	154,124,199	3,907,104	844
Baixa Sorocabana	1,225	1,354	0.2%	1,626	2,045,197	208,001	
Santos	797	1,087	0.2%	1,013	1,010,375	89,956	
Total	65,457	719,663	100.0%	72,333	1,071,263,074	20,905,444	672

SOURCE: Instituto Brasileiro de Geografia e Estatística, *Recenseamento geral do Brasil, 1940*, regional series, part 17, vol. 3, pp. 41–180.

establishments that produced 1.3 million metric tons. In the case of these three cereals and pulses, São Paulo production represented 23 percent of national output in 1940. It also produced a quarter of the national harvest of English potatoes on 13,000 farms. Though sugar production and its derivatives remained important, the state produced 2.2 million metric tons of sugarcane, or 12 percent of national production. From this cane were produced 36,936 metric tons of refined sugar and 337,763 hectoliters of aguardente, which were 13 percent and 35 percent, respectively, of total Brazilian output. Between the census of 1920 and 1940, Paulista sugar production had increased by a quarter, but only aguardente production had an unusually large share of national production.

Between 1920 and 1940 the number of farms tripled, but the cultivated area grew by only a third, from 13.8 million hectares to 18.6 million hectares. The number and relative importance of small farms increased in the twenty years between 1920 and 1940. There were more small farmers in 1940, and they increased their farmland ownership to 28 percent of the land. In contrast, there was little change among the farms of over 1,000 hectares. All of this led to a reduction in midsize farms, those between 100 and 999 hectares, which went from holding 50 percent of the land to just 39 percent of it in 1940 (see Table 4.10).

While all areas in 1940 produced the basic cereals and pulses, once again there was some specialization by region. Rice was mostly produced in the Northwest (34 percent of all production), beans in the Central region (15 percent), and corn in Alta Sorocabana (24 percent). The Northwest was also the largest producer of cotton (28 percent), followed by Araraquarense and Alta Sorocabana, this latter being a traditional area of cotton cultivation. The Vale do Paraíba region was important only for manioc, which was of little importance in state agriculture though of fundamental importance within the rest of Brazil (see Table 4.11). Manioc was not a major consumption item in the state and was mostly confined to the poor soils on the coast. Given that the Vale do Paraíba region had the poorest and most exhausted lands in the state, it was inevitable that this easily produced and very cheap crop would become a local food staple unique to this region.

Refined-sugar and alcohol production was increasingly concentrated where usinas were located. Cane and refined sugar was concentrated in the Central and Mogiana regions. Although Brazil was still not among the most advanced sugar-producing countries, significant increases had been made in total volume and quality. New varieties of cane resistant to disease and with higher sugar content were introduced, and after the 1930 revolu-

TABLE 4.10
Number, Area, and Value of Farms in São Paulo, 1920 and 1940

	1920			1940		
Characteristics	Farms	Area (ha)	Value (mil réis)	Farms	Area (ha)	Value (mil réis)
Total properties	80,921	13,883,269	2,887,244	252,615	18,579,827	6,497,940
Individual-owned farms	76,438	11,752,979	2,340,353	201,225	13,005,685	4,553,253
Brazilians	54,245	9,824,428	1,834,402	136,256	9,543,629	3,009,938
Foreign born	22,065	1,914,458	503,142	64,969	3,462,056	1,543,315
Less than 100 ha	59,600	2,113,707	545,303	222,533	5,191,288	2,543,350
100–200 ha	9,345	1,344,614	326,597	14,848	2,114,048	809,419
200–1,000 ha	9,977	4,199,564	1,100,673	12,855	5,176,954	1,809,687
1,000–5,000 ha	118	838,653	660,888	2,015	3,807,738	962,944
5,000–10,000	118	838,653	115,847	138	960,848	198,202
10,000+ ha	73	1,831,127	137,976	69	1,328,951	172,699
Total	79,231	11,166,318	2,887,284	252,458	18,579,827	6,496,301
Participation						
Less than 100 ha	75.2%	18.9%	18.9%	88.1%	27.9%	39.2%
100–200 ha	11.8%	12.0%	11.3%	5.9%	11.4%	12.5%
200–1,000 ha	12.6%	37.6%	38.1%	5.1%	27.9%	27.9%
1,000–5,000 ha	0.1%	7.5%	22.9%	0.8%	20.5%	14.8%
5,000–10,000	0.1%	7.5%	4.0%	0.1%	5.2%	3.1%
10,000+ ha	0.1%	16.4%	4.8%	0.0%	7.2%	2.7%

SOURCE: Instituto Brasileiro de Geografia e Estatística, *Recenseamento geral do Brasil, 1940*, regional series, part 17, vol. 3, pp. 1–37.

tion the Getúlio Vargas government carried out a major intervention in the industry, culminating in the creation of the federal Institute of Sugar and Alcohol (IAA) in 1933. The institute's aim was to regularize the market in terms of prices and to stimulate production of ethanol fuel.[58] The activity of the IAA was quite extensive. It fixed output quotas for the usinas and withdrew excess alcohol from the market and turned it into ethanol fuel. It also subsidized the installation of new equipment and even manipulated prices by reducing production and purchasing stocks.

World War II would lead to a major decline in the availability of fuels on the international market and the search in Brazil for alternative solutions. Locally produced anhydrous alcohol was blended with gasoline for the growing fleet of cars, buses, and trucks in the country.[59] Though this biofuel was most intensely used in the 1940s, Brazil would continue to develop ever more refined motors and ethanol manufacturing processes and slowly and steadily increase the usage of ethanol mixed with gasoline, until the twenty-first century, when flex motors were finally and universally

TABLE 4.11

Number of Farms and Principal Agricultural Products in São Paulo, 1940

	RICE		BEANS		CORN		COTTON		MANIOC AND CASSAVA		SUGAR	
Region	Farms	Production (t)	Farms	Production (t)	Farms	Production (t)	Farms	Production (t)	Farms	Production (t)	Farms	Production (t)
Capital	680	917	3,651	1,927	4,958	21,206	95	1,552	1,161	4,467	136	10,727
Vale do Paraíba	5,514	17,380	11,601	9,021	14,049	54,134	18	5	5,723	48,438	4,253	87,320
Central	21,673	29,230	29,753	17,549	36,258	178,147	17,888	104,499	2,677	36,345	2,130	1,149,993
Mogiana	13,233	40,335	12,900	15,704	16,411	153,045	7,092	81,943	2,378	20,572	1,304	406,033
Baixa Paulista	7,760	15,331	6,027	6,408	9,615	104,014	5,914	76,883	1,833	43,928	691	170,362
Araraquarense	26,412	53,036	21,420	18,551	29,783	187,329	20,738	167,983	4,144	11,438	697	118,573
Noroeste	20,706	106,055	21,062	19,543	26,452	147,276	21,708	237,933	5,038	34,682	1,212	90,137
Alta Sorocabana	19,788	26,590	22,936	19,453	29,378	290,575	18,888	143,089	4,209	52,662	1,508	81,266
Baixa Sorocabana	9,353	8,469	14,482	5,888	16,141	86,931	7,583	24,015	4,524	41,532	2,397	24,015
Santos	6,082	12,459	4,199	1,033	5,057	6,181	6	15	3,977	22,524	1,551	20,539
Total	131,201	309,802	148,031	115,077	188,102	1,228,838	99,930	837,917	35,664	316,588	15,879	2,158,965

SOURCE: Instituto Brasileiro de Geografia e Estatística, *Recenseamento Geral do Brasil, 1940*, regional series, part 17, vol. 3, pp. 41–180.

introduced that enabled all cars to use either ethanol-gasoline mixture or pure ethanol alone.[60]

In the harvest of 1940/1941, São Paulo accounted for 12 percent of national production, which was more or less its average output for most of the 1930s. What is impressive, though, is that while usinas refined only some two-thirds of national sugar, in São Paulo 100 percent of refined sugar was milled in usinas from the middle of the decade and onward. By the time of the 1940 agricultural census São Paulo had thirty-four operating usinas, the largest number of any state.[61] Moreover, these were the most profitable in the country. For all this growth, however, the leading sugar-producing state was Pernambuco, which produced 4.6 million bags, followed by Rio de Janeiro.[62]

We should stress that the 1940 census was influenced by the war period. In contrast, the census of 1950 was carried out when the world economy was in a period of massive reconstruction that would turn into a long period of accelerated growth and in turn foster an extraordinary growth in Paulista agriculture.[63] By 1950 São Paulo had increased production and its relative standing within national agro-industry. It now listed 221,000 agricultural establishments with 19 million hectares, or 8 percent of such land in Brazil. Of these São Paulo cultivated lands, 1.5 million hectares were in permanent crops and 2.7 million hectares in seasonal plantings. This represented 38 percent of all Brazilian lands dedicated to permanent crops and 18 percent of all seasonal croplands—both ratios well above its 8 percent share of cultivated lands. Paulista agriculture now employed 1.5 million rural workers (13 percent of the national rural workforce), and their salaries represented 19 percent of all national rural worker income, greater than that paid by all other states.

Although Brazilian agriculture in general still used relatively little machinery and fertilizer, the state of São Paulo was the most advanced user of them. It accounted for two-thirds of all money spent on fertilizers in Brazil and had half the nation's tractors and a third of its plows.[64] Although productivity was increasing, even as late as 1950 Brazil was still not at the level of the leading agricultural countries of the world and would not reach them until the last quarter of the century.[65] In tractors or plows to hectare, São Paulo still showed that its mechanization was incomplete.[66] According to one study, the modern sector of Paulista agriculture in the quinquennium 1948–1952 represented only 26 percent of the total value of state production, the sector in transition 43 percent, and the traditional sector 31 percent.[67] But for all the increase in mechanization, there was still no agro-industrial integration, whether in the processing of agricultural products or in the generation of a national industry to supply machines, equipment, fertilizers, and pesticides. All this would occur only in the last quarter of the century. In 1950 São Paulo had only 3,800 tractors, or 1 tractor for a thousand cultivated alqueires, or 1 per 400 rural workers. The state still employed 1.5 million agricultural laborers, a figure that would progressively decline as mechanization increased in subsequent decades.

The trends seen in coffee production in the censuses of 1920 and 1940 were even more evident in the agricultural census of 1950. Paulista coffee had accounted for 60 percent of national output in 1940 and was now down to 44 percent of national production. It had 49 percent of the coffee plantings and 44 percent of the coffee trees in production, but only 25 percent of its trees were newly planted. Paraná, for example, had only 6 percent of all the coffee trees in Brazil, but its trees were primarily recent plantings. Clearly, the north of Paraná would soon be a major coffee zone, along with Espírito Santo. Moreover, in São Paulo, production was concentrated in municípios in the regions of Baixa Paulista, Araraquarense, and Northwest (see Map 4.3).

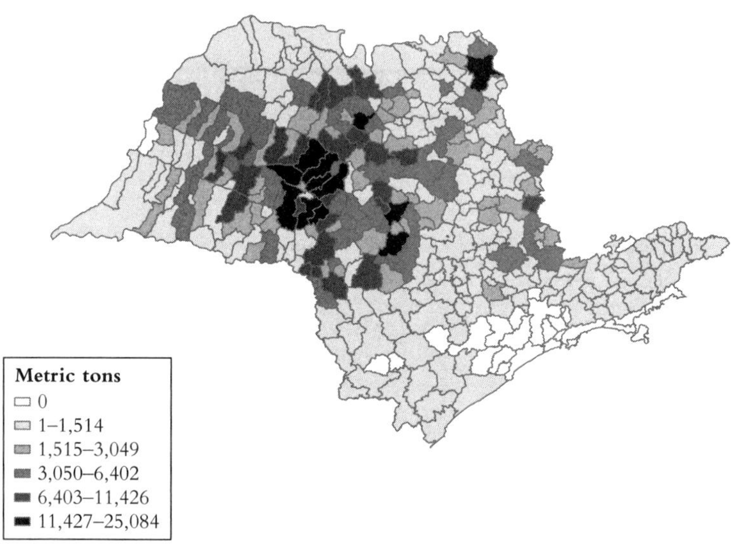

Map 4.3 Coffee Production by Município in São Paulo, 1950

But São Paulo increased its leadership in the production of other crops. Its cotton crop by 1950 accounted for over half of all Brazilian cotton grown, producing in the 1949/1950 harvest 441,000 metric tons. In fact, so important had cotton become that it occupied roughly the same amount of cultivated land as the amount of land devoted to corn and rice each. The state also harvested 912,000 metric tons of corn (16 percent of national production), 688,000 metric tons of rice (25 percent of Brazil's corn), and 52,000 metric tons of beans (just 6 percent of the national harvest). It now became the second-most-important sugar state after Pernambuco, and it was still the leading producer of alcohol.[68] Although it contained a still-modest ranching economy, the state produced 19 percent of all milk in the country (see Table 4.12). But there was still no indication that oranges and soybeans would soon become among the most important agricultural products of the state. Overall, the state accounted for over a third of workers employed despite having only 8 percent of the nation's farms. Its principal products also accounted for over a third of such products in the nation—this despite the fact that the state contained only 18 percent of the national population.

The 1950 census also reveals Paulista agriculture at a moment of fundamental change in crop mix. Coffee had expanded in the state until the 1920s and then went into a long-term decline that was especially marked after 1960, when official tree eradication programs cut production and stimulated the move to alternative crops.[69] Cotton grew rapidly through the first half of the century and then systematically declined in the second half of the century.[70] World War II had been a particularly stimulating period for local production, which expanded to meet local demand in the face of falling textile imports and the growth of the local textile industry. But in the decade of the 1980s the local crop was hit by a plague that almost totally destroyed Brazilian production. Not until the end of the last century did cotton once again become a significant crop, but it never reached its previous levels. In 1950 São Paulo harvested 400,000 metric tons, but by the first decade of the twenty-first century harvests were averaging less than 100,000 metric tons. In contrast, sugar production showed long-term steady growth in the first half of the twentieth century and would continue to grow quite dramatically in the second half. On the other hand, the major food crops, like corn, rice, and beans, from 1905 to 1950 showed no clear secular trend in total production (see Table 4.13).

One factor to emphasize is that agricultural productivity per area in the first half of the twentieth century was low. None of the principal products,

TABLE 4.12

Agricultural Production in São Paulo and Other Leading States, 1950

Product	São Paulo	São Paulo (% of nation)	Brazil	Minas Gerais	Rio de Janeiro	Paraná	Rio Grande do Sul
Coffee							
Farms	65,114	21%	311,781	79,641	9,111	21,106	979
Production (t)	864,862	44%	1,952,774	364,913	58,451	303,015	232
Area planted (ha)	1,195,928	49%	2,465,450	500,402	90,918	253,942	367
Trees in production	933,344,186	44%	2,120,036,210	457,607,157	94,988,206	141,257,813	116,964
New trees	137,936,022	25%	543,566,978	117,243,103	11,651,061	118,525,213	36,477
Cotton							
Farms	71,505	20%	349,359	15,203	1,186	4,036	
Quantity (t)	441,353	58%	763,259	18,753	4,264	17,158	
Area planted (ha)	619,623	30%	2,037,413	50,976	7,826	27,192	
Corn							
Farms	132,290	9%	1,483,535	219,187	22,547	79,967	275,025
Quantity (t)	911,757	16%	5,565,580	1,267,183	107,818	709,450	1,085,846
Area planted (ha)	777,989	15%	5,311,799	1,077,214	128,218	522,604	927,232
Rice							
Farms	115,054	17%	660,400	128,853	8,993	32,108	89,157
Quantity (t)	688,471	25%	2,703,228	513,257	57,469	73,615	562,139
Area planted (ha)	611,019	28%	2,163,653	484,999	49,627	78,260	254,048
Beans							
Farms	60,859	5%	1,116,837	160,902	12,821	61,718	188,464
Quantity (t)	52,323	6%	945,230	224,849	14,528	90,694	130,171
Area planted (ha)	134,164	6%	2,363,631	560,303	28,074	193,931	199,098
Sugarcane							
Farms	5,887	3%	208,144	49,821	11,398	1,711	50,987
Quantity (t)	4,773,607	21%	22,774,617	2,213,385	3,000,604	240,024	654,554
Area planted (ha)	137,135	16%	846,032	104,905	128,650	8,691	44,798
Sugar produced (t)	1,366	4%	35,419	6,345	875	147	3,093
Aguardente produced (t)	28,911	7%	412,810	104,750	14,733	8,295	76,231

TABLE 4.12 (CONTINUED)

Product	São Paulo	São Paulo (% of nation)	Brazil	Minas Gerais	Rio de Janeiro	Paraná	Rio Grande do Sul
Potatoes							
Farms	6,016	5%	128,983	5,141	884	18,426	69,574
Quantity (t)	138,502	43%	323,746	19,163	3,081	50,979	83,839
Area planted (ha)	27,670	29%	94,561	5,237	634	17,025	29,030
Oranges							
Farms	10,104	4%	260,267	29,067	4,781	12,489	99,461
Oranges produced (100s)	4,259,729	10%	43,774,507	3,727,516	8,285,253	1,501,849	8,327,906
Area planted (ha)	12,505	22%	57,135	4,551	9,692	1,613	8,134
Trees in production	2,805,287	13%	22,003,869	1,219,392	5,689,370	368,077	2,319,292
New trees	1,427,204	23%	6,298,467	319,160	764,104	279,057	717,952
Peanuts							
Farms	15,822	18%	89,569	5,402	827	4,423	39,442
Quantity (t)	58,512	73%	79,882	4,675	1,015	1,537	7,382
Area planted (ha)	53,998	66%	81,632	5,918	964	1,730	10,755
Ranching							
Cows	5,721,977	13%	44,600,159	9,790,100	777,780	795,821	8,617,587
Pigs	2,670,812	12%	22,970,814	3,689,964	345,458	2,040,411	4,164,470
Milk (hL)	5,147,101	19%	27,508,924	8,747,294	1,164,158	564,392	4,488,460

SOURCE: Instituto Brasileiro de Geografia e Estatística, *Censo agrícola de 1950*, national series, vol. 2, pp. 59–101.

whether corn, rice, or beans, destined for the internal market, products going to industrial processing like cotton and sugarcane, or even coffee, changed output per unit. When production increased it was because of new plantings rather than increased productivity (see Figures 4.3 and 4.4).

Thus, São Paulo agriculture, although it became somewhat more diversified and was beginning to modernize during the first half of the twentieth century, remained an economy dominated by coffee. It was partly the defense of this coffee agriculture that led the state to rebel against the federal government, and it was this important role of coffee that finally forced the federal government to come to the aid of the planters, even as it reduced their political power.

TABLE 4.13

Volume of Principal Crops Produced in São Paulo, 1905–1950

Year	Coffee (sacks)	Cotton (t)	Sugarcane (t)	Corn (t)	Rice (t)	Beans (t)	Oranges (boxes)
1905	8,903,011	7,758		685,976	70,259	94,451	
1920	5,569,820	104,584	1,110,749	1,192,250	348,019	213,507	
1931	12,908,793	18,933	1,134,420	1,111,584	453,938	201,182	6,456,384
1932	18,261,448	47,835	1,314,730	1,591,425	664,602	242,208	9,294,208
1933	18,670,640	84,740	1,535,510	1,554,525	596,046	244,390	10,031,859
1934	20,159,000	238,690	2,414,140	1,099,776	560,040	173,184	10,839,840
1935	12,600,000	229,150	1,545,000	1,365,000	630,840	210,258	10,109,651
1936	17,505,000	416,500	1,675,230	1,161,066	451,051	183,618	9,364,256
1937	15,687,000	472,776	1,602,560	1,200,000	480,000	163,941	7,438,534
1938	15,615,066	579,357	1,561,085	1,399,060	467,708	189,119	7,782,452
1939	12,370,778	637,616	2,708,000	1,320,000	468,000	180,000	8,448,000
1940	10,234,298	717,212	2,576,134	601,077	207,830	83,265	8,448,000
1941	9,283,739	889,000	2,451,608	900,000	487,819	150,000	9,152,000
1942	8,528,472	659,552	2,800,000	722,576	504,480	96,098	8,940,800
1943	8,187,379	875,229	3,000,000	1,090,500	629,752	161,936	8,588,800
1944	4,892,117	877,641	4,301,657	994,912	494,553	144,551	5,123,552
1945	5,973,033	489,488	4,090,065	994,827	677,934	155,718	5,113,564
1946	7,443,900	476,346	4,487,260	1,310,709	949,155	191,729	4,749,736
1947	7,365,367	382,719	5,792,007	1,216,780	838,456	172,400	4,217,996
1948	9,152,317	344,128	6,045,769	1,149,314	832,650	173,930	4,374,764
1949	8,124,967	458,267	5,984,171	1,097,870	781,899	181,772	4,404,304
1950	7,820,483	404,627	6,913,524	1,262,451	992,772	177,421	3,963,192

SOURCE: *O crescimento da agricultura paulista*; Instituto de Economia Agricola, *Censo agrícola de São Paulo, 1905*.
NOTE: Sacks are 60 kg each. Boxes are 40.8 kg each.

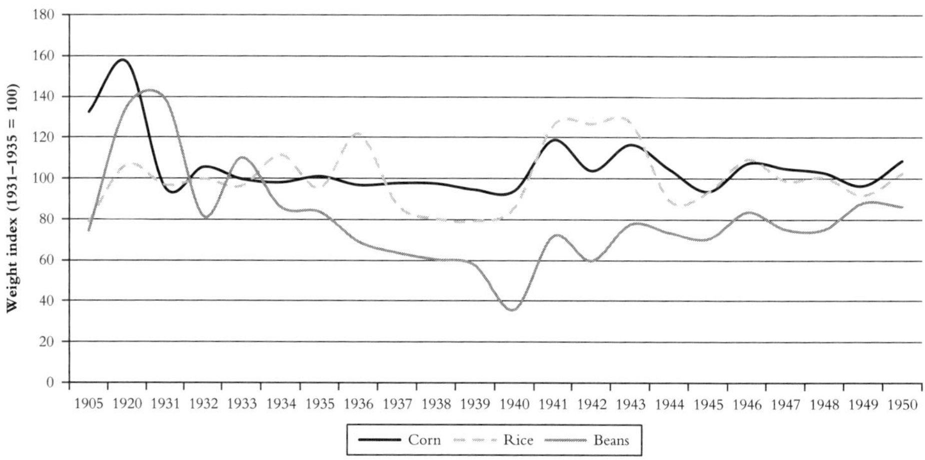

Figure 4.3 Production per Hectare of Corn, Rice, and Beans in São Paulo, 1905–1950

NOTE: The base for the calculation of weight is the five-year average of 1931–1935.

SOURCE: Araujo et al., *O crescimento da agriculltura paulista.*

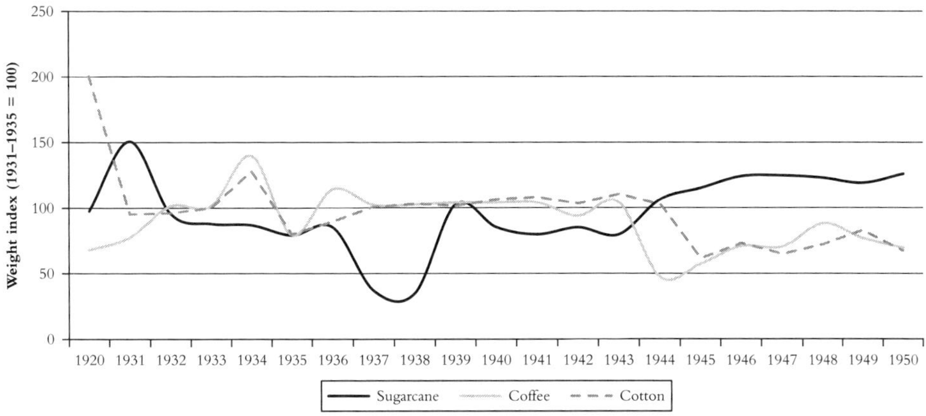

Figure 4.4 Production per Hectare of Sugarcane, Coffee, and Cotton in São Paulo, 1920–1950

NOTE: The base for the calculation of weight is the five-year average of 1931–1935.

SOURCE: Araujo et al., *O crescimento da agricultura paulista.*

Chapter 5

Crisis of the Paulista State and the Loss of Hegemony of the Paulista Elite

The international crisis of the 1930s not only had a profound impact on the Brazilian economy but also ushered in a major change in the political structure of the nation, which directly affected the state of São Paulo. The Old Republic fell, and the liberal federal system was replaced by an authoritarian, centralist, and interventionist regime, thus breaking the power hold of the Paulista elite on the central government and even reducing their control over the state government.

The Old Republic was based on the coalition of regional oligarchies who commanded policy in their respective states and the coffee bourgeoisie who controlled the central government. This federal system was highly decentralized, even in relation to its tax regime. Representatives of Minas Gerais and São Paulo, the most populous states in Brazil, mostly dominated the presidency of the republic. In the economy the interests of the coffee elite predominated. The emerging industrial sector depended largely on the dynamics of the agro-export economy and thus did not oppose or enter into conflict with the interests of the coffee elite or with the policies of the liberal regime then in force. But over the years areas of conflict emerged in some social segments and divisions within the hegemonic coalition itself. The dynamics of the expanding agro-export economy led to diversification of the domestic market and also created new social actors, particularly in the urban middle class, with their own aspirations and demands, underserved by the existing regime.

In the late 1920s the Paulista elite divided politically. In 1926 the Democratic Party of São Paulo was established, consisting of professionals and some representatives of the coffee bourgeoisie. The Democratic Party of São Paulo opposed the traditional Republican Party, which controlled São Paulo politics and through which the Paulista elite wielded their power at the federal level. The Democratic Party demanded secret and compulsory voting, minority representation, and electoral oversight by the judiciary.[1] The split in the dominant group in power took place over the succession of President Washington Luís (1926–1930), a representative of the São Paulo bourgeoisie. Traditionally, the presidency had alternated between São Paulo and Minas Gerais. Thus, to maintain that balance, the candidate should have been from Minas Gerais. However, the refusal of the São Paulo elite to support this transition led to the formation of an opposition alliance of the states of Minas Gerais and Rio Grande do Sul and the launching of the southern politician Getúlio Vargas as presidential candidate. This movement had the support of the Democratic Party of São Paulo.

During the election the overproduction crisis of the coffee market intensified, and the election of the governor of São Paulo, Julio Prestes, as president seemed to be the elite response to the need to both control the presidency and resolve the market crisis. But the old elite no longer could command all the traditional forces, and to their shock, the defeated Vargas led a coup and overthrew the government.[2]

The revolution of 1930 would prove to be a profound change for Brazil and even more so for São Paulo. The old federalist system was dissolved and Brazil returned to a far more centralized and authoritarian government. Vargas dismissed the national Congress and all the state and local legislatures and replaced the state governors with federally appointed interventors, radically reducing the power of the states.[3] There was resistance to the political and administrative centralization imposed by the new regime. The most extreme resistance occurred in São Paulo. The Paulista elite, divided at the moment of the Vargas revolt, united to defend its interests against the interventionism of Vargas. This growing resistance eventually led a full-scale military rebellion in 1932, which was crushed by the central government when the other states refused to follow the Paulista elite in open rebellion.[4]

Thus, Vargas was able to consolidate his regime ever more firmly after 1932. He was elected to another term in 1934 by an indirect vote in a controlled national legislature for a term that would have lasted to 1938. But in November 1937, when the electoral process for the presidential succession was in full swing, Vargas carried out another coup and imposed a nondemocratic constitution. Thus, the authoritarian, centralized, and repressive Estado Novo regime was inaugurated,[5] and until his overthrow in 1945 Vargas governed by decree without legislative representation. Although the Estado Novo resembled a fascist state, and several of its members professed sympathy for the Italian and German models, it rejected identification with the fascist movements in Brazil and maintained its support for the Allied nations in World War II and even supported the Catholic Church. The *integralistas*—the major representative of fascism in Brazil—who had hoped to be incorporated into the government, were also jettisoned in the Estado Novo. After closing Congress, dissolving political parties, and repressing the left, Vargas also banned the integralistas.[6]

Despite this change in the power structure, which removed the influence of the coffee bourgeoisie over the central government, the coffee economy was of such fundamental importance to the nation that the government could not ignore planter interests. In the mid-1920s Brazil had adopted a policy regulating coffee prices by controlling exports and purchasing unsold stocks.[7] In this period the Mortgage and Agricultural Bank was transformed into the State Bank of São Paulo (Banco do Estado de São Paulo), with a capital of 50,000 contos (approximately US$5 million), controlled by the Coffee Institute and the state treasury. The State Bank became the main financial backer of coffee defense operations.[8]

From the harvest of 1923–1924 to that of 1929–1930, São Paulo produced 85.8 million bags of coffee: 59.1 million were exported through the port of Santos, 1 million were exported through the port of Rio de Janeiro, and 8 million were consumed in the state. Thus, the Coffee Institute had to purchase 17 million bags of excess coffee, which were added to the world inventory, then around 5.5 million bags.[9] In addition, the stimulus of the high prices of the second half of the 1920s spurred planting in Brazil and in competing countries, which led to higher yields in subsequent years. This was the picture of the coffee market when the Great Depression of the 1930s occurred. In July 1930, Heitor Penteado, vice president of the state, reported problems in obtaining funds in the international financial market because of the reduction of loans, the increasing interest rates, and even the prevention of the outflow of capital. So scarce was credit that the government was forced to stop purchasing coffee, leading to a crisis. Compounding the problem, the Great Depression caused a swift and sudden fall in the price of all consumer goods.

By September 1929 14.9 million bags of coffee were in buffer stocks. In November the government negotiated a short-term external loan of £2 million, but this was insufficient to meet the needs of coffee producers.

It negotiated another loan of £20 million in April 1930, which required the creation of a special tax of three shillings for each bag of 60 kilos exported.[10]

But Brazilian overproduction continued, and the crisis deepened, adding to the general deterioration of coffee prices in the international market. In the last years of the 1920s the coffee defense program stimulated new plantings and thus generated a supply of coffee incompatible with the absorptive capacity of the market. After getting foreign loans to meet short-term commitments, the state requested funds from the federal government, which were denied. President Washington Luís was unable to obtain loans abroad, and he refused to help the coffee sector through new monetary issues that could destroy the exchange rate stability achieved by the end of his administration. But the central government leaders seemed to be unaware of the seriousness of the situation. The deepening crisis reduced exports, caused capital flight, and led to the closure of the Stabilization Board. The newly installed Vargas government, however, recognized the serious nature of the situation and was forced to support the industry by preventing the crisis from destroying the coffee economy and deepening the economic and social crisis that was spreading through the country. In addition to forgiving the debt of the coffee farmers, Vargas established a mechanism for destroying excess stocks of coffee, preserving the structure of the coffee market, and reducing the impact of the crisis on planters. The government's anticrisis policy preserved the income of the coffee planters and reduced the effect of the crisis on the economy.[11]

To develop the aid program for coffee, the federal government took over the operations of the Coffee Institute from São Paulo. To discourage new plantings and finance purchases of stocks, it created two taxes, one focused on new plantings, the other on coffee exports. Part of the government-purchased coffee was destroyed. The federal government also established the National Coffee Board and later the National Coffee Department, which would be the effective operating arm of the coffee defense program. In 1933, faced with the largest crop ever produced, the federal government banned both new plantings and replantings and set up an export quota: 30 percent would be exported; 30 percent would be retained in government stocks, and 40 percent would be destroyed.[12] The system was maintained, with occasional adjustments, until 1944, by which time 78.2 million bags of coffee had been burned, the equivalent of three times global consumption in one year.[13] Coffee production in Brazil, after peaking in 1933, was reduced gradually, the disincentive to new plantings and replant-

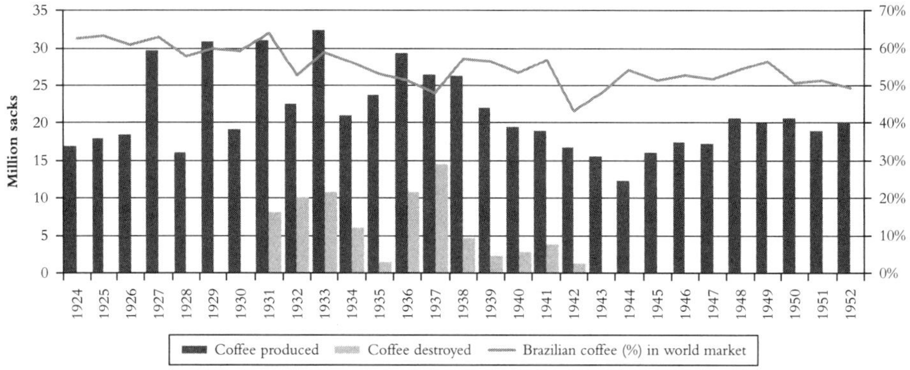

Figure 5.1 Brazilian Production and Destruction of Coffee and Participation in World Market, 1924–1952

SOURCE: Bacha and Greenhill, *150 anos de café*, apendice estatístico, tables 1.6 and 1.8.

ing having an effect. The price remained quite low until the end of the 1930s, recovering only with the outbreak of World War II (see Figure 5.1).

Despite the severity of the international situation during the Great Depression and the continuation of the coffee crisis throughout the decade, there was relatively little decline in domestic product in the first two years of the Great Depression, and the local economy maintained persistent growth in the following years. The agro-export economy, the dynamic element of the Brazilian economy since the beginning of colonization, was now slowly being replaced by the domestic market as a major factor in national growth. Given the international economic crisis and the new direction of the economy, the Vargas government implemented sweeping reforms in the structure of the state and the economy. These reforms were aimed at modernizing both but were also authoritarian and conservative. One important part of this reform was major support for the development of national industry, a theme maintained throughout the Vargas period.

Formal structural changes in the government and its administration, implemented from the beginning of the Vargas government, increased after the second coup and Estado Novo, including executive control over all new legislation. Congress was closed and the opposition muzzled, and the power of the states was replaced by an all-powerful central government. These administrative changes at the national level were consolidated by the end of 1941 and allowed a major centralization of power.[14]

Between 1934 and 1946 the country had three different constitutions, two under Vargas and one in the immediate post-Vargas democratic period. The constitution of 1934, enacted by a conservative constitutional assembly, was a basic reversal of the Old Republic structure, emphasizing a more unitary state, with the federal government taking over many functions that had been under state control.[15] This constitution was replaced by the 1937 constitution, which was designed along European fascist models. It suppressed political parties and annulled the separation of powers and the autonomy of the states. With the overthrow of Getúlio Vargas and the redemocratization of the country came the constitution of 1946, which reestablished individual rights and returned autonomy to states and municípios. This constitution was replaced by the constitution of 1967, promulgated under the military regime that assumed power in 1964.[16] But none of these constitutions allowed the extreme state autonomy of the Old Republic.

In the constitution of 1934, the states had the right to tax rural property; the sale, transfer, and inheritance of property; gasoline consumption; and sales and consignments carried out by traders and producers, including industrial ones. They also could tax industries and occupations within their boundaries, charge fees for state services, and tax local-production exports to a maximum of 10 percent of value. But the states were specifically prohibited from imposing any other additional taxes. In the case of obligations, the constitution specified that the states were to concern themselves with health care and social assistance and with colonization and public education at all levels.

The authoritarian constitution of 1937 gave the president of the republic, in periods of recess of parliament or dissolution of the chamber of deputies, the power to make laws that could even change the constitution. Moreover, the federal government had the exclusive power to legislate on many subjects, for which the states could legislate only in a complementary way. On fiscal issues, states had practically the same jurisdiction defined in the constitution of 1934, including the right to impose local-production export tax and the prohibition to impose additional taxes. The constitution provided that a state export tax could be temporarily increased beyond the 10 percent limit in exceptional cases.[17]

The constitution of 1946 marked the return to democratic rule, reinstating essential human rights and returning to a federal system. But the federal government maintained greater powers than given in the first republican constitution of 1891. It provided, for example, for the federal government's right to intervene in the economic domain, including the right to create monopolies in industry or other activity.[18] States lost their right to tax industries and professions and urban properties, which was given to the municípios, and taxation on exports was reduced to a maximum of 5 percent.[19]

In terms of education, both the state and federal governments could now operate at all levels, with the proviso that education be free and nonreligious but could also involve private efforts.[20] Primary education was compulsory and free to all; further education was free if there were funds to support it. Industrial, commercial, and agricultural enterprises with over a hundred workers would be required to provide free primary education for workers' children (article 168).[21] But the constitution made no mention of the other major area of fiscal responsibility, that of providing health care to all citizens.

In the next several decades the economy and the state government were in constant expansion. To coffee production was now slowly added a major industrial system, which attracted to the state ever-increasing flows of immigrants from other states, who slowly replaced foreign immigrants after 1920. The growing population required state investments in health, urban sanitation infrastructure, and education. There was also the need for major investments in interurban infrastructure, particularly roads and railways. The state population grew at an annual rate of 3.2 percent from 1890 to 1950, compared to a national growth rate of only 2.2 percent, and by 1950 was double that of Minas Gerais, previously Brazil's most populous state. The population of the state of São Paulo was only 43 percent of Minas Gerais's in 1890, but by 1950 it was 17 percent greater and had the largest population in the union. In the same period the city of São Paulo grew at extraordinary rates, on the order of 6.1 percent per annum, which soon made it the second-largest urban center in the country. In 1890 the city's population was only 16 percent that of the imperial capital of Rio de Janeiro, but by 1950 it was at 92 percent of the population of Rio and would soon surpass that city.[22]

The centralization and authoritarianism of the Vargas government and the major changes in the structure of the Brazilian government enormously influenced the economy and administrative organization of the state of São Paulo and its fiscal resources. For long periods the government of the state of São Paulo was ruled by interventors appointed by the federal government.[23] The federal government reorganized both the federal and the state governments. At the federal level it created the Department of Administration and Public Services (Departamento Administrativo do Serviço Público; DASP) in 1938, whose task was to reorganize the national administrative structure and provide the state with a competitive and modern civil service and a technically prepared bureaucracy.[24] DASP also controlled the public budget and advised the government in general. It had branches in the states and, together with the interventors, administered the states and contributed to the political and administrative centralization of power in the central government.

Other numerous executive and advisory bodies of the federal government were also created. Key productive areas of the economy were given attention through the Institute of Sugar and Alcohol, the National Coffee Department, the Institute of Mate, the Pine Institute, the National Salt Institute, and the Institute of Bahian Cacao. Moreover, the agricultural sector was endowed with some essential tools, including the Agricultural and Industrial Credit Department of the Banco do Brasil (CREAI) and the Commission on Funding for Production (CFP), which would be in charge of price policy. In the area of mineral resources, the regime created the National Department of Mineral Production, the National Petroleum Council, the Board of Water and Electrical Power, and the National Council of Mining and Metallurgy. Legal codes were established to regulate economic, social, and political relations, such as the Water Code, the Mining Code, the Brazilian Air Code, the Code of Industrial Properties, the Forest Code, and Corporation Law. In the industrial area, it created such supportive institutions as the Textile Executive Committee, the National Committee on Fuels and Lubricants, the National Commission on Railways, and the Vale do Rio Doce Commission.[25]

The São Paulo revolt of 1932 had shown the central government the power of the opposition that had emerged against these new central government activities.[26] Thus, the Vargas regime was forced to make various concessions to reduce this opposition. It did so by naming a Paulista as interventor,[27] responding to the demands of the coffee elite for market protection, and consulting the local elite when writing the constitution of 1934.[28] Changes were also made in the state administrative structure.[29] The principal changes occurred after 1934 when the Institute for the Rational Organization of Labor (Instituto de Organização Racional do Trabalho; IDORT) developed a major reorganization plan for the state government of São Paulo.[30] IDORT was founded in 1931 by Roberto Simonsen, a leader of Paulista industry,[31] and was designed to rationalize the industrial process.[32] Before undertaking administrative reform, IDORT carried out a complete review of the government as it existed in 1935. Before the reform just five departments were called secretariats (*secretarias*). They had a total of some 50,000 employees under the command of the governor. IDORT proposed completely reforming the secretariats.

After a comprehensive review of the organizational structure of the public administration of the state, IDORT suggested several changes in the structure of departments, moving to create a uniform standard. This meant creating a superior council in each department, or secretariat, and section or department administrations in all the secretariats that would be in charge of accounting, materials, control of personnel, vehicles, and other services. Given the cost and complexity of reform, even in general administrative areas, changes were to be made gradually.[33] The Finance Secretariat was the first to be entirely remodeled along the lines of the IDORT plan.[34] The Finance Secretariat would contain a new administrative directorate general and such general directorates would be established in the subbranches of the Finance Secretariat: these included Revenue, Expenditure, Treasury, the office of the Tax Attorney of Finance, and the Central Accounting Office.[35] The savings banks (*caixas econômicas*) and the pension funds (*montes de socorro*), which had been separate, semiautonomous agencies with their own finances, were combined and now called the Caixa Econômica do Estado de São Paulo. The Caixa Econômica do Estado de São Paulo and the Court of Taxes and Fees, the Official Coffee Exchange of Santos, the official Stock Exchanges of São Paulo and Santos, and the various pension programs for Finance Secretariat employees were placed under the control of the Finance Secretariat.[36]

Other reforms were proposed for education, health, and public safety. A major reform proposed by IDORT involved the development of vocational and professional education.[37] This led to the creation of the Railway Center of Vocational Education (Centro Ferroviário de Ensino e Seleção Profissional; CFESP), which was the precursor of the National Industrial Learning Program, known as SENAI (Serviço Nacional de Aprendizado Industrial).[38]

The São Paulo elite also supported primary education and teacher preparation, promoted numerous reforms, and actively expanded state education, especially in the 1930s. A broader conception of secondary education led to the formulation of a more modern system; professional education received an impetus and made major advances into higher education. All these reforms found expression in the Education Code promulgated in 1933.[39] This decree stipulated that public education in the state would encompass preprimary education, taught in nursery schools in courses of two years for children two to four years old and in kindergarten courses of three years for children four to seven years old. Primary education was to be given to all children over seven years old in free-standing schools in a first level for three years and then in a second four-year course in multilevel schools. Prevocational education was to be provided in the fifth year of schooling for those who wanted it. It also established complex multilevel training courses for teachers with different years of study and different types of normal schools for each level of school, from preprimary to secondary. The profession of pedagogy at the tertiary level at the Institute of Education (Escola de Professores do Instituto de Educação) was also proposed. Even special education of children and teenagers was contemplated in the law and was to be made available at various schools. In the case of primary education, the law stated that wherever there were at least two hundred school-age children within a two-kilometer radius, a school group would be created. The government would give preference to areas where individuals or municipalities donated the building in accordance with the requirements of the Department of Education.[40]

Although secondary education had advanced only modestly in this period, there was a major breakthrough in tertiary education. The 1930s would finally see the development of modern universities in Brazil, and this would occur most successfully in the state of São Paulo. In 1934 the University of São Paulo was created at the initiative of interventor Armando Salles de Oliveira. The preamble to the decree that established the university affirmed that the development of a philosophical, scientific, literary, and artistic culture constituted the basis on which rested the freedom and greatness of a people. It declared that, to form a ruling class, especially in countries with heterogeneous populations and diverse customs, it was essential to have a cultural and academic institution that could offer opportunity to all capable people regardless of origin. The University of São Paulo initially consisted of faculties of law, medicine, dentistry, pharmacy, engineering (the polytechnic school), philosophy, and letters and science and the Institutes of Education, Economic and Commercial Sciences, School of Fine Arts, School of Veterinary Medicine, and the College of Agriculture.

As in primary and tertiary education, the political and administrative centralization that occurred during the Vargas period was strongly felt in health and social security within the state. The creation of the National Department of Health in the new Ministry of Education and Health in 1931 gave the central government significant influence over state health offices.[41] In São Paulo this process occurred through the reorganization of the state sanitary service.[42] Then in 1938 the state Department of Health replaced the sanitary service and was given control over the rural and urban health centers and health stations.[43] It appears that this was a well-run institution and reorganized all the state's public health activities, including planning and public programs, and was considered the most modern of such institutions in the country.[44] Finally, in 1947 the state Public Health and Social Assistance Secretariat was created and made equal to all the other major state ministries.

The central and state governments also concerned themselves with the delicate issue of reforming the autonomous state police, which had been an important element in the rebellion of 1932. In 1934 the police were taken out of the state justice department and put into an independent Secretariat of Public Safety (Secretaria de Segurança Pública), along with penitentiaries, fire departments, and other services. By 1937 the Public Safety department was composed of 8,880 men, of whom 6,000 were soldiers.[45] The 1934 decree also created the Agency for Social and Political Order (Superintendência de Ordem Politica e Social), which would eventually become the Department of Political and Social Order (DOPS), basically a political police force representing some of the more authoritarian aspects of the Vargas period.

These changes in the structure of state government can be seen in the far larger number of departments that existed in the state government in 1950 and the new orientation in terms of health, education, and public safety. There were now seven secretariats in the state, with labor being a new important component. The state paid for this increasingly complex structure through reorganization of its taxes. The tax revenue would be much influenced by changes in the organization of the Brazilian nation-state as well as in local government. Between 1930 and 1950 taxes and fees entering the state coffers grew significantly, at approximately 14 percent per annum (nearly 6 percent in real terms). But the budget consistently showed major deficits, particularly in the 1930s, when the deficit in relation to realized revenue was mostly between 30 and 50 percent, although it reached 73 percent in 1932 and was only 8 percent in 1938. The crisis of the 1930s affected all economic activities, not just coffee, and lowered overall tax and state fee collections. Also, the 1932 rebellion against the federal government led to extraordinary expenditures for that year. All this resulted in increased indebtedness of the state.

From 1930 to 1939 we have complete data on both budgeted and actual collections and disbursements by the state treasury. To examine the period after 1939 and up to mid-century, we have the totals budgeted and totals actually obtained or disbursed, as well as detailed income received by category. But we no longer have available the actual expenditure data by item, only annual estimates of specific items of expenditure proposed in the budget for that year.

The state revenue collected was usually lower than estimated in the proposed budgets throughout the 1930s and 1940s, while actual expenditure often significantly exceeded that proposed (see Table 5.1 and Figures 5.2 and 5.3). While this guaranteed that a supposed balanced budget was pre-

TABLE 5.1

Budgeted Income and Expenditure and Balance of the State of São Paulo, 1928–1950 (mil réis and cruzeiros)

	ESTIMATED BUDGET		ACTUAL BUDGET				RATIO OF ESTIMATED AND ACTUAL	
Year	Income	Expenditure	Income	Expenditure	Balance (income – expenditure)	Deficit or surplus (%)	Income	Expenditure
1928	378,237,200	378,237,200	408,424,343	436,914,806	-28,490,463	-7%	1.08	1.16
1929	453,606,980	453,606,980	438,459,497	457,564,937	-19,105,440	-4%	0.97	1.01
1930	495,772,019	493,816,030	400,204,311	616,197,209	-215,992,898	-54%	0.81	1.25
1931	444,390,000	495,081,800	429,571,365	662,905,834	-233,334,469	-54%	0.97	1.34
1932	400,920,000	407,558,552	382,424,183	662,668,566	-280,244,383	-73%	0.95	1.63
1933	447,760,000	474,041,994	432,283,128	593,139,150	-160,856,022	-37%	0.97	1.25
1934	492,600,000	513,936,552	475,919,306	656,967,185	-181,047,879	-38%	0.97	1.28
1935	596,971,139	661,310,879	582,142,193	745,582,541	-163,440,348	-28%	0.98	1.13
1936	608,508,506	718,370,859	593,727,543	747,757,705	-154,030,162	-26%	0.98	1.04
1937	634,425,151	749,909,858	549,744,145	837,684,217	-287,940,072	-52%	0.87	1.12
1938	692,050,764	722,551,198	626,682,120	678,508,642	-51,826,522	-8%	0.91	0.94
1939	949,573,369	749,909,858	843,231,267	1,035,385,661	-192,154,394	-23%	0.89	1.38
1940	949,838,084	940,829,273	878,204,189	914,606,665	-36,402,476	-4%	0.92	0.97
1941	1,018,141,480	1,059,958,944	1,095,055,015	1,020,625,829	74,429,186	7%	1.08	0.96
1942	1,192,399,433	1,229,235,105	1,164,731,891	1,245,651,793	-80,919,902	-7%	0.98	1.01
1943	1,284,719,051	1,287,961,051	1,554,371,049	1,477,218,834	77,152,215	5%	1.21	1.15
1944	1,554,580,292	1,554,164,293	2,052,365,056	1,993,124,749	59,240,307	3%	1.32	1.28
1945	2,322,440,768	2,322,440,770	2,428,108,785	2,793,419,399	-365,310,614	-15%	1.05	1.20
1946	2,575,752,011	2,575,752,035	3,069,909,911	3,210,055,178	-140,145,267	-5%	1.19	1.25
1947	3,265,850,000	3,265,849,978	3,147,485,000	3,780,554,000	-633,069,000	-20%	0.96	1.16
1948	3,911,860,000	3,911,860,000	3,818,852,000	4,636,396,000	-817,544,000	-21%	0.98	1.19
1949	5,331,319,998	5,326,579,493	5,102,146,997	5,618,497,648	-516,350,651	-10%	0.96	1.05
1950	5,794,559,998	5,739,381,296	5,966,324,231	7,778,463,069	-1,812,138,838	-30%	1.03	1.36

SOURCE: Assembleia Legislativa do Estado de São Paulo, leis orçamentárias, various years; Instituto Brasileiro de Geografia e Estatística, *Anuário estatístico do Brasil, 1950.*

NOTE: In 1929, 1930, 1937, and 1948–1950 the budget was approved by the legislature; in all others, by executive decree. In 1935 and 1938 we do not consider loans as income.

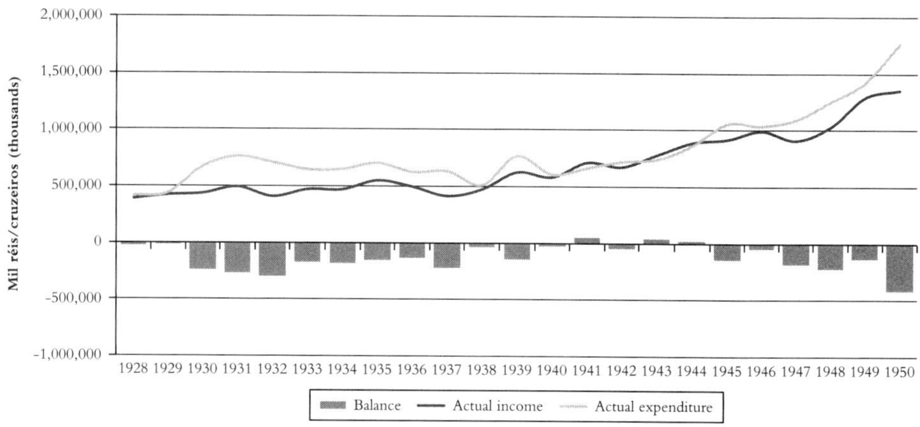

Figure 5.2 Actual State Income, Expenditure, and Balance, 1928–1950 (constant values)

SOURCE: Assembléia Legislativa do Estado de São Paulo, leis orçamentárias, various years, http://www.al.sp.gov.br/leis; Departamento de Estatística do Estado, *Anuário estatístico de São Paulo*, various years; Secretaria da Fazenda do Estado de São Paulo, *Contas do exercício*, various years.

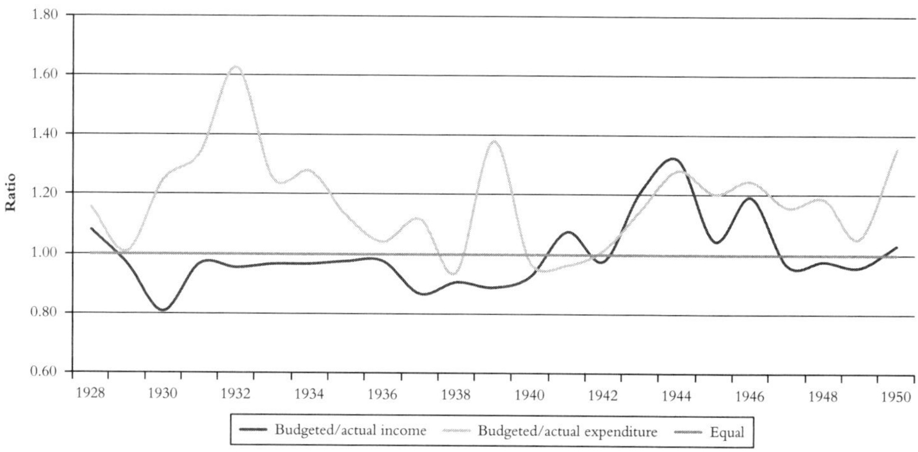

Figure 5.3 Relation Between Budgeted and Actual Income and Expenditure, 1928–1950

SOURCE: Assembléia Legislativa do Estado de São Paulo, leis orçamentárias, various years, http://www.al.sp.gov.br/leis; Departamento de Estatística do Estado, *Anuário estatístico de São Paulo*, various years; Secretaria da Fazenda do Estado de São Paulo, *Contas do exercício*, various years.

sented to the legislature, it meant that the projected budget often bore little resemblance to the actual income and expenditure and that deficits were the norm.

In the post-1930 period there was also a major change in the base of state finances. Until 1930 the tax obtained on coffee exports was the most important realized income item, accounting for more than half of revenue received by the state until the mid-1910s, and between 30 percent and 50 percent of income received in the 1920s.[46] In 1930 and 1931 the percentage was still relatively high (34 percent and 28 percent, respectively), but in late 1932 the interventor suppressed all state taxes on coffee produced in the state on the grounds that they increased coffee costs and decreased exports. But the continuing need to repay the previous foreign loan taken out for the defense of coffee forced the interventor to abandon this drastic position and create an emergency fixed tax of 5 mil réis per bag of coffee produced in the state.[47] Like the old tax on coffee exports, this new one primarily serviced the foreign loan of 1921.[48]

But from 1936 onward the state no longer collected a regular export tax on coffee. In 1935 the Tax on Sales and Consignments (IVC) would become the main source of revenue for São Paulo and remain so until the tax reform carried out by the military government in 1965, when it was replaced by the Tax on Circulation of Goods (ICM).[49] This sales tax, initially set at 1 percent, was levied on all sales and consignments by industries and traders. This represented 38 percent of all tax revenues in 1938 and reached approximately 60 percent of total state income in 1949 and 1950. In 1936 the tax on industries and professions was charged on all natural or legal persons who participated in industry or trade or exercised any profession, art, or craft.[50] This tax accounted for between 5 and 10 percent of state income until 1946, when it was given to the municipalities as their source of income in the new constitution of that year. In aggregate, the taxes levied on real property (houses and rural lands) or property sales and inheritance remained a relatively stable share of the state's revenue of about 15 percent throughout the period. The traditional stamp duty remained at around 3 percent of revenues. The group of taxes on railroad and road movement of goods and passengers was relatively unimportant, usually accounting for less than 3 percent. The collection of outstanding debt contributed a variable percentage of between 2 and 6 percent in any given year.

There are two important items of so-called industrial revenue: the fees charged on water and sewage services and the rents and income obtained from the railroads controlled by the state government, which had been acquired by expropriation.[51] Revenue from water and sewage services in the capital and the cities of Santos and São Vicente accounted for 3 to 6 percent; revenue from railways, between 15 and 20 percent of total state income received. Income called "industrial receipts" had a corresponding expenditure in the budget since the state had to pay for the rail, water, and sanitation services being provided. To get an idea of the ratio between revenue and expenditures on these fees we consider the year 1937. In that year the Sorocabana railroad had revenue of 120,000 contos and expenses of 94,000 contos, which provided the state with a positive income of 26,000 contos; the Araraquara railroad, with revenues of 16,200 contos and expenses of 11,438 contos, also gave a positive result, of 4,762 contos; and water and sewage services for the capital and the cities of Santos and São Vicente had an income of 49,601 contos and expenses of 33,983 contos. The railroads of Campos de Jordão, the São Paulo–Minas, and the Tramway of Cantareira, however, had more expenses than income, but their negative numbers were much lower than the positive results of the three largest industrial operations. During the period analyzed, these fees for water and sanitation and railroad services accounted for some 20 to 30 percent of realized income, and the funds from the active debt did not exceed 5 percent (see Table 5.2 and Figure 5.4).

In relation to expenditures made by the state from 1930 to 1940 we see two distinct phases. In the first, in 1931–1938, there was low nominal realized spending growth, including nominal and real drops in expenditures in 1933 and 1938, which were explained by the crisis in the coffee economy and affected the collection in general. Only with the creation and consolidation of sales and consignments taxes, which became the main source of revenue obtained by the state government after 1936, was there a strong recovery in revenue growth, even in real terms. In general, the actual expenses exceeded the budgeted expenses, particularly in some years, like 1932 and 1939. In 1932 the fiscal performance was strongly affected by the extraordinary "expenses of the revolution," made by the Secretariat of Justice for costs incurred with the Constitutional Revolution of 1932.[52]

When we examine the detailed categories of expenditures, we have actual expenditure information only for 1930 to 1939 and must rely on the budgeted estimates for the 1940s. It is evident that the major expenditure was for collections and debt service, accounting for 20 to 30 percent of state expenditures and even reaching 45 percent in 1931. The plans to support coffee production created extremely onerous liabilities, requiring rescheduling of loans or new loans to consolidate liabilities that burdened the treasury in the short term. In 1930, when the largest share of debt service on the public budget occurred, the state allocated 156,442 contos for debt service in the budget but then was forced to spend in 1931 an additional 104,249 contos to service the debt. In that year the export tax on coffee totaled only 118,144 contos, and even with all other revenues, total expenses were 54 percent higher than the revenue in 1931.

Expenditures on public safety and justice were relatively stable for most of this period and accounted for between 10 and 15 percent of all expenditures. Education, culture, and sciences accounted for a growing share of expenses, beginning at 12 percent in the early period and ending at 17 percent by the late 1940s, with primary education being the most important item in this group. Expenditures for public health, sanitation, and social assistance also grew, going from around 5 percent in the first years of the 1930s to around 15 percent in the last years of the 1940s, with public health being the largest share of this category of expenses. The items listed as means of communication and transport also grew to around 20 percent of all expenses by the late 1940s, with railroad costs being the biggest single item of this group. This was also a period of major road construction as trucks slowly replaced railroads in the movement of goods and persons both within the state and across state lines. But fortunately for the state, the revenues and expenses of the railway companies taken over by the state government of São Paulo in the aggregate generated positive operating results. However, as expropriation usually required the state to borrow funds, the debt service that annually burdened the public coffers was partly from this initial indebtedness for the acquisition of the railroad companies, acquired by the government when they were in precarious financial conditions (see Figure 5.5).

By the mid-1940s the debt service alone represented the main item of expenditure, with railroads and primary education following in importance. Thereafter, the share for servicing the debt declined. At constant prices debt service presented a relatively stable amount. The actual expenditures on railways, public health, and education showed a strong increasing trend in real terms, while funds spent on law enforcement remained relatively stable throughout the period.

Because of recurring budget deficits of a large magnitude, the government of the state was forced to increase its debt, though in contrast to earlier times this funding came primarily through internal sources rather than the international market that had been the prime source of such borrowed capital in the earlier period. By 1950 the balance of credit operations totaled 7,336 million cruzeiros, or approximately US$390 million at the then exchange rate of 18.8 cruzeiros to the dollar, a value five times as high as that in 1930. The balance exceeded the realized revenues in 1950

Table 5.2

Principal Actual Taxes and Fees Collected by the Government of the State of São Paulo, 1929–1950 (contos and cruzeiros)

	1929	1930	1931	1932	1933	1934	1935	1938	1939
Export tax	146,974	134,365	118,145	64,079	40,245	45,971	54,151		
Property tax	73,726	55,706	68,013	56,749	71,203	79,717	115,271	99,466	109,944
Sales tax								263,768	290,492
Industrial and professional taxes								72,326	83,935
Commerce and industry taxes	23,168	20,612	19,850	19,385	21,340	23,807	34,502		
Stamp tax	14,432	11,003	14,342	15,304	18,930	22,720	22,340	16,041	30,506
Transport tax	13,947	10,696	8,953	7,455	36,967	48,189		27,232	6,561
Additional fees	6,431	12,477	14,675	19,641	28,435	18,267			
Water and sewage fees, capital and Santos	25,459	28,048	28,057	27,438	28,198	31,718	39,890	55,916	
Railway income	69,702	72,590	73,279	83,954	71,678	99,472	103,005		
National Coffee Department							83,442		
Fines, delayed taxes, and active debt	23,056	10,047	12,923	17,792	15,571	26,800	24,547	16,157	
Subtotal	396,896	355,545	358,235	311,797	332,567	396,661	477,147	550,905	521,437
Total income, excluding loans	438,460	400,204	429,571	382,424	432,283	475,919	657,142	696,033	843,231
Percentage of income	91%	89%	83%	82%	77%	83%	73%	79%	62%

	1940	1941	1942	1943	1944	1945	1946	1949	1950
Export tax									
Property tax	107,077	132,460	147,518	212,538	293,218	319,345	469,846	606,038	757,250
Sales tax	311,160	376,742	434,619	633,392	824,514	930,248	1,259,940	3,000,510	3,639,793
Industrial and professional taxes	75,217	76,659	80,675	93,166	105,686	114,324	128,075		
Commerce and industry taxes									
Stamp tax	25,192	30,023	30,441	30,800	35,918	35,009	39,311	80,488	92,101
Transport tax	6,307	7,888	7,846	4,979	5,649	6,884	10,616	28,539	77,122
Additional fees									
Water and sewage fees, capital and Santos	58,846	64,127	69,511	75,960	80,049	83,117	92,831	205,229	196,744
Railway income	152,010	187,623	167,697	222,321	315,119	362,806	548,671	617,997	694,769
National Coffee Department		38,245	24,679	37,683	54,888	48,983	46,743		
Fines, delayed taxes, and active debt	19,959	20,056	21,632	19,467	18,128	16,371	20,550	50,076	59,319
Subtotal	755,768	933,823	984,618	1,330,306	1,733,168	1,917,087	2,616,582	4,588,876	5,517,098
Total income, excluding loans	878,204	1,095,055	1,164,732	1,554,371	2,052,365	2,428,109	3,069,909	5,102,147	5,966,324
Percentage of income	86%	85%	85%	86%	84%	79%	85%	90%	92%

SOURCE: Assembleia Legislativa do Estado de São Paulo, leis orçamentárias, various years; Instituto Brasileiro de Geografia e Estatística, *Anuário estatistico do Brasil, 1950.*

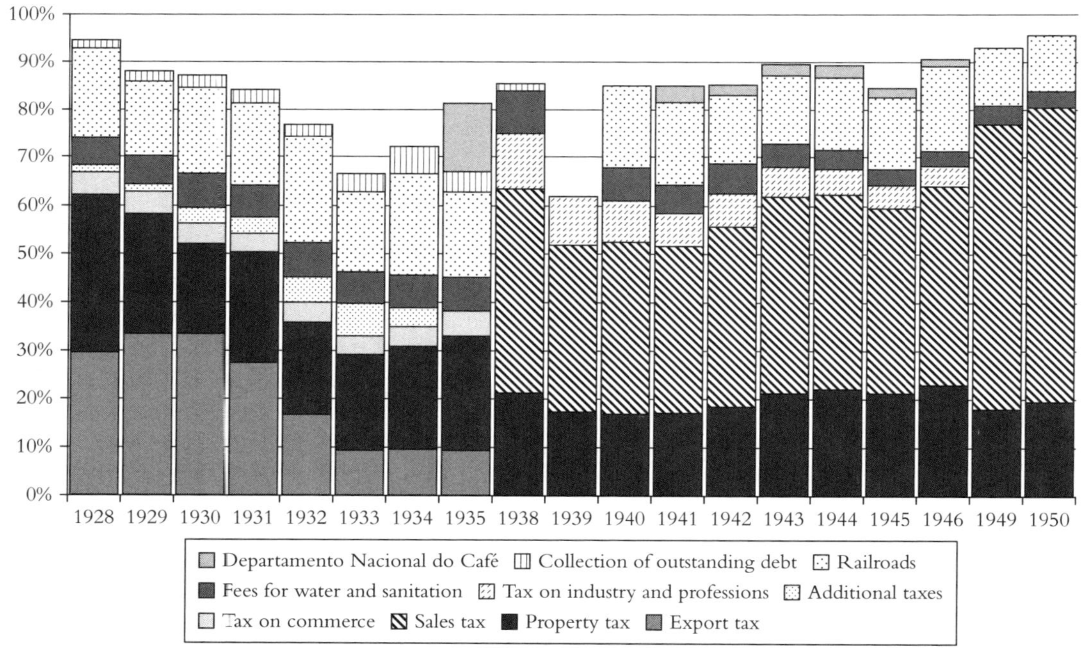

Figure 5.4 Breakdown of the Principal Taxes, Fees, and Revenues in the Income Obtained by the State, 1928–1950

SOURCE: Secretaria da Fazenda do Estado de São Paulo, *Contas do exercício*, 1928–1950.

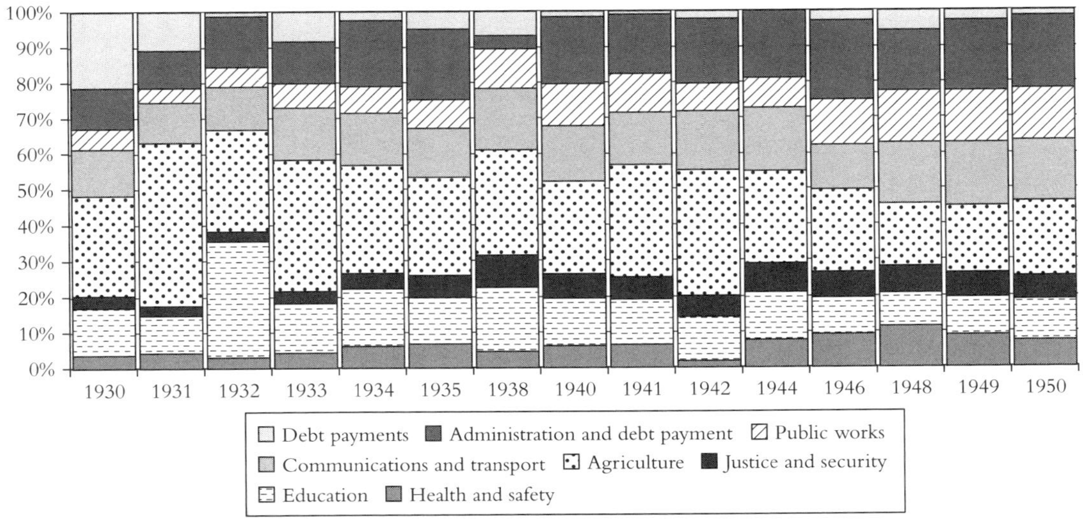

Figure 5.5 Percentage of Major Expenditures of Total Expenditures, 1930–1950

SOURCE: Assembléia Legislativa do Estado de São Paulo, leis orçamentárias, various years, http://www.al.sp.gov.br/leis; Departamento de Estatística do Estado, *Anuário estatístico de São Paulo*, various years; Secretaria da Fazenda do Estado de São Paulo, *Contas do exercício*, various years.

by 23 percent, much lower than the percentage of 1930 when the balance of loans was three times the revenues realized in that period. Another major difference was that 91 percent of these loans were now in local currency in 1950, compared with 27 percent in local currency in 1930. All the existing loans in foreign currency in 1950 were remnants of the pre-1930 period (see Tables 5.3 and 5.4).[53]

Tax collections in São Paulo showed increasing importance on the national level and in the total income generated by the state governments. São Paulo's share of taxes collected by states went from 32 percent in 1940 to 40 percent in 1949. It also expanded its share of taxes sent to the federal government by the states. São Paulo's contribution went from 28 percent to 34 percent of federal state receipts in the same years. Paulista municípios also accounted for a significant amount, 40 percent, of all município taxes collected in the nation in 1949 (see Table 5.5). These numbers show the increasing importance of the state in the national context. Its increasing revenues benefited the three levels of government—the central, state, and município governments.

The relative importance of São Paulo was due to its dynamic expansion but also to its systematic creation of a relatively efficient public administration that could tax this growing economy. Despite the recurring deficits, the evolving fiscal system of first the province and then the state allowed the Paulista government to meet the growing demands for education, health, sanitation, and security. It allowed the state government to systematically support the local economy by building a modern railroad and road infrastructure. The state also took the initiative with an immigration subsidization program, which was crucial for the survival of the coffee economy after the abolition of slavery. Finally, the systematic market intervention to sustain coffee prices was initially a fundamental state activity supported by the state fiscal system.

Under the Old Republic a very modern state administration had been created not only to tax the population and its resources but also to provide detailed studies of the evolution of all the social and economic developments in the state and provide the government with a sophisticated knowledge of the local economic and social conditions. Thus, state development policies were based on very well developed plans resting on accumulated statistical data of the highest order. Even during the authoritarian and centralizing Vargas period, no setback in the consolidation of state organization occurred. But government costs remained above government income for most of this period. Particularly after 1930 there were frequent government deficits that were successfully financed by local and foreign loans, which

TABLE 5.3

Internal and External Debt of the State of São Paulo, 1950 (thousands of cruzeiros)

Year	Series	Term (years)	Actual value	Balance in December 1950	Purpose
1905	3rd	50	5,000	3,114	Extension of the EF Sorocabana railway
1905	4th	50	4,000	2,057	Extension of the EF Sorocabana railway
1905	5th	50	4,000	2,070	Extension of the EF Sorocabana railway
1907	6th	50	8,000	5,367	Extension of the EF Sorocabana railway
1909	8th	50	10,000	6,664	Consolidation of floating debt
1910	9th	50	10,500	6,717	Acquisition of school buildings
1917	11th	50	2,500	1,971	Liquidation of judicial sentence
1919	12th	40	48,694	23,763	Termination of rental of EF Sorocabana railway
1920	13th	40	18,000	11,101	Commemoration of centenary of Independence
1920	14th	50	5,000	3,415	Payment of judicial judgments
1927	15th	30	31,348	11,151	Purchase of the EF Santos a Juquiá railway
1920		25	150,000	106,586	Redemption of floating debt, conversion unification of funded debt
1920		30	116,700	71,998	Redemption of floating debt, conversion unification of funded debt
1926		30	5,740	3,932	Empréstimo à Bolsa de Mercadorias de São Paulo
1926		30	10,000	7,349	Leper care
1921		30	581	495	Aid to the Cia. Melhoramentos de Monte Alto
1921		30	6,361	5,535	Aid to the Cia. Eletrometalurgica Brasileira
1921		30	2,416	2,194	Aid to the EF Morro Agudo railway
1921		20	8,913	3,336	Municipal credit
1935		40	300,000	289,323	Unification and conversion of funded internal debt
1935		40	300,000	293,232	Unification and conversion of funded internal debt
1935		40	300,000	294,333	Unification and conversion of funded internal debt
1935		40	200,000	173,768	Consolidation of the floating debt and public works
1942	1st	30	30,000	30,000	Construction of road network improvements and duplication
1942	2nd	30	40,000	40,000	Construction of road network improvements and duplication
1942	3rd	30	50,000	50,000	Construction of road network improvements and duplication
1942	4th	30	60,000	60,000	Construction of road network improvements and duplication
1942	5th	30	51,342	51,342	Construction of road network improvements and duplication
1945		50	4,199,663	4,199,663	Unification of public debt
1945		20	899,890	899,890	Improvements and electrification of the EF Sorocabana railroad
1945		30	30,594	30,594	Works and public services relevant to state offices
Balance			6,909,242	6,690,960	

SOURCE: Secretaria da Fazenda do Estado e do Tesouro do Estado de São Paulo, *Contas do exercício de 1930*, tables 8, 9.
NOTE: The table does not include the outstanding balance for coffee.

TABLE 5.4
Internal and External Debt of the State of São Paulo, for Loans as of December 1950 (foreign currency)

Year	Currency unit	Original amount	CRUZEIROS (THOUSANDS) Exchange at par	Official exchange
1904	Libra	30,020	266,817	1,573,528
1905	Libra	1,421,477	12,634,095	74,508,185
1907	Libra	1,027,401	9,131,544	53,852,277
1921	Libra	769,700	6,841,093	40,344,595
1926	Libra	1,170,550	10,403,848	61,355,548
1928	Libra	1,660,550	14,758,968	87,039,388
Total	*Libra*	*6,079,699*	*54,036,368*	*318,673,523*
1921	Dollar	1,583,000	2,898,473	29,633,760
1925	Dollar	6,237,750	11,421,320	116,770,680
1926	Dollar	2,641,750	4,837,044	49,453,560
1928	Dollar	5,310,000	9,722,610	99,403,200
Total	*Dollar*	*15,772,500*	*28,879,447*	*295,261,200*
1921	Florin	6,428,100	4,731,081	31,587,683
Balance			87,646,897	645,522,406

SOURCE: Secretaria da Fazenda do Estado e do Tesouro do Estado de São Paulo, *Contas do Exercício de 1930,* tables 8, 9.

TABLE 5.5
Income Generated by the Principal States and Federal District, 1940 and 1949

	1940			1949		
	Federal	State	Municipalities	Federal	State	Municipalities
Minas Gerais	102,868	326,366	119,230	639,853	1,285,497	382,165
Federal District	2,450,119	423,379		7,464,843	2,548,593	
Rio Grande do Sul	2,033,039	349,207	142,954	1,107,713	1,684,125	523,514
São Paulo	1,304,399	878,204	363,626	6,104,422	5,794,560	1,499,928
Total Brazil	4,644,813	2,718,021	936,558	17,916,540	14,657,450	3,736,411
São Paulo's percentage of Brazil	28%	32%	39%	34%	40%	40%

SOURCE: Instituto Brasileiro de Geografia e Estatística, *Anuário estatistico do Brasil, 1950.*

demonstrated the quality of the credit of the state of São Paulo. Although the federal government had reorganized the tax system, and the balance between the federal and state governments had once again shifted toward the central government under Vargas, São Paulo still continued to increase its collections. But expenses still outran income, and repeated borrowing by the government was gradually burdening the public budget, which in turn reduced state investments in basic services. Nevertheless, despite these limitations, such services expanded at a pace well above that of other states, as we see in the following chapters, which show that the state took the lead in the nation in almost all economic and social indices by the middle of the twentieth century.

Chapter 6

The State in National and International Commerce

The growth of the coffee economy in São Paulo finally permitted the state to become a significant participant in the international economy. It also allowed the state to achieve independence from the port of Rio de Janeiro, which had been its primary contact with the outside world. Although the extensive farmlands of the state supplied most of the food and raw materials it needed, São Paulo was increasingly an importer of sugar and raw cotton from other states of Brazil, wheat from Argentina, and industrial products and raw materials from Europe. These basic imports and increasingly sophisticated European imports were paid for with the increasing exports of coffee. This expansion of coffee plantations and integration into the world market began in the middle decades of the nineteenth century, with mule trains carrying São Paulo's coffee and sugar to the coast.

In 1850 the province still shipped most of its coffee and sugar to the port of Rio de Janeiro, there to be transshipped to Europe or other Brazilian provinces or American republics. Since the early coffee industry was concentrated near the province of Rio de Janeiro in Vale do Paraíba, most coffee exports were initially sent by mule trains either overland directly to the city of Rio de Janeiro or to nearby northern coastal ports of the state, such as São Sebastião, Ubatuba, Vila Bela, Iguape, and Cananéa. From these Paulista ports the sugar and coffee were then shipped via coastal trading vessels to the imperial capital. Even Santos, which initially dealt primarily with sugar exports, remained primarily a transshipment center, sending its goods on to Rio de Janeiro. Santos was the natural port of exit for goods produced in the central and western parts of the province, but these zones were still primarily sugar producers at mid-century.

The center of Paulista sugar production at this time was Campinas, whose natural port of exit was Santos. As of 1850–1851 Santos accounted for 79 percent of all the sugar exported from all ports in the province but shipped only 26 percent of all coffee in that year. At this point the only major coffee-producing municípios outside Vale do Paraíba were Campinas and Limeira. At the minimum, the municípios of Vale do Paraíba were still producing at least 40 percent of 51,000 metric tons of Paulista coffee as late as the crop year of 1857, which meant that Rio de Janeiro was still taking the bulk of coffee being shipped from the state. But it was evident from the export data from all the provincial ports that coffee as early as the 1840s had come to dominate provincial exports, far surpassing in bulk and value the sugar that had been the leading São Paulo export up to that time.[1]

Even Santos by the 1850/1851 crop year was finally exporting more tons of coffee than sugar. In that year almost 7,000 metric tons of coffee left the port compared to just 5,000 metric tons of sugar. In the next few decades the opening of the western Paulista coffee fields and the slow decline of Vale do Paraíba in coffee production meant that Santos would emerge as the premier coffee-exporting port of Brazil. Santos would also stop transshipping its output to Rio de Janeiro, becoming instead an independent exporter to the world with direct connections to overseas ports. Thus, from the early 1850s coffee exports from the port grew rapidly, reflecting the rise of these new coffee counties in the western Paulista plains for which it was the natural port of exit. Coffee exports from all the ports of São Paulo went from an annual average of 10,600 metric tons in the 1850s to 24,000 metric tons in the 1860s, just before the rail link was opened between the highlands and Santos (see Figure 6.1).

Until the 1870s, this growing volume of coffee was carried by mules in long mule trains (*tropas*). In 1855/1856, for example, Santos exported 11,000 metric tons of coffee and 1,400 metric tons of sugar, in addition to smaller amounts of numerous other agricultural products. According to most contemporary observers, an average mule carried at least 8 arrobas of coffee or other products per trip.[2] This would have required at least 108,000 mule trips to move the coffee and sugar to the coast. In fact, the Barreira de Cubatão, the customs house at the entrance to the port of Santos, reported that some 166,000 cargo mules had passed through to the port in that year.[3] Even after the arrival of the railroads, mules still carried coffee up to 1880. Thus, in the five crop years of 1875/1876 to 1879/1880, some

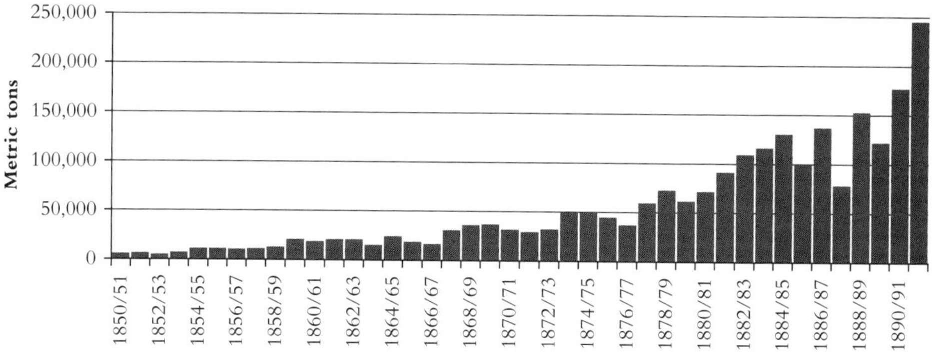

Figure 6.1 Coffee Exports from Santos, 1850–1892

SOURCE: Departamento de Estatística do Estado, *Anuário estatístico de São Paulo, 1908*, 2:117.

56,000 metric tons on average were shipped per annum from the port of Santos, of which 48 percent still arrived on the backs of mules.

Change was now quite rapid. In 1865 the Estrada de Ferro D. Pedro II railroad reached Vassouras from the port of Rio de Janeiro, thus eliminating the role of the small northern coastal ports in transshipping Vale do Paraíba coffee to this port. There soon followed the first and most important rail connection to the port of Santos. In 1867 the São Paulo Railway Company connected Santos to the highland city of Jundiaí passing through the capital in route, which was the traditional entrance to the interior plains of western Paulista. In turn, the interior zones were progressively linked to Jundiaí via the new Companhia Paulista de Estrada de Ferro, which connected that city to Campinas in 1872 and then to Rio Claro in 1876. Then the Companhia Mogiana de Estrada de Ferro opened up several coffee zones, including Ribeirão Preto via rail to Jundiaí in the 1870s and 1880s. Finally, the more southern zone of Sorocaba also became linked to the Jundiaí railhead via the Estrada de Ferro Sorocabana. These connections guaranteed that coffee was now being shipped rapidly to market, and the railroads became the basis for the entire Santos economy. Each of these railroads began shipping coffee in the late 1870s, and by the 1880s the railroads had eliminated mules and together were bringing in an impressive average of over a hundred thousand metric tons of coffee per annum, as can be seen from the shipping data from three of the four major lines connecting the interior to the port (see Table 6.1).[4] The São Paulo Railway Company, the

TABLE 6.1
Average Annual Shipments of Coffee Carried by Principal Railroads Connecting to Santos, 1875–1940 (metric tons)

Years	Companhia Paulista	Companhia Mogiana	EF Sorocabana	Total
1875–1880		14,588	14,146	28,734
1881–1885	83,353	36,556	23,691	143,600
1886–1890	104,696	48,158	61,210	214,064
1891–1895	195,189	80,270	140,672	416,131
1896–1900	315,391	165,814	248,394	729,599
1901–1905	404,338	261,357	269,598	935,293
1906–1910	531,774	314,191	411,883	1,257,848
1911–1915	505,783	329,180	588,709	1,423,672
1916–1920	415,869	271,656	838,267	1,525,792
1921–1925	413,148	253,314	1,076,403	1,742,865
1926–1930	501,830	291,376	1,442,270	2,235,476
1931–1935	757,239	344,625	1,683,897	2,785,761
1936–1940	534,596	188,774	2,887,845	3,611,215

SOURCE: Saes, *As ferrovias de São Paulo*, 92, table 2.3.

biggest of the four major railroads carrying coffee and the only one to directly link to Santos, moved large numbers of passengers as well as products for the internal market, as did all the others and as can be seen in the more detailed breakdown of their goods shipped in 1900 (see Table 6.2).[5] But given the initial poor quality of the roads, most of the goods still arrived at the railheads on the backs of mules or in ox-drawn carts until well into the twentieth century.

As expected, coffee overwhelmingly dominated these exports. But even in 1900 some manufactured goods were exported from Santos as well, probably to the other regions of the country. Thus, there were shipped from Santos 151 metric tons of cotton textiles, 4 metric tons of woolens, and 17 metric tons of fedora hats plus shoes, leather soles, beer, and some grains. In all, the state exported from Santos 248,478 contos of locally produced goods, but noncoffee exports represented less than 2 percent of the value of these exports.[6] Although cotton and sugar continued to be produced in the state, they were less and less exported as the local market expanded. The local textile industry absorbed almost all locally produced cotton and still needed to import even more from the Northeast. Sugar was consumed by the growing state population, and less and less of it entered the export market. In fact, the state by the turn of the century had to import sugar from the northeastern states, above all from Pernambuco. These two products were exported until the first years of the 1890s, but from 1883 to 1905

TABLE 6.2
Transportation of Major Products and Characteristics of the Railroads in São Paulo, 1900

	Mogiana	Paulista	São Paulo Railway	Others[a]	Total
Passengers	1,156,186	1,052,900	1,066,638	239,502	3,515,226
Telegrams	513,033	214,321	134,642	19,071	881,067
Baggage	9,791,197	10,162,000	14,650,874	2,608,603	37,212,674
Goods (kg)					
Aguardente	5,667,839			1,304,771	6,972,610
Cotton	44,451		1,295,000	3,815	1,343,266
Sugar			32,605,000	885,727	33,490,727
Rubber			179,000		179,000
Coffee	203,826,416	338,453,000	390,994,000	37,834,216	971,107,632
Cereals	67,785,915			9,575,085	77,361,000
Coal			79,361,000	–7,000,000	72,361,000
Leather	495,295			27,674	522,969
Tobacco	280,657			332,115	612,772
Salt	28,789,913		36,043,000	2,293,457	67,126,370
Miscellaneous	115,949,549	338,359,000	631,482,000	22,432,463	1,108,223,012
Total goods	421,949,549	676,812,000	1,164,959,000	76,192,657	2,339,913,206
Animals	49,748	31,819	14,170	6,922	102,659
Rail in use (km)	909	1,023	139	313	2,384
Rail under construction (km)	119	68		28	215
Stations	86	82	26	40	234
Wagons	1,156	1,093	2,621	262	5,132
Employees	3,231	3,395	3,563	444	10,633
Income from goods (mil réis)	13,464,214	17,950,533	16,905,012	776,585	49,096,344
Total income (mil réis)	16,663,032	22,071,945	20,122,024	1,403,028	60,260,029
Net income (mil réis)	8,215,673	12,939,589	10,955,926	275,411	32,386,599

SOURCE: Departamento de Estatística do Estado, *Anuário estatístico de São Paulo, 1900*, 605–611.
[a]Other railroads include the Bragantina, Carril Agrícola Funilense, Araraquara e Ribeirãozinho, Rezende e Bocaina, Bananalense, Ramal Dumont, Carril Itatibense, and Dourados. There were no data for the União Sorocabana–Ytuana or the São Paulo–Santo Amaro railroad.

they no longer were significant in the export mix. The same occurred with flour, beans, corn, bacon, and wine. These were still being produced, but the local market was absorbing all local production (see Table 6.3).

In fact, the state was a major importer of goods from other states as well as machinery coming from Europe in 1902. It imported some 35,000 metric tons of sugar, most of it from Pernambuco. In the same year, it produced just 16,000 metric tons of sugar. This meant that two-thirds of the

Table 6.3

Principal Agricultural Products Exported from São Paulo, 1883–1905

												Value of exports (contos)	
Year	Aguardente (L)	Cotton (kg)	Rice (L)	Sugar (kg)	Animal horns (kg)	Leather (kg)	Flour (L)	Beans (L)	Tobacco (kg)	Corn (L)	Lard (kg)	All but coffee	Coffee
1883–1884	45,824	293,960	2,577,139	151,920	44,016	476,686	179,024	278,885	343,789	299,988	154,472	1,286	138,173
1884–1885	5,980	939,004	1,854,006	1,170	76,364	511,526	97,996		283,584	105,016	262,287	1,659	140,687
1885–1886	148,703	15,835	2,152,194	42,628	53,658	68,640	31,490	393,780	240,262	179,495	237,567	1,261	112,408
1886–1887		404	1,386,883	25,692	56,191	237,377	8,630	67,173	94,121	79,925	183,423	749	168,491
1887–1888		5,366	1,631,752	5,640	76,437	160,021	4,567	99,381	179,950	76,024	183,282	758	84,775
1888–1889	89,463	64,241	1,109,177	250,380	76,180	259,995	10,421	32,080	112,190	69,950	133,949	881	169,175
1889–1890	153,986	147,917	1,471,585	488,790	44,750	348,472	347,795	195,071	96,624	19,382	69,989	1,171	137,898
1890–1891	130,728	235,885	1,705,293	222,152	26,000	368,730	42,812	85,307	102,202	315,562	41,625	1,259	195,448
1891	42,594	55,227	1,144,866	216,440	35,900	80,908	2,880	20,848	23,535	46,557	10,298	914	119,166
1892	61,790		829,067	64,32	68,000	357,665	800	61,717	128,011	15,080	23,489	783	245,457
1893	717		167,305		49,000	229,556	44,640	51,858	67,597	28,120	8,406	591	169,217
1894	4,948		637,600		111,900	257,237	35,378	47,632	48,197	71,210	5,777	926	174,415
1895	18,230		831,195		69,890	463,360	165,369	170,469	80,081	37,012	10,410	1,033	262,375
1896	26,252		850,100		97,000	415,509	69,877	816,858	106,904	18,950	20,981	1,339	240,396
1897	33,765		759,438		87,405	1,109,321	2,250	465,329	125,780	61,134	17,520	1,418	343,522
1898	14,558		627,536		156,316	1,492,175	156,064	1,746,335	319,832	451,882	42,424		346,077
1899	32,388				123,252	759,145			381,480			1,294	363,465
1900	31,906				95,639	530,131			334,399			1,260	366,701
1901	460				122,881	203,601			251,737			3,390	602,006
1902					107,982	422,836			3,436			305	508,290
1903					154,936	926,528			417,409			927	473,667
1904					121,426	674,771			589,742			1,053	380,080
1905					70,603	373,075			259,457			564	450,732

SOURCE: Departamento de Estatística do Estado, *Anuário estatístico de São Paulo, 1905*, 2:150–152.

NOTE: In 1883–1905 there were also some minor rubber and wine exports. Numbers for 1891 are only for July through December.

sugar consumed in the state had to be imported. As for cotton, in that same year the state produced 3,000 metric tons and had to import another 3,000 metric tons to satisfy local demand. The state also imported lard, onions, and manioc flour coming from Rio Grande do Sul. It even imported food products internationally, with salt and wheat flour coming from Argentina via the port of Rio de Janeiro. Unusually, there was also a deficit in that year of some types of beans, more of which were imported in that year than were exported.[7] The growth of the interior rail lines also meant that by the late 1880s Santos exported even some products from the neighboring states of Minas Gerais and Paraná, though nothing on the scale of the port of Rio de Janeiro in terms of shipping to other states.[8]

The port itself received a major modernization when the Melhoramentos do Porto de Santos company built the city's first modern docks in the 1890s. By 1905 these modern facilities were able to handle the entire coffee export of that year, allowing oceangoing vessels to directly load from these docks without using lighters or barges. Already by the end of the nineteenth century and the beginning of the new century, Santos had become the prime exporting port of the state, accounting for 70 percent of all Brazilian coffee shipments. Rio de Janeiro now accounted for only a quarter of all coffee exports on average in the first decade of the new century, while the ports of Bahia and Victoria along with much smaller ports shipped the rest.[9]

In the 1870s the shipping arriving in the port of Santos still included a large number of sailing ships, even in long-distance trade, though this was changing. Already in the period from 1877 to 1887, steamships represented about 70 percent of the total shipping in long-distance trade and about half the ships in cabotage, or coastal trading, within the national borders.[10] But as yet the vast majority of ships were tramp steamers or sailing boats with no fixed routes or schedules. The delay in setting up scheduled routes to Santos and other Brazilian ports, according to the British, was the competition of tramp steamers and sailing ships, which took a significant share of the coffee trade.

But in the second half of the century, it was the British and then the Germans who finally established the first scheduled lines to Brazil, with the two dominating the export of coffee from Santos. In 1851 the Royal Mail shipping company established the first scheduled lines to Brazil, a decade after the company had established regular liner schedules for the Caribbean (with Cunard opening up the US-British route and the Peninsular and Oriental to the Far East in the 1840s). It initially opened up scheduled arrivals to the ports of Rio de Janeiro, Montevideo, and Buenos Aires from England and the Continent, with significant subsidies for carrying mails from the British government. These were the three busiest ports of the South Atlantic. Soon competition developed from two other British companies: the Pacific Steamship Company opened the route to the Pacific through the Strait of Magellan in 1868, and the Liverpool firm of Lamport and Holt became very active in the port of Santos. It was the *Haley*, a boat owned by Lamport and Holt, that carried the first steam-driven shipment of coffee from Rio de Janeiro to New York City in 1865.[11] And it was the Lamport and Holt line that took over a large share of the shipping of coffee from Santos to North America and Europe. Quickly, two German lines came to compete in the port of Santos, these were the Hamburg Süd, founded in 1871, and the Bremen-based North German Lloyd, founded in 1856. It was Hamburg Süd that became a major coffee shipper along with Lamport and Holt, and it was their representative, the commercial house of Theodor Wille, that was the biggest German factor and one of the largest exporters of coffee in Brazil. Theodor Wille was a Hamburg-Rio-Santos–São Paulo company, founded in Santos in 1844. Theodor Wille even owned coffee fazendas and also supplied credit to Brazilian planters. Wille himself was also instrumental in founding a coffee exchange in Hamburg, which had become the principal European port of entry for Brazilian coffee.[12] To these early British and German initiatives were added the Italian and French lines after 1880, with the French being third in importance after the English and the Germans. The Scandinavian shipping entering the port of Santos in this period was still essentially sporadic tramp steamers or sailing vessels with no regular schedule.

The arrival of ever-larger numbers of immigrants from Europe was also facilitated by the increasing size of the steamships arriving in Santos. These newer late-nineteenth and early-twentieth-century steamships now carried hundreds of passengers in third class. Thus, for example, between August 4, 1899, and July 12, 1900, some 105 steamships left the port of Santos for Europe or North America, with one sailing to Europe approximately every three and a half days. The Italian lines had particularly large passenger ships. Thus, the *Perseo* of the Navigazione Generale Italiana, built in 1891, had a capacity of 1,200 passengers in third class, and the *Minas* of the La Ligure–Brasiliana line, built in the same year, carried 900 passengers in steerage. The *San Gottardo* of the La Veloce–Navigazione Italiana line, built in 1884, had capacity for 1,290 persons in third class.[13] The Hamburg Süd lines had nineteen ships leaving Santos and forty-two sailings in this period, with a standard route to Hamburg and Copenhagen often via Rio de Janeiro and Bahia before crossing the Atlantic to Cherbourg and Rotterdam. As in the case of the Italian lines, these vessels made multiple crossings in this period. The Hamburg Süd ships also had significant passenger capacity. Thus, the *Pernambuco*, built in 1897, carried 440 passengers in third class, and the *Paranagua*, built in 1895, carried 300 passengers in steerage. While their tonnage was comparable to the Italian ships making this route, the Germans seem to have used most of their space for cargo.[14] There was also a third German company taking passengers, the Robert M. Sloman Line, which had four ships making a direct run between Santos and New York. There were three distinct Italian lines with thirty-one sailings using fourteen ships in this period: La Ligure–Brasiliana, La Veloce–Navigazione Italiana, and the Navigazione Generale Italiana. All these companies stopped in Rio de Janeiro before crossing to Genoa and Naples. The Navigazione Generale Italiana's steamships *Orione* and *Perseo* were claimed to have done the Atlantic crossing in fourteen days. Finally, there were fifteen sailings in this period from the English Royal Mail company using nine ships, which stopped at Rio, Bahia, Lisbon, Cherbourg, and Southampton. At the end of the period the English Pacific Steam Navigation Company, which primarily used the port of Rio de Janeiro, also began to have direct shipping from Santos to Liverpool via the ports of Portugal and Spain. Two other late entrants but with few sailings in this period were the French-owned Société Générale de Transportes Maritimes, which had two ships going to France and Italy, and the Mala Real Portuguesa, which had only two sailings in the entire period. Both the Royal Mail and the Hamburg Süd lines had two or three separate routes for different ships that ended in either Hamburg or Southampton but included various French, Dutch, or Danish ports as regular ports of call. Also, the Italian lines offered transshipment from Genoa to northern European ports. The price for third-class passage to Europe varied from 150 mil réis in the Hamburg lines to 163 mil réis for the passage to Europe on the Royal Mail ships.[15]

A second major part of the Santos activity was coastal shipping. In the early part of the century, this was the major activity of the port but became secondary after Santos was opened to international trade. Nevertheless, the coastal trade of Brazil was sufficiently important that Brazil's commercial fleet ranked first in size in Latin America and fifteenth in the world in the late nineteenth century.[16] Although the empire had opened up the coastal trade to foreign vessels in the 1860s, only the British company Lamport and Holt provided a regular coastal service, that between Rio and Porto Alegre. While foreign vessels occasionally picked up coastal cargoes, this essentially remained a trade under subsidized imperial companies. Until 1850 local Brazilian shipping also participated in the Atlantic slave trade. But once the slave trade was effectively ended in 1850, Brazilian-owned vessels no longer engaged in transatlantic or international trade. In 1890, a Brazilian investor obtained state support to found the national company of Lloyd Brasileiro, which soon absorbed the main coastal shipping lines. And the new republican constitution of 1891 returned coastal shipping to exclusively national shipping after 1906, which eventually aided the new company when it attempted to develop an international route between New York and Santos in the period between 1906 and 1914. But this effort eventually failed after fierce competition from both Lamport and Holt and Hamburg Süd on this same run.[17]

Santos did not become a major part of the regular liner schedules until British mail steamers started a regular service between Southampton and Santos in 1878.[18] Moreover, despite significant growth of shipping in the next two decades, Rio de Janeiro remained the predominant Brazilian port. In the decade 1877–1887 some 652 ships with a combined average tonnage of 458,000 metric tons arrived annually in Santos. In the nine years from 1878 to 1887 the port of Rio de Janeiro averaged per annum 1.2 million metric tons of shipping and close to 1,300 ships.[19] But by 1902 the total of ships arriving in Santos reached over a thousand, and the total tonnage of shipping was over a million metric tons; it had now become a serious competitor to the port of Rio de Janeiro.

As Santos became an ever more important port in international trade, the shipping arriving at the port also changed. Not only did steam replace sail and irregular schedules become regular routes but the size of shipping also changed. This was the period when specialized and ever-larger ships were developed. In the 1880s came the first tanker and refrigerated ships and, in the 1890s, specialized bulk carriers for grains and ore. Moreover, even the average size of regular cargo vessels went from 1,500 to 2,000 deadweight tons (dwt) in 1870 to 5,000 to 7,000 dwt by 1900 and then doubled again by 1910.[20] By the 1890s the large transatlantic steamers were entering the Europe–Santos run and bringing ever-higher numbers of passengers in steerage class as many of the lines became standard carriers of subsidized immigrant workers. In turn, the passenger liners that arrived in the 1899–1900 period—most built within the five years prior to their usage in Santos—ranged from 2,000 gross register tons (grt) to 5,891 grt. One of these latter ships was the *Danube* of the Royal Mail, and in fact all the Royal Mail's ships used in Santos were over 5,000 grt. By 1910 the port of Santos was handling over 1,400 steamships with a total of 3.1 million tons and received only 38 sailing ships weighing just 19,000 tons. Moreover, even the Brazilian coastal fleet was essentially using only steamships, with 558 arriving in the port in that year compared to only 18 national sailing ships using the port.[21]

The two leading long-distance cargo shippers were the English and the Germans, who had the largest number of ships, crews, tonnage, and volume of goods exported. As many have noted, US shipping was totally absent except for a few sailing ships. Although the United States was a major market for Brazilian coffee, it obtained its Santos coffee from mostly English and German ships that transshipped it to the United States. The largest shipper was Lamport and Holt, which developed a regular schedule of sailings between Santos, New York, and London. It brought Santos coffee directly to New York, picked up wheat in the United States for the English market, and then picked up English manufactured goods for sale in Brazil.[22]

By 1886 the English and European liners and some tramp steamers had formed the West African and Northern Brazil Conference—meaning a unified group of shipping companies providing common prices and guaranteed times and routes—and in 1896 came the River Plate Conference of shipping going to Rio, Montevideo, and Buenos Aires and now finally including the port of Santos.[23] Though monopoly prices were charged, it appears that freight prices were declining over the century and coffee was a high-value product whose rates dropped significantly in the second half of the century. It was the liners that brought out the coffee and brought in immigrants and valuable manufactured goods individually wrapped by smaller firms. It was the tramp steamers that moved the cheap bulk cargo goods to and from Brazilian ports (see Table 6.4). While wheat and wool shipments to Europe from Argentina and Uruguay were highly seasonal in nature, it turned out that coffee shipments, at least until the first valorization schemes, were better distributed over the whole year, meaning that international shipping tended to be more evenly spread over the year for Brazil compared to the River Plate ports.[24]

Although international trade for São Paulo had been growing from the 1850s, there was a quantitative change in the 1890s. The average value of exports in Brazilian contos increased by a factor of three in the quinquennium of 1886/1890–1891/1895, from 69,000 contos to 228,000 contos.[25] This was driven by both the growth of the new coffee areas in western Paulista and the full integration of these new coffee fazendas into the railroad network, which efficiently and quickly brought the coffee to the port of Santos.

In the late 1870s and in the 1880s, São Paulo was still exporting raw cotton, hides, and some sugar, but it was the coffee that dominated its exports. Although of considerable volume, these other products were of insignifi-

TABLE 6.4
Characteristics of Ships Exporting Goods from Santos, 1902

Flag	Ships	Tonnage	Crew	Goods exported (t)	Goods arriving in cabotage (t)
Steamships					
Brazilian	322	180,166	12,574	3,068,680	98,039,672
English	202	430,642	9,824	171,527,180	
German	119	280,740	5,579	228,246,740	
French	97	183,092	6,528	68,935,960	
Italian	62	145,526	4,607	8,646,840	
Austrian	15	24,132	532	33,143,140	
Belgian	11	29,016	411	13,891,720	
Spanish	8	16,235	445	2,237,660	
Argentine	2	1,215	39		
Swedish-Norwegian	2	2,483	49		
Danish	1	2,159	26		
Dutch	1	2,284	27	435,120	
Total	842	1,297,690	40,641	530,133,040	
Sailing ships					
Brazilian	52	3,969	293	9,580	3,782,080
English	16	8,988	8	1,052,540	
Swedish-Norwegian	8	4,828	16	1,428,980	
Danish	4	1,907	1,410	742,640	
German	3	1,065	32	1,513,020	
American	2	2,018	29	480	
Dutch	1	462	37	376,000	
Russian	1	1,173	180	60	
Total	87	24,410	2005	5,123,300	

SOURCE: Departamento de Estatística do Estado, *Anuário estatístico de São Paulo, 1902*, 608.
NOTE: Tonnage in the source table for sailing ships was 200 less than these corrected numbers.

cant value. In no year in this period did the value of coffee fall below 99 percent of the total value of exports. This growth in the volume and value of exports was matched by a growth in imports. But throughout most of this period, the province maintained a positive annual trade balance, as shown in the statistics. In 1890, for example, exports from the port of Santos reached £13.4 million, and imports were just £2.2 million. This positive balance had reached £18.8 million by 1912 (see Table 6.5).

The principal nations that consumed Santos's exports were the United States, Germany, France, and the Netherlands. England controlled the shipping of coffee to the United States, and Germany took the bulk of the coffee shipped from Santos for northern European consumption. The Dutch and French ports also served as transshippers to eastern and southern European regions. The biggest consumers of coffee per capita in Europe in the

TABLE 6.5
International Commerce of São Paulo, 1890–1912 (£)

Year	Exports	Imports	Balance
1890	13,429,972	2,186,237	11,243,735
1895	11,505,404	2,979,980	8,525,424
1900	11,746,568	3,341,168	8,405,400
1905	14,549,510	5,151,494	9,398,016
1910	19,745,474	9,047,760	10,697,714
1912	35,337,919	16,577,814	18,760,105

SOURCE: *Boletim da Diretoria de Industria e Comercio*, suplemento dados econômicos, 1912, p. 3.

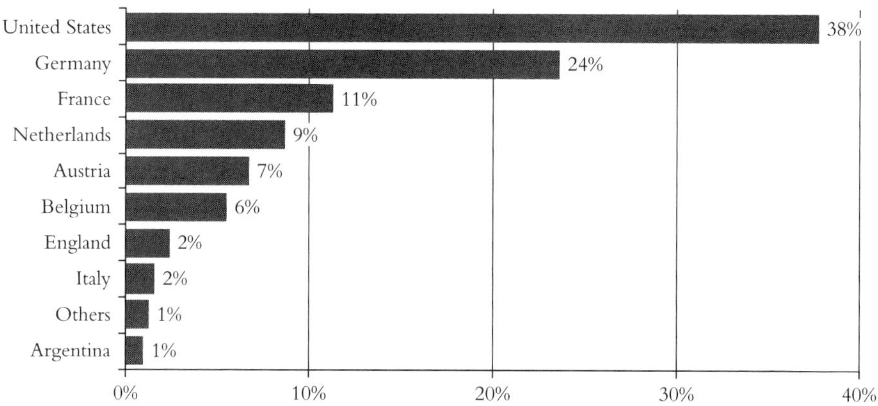

Figure 6.2 Share of the Value of Exports from Santos by Destination, 1904–1908

SOURCE: Departamento de Estatística do Estado, *Anuário estatístico de São Paulo, 1908*, 2:104.

late nineteenth and early twentieth centuries were the Nordic countries, which drank almost as much coffee per capita as the United States. Hamburg was the major importer of Brazilian coffee for this northern European trade.[26] But the Netherlands, Belgium, and France were also significant consumers, as can be seen in the relative importance of national destinations for coffee shipped from Santos at the beginning of the twentieth century (see Figure 6.2). In 1911 officials finally broke down coffee exports by the actual city of destination, and the results confirm the earlier data. In that year Santos shipped 8.7 million sacks of coffee (at 60 kilograms per sack). The leading receiving ports were New York (which received 25 percent of the total shipped) and Hamburg (17 percent). But the third was

New Orleans, which together with New York took 37 percent of all the coffee shipped. Next came Rotterdam (10 percent), Trieste in the Austro-Hungarian empire (9 percent), the Panama Canal (possibly to reship to the US West Coast), Le Havre (6 percent), and Antwerp (3 percent).[27]

In terms of imports to Santos, the majority of machinery and luxury goods that were being imported came from England, Germany, Italy, the United States, and France, while Argentina supplied the crucial wheat that was a basic consumption item in the state and was always an important international food import for São Paulo as well as for all of Brazil. Portugal sent olives and other traditional Portuguese food products (see Figure 6.3).

The major imports into Santos by the first decade of the twentieth century were manufactured goods, food, and primary materials for construction and industry. Though there were big variations by year, 1906 and 1907 can be considered normal years, and on average for these two years some 44 percent of the value of imports was in manufactured goods, 32 percent in food, and 21 percent in primary materials (see Table 6.6). Moreover, despite the impressive growth of local textile manufacturing, cotton and woolen cloth still represented on average 8 percent of the value of all imports. Though no detailed data are provided for 1906 for food imports,

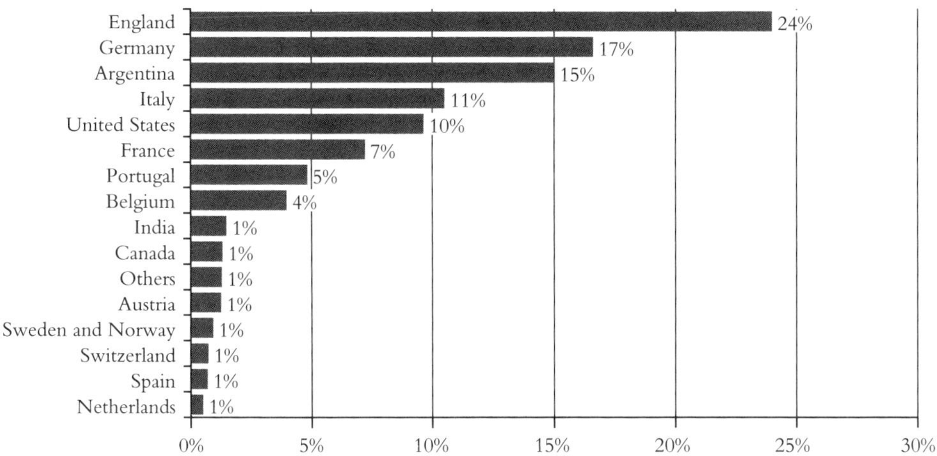

Figure 6.3 Share of the Value of Imports into Santos by National Origin, 1904–1908

SOURCE: Departamento de Estatística do Estado, *Anuário estatístico de São Paulo, 1906*, 2:126; Departamento de Estatística do Estado, *Anuário estatístico de São Paulo, 1908*, 2:111.

TABLE 6.6
Major Categories and Types of Products Imported into Santos, 1906–1907 (contos)

Major categories	1906	1907
Live animals	310	486
Primary materials	21,362	29,233
Jute	5,055	6,466
Stones and building materials	5,272	7,032
Unprepared hides and leather	2,002	2,575
Chemicals and perfumes	1,017	1,344
Iron and steel	1,353	1,334
Wool	1,084	2,052
Fruit and vegetable juices	1,303	2,420
Manufactured goods	40,340	63,588
Cotton cloth, mixed or not	5,468	9,260
Finished iron and steel	9,637	13,958
Machines and diverse tools	6,363	12,216
Drugs and chemical products	1,969	2,753
Woolen cloth, mixed or not	1,906	3,229
Food	34,378	41,368
Coins and bank notes	6,270	1,415
Total	102,659	136,089

SOURCE: Departamento de Estatística do Estado, *Anuário estatístico de São Paulo, 1907*, 2:94–97.

there are detailed data for such imports into Santos in 1907 and 1908. In these two years wheat (27 percent) and wheat flour (15 percent) together made up 42 percent of the value of food imports in those two years. This was followed in importance by wines (23 percent), codfish and other fish products (9 percent), and then cheese and olive oil, both of which represented 3 percent of the total.[28] Argentina, Portugal, Norway, the Netherlands, and France were the key suppliers of these foods.

Although São Paulo generally had a positive international trade balance, it had a mostly negative trade balance with the other provinces and states of the empire and republic. São Paulo from the mid-nineteenth century was always in a negative balance of trade with other Brazilian provinces, principally for sugar, which it no longer produced in sufficient quantities to feed its own population, and eventually for raw cotton, which was becoming essential for its evolving textile industry. Cotton and lard, which had been major exports for most of the nineteenth century, now became major items of importation from the other states of Brazil. In the case of raw cotton, Paulista exports stopped in 1882, and for lard they ended in 1899. São Paulo shipped coffee, beer, hats, and textiles to the other Brazilian states but in quantities less than the value of these imports.[29] This deficit in its commercial balance with the empire did not stop with the end of the nineteenth century but continued well into the new century even despite the increase in manufactured goods coming from São Paulo. Thus, from 1905 to 1917 São Paulo was in continuous commercial debt to the other states of Brazil (see Table 6.7).

The principal item of importation from the other states, both in terms of volume and value, was sugar, obtained primarily from Pernambuco and the other Northeast states. It represented 36 percent of all the goods imported in a sample of four years from 1900 to 1917. Next in importance was raw cotton, coming mostly from Alagoas, which represented a third of all Brazilian imports into Santos and supplied the basic raw material for the Paulista textile industry, supplementing the limited local production. Clearly, the production of pigs in São Paulo was insufficient to supply the important lard, which represented a significant 18 percent of the value of all these national imports. Together, these three items represented 87 percent of the total imports (see Table 6.8).

The states and regions supplying goods to Santos were the major producers of these goods. Pernambuco supplied the sugar, Alagoas the cotton, and Rio Grande do Sul the animal products. The one exceptional source of imports was the federal capital, the port city of Rio de Janeiro. Still

TABLE 6.7

The Volume and Value of Imports and Exports from Santos in the Coastal Trade with Other States of Brazil, 1905–1917

	IMPORTS		EXPORTS		
Year	Volume (t)	Value (contos)	Volume (t)	Value (contos)	Commercial balance (contos)
1905	129,728	29,518	20,157	9,430	-20,087
1906	123,632	37,492	20,980	12,488	-25,004
1907	134,722	52,189	18,106	18,857	-33,333
1908	104,470	41,497	11,779	13,207	-28,290
1909	107,921	44,152	14,933	17,985	-26,167
1910	122,505	42,514	14,698	20,103	-22,411
1911	141,763	44,985	15,273	21,753	-23,232
1912	181,086	74,397	19,946	23,018	-51,380
1913	166,353	77,179	22,794	29,074	-48,106
1914	159,039	77,186	18,482	27,527	-49,659
1915	180,227	90,810	41,500	51,925	-38,886
1916	165,906	99,871	52,887	66,870	-33,001
1917	152,230	127,060	45,247	78,905	-48,155

SOURCE: *Boletim da Diretoria de Indústria e Comércio* 9, nos. 10–11 (1918): 447.

TABLE 6.8
Principal Products Imported in the Coastal Trade, 1900–1917

	1900	1910	1915	1917	Total
Volume (t)					
Sugar	25,781	49,575	63,514	45,300	184,170
Salt		31,848	43,481	36,173	111,502
Cotton	1,486	7,133	12,733	14,246	35,598
Lard	779	3,541	6,437	10,453	21,210
Flour	3,283	4,079	4,062	3,089	14,514
Onions	1,508	2,717	3,372	5,272	12,869
Rice	576	351	6,865	621	8,413
Jerked beef	999	1,501	578	147	3,224
Value (contos)					
Sugar	3,867	12,157	24,135	24,462	64,621
Cotton	1,115	9,272	13,497	35,614	59,498
Lard	569	3,788	10,656	17,770	32,783
Salt		1,911	4,348	7,235	13,494
Onions	603	543	1,349	2,109	4,604
Flour	493	612	810	1,236	3,150
Rice	173	158	3,776	311	4,417
Jerked beef	549	976	751	161	2,437

SOURCE: *Boletim da Diretoria de Indústria e Comércio* 9, nos. 10–11 (1918): 448–449.

the leading industrial center at this time, it supplied manufactures of various kinds and probably acted as a transshipping source of European goods as well. The relative importance of these states and ports can be seen in the import figures for cabotage by origin in the period 1911–1913 (see Figure 6.4). If land transport to other states is included, this increases the influence of the neighboring states of Minas Gerais and Paraná. While this trade overland might have been a minor part of the total national trade of the state in this early period, it would become dominant by the 1930s when motor traffic became more important.

For its part São Paulo essentially shipped out manufactured goods to the rest of the nation, though clearly not of the value of these imports. Some 60 percent of the value of the exports to the other states in four select years from 1900 to 1917 was made up of finished cotton textiles, the key industry in the state. Sackcloth, shoes, hats, and beer made up just under a third, and beans were the only significant export coming from the local farm sector (see Table 6.9).

The states with which São Paulo mostly traded were still roughly the same in the 1920s. Some 70 percent of imports came from three places in

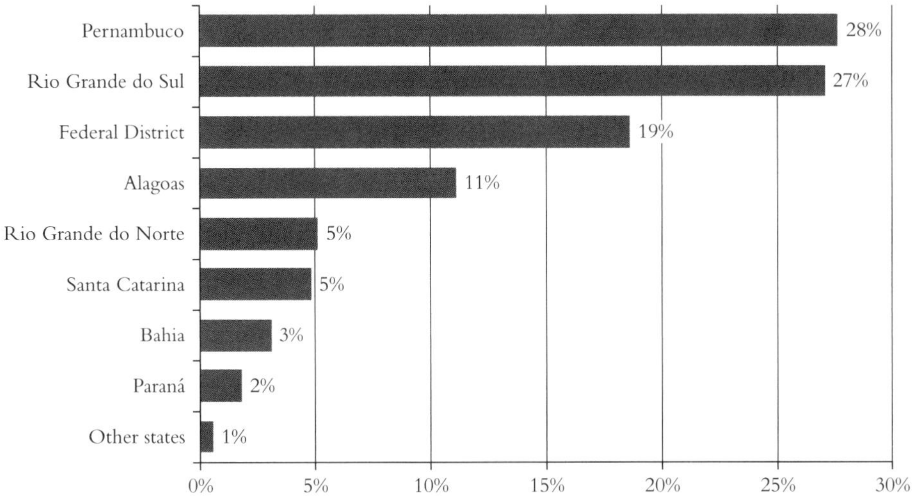

Figure 6.4 Share of the Value of Imports into Santos from Brazilian States, 1911–1913

SOURCE: Departamento de Estatística do Estado, *Anuário estatístico de São Paulo, 1913*, 2:143.

TABLE 6.9

Principal Products Exported from Santos in the Coastal Trade, 1900–1917

	1900	1910	1915	1917	Total
Volume (t)					
Beans	1,023	3	12,800	6,089	19,916
Textiles	160	1,923	3,152	3,187	8,422
Beer	897	2,659	964	2,283	6,803
Sackcloth	110	277	1,184	1,037	2,609
Shoes	3	123	225	398	749
Hats	17	146	276	242	681
Value (contos)					
Beans	244	3	3,948	1,907	6,101
Textiles	1,011	7,172	16,468	17,661	42,312
Beer	557	1,287	662	1,217	3,722
Sackcloth	141	197	2,366	4,104	6,807
Shoes	22	811	1,255	2,589	4,677
Hats	319	1,154	2,146	2,842	6,461

SOURCE: *Boletim da Diretoria de Indústria e Comércio* 9, nos. 10–11 (1918): 448–449.

the two years of 1926 and 1927: Rio Grande do Sul, the port of Rio de Janeiro, and Pernambuco. Alagoas, while still an important exporter to São Paulo, was displaced by Rio Grande do Norte and Bahia. From Rio Grande do Sul came meats and hides and possibly some manufactured goods, from the Federal District came mostly manufactures, and from Pernambuco came sugar. While São Paulo was not in negative balance of trade with these big suppliers in all years, overall, even in the 1920s, it still imported more goods in value than it shipped to the rest of Brazil (see Table 6.10).

Given its neutrality and the fact that its prime export product was a popular international consumption product, Brazil did not suffer any serious decline of its exports during World War I. As can be seen in the comparison of the prewar period (1900–1914) and the war years (1915–1917) in Table 6.9, São Paulo was able to increase its exports during the war years. Of course, destinations changed and various markets were blocked, but it was evident that new markets were able to compensate for the loss of traditional Continental consumers. There was also a profound change in importers and the goods they brought in to Santos as a result of the European war. Such major importers as Germany declined along with the Continental powers fighting for or against Germany. Even Great Britain, although it shipped goods from its colonies as well, experienced declining values of imports in this war period. It was the United States that replaced them as the primary importer into the state, and once it achieved this advantageous position, it replaced Britain and Germany as the prime supplier of the Paulista market even after the war had ended.[30]

Even though imports remained high, there was an obvious shift in sources of supply and even of availability of basic prime materials, and there was most definitely a severe drop in manufactured goods being imported because of the diversion of European and North American industries toward war production. In fact, manufacturing dropped below the share of foods in 1915 at the beginning of the war and did not fully recover its prewar importance until 1919.[31]

With the end of the war, the Continental European nations returned to Santos and slowly recovered their previous positions. The United States, which looked to dominate local markets by 1919, had another spectacular year in 1920 but lost its share with the return of France and Germany and the expansion even of Canadian imports in the middle years. The only prewar major player no longer involved in this trade was Austria, which with the fall of the Austro-Hungarian Empire and the loss of Trieste to Italy seemed to abandon direct trade with Santos in the 1920s. As usual,

TABLE 6.10

Trade Balance of São Paulo with Other Brazilian States, 1926 and 1927 (mil réis)

	Imports	Exports	Trade balance
1926			
Rio Grande do Sul	91,968	61,224	-30,744
Pernambuco	90,087	25,085	-65,003
Federal District	70,855	70,464	-391
Rio Grande do Norte	17,937	3,427	-14,510
Bahia	15,299	25,301	10,002
Parahyba	14,506	3,869	-10,637
Alagoas	13,689	4,520	-9,168
Santa Catarina	11,812	19,383	7,571
Paraná	10,050	14,308	4,258
Sergipe	6,592	2,585	-4,007
Pará	2,745	5,257	2,512
Maranhão	2,711	4,415	1,704
Ceará	2,365	6,645	4,280
Espírito Santo	1,332	7,537	6,204
Piauhy	646	2,611	1,965
Amazonas	587	3,596	3,009
Mato Grosso	0	1,199	1,198
Total	353,182	261,426	-91,756
1927			
Federal District	121,709	131,089	9,379
Rio Grande do Sul	100,814	108,052	7,238
Pernambuco	100,461	33,711	-66,750
Rio Grande do Norte	32,987	4,197	-28,790
Parahyba	27,190	2,359	-24,831
Alagoas	18,353	3,783	-14,570
Bahia	18,346	40,978	22,632
Ceará	15,261	9,248	-6,014
Santa Catarina	10,710	21,392	10,681
Sergipe	6,123	1,583	-4,540
Paraná	5,304	13,642	8,338
Pará	3,794	7,441	3,648
Piauhy	1,692	2,065	373
Maranhão	1,491	3,052	1,561
Amazonas	291	2,506	2,215
Espírito Santo	95	3,922	3,827
Mato Grosso	5	530	525
Total	464,628	389,552	-75,076

SOURCE: *Boletim da Diretoria de Industria e Comercio* 19, nos. 1–2 (1928): 5.

Argentina remained a steady supplier, always occupying third place among the foreign nations because of its supply of wheat to the Paulista market.[32]

Growth in trade continued in the next decade until the crisis of the Great Depression of 1929 finally slowed the steady rise of ships into the port of Santos. By the late 1920s and early 1930s all the traditional European shipping had returned to the port. The major changes were the increased importance of Brazilian flag shipping, now second only to the English, and the emergence of US ships as significant contenders for the first time. Also new was the beginning of Japanese shipping, which by 1938 had reached sixty-seven ship arrivals in Santos with a still-modest total of 327,000 metric tons. But this trade was clearly growing, since Japan in 1921 had only twenty-five ship arrivals and a total tonnage of 87,000 metric tons (see Figure 6.5).

The progressive growth of the shipping into Santos reached a peak in 1930, with 3,781 steamships arriving in the port having a tonnage of 10.6 million metric tons. But in the next year the Great Depression began to affect Santos trade. Starting in 1931 tonnage arriving began to decline, reaching a low point in the following year. In 1933 tonnage began to increase, but it did not return to the precrisis level until 1936.[33]

There were also long-term changes in the export trade, especially among the European importers of coffee. Although Santos by 1933 was again exporting at precrisis levels of coffee exports, there were some serious changes in regional participation in the trade, as the European countries

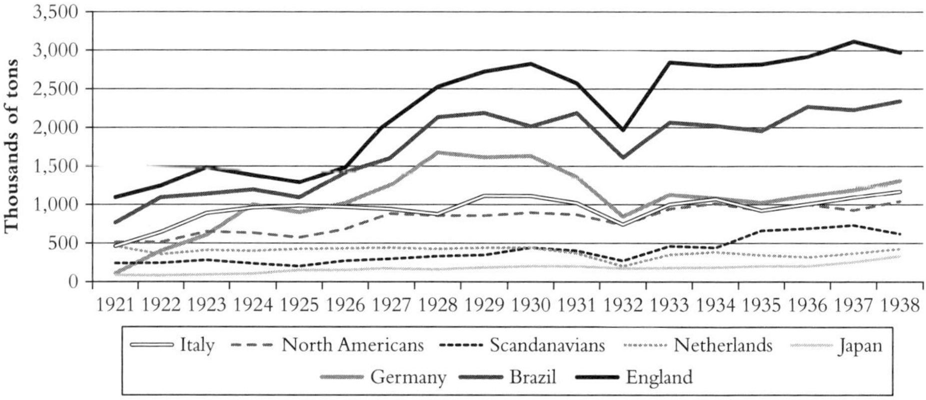

Figure 6.5 Tonnage and Flag of Ships of the Principal Traders Arriving in Santos, 1921–1938

SOURCE: *Boletim da Diretoria de Indústria e Comércio* 8 (1939): 168–171.

experienced a slow decline, while the Americas were importing ever-larger shares of Santos coffee exports. But the two regions together dominated the trade, accounting for between 90 and 95 percent of all exports from 1919 to 1939.

European consumption changed both by a relative decline in volume and also in major shifts among the principal traders. France, which was a dominant player at the beginning of the century, lost its leadership to Germany, and both suffered declines in the 1920s. Such countries as Belgium and Sweden kept up their shipments through most of this period. The big steady consumer that dominated the market was the United States, which until 1939 consistently took between 58 and 68 percent of the exported coffee (see Table 6.11).

TABLE 6.11
Major Recipient Countries of Santos Coffee Exports (sacks, 60 kg each), 1923–1950

Year	Germany	France	Holland	Belgium	Italy	Sweden	US	Total
1923	244,772	1,354,590	737,962	241,911	516,060	255,764	5,817,865	9,668,183
1924	413,947	1,466,015	918,812	266,843	451,914	15,487	5,553,320	9,505,808
1925	374,533	1,254,731	702,214	226,592	374,250	218,064	5,587,179	9,101,065
1926	498,543	720,022	733,931	168,988	324,280	292,265	6,102,140	9,218,301
1927	721,286	1,008,750	690,151	223,532	342,876	289,006	6,603,432	10,284,538
1928	713,429	614,439	579,359	156,406	224,902		6,056,078	8,956,041
1929	552,935	1,314,438	560,686	243,616	288,831		5,608,104	9,311,508
1930	612,420	857,856	662,022	283,901	292,015	51	5,842,667	9,318,260
1931	876,929	1,029,105	846,356	297,477	257,379	384,010	6,700,904	10,865,120
1932	652,459	419,496	402,213	139,707	125,131	190,251	3,895,278	6,152,986
1933	1,004,535	1,149,603	699,184	314,400	244,495	387,985	6,106,570	10,383,667
1934	1,573,700	786,585	506,776	254,035	284,449	387,103	5,928,994	10,184,660
1935	708,561	954,238	459,874	335,582	241,221	394,682	6,839,067	10,433,748
1936	985,709	722,996	406,331	254,769	237,075	356,346	6,254,947	9,677,009
1937	1,067,753	469,599	229,757	144,311	142,359	351,070	4,765,499	7,622,531
1938	1,594,657	569,141	537,299	272,385	287,297	526,269	6,848,829	11,357,955
1939	877,235	492,423	511,289	338,929	211,566	653,605	7,120,270	11,063,128
1940			41,377	119,741	124,673	117,823	7,165,224	8,392,817
1941						65,613	7,154,115	7,550,380
1942						100,893	4,146,512	4,510,982
1943						321,865	6,594,686	7,392,622
1944						341,533	9,871,359	10,857,937
1945			83,261	310,902	115	468,503	8,544,383	10,278,933
1946		56	248,523	590,089	271,361	581,476	8,693,221	11,437,981
1947	15	8	188,042	260,999	98,759	531,630	7,592,904	9,772,999
1948	48,819	24,201	24,789	335,283	165,177	273,870	8,962,718	11,222,875
1949	49,419	159,719	310,555	416,805	198,110	449,599	8,484,653	11,439,756
1950	36,501	134,686	124,256	166,311	85,059	479,106	6,445,162	8,377,062

SOURCE: Superintendência Serviços do Café, *Anuário de café, 1952*, 106–112.

Again, all of this changed with World War II, an international crisis that had far more influence on Santos exports than World War I or the Great Depression of 1929. The most obvious impact was the total elimination of all major European importers. Only the neutral country of Sweden imported coffee from 1940 to 1944, and even its shipments were down from historic levels. This meant that the only serious importer was the United States. Even when imports began to rise in the late 1940s, France, Germany, and Italy were no longer serious importers and were being replaced by the Netherlands and Sweden. Now the United States was taking 70–80 percent of all coffee exports from Santos, and the Europeans had fallen to less than 20 percent, with Asian and African countries beginning to pick up some of the trade lost to Europe.

These changes can also be seen in the value of coffee destined for international export placed on board ships from 1903 to 1939. The war years 1914–1917 clearly slowed the growth in the value of exports, with 1914 and 1917 being the worst years, and values did not return to prewar levels again until 1919. In turn, the period after 1929 also saw an abrupt drop in the value of these exports, which had not recovered to pre-1929 levels even as late as 1939 (see Figure 6.6).

For all the fluctuations in international trade in this period, what did not change significantly was the origin of the coffee arriving in Santos. In most years some 90 percent of the coffee came from the state of São Paulo, with the rest divided between Minas Gerais and Paraná. There was a peak of Minas Gerais shipments in the late 1910s and again in the mid-1940s, but by the 1950s Paraná would progressively replace Minas Gerais as the port's second-most-important source of coffee. But for both these

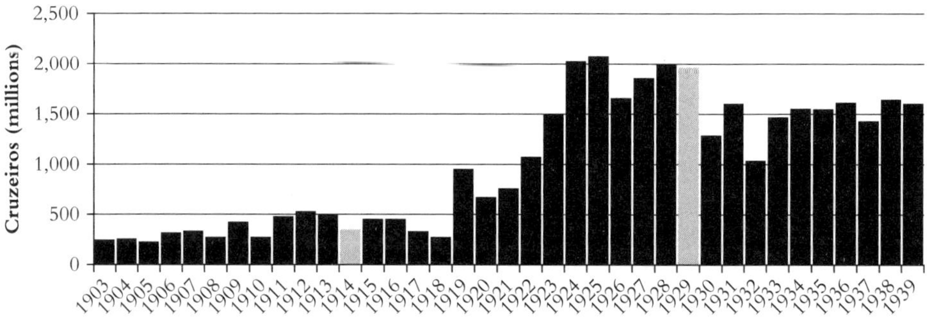

Figure 6.6 Value of Santos Coffee Exports, 1903–1939

SOURCE: Superintendência Serviços do Café, *Anuário do café, 1952*, 66.

states, most of their exports went to other ports. The growing Paraná coffee exports went through the port at Paranaguá, and most of the Minas Gerais exports went through Rio de Janeiro. While losing its total share of exports, Santos still maintained its leadership as the premier coffee port by mid-century. Thus, for the harvest of 1950/1951 Santos exported 8.5 million bags of coffee, Rio de Janeiro exported 4.3 million bags (mostly from Minas Gerais), and Paranaguá now exported 3 million, whereas as late as the harvest of 1947/1948, this latter port had exported only 682,000 bags of coffee. Of this 1950/1951 harvest, Santos received only 461,000 bags of coffee sent by Minas Gerais and 392,000 bags sent by Paraná.[34] Clearly, these small quantities were coming from frontier districts in both states that were better served by the railroads going to Santos.

There were also significant changes in this period in the role the port now began to play in the coastal trade. Whereas the bulk of internal trade moved by sea in the first decade of the twentieth century, by the 1930s most of the state's exports to the other states moved by land and did not use the port of Santos. This was a clear reflection of the revolution in infrastructure and technology that had occurred in the first half of the twentieth century. The construction of paved roads to all the neighboring states and the development of a major fleet of trucks meant that moving goods by land was now competitive to seaborne trade in all but large bulk products such as sugar. Thus, by 1939 almost two-thirds of the state's exports destined for consumers in other states went by land. Moreover, the new industrial might of the state was evident in 72 percent of its national exports by sea and by land being in manufactured goods (see Table 6.12). This transport revolution also had an impact on São Paulo's international trade. By the 1950s, Venezuela had replaced Argentina as São Paulo's primary South American trading partner. While Argentine wheat continued to arrive in steady volume and value, petroleum imports, coming largely from Venezuela, now exceeded in value the wheat imports, often by a considerable margin.[35]

TABLE 6.12

Value of São Paulo's National Exports by Sea and Land, 1939 (contos)

	Port of Santos	Land	Total
Live animals	394	4,969	5,363
Primary materials	118,159	124,087	242,246
Food products	101,745	314,552	416,297
Manufactures	598,516	1,075,455	1,673,971
Total	818,814	1,519,063	2,337,877

SOURCE: Departamento de Estatística do Estado, *Anuário estatístico de São Paulo, 1939*, 562–563.

World War II also changed the volume of international trade leaving and arriving in the port, which dropped precipitously in the early 1940s and had not quite recovered its prewar levels by mid-century. International exports from Santos reached 1.7 million metric tons in 1939,[36] but this volume of exports did not reach prewar levels even by 1951 (see Table 6.13).

The century from 1850 to 1950 was thus one of profound changes in international commerce for São Paulo. It began in the era of mule transport and dependence on the port of Rio de Janeiro to reach the outside world and ended with Santos being one of the major Atlantic ports and the primary outlet for São Paulo–grown coffee, which in turn dominated the world market. The introduction of rail transport in the late 1870s profoundly changed the port of Santos, tying it by modern communications to the new interior central zones of Paulista coffee production. The countries whose shipping carried these millions of coffee sacks to the world were primarily European until well into the twentieth century. It was English, German, French, and Italian shippers along with the Scandinavian countries who dominated the foreign trade entering and leaving the port of Santos. Yet it was the United States that consumed some 60 percent or more of the coffee that was exported by the state. It was not until the multiple crises of world wars and a great depression that North American merchant shipping finally began to dominate the supply of coffee to the United States.

In turn, these rail and port facilities by the end of the nineteenth century were also São Paulo's primary connection to the rest of Brazil via cabotage. With increasing dependence on sugar and raw cotton imports, São Paulo received many of its primary materials from other Brazilian states. But the

TABLE 6.13
Value of Foreign Imports and Exports, and Tonnage of Foreign Exports in the Port of Santos, 1942–1951 (cruzeiros)

Year	Exports	Imports	Trade balance	Quantity (t)
1942	3,145,760	1,701,976	1,444	746,847
1943	3,885,773	1,834,366	2,051	895,619
1944	5,327,937	2,716,104	2,612	1,054,448
1945	6,096,362	3,386,304	2,710	1,194,826
1946	9,607,565	5,536,454	4,071	1,542,819
1947	10,623,982	9,807,419	817	1,316,812
1948	10,803,515	9,047,133	1,756	1,328,563
1949	10,198,962	8,653,132	1,546	1,164,383
1950	12,300,405	8,791,174	3,509	993,509
1951	14,195,037	17,853,724	-3,659	1,216,398

SOURCE: Departamento de Estatística do Estado, *Anuário estatístico de São Paulo, 1951*, 3:37.

role of Santos changed dramatically for this internal trade with the development of interstate paved roads and the development of auto trucking routes. By the late 1920s the port of Santos was reduced to working with bulk cargoes like sugar and coffee, while the manufactured goods and even food products of São Paulo went to the rest of the nation by rail and truck. This was a trade that by 1950 was becoming more of a manufacturing trade than in previous periods as São Paulo industry become ever more dominant on the national scene. Although coffee exports as late as 1950 were of far more value than the interstate trade, that trade was progressively growing. Moreover, the absolute dominant role of Santos, even in the Brazilian coffee trade, was declining by 1950 as coffee production moved out of the state to neighboring Paraná and Minas Gerais, which in turn were shipping their coffee out of the ports of Paranaguá and Rio de Janeiro. By the crop year of 1950/1951 Santos was down to exporting half the Brazilian coffee exports, by the next crop year it had dropped to exporting less than half the total Brazilian coffee crop, and by the end of the decade just the two ports of Paranaguá and Rio de Janeiro combined now shipped more coffee than Santos.[37] By the middle of the twentieth century, the era of coffee dominating the international commerce of São Paulo was slowly coming to an end, to be replaced by an era in which agriculture now shared a place with a dynamic manufacturing industry primarily geared to the home market.

Chapter 7

Industrial Growth in São Paulo

Although the creation of a dynamic agricultural economy was explained by the extraordinary quality of the soils of the state and their excellent conditions for the growth of coffee, the same was not the case with industry. There was nothing inevitable about the emergence of São Paulo as the industrial heartland of Brazil. The coastal plains of Rio de Janeiro and of Rio Grande do Sul seemed to be more propitious for such an evolution, and yet by the early decades of the twentieth century it was clear that the state had surpassed these alternative industrial centers and become the core national zone for industrial growth that it has maintained until today. The cause for this emergence of São Paulo as an industrial powerhouse has generated a great deal of debate and discussion.[1]

Much of this early debate on the emergence of industry in São Paulo and the rest of Brazil was influenced by the discussion in the post–World War II period about the viability of the traditional models of comparative advantage. Led by Latin American economists, there emerged a school of thought associated with CEPAL (Comisión Económica para América Latina y el Caribe), the Latin American research center of the United Nations, that held that, over the long term, primary goods producers were at a disadvantage to industrial producers in their trade relations and that only through their own industrialization could these primary producers develop and expand their own economies. This in turn required either direct governmental intervention to create protected markets or the existence of external shocks that forced primary producers to replace missing imports through locally developed industries.

It was clear in the Brazilian case that industrialization began before formal protection was established. The Brazilian state had no coherent industrialization program until the early 1940s, long after industries had been firmly established in the country.[2] But as Celso Furtado and others had initially argued, it was the disruption of international trade in World War I and the Great Depression that established de facto protection and permitted the emergence of these industries.[3] But in the past few decades scholars have shown that industry was already evolving quite well before 1914 and that it was not so much protected markets as it was comparative costs, the emergence of an expanded market, and the abundance of local capital that explain the early emergence of industry in Brazil.[4] Moreover, as could be expected given the local production of raw cotton in the state and the nation and the high costs of transport, it would be the textile industry producing low-cost cotton cloth that would first emerge as a serious industrial activity. It was soon followed by a vibrant food-processing industry, which developed to satisfy local consumption of processed food produced by local agriculture.

That local industry would evolve to supply the agricultural sector and its workers was to be expected. That the agro-export sector was fundamental in initiating industrial activity can be seen both in the first products produced by Brazilian factories and in the association of industrial activity with cycles in the export economy. Before the crisis of 1929, industrial expansion corresponded to the most dynamic periods of the agro-export economy. Thus, a textiles industry emerged to provide cotton clothing for slaves and jute bags to hold coffee being exported. It expanded even more rapidly with the arrival of the European coffee workers after slaves were emancipated in 1888. This new salaried workforce greatly expanded the domestic market.[5] In turn, a food-processing industry evolved to meet this ever-expanding free labor market, and a sugar-refining industry developed with the growth of a revitalized cane sugar sector in the late nineteenth century. Finally, metallurgy evolved along with the railroad expansion in the last half of the century, which in turn was tied to the expansion of the coffee economy. All this growth in turn was aided by the provision of abundant and cheap hydroelectric power, cheaper transport from the new railroads, and lower costs for textile and machinery imports in this period.[6] It was also primarily financed by local coffee capital, rather than foreign funding. As Wilson Cano has stressed, even in funding the railroads, São Paulo used more local capital than any other province in the nation, and by the end of the century it was systematically generating huge trade surpluses. With the beginning of a regulated coffee market in 1906, much of the capital involved in new plantings would be applied to industrial development by the planter class.[7]

Unfortunately, data on early industrial activity is limited for Brazil. However, the economic historian Wilson Suzigan was able to calculate the amount of English-produced machinery and equipment exported to Brazil in this early period.[8] These figures show the growth in investment in industry first occurring in 1890–1896, during the Encilhamento, or economic bubble, which clearly had real consequences in the economy. This was a period of euphoria and financial speculation. A major monetary expansion occurred, legal changes were made that facilitated the creation of companies, the coffee market was experiencing major growth and good prices, and the fall of the empire seemed to usher in a new age.[9] Finally, the inflow of immigrants and the expansion of the wage market generated a climate conducive to new businesses, with the creation of hundreds of companies in all sectors. Although many of these companies did not survive, this phase represented the first intensification of investment in industry. This was the period that saw a major expansion in the cotton industrial sector, with many of Brazil's largest firms being founded in this period of easy credit and abundant capital.[10]

The high level of machinery imports reached in 1896 was surpassed only in 1906, and from then until 1913 there was an accelerated expansion of investments that corresponded to a new cycle of high exports of coffee generated by the first valorization scheme. The period from 1905 to 1912 was a particularly active period of industrial growth.[11] There was an abrupt decline during World War I but recuperation occurred in the early 1920s aided by elevated coffee exports and sales. With the world economic crisis that began in 1929 occurred another major retraction in machinery imports. From their relative importance in total imports and their high correlation with the movement of total machinery imported, it is evident that the machines and equipment for the textile industry were of fundamental importance in the stream of imported European industrial products (see Figure 7.1). The curves of the consumption of cement and steel during this period, as well as of the importation of capital goods, also show these three cycles of investment during the Old Republic—that of 1889–1896, 1901–1913, and 1921–1929 (see Figure 7.2).

The lead industry was unquestionably textiles. Brazilian industrial textile production grew systematically from the late nineteenth century until 1923 and then fell for the rest of the 1920s, only recovering again in the 1930s.[12] The growing importance of the national textile industry is reflected in the decline of imported textiles (see Figure 7.3). These Euro-

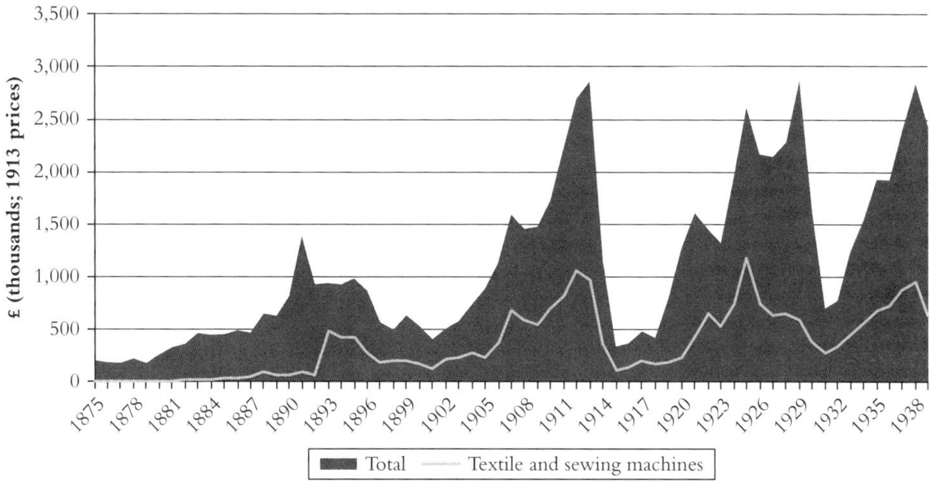

Figure 7.1 British Machines and Equipment Exported to Brazil, 1875–1938

NOTE: We added sewing machines to Suzigan's data.

SOURCE: Suzigan, *Indústria brasileira.*

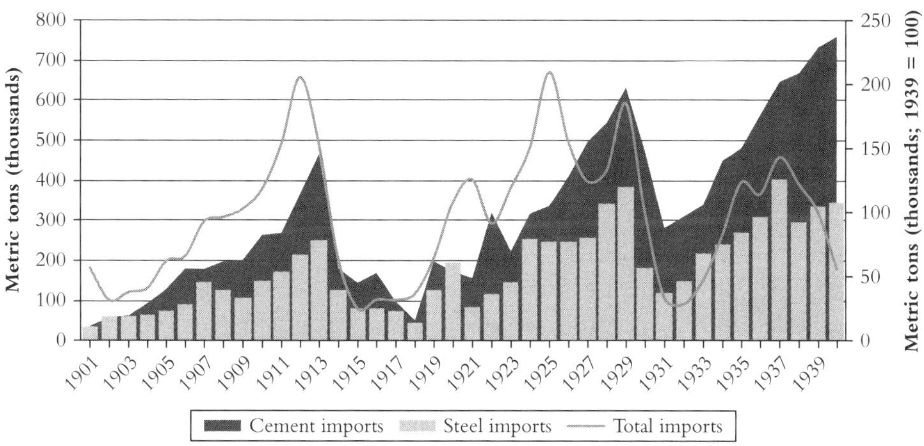

Figure 7.2 Investment Indicators for Brazil, 1901–1939

NOTE: The base year for the calculation of constant weight is 1939.

SOURCE: Suzigan, *Indústria brasileira.*

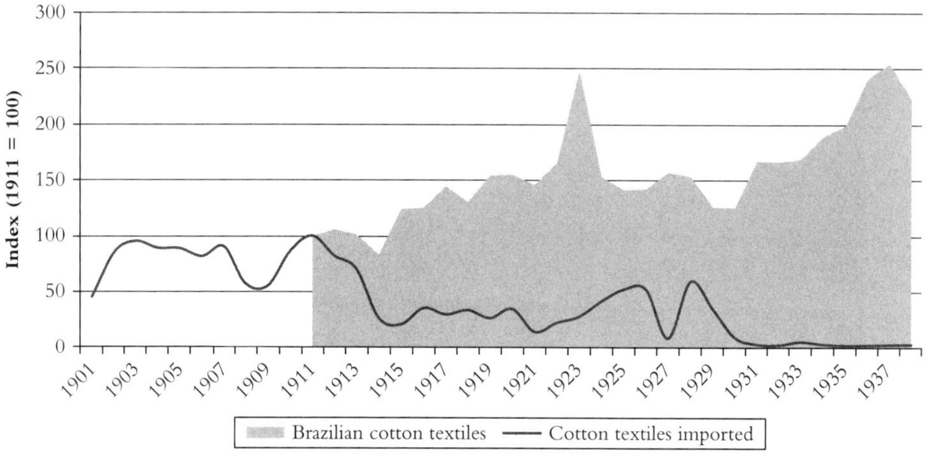

Figure 7.3 Brazilian Production and Importation of Cotton Textiles, 1901–1938

NOTE: The base year for the index calculation is 1911.

SOURCE: Stein, *Vassouras*, app. 3.

pean textiles had represented an important part of Brazilian imports in the nineteenth century (accounting for 29 percent of all imports in the period 1870–1875) but now slowly declined in the twentieth century as imported cloths were replaced by national production. By 1911 textile imports accounted for only 18 percent of all imports and dropped to 7 percent in 1914, a level that was maintained until the 1929 crisis.

Already by the industrial census of 1907 the national industry supplied two-thirds of the local market. But this was not the only area where national production slowly replaced foreign industrial manufactures. According to the industrial census of 1907, there were numerous food and light manufacturing areas for which Brazilian factories satisfied most of national demand.[13]

But some basic and luxury goods continued to be imported and in fact grew in volume and value as the national economy expanded in the twentieth century. Food products such as wheat and wheat flour, as well as machines and more expensive textiles along with raw materials for industries, were on the list of imports. There was also increasing demand for higher-quality consumer goods produced in North America and Europe. Of these imports, manufactured goods dominated until the crises of World War I and the Great Depression, with food imports declining in importance over time, just as primary materials for local industry kept increasing as a part of the total goods being brought into the country.[14]

Much of this national industry was well established by the time of the industrial census of 1920. In that year there existed in Brazil some 13,336 industrial firms, 30 percent in the food sector, 15 percent in clothing, 12 percent in ceramics, and the rest primarily in wood and textiles. Broken down by value, firms producing food products made up 41 percent of the total value of industrial production and textiles 27 percent.[15] Nevertheless, the largest employer of industrial workers and the largest user of motors in factories was still the textile industry, followed by food and finished clothing. In terms of factory size, the preponderance of textiles was evident, averaging ninety-three workers per plant compared to an average of twenty-one workers per factory in all industries. Although there was a sharp increase in the total number of employees in industry in general by 1920, there was a reduction in the average number of workers by industry compared to the industrial census of 1907, probably as a consequence of the increasing diversity of the industry in general.[16]

Despite the existence of large factories, national industry was defined by numerous small enterprises. In 1920, of the 9,450 enterprises subject to the consumption tax,[17] the majority of factories (89 percent) employed just nine workers or fewer and accounted for only 15 percent of all workers. At the other extreme were sixty-one companies with more than five hundred workers, representing less than 1 percent of all enterprises but accounting for 42 percent of the industrial workforce. These large companies had on average a thousand workers per unit. Although this indicates a relative concentration within the industrial sector, the few factories of this large size indicated the relatively modest nature of Brazilian industry. Local industry still produced primarily mass-consumption articles of low aggregated value and high volume that were too expensive to import.[18]

The new industrial workforce was made up primarily of men. But in the new textile industry it was women who dominated, accounting for 51 percent of the workforce. Women and children made up a total of 60 percent of the workforce in textiles and 49 percent in all industries. All industries, however, used child labor (workers under fourteen years of age) at roughly the same ratio, so that somewhere between 6 and 12 percent of their workers were children.[19]

In the context of the history of Brazilian industry, the state of São Paulo stands out as a major player whose growth soon outstripped all other states in the twentieth century. The early evolution of state industry can be seen in the first industrial census of Brazil in 1907. Although the Federal District (the city of Rio de Janeiro) was then the most important manufacturing zone in the republic, and the state of Rio de Janeiro (including the

Federal District) was the leading industrial state in Brazil, São Paulo was quickly emerging as the second-most-important zone. Other areas, such as Rio Grande do Sul and Pernambuco, were also important industrial centers, and while Minas Gerais had a significant number of factories, it had little influence in terms of national production or industrial workers (see Table 7.1).

The growth of São Paulo can be seen in the crucial textile industry. Although in 1907 the Federal District was the leader in the average output per mill and the average number of workers per factory (see Table 7.2), by 1905 São Paulo's eighteen textile companies represented some 15 percent of Brazil's factories, production, and workers. Two years later there were thirty textile factories in production. By 1915 the state's fifty-one such companies had increased their share of national production and workers to over a quarter of all Brazil's textile factories and had the same share of finished output.[20]

TABLE 7.1
Brazilian Industries: Factories, Capital, Production, and Workers, 1907

State	No. of factories	% of total capital	% of total value of production	% of factory workers	Average no. of workers per factory
Rio de Janeiro	877	38%	38%	32%	56
São Paulo	326	19%	16%	16%	74
Rio Grande do Sul	314	7%	13%	10%	49
Pernambuco	118	9%	7%	8%	102
Paraná	297	3%	4%	3%	16
Minas Gerais	531	4%	4%	6%	18
Bahia	78	4%	3%	7%	128
Pará	54	2%	2%	2%	47
Sergipe	103	2%	2%	2%	29
Santa Catarina	173	1%	2%	1%	12
Amazonas	92	1%	2%	1%	13
Alagoas	45	2%	1%	2%	84
Maranhão	18	2%	1%	3%	253
Mato Grosso	15	2%	1%	3%	258
Paraiba	42	1%	1%	1%	35
Rio Grande do Norte	15	1%	0%	1%	137
Ceará	18	1%	0%	1%	67
Goiás	135	0%	0%	1%	6
Piaui	3	0%	0%	0%	118
Espírito Santo	4	0%	0%	0%	23
Total	3,258	100%	100%	100%	47
Total (contos)		665,576	741,536	151,841	

SOURCE: Instituto Brasileiro de Geografia e Estatística, *Séries estatísticas retrospectivas*, vol. 2, bk. 3, p. 265.
NOTE: Here the state of Rio de Janeiro includes the Corte (city of Rio de Janeiro).

TABLE 7.2
Textile Factories and Their Value of Capital, Production, and Workers, 1907

State	No. of factories	% of total capital	% of total value of production	% of factory workers	Average no. of workers per factory
Federal District	22	20%	26%	19%	467
Rio de Janeiro	25	28%	25%	20%	286
São Paulo	30	17%	13%	14%	371
Minas Gerais	37	7%	8%	9%	130
Bahia	13	6%	6%	8%	314
Pernambuco	8	7%	6%	7%	463
Rio Grande do Sul	9	3%	5%	5%	269
Maranhão	13	4%	3%	7%	289
Alagoas	5	2%	2%	4%	416
Sergipe	4	2%	2%	2%	322
Ceará	6	1%	1%	2%	160
Paraíba	1	1%	1%	1%	561
Piaui	1	0%	1%	1%	289
Rio Grande do Norte	1	0%	0%	1%	320
Santa Catarina	13	1%	0%	1%	28
Espírito Santo	1	0%	0%	0%	50
Paraná	5	0%	0%	0%	34
Total	194	100%	100%	100%	268
Total (contos)		268,370	171,088	51,992	

SOURCE: Instituto Brasileiro de Geografia e Estatística, *Séries estatísticas retrospectivas*, vol. 2, bk. 3, p. 265.

From 1905 to 1915, the capital involved in just the cotton textile mills went from 28,000 contos to 81,000 (or £4.3 million)[21] and the number of workers from 6,296 to 17,989 workers.[22] After a rapid expansion, local cloth production stabilized during the early 1910s but grew dramatically again after 1915. All the cloth went to the national market, which by 1919 was consuming 520 million meters of cotton cloth;[23] this meant that São Paulo was supplying roughly a third of national needs.

The driving force for this growth was cotton textiles, followed by jute, and then woolen production. From 1910 to 1927 local cotton production increased by a factor of three, going from 76 million meters to 239 million meters.[24] Woolens grew even more dramatically, going from just 218,000 meters to production of over 3 million meters of cloth by 1927. Clearly, both industries were increasing their share of local and national markets and responding to an expanding population. Jute cloth grew less systematically and in fact fluctuated significantly year by year, largely responding to changes in coffee production, since the primary use was the coffee industry's jute sacks. Jute producers went from accounting for 14 percent of all textile production in 1910 to a more significant 39 percent in the coffee boom year of 1927. In terms of value, although woolen cloth grew dramatically in output in this period, its relative share of total value of production remained relatively stable at 10 to 20 percent of all textiles produced, even combining woolen cloth's value with the value of woolen quilts and blankets (see Table 7.3).

The Paulista textile industry mainly consumed nationally produced cotton, grown either in São Paulo or in Pernambuco and the other northeastern states. Thus, its primary import from abroad was machinery. Moreover, the growth of this industry was so rapid that Paulista cloth not only supplied the local Paulista market and reduced its dependence on imports but allowed São Paulo to export its cloth to the other states of the nation (see Figure 7.4).

As could be expected, the city of São Paulo, now a metropolis of 389,000 persons in 1911,[25] contained a large share of the local textile industry. But the industry was well distributed throughout the state. Of the thirty-two textile factories analyzed in a state industrial census of 1911, ten were in the city of São Paulo, though they were among the largest in the state. These São Paulo city factories were worth a third of the 54,000 contos (£3.6 million) invested in the state's textile industry, had a third of the looms and spindles, and had 42 percent of the 15,000 workers in the

TABLE 7.3
Textile Production in the State of São Paulo, 1910–1926

Year	Cotton cloth (m)	Wool cloth (m)	Jute cloth (m)	Blankets, quilts, etc. (no.)
1910	75,833,740	218,331	19,087,755	29,811
1911	83,552,394	216,224	25,379,878	426,037
1912	84,040,528	404,354	28,184,264	657,859
1913	81,962,739	502,647	23,616,814	611,925
1914	70,187,985	619,110	14,203,058	471,978
1915	121,589,728	616,723	33,462,805	710,214
1916	134,650,629	1,104,462	31,700,943	1,171,744
1917	160,554,139	1,317,327	42,681,010	807,479
1918	147,072,191	1,469,704	41,555,668	651,420
1919	175,255,068	1,253,942	9,177,963	1,601,353
1920	186,519,883	1,572,776	25,366,810	1,684,160
1921	197,784,698	1,870,611	35,561,482	766,973
1922	217,263,750	2,673,280	45,756,165	2,717,177
1923	488,380,084	2,258,017	32,194,878	2,527,395
1924	230,752,600	2,615,331	52,994,721	2,354,641
1925	206,148,127	3,505,960	86,150,789	1,891,513
1926	238,932,628	3,083,235	97,852,063	2,046,741

SOURCE: *Boletim da Diretoria de Industria e Comercio* 18, no. 9 (1927): 197.

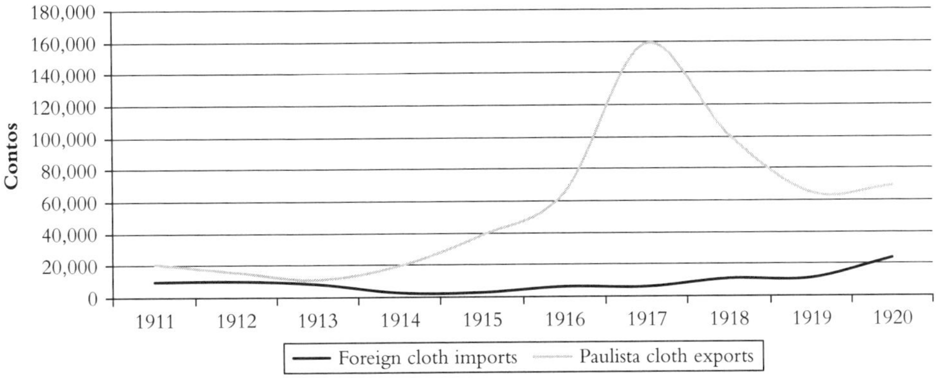

Figure 7.4 Value of Foreign Cloth Imports and Paulista-Produced Cloth National Exports, 1911–1920

SOURCE: *Boletim da Diretoria de Indústria e Comércio* 12, no. 1 (1922): 4.

industry. Sorocaba, the next-largest center, with five textile mills, had 21 percent of the capital, only 14 percent of the workers, and about a quarter of the state's textile machines. Salto de Itú and Tatuí also had multiple factories. The largest factory in terms of labor force was the Matarazzo textile mill in the capital city, with 1,900 workers, but the largest in terms of spindles and looms was the Votorantim textile mill in Sorocaba, which was the second-best-capitalized mill in the state, employed 812 workers, and primarily consumed cotton grown in São Paulo.[26] Thus, the industry, thanks to the ever more sophisticated railroad linkages, was able to set up in numerous areas of production within the state (see Table 7.4).

But this was not all that was produced in significant quantities in the state. Already by 1911 São Paulo was producing 31 percent of the total national cloth production, 39 percent of hats, 37 percent of shoes, and a third of all drinks.[27] Thus, it began to show early in the new century significant representation in all the industrial activities, and its important role in the national economy would grow even more in the next several decades.

A new expansion of the industry occurred in the next decade as indicated by a survey of 1920, which showed that 72 percent of the local textile mills then in production had been founded after 1910.[28] By the industrial census of 1920, the interior of the state had twenty-nine textile mills, up from twenty-three just nine years previously, and had roughly the same capital valuation as the twenty-five textile mills inside the city of São Paulo—in turn, up from just nine in the city in the earlier census. But now

Table 7.4
Cotton Textile Mills of São Paulo, by Size of Workforce, 1911

Company	City	Owner	Capital and debentures (contos)	Workers	Looms	Spindles
Fabrica de Tecidos Mariangela	S. Paulo	Industrias Reunidas F. Matarazzo	2,000	1,903	1200	30,000
Cotonificio Rodolpho Crespi	S. Paulo	Sociedade Anonyma Cotonificio Rodolpho Crespi	6,000	1,305	500	14,000
Fabrica de Tecidos Jupiter e Fortuna	Salto de Itú	Società per l'Export e per l'Industria Italo-Americana	2,491	1,019	364	13,436
Fabrica de Tecidos Votorantim	Sorocaba	Banco União de S. Paulo	5,000	812	1,109	36,000
Fabrica de Tecidos "Labor"	S. Paulo	Sociedade Anonyma Labor	1,200	800	313	7,000
Fabrica de Tecidos Ipiranga	S. Paulo	Nami, Jalet & Irmão	4,000	785	444	14,000
Fabrica de Tecidos Santa Rosalia	Sorocaba	Oetterer, Speers	3,410	755	625	20,732
Industrial de S. Paulo	S. Paulo	Companhia Industrial de S. Paulo	4,000	600	318	11,000
Fabrica de Tecidos S. Bento	Jundiai	Companhia Fiação e Tecidos S. Bento	3,500	582	406	12,044
Fabrica de Tecidos Carioba	Vila Americana	Rawlinson, Müller	1,700	550	366	8,000
Fabrica de Tecidos Taubaté Industrial	Taubaté	Companhia Taubaté Industrial	1,214	550	336	10,000
Fabrica de Tecidos Anhaia	S. Paulo	Companhia Fabril Paulistana	2,000	500	300	8,254
São Bernardo Fabril	S. Bernado	Companhia S. Bernardo Fabril	1,500	500	180	8,600
Fabrica de Tecidos S. Roque	S. Roque	Società per l'Export e per l'Industria Italo-Americana	783	487	305	
Est. Fabril Pinotti Gamba	S. Paulo	Sociedade Anonyma Est. Fabril Pinotti Gamba	1,200	400	200	4,000
Fabrica de Tecidos S. Martinho	Tatuí	Companhia Fiação e Tecidos S. Martinho	3,700	374	325	8,312
Fabrica de Tecidos Arethusina	Piracicaba	Rodolpho Miranda & Filho	1,940	300	180	8,600
Fabrica de Tecidos Belemzinho	S. Paulo	Boyes & Kirk	200	252	204	6,500
Fabrica de Tecidos Magdalena	S. Carlos	Companhia Industrial S. Carlos	1,000	250	112	4,754
Nossa Senhora da Ponte	Sorocaba	M. J. da Fonseca	365	250	112	3,500
Fabrica de Tecidos Santa Maria	Sorocaba	Companhia Fiação de Tecidos S. Maria	1,500	200	205	

TABLE 7.4 (CONTINUED)

Company	City	Owner	Capital and debentures (contos)	Workers	Looms	Spindles
Fabrica de Tecidos S. Pedro	Itú	Companhia Fiação e Tecelagem S. Pedro	500	200	150	3,000
Fabrica de Tecidos Salto Fabril	Salto de Itú	Companhia Fiação e Tecelagem Salto Fabril	420	200	100	2,000
Fabrica de Tecidos S. Luiz	Itú	J. E. Corrêa Pacheco	250	180	65	1,200
Fabrica de Tecidos Monte Serrat	Salto de Itú	Pereira Mendes	100	172	131	
Fabrica de Tecidos Mogyana	Mogi das Cruzes	Companhia Industrial Mogyana de Tecidos	700	160	106	3,200
Fabrica Alpargatas	S. Paulo	S. Paulo Alpargatas	1,000	150	40	480
Fabrica Kenworthy	Sorocaba	Companhia Nacional de Estamparia	936	130	400	
Fabrica de Tecidos S. João	Atibaia	Companhia Fiação e Tecidos S. João	200	130	56	1,630
Fabrica de Tecidos Santa Cruz	Tatuhy	Campos Irmãos	240	122	100	3,204
Fabrica Nacional	S. Paulo	Companhia Nacional de Tecelagem	300	120	53	1,000
Pinhal Fabril	E. S. Pinhal	Companhia Pinhal Fabril	500	100	52	
Total			53,848	14,838	9,357	244,446

SOURCE: *Boletim da Diretoria de Industria e Comercio* 4, no. 4 (1913): 124–125.

the interior mills employed more workers than the capital city ones, some 15,442 compared to some 12,381 in the city, and they had slightly more spindles and looms as well. Votorantim of Sorocaba was still the largest interior factory and now employed 1,800 workers, but the Taubaté textile mills in the same city now employed 1,200 workers. These were the only two companies to employ more than a thousand textile workers in the interior. In the capital there were now five mills that employed a thousand workers or more, with Matarazzo's Mariangela textile mill using some 2,000 workers (see Table 7.5).[29]

Of later development was the woolens sector. The first woolen weaving factory run with a steam engine was founded in the state in 1897. It had 8 spindles and 32 workers. By 1900 there were three mills dedicated to woolens with a total of 112 spindles and 272 workers, and production reached 255,000 meters of woolen cloth. By 1920 there were 1,478 workers producing 617,000 meters of various types of woolen cloths (cashmeres,

TABLE 7.5

Cotton Textile Mills of São Paulo, by Size of Workforce, 1920

Company	City	Owner	Capital and debentures (contos)	Workers	Looms	Spindles
Mariangela	S. Paulo	Industrias Reunidas F. Matarazzo	4,500	2,000	1,463	41,392
Cotonificio Rodolpho Crespi	S. Paulo	Sociedade Anonyma Cotonificio Rodolpho Crespi	7,728	1,800	720	25,000
Votorantim	Sorocaba	Sociedade Anonyma Fabrica Votorantim	6,000	1,800	1,300	46,000
Taubaté	Taubaté	Companhia Taubaté Industrial	4,000	1,600	780	34,000
Maria Zélia	S. Paulo	Companhia Nacional de Tecidos de juta	10,000	1,350	1,000	42,000
Jupiter	Guaratinguelá	Sociedade Anonyma Brasital	0	1,300	364	32,000
Jafet	S. Paulo	Sociedade Anonyma Fiação Tecelagem e Estamparia Jafet	6,420	1,130	1,027	32,000
Belemzinho	S. Paulo	Industrias Reunidas F. Matarazzo	700	1,000	768	20,000
Santa Rosalia	S. Roque	Oeterer, Speer	4,420	860	1,033	35,542
Luzitânia	S. Paulo	Pereira Ignacio	3,000	810	394	11,344
Lucinda	S. Bernardo	Sociedade Anonyma Scarpa	4,000	780	368	15,000
Labor	S. Paulo	Sociedade Anonyma Fabrica de Tecidos Labor	7,600	750	380	9,500
Carioba	Vila Americana	Rawlinson Millier	2,600	700	400	10,000
São Paulo	Vila Americana	Companhia Nacional de Estamparia	2,000	700	400	15,800
Cotonifício Gamba	S. Paulo	Sociedade Anonyma Estabelecimento Fabril Pinotti Gamba	2,223	650	350	12,000
S. Paulo Alpargatas	S. Paulo	Sociedade Anonyma S. Paulo Alpargatas	2,000	600	110	5,570
Nossa Senhora da Ponte	S. Bernardo	Sociedade Anonyma Scarpa (previously Fonseca)	4,000	600	308	12,000
São Bento	Jundiahy	Companhia Fiação e Tecidos São Bento	3,746	600	422	12,000
Santa Cruz	Vila Americana	Campos lrmãos	2,200	600	320	10,000
Santo Antonio	Vila Americana	Companhia Nacional de Estamparia	2,000	600	320	10,000
Santa Maria	Vila Americana	Companhia Fiaçao e Tecidos Santa Maria	1,500	600	320	10,010
Arethusina	Piracicaba	Boyes & lrmaos	500	600	150	4,000
São Martinho	Tatuhy	Companhia Fiação e Tecidos São Martinho	3,068	550	401	6,720
Lapa	S. Paulo	Sociedade Anonyma Fábrica de Tecidos e Bordados Lapa	2,000	520	156	4,500
São Simeão	S. Paulo	S. Boyes	2,000	500	500	18,000
Fortuna	S. Roque	Sociedade Anonyma Fabrica Votorantim	5,000	500	305	
Trevisoli	S. Carlos	Trevisoli Borini	800	500	173	6,500
Paulistana	S. Paulo	Companhia Fiação e Tecidos Fabril Paulistana	3,400	483	385	12,000

TABLE 7.5 (CONTINUED)

Company	City	Owner	Capital and debentures (contos)	Workers	Looms	Spindles
São Pedro	Itú	Companhia Fiação e Tecidos Sao Pedro	700	450	300	5,500
Magdalena	S. Carlos	Companhia Fiação e Tecidos Sao Carlos	1,000	400	120	4,000
Saito Fabril	Salto de Itú	Companhia Saito Fabril	761	315	100	2,700
Japy	Vila Americana	Sociedade Anonyma Fabrica Japy	1,000	300	200	7,000
Brasilissa	Bragança	Companhia Fabril Brasilissa	700	280	150	
Mont Serra	Salto de Itú	Boyes & lrmaos	400	200		3,600
Fiação de Algodão da Saúde	S. Paulo	Pereira, Estefano	600	180		
Victoria	S. Paulo	Giorgi & Cataldi	600	180	57	
Mogyana	Mogy das Cruzes	Companhia Industrial M. de Tecidos	763	180	100	2,500
São João	Atibaia	Companhia Fiação e Tecidos São João	502	150	60	1,875
São Luiz	Salto de Itú	G. E. Correia Pacheco	250	138	90	1,500
Sociedade Commercial de Genova	S. Paulo	Maluf, Mussali	600	120	45	
Cotonificio Italia	S. Paulo	Define, Frasca	200	80	70	
Indústrias Textis	S. Paulo	Companhia de Industrias Textis	200	80		1,500
Tisso	S. Roque	A. Tisso	40	70	40	300
Ermelinda	Salto de Itú	Companhia Industrial Atibaiana	200	60	24	200
Fábrica de Toalhas e Estopa	S. Paulo	Angelo Livio	100	50	2	400
Sociedade Commercial de Genova	S. Paulo	Maluf, Mussali	0	30	12	
Cotonificio Paulista	S. Paulo	P. Frasca & Beltram	50	30	48	
Barra funda	S. Paulo	lrmaos Martini	30	12	6	
Fabrica de Tecidos	S. Paulo	Henrique Carbone & Filho	10	10	9	60
Fábrica de Tecidos de Algodão	S. Paulo	Evaristo Bezonini	10	9	10	16
Bezonini	Guaratinguetá	Evaristo Bezonini	10	9	10	
Fábrica de Ponto Russo	S. Paulo	Gonzalez	15	5		
ltalo-Americana	S. Paulo	Halo. Americo Terlera	10	2	1	
A. Brazil	Jacareí	Adamastor Brazil	30			
Total			106,186	27,823	16,071	524,029

SOURCE: *Boletim da Diretoria de Industria e Comercio* 13, nos. 2–3 (1922): 60–63.

tweeds, twills, and flannels) in ten factories,[30] and by 1927 there were twenty-four factories with almost double the number of workers producing five times the cloth (see Table 7.6). Though there were factories to be found throughout the state, this was an industry more concentrated in the capital, which in 1927 had nineteen of the state's twenty-four woolen factories and 65 percent of the workforce dedicated to woolens.

Even more concentrated than woolens was the jute cloth industry. This cloth was produced in just four factories, of which three were in the capital and one in Santos. Yet it had roughly the same capital invested in it as the woolen industry. The dominant factory was Sant'Anna in the city of São Paulo, which alone produced half the state's jute cloth and all the jute sacking for coffee, and it had half the looms and more than half the workers and spindles in the state employed in this sector (see Table 7.7).

Although cloths made of cotton, wool, and jute had been produced in factories in the state from early in the nineteenth century, a new element in the textile industry in the late nineteenth century was the development of a silk cloth industry using locally produced silk. The first Paulista factory producing silk cloth dated from only 1895, and it was still the only one functioning in 1900, with just 150 workers. By 1910 there were six factories with 395 workers producing 1,000 contos' worth of cloth. The industry in 1920 grew to ten factories, with the value of output increasing to 5,000 contos. In the next five years there was a major growth in the industry. By 1925 there were thirty factories (of which five were in the interior) capitalized at 32,000 contos, or six times the capital invested in the industry just five years previously. The number of workers producing silk cloth went from 1,400 to 3,800, the number of looms tripled to almost 1,200, and spindles went from just 360 to close to 6,400. The value of production increased dramatically in the early 1920s, and by 1925 output of silk cloth was valued at 20,000 contos (see Table 7.8).[31]

It was evident that by the time of the national industrial census of 1920 the entire textile industry producing cloths from various types of natural fibers was the dominant industry in the state. São Paulo had some 247 cloth- and thread-producing factories employing 34,825 wage laborers, which represented 6 percent of all industrial establishments but accounted for 41 percent of all such wage workers. The average textile factory employed 141 workers. Their nearest competitor was the 142 metallurgy shops of the state, which averaged 39 workers per establishment.[32] Moreover, the 83,000 industrial workers employed in São Paulo in 1920 now exceeded that of any other state, including the combined Rio de Janeiro and Fed-

TABLE 7.6

Factories Producing Woolen Textiles in the State of São Paulo, by Size of Workforce, 1927

Company	City	Owner	Capital (contos)	Workers	Looms	Spindles
F. Kowarick	S. Bernardo	F. Kowarick	4,800	489	70	5,270
Companhia de Indústrias Textis	S. Paulo	Indústrias Textis	600	300	76	2,200
Antonio de Camillís	S. Paulo	Lanificio Halo-Paulista	1,800	250	65	3,200
Sociedade Anonyma Cotonificio Crespi	S. Paulo	Crespi (Secção de Lan)	2,000	250	120	8,000
Lanificio Anglo-Brasileiro	S. Paulo	Lanificio Anglo-Brasileiro	3,000	220	47	2,840
Sociedade Anonyma Fábrica de "Manchester"	Jacareí	Manchester (filial)	500	155	80	
Clemente Bernacchi	S. Paulo	Fábrica de Tecidos Belém	500	140	28	420
Biola, Amósso	S. Paulo	Tecelagem de Lan	300	130	173	
Companhia Fiação e Tecidos Plastira	Guaratínguetá	Plastira	600	106	48	500
Companhia de Tecidos Guaratinguetá	Guaratínguetá	Guaratínguetá	800	100	40	1,220
Ubaldo Fronzi	S. Paulo	Fábrica de Tecidos S. Paulo	240	80	15	
José Mortari	S. Paulo	Lanificio José Mortari	630	60	45	1,000
José Maluf & Irmão	S. Paulo	Lanificio S. Jorge	400	55	19	
Companhia Lanificio de Pirituba	Pirituba S.P.R.	Lanificio de Pírituba	800	50	20	
Lanificio de Leduar Kncese	S. Paulo	Lanificio de Leduar Kncese	250	35	17	
Mendes & Fernandes	S. Paulo	Adamastor	300	30	12	
Camillo Sinfi	S. Paulo	Adamastor	50	20	6	
Dante Passione	S. Paulo	Adamastor	100	20	6	
Masi & Covelli	S. Paulo	S. José do Belém	50	16	6	
Varan & Filepo	S. Paulo	Lanificio Italo-Armenio	100	13	6	
Halo Adami & Irmão	S. Paulo	Tecelagem Brasil	20	12	9	54
Graziani & Graziani	S. Paulo	Gina	30	9	7	
Lofredo & Paccioni	S. Paulo	Tecelagem de Lan	30	6	7	
Edoardo Parisi	S. Paulo	Independencia G. Terlera	80	6		
Total			17,980	2,552	922	24,704

SOURCE: *Boletim da Diretoria de Industria e Comercio* 19, nos. 7–8 (1928): 164–165.

TABLE 7.7
Jute Cloth Factories in the State of São Paulo, 1922

Company	City	Owner	Capital (contos)	Workers	Looms	Spindles	ANNUAL PRODUCTION Jute cloth (m)	Sacks	Covers
Sant'Anna	S. Paulo	Companhia Nacional de Tecidos de Juta	8,000	2,800	750	15,000	24,756,165	11,531,934	194,603
Paulista	S. Paulo	Companhia Paulista de Aniagens	5,000	1,500	250	6,000	15,000,000		
Anglo-Brasileira	S. Paulo	Companhia Anglo-Brasileira	3,000	900	200		6,000,000		
Santista	Santos	Companhia Santista de Tecelagem	800	240	180		5,000,000		
Total			16,800	5,440	1,380	21,000	50,756,165	11,531,934	194,603

SOURCE: *Boletim da Diretoria de Industria e Comercio* 15, nos. 7–8 (1923): 175.

eral Capital totals. The same went for the total value of industrial production.[33] The state's total value of industrial production now accounted for a third of the almost 3 million contos of Brazilian industrial sales, surpassing the 850,000 contos produced by the Federal District and the State of Rio de Janeiro combined. Moreover, in several key industries São Paulo dominated national production, accounting for over 40 percent of national production in metallurgy, ceramics, construction of transport vehicles, and luxury items.

By 1920 the value of São Paulo industrial production had reached 83 percent of the value of the state's agricultural production in that year (which was almost 1.2 million contos), making it a major contributor to the São Paulo economy.[34] There were also some significant structural changes within Paulista industry. In 1920 the food industries now took first place in the value of total industrial production, accounting for 35 percent of the state industries (see Figure 7.5). But these food-processing establishments were much smaller enterprises and accounted for only 13 percent of the wage workers. In contrast, the textile industry employed 41 percent of the state's industrial workers. If the cloth spinning industry is combined with the clothing industry, they accounted for 40 percent of the value of São Paulo's industrial products, and along with the food industry these two sectors accounted for three-quarters of the total industrial value.

TABLE 7.8

Manufacturers of Silk Textiles in the State of São Paulo, 1925

Company	Owner	Capital (contos)	Workers	Looms
Capital of São Paulo				
Italo-Brasileira	Sociedade Anonyma Tec. de Seda Italo-Brasileira	15,652	1,440	439
Santa Branca	Companhia de Tecidos Santa Branca	3,370	75	32
Libaneza	Farcs Irmãos	1,000	70	24
Secção de Seda	Companhia Prada	600	126	39
Anglo-Brasileira	Companhia de Tec. de Seda Anglo-Brasil	600	120	60
Socied. Industrial de Seda	Jorge Malnf	500	110	80
Marcoz	Alfredo Marcoz	500	40	24
Paulista	Almeida Sampaio	450	50	38
Sant'Anna	Sociedade Anonyma Tec. de Seda "Santa Anna"	400	40	36
Esperança	Salomão	300	15	20
Santa Mathilde	Nasser & Malta	200	20	
Paulista	Chani Maluf & Irmão	160	40	16
Santa Magdalena	S. Lunardi	150	85	67
Fitas de Seda e Algodão	Lenci, Cinquini	150	50	
N. Jafet	David Jafet	100	30	16
Brasitania	M. A. Maluf	100	60	30
Tres Irmãos	Abrahão Andraus & Irmãos	90	36	
Ideal	Baptista lmparati	80	5	5
Braz	Bressan	80	12	7
Tecelagem de fitas	C. Peterson	60	40	12
Oriente	F. Frigerio	45	12	15
Assumpta	Magnanini & Irmão	40	12	8
Passamanarias	O Caielli	30	12	
Mercedes	Julio Resende	29	120	5
Michele Noschese	Michele Noschese	190	30	20
Interior				
Indust. de Seda Nacional	Sociedade Anonyma Indust. de Seda Nacional	4,000	700	
Carioba	Companhia Leyen (Villa Americana)	2,250	250	55
Villa S. Bernardo	Companhia de Tecidos S. Bernardo	602	140	78
Americana	Tec. de Seda. Sul Americana	310	36	28
Manufactura Botucatú	Schlossarek, Zanotti & Tortori	200	27	12
Total		32,238	3,803	1,166

SOURCE: *Boletim da Diretoria de Industria e Comercio* 17, no. 9 (1926): 192.

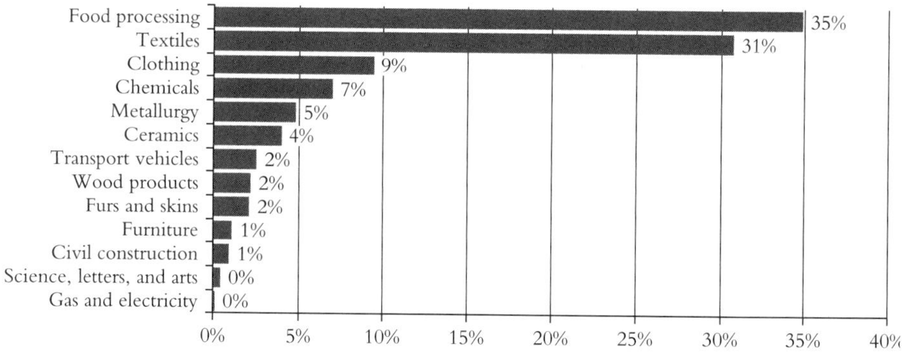

Figure 7.5 Percentage of Major Industries in the Value of São Paulo Industrial Production in 1920

NOTE: Only in 1920 and 1940 is civil construction listed in the census.

SOURCE: Instituto Brasileiro de Geografia e Estatística, *Recenseamento geral do Brasil, 1920,* vol. 5, part 1a, p. 409, table xxiv.

This major growth of industries in the first three decades of the twentieth century tended to evolve in most of the major urban centers and counties of the state. The existence of a major rail network permitted easy distribution of finished products and allowed many processing plants to be close to their raw material supplies. While much of the textile industry was highly concentrated in large factories in a few major interior cities and the capital, most other early industrial workshops and plants in São Paulo were quite local and artisanal for most of the nineteenth and early twentieth centuries. Industries related to construction such as sawmills and brickyards, which provided the basic materials for housing and commercial buildings, were still the most numerous in the state. As late as the 1915 industrial census, there were some 558 sawmills (and 45 percent of the 184 municípios had one) and 972 brickyards (found in 43 percent of these municípios).[35] Milling of cereals was always important for the production of local foods, and the next most widely distributed factories were those that produced beer (270 factories found in 38 percent of the municípios) and the 200 producing other beverages (located in 32 percent of the municípios). While there were eighteen railroad workshops in the principal marshalling yards of the major railroads, the state of São Paulo still used horses as a means of transport. There were 248 workshops producing harnesses and saddles (in 36 percent of the municípios) and 383 workshops making wagons and carts (in 38 percent of the municípios). As early as 1907 there were also twelve large central sugar mills (*usinas*), and these sugar mills had increased to fourteen by 1920 and were capitalized at 22 million contos.[36] Finally, there were numerous mills producing cereals and others refining the food produced in the state.

But in the capital was concentrated the Paulista clothing manufacturers. Although the city had only 53 percent of textile manufactures, it was the major center for the state's production of all types of hats, especially felt fedoras and homburgs, accounting for 93 percent of local production in 1915, and shops in the capital made over 60 percent of the ribbons, lace, stockings, and shirts produced in the state. The city produced two-thirds of the state's paper products and had three-quarters of its machine shops and half of the state's foundries. Though the food industry was widely dispersed throughout the state, the capital dominated the canning industry.[37]

In addition to the textile, clothing, and food and drink industries there were a few pioneer industries in this period that would later become dominant actors within both the state and the national industries. São Paulo had a significant papermaking industry by the 1920s that fed on national forests both natural and manmade. The first paper factory was founded in the state at Salto de Itú in 1888, and there were two operating in the state by 1890 producing 700 metric tons of paper per annum. By 1910 there were four such factories in the state and production was up to some 3,300 metric tons per annum, and by 1924 production reached 13,000 metric tons of paper annually. Not only did this production satisfy the needs of the state, but half was exported to the other states of the nation, though finer papers were still being imported from Europe.[38] As could be expected the factories were spread throughout the state, producing both paper and cardboard, and had a total capital of some 19,000 contos, roughly the same capitalization as the jute and woolen industries, though with many fewer workers (see Table 7.9).

Another such pioneer industry closely associated with the food and drinks industry was the glass industry. The first glass-producing factory dated from 1852 in the município of Ubatuba, but it did not survive, and by 1900 there were just four such factories in the state. By 1922, however, there were sixteen factories in the capital capitalized at 6,000 contos, with some 3,000 workers, and producing 3 million kilograms of glass, as well as numerous glass vessels for drinks and laboratory usage (see Table 7.10). By 1927 the capital was producing 38 million beer bottles. These factories satisfied local needs and produced enough extra glass to export to the other states of Brazil. Moreover, the majority of the raw materials used in the production of glass were of local origin.[39]

TABLE 7.9
Paper and Carton Factories in the State of São Paulo, 1924

Owner	City	Capital (contos)	Workers	ANNUAL PRODUCTION (T)	
				Paper	Cardboard
Companhia Melhoramentos de S. Paulo	Cayeiras	6,500	700	6,396	
Companhia Ind. de Papel e Cartonagem	Salto and Osasco	5,000	88	1,500	1,300
Companhia Fabricadora de Papel	S. Paulo	3,050	320	2,500	1,500
Companhia Industrial Paulista de Papeis e Papelão	S. Paulo	700	70		1,250
Companhia Fabril do Cubatão	Cubatão (Santos)	3,778	125	2,621	
Oliveira Ribeiro	S. Paulo and Limeira	200	210		840
Total		19,228	1,513	13,017	4,890

SOURCE: *Boletim da Diretoria de Indústria e Comércio* 16, no. 6 (1925): 105.

The food-processing industry mostly occurred in small artisanal shops. But there were a few very large establishments that had emerged by the 1920s. One type of these larger food-processing factories was the modern meatpacker. Early in the twentieth century this major food area underwent an industrialization process with the opening up of the first meat-processing plants that produced fresh, frozen, chilled, and canned beef, pork, and other animal products for local consumption and export. Many of these *frigoríficos* started with foreign capital, and by 1924 there were four such factories scattered throughout the state, with the North American–owned Companhia Armour do Brasil in the city of São Paulo (founded the year before) being the largest with 700 workers, followed by the Osasco-based Continental Products Company with 600 workers. In total, the four frigoríficos had 1,702 workers and produced 109,000 contos' worth of meat products, up from just 11,000 contos in 1922, and now processed some 400,000 animals.[40]

There was an equally significant modernization and continued expansion in one of the oldest industries in the state of São Paulo, that of refining sugar. From the colonial period sugar had been processed in simple animal- or water-driven mills called *trapiches*. The big steam-driven modern mills emerged in São Paulo only in the late nineteenth century, and it was only in the twentieth century that modern milling occurred in the usinas. These central mills had expanded to seventeen by 1926, and production of refined sugar was close to 40,000 metric tons.[41] By 1926 capital invested in these enterprises had risen to 32,000 contos, and they employed some 3,400 workers. As could be expected these mills were closely associated

TABLE 7.10
Glass Factories in the Capital of São Paulo, 1922

			ANNUAL PRODUCTION				
Owner	Workers	Capital (contos)	Glass (kg)	Bottles	Boxes containing glass	Laboratory glass	Mirrors
Companhia Crystalleria Barone	600	1,500	950,480				
Companhia Vidraria Santa Marina	1,350	2,000		26,000,000	20,000		
Companhia Crystalleria Brasil	200	550	300,000			5,780,000	
Ribeiro Sobrinho	120	550		1,000,000			
Emp. Chimica Industrial	80	250					
Sociedade Anonyma Vidraria Paulista	200	400	2,000,000				
Scarrone (F. Colombo)	178	200	250,000				
Renato E. Souza Aranha	15	100				4,800,000	
Milhas	80	100					
Antonio Joaquim dos Santos	10	40					1,200
Assao Aun & Farah	2	4					2,400
Irmãos Gallo	5	3					
João de Oliveira Salvador	2	2.5					
Henrique Jacobi	20	10					
Irmãos Alfano (Crystálleria Progresso)	130	100	1,200				
Conrado Sorgenicht	60	52					
Total	3,052	5,862	3,501,680	27,000,000	20,000	10,580,000	3,600

SOURCE: *Boletim da Diretoria de Indústria e Comércio* 13, no. 6 (1922): 191.

with the sugar harvest and thus were built close to the sugar-growing areas, all of which slowly began to expand with the relative decline of coffee plantings in the middle decades of the twentieth century. These seventeen usinas produced some 393,000 sacks of sugar, 2.9 million liters of alcohol, and 1.7 million liters of aguardente (see Table 7.11). But despite this return to growth in sugar planting and refining, São Paulo before World War II still consumed more sugar than it produced, getting its imports from the Northeast states of Brazil such as Pernambuco and Alagoas (see Figure 7.6). Its role as a world-dominant sugar producer was still in the future.

TABLE 7.11

Size and Production of São Paulo Usinas, by Sacks of Sugar, 1926

Usina	Município	Owner	Capital (contos)	Workers	Horsepower	Cane milled (t)	Production (sacks)	Alcohol (L)	Aguardente (L)
Fortaleza	Araraquara and S. Carlos	Refinadora Paulista	7,000	300	1,000	57,004	59,831	672,932	62,315
Villa Rafard	Capivari	Société Sucreries Brésiliennes	1,500	380	800	48,154	48,615	738,000	
Amalia	Santa Rosa	Socied. Agric. Fazenda Paulista	1,000	300	600	36,192	41,556	284,000	10,000
Santa Barbara	Santa Barbara	C. E. de Ferro Agrícola	2,500	90	350	36,150	41,161	429,326	
Monte Alegre	Piracicaba	Companhia União dos Refinadores	2,000	60	2,000	34,420	37,275	229,861	630,326
Vassununga	S. Rita do Pas Quatro	Companhia Uzina Vassununga	1,500	30	100	24,663	34,459		
Junqueira	Igarapava	Francisco Maximiano Junqueira	1,500	500	800	18,000	22,000	90,000	
Schmidt	Sertãozinho	Guilherme Schmidt & Irmãos	600	310	280	13,350	15,000		160,000
Itahyquara	Caconde	Joâo B. de Lima Figueiredo	100	70	400	10,642	14,201	40,260	19,400
Albertina	Sertaozinho	Guilherme Schmidt & Irmãos	400	250	250	10,572	10,944		90,000
Piracicaba	Piracicaba	Société Sucreries Brésiliennes	2,000	400	740	10,310	10,939	160,400	

Porto Feliz	Porto Feliz	Société Sucreries Brésiliennes	1,000	300	500	10,200	11,763	190,388	353,600
Lorena	Lorena	Société Sucreries Brésiliennes	800	150	550	10,000	15,759	65,000	
Barbacena	Araraquara	Bigheti & Biagi	500	35	100	8,000	10,000		200,000
Miranda	Pirajuí	Sociedade Anonyma Uzina Miranda	6,000	60	540	7,498	10,000		90,000
Esther	Campinas	Sociedade Anonyma Uzina Esther	2,000	130	400		5,731		80,000
Pimentel	Jaboticabal	Dr. Alvaro Pimentel	1,250	24	200	4,116	3,421	3,200	20,000
Total			31,650	3,389	9,610	339,271	392,655	2,903,367	1,715,641

SOURCE: *Boletim da Diretoria de Indústria e Comércio* 18, nos. 7–8 (1927): 135–136.

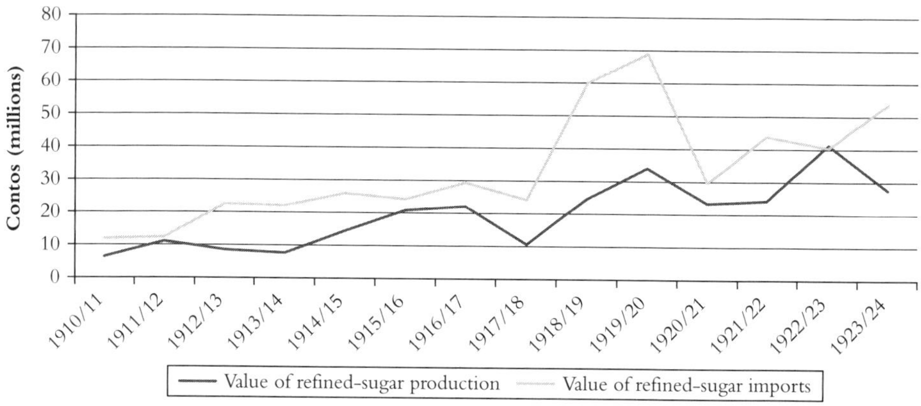

Figure 7.6 Value of State Production of Refined Sugar by Crop Year, 1910–1924, and Sugar Imports by Year, 1911–1924

SOURCE: *Boletim da Diretoria de Indústria e Comércio*, nos. 11–12 (1922): 354–355; *Boletim da Diretoria de Indústria e Comércio*, nos. 1–2 (1925): 3–4; *Boletim da Diretoria de Indústria e Comércio, 1922–1926 Summary*, 540; *Boletim da Diretoria de Indústria e Comércio*, nos. 7–8 (1927): 4.

In terms of industrial workers, the state was also the leader in the nation by 1920. In 1907 the state of Rio de Janeiro and its Federal District contained 32 percent of the nation's 149,000 industrial workers, and São Paulo had 16 percent. By 1920 Rio de Janeiro and the Federal District held only 26 percent of the nation's 294,000 industrial workers, whereas São Paulo's 84,000 workers increased their national share to 29 percent.[42] Industrial workers in São Paulo in terms of sex and age were similar to all other states. Spinning and weaving of cotton textiles and the clothing industry tended to use more women than most other industries.[43] All factories used a relatively small number of children in their workforce, though furniture and wagon construction seemed to have employed the most youths, and then it was overwhelmingly boys (see Table 7.12).

The distribution of these semiskilled or unskilled *jornaleiros* or *operários* (weekly workers or day laborers), both paid by the day or hour, accounted for 88 percent of all workers, owners, and managers in industry. There were also major differences in size of the workforce by industry. Factories employing fewer than 20 workers made up 62 percent of the textile mills but contained only 3 percent of these textile workers. But for all factories, those employing fewer than 20 workers made up 89 percent of all industrial establishments and accounted for 19 percent of the workers, suggesting less concentration in nontextile sectors (see Table 7.13).

TABLE 7.12

Category, Age, and Sex of All Workers in São Paulo Industries in the Census of 1920 (sorted by value of production)

	ALL EMPLOYEES AND WORKERS						ALL DAILY AND WEEKLY WORKERS (*OPERARIOS* AND *JORNALEIROS*)			WORKERS UNDER AGE 14 (%)			
Industry	Total	Men (%)	Women (%)	Owners (%)	Administrators (%)	Monthly employees (%)	Total	Men	Women	Total	Male	Female	Value of industrial production
I. Food industries	14,630	47.2	52.8	2.5	2.9	5.8	11,213	9,189	2,024	24.3	11.1	13.2	343,783
II. Textiles	36,477	98.3	1.7	0.4	0.1	0.2	34,825	15,596	19,229	0.2	0.2	0.0	302,504
III. Clothing and toiletries	12,316	99.6	0.4	2.0	0.8	0.8	10,494	6,501	3,993	1.2	1.2	0.0	93,432
IV. Chemical products	5,521	94.5	5.5	3.4	2.9	5.1	4,748	3,360	1,388	9.0	8.3	0.7	69,031
V. Metallurgy	6,146	89.1	10.9	13.4	2.3	2.8	5,514	5,183	331	9.0	7.3	1.7	47,092
VI. Ceramics	10,499	74.4	25.6	3.5	1.1	2.8	9,360	8,257	1,103	2.7	1.8	0.9	39,192
VII. Construction of transport vehicles	1,894	85.3	14.7	87.4	23.4	69.6	1,458	1,454	4	61.3	42.9	18.4	24,180
VIII. Wood	2,534	66.6	33.4	37.3	9.0	25.6	2,089	2,083	6	47.8	26.8	21.0	21,176
IX. Leather and skins	1,341	93.3	6.7	20.1	3.1	6.6	1,104	1,083	21	22.8	20.7	2.1	20,511
X. Furniture	2,430	99.3	0.7	2.6	0.5	0.9	2,030	1,872	158	1.0	1.0	0.0	11,080
XI. Building construction	822	99.7	0.3	37.7	3.8	11.6	726	721	5	21.9	21.9	0.0	9,335
XII. Luxury goods and science and letters	471	98.9	1.1	3.4	1.3	1.7	373	300	73	0.8	0.8		4,301
XIII. Electricity	94	83.9	16.1	17.0	10.6	76.6	64	64	0	34.4	34.4	0.0	483
Total	95,175	69.8	30.2	5.7	1.8	4.2	83,998	55,663	28,335	7.7	4.8	2.9	986,100

SOURCE: Diretoria Geral de Estatística, *Recenseamento do Brasil realizado em 1 de setembro de 1920*, vol. 5, part 1a, pp. 270–271, 382, table xxiv.

TABLE 7.13
Cumulative Percentages of Factories and Workers by Size of Unit in Textiles and All Factories in São Paulo, 1920

	TEXTILES				ALL FACTORIES			
Size of workforce	Factories	Workers	Factories (%)	Workers (%)	Factories	Workers	Factories (%)	Workers (%)
0–4	41	116	16.6	0.3	2,376	5,385	57.3	6.4
5–9	74	502	46.6	1.8	901	5,642	79.1	13.1
10–19	38	463	61.9	3.1	407	5,295	88.9	19.4
20–49	19	638	69.6	4.9	212	6,627	94.0	27.3
50–99	14	1,003	75.3	7.8	102	6,926	96.5	35.6
100–199	21	2,860	83.8	16.0	68	9,122	98.1	46.4
200–499	16	5,539	90.3	31.9	47	14,413	99.2	63.6
500–999	17	12,518	97.2	67.9	23	16,590	99.8	83.3
1,000+	7	11,186	100.0	100.0	9	13,998	100.0	100.0
Total	247	34,825			4,145	83,998		

SOURCE: Diretoria Geral de Estatística, *Recenseamento do Brasil realizado em 1 de setembro de 1920*, vol. 5, part 1a, pp. 294–295, table xx.

The 1920 industrial census also provides information on the types of expenditures made by all industries in São Paulo. The buildings and land category and stocks of raw materials category accounted for 30 to 40 percent of investment in almost all the industries, with machinery and tools accounting for about 20 to 30 percent. The major exception was in the electricity-generating industry, in which machinery made up an extraordinary 60 percent of expenditures (see Table 7.14). In turn, the ceramics industry spent the most on buildings and land, and the transport, vehicle construction, and clothing industries spent the most on stocks of materials needed to produce goods. Given the dominance of the textiles and food-processing industries, their relative expenditures were close to the norm for all industries in the state. Although more detailed breakdowns do not exist for the state, the industrial census does supply costs of salaries and taxes at the national level. Excluding the costs of buildings and land, of the expenditures for all industries in Brazil, the percentage paid in salaries was 16 percent (and 18 percent for all the textile mills in Brazil); 5 percent of expenditures were for federal, state, and município taxes (4 percent for textiles); transport costs averaged 4 percent (only 2 percent for textiles); stock of materials represented 73 percent (72 percent for textiles); and just 3 percent was for fuel and energy (3 percent for the cloth-producing mills).[44]

The 1920 census, as well as some later surveys, also presents data on ownership of these factories. All these surveys suggest that the foreign born

TABLE 7.14

Components of Expenditures in Principal São Paulo Industries in the Census of 1920

Industry	Factories	Total expenditures (contos)	Buildings and land (%)	Machinery and tools (%)	Raw materials stock and fuels (%)
I. Textiles	247	223,646	36.2	28.6	35.2
II. Leather and skins	86	15,941	35.8	14.7	49.6
III. Wood	183	13,053	45.5	33.8	20.7
IV. Metallurgy	142	28,491	29.4	30.3	40.3
V. Ceramics	696	26,201	61.2	23.6	15.3
VI. Chemical products	265	39,139	41.9	25.0	33.2
VII. Food industries	1,267	127,258	38.2	29.1	32.7
VIII. Clothing and toiletries	736	42,917	20.9	18.8	60.3
IX. Furniture	207	5,380	34.7	27.6	37.8
X. Building construction	55	3,819	49.7	20.4	29.9
XI. Construction of transport vehicles	239	8,512	18.9	18.2	62.9
XII. Electricity	11	392	30.8	59.9	9.4
XIII. Luxury goods and science and letters	11	3,071	12.5	16.9	70.7
Total	4,145	537,817	36.6	27.0	36.5

SOURCE: Diretoria Geral de Estatística, *Recenseamento do Brazil realizado em 1 de setembro de 1920*, vol. 5, part 1a, pp. 222–223.

were a significant group in industry ownership in São Paulo, especially compared to agriculture. In rural land ownership foreign ownership was very limited, especially as concerned the coffee fazendas.[45] Although Brazilians accounted for the majority of the value of capital and workers and motor force employed in the factories of the state—contributing between two-thirds and four-fifths of all three factors of production—foreigners made up a substantial minority of owners. Italians were second among factory owners at a significant 25 percent share. Nevertheless, the few companies that the English or the Canadians owned were quite large. The largest factories in terms of workers were owned by Canadians, which were the electricity-producing companies and averaged 730 workers in four companies. This was largely due to one company that they owned, the São Paulo Tramway, Light, and Power Company, or "Light," which electrified the capital city, owned the tramways in the capital, and was important everywhere in the state because of its dams and electricity-producing generators. The twenty-seven factories owned by the English averaged 145 workers, the second-highest level, whereas the Brazilian factories had on average only 39 workers per factory. In turn, foreign capital invested in industry outweighed direct foreign ownership of factories in São Paulo.

In most of the census surveys this foreign capital accounted for between 40 and 45 percent of capital invested in industry.[46] While a state industrial census of 1934 clearly understates foreign ownership (assuming that 56 percent of the factories were Brazilian owned), it is the only source that details the national origins of this foreign capital. As could be expected, it was the Italians who were the most important foreign investors in industry, in general accounting for a quarter of all factories, followed by the Portuguese, who accounted for 5 percent of the total. Although the Syrians held only 3 percent of the factories, they were significant in the production of textiles. After Brazilians, who accounted for 69 percent of the invested industrial capital, it was the Canadians who had the highest investments in industry, accounting for 18 percent of all capital invested, which was due to their control over the production of electricity.[47]

Finally, the factories in São Paulo and in all of Brazil by 1920 had completely converted to obtaining their power by electricity from outside sources. Some 90 percent of the Paulista factories used electricity, while the national total was 88 percent. In São Paulo only the textile, leather, and furniture industries were below this average, and of these it was only the furniture and leather industries (at 61 percent and 79 percent, respectively, of their factories with electricity) that were significantly below the norm with some still using their own steam engines to generate power.[48]

This massive shift to electric power had come through major investments in hydroelectric power and to a far lesser extent in coal and oil plants, all established in Brazil primarily after 1900. Only 2 electricity-generating companies existed before 1890, and another 8 were established in the 1890s, but they generated only some 17,000 horsepower. But in the first decade of the new century another 77 companies entered the field, and they added 187,000 horsepower to the system, and in the 1911–1920 period there was a massive expansion with 256 new installations built that produced 272,000 horsepower.[49] By 1920 there were some 337 generating plants producing 431,000 horsepower. This explains how Brazil went from producing 10 megawatts of power in 1900 to 157 megawatts in 1910 and 367 megawatts by 1920. From 1901 onward four-fifths of this power came from hydroelectric sources as all of Brazil, but especially São Paulo, went on a major dam-building program.[50] São Paulo accounted for 51 percent of the 346,000 horsepower generated by hydroelectric plants, which meant that it alone accounted for 43 percent of all electricity generated in the country. The nearest competitors were the Federal District and the state of Rio de Janeiro, which combined accounted for only 26 percent of all national electricity generation.[51]

New industries now entered the state in this period. In the late 1920s the first cement plants in Brazil were built, in the state of São Paulo.[52] From 1927 to 1931 these state producers went from providing 3 percent of national consumption to 93 percent.[53] But in one area, that of steel construction, it took the direct effort of the federal government to finally establish a national industry in the 1940s. Until the late 1940s two-thirds of Brazil's steel needs were met by imports. In the end the Getúlio Vargas regime decided to build its own steel mill and created the Companhia Siderúrgica Nacional at Volta Redonda in Rio de Janeiro in 1941. When this steel mill finally went into operation in 1946 it became one of the largest steel plants in the world.[54]

The next twenty years saw increasing complexity of Paulista industries and growth of traditional industries. By the census of 1940 there was very substantial development of the food-processing industry, which maintained its role as one of the two primary industries in the state. Textiles, at 30 percent of the value of the state's industrial production, was now the leader in the census of 1940, and if clothing is added, it now accounted for 35 percent of total value (see Figure 7.7). Textiles alone accounted for 31 percent of the state's workforce. The two leading industries, manufacture of cloth of all kinds and food processing, accounted for half the total value of the state's industrial production and 45 percent of its workforce. Given their importance in the local market, it is not too surprising to see that these

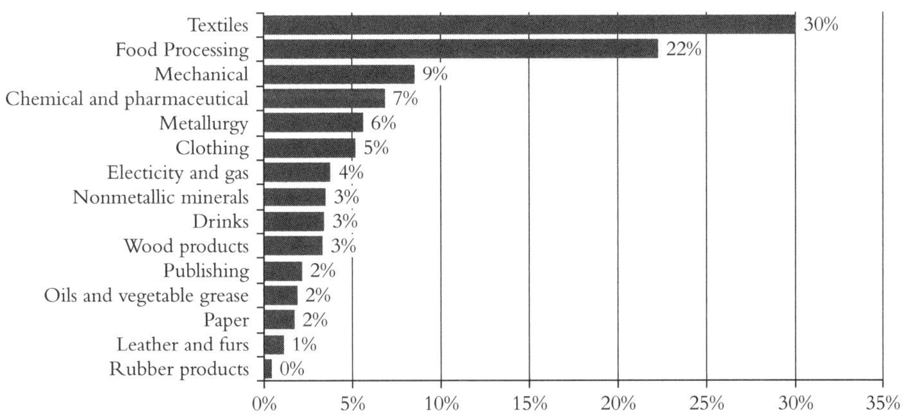

Figure 7.7 Relative Importance of Industries in the Value of Industrial Production of São Paulo in 1940

SOURCE: Instituto Brasileiro de Geografia e Estatística, *Recenseamento geral do Brasil, 1940*, regional series, part 17, vol. 3, p. 481, table 15.

were among the Paulista industries with the most national capital investments, 65 percent of the total. This compares to the industry with the most foreign capital, gas and electricity production, which had only 22 percent of its invested capital coming from national investors.[55]

By 1940 the value of São Paulo's industrial production reached 7.4 million contos (US$438 million). The number of industrial workers had increased by a factor of three since 1920, to 325,000 in 1940. There were also some structural changes in the labor force. There was a slight decline in the number of women and a significant increase in administrators and monthly employees in the total labor force, suggesting that a more sophisticated industrial structure had been achieved by the 1940s (see Table 7.15).

Of the total industrial workforce employed in the state, the city of São Paulo was overwhelmingly the dominant place of industrial activity, especially if the neighboring município of Santo André is included. The capital city of São Paulo accounted for 54 percent of the industrial workers and 63 percent of the capital absorbed in industry. Including Santo André, the figure rises to 61 percent of all the state's industrial workers. Sorocaba, Santos, and Jundiaí were also major industrial centers, though not comparable in size to the capital (see Table 7.16).

There is little question that São Paulo industry grew faster in the twentieth century than any other state of the nation.[56] By 1928 São Paulo alone accounted for 38 percent of all industrial companies, and this dominance would increase in the 1930s. By 1938 it accounted for 49 percent of the value of all nationally produced cloth and artifacts, 88 percent of all spun and woven cotton, 81 percent of the nation's dyed and printed cloth, and 61 percent of the total value of all textile production. The Federal District of Rio de Janeiro now accounted for only 17 percent of the total of national textile production.[57] By 1938, São Paulo dominated the clothing industry, from hats to shoes, and even made 53 percent of the ready-made clothes sold in the national market.[58]

If World War I was a stimulus to local production, the extension of it occurred because of the lack of imported products or their high cost. The postwar period saw major investments, stimulated by the great expansion of the national market. While a consistent industrial policy was not applied in the state even as late as 1950, there is little doubt that the blockade of trade in World War II also had an impact on industrial growth in the state. In the decade from 1940 to 1950, for example, the number of industrial workers employed in the state almost doubled, to 498,000.[59] Especially after the end of the war in Europe and Asia, there was major growth in industrial

TABLE 7.15

Structure of the Labor Force in Industry in São Paulo, 1940

			PERCENTAGE OF TOTAL WORKFORCE					
Industry	No. of factories[a]	Total no. of workers	Men	Administrators	Monthly salaried	Day laborers	Children[b]	Average no. of workers per factory
Textiles	397	100,867	42.3	1.6	5.0	93.4	21.0	254
Food production	4,495	45,786	87.1	12.8	18.1	69.1	8.1	10
Transformation of nonmetallic minerals	1,579	23,337	90.4	8.2	9.3	82.5	13.1	15
Metallurgy	570	22,735	93.5	4.1	8.0	87.8	13.6	40
Wood products	1,385	19,964	97.9	9.7	12.3	78.0	9.8	14
Clothing manufacturers	1,121	19,442	69.4	7.1	12.3	80.6	16.9	17
Chemicals and pharmaceuticals	477	17,113	60.9	4.5	12.1	83.4	18.8	36
Mechanical products	402	14,762	96.0	4.5	11.0	84.5	9.5	37
Civil construction	412	11,257	99.6	4.9	7.4	87.7	2.8	27
Publishers and printers	719	10,981	88.3	8.3	17.1	74.6	14.6	15
Electricity and gas	488	10,125	99.7	1.5	52.3	46.2	0.8	21
Drinks and stimulants	369	7,080	78.3	7.2	18.9	73.9	9.9	19
Mixed industries	271	5,803	73.7	6.7	6.8	86.5	20.4	21
Paper and cardboard	93	5,685	64.1	2.3	10.7	87.1	22.6	61
Leather and skins	281	3,492	92.6	10.9	7.6	81.5	8.8	12
Oils and vegetable oils	28	3,426	95.0	0.5	6.9	92.6	2.7	122
Rubber products	33	2,665	61.8	2.4	15.3	82.2	9.3	81
Animal hair, feathers, and other remains	8	149	89.3	7.4	8.1	84.6	10.1	19
Total	13,128	324,669	72.5	5.6	11.4	82.9	14.4	25

SOURCE: Instituto Brasileiro de Geografia e Estatística, *Recenseamento geral do Brasil, 1940*, national series, part 17, vol. 3, p. 458, table 3.
[a] This is the category *estabelecimentos*, which the census defines as units of production rather than companies (*empresas*).
[b] Children are found only in the day laborer category, and they are defined as anyone under eighteen years of age.

TABLE 7.16
Industry in São Paulo by Município, by Size of Workforce, 1940

Município	No. of factories	Capital applied (contos)	No. of workers	% workers
State total	*14,225*	*7,721,014*	*323,342*	*100.0*
São Paulo	4,876	3,386,160	174,367	53.9
Santo André	376	485,695	22,183	6.9
Sorocaba	192	302,642	10,921	3.4
Santos	267	879,313	9,173	2.8
Jundiaí	139	104,986	7,000	2.2
Campinas	284	141,732	6,627	2.0
Taubaté	78	26,900	4,522	1.4
Piracicaba	170	708,000	3,467	1.1
Limeira	119	31,236	3,299	1.0
Araraquara	158	127,259	2,880	0.9
Ribeirão Preto	181	98,476	2,739	0.8
Salto	48	60,363	2,722	0.8
Barretos	94	23,984	2,623	0.8
São Carlos	117	29,237	2,566	0.8
Americana	100	32,180	2,414	0.7
Tatuí	92	12,523	2,256	0.7
Itú	71	17,892	2,204	0.7
Rio Claro	155	19,497	2,178	0.7
São José dos Campos	45	14,216	2,034	0.6
Porto Feliz	22	33,026	1,980	0.6
Bauru	80		1,763	0.5
Franca	112	22,911	1,742	0.5
Mogi das Cruzes	80	16,091	1,622	0.5
Jacareí	46	26,048	1,620	0.5
Guaratinguetá	46	14,380	1,360	0.4
Juquerí	12	23,430	1,303	0.4
Itatíba	42	17,616	1,229	0.4
Pinhal	55	12,856	1,177	0.4
Amparo	76	29,179	1,111	0.3
Santa Barbara	41	25,732	1,093	0.3
Marília	94	39,266	1,062	0.3
Bragança	85	5,967	1,054	0.3
Capivarí	75	39,826	1,029	0.3

SOURCE: Instituto Brasileiro de Geografia e Estatística, *Recenseamento geral do Brasil, 1940*, national series, part 17, vol. 3, pp. 485–489, table 16.

companies within the state. Most of the firms operating in 1950 had been recently founded, and two-thirds of them were established in the decade of the 1940s. But large firms founded before 1940 still were important since they accounted for more than half the value of industrial production in that year. Moreover, most of the heavily capitalized firms had been in existence for several decades. This was especially the case with textiles and food-processing plants in terms of capital invested, which still had major plants functioning in 1950 that had been founded in the first three decades of the century. Thus, only a little over a third of the invested capital in textiles was coming from firms founded in the 1940s, while food-processing plants, machine tool workshops, and metallurgy firms had over half their invested capital coming from earlier periods (see Table 7.17).

The two classic industries, food processing and textiles and clothing, still continued to dominate the local industrial sector. The future growth industries of metallurgy and machine tools accounted for only 8 percent of the total value of industrial production in the state in 1950. But if the industries producing electrical fixtures and machines, those building transport vehicles, and the chemical industry are included in the modest heavy-industry sector, then its share of total production rises to a quarter of the value of the state's total industrial production (see Figure 7.8). However modest their production, São Paulo's metallurgy companies represented half of those operating in Brazil in 1950.[60] They produced over half the value of Brazil's metallurgy, mechanical, and chemical-producing industries and accounted for two-thirds of the value of all the nation's transport construction and 78 percent of its electrical and communication materials output. It was also the tire capital of the nation, accounting for 68 percent of workers in this field and 84 percent of the total value of production.[61] Thus, while São Paulo industry in 1950 was still primarily producing consumer goods for the national market, it was emerging as the principal state for the capital's goods and machine-tool industry, which would become increasingly important after mid-century.[62]

The industrial sector was dominated by well-financed large firms, but as could be expected in an economy that predominantly produced consumer goods, there was a large number of very small firms in terms of income, capital invested, and the number of workers employed. But it was the very large firms that accounted for the majority of workers, capital, energy consumed, and value of industrial production. Those industrial companies capitalized at less than 100,000 cruzeiros (approximately US$5,000 at the time) made up over half the firms but had just 2 percent of the capital in 1950 and employed just 11 percent of the total workforce. They consumed just 5 percent of the electrical power. At the other extreme, the 701 companies with capital of over 5 million cruzeiros (US$266,000) accounted for less than 2 percent of the firms but had 62 percent of the invested capital and 38 percent of all workers. They also used over half the total energy consumed by industry. The firms that generated an annual value of production of 5 million cruzeiros or more by 1950 made up 4 percent of the firms

TABLE 7.17

Cumulative Percentages of Industrial Firms in São Paulo in 1950, by Type of Industry, Date of Establishment, and Capital Invested

	ALL INDUSTRIES		METALLURGY		MACHINERY		TEXTILES		FOOD PROCESSING	
Year founded	Established (%)	Capital invested (%)	Established (%)	Capital invested (%)	Established (%)	Capital invested (%)	Established (%)	Capital invested (%)	Established (%)	Capital invested (%)
Before 1900	0.5	4	0.4	2	1	11	0.6	2	0.3	2
1900–1909	0.6	8	0.4	6	1	0	0.6	9	0.5	21
1910–1919	1.5	9	1.2	6	3	7	1.9	15	1.4	7
1920–1929	5.5	16	5.3	11	8	16	5.7	19	6.0	14
1930–1939	16.3	21	15.7	30	17	20	15.8	20	16.2	15
1940–1949	75.7	42	77.1	45	71	46	75.4	35	75.5	41
Total percentage	100.0	100	100.0	100	100	100	100.0	100	100.0	100
Total number of firms and invested capital	19,011	15,377,535	1,003	1,668,612	401	410,891	1,256	4,260,406	6,127	2,777,244

SOURCE: Instituto Brasileiro de Geografia e Estatística, *Recenseamento geral do Brasil, 1950*, regional series, vol. 25, bk. 3, pp. 8–9, table 6.

NOTE: In 1950, there were 465 firms with invested capital of 998 million cruzeiros whose founding date was unknown. Total invested capital is listed in cruzeiros.

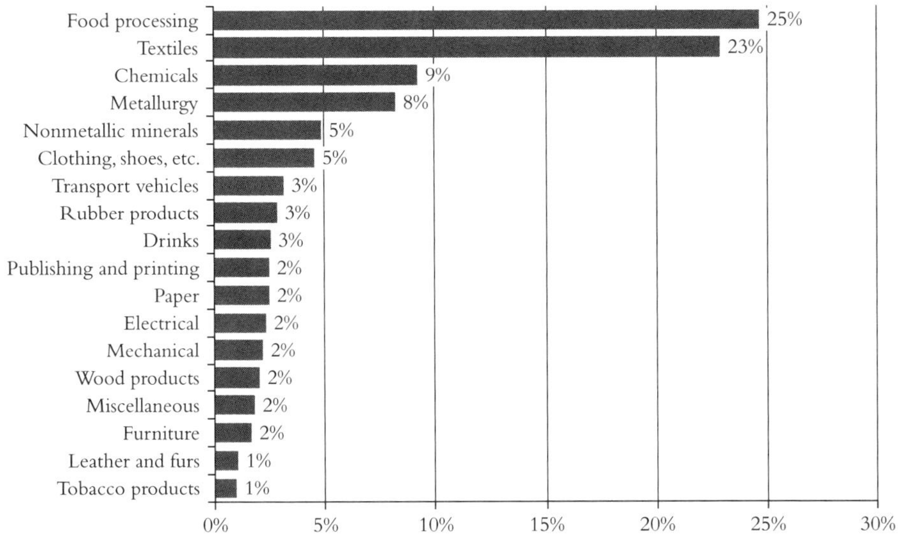

Figure 7.8 Relative Importance of Industries in the Value of Industrial Production of São Paulo in 1950

SOURCE: Instituto Brasileiro de Geografia e Estatística, *Censo agrícola de 1950*, regional series, part 35, vol. 3, p. 45.

but accounted for almost two-thirds of the capital invested and energy consumed and employed over half the workforce (see Table 7.18).

The dominance of large factories can be seen in the distribution of workers among the industrial establishments. The 14,218 factories that had five employees or fewer (salaried and daily wage workers combined) accounted for over half of all factories. But they contained only 6 percent of the industrial workforce. In turn, the 1,796 factories employing more than fifty employees accounted for only 4 percent of manufacturing companies but contained well over half the employees and daily wage workers.[63]

In relation to the rest of Brazil, there was little question that by 1950 São Paulo was the industrial giant of the nation. The recent growth of the industrial plant of the state exceeded the growth of industry everywhere else in the nation. From 1940 to 1950 the state increased its share of industrial wage laborers from 35 percent of the national total to 40 percent. In turn, the value of local industrial production went from 43 percent of national industrial production in 1940 to 47 percent by 1950.[64] At mid-century São Paulo's industrial firms used 40 percent of the power consumed by industry and generated 47 percent of the total value of Brazilian industrial

TABLE 7.18
Characteristics of Industrial Firms in São Paulo in 1950, by Amount of Capital Invested and Value of Production

	Factories	Capital invested (cruzeiros)	Total employees	Motor force (CV)
By capital invested (cruzeiros)				
Less than 50,000	9,044	194,524	35,782	26,140
50,000–99,999	4,353	309,747	25,825	34,758
100,000–499,999	7,450	1,655,110	88,058	124,387
500,000–999,999	1,456	1,019,102	43,000	62,545
1,000,000–2,499,999	1,138	1,784,827	59,934	105,989
2,500,000–4,999,999	428	1,507,606	42,776	77,685
5,000,000–9,999,999	308	2,171,397	57,684	100,493
10,000,000–49,999,999	331	7,195,199	140,483	373,500
50,000,000–99,999,999	39	2,503,948	32,114	123,177
100,000,000+	23	4,636,143	48,661	102,252
Total	24,570	22,977,603	574,317	1,130,926
By value of production (cruzeiros)				
Less than 50,000	4,319	229,991	9,071	16,390
50,000–99,999	3,181	245,693	12,958	13,547
100,000–499,999	4,747	535,435	22,104	34,429
500,000–999,999	3,492	562,178	23,979	36,690
1,000,000–2,499,999	3,115	751,333	32,407	48,935
2 500,000–4,999,999	4,226	2,938,478	111,397	170,409
5,000,000–9,999,999	823	1,978,945	59,200	97,787
10,000,000–49,999,999	769	6,459,373	152,676	344,062
50,000,000–99,999,999	101	2,768,178	67,957	152,247
100,000,000+	66	4,473,872	80,577	221,268
Total	24,839	20,943,476	572,326	1,135,764

SOURCE: Instituto Brasileiro de Geografia e Estatística, *Recenseamento geral do Brasil, 1950*, vol. 25, bk. 3, p. 28, table 6.

NOTE: For the 25,016 factories we examined, 446 did not have data on capital invested, and 177 had no production value listed.

production; they accounted for 37 percent of the wage workers, 45 percent of the invested capital, but just 27 percent of the firms, clearly indicating a more efficient and dominant industrial establishment.[65] Clearly, São Paulo had become the dominant force in Brazilian industry and, excepting Rio de Janeiro, Rio Grande do Sul, and Minas Gerais, the other states were of minimal importance (see Figure 7.9).

The reasons for the emergence of the supremacy of São Paulo have been well studied and are essentially related to the rise of the coffee economy and its impact on the state economy. The dramatic growth of coffee led to both the creation of an important internal market and important backward links to everything from transport and manufacturing to the development

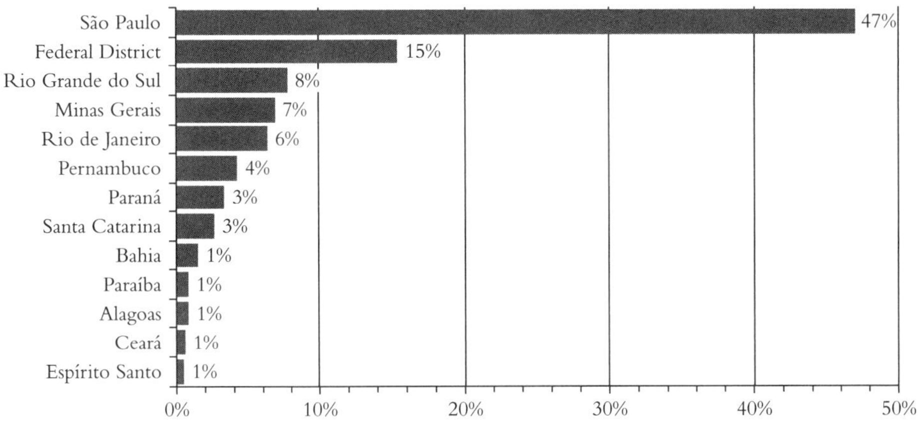

Figure 7.9 Share of the Value of Brazilian Industrial Production by Major Industrial States in 1950

NOTE: States with a share of less than 1 percent are not shown.

SOURCE: Instituto Brasileiro de Geografia e Estatística, *Recenseamento geral do Brasil, 1950*, national series, part 3, vol. 1, pp. vi–vii, table 2.

of a service sector. It was the income from coffee exports that provided the funds needed to develop the necessary infrastructure to promote the basic transport infrastructure.[66] São Paulo's 7,000 kilometers of railroad were Brazil's most complete rail network, and this railroad built for coffee exports also facilitated the integration of an internal market and thus promoted the industrial growth of the state. The booming coffee industry provided the capital needed to get the process started. Finally, the creation of a large, free, wage-labor force in coffee after the abolition of slavery enabled São Paulo to create a significant internal market, and the arrival of a mass of better-educated immigrants also provided the basis for a modern industrial labor force.

São Paulo clearly benefited from the massive introduction of foreign workers and foreign capital. By the census of 1900 it housed 44 percent of the foreign-born migrants arriving in Brazil and quickly reached over half of all foreign born in every census to 1950, absorbing something like 2.4 million overseas immigrants between 1880 and 1950, or 57 percent of all foreign-born immigrants who arrived in Brazil.[67] Better educated than the native-born population, many of these foreign immigrants entered as skilled and semiskilled workers in the industrial sector. It has been estimated that the European-immigrant component of the industrial labor force grew at 4.7 percent between 1872 and 1920, far faster growth than that for the native-born industrial workers, which meant that the foreign born accounted for at least a quarter of the industrial labor force by the 1920s.[68] In turn, well-educated and richer foreign-born immigrants proved willing to invest in this growing Paulista market along with the wealthiest coffee planters, who became entrepreneurs in a wide variety of businesses, especially those derived from or dependent on coffee. These businesses included railroads, electricity generation, import merchant houses, financial services, coffee brokers, and the new industries supplying the expanding internal market.

Various studies suggest that there were several groups that invested the capital to develop the Paulista industrial sector. Warren Dean, in a classic work on the pioneers of industrialization in São Paulo, stressed the existence of three different groups of entrepreneurs. The first were the importers, who supplied the local market with imported goods that were not produced locally.[69] These importers had multiple operations in the country, including even assembling and maintaining imported machines and equipment since some imported products still needed finishing or parts that were not imported and had to be produced in the local market. Moreover, these importers knew the internal producers and were also furnishers of raw materials and manufactured parts and equipment for these new factories and had access to foreign capital. In many cases this permitted them to shift from being distributors of a given product to national manufacturers of that product. Thus, at the margin of the importation process there developed a segment of the industrial plant in Brazil headed by these importers.

The coffee planters represented another important group who promoted Brazilian industrialization. Earlier sugar producers had promoted agro-industries, and this occurred in coffee as well. Equipment and agricultural machines needed by growers, initially imported, were then assembled, adjusted, repaired, and finally constructed in part in Brazil. Thus, coffee planters participated in innumerable manufacturing activities in all sectors, including in textiles. They were also heavy investors in the railroad companies and even administered them.[70]

The third important initiators of early industrialization in São Paulo were the immigrants. In this case we can divide the immigrants into two large groups. There were those who came to work in the countryside, beginning as colonos on the coffee fazendas, and through their own efforts became small, medium, and large farmers or small-factory owners. Another immigrant group emphasized by Dean was foreigners who had relatively high-status positions in Europe and arrived in Brazil as specialized workers or with the capital needed to establish themselves in Brazil. These elite immigrants founded an important share of the early great factories. According to Dean both of these entrepreneurial immigrants and the big importers took advantage of "the ready-made market that the rural and urban European-born masses provided for those who were familiar with their tastes and habits."[71]

Thus, native and foreign capital as well as native and foreign industrial workers were turning São Paulo into both the largest and the most dynamic industrial state of the country in the first half of the twentieth century. By the middle of the century São Paulo had already created a significant industrial structure unmatched by any other region that was unchallenged until the very end of the century. After 1950 it would also be the first state to develop a modern durable and capital goods sector along with the traditional consumer goods industries. It was during the second half of the 1950s, under the government of Juscelino Kubitschek, that an intense process of induced government-supported industrialization occurred, which involved, among other areas, the establishment of a modern automobile industry in Brazil. Under this policy, São Paulo would further strengthen its role of industrial leadership because it housed most of this new automotive industry with its complex supply chain, and in turn this industry would become the main dynamic element of the Brazilian economy.[72]

All this industrial and agricultural dynamism was due to the state undertaking massive investments in infrastructure. From railroads to modern road networks the state would prove to be the leader in the nation. While this investment in infrastructure was driven by the need for exporting coffee cheaply and efficiently, it also led to the major integration of the state, as the frontier finally came to an end by the 1940s. It also led to the emergence of São Paulo as one of the leading metropolises in Brazil and eventually its single largest urban center.

Chapter 8

Infrastructure and Urbanization of the State

If the period of growth for the state of São Paulo can be defined by the maturation of the coffee economy and the entrance of São Paulo into the world economy, it is also distinguished by the creation of a modern communications network, the construction of a massive hydroelectric complex, and the birth of a major world metropolis from a previously undistinguished urban center. All of these developments were made possible by major investments of the state and of the private sector in the basic infrastructure.

As we emphasize in previous chapters, modern and cheap transport was one of the crucial factors that the planter aristocracy needed to resolve if the Paulista economy was to grow and meet international demand for coffee. But the arrival of the railroad age to Brazil was a slow and costly project that really did not get started until the middle of the nineteenth century. The first railroad law in Brazil was issued in October 1835 by the imperial government and offered a concession to any private company that would build a railroad from Rio de Janeiro to the state capitals of Minas Gerais, Rio Grande do Sul, and Bahia. In 1838 it was the turn of the provincial assembly of São Paulo that in this case authorized a particular group of investors to build a railroad from Santos to the interior.[1] From the middle of the nineteenth century the necessity of creating an efficient rail transportation system to ship coffee to the coast was recognized as a fundamental necessity. The traditional system of transporting the crop by thousands of mules was costly and limited the potential expansion of the system. But all these early railroad concession laws and private attempts to construct railroad lines in the 1830s and 1840s ended in failure.[2] The key problem they all faced was lack of funding. These first frustrated projects were just concessions of zones of exclusion along the railroad lines. But this exclusivity was not sufficient to guarantee the economic viability of the enterprises. The solution came in 1853 when the government decided to guarantee interest on the funds invested in railroad construction.[3] The Estrada de Ferro D. Pedro II, which went from Rio de Janeiro to Cachoeira, in the province of São Paulo, was the first railroad to be successfully built. Along with granting an exclusive control over the length of the railroad line, the central government guaranteed a return of 7 percent to investors, of which 2 percentage points came from the provincial government of Rio de Janeiro. This railroad finally reached Vassouras in 1865 but did not arrive in Cachoeira until twenty years later.[4] The railroad proved to be a crucial one since it served the major coffee region of Vale do Paraíba, permitting the export of coffee by rail to the port of Rio de Janeiro.[5]

The western Paulista coffee zones continued to rely on mule transport to reach their natural export port of Santos until the late 1860s.[6] In 1867 the São Paulo Railway was finally inaugurated, which connected Santos to the city of Jundiaí, which was the traditional entrance to the western Paulista region. The English company that built the railroad had the same guarantee of 7 percent return on its investment, with 2 percentage points of that interest coming from the province of São Paulo.[7] Now the pace increased everywhere in Brazil, with the most concentration of railroad lines occurring in the province of São Paulo. Using local planter funds as well as foreign capital, a complex railroad network was created that spread through the interior of the province and even reached the unexplored backlands.[8] The railroads permitted the exploitation of lands of exceptional quality, particularly suited for coffee cultivation.

Once strong financial guarantees were established, capital arrived quickly, and the second half of the nineteenth century and first decades of the twentieth century can be described as the railroad era in the history of the state. São Paulo quickly became the leader of rail construction in Brazil, outpacing all other state systems.[9] In 1860 the British-owned São Paulo Railway Company was formed to construct a line from the port of Santos to Jundiaí in the highlands. Construction began in that year and the railroad was completed in 1867—a total of 139 kilometers that also passed through the capital city of São Paulo. This would become one of the most important railroads carrying coffee. The railroads that opened up the interior regions were the Companhia Paulista de Estrada de Ferro, which was founded with Brazilian and English capital in 1868, and the Mogiana railroad.[10] When the São Paulo Railway Company rejected initial requests to extend its lines beyond Jundiaí, the Paulista and the Mogiana companies were given concessions to extend the line from Jundiaí to the interior or to connect interior cities to Campinas and other major terminal centers. By 1872 the Companhia Paulista finished its line from Jundiaí to Campinas and then reached Rio Claro by 1876. This railroad was continually extended in the 1880s until it reached the Mogy-Guassú region, just behind the Mogiana railroad, which extended its line also from Campinas to this thriving coffee município in 1875. Eventually, it was the Mogiana that continued on to Ribeirão Preto, and in response the Companhia Paulista initially opened up a steamer service in 1884 to these same towns along the Mogy-Guassú River and then in 1891 bought the Rio Claro Railway Company.[11] By 1893 the Companhia Paulista was moving over 1 million passengers and 121,000 metric tons of coffee.[12] In a complex history of smaller lines created and concessions granted to wealthy individuals as political gifts, the various smaller railroads were eventually incorporated into the Companhia Paulista and the Mogiana, and these two lines were able to open up the entire northern and western coffee regions. The Companhia Mogiana de Estrada de Ferro connected the regions to the northeastern part of the state and into the neighboring state of Minas Gerais and proved to be the second-most important of the interior coffee railroads.

The Companhia Mogiana was established in 1872 to run a line from Campinas to Mogi Mirim that was completed three years later. This company then obtained new concessions in 1880 to extend its line farther into the interior, one branch reaching Itapira and the main line reaching Ribeirão Preto in 1883. Other branches were constructed by this company in the late 1880s, one of which reached Franca in 1887 and others reached Canoas in 1891 and Serra Negra in 1892 with a branch line (Ramal Fazenda Dumont) finished in 1900.

Finally, the Companhia Sorocabana was founded in 1870 and completed most of its basic network by the 1880s, and it opened up the southern and western regions to coffee production. Several new smaller companies were formed in the 1880s that constructed local lines. Then in the 1890s the São Paulo Railway Company was granted the right to build a second set of tracks from Santos to Jundiaí.[13] Another important route was the construction of a branch line from the capital through Vale do Paraíba, connecting with the Dom Pedro II line from Cachoeira, Rio de Janeiro, which was begun in 1875 and completed in 1877. Between this railroad link and the

São Paulo Company lines, railroads now connected the ports of both Rio de Janeiro and Santos with the capital of São Paulo.

Once state subsidies were firmly established, expansion was rapid. It was estimated that by 1895 British nationals had invested £33 million in Brazilian railroads—their largest nonpublic investment in the country.[14] In the 1870s over a thousand kilometers were constructed, and the same occurred in the 1880s. Even in the 1890s some 984 kilometers were built.[15] Each decade saw almost a doubling of tracks. By 1877 the state railroads reached close to two thousand kilometers and by 1897 the railroads exceeded three thousand kilometers.[16]

The network of railroads completed in the last quarter of the century created a transport revolution within the state and reduced costs sufficiently so that Brazilian coffee could successfully compete on the world market. Already by the late 1870s the railroads had displaced mules as the basic transport in the state and the majority of Paulista coffee now moved by rail to the port of Santos. With this change, the port of Rio de Janeiro no longer took any significant share of Paulista production, especially with the progressive decline of Vale do Paraíba, whose natural outlet had been the ports of São Sebastião and Rio de Janeiro. The bulk of these coffee exports to Santos was dominated by just three companies—the Paulista, São Paulo Railway, and the Mogiana, which together carried 92 percent of the state's 800,000 metric tons of coffee produced in 1898 to the port of Santos (see Table 8.1).

Along with moving coffee, these railroads opened up previously unsettled land—that is, land not exploited by the non-Indian populations—and they essentially defined the placement of both cities and farms within the central and western parts of the state. Moreover, while the logic of their implementation was to reduce the transport costs of coffee from the most fertile lands, the railway moved other types of goods between ports and between different regions of the state, thus creating more integrated regional markets, for domestic production as well as for imports.[17] The railroads also played an essential role in the movement of passengers. Previously, goods and passengers had been transported by an extremely precarious mule transport system because there were few wagon roads available in the state. Thus, the emergence of the rail system had an important modernizing social, as well as economic, impact. In this same year of 1898 all the railroads, besides moving coffee, carried 5.4 million passengers, and the Mogiana and Sorocabana lines—at two different ends of the state—moved almost 145,000 metric tons of cereals. It is estimated that in this year some 17 percent of the income of these railroads came from their passenger service and

TABLE 8.1
Coffee, Cereals, and Passengers Carried by São Paulo Railroads, 1898

Railway	Coffee (t)	Coffee (%)	Number of passengers	Passengers (%)	Cereals (t)	Cereals (%)
São Paulo Railway	327,715	40.9%	1,267,404	23.1%		
Paulista	260,557	32.5%	1,248,553	22.8%		
Mogiana	151,033	18.9%	1,219,398	22.3%	76,531	52.9%
Sorocabana e Ituana	44,976	5.6%	573,698	10.5%	65,817	45.5%
Ramal Dumont	6,929	0.9%	30,534	0.6%	588	0.4%
Ramal Ferreo Campineira	5,857	0.7%	73,689	1.3%		
Rezende a Bocaina	1,381	0.2%	16,469	0.3%		
Carril Itatibense	1,275	0.2%	35,585	0.6%	1,151	0.8%
Bananalense	655	0.1%	8,581	0.2%	363	0.3%
Araraquarense e Ribeirãozinho	167	0.0%	3,948	0.1%	176	0.1%
Bragantina			42,203	0.8%		
Estrada Ferro São Paulo a Santo Amaro			957,003	17.5%		
Total	800,545	100.0%	5,477,065	100.0%	144,626	100.0%

SOURCE: Departamento de Estatística do Estado, *Anuário estatístico de São Paulo, 1898*, 508–509.

another 4 percent from their baggage, parcel, and telegram service, whereas the movement of agricultural products accounted for 77 percent of their total income.[18]

The Paulista railroads were also major employers of salaried workers and established machine shops and other advanced technical facilities and were thus on the frontier of early mechanization. By 1900 its railways employed over ten thousand permanent workers and used several thousand more as part-time construction workers.[19] These several thousand temporary free immigrant and native-born workers were hired through labor contractors for the constructing of new lines.[20] These São Paulo rail lines in the same year of 1900 used 268 steam locomotives and had rolling stock of over 5,000 cargo wagons and coaches. But unlike other countries that established their railroads at more advanced stages of their industrialization, the railroad's backward linkage was reduced in Brazil, since most inputs for the construction and operation of the railroads were imported.[21] Moreover, the state played an extremely important role even as an owner of railroads. Not only did the state guarantee a return on the private capital invested, but over time the government began to take control of the companies themselves because the railroads were often in deficit.

Once the railroads had connected to the ports, there was also a fundamental necessity to construct modern docks and dredge canals in order to accommodate oceangoing vessels. After numerous plans and projects, the first modern dock was constructed in the port of Rio de Janeiro under the direction of André Rebouças, and it was the first project in Brazil to use portland cement. In the 1870s further docks were constructed in the imperial capital, and the major expansion of docks was completed by a foreign company between 1890 and 1910. After numerous studies and abandoned projects, in 1888 the private national company Melhoramentos do Porto de Santos was finally incorporated. The first docks were built in the port by the 1890s, and the basic structure of some 4,719 meters of docks was reached by 1909. With the completion of these extensive docks, sixteen warehouses, and the dredging of the canal to ten meters below low tide, Santos became the most modern port in the country.[22] Already in 1905 these docks displaced the older barge system and were able to handle the entire coffee crop of São Paulo of that year, directly uploading to oceangoing vessels moored to these docks. The port also now became a major center for passengers and between 1901 and 1909 had an annual average of 47,000 passengers arriving in and 41,000 leaving from Santos.[23]

This construction of a modern port at Santos was a fundamental link in the communications infrastructure since it eliminated costly and time-consuming offloading of ships to barges and permitted ships to directly load from the land. Also, the dredging allowed ever-larger ships to dock in the port, which could now accept the largest ocean liners. By the 1880s Santos, a late entry among the major Atlantic ports, had become one of the four busiest ports of the South Atlantic, along with Rio de Janeiro, Montevideo, and Buenos Aires.[24] In that period it received 277,000 metric tons of foreign shipping, of which 40 percent was English, 39 percent German, and 11 percent French. Nevertheless, this was less than a quarter of the tonnage of foreign vessels arriving in Rio and less than half the tonnage going to Montevideo. At this point Buenos Aires received the most tonnage. But by 1913 Santos was receiving 4.4 million metric tons of foreign shipping.[25] The docks of Santos were completed just as the regular steamship routes were being established to South America.[26] All these factors—direct rail connection from Santos to the interior, modern docks, and regular steamship arrivals from Europe—came together in this period and resulted in Santos becoming a major South Atlantic port and the primary port for the arrival of immigrants and the exporting of coffee.[27]

Along with speedy trains, modern docks, and dredged ports that could accommodate transatlantic vessels, electric wires soon replaced flags, signal stations, and horses. Modern communications began in Brazil in 1852 with the introduction of the first electrical telegraph system. By 1858 the first intercity line opened between the imperial capital and Petrópolis—a distance of 50 kilometers. But expansion was relatively slow, and it took the war with Paraguay to finally convince the government to expand the system. A telegraph line was built from Rio de Janeiro to Porto Alegre in 1866. In 1869 the telegraph was declared a state monopoly, though private companies were invited to construct the system. In the 1870s foreign companies were granted sixty-year concessions to construct marine cables linking the entire coast, and by the end of the decade there were over 2,000 kilometers of telegraph lines with 51 stations within the empire. In this same decade lines crossed the frontier into Uruguay and Argentina. In 1874 a marine cable linking Brazil to Portugal was opened, and the line to the United States was finished in 1886. By the end of the empire there were some 19,000 kilometers of lines and 182 stations, with volume reaching 637,000 telegrams in a year. In 1891 the new republican government gave the states control over their own lines and the ability to construct new ones—now mostly built by the expanding railroads—and further connected Brazil with new submarine cables to Africa and the United States. By this decade average volume of traffic had tripled. Most of the basic system connecting almost all parts of the country had been completed by the first decade of the new century.[28]

The telephone era began soon after. Private and public telephone lines were built in the 1870s in Rio de Janeiro. The first concession was granted in 1879, and by 1881 it, along with the telegraph lines, was now considered a state monopoly, though as usual private concessions were granted to foreign and national companies to build lines. But growth was relatively slow even though both state and federal governments after 1889 were establishing telephone lines. Eventually, most of the local companies were taken over by the Canadian Brazilian Traction, Light, and Power Company, which was the big electricity company that served the cities of Rio de Janeiro and São Paulo. But real growth occurred only after World War I. In 1915 there were some 40,000 telephone subscribers in Brazil, and by 1921 that figure had more than doubled to 85,000.[29]

What is evident from this general history of these two key infrastructural networks is that most of the initial development under the empire was concentrated in Rio de Janeiro. Thus, São Paulo was always behind the developments of its neighbor until the republic was established. But once the state had the power to develop its own systems under the new republican constitution, São Paulo quickly began to expand and achieve comparable rates to Rio de Janeiro. Given that most of the telegraph system was developed by the railroads, the fact that São Paulo was the leading railroad state in terms of the size of its network by the beginning of the twentieth century meant that it had one of the more extensive telegraph systems in the country. By 1910 it contained 11 percent of the 31,000 kilometers of telegraph lines in the country and conveyed some 11 percent of the total telegrams.[30]

But it expanded even faster with telephone installations. In 1907 the state of Rio de Janeiro and the associated Federal District had less than 500 kilometers of telephone lines, compared to 12,000 kilometers for São Paulo and 5,000 kilometers for the state of Rio Grande do Sul. In the entire country at this time there were only some 20,000 kilometers. São Paulo was also the leading state by far in the number of telephones used, having a third of the 15,000 in all of Brazil at this time.[31] By 1920 the state figure had risen to some 37,000 telephone subscribers—or roughly 44 percent of all the Brazilian subscribers existing in the previous year.[32] But just as telephone distribution within Brazil was highly skewed toward a few states, so too was the distribution of telephones within the state highly biased. The capital and the coastal region around Santos had 69 percent of the 137,000 telephones in the state in 1940 but contained only 29 percent of the state population. This meant that in the capital region there were 31 telephones per thousand resident population, and the Santos coastal region had 27 telephones per thousand residents. But the state as a whole averaged only 13 telephones per thousand population.[33]

This growing communications network, as well as São Paulo's industrial growth, was increasingly dependent on the installation of a modern network of electricity generation and distribution that could produce electricity and deliver it throughout the state. This was a need well recognized by the Paulista elite even in the imperial period. The earliest activity in this area was nighttime illumination, and the first product to be used after oil lamps was gas. The first gas lamps were introduced in London in the 1810s and 1820s. For most of the nineteenth century it was gas that lit the streets of Europe and America. By the 1870s English companies began producing gas and illumination for several of the cities in the state.[34] But the discovery and development of electricity in the first half of the nineteenth century would lead to the eventual emergence of electric motors and an electricity-generating industry in the second half of the nineteenth century. By the 1870s electric lamps were slowly emerging as competitors to gas, and by the 1870s and 1880s electric incandescent lamps were appearing in European and North American cities. In the 1880s several inventors finally created central electricity-generating plants based on both steam and hydroelectric power. It was also in the 1880s that the first electric motors were introduced to tramways and trolleys in Europe and the United States, and it was in the 1890s that Europe and North America finally established the first long-distance power lines. While both types of generation were used worldwide, in the case of São Paulo its abundant rivers guaranteed that it was hydroelectric power rather than steam engines that fueled most of the electricity-generating plants. The state experienced a veritable boom in hydroelectric power plant construction in the period from the 1890s to 1914.[35] Thus, Brazil entered the electricity age at roughly the same time as all other nations and was to depend more on hydroelectric power than most other nations. Even today, 83 percent of Brazil's electricity consumption comes from hydroelectric plants.[36]

Just as with the railroads, European and North American innovation soon reached the shores of Brazil. The growth of electricity-producing companies was fairly chaotic in the early period with concessions being granted, revoked, or purchased by other early investors. Brazilian, European, and North American capitalists became involved in electricity-generating projects throughout Brazil, usually evolving out of the provision of public lighting contracts, for the establishment of tramways or for telephone installations, all of which required the generation and distribution of electricity. A branch of the German company Siemens first started in the Federal District, and Canadian companies received the early contracts in the case of São Paulo. The two Canadian investors who created the São Paulo Tramway, Light, and Power Company had been investors in the Canadian Pacific Railway and had participated in establishing streetcar service in Toronto, Canada, and Birmingham, England. In coming to Brazil these associates also had close contacts with the Paulista elite, several of whom became members of their company when it was founded in April 1899. The company was granted statewide rights to generate electricity for its trams. The Canadian group soon brought in Frederick Stark Pearson and his group of New York electrical engineers, who had built numerous power-generating systems throughout the United States and Europe, as an associate to build a hydroelectric plant at Parnaíba on the Tietê River some thirty-six kilometers from the capital city.[37] Rights to that site were given by the local municípios in return for public illumination. The São Paulo Light company engineers had surveyed the site in 1898, and using equipment made by General Electric in the United States, they were able to finish the dam and generating station and start producing electricity in 1901. By 1902 this station was proving to be the major source of electricity in the state.[38]

This was not the first such hydroelectric generating plant in Brazil; that distinction went to the city of Juiz de Fora in Minas Gerais, where in 1889 a plant generating 250 kilowatts was constructed by a local textile company for its own energy source. This was soon followed by several other local municipal plants and private-company generators—all using water power given the lack of coal in the country and the abundant availability of water. By 1900, the year that the Parnaíba plant went into production, there were already ten such generating plants with a capacity of some 12,000 kilowatts of power in the country. But the Parnaíba plant with its initial 2,000-kilowatt output (later doubled to 4,000 kilowatts in 1903) was the largest single electricity-generating plant built up to that time in the country. Its capacity was increased by a factor of three when a new dam at Guarapirangá was built in 1912. By then the Parnaíba plant had reached capacity, and in 1911 the company decided to build this new dam and generating station on the Sorocaba River. A third company was organized by the Canadians, called the São Paulo Electric Company, to build this plant, which began to produce electricity in 1912 and by 1914 was generating 37,000 kilowatts. With these two plants in operation São Paulo Light was able to offer more energy than was consumed in the state up until the 1940s. By 1920 some 95 percent of the power produced in the state came from its dams, and in turn São Paulo quickly passed Rio de Janeiro as the leading producer of electricity. In that year it produced 43 percent of Brazil's electricity and accounted for over half of all hydroelectricity produced in the country.[39]

The construction of the first electrical tramway lines began in the city of São Paulo in June of 1899. In that same year the Canadians bought the Companhia Água e Luz and a year later the Viação Paulista, which in turn had absorbed earlier tram companies mostly started in the 1870s that had used animal traction.[40] By 1905 São Paulo Light was transporting 20 million people in its electric motor trolleys in the capital, and in 1913 it took over the English-owned San Paulo Gas Company, which had been founded in 1872. With this purchase São Paulo Light finally had a monopoly on the provision of gas and electricity for the city of São Paulo and was now its only provider of trolleys and trams. So successful was the company in São Paulo that in 1904 it founded the Rio de Janeiro Light and Power Company, which eventually bought the local tramway and gas companies and all other competitors there and became the same type of dominant player in the federal capital as it was in São Paulo. Moreover, given the initially much larger size of the city of Rio de Janeiro, which was also the federal capital, Rio de Janeiro Light was at first a much larger entity than São Paulo

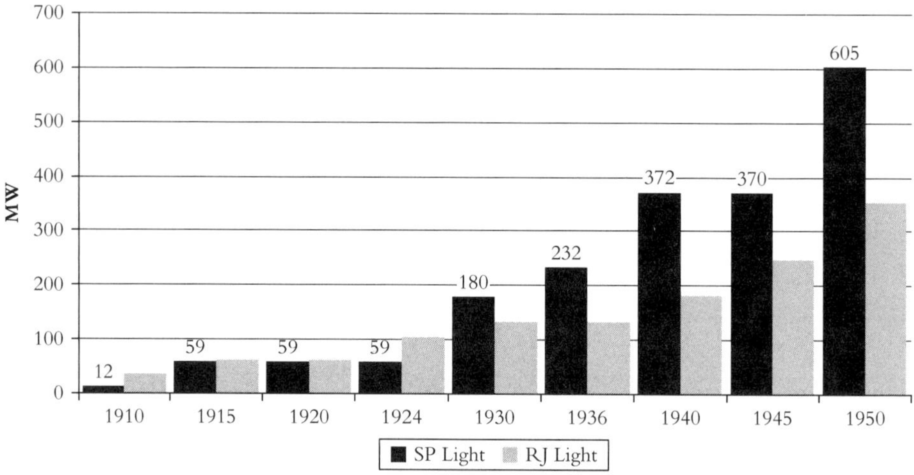

Figure 8.1 Comparative Growth of Electricity Production of the São Paulo and Rio de Janeiro Light Companies, 1910–1950

SOURCE: Jourdan, "A Light, investimentos estrangeiros no Brasil," 68.

Light, though this would change by the 1930s (see Figure 8.1).[41] All these various distinct units were finally integrated into the Canadian-based Brazilian Traction, Light, and Power, which was founded in Canada in 1912.[42] Although a dominant player, Brazilian Traction was not the only producer of electricity in the state. In a state industrial survey of 1932, there were listed 85 electricity-generating companies operating in the state, producing 412,000 horsepower of electricity and employing 8,277 workers. Out of this total the two major Paulista firms of the Canadian company accounted for 55 percent of the generated electricity and 72 percent of the workers employed by the industry.[43] By 1950, the companies in São Paulo and Rio de Janeiro that made up Brazilian Traction produced 50 percent of the nation's electricity.[44]

All this electricity was initially directed toward urban illumination, urban transport, and industrial production. The lighting of cities had been a fundamental concern of the imperial government and then the state government after 1889. Lighting was done with oil and then gas by the middle decades of the nineteenth century. By the end of the century electrical lighting of various kinds was becoming more common. By 1902, for example, the 172 municípios of the state had almost 17,000 public lamps, of which 18 percent were now powered by electricity, compared to 36 percent still powered by gas and 46 percent by kerosene.[45] This same slow process was also seen in the evolution of the tramway system in all the cities. Horse-drawn trolleys had become the norm even before the end of the empire. It was not until the late 1870s that European inventors had created electric motors small enough to run such trolleys, with the first successful trains established in the next decades. By the 1890s such electric trolleys were still a minority in Europe and North America, but by the first decade of the twentieth century they had replaced animal-powered trolleys everywhere.[46] Thus, Brazil was not far behind when in 1897 and again in 1899 the municipality of São Paulo granted to two different groups the right to construct the first electrified system in the city. Eventually, São Paulo Light took over both these concessions,[47] and in May 1900 the first electric trolley began to function in the city of São Paulo.[48] Growth of this trolley system was rapid, and by 1907 it was all electrified. In that year the company had over 800 workers, ran some 144 passenger trolleys, and transported 23 million persons. There was also a horse-driven system in Campinas that moved 353,000 passengers in a year and functioning trolleys in Santos and Taubaté.[49] By 1910 the São Paulo Light tramways had 1,200 workers, moved 33 million persons, and had 165 kilometers of rail, which was on a vastly different scale from other tramways in the state. The Campinas trolleys extended only 11 kilometers, and the Taubaté to Tremembé line had just 9 kilometers.[50]

Along with transport and power networks, the São Paulo elite was also concerned with creating a healthy environment in the state. Thus, along with railroads, streetcars, electricity, and public illumination, the proper elimination of sewage as well as the provisioning of potable water became prime concerns of the Paulista elite for the newly developing urban centers. That elite was concerned with not only its own welfare but also that of the newly arriving immigrants, who would be more susceptible to local disease environments than the native born, and their higher death rates potentially could be a negative factor in attracting the vital labor force needed to work the coffee estates.[51] This concern went back to the imperial period and would become a dominant interest of the new republican state government, which actively invested funds in this area.[52] The state was particularly susceptible to air- and waterborne diseases—above all, yellow fever, malaria, bubonic plague, and tuberculosis, which spread more easily once the railroads connected all the urban centers of the state.[53] While malaria was spread from the coast to the interior and became endemic, yellow fever epidemics were short-term events and massive killers. They were an almost annual scourge in the port of Rio de Janeiro in the late nineteenth century, and the one in Santos in 1892 is said to have killed 6 percent of the population. A major outbreak occurred in Campinas in the 1880s and 1890s, and another in Ribeirão Preto in 1901 led to the first systematic quarantine of that city under the leading medical researcher of the state, Emílio Ribas.[54] Bubonic plague was associated with grain imports from Argentina and affected all the railroad cities where grain was stored. In 1902, for example, Oswaldo Cruz led a campaign against rats in the port of Santos.[55]

Even before the bacteriological revolution that finally led to the control of yellow fever and bubonic plague by the first decade of the twentieth century, the sanitation movement of the late nineteenth century had argued that these contagious diseases were associated with improper water sources and sewage disposal. Influenced by these European ideas, the local elite pushed for changes in all the cities. No modern water or sewage works were built in Brazil before 1860. Although aqueducts and public water fountains (*chafarizes*) were constructed in the colonial and early nineteenth century, they were fed by ducts open to the sky from natural sources of water, with no attempts made at purification. Similarly, human waste was deposited in jars or in simple wells, and rainwater was not controlled.[56] But influenced by European ideas on sanitation, the Paulista political class became committed to adopting these hygiene programs in the state. These groups had pressured the old imperial government for change, but they had more influence in the new state republican regime. Their aim was to create safe water, sewage, and rainwater control for the major urban centers of the state. Moreover, they held that if private capital could not accomplish these ends, then the state should provide the funds. This sanitation movement also sought to create public awareness of personal and familial hygienic issues and, in the case of São Paulo, even succeeded in influencing housing laws in the cities.[57]

The result of their efforts was the beginning of sewage and water system construction throughout the state in the late nineteenth century that would eventually have a significant impact on reducing infant and child mortality.[58] They also paid for the establishment of a complex of research institutes, hospitals, and medical school and a state department of health in the new republican era, all of which had a major impact on the urban and rural health of the state.[59] Already under the empire major engineering efforts were begun to bring pure water into the cities of São Paulo, Santos, and Campinas—that activity was now recognized as an essential obligation of the state.[60] As early as 1877 the mixed public-private Companhia Cantareira de Águas e Esgotos was established to provide water and sewage facilities for the capital. This company was able to deliver pure water to the capital city in 1881 and to build its first sewers in 1883. By this decade the company was able to provide canalized water to 3,000 buildings in the capital and carried 3,000 cubic meters of water per day. But unsatisfied with the results, the state government annulled the contract and created its own Repartição de Águas e Esgotos da Capital (RAE) in 1892.[61] By the 1890s this state organization had built 90 kilometers of sewage piping for the capital city. In 1887 a private company, Companhia Campineira de Águas e Esgotos, was granted the concession for Campinas, but by the new century it too would become a state enterprise. In 1892 the state also created the Comissão de Saneamento de Santos, which in the first decade of the new century constructed a complex system separating rainwater from human waste in this crucial port city. Despite debates about direct purification versus opening up new pure water sources, the latter activity was encouraged, and it was not until the 1920s that there was undertaken the first systematic use of chemicals to purify water in Brazil. By then the polytechnic schools of Rio de Janeiro, São Paulo, and Porto Alegre were producing civil engineers capable of building water and sewage systems, and a national industry of iron pipes was established that could compete with imported products. As early as 1903 some twenty-five Paulista cities had enclosed water piping systems in operation with more in construction, and by the 1910s practically all the state's major cities had piped-in water going to private homes. In 1910 Santos was the first Brazilian city to begin treating human waste, followed by São Paulo in 1911.[62] By 1945 the state had built 2.5 million kilometers of sewers that went to 262,000 buildings, and it was supplying 6.8 billion gallons of water every twenty-four hours to 376,000 buildings in its various cities and towns.[63] While this is significant, it was still not adequate coverage. It was estimated that the capital alone had 248,000 buildings in 1947.[64] Nevertheless, even despite their incomplete coverage, these impressive public works, when accompanied by vaccination and health campaigns, finally rid the cities of the state from plagues and most infectious disease epidemics.

The state also began a serious effort to create major institutions of public health to deal with this issue on a long-term basis. Although smallpox vaccination had been introduced to Brazil early in the nineteenth century, vaccination was not universal and was little applied until the emergence of the republic.[65] In late 1891 the São Paulo government passed a law mandating vaccination for all citizens for smallpox and provided for the creation of vaccine-producing laboratories. In 1892 came the previously mentioned government funding for municipal water and sewage projects, and in 1893 the provincial government finally created the important State Sanitary

Bureau (Serviço Sanitário do Estado) that scholars consider to be the beginnings of the modern state public health system in Brazil. The service was led by the distinguished scientist Adolfo Lutz and had considerable government funding. Lutz set up a vaccine-producing laboratory and in the next year came the Instituto Bacteriológico. This became a major laboratory for studying epidemic diseases, and in 1901 an autonomous laboratory was spun off from the Biological Institute for the analysis of venomous toxins and the production of antitoxins, which would eventually become known as the Instituto Butantan.[66] Numerous other institutions were supported by the state in the area of public health, and the control of epidemics became a central concern of the state officials.[67] In fact, a pioneering local medical leader, Emílio Ribas, who became head of the state's *serviço sanitário* in 1898, is credited, along with Adolfo Lutz, with controlling yellow fever throughout the state via elimination of the breeding grounds for the mosquito carrying the disease. Ribas and Lutz proved by rigorous testing in 1902–1903 that previous findings in Cuba that mosquitoes were the vector were accurate, and they thus implemented an eradication campaign. As late as the 1880s yellow fever had struck the coast and highland cities. But through their efforts the disease had disappeared from the cities of São Paulo and Rio de Janeiro by 1908.[68]

These early state efforts continued to evolve in the 1930s and 1940s, which was a new period of expansion in the area of public health for both private and public funding, an area in which the state was already a leader in the nation. Already in 1934 São Paulo had the largest number of hospitals and clinics, with capacity to house patients greater than any other state in the country. Its 165 hospitals housed some 125,000 patients, and these represented 23 percent and 28 percent, respectively, of the national totals, this when the state had only 16 percent of the national population.[69] By 1942 it had 281 such hospitals.[70] But most of this hospital growth was from private organizations, with the state participating with only a modest investment. Of the total of 580 hospitals and clinics listed for São Paulo in 1950 (now 31 percent of these establishments in the nation), only 61 were maintained by the state. But there was now a more even distribution of these health facilities within the state, with the capital having only 161 such units and the interior municípios having the rest.[71] São Paulo also had the most doctors. By 1950 its 1,043 doctors accounted for 34 percent of the national total (when the state accounted for 18 percent of the total population), and their distribution was much like the hospitals, with only 10 percent of them working in the capital.[72] Nurses in São Paulo accounted for 22 percent of the 1,239 in the nation, but unlike doctors São Paulo's 275 nurses were concentrated in the big hospitals in the capital of São Paulo, which accounted for the fact that 45 percent of the nurses in the state were in the city of São Paulo. The capital also had an unusual concentration of dentists. Some 42 percent of the 780 dentists in the country in 1950 resided in the state, and like the nurses, they were mostly (87 percent) in the capital city.[73] Clearly, the rural areas of the state and most of the nation lacked dentists and nurses, though the lack was less for doctors. By 1950 São Paulo was thus the state with the most important set of hospitals and health professionals in the nation.

The republican government equally promoted advanced engineering, medical, and agricultural education. A Politécnica de São Paulo school was founded in 1893 to train engineers and agronomists, and it was Antônio Francisco de Paula, a European-trained engineer and at the time president of the provincial assembly, who pushed through the creation of this key institution, which educated an important group of engineers, many of whom played key roles in state and local governments. Then in 1899 the state established pharmacy and dental schools. A medical school, the Faculdade de Medicina e Cirurgia de São Paulo, was established in 1913, and in 1918 a public health school, the Faculdade de Higiene e Saúde Pública, was established. By 1913 the Faculdade de Medicina e Cirurgia de São Paulo had 180 students, of which 6 were women, and the Escola Politécnica de São Paulo had 359 students in all courses. Along with this state activity, a group of private physicians in the early 1930s created the Escola Paulista de Medicina. The state also supported some ten normal schools to train teachers, only two of which were in the capital. However, these two capital schools matriculated 44 percent of all students studying for a teaching degree. This was, unlike medicine and engineering, primarily a field for women. Of the 3,704 students enrolled in these teacher training programs, three-quarters were women. As part of this expansion of higher education, private individuals even established the Escola Livre de Sociologia e Política.

Several of these faculties and schools would eventually be incorporated into the Universidade de São Paulo, which was established in 1934 and credited with being among the first modern research and educational universities in Brazil.[74] The local elite had been promoting the creation of a formal university under state control since the founding of the republic. Although Brazil had medical, law, and engineering schools early on, there was no single university established. But leading political leaders and industrialists in São Paulo succeeded in establishing the University of São Paulo by combining these various earlier faculties with a new Faculty of Science and Letters. The university was to be liberal, lay, and public and was initially modeled along the lines of a standard French university. France sent a mission of distinguished French academics to help establish the school, among whom were Claude Lévi-Strauss and Fernand Braudel. In its first year the Faculty of Science and Letters had scholars who came from France, Italy, and Germany teaching in all the sciences and social sciences. This was a revolutionary concept in Brazilian higher education, and it would take several years before this core faculty became a major part of the university and could finally establish its independence from the engineering, mining, law, and medical schools. But eventually this new Universidade de São Paulo and the Instituto Osvaldo Cruz of Rio de Janeiro developed as the true pioneers of modern Brazilian science.[75] Thus, very early in the new republic a well-educated technical elite was established in the state, and they were important in promoting a modern state government with a distinctly social vision of how the state could and should develop.[76]

Primary education also became a basic priority of the state government. Educational expenditures for the province of São Paulo had grown slowly through the nineteenth century and were still modest at the end of the empire. In contrast, the republican state government now put in a considerable effort to improve public education, from expanding schools to establishing normal schools for teacher education. By the quinquennium of 1902–1906, the state was spending almost seven times as much on education as it had spent in the last quinquennium of the empire. Three-quarters of this expenditure went to pay the costs of over a thousand primary schools, with funding also provided in 1905 for a normal school that had 309 students, the engineering school (escola politécnica), and two high schools (*ginásios*), one in the capital and the other in Campinas.[77] But the results were still modest. There were only 28,635 primary students matriculated in public schools in this year, although girls now represented 48 percent of all primary students.[78] Of concern to educators was the low level of attendance. It was estimated that only two-thirds of the students registered for state primary day school in 1913 attended classes, and the ratio for the state primary night schools was even lower, with just 31 percent who initially registered being in actual attendance.[79] Clearly, the costs of even primary education in an economy with a major component of child labor were too high for many families.

By 1909 the number of matriculated primary school students rose to 123,000, but this was out of some 433,000 children of school age, which meant that only 28 percent of the children of the state were receiving an education. Of those attending school, some 66 percent were in state elementary schools, 23 percent in private schools, and the remaining

11 percent were in municipal public schools. In addition, primary education was not evenly spread across the state. An estimated three-quarters of the children in the capital were in school, whereas the figures for Campinas and Santos were around half the school-age children; several of the other secondary cities were even lower (see Table 8.2).

What is evident from the data is that the state concentrated most of its resources on primary and professional education and left secondary education mostly to private groups. In a survey of institutions that supported education in the state in 1912, some 83 percent of the 178,000 primary students were in state or municipal schools, and if state-subsidized private schools are added, the state accounts for 90 percent of the primary school enrollments. Of these primary students 46 percent were girls. But in secondary education, even with state-supported private institutions, the state accounted for only 30 percent of the students. It had a larger role, however, in providing professional schools, accounting for 83 percent of students, although fewer in higher education, there accounting for less than half of all students. The capital received heavy state support and had a greater proportion of the secondary, professional, and higher education institutions than its population justified. While just under a quarter of the primary students in the state were enrolled in the capital, half of the secondary school students, two-thirds of the professional students, and 88 percent of those in higher education resided there.

For most of the first half of the twentieth century, the principal educational investment of the state was in basic primary education. In 1945, for example, in the middle schools, high schools, and normal schools, there were only some 35,000 students matriculated, compared to 833,000 primary school enrollments—in short, just 4 percent of those enrolled in elementary school were in middle schools. Moreover, the state paid for only

TABLE 8.2
School-Age Children and Types of Primary Schools, 1909

Major cities	School-age population	State schools	Municipal schools	Private schools	Total students	Children in school (%)
Capital	42,857	17,974	0	14,014	31,988	75%
Campinas	12,571	2,482	751	2,783	6,016	48%
Santos	11,571	1,603	889	3,530	6,022	52%
Ribeirão Preto	7,428	1,005	0	879	1,884	25%
Piracicaba	6,857	1,548	314	584	2,446	36%
State total	432,807	80,469	13,561	28,648	122,678	28%

SOURCE: Departamento de Estatística do Estado, *Anuário estatístico de São Paulo, 1909,* 2:202–204.

half of the schools that enrolled these secondary students.[80] In contrast, the state was the principal supplier of basic primary education. As late as 1949 it was estimated that the state schools had 83 percent of the close to 1 million of these matriculating elementary school students, with local municipal schools taking another 9 percent and private schools absorbing only 8 percent of them. In fact, it was mostly in the capital where these private schools flourished. Here the private primary schools accounted for 24 percent of the students, and the city had no municipally subsidized schools. It would appear that normal schools produced sufficient teachers to meet state demands, since 90 percent of the state's teachers were *normalistas*, or graduates of the normal schools. There appeared to be little sex bias among the students matriculating, girls being 46 percent of all students in the state and 48 percent of those elementary school students in the capital. But there continued to be a strong geographic bias in the state's educational effort and a neglect of the rural areas.[81] In the census of 1950, São Paulo had only 40 percent of its population living in cities, yet these cities accounted for 64 percent of the total of all elementary matriculated students in the state.[82] Nor did this ratio differ greatly over time. It was 64 percent in 1934 and the same in 1949 and never dropped below 59 percent in this sixteen-year period.

Although primary education remained the prime area of state investment for the early decades of the twentieth century, with significant investments in tertiary education, there was only a modest effort in secondary education. But late in the period there was a significant development with public and private funds in vocational training programs. In 1939, when decreeing that large companies with five hundred or more workers had to provide commissary facilities, the Getúlio Vargas government also required that such companies would maintain "courses of professional development" for their workers.[83] This idea of private industry-sponsored education was being pushed both by the new Ministry of Labor and also by the São Paulo industrial federation (Federação das Indústrias do Estado de São Paulo; FIESP) under the leadership of Roberto Simonsen, largely against the wishes of the Education Ministry.[84] Influenced by the German ideas of a modern industrial apprenticeship, the industrialists pushed for control over an area totally neglected by the state until that time. The result was the creation in 1942 of what would become one of the world's largest, modern, privately run industrial education systems. The first organization founded was the Serviço Nacional de Aprendizagem Industrial (SENAI) for training skilled workers for industry, and then in 1946 was established the Serviço Nacional de Aprendizagem Comercial (SENAC) for training workers for commerce. The industrialists convinced the federal government to create a payroll tax to develop a school system administered by the private industrial associations in each state. SENAI quickly established training courses and would enroll many thousands of students in short- and long-term programs and would even educate a future president of the republic. It was the state of São Paulo that led all this educational reform for the nation and it was here that the largest industrial educational training programs occurred.[85]

It was this concentration of educational resources in the city that primarily explains the unusually high literacy rate achieved by the capital well before the rest of the state. The state government provided the capital with far greater resources than the rest of the state in terms of primary education, which attracted a large share of the primary graduates from the interior of the state given the capital's dominant role in secondary, professional, and higher education. Thus, by the census of 1920, the city had a literacy rate for persons fifteen years of age and older of 71 percent, compared to 42 percent for the state as a whole.[86] This sharp difference continued into the next decade. In a state census carried out in 1934, the capital came in at an even higher rate of literacy (this time using the base of age six and older) than did the state as a whole, where the majority of persons were still illiterate. This gap between the city and the rest of the state was still evident in the census of 1950. In fact, this difference occurred in all the urban centers of the state, which were almost twice as literate as the rural areas and with the gap being even greater for women. Moreover, despite the increasing education of women, all regions of the state still had a 9 to 14 percentage point difference between male and female literacy rates (see Table 8.3). Although the state was the leader in literacy within the nation by 1950, São Paulo's total literacy rate was below the total literacy rate of nine Latin American countries.[87]

The provisioning of basic hygiene in the more important urban centers of the state, establishment of institutions of research and education, improvement in transport, availability of electricity, and introduction of tramways all favored the growth of one major urban center and numerous smaller cities. With the need for capturing local capital, and an elite of absentee coffee barons who wanted a convenient place to enjoy their new wealth, it was inevitable that a major urban center would develop to concentrate the resources and elite residence in the state. Although the capital of the state would ultimately become one of the world's largest metropolises, this was not an inevitable outcome, according to the geographer Pierre Monbeig. For a time in the 1870s it looked as if Campinas, which then had roughly the same number of inhabitants as São Paulo, would surpass the capital.

TABLE 8.3
Literacy of São Paulo Population Five Years of Age and Older by Sex and Location, 1950

	Literate	Illiterate	Total	% literate
State				
Men	2,563,437	1,406,250	3,969,687	64.6%
Women	2,063,892	1,763,278	3,827,170	53.9%
Total	4,627,329	3,169,528	7,796,857	59.3%
Capital of São Paulo				
Men	754,846	126,507	881,353	85.6%
Women	705,333	214,096	919,429	76.7%
Subtotal	1,460,179	340,603	1,800,782	81.1%
All cities				
Men	1,614,767	344,794	1,959,561	82.4%
Women	1,475,543	571,702	2,047,245	72.1%
Subtotal	3,090,310	916,496	4,006,806	77.1%
Villages				
Men	76,901	31,395	108,296	71.0%
Women	59,251	45,093	104,344	56.8%
Subtotal	136,152	76,488	212,640	64.0%
Rural				
Men	871,769	1,030,061	1,901,830	45.8%
Women	529,098	1,146,483	1,675,581	31.6%
Subtotal	1,400,867	2,176,544	3,577,411	39.2%

SOURCE: Instituto Brasileiro de Geografia e Estatística, *Recenseamento geral do Brasil, 1950*, regional series, vol. 25, bk. 1, pp. 188, 192, table 46.

Campinas was the jumping-off city for the expansion of coffee to the west and was well connected to Santos by all the major new railroads being constructed. But the successive epidemics of yellow fever that struck Campinas in the 1880s led to its relative decline and the decision to concentrate all the capital and resources in the more climatically favorable city of São Paulo.[88]

The city of São Paulo, situated in a relatively poor agricultural region, did have some significant geographic advantages. In contrast to most of the Brazilian coastline, which easily opened up into the interior, the Atlantic littoral of the province of São Paulo was quite narrow, and its access to the rich highlands of the interior was blocked by a major mountain range, the Serra do Mar. Of the few valleys that connected the coast with the highland interior of the state, the best one was the valley leading up from Santos, and at the head of this easily ascending valley at the edge of plateau some thirty miles from the port in open plains with no forest growth was established the town of São Paulo in 1554. The settlement of São Paulo was in turn situated on a major waterway, the Tietê River, which served as a natural gateway to the rich interior highland grasslands and forests that would be settled by the coffee barons in the nineteenth and early twentieth centuries. This coast-to-highland valley and river system had been in use by Indian groups long before the arrival of the Portuguese, and in turn the river would be the major gateway of the *monções* (canoe convoys) expeditions that moved from the settlement of São Paulo deep into the interior in the colonial period in search of Indian slaves and mineral deposits. This same river in the late nineteenth and early twentieth centuries would also provide a ready source for hydroelectric power for the growing metropolis. Given its close ties to the coast, the capital would also grow in coordination with the port of Santos, one of the best natural ports on the Atlantic coast of Brazil. From a sleepy secondary port town primarily engaged in coastal trading and some fishing, Santos in the late nineteenth century would finally emerge as a major national and international port, surpassed only by Rio de Janeiro. By 1900 it had regular transatlantic service to Europe and even to North America, and it was growing as fast as the national capital.[89]

The richest new coffee lands opened up in the late nineteenth century by the railroads all connected to the capital and Santos as their natural outlet to the sea. Thus, the city of São Paulo became the secondary residence of the coffee fazendeiros, and with their wealth came theaters, restaurants, regal homes, and other amenities of a growing wealthy metropolis. Banks emerged to recycle the profits being generated in coffee, and the city quickly became the financial center of the state and the home of most of its industries. It also became the place of residence for foreign merchants who catered to the growing wealth of the planter class and the increasing consumption of the immigrant workers. Then in 1888 the government built the Hospedaria dos Imigrantes, which became the official and unique residence for recently arrived immigrants and a formal labor exchange for moving them into the interior coffee estates. The city thus became the focal point for the mass of European immigrants arriving into Santos, and while most moved to the coffee estates, a significant number of these European workers remained in the city and provided a more skilled and better-educated labor force.[90]

In the early days of its growth the capital drew more women to its urban districts than men, typical of a nineteenth-century city with a major domestic-servant labor market. Thus, in 1854 when the city had 25,000 residents, the ratio of its population was 95 males per 100 females, compared to the rest of the state's ratio of 109 males for every 100 females. As also could be expected, it had a much higher ratio of single persons over the age of ten compared to the rest of the state (66 percent in the city compared to 50 percent for the rest of the state).[91] The capital also had fewer slaves than the norm for the rest of the municípios, largely due to the lack of a significant agriculture either within the city limits or within the nearby rural districts. In 1872, for example, only 12 percent of its 31,000 residents were slaves, whereas the ratio in the rest of the state was 19 percent.[92] Most of these slaves were either domestics or artisans and unskilled laborers. Because it contained fewer slaves and more Europeans, the city was more "white" than the other urban and rural centers of the state. In a census of 1890, some 82 percent of the 65,000 residents were considered white, compared to only 62 percent of the state's population. As the city grew, it became a city even more dominated by the foreign born until the 1940s. Some 8 percent of the capital residents were foreign born in 1872, 22 percent in 1890, and 36 percent in 1920.[93] By 1920 the foreign born could be found throughout the city but were especially important in Brás, Bela Vista, Moóca, and Osasco, which had over 40 percent of their residents listed as foreign born.

With its growing wealth, its absorption of Asian and European immigrants, and its increasing attraction for native-born rural migrants, the urban population of the capital would expand at an ever more rapid pace. In the 1870s the city of São Paulo was still a small town with only some 26,000 residents and around 3,000 buildings being taxed. By the mid-1880s, it had increased its stock of housing to 7,000 buildings and its population to almost 50,000. By 1900 it had 22,000 buildings and a population of some 240,000 persons. It was the first city in the state to have electric tramways and was quickly following the pace of the Federal District of Rio de Janeiro in trolleys, electric lights, and telephones.[94] By 1912, when the city held about 411,000 persons, it had 39,000 buildings. One of the earliest detailed analyses of the housing stock of the city is provided by the results of the building tax of 1912. Of the eleven districts that made up the city in that year, the overwhelmingly wealthiest district was that of Sé, which housed all the principal government institutions and the cathedral. It had 40 percent of its buildings listed at the highest tax category (6 contos or more) and only 1 percent valued at the lowest rate (120–600 mil réis). In fact, no other district had even 2 percent of its buildings listed as the most expensive buildings, whereas more than half the buildings in each of five districts (Belémzinho, Villa Marianna, Cambucy, Sant'Anna, and Penha) were listed in the lowest valuation. Sé also had almost all the two-story buildings in the city.[95]

Little had changed by 1915 except in terms of the number of buildings and the increasing concentration of wealth. The district of Sé increased its share of the wealthiest structures, its district now containing 47 percent of its buildings being taxed at the highest rate. The next-closest districts were Santa Ephigenia and Consolação, with just 4 and 3 percent, respectively, of buildings valued at more than 6 contos. Sé had less than 1 percent of its buildings listed in the poorest categories, while of the fifteen districts that now made up the city, six had over half their buildings valued at the lowest level (120–600 mil réis).[96]

By 1920 the city contained 579,000 persons and listed 58,000 buildings being taxed. As usual Sé was by far the wealthiest district, with 48 percent of its buildings now taxed at the highest rate, and Santa Ephigenia and Consolação followed with just 3 percent each of such buildings. There were now twenty-one districts in the city, twelve of which had more than half their buildings taxed at the lowest rate, with the poorest being Casa Verde, where 95 percent of its buildings had the lowest tax valuation.[97]

Within a decade the city's population had passed a million persons. By the 1930s it was consuming more electricity than Rio de Janeiro because of its increasingly dominant industrial sector, though total population did not pass that of Rio de Janeiro until the late 1950s.[98] But the growth of the capital city of São Paulo was not initially matched by growth of urban centers in the rest of the state. Smaller cities began to expand, especially after the construction of the railroad opened up new regions or revitalized old ones as transit centers. But even with this slow urban growth of interior cities, a survey of 1937 found that only four other cities had populations of 25,000 or more residents. Of these urban centers, only Santos and Campinas had more than 50,000 residents. As late as 1940, in the census of that year only 38 percent of the state's population were listed as being urban.[99] Only Santos was now a significant urban center, with 156,000 persons compared to the 1.3 million now living in the capital city. In turn, Campinas, the third-largest city, was only half the size of Santos. Thus, the spectacular growth of the capital was not initially matched by the state's other cities, which grew at only moderate rates in the first four decades of the twentieth century (see Table 8.4).

Although the capital of São Paulo was still not that dominant within the nation, accounting for just 4.2 percent of the total Brazilian population in 1950, it was totally dominant in the state until late in the twentieth century. Nationally, it finally surpassed Rio de Janeiro as Brazil's largest city in 1960, and then, because of massive immigration, it reached 10.2 percent of the total national population by 1980. Its dominance also increased with each census within the state. In 1940, for example, the capital contained 18.5 percent of the state's residents, a figure that rose to 24.1 percent in

TABLE 8.4
State Cities with Populations Greater than 30,000, 1940

	URBAN			SUBURBAN			
Município	Male	Female	Total	Male	Female	Total	Grand total
São Paulo	569,647	592,246	1,161,893	49,683	46,906	96,589	1,258,482
Santos	60,952	57,944	118,896	19,178	17,820	36,998	155,894
Campinas	39,925	39,535	79,460	526	696	1,222	80,682
Sorocaba	22,784	24,002	46,786	682	643	1,325	48,111
Ribeirão Preto	21,811	24,103	45,914	535	497	1,032	46,946
Piracicaba	13,627	14,802	28,429	1,722	1,772	3,494	31,923

SOURCE: Instituto Brasileiro de Geografia e Estatística, *Recenseamento geral do Brasil, 1940,* regional series, part 17, vol. 2, pp. 545–560, table 63.

1950 and peaked at 33.8 percent by the end of the century.[100] This was occurring despite the significant growth in the next several decades of cities in the interior, which, however, were growing less quickly than the capital. As early as 1950 several cities began to approach the 20,000 level, and the number of cities that possessed 30,000 persons or more had increased two and a half times since 1940. New places emerged as important urban centers, but two of these new cities, Santo André and São Caetano, were part of greater metropolitan São Paulo and were centers for new industrial activity. Two autonomous cities were now becoming serious metropolitan centers: Campinas approached 100,000 and the port of Santos came close to 200,000 persons. Given the increasing industrialization within the state, some of these expanding cities had local industries that were attracting male workers, so that, unlike the capital, some of the interior cities and the port of Santos had a higher ratio of males than females, whereas the capital and most other cities had a larger female population (see Table 8.5). The urban centers of the state were still drawing in larger numbers of women than men. This explains the distribution of women and men in the 1950 census. In the state as a whole, the rural areas had 111 males per 100 females and the towns and cities had a ratio of 95 males per 100 females.[101]

A big factor in the rise of new urban centers in the state was the creation of a new means of transport. Whereas railroads were dominant from the end of the empire, by the 1920s and 1930s there was also beginning to occur a profound change in the state's transport infrastructure. Railroads were now being replaced by cars and trucks. In response to this new means of transport, the state began to construct a major network of highways and roads that moved goods and people that formerly had moved only by train. From the 1920s onward the local government would create a modern road system

TABLE 8.5
State Cities with Populations Greater than 30,000, 1950

Município	Male	Female	Total
São Paulo	991,201	1,025,824	2,017,025
Santos	101,990	96,415	198,405
Campinas	47,451	51,705	99,156
Santo André	49,040	48,404	97,444
Sorocaba	33,481	35,330	68,811
Ribeirão Preto	30,117	33,195	63,312
São Caetano do Sul	28,444	26,955	55,399
Bauru	25,315	26,419	51,734
Piracicaba	22,069	23,713	45,782
Jundiaí	19,048	19,966	39,014
São José do Rio Prêto	17,675	19,267	36,942
Taubaté	16,522	18,627	35,149
Guarulhos	18,198	16,485	34,683
Rio Claro	16,641	17,977	34,618
São Carlos	14,699	16,131	30,830
Subtotal	1,431,891	1,476,413	2,908,304
Total state	4,648,606	4,485,817	9,134,423

SOURCE: Instituto Brasileiro de Geografia e Estatística, *Recenseamento geral do Brasil, 1950*, regional series, vol. 25, bk. 1, pp. 188–222, table 46.

throughout the state. São Paulo's road network continued to grow long after mid-century. By the end of the century the state had 195,000 kilometers of highways, of which 22,000 kilometers were paved roads (some 95 percent built by the state or municipalities), and they eventually reached all areas of the state, even those not served by railroads.[102] By the late twentieth century, São Paulo's paved roads were three times the length of the total railroad network in the state.[103] By the end of the century it was estimated that 81 percent of Brazil's soybeans moved to port by truck and highways and at least 60 percent of all goods were moving by roads instead of trains.[104]

This well-developed system of first-class roads in the state permitted the progressive decentralization of heavy industry from the core metropolitan region of the capital to new regional centers. At first these industrial centers were located in the region between the capital and the port of Santos, the so-called ABC districts (Santo André, São Bernardo do Campo, and São Caetano do Sul, along with Diadema), and they became the center of Brazilian and Paulista industry from the 1940s to the 1970s. Then, after 1970, industry slowly and steadily began to move into the interior.[105] Crucial to these initial changes was the completion of the Rodovia Anchieta (SP 150), 56 kilometers of highway that was initiated in 1939, partly completed in 1947, and with a southern extension added in 1953. This 56-kilometer stretch of modern highway (the first such modern road built in Brazil) tied the city to the port of Santos and connected it to the major ABC industrial suburbs.[106] Eventually, this route became so congested that a new parallel highway would be constructed in the 1970s, the Rodovia dos Imigrantes (SP 160), that crossed from the high plateau to the Paulista coast in a major feat of modern engineering with the construction of numerous tunnels. Roads stretching from São Paulo west to the interior of the state received major support from the 1930s onward by the state's Department of Road Transport (DER), founded in 1934.[107]

A few autos were already being imported into the state at the end of the nineteenth century. In 1903 the state began to use license plates and in 1906 it required an examination for all drivers. In 1907 the Automóvel Clube do Brasil was founded. Then in 1908 came the first successful trip made by auto between Rio de Janeiro and the city of São Paulo. In 1910 São Paulo was the first state to offer incentives for road construction and also provided subsidies for companies transporting cargo and passengers by road. In 1919 Ford Motor Company built its first Model T in São Paulo, and by the 1920s a frenzy of road building occurred, especially in the rural areas as farmers moved their products to market with the new trucks, which replaced animal-drawn wagons and carts.[108] Then in 1928–1929 an asphalt road between the port of Rio and the capital city of São Paulo was built by the federal government.[109] The crisis of World War II closed replacement part imports for the railroads for many years, which also led to their relative decline. By 1950 it was estimated that, of all goods transported in Brazil, 38 percent moved by truck, 32 percent by water, and only 29 percent by rail. By 1954 the road system had been so extended that trucks now accounted for 52 percent of the movement of all goods in Brazil, and railroads moved only 22 percent of these cargos.[110]

Along with the roads, the stock of automobiles, trucks, and buses expanded rapidly in the state. Already in 1939 the state listed some 41,000 cars (of which 879 were public vehicles), 2,476 buses, and 27,000 trucks. But two- and four-wheeled wagons drawn by animals still outnumbered the trucks by almost two to one.[111] The increasing number of buses in turn led to the establishment of fixed and frequent bus routes. In 1939 there were close to 700 bus routes in the state, which were run by half that number of companies. These routes covered 32,000 kilometers in the state, used 2,420 buses, and carried 156,000 passengers.[112] In that same year of 1939 the trains still carried 549,000 passengers.[113] By the middle of the century there were 853 bus companies, using some 5,600 buses to move 897,000 persons, though trains still carried more passengers.[114] Nevertheless, roads and buses were not the only new entrant to the transport sector. By 1950 the airport of São Paulo was handling some 35,000 flights a year and carrying 395,000 passengers, 11,000 metric tons of cargo, and 95,000 pieces of mail.[115] Thus, by the middle of the twentieth century the railroads, now all state companies, were losing their monopoly of transport to trucks, buses, and planes.

A late development of the basic infrastructure of the state was the financial sector. It has been argued that the entire Brazilian banking system was underdeveloped in this period because of political barriers created by the highly centralized imperial government, which was relatively hostile to new bank formation.[116] At the same time, this centralization guaranteed that the empire was one of the few Latin American nations able to pay its international obligations and fund its debts in the international capital market.[117] This explains why the first bank in São Paulo did not began to operate in the state until 1856 and why there were just nine joint-stock banks and five private banking houses by the end of the empire. But all of them were engaged in very short-term credit operations and were of little assistance to the development of long-term enterprises.[118] But with the fall of the empire came the elaboration of new commercial codes, and joint-stock companies were allowed to flourish, and among them were local banks. Thus, for a large part of the nineteenth century the Banco do Brasil, a Rio de Janeiro–based company, was the major local bank and primarily issued imperial banknotes and carried out credit operations that were typically less than one year in duration. The English Bank was a second Rio de Janeiro–based bank that was established in the 1870s in the capital and Santos and was closely tied to the export coffee market. But the republic and its probusiness climate along with the ongoing economic expansion of the state's coffee exports led to far more banks being created, with primarily local capital. Although foreign banks began to appear, they never accounted for much more than a quarter of all banking, and these domestic banks were funded by local capital. It was Paulista investors who made up a large share of the stock owners of these banks, even those headquartered in Rio.[119] Over time more of the credit operations involved guaranteed lines of credit, secured by collateral, to planters, merchants, and manufacturers rather than the previously dominant activity of discounting bills of exchange. By the 1890s long-term credit arrangements began, along with investments in stocks and bonds of joint-stock companies. One of the first new banks of the 1880s, Banco da Lavoura, even began offering agricultural credit secured by harvests and other assets and was soon followed by a full-time agricultural bank, the Banco de Crédito Real, a local Paulista bank founded in 1882.[120]

These new banks and banking houses fit well into the capital investments of the coffee planter class, whose multiple investments included railroads, utilities, and even manufacturing activities.[121] Credit was short term to meet the needs of the harvest and was not initially directed to the investment needed to develop new coffee tree plantings with their long maturation period.[122] The very characteristic of the coffee activity with its long lag between planting and the start of production made financing coffee production a high-risk operation for potential funders. In 1886, loans of São Paulo banks totaled 30,865 contos and deposits 25,453 contos, with only the Banco de Crédito Real de São Paulo providing mortgage loans.[123] In that year, the national banks accounted for 80 percent of the total loans (Table 8.6).

When we analyze the information of the banks in São Paulo at the end of the nineteenth century, we see a reduced participation of foreign banks in the banking activity within the state, but this was not the only role of foreign capital in São Paulo development. Foreign banks were active in the foreign exchange market as well as in financing the federal and state governments, in operations carried out in the country but particularly in trans-

TABLE 8.6

Credit Establishments in the Province of São Paulo, December 31, 1886 (contos)

	Money on deposit	Discount of letters and loans	Mortgage loans	Money on deposit in interest-bearing accounts
National				
Banco Commercial de S. Paulo	499,750	2,775,272		2,396,192
Banco Crédito Real S. Paulo	65,750	5,857,209	12,880,129	84,668
Banco da Lavoura	81,943	427,119		218,170
Banco Mercantil de Santos	511,109	4,401,816		2,634,738
Caixa Filial do Banco do Brasil	412,663	7,357,201		8,539,470
Caixa Bancária da Província de S. Paulo	413,483	4,800,628		4,968,748
Subtotal	1,984,698	25,619,245	12,880,129	18,841,986
Foreign				
English Bank of Rio de Janeiro	364,548	3,721,687		4,083,416
London Brazilian Bank	840,639	1,524,713		2,527,661
Subtotal	1,205,187	5,246,400		6,611,077
Total	3,189,885	30,865,645	12,880,129	25,453,063

SOURCE: *Relatório apresentado ao Exmo. Sr. presidente da província de São Paulo pela Comissão Central de Estatística*, 170.

actions carried out directly abroad. In this case, such foreign banks could be domiciled or not in Brazil.[124] The state of São Paulo especially would borrow extensively abroad during the Old Republic, primarily for operations related to its coffee policies. The first foreign loan to São Paulo occurred at the end of the empire (September of 1888) for the sole purpose of consolidating the floating debt of the province and meeting the needs of the subsidization immigration service. This loan of £787,500 (corresponding to 22,000 contos) was contracted with London bank Louis Cohen and Sons and would be represented by bearer bonds of £100, £500, and £1,000 amortized annually by draw at 5 percent per annum, with the bonds yielding 5 percent per annum.[125] Between 1888 and 1930, São Paulo obtained twenty-five foreign loans, totaling £68,752,500, or US$82.5 million.[126]

Aside from bank loans, private companies also issued debt securities such as bonds, also using the international market to introduce such types of financial instruments even during the empire. Thus, for example, in 1888 several companies had already issued bonds in other currencies such as pounds sterling. These were primarily the railway companies but also included utilities such as the Cantareira de Águas e Esgotos Company and several production companies. Some fifteen different issues were reported, totaling about £2 million. The railways were the major issuers of bonds, accounting for 82 percent of those listed in pounds sterling and 77 percent of issues in mil réis (Table 8.7).

TABLE 8.7

Bonds Issued by São Paulo Banks, 1888

Company	Bond amount	Currency	Interest rate
Companhia S. Paulo Railway	750,000	Libras	5.5%
Companhia Cantareira de Águas e Esgotos (1st series)	121,000	Libras	6.0%
Companhia Cantareira de Águas e Esgotos (2nd series)	200,000	Libras	7.5%
Companhia Paulista de Vias Ferreas e Fluviais	150,000	Libras	7.0%
Companhia Sorocabana, Ouro	230,000	Libras	6.0%
City of Santos Improvements Co.	30,000	Libras	6.0%
Companhia Mogyana	488,000	Libras	5.0%
Caris de Ferro S. Paulo a Santo Amaro	300,000	Mil réis	8.0%
Engenho Central de Piracicaba	250,000	Mil réis	8.0%
Engenho Central de Lorena	250,000	Mil réis	8.0%
Engenho Central de Porto Feliz	300,000	Mil réis	8.0%
Engenho Cental de S. João de Capivary	370,000	Mil réis	
Companhia Sorocabana, Papel	3,982,900	Mil réis	6.0%
Companhia Bragantina	1,300,000	Mil réis	8.0%
Companhia Gaz e Óleos Minerais de Taubaté	100,000	Mil réis	10.0%

SOURCE: *Relatório apresentado ao Exmo. Sr. presidente da província de São Paulo pela Comissão Central de Estatística*, 170.

But the real growth in the financial market occurred with the republic and legal reforms that occurred in 1890.[127] By 1895 the eight banks of the previous decade had increased to eighteen banks, which remained the total number until the 1920s. In that decade they increased to thirty, and after 1927 there was a major expansion of banking both in the capital and interior cities, to fourteen foreign banks and twelve national ones in the capital and five more in the interior. Aside from the large banks there were another fourteen of smaller size.[128] During the Old Republic, at constant prices, bank loans had distinct phases. Between 1895 and 1910 the balance of loans in banks based in São Paulo showed relative stability, perhaps reflecting the banking crisis caused by the stabilization policy implemented by President Manuel Ferraz de Campos Sales. After that came strong growth until 1914, when there was a sharp drop that coincided with World War I; in the 1920s the growth was continuous until 1928. In the period from 1895 to 1928, the banking companies multiplied by a factor of five (see Figure 8.2).

During the Old Republic there was a change in the relative importance of foreign and national banks resident in both the capital and the interior. In the late nineteenth century there was still a significant participation

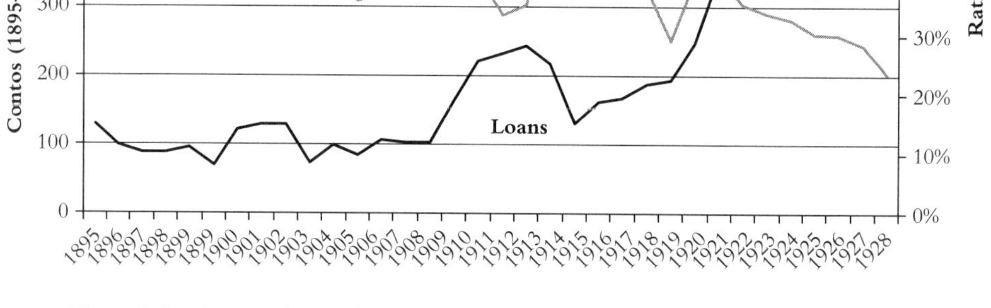

Figure 8.2 São Paulo Bank Loans and Ratio of Cash to Deposits, 1895–1928

NOTE: The base for the calculation of constant prices is the five-year average of 1895–1899.

SOURCE: Saes, *A grande empresa de serviços públicos na economia cafeeira*, 205–238; Ipeadata database, at http://www.ipeadata.gov.br/Default.aspx.

of national banks headquartered in the interior in the ratio of total loans of the state banking system, reaching about a fifth of the total loans until 1902, when their absolute amount and relative position declined precipitously. The foreign banks had an opposite change, systematically growing in value and relative participation in state banking until the middle of the 1910s, when they reached a loan rate of 50 percent, which they would maintain until the 1920s. The national banks headquartered in the capital, however, made half the state loans throughout the period (see Figure 8.3).

But the relative shares of foreign and national banks changed again after 1940. In the decade of the 1940s, the banking system of the state experienced major growth, practically duplicating itself in real terms. In this period approximately 70 percent of the loans and deposits in Brazil were in the Federal District and the capital of São Paulo, with the Federal District (city of Rio de Janeiro) continuing as the leading center but only moderately ahead of São Paulo. But the foreign banks now had a much reduced role in this much larger banking system. In the case of São Paulo they represented only 10 percent of the deposits and loans (see Table 8.8). By mid-century, São Paulo had 103 different banks (of which only 15 were foreign owned) that operated a network of 805 establishments. At this point São

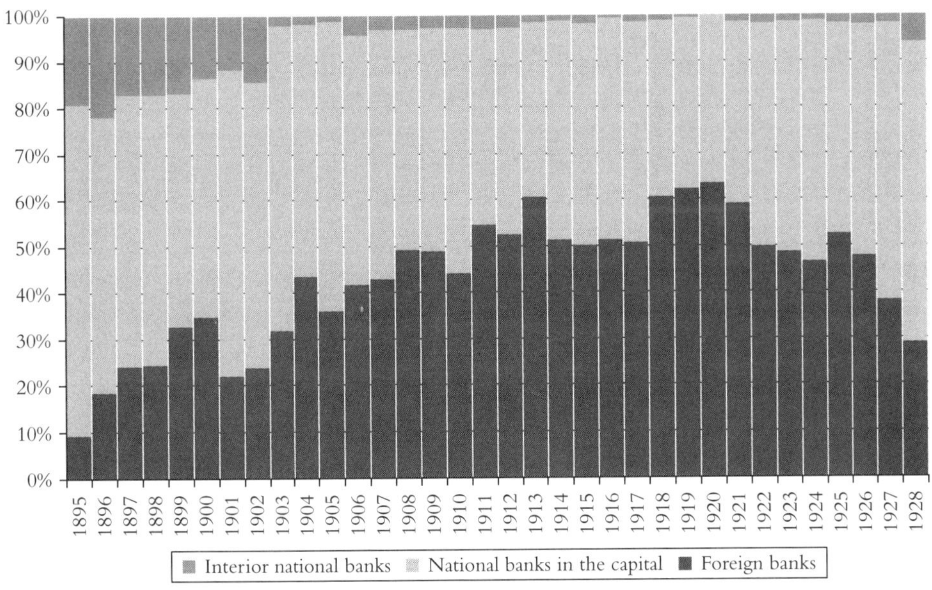

Figure 8.3 Bank Loans in São Paulo by Type of Bank, 1895–1928

SOURCE: Saes, *A grande empresa de serviços públicos na economia cafeeira*, 205–238.

TABLE 8.8

Loans by and Deposits in the Banks of Brazil, 1940–1949

	SÃO PAULO				FEDERAL DISTRICT				BRAZIL			
Year	Total loans	National loans	Foreign loans	Deposits	Total loans	National loans	Foreign loans	Deposits	Total loans	National loans	Foreign loans	Deposits
1940	4,281,845	3,613,868	667,977	3,819,484	4,726,414	4,127,640	598,774	3,182,636	12,836,700	11,256,748	1,579,952	10,247,670
1941	5,088,697	4,334,701	753,996	4,416,467	6,059,507	5,494,227	565,280	4,993,902	15,894,145	14,235,081	1,659,064	13,108,166
1942	5,949,523	5,375,377	574,146	5,130,112	6,519,967	6,026,727	493,240	5,817,175	18,206,336	16,893,523	1,312,813	15,597,134
1943	7,660,602	6,935,143	724,459	7,511,960	13,447,997	12,537,771	910,226	7,851,199	28,756,587	26,800,636	1,955,951	22,426,193
1944	10,168,830	9,236,343	932,487	10,809,079	18,473,935	17,776,327	697,608	9,701,813	40,106,538	38,125,079	1,981,459	30,262,375
1947	13,817,255	12,240,470	1,576,785	17,310,188	16,002,398	14,689,198	1,313,200	19,071,944	46,538,533	43,161,230	3,377,303	51,808,893
1948	15,537,898	14,240,760	1,297,138	18,982,679	17,843,798	16,632,997	1,210,801	20,958,253	51,309,283	48,197,996	3,111,287	57,217,860
1949	18,648,036	17,141,147	1,506,889	21,956,924	22,711,670	21,379,882	1,331,788	22,430,040	62,418,881	58,901,650	3,517,231	64,026,428

SOURCE: Instituto Brasileiro de Geografia e Estatística, *Anuário estatístico do Brasil*, 1940–1949.

TABLE 8.9
Number of Banking Establishments in São Paulo, the Federal District, and Brazil, 1949

	NUMBER OF ESTABLISHMENTS					CAPITAL (CRUZEIROS)		
	Total	National	Foreign	Headquarters	Subsidiaries and branches	Total	National	Foreign
São Paulo	805	790	15	103	702	1,332,313	1,277,313	55,000
Federal District	272	262	10	156	116	1,706,802	1,405,802	301,000
Brazil	2,430	2,388	42	418	2,012	4,823,347	4,451,347	372,000

SOURCE: Instituto Brasileiro de Geografia e Estatística, *Anuário estatístico do Brasil, 1950*, 229–230.

Paulo had a third of Brazil's banks and the same ratio of loans and deposits (see Table 8.9).

Thus, by 1950 São Paulo looked more and more like an advanced, developed society. It had already established a complex and modern rail and road network and had begun to modernize its cities with services for electricity, sewage, and potable water. It had finally provided a primary public education for the majority of its citizens and had achieved an enviable literacy rate by Brazilian standards, if not by the standards of the modern advanced societies in the Southern Hemisphere. Its regional cities at mid-century were finally beginning to grow faster, thus ending the fear that the capital would become a megalopolis that overwhelmed the urban sector. Because of the new road network and rather well-developed electricity-generating system it began to spread its newly developing heavy industrial plants throughout the state with a consequent growth of regional urban centers. Finally, more than half the state population now resided in its towns and cities.[129] Although it was in these respects more advanced than any other state in Brazil, it was still far behind in levels of education and urbanization compared to the advanced economies of the world. Moreover, though the state grew impressively from immigration and high natural population growth, it also had far higher mortality rates than its neighbors Uruguay and Argentina and was still a society that was, in demographic terms, a pretransition state.

Chapter 9

Population Growth and Structure

The São Paulo population between 1850 and 1950 would grow from half a million persons in the middle of the nineteenth century to over 8 million a century later. This growth of the resident population through births and immigration was accompanied by major internal migrations within the state, as well as alteration in the ethnic and racial composition of the population. All of this demographic change was profoundly influenced by the dynamic expansion of the economy and above all of coffee production.

São Paulo in 1850 was still a province in which over half the territory was unexplored and under the control of Amerindian tribes. The majority of the Brazilian population, made up of whites, colored, and *caboclos* (Indian-white mestizos), primarily resided along the coast, only a few hundred kilometers inland from the Atlantic. There were few towns and they were quite small, and thus most of the population resided in rural areas. The majority of farms were family-run units, with only a few major plantations developing sugar and coffee appearing in select areas. Labor was primarily free, though African slaves could be found in most areas as a minor part of the economy and society. This would all change in the next half century as São Paulo slowly emerged as the premier coffee plantation zone of the empire and the world. With that change the African-origin population would increase and the ethnic and racial mixture would become more complex.

A first partial census for this period appeared in 1854. By then the provincial officials were able to count some 419,000 persons. But there were four municípios, or counties, with no population reported and numerous others among the fifty-odd municípios that reported only partial totals. Given these lacunae it is probable that the province had between 450,000 and 500,000 inhabitants.[1] The major urban centers in 1854 were the capital of São Paulo, which had only 25,000 persons; Campinas, which had an estimated 14,000 persons; and Santos, with less than 10,000. Thus, the urban population was probably no more than 10 percent of the total population.[2]

The two major demographic developments in this early period were the massive internal migration of the population within the province and the major introduction of African- and Brazilian-born slaves into this region. The analysis of this internal migration in the nineteenth-century period is based on the reconstruction of the population carried out by José Francisco Camargo from local provincial censuses in the period from 1835 to 1887.[3] It is evident from these censuses that there was a migration of the total population ever more inland and westward. Almost all of the state, except the far Northwest and Alta Paulista zone, was settled in this period and most of the Indians removed. New regions were inhabited to the north and west of the capital, and the population of the state moved well beyond the coastline, which in turn progressively declined in importance.

But even more dramatic was the geographic shift of the slave population, which was the group most sensitive to changes in the economy. This migration was driven by planters and their slaves opening up virgin lands to coffee production. Even though the total population of slaves would decline after the freeing of all children born after 1872, there were still zones within the province that continued to gain slave population at the expense of older regions of development. Thus, the number of slaves in the Vale do Paraíba, which had increased steadily to 1874, by the eve of emancipation had declined by some 20,000 from the previous decade. The Central region also followed this same pattern of growth and decline. In contrast, Mogiana and Baixa Paulista, the newly settled western zones, grew from less than 3,600 slaves in 1836 to some 39,000 slaves in 1886 and by that date accounted for half of all the slaves remaining in the province. All of these immigrations and natural growth led to a steady expansion of the provincial population from 1836 to 1886 (see Table 9.1).

By the time of the first national census in 1872, São Paulo had a population of some 837,000 persons distributed in eighty-nine municípios.[4] There were now thirty-nine municípios created since the last census of 1854, and all were established in the western frontier now being opened to exploitation. This population increase and movement was directed primarily to the rural areas, and urban settlement remained limited. There was also a major

TABLE 9.1
Distribution of the Population in São Paulo by Region, 1836–1886

Region	1836 (%)	1854 (%)	1874 (%)	1886 (%)
Capital	10	9	6	6
Vale do Paraíba	37	30	30	28
Central	36	31	27	24
Mogiana	7	14	15	15
Baixa Paulista	1	5	8	11
Araraquarense			2	3
Noroeste				
Alta Sorocabana			4	6
Baixa Sorocabana	2	6	5	4
Santos	7	6	4	3
Total	100	100	100	100
Total population	284,312	417,149	837,354	1,221,380

SOURCE: Camargo, *Crescimento da população no Estado de São Paulo e seus aspectos econômicos*, 1:61–101.
NOTE: Blank cells indicate no population in the region.

change in the ethnic composition of the population. By 1872 São Paulo had become the fourth-largest slave province in Brazil, with the same ratio of slaves to total population as the largest slave province in the empire—Minas Gerais. But despite this growth, there was also an increase of the nonslave population, primarily through natural growth. This meant that São Paulo was one of the few Brazilian provinces where the black and mulatto populations were still a minority, and at the same time it was becoming one of the most important slave provinces with an ever-rising share of African-born population.

The African slaves brought to Brazil through the Atlantic slave trade were predominantly male, and the steady inflow of such migrants influenced overall population structures throughout the region.[5] The 157,000 African- and Brazilian-born slaves residing in the province of São Paulo in 1872 had a sex ratio of 128 males per 100 females, the highest in the empire. Moreover, if we take just the *pretos* (persons of pure African ancestry), their sex ratio was 138 males per 100 females. In this it was much like the neighboring province of Rio de Janeiro to the north, suggesting that these two provinces were centers of recent African arrivals, compared to most of the other principal slave states, which had lower ratios of males to females among this population group. Even though the census found relatively few Africans among the pretos in the provincial population, this may be the result of counting many Africans as Brazilian born, given the illegality of all African slaves arriving after 1830 when the slave trade officially ended, even though the trade did not actually terminate until 1850. Although the predominance of male slaves influenced the overall sex ratio of the total population, the more adult nature of this Atlantic slave migration had less impact on the age structure of the total Paulista population in 1872. The average age of the provincial population, estimated to be twenty-five, was the same as the imperial norm.[6]

The seven largest slave provinces (with at least 50,000 or more slaves) in this first national census year of 1872 together held 88 percent of all the imperial slaves though only two-thirds of the total population. Between them, Rio de Janeiro and São Paulo had a third of the imperial slaves (see Table 9.2). Although the African component seemed to be highest in these two slave-expanding provinces, they differed not only in the high ratio of whites and the ratio of slaves to total population but also in the ratio of free persons of color to the total population and their importance within the total colored population. Given the more recent nature of the settlements and plantations in São Paulo compared to the province of Rio de Janeiro, it is surprising that the 200,000 free colored in São Paulo were already more than half (57 percent) the total colored population in São Paulo, whereas the 252,000 freedmen were just 42 percent of the total colored in the more settled province of Rio de Janeiro. Equally impressive is that these freedmen made up 31 percent of all free persons in São Paulo and that caboclos were still a significant part of the population.

Although pretos and *pardos* (mulattos) could be found everywhere in the province, the general tendency was for the urban centers to be whiter than most of the rural areas. Thus, in the capital and Santos, over half the population was white. Of the nineteen *comarcas* (judicial districts containing several municípios) some four had a majority of colored population. These in general were the major plantation areas of the province. Thus, Bananal, the first of the major coffee plantation areas, had only 36 percent of its population listed as white, while the sugar and coffee plantation region of Campinas had only 40 percent whites, and both had the highest ratio of pretos in the province. Constituição (Piracicaba) and Guaratinguá were third- and fourth-largest coffee producers in this period, behind Bananal and Campinas. Mogi Mirim and Campinas were the largest sugar producers, which explains their high ratio of slaves. But all the comarcas had a significant colored population, none of these comarcas had less than 35 percent of the population made up of blacks and mulattos of whatever legal status, and blacks and mulattos made up 43 percent of the province's total population (see Table 9.3). Moreover, free colored outnumbered slaves in all but five of the nineteen comarcas. The caboclo population, though relatively small, was also present everywhere with a very significant representation only in Bragança.

Table 9.2

Slave and Total Populations in Major Provinces, 1872

	SLAVE POPULATION		TOTAL POPULATION						
Province	Number	Sex ratio[a]	Number	Sex ratio[a]	Mean age	% African	% White	% Slave	% Caboclo
Minas Gerais	370,459	117	1,669,276	106	28	2%	41%	18%	2%
Rio de Janeiro (Court + province)	341,576	121	1,057,696	115	23	8%	39%	37%	1%
Bahia	167,824	113	1,379,616	109	26	1%	24%	12%	4%
São Paulo	156,612	128	837,354	109	25	2%	52%	18%	5%
Pernambuco	87,561	112	834,314	104	23	1%	35%	10%	1%
Maranhão	74,939	97	359,040	99	23	1%	29%	21%	3%
Rio Grande do Sul	67,791	111	434,813	109	25	2%	59%	16%	6%
Empire	*1,509,339*	*114*	*9,923,253*	*107*	*25*	*3%*	*38%*	*15%*	*4%*

SOURCE: Puntoni, *Os recenseamentos gerais do Brasil no século XIX: 1872 e 1890.*

[a]Number of men per 100 women.

TABLE 9.3

Characteristics of the Population of São Paulo by Comarca, *1872*

				PERCENTAGE OF TOTAL POPULATION				
Comarca	Total population	Total colored	Free colored/total colored (%)	Slave	White	Caboclo	Free colored	Preto
Araraquara	34,801	13,946	54%	18%	56%	4%	22%	17%
Bananal	30,180	17,965	31%	41%	36%	5%	19%	39%
Bragança	62,537	26,260	73%	12%	47%	11%	30%	15%
Campinas	45,862	25,546	32%	38%	40%	4%	18%	36%
Capital/São Paulo	50,113	17,489	70%	11%	62%	3%	24%	14%
Constituição	50,760	26,079	45%	28%	43%	5%	23%	27%
Franca	45,829	17,397	58%	16%	59%	3%	22%	16%
Guratinguetá	28,710	12,682	51%	22%	50%	5%	23%	21%
Iguape	27,651	12,940	78%	10%	49%	4%	36%	17%
Itapetininga	37,908	16,531	80%	9%	52%	5%	35%	16%
Itapeva	62,754	24,383	80%	8%	56%	5%	31%	12%
Itú	53,434	22,973	49%	22%	54%	3%	21%	21%
Jacarehy	74,269	26,875	67%	12%	60%	4%	24%	14%
Lorena	37,814	16,248	54%	20%	53%	4%	23%	20%
Mogy Mirim	59,716	28,000	51%	23%	47%	6%	24%	25%
Parahybuna	15,413	4,760	71%	9%	65%	5%	22%	13%
Rio Claro	51,160	21,759	47%	23%	54%	4%	20%	20%
Santos	33,035	12,625	62%	14%	58%	4%	24%	16%
Taubaté	50,512	25,758	61%	20%	40%	9%	31%	25%
Total	852,458	370,216	58%	18%	51%	5%	25%	20%

SOURCE: Puntoni, *Os recenseamentos gerais do Brasil no século XIX: 1872 e 1890.*

Given its later evolution, it is worth noting that São Paulo in 1872 was a province with as yet few foreign-born residents compared to the rest of the provinces of the empire—in fact, it had fewer foreign born than the national average. The census shows that only 4 percent of the population—or some 30,000—were born outside the empire. Of these foreign-born residents the most significant group was the 15,000 or so African born, some 14 percent of whom were already free persons. The most significant European group was the Portuguese, followed by small groups of Germans and Italians. Moreover, even among native born, only 4 percent (or 1,700 persons) of the Brazilian-born residents were born outside the province, with the majority of these migrants coming from Minas Gerais, Rio de Janeiro, and Bahia.[7]

Assuming that the 1854 São Paulo population was approximately 500,000 persons, the provincial population in the 18 years between 1854 and 1872 grew at a very high 2.9 percent per annum. By the late 1870s the population would increase by 3.5 percent per annum and increase again by 3.9 percent in the next decade of the 1880s, which would be its highest growth rate of the second half of the nineteenth century. This rate would mean that the population was doubling every 17.7 years. Moreover, the state was growing faster than the rest of the empire, which as a whole grew at only 2.0 percent per annum between the first national census of 1872 and 1890.[8] In the 1880s there was a net increase of thirty municípios in the state and another forty in the 1890s.[9]

According to the estimates of José Francisco Camargo, the Paulista population in 1887 on the eve of emancipation had reached 1.4 million persons. The internal migration was now even more pronounced and newer regions were absorbing more of the total and far more of the slave population. The Vale do Paraíba and the north littoral, as well as the Central zone, had lost share of provincial population, just as the newly settled western Paulista region, then made up of the two zones of Mogiana and Baixa Paulista, grew significantly. The capital and the southern and littoral municípios all lost shares as well, primarily because of the movement of slaves in the pre-emancipation period (see Table 9.1 and Map 9.1).

The partial census of 1880, taken just before the abolition of slavery, counted only 750,000 persons in the province out of a probable 1 million population. But it does contain some interesting material on the capital, which now stood at 48,000 persons, of whom 76 percent were white. Whites represented 68 percent in the eighty-five municípios that did provide information on population, while colored represented 24 percent of the total.[10] As in the previous census the capital had fewer caboclos, pardos,

Map 9.1 Population Distribution of São Paulo by Region, 1886

and pretos than did the rural municípios. Finally, a late slave registration (*matrícula*) of 1888 shows that São Paulo had now become the third-leading slave state, just behind Minas Gerais and Rio de Janeiro. Moreover, its slave population was the most highly biased toward men of any provincial slave group, suggesting a higher ratio of African born among its residents (see Table 9.4).

The end of slavery in 1888 resulted in the influx of ever-larger numbers of European immigrants to replace the slave labor on the coffee estates. This new immigration plus the high rate of natural increase meant that by 1900 the state population reached 2.2 million persons, and though growth slowed in the next decades, it still reached 9 million persons by the middle of the twentieth century.[11] This was the highest sustained growth rate of any state in Brazil in this entire period and explains why São Paulo moved from being the fourth-most-populated province in the empire in 1872 to being Brazil's largest state by far, with 18 percent of the national population, in 1950.[12]

This extraordinarily rapid population growth would be driven primarily by changes in the rates of native births and deaths and secondarily by the

TABLE 9.4
Slave Census, 1888

Zone/province	Men	Women	Total
North			
Pará	5,196	5,339	10,535
Maranhão	15,991	17,455	33,446
Northeast			
Piauí	4,317	4,653	8,970
Ceará	54	54	108
Rio Grande do Norte	1,584	1,583	3,167
Paraíba	4,210	5,238	9,448
Pernambuco	20,531	20,591	41,122
Alagoas	7,449	7,820	15,269
Sergipe	8,147	8,728	16,875
Bahia	37,966	38,872	76,838
Center-South			
Espírito Santo	7,112	6,269	13,381
Court	3,653	3,835	7,488
Rio de Janeiro	87,767	74,654	162,421
Minas Gerais	104,748	87,204	191,952
São Paulo	62,557	44,528	107,085
South			
Rio Grande do Sul	1,770	1,743	3,513
Santa Catarina	2,769	2,158	4,927
Paraná	4,591	3,851	8,442
West			
Goiás	2,430	2,525	4,955
Mato Grosso	1,642	1,591	3,233
Brazil	384,484	338,691	723,175

SOURCE: Ministerio da Agricultura, *Relatório 14 Maio 1888*, 24.

flow of international immigrants both slave and free. São Paulo had close to the same high birth rates as the other areas of Brazil, but it had among the lowest death rates during both the empire and the republican years, which led to a growth rate above the national average. In turn, this natural growth was significantly enhanced by immigration that was almost unique to São Paulo. In fact, the state had the largest foreign-born population by 1900, with immigrants making up 23 percent of the state population compared to the national average of just 7 percent, and no other state came close to this ratio in 1900. It alone absorbed over half the 4 million immigrants from Europe who arrived in Brazil from 1880 to 1930.[13] It was the progressive decline of this foreign-born immigration after 1920 that accounts for the progressive decline in the growth rates of the total state population. A rough estimate of crude birth, death, and immigration rates for 1900, a key year of this foreign immigration, suggests that the natural growth rate (births less deaths) accounted for just over half the population growth in that extraordinary year with the rest being explained by immigrant arrivals from Europe.[14] For the empire as a whole, however, it has been estimated that the immigrants and their children—the so-called immigrant stock—accounted for 12 percent of Brazilian population growth in this period, compared to 22 percent in the United States, 41 percent in Canada, and 58 percent in Argentina.[15] This growth of immigrants also shifted the color balance of the population of the state toward a white majority—whites being 63 percent in the census of 1890 and 85 percent in 1940 when color was again registered in the census.[16]

The impact of the immigrants on São Paulo growth continued until the end of the twentieth century. Although foreign-born migration slowed considerably, it was replaced by native-born migrants attracted to the rapidly expanding local economy. With the end of significant international migration after 1920, the foreign born declined to just 14 percent in the state census of 1934 and to only 8 percent by the time of the national census of 1950.[17] The native-born migrants began arriving in the state after 1920 and passed the volume of foreign immigrant arrivals after 1931. By the late 1930s, 59,000 native-born migrants entered the state per annum, and this volume increased to 77,000 just after World War II and finally averaged over 100,000 per annum after 1950.[18] In the period 1940–1950 migrants still accounted for only a quarter of the growth of the state's population.[19]

Aside from a few decades of exceptional immigration, there is little doubt that the single most important factor influencing growth in the century from 1850 to 1950 was the decline in mortality. This mortality decline was initially due to both campaigns of immunization and to the state's investment in modern sanitation to deal with sewage and drinking water. Beginning in the last quarter of the nineteenth century, São Paulo had initiated a modern sanitation system more quickly than any other state in Brazil and was ahead in the installing of this system throughout the state. It was this factor that accounted for the state's death rates slowly declining from the 1890s to the 1920s.[20] After 1930 it was improved public health and medicines that were the prime causal factors, as these rates of mortality declined even faster, especially for infants and children. In this period São Paulo and the Southeast region also led the nation in declining fertility, but the total fertility rate was still at 35 births per thousand resident population (or approximately 5.5 children per woman ages fourteen to forty-nine) in 1950.[21] Brazil would not enter the period of demographic transition until the decade of the 1970s when fertility began to decline to below the replacement level of a total fertility rate of 2.1 births. Thus, it was this increasing decline in mortality that drove the high population growth rates until well into the second half of the twentieth century.

This is the general pattern of population growth within the state in this century of its history. But given the paucity of data it is extremely difficult to reconstruct these vital statistics of births and deaths of the São Paulo population in greater detail before the late twentieth century and thus better refine the evolution of these causal relationships. We do not as yet have any data on peoples' heights over time, which has become a major tool for analyzing changing standards of living of historic populations. We do have estimated life tables that have been produced for the first national census of 1872 for the nation as a whole, and in this case São Paulo probably differed only moderately from the rest of Brazil.[22] The Eduardo E. Arriaga reconstruction of a life table for 1872 suggests an infant mortality rate of 267 deaths per thousand live births for males and 249 deaths for females and gives a life expectancy of 27.1 years for men and 27.6 years for women.[23] These estimated Brazilian infant mortality rates in 1872 are quite high by most European and North American standards in the 1860s but equal to the Italian rates and better than those of Chile in the same period (see Table 9.5).

Along with generally very high rates of mortality, Brazil until the first decade of the twentieth century also suffered from periodic epidemics, which included the cholera epidemic of the 1850s, several malaria outbreaks, major bouts of yellow fever, and even rat-borne bubonic plague.[24] Giorgio Mortara has estimated that Brazil in the last half of the nineteenth century still had a very high crude birth rate of 47–48 births per thousand resident population but a declining crude death rate of 31–32 deaths per thousand resident population. These rates were high by European standards but were common to Latin America at the time. It is suggested that the birth rate fell slowly at the beginning of the twentieth century to a crude birth rate of 44–45, whereas the crude death rate fell to 24–25, which meant that Brazil had a high natural growth rate of 20 persons per thousand resident population.[25]

The data available for the state of São Paulo would confirm Mortara's estimates, though it would appear that São Paulo experienced changes in vital rates earlier than the rest of the country. By the second half of the nineteenth century the Paulista crude birth rate was probably the same as the rest of the empire—that is, in the lower 40s for births per thousand

TABLE 9.5
Infant Mortality Rates for Selected Countries in the Mid-Nineteenth Century

Country	Year	Infant mortality[a]
UK and Wales	1861	160
France	1861	204
Belgium	1851–1855	161
Italy	1861–1862	270
Spain	1860–1862	184
Denmark	1860–1862	129
Holland	1860	209
Finland	1851–1860	183
Norway	1856–1860	100
Sweden	1858–1862	138
Canada	1861	178
US	1860	197
Australia	1856–1865	106
New Zealand	1881	89
Chile	1863–1869	318

SOURCE: Pérez Moreda, Reher, and Gimeno, *La conquista de la salud*, 209–210.
[a]Deaths per thousand live births.

resident population—with the crude death rate in the lower 30s per thousand resident population. Given these crude vital rates, life expectancy was probably in the upper 20s to lower 30s for men and women in the late nineteenth century and first decade of the twentieth. In all available annual mortality data by age, over half the total numbers of deaths were of infants and children under five years of age.[26] This probably indicated an infant mortality rate above 200 deaths of infants under one year of age per thousand live births.

Unfortunately, most of the data on births, deaths, and marriages reported for São Paulo in this period are for selected municípios and relatively less is available for the state as a whole. Our best data for the late nineteenth century comes from four major districts, two of which were predominantly urban centers.[27] These are the capital, the port of Santos (both primarily urban), and the interior districts of Campinas and Ribeirão Preto, which were dominated by large rural populations though each had small urban centers as well.

In the mid-1880s, the crude death rate in the capital and Santos was in the lower 30s deaths per thousand resident population, in agreement with Mortara's estimates, but then quickly dropped to the upper 10s by the beginning of the new century—a faster rate of decline than Giorgio Mortara estimated for Brazil as a whole. It was only the influenza epidemic of the 1910s that sent rates back into the upper 20s in both the capital and Santos. But Santos was more prone to epidemic diseases, and its crude death rate tended to fluctuate more dramatically than the capital.

This same trend of falling rates was also to be seen in the crude birth rate. Starting at around 40 births per thousand residents in 1894, the crude birth rate of the capital dropped to the upper 30s during the first decade of the new century and then began a slow decline toward the upper 20s in the decade of the 1920s (see Figure 9.1). The birth rates recorded for Santos were more erratic and lower than those estimated for the capital, but the trend was the same—the crude birth rates of the port also began a secular decline in the 1920s. The rural-dominated municípios of Campinas and Ribeirão Preto both had higher crude birth rates and lower crude death rates than the capital and Santos. Their birth rates remained in the high 40s far longer, and their death rates dropped more quickly into the lower 20s and upper 10s sooner. By the 1920s their crude death rates were in the mid-10s of deaths per thousand resident population (see Figure 9.2). This finding is consistent with other nineteenth-century American nations. In general,

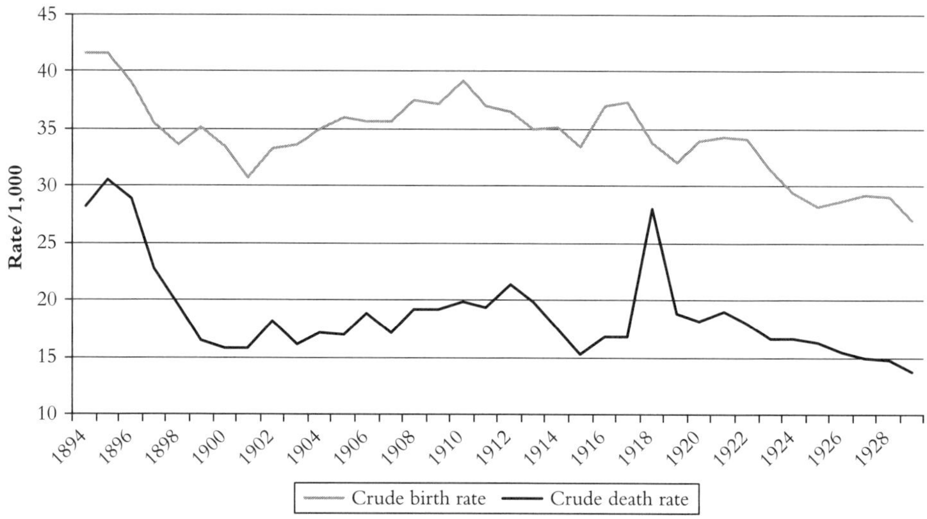

Figure 9.1 Estimated Crude Birth and Death Rates for the Capital Population, 1894–1929

SOURCE: Directoria do Serviço Sanitario do Estado de São Paulo, *Annuario demographico, 1929*, 1:72.

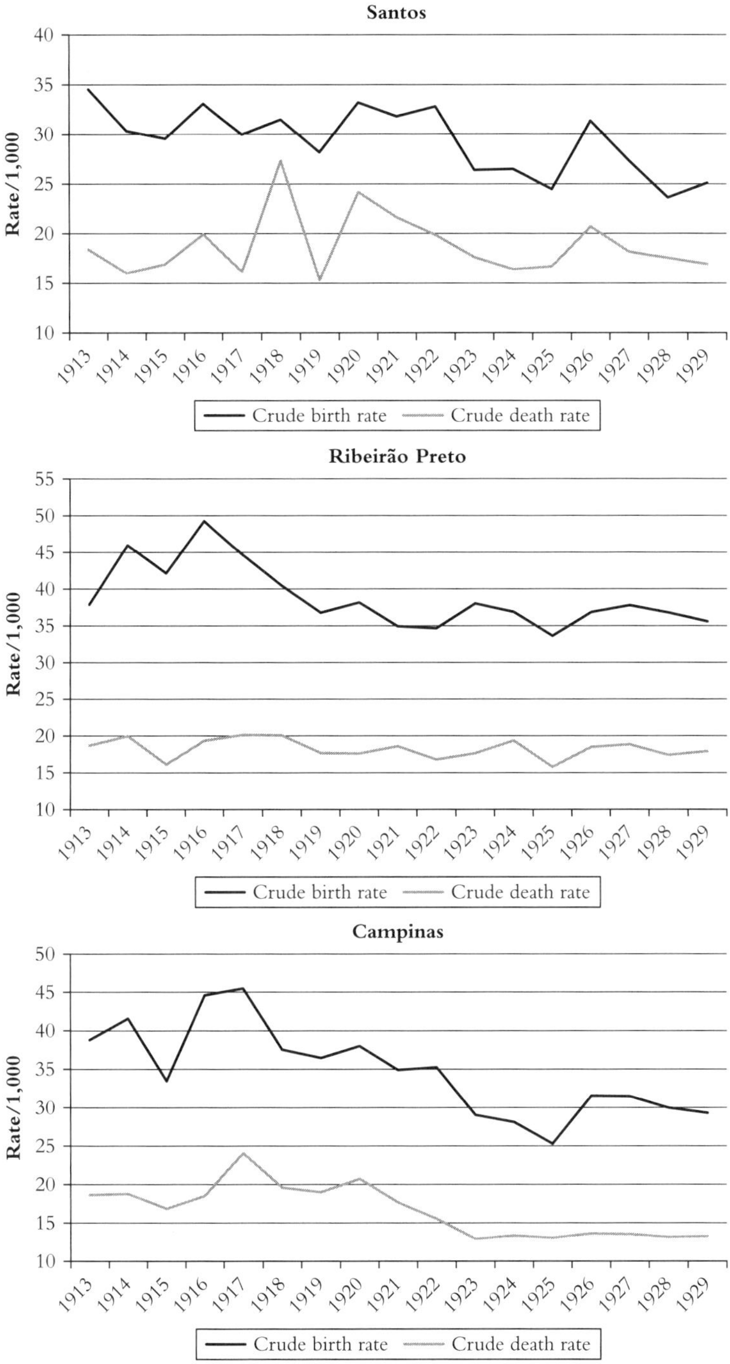

Figure 9.2 Estimated Crude Birth and Death Rates for Selected Cities of São Paulo, 1913–1929

SOURCE: Directoria do Serviço Sanitario do Estado de São Paulo, *Annuario demographico, 1929*, 1:271, 499.

urban centers tended to initiate falling fertility rates, while the rural areas tended to maintain them far longer at high levels. In turn, there was an urban penalty in mortality—deaths were higher in cities than in the rural areas—which does not disappear in most regions of the Americas until the mid-twentieth century. Until then, rural areas were consistently healthier places than the urban centers with their crowding and poor sanitation.[28]

These leading urban centers and most especially the city of São Paulo were ahead of the state trends in the decline of the crude birth and death rates. Whereas we have data for only a few select counties before 1900, after that date we have reasonable statistics for the entire state. It would appear that the crude birth and death rates for the state as a whole moved much more slowly than in the selected municípios. From 1900 to 1950, crude birth rates also dropped from their late nineteenth-century highs, but they then remained remarkably stable for the next seventy years, staying in the mid- to low 30s in births per thousand residents into the 1960s.[29] Death rates, though slowly declining, remained stubbornly in the upper teens and lower 20s until the 1940s, which meant that they were at least a decade behind the capital declines (see Figure 9.3). The stability of these patterns meant that there was a high natural growth rate throughout most

Figure 9.3 Crude Birth and Death Rates for the State of São Paulo, 1904–1950

SOURCE: Calculated from data in *Boletim do Departamento Estadual de Estatística*, no. 1 (1956): 23–24.

of the twentieth century. In the last three decades of the nineteenth century and the first decade of the twentieth century the state population grew at over 3 percent per annum. But in the next three decades, growth declined, and it was only in the 1950s, with the serious decline of death rates combined with the steady maintenance of high birth rates, that the state population again increased at such a high rate of natural increase. Between the 1950s and the 1970s the state grew at above 3 percent per annum but dropped below 2 percent in the 1980s, and the rate has continued to decline ever since then as the fall in birth rates outpaces the decline in both death rates and the rates of migration.[30]

Nevertheless, all these vital statistical rates for the state of São Paulo were lower than the national rates throughout this period. Thus, the national crude birth rate stayed in the mid-40s until the late 1950s, and the death rate did not fall below 20 until that date as well.[31] Comparable data exist for the state of São Paulo and the nation from 1910 to 1955. In that period the difference in births peaked at 12 births per thousand resident population in 1945, and the largest spread was 8.9 deaths as of 1930. By 1955 the spread was declining as the rest of the nation followed São Paulo, but the differences in the crude rates were still 6.3 fewer births in São Paulo and 3.1 fewer deaths than the national averages (see Figure 9.4).[32] Clearly, the state preceded the nation in terms of declining birth and death rates throughout

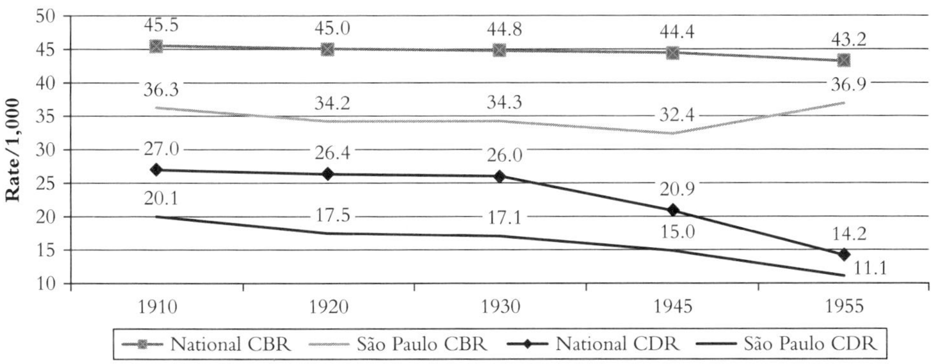

Figure 9.4 Crude Birth Rate (CBR) and Crude Death Rate (CDR) in Brazil and São Paulo, 1910–1955

SOURCE: For Brazil data: Instituto Brasileiro de Geografia e Estatística, "Taxas brutas de natalidade e de mortalidade." For São Paulo data: Directoria do Serviço Sanitario do Estado de São Paulo, *Annuario demographico, 1929*, 1:161; Departamento de Estatística do Estado, *Anuário estatístico de São Paulo, 1957*, 1:41.

the first half of the twentieth century, though by mid-century the national rates were finally dropping faster than those for São Paulo, and the differences were thus declining.

Despite it being a leading state in declining vital rates, there is no question that São Paulo was still a premodern society in terms of mortality no matter where people resided. Epidemic diseases rather than chronic or degenerative ones were the prime killers, and because of that, children died in significant numbers, especially when malnutrition and contaminated water led to extraordinarily high deaths from dysentery. A study of the capital population in 1901 found that 46 percent of the deaths in the city in that year were due to infectious diseases, with an infant mortality rate of 178 deaths per thousand live births. Diarrhea and enteritis alone were the largest killers, primarily affecting infants and children, and accounted for 20 percent of all deaths in the city, with the next two largest infectious diseases, tuberculosis and pneumonia, together accounting for 30 percent of all deaths.[33] Infectious diseases remained a major contributor to deaths in the capital well into the twentieth century, with the 1918 influenza attack explaining the unusual high rate of that year.[34] Through sanitation efforts, yellow fever, which had been a significant killer as late as the 1890s, virtually disappeared by the first decade of the twentieth century in all the major cities. Another infectious disease that slowly lost its impact was malaria. A major killer in all Paulista cities from the 1890s to the 1910s, malaria finally was reduced to a minor killer in the 1920s in all the studied municípios except the port of Santos, where it remained a major cause of death. But at the same time tuberculosis remained the single largest killer throughout the period from the late 1890s until 1940s. Measles, whooping cough, and dysentery, particularly fatal for infants and young children, were also constant causes of death throughout the period.[35]

The majority of the people dying in the capital until the end of the 1920s were children. Infants and children under 5 years of age represented more than half the deaths in the capital until 1929, though even then half the deaths were of persons younger than 20. These capital death rates by age appear not to have differed from that of the province as a whole, despite the supposedly higher mortality of this urban concentration. Thus, a listing of deaths by age for 171 interior municípios in the state listed a total of some 50,000 deaths in the year 1905. Of these deaths, we can eliminate those unknown as to age and those dying before birth (stillbirths), which leaves 49,704 deaths, of which 57.2 percent were infants and children under 5 years of age.[36] While life tables are not available for this early period, it is evident that average life expectancy at birth in 1900 given these high infant and child mortality rates was at best only in the mid-30s for both sexes.[37] It has also been suggested that in periods when infectious diseases accounted for the majority of deaths, as in São Paulo until the late 1920s, life expectancy remained in the 30s. Thus, a recent calculation of life tables for the capital in 1920 showed a life expectancy at birth for men of 30.9 years and for women of 36.6 years. Just how important infant mortality was in affecting life expectancy is shown by the fact that life expectancy increased by 16.5 years for men (to 47.4 years) and just under 16 years for women (to 52.4 years) for those who survived in the capital to 5 years of age in 1920. It was the change in infant and child mortality in the next few decades that finally caused most of this dramatic change in life expectancy at birth. By 1935 life expectancy for *Paulistano* (residents of the capital) men finally reached into the lower 40s, whereas Paulistano women living in the city had achieved this rate by 1930. In turn, life expectancy for Paulistano women reached into the lower 50s by 1940, and for Paulistano men this occurred five years later. In 1950 the average life expectancy for these urban residents of the capital was 60.3 years at birth for women and 55.7 years at birth for men.[38]

Life expectancy for the state population increased at a slower pace. It reached 44.3 years for Paulista men and 46.7 for Paulista women in the census year of 1940 and then increased again in the next decade to 52.8 years for men and 55.9 for women.[39] In 1949–1951 the state statistical bureau estimated that in the interior of the state (all municípios except the capital city) life expectancy at birth had reached 52.3 years for men and 54.6 years for women.[40] Clearly, by 1950 the urban penalty had disappeared and the cities were now better places in terms of health than the rural municípios. Almost all this change in life expectancy in the period up to the 1940s was driven by decline in infant and child mortality. Although we lack data for the entire state for most of this period, there does exist good data on this for the capital from 1894 to 1929. In the earliest period, 54 percent of all the deaths registered were accounted for by infants and children under 5 years of age, and it is only in 1929 that the rate of infant and child deaths to total deaths fell below 50 percent of all deaths (see Table 9.6). The trend noted in 1929 in infant and child deaths continued, and by the 1930s infant and child mortality was down to 37 percent of all deaths.[41]

These changes in rates of child and infant deaths in the capital reflected changes in the diseases that killed the *Paulistana* population. What is evident from the data is that there was a major demographic transition in the capital between the 1920s and the 1930s that established a trend in both declining rates of mortality and basic changes in the diseases that influenced the death

TABLE 9.6

Mortality by Age in the Capital, 1894–1929

Ages	Men	Women	Total	Cumulative %
1894				
0–5	1,180	1,092	2,272	54.2
5–10	53	51	104	56.7
10–20	114	83	197	61.4
20–50	728	408	1,136	88.5
>50	262	219	481	100.0
Total	2,337	1,853	4,190	
1906				
0–5	1,614	1,453	3,067	56.8
5–10	74	65	139	59.3
10–20	108	87	195	62.9
20–50	687	497	1,184	84.9
>50	451	367	818	100.0
Total	2,934	2,469	5,403	
1912				
0–5	2,634	2,322	4,956	57.7
5–10	113	107	220	60.3
10–20	192	180	372	64.6
20–50	1,066	721	1,787	85.4
>50	723	526	1,249	100.0
Total	4,728	3,856	8,584	
1920				
0–5	2,910	2,659	5,569	52.8
5–10	127	139	266	55.3
10–20	312	250	562	60.6
20–50	1,316	936	2,252	82.0
>50	1,118	782	1,900	100.0
Total	5,783	4,766	10,549	
1929				
0–5	3,736	3,293	7,029	48.1
5–10	133	111	244	49.7
10–20	308	320	628	54.0
20–50	2,040	1,385	3,425	77.5
>50	1,827	1,468	3,295	100.0
Total	8,044	6,577	14,621	

SOURCE: Directoria do Serviço Sanitario do Estado de São Paulo, *Annuario demographico*, various years; Directoria do Serviço Sanitario do Estado de São Paulo, *Boletim annual de estadistica demographo-sanitaria da Capital e de Santos, 1894*, 10–11.

rates that has continued to the present day.[42] Some of these trends, such as the decline of infectious diseases and the rise of diseases related to older ages such as cancer, can be seen in the percentage of annual deaths by cause listed in the capital from 1920 to 1950, which showed a steady decline in dysentery and pneumonia and a slow rise in deaths from cancer, though there seemed little variation in tubercular deaths in this period (see Figure 9.5).

The decline of infectious diseases in the city occurred at a faster pace and reached lower levels than in the city of Rio de Janeiro during this same period.[43] It also dropped much faster than in the rest of the state. In the interior of the state (all municípios but the capital) diarrhea and enteritis were still the largest single causes of deaths in 1940, accounting for 22 percent of the 78,000 deaths in the state for which the cause was known. In contrast, tuberculosis and pneumonia accounted for just 16 percent of total known deaths in the rest of the state. By then diarrhea and enteritis had dropped to 17 percent of all deaths in the capital, whereas tuberculosis and pneumonia now accounted for 19 percent of the 17,000 deaths recorded.[44] Clearly, the crowded conditions in the cities were a factor in these two airborne diseases.

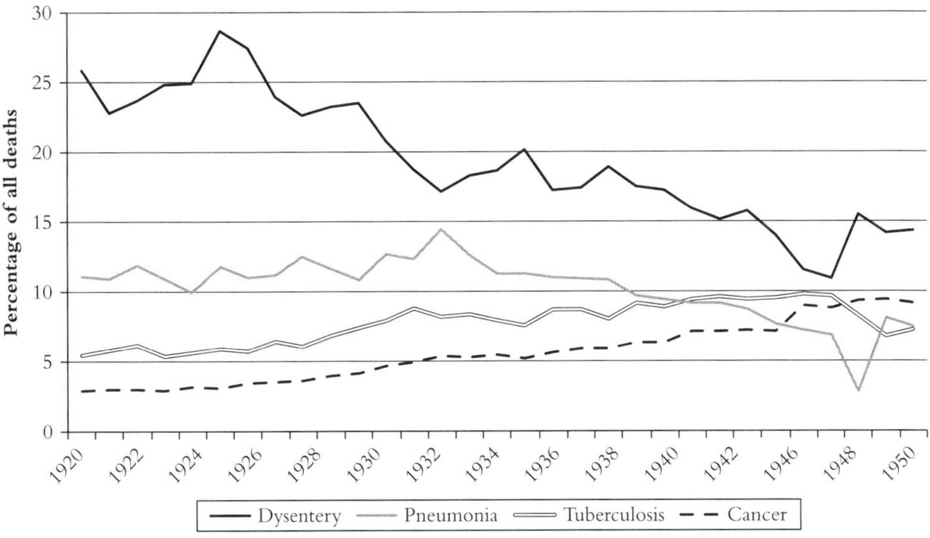

Figure 9.5 Changing Importance of Principal Deadly Diseases in the Capital, 1920–1950

SOURCE: *Boletim do Departamento de Estatística do Estado de São Paulo*, no. 1 (1956): 8–10.

This decline in mortality in the state and city of São Paulo, although occurring earlier than in the rest of the country, was still a relatively late change compared to the more advanced countries of the world. But it was similar to the pace of change in other advanced Latin American countries.[45] Some of this change had to do with the dramatic growth of the economy, but most resulted from the establishment in São Paulo of one of the most advanced public health systems in Brazil and probably in all of South America. The sanitation movement in Europe and North America had begun in the mid-nineteenth century in response to increased waves of epidemic diseases brought on by growing international trade. Water and sewage control were seen as fundamental in controlling their impact. Then came the new science of bacteriology emerging in the 1880s in which most of the major epidemic diseases were defined and their vectors of infection understood. This led the Paulista elite on its own initiative, without the usual leadership of the medical profession, to propose fundamental reforms in public health, from control of rats and mosquitoes to vaccination of the entire population.[46] Important for arousing public concern was a devastating yellow fever epidemic that caused high death rates in Campinas in 1889, just one of numerous epidemics that reached the central part of the state from Santos.[47] Even before the end of the empire, the city of São Paulo had extended water service to over five thousand homes. In 1892 the state legislature passed a bill that provided state funding for municipal sanitation projects for water and sewage in Santos, Campinas, and smaller cities, and the next year it took over the task of providing both services for the capital as well.[48] By the end of the 1890s it was said that the state had the best water and sewage systems in Brazil.[49] The major ports of Recife, Rio de Janeiro, and Santos in the first decade of the twentieth century also had major sanitation campaigns, which had become more active after bubonic plague reached Santos in 1889.[50] All this urban sanitation construction had its impact on slowly reducing mortality even before the introduction of childhood vaccinations in the early twentieth century.

But even with all this effort, the traditional causes of mortality in a premodern society remained throughout most of this period, with infectious diseases and nutritional and sanitation problems leading to high mortality rates for infants, children, and teens. The official data on infant mortality, the ratio of deaths of infants younger than one year of age to all births in a given year, show very high rates well into the twentieth century (see Figure 9.6). Rates remained above 200 deaths per thousand live births until the second decade of the twentieth century and did not drop below 150 deaths until the 1930s, with the state as a whole usually above the

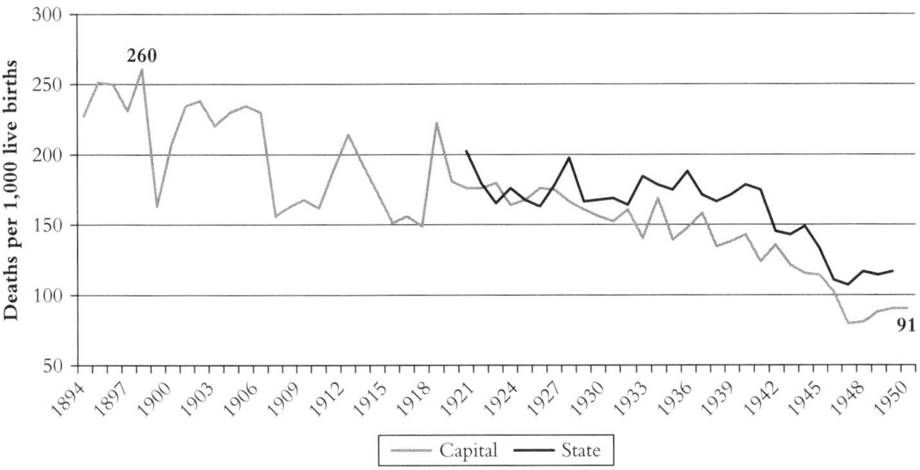

Figure 9.6 Infant Mortality in the State and Capital, 1894–1950

SOURCE: Fundação Sistema Estadual de Análise de Dados *Estatísticas Vitais* database, at http://produtos.seade.gov.br/produtos/500anos/index.php?tip=esta.

rates found for the capital. The state's infant mortality level remained quite high until the late 1940s. The infant mortality rate for the state remained relatively stable until the mid-1940s, a pattern also evident in the capital, whose rate also started to decline in this period (in 1940 the state was at 170 deaths and the capital at 124 deaths). The infant mortality rate finally dropped below 100 deaths per thousand live births in the capital in 1946, and in the state this occurred a decade later.[51]

Even as these rates declined, they were still above many other South American societies in this period, marking Brazil as a particularly poor society. However, in Brazilian terms the capital of São Paulo had one of the lower infant mortality rates. In 1920, for example, of all the state capitals, only Curitiba had a rate lower than São Paulo's rate of 174 deaths per thousand live births.[52] Moreover, even within the state, its rate was not excessive. A comparative survey of 1929 of infant mortality rates in the major districts of the state showed that in this respect the capital was not unusually high. Thus, while Campinas's and Ribeirão Preto's rates were much lower than the capital's, Santos's and several rural municípios' were higher (see Figure 9.7).

Another indicator of mortality is the unusual one of stillbirths recorded by state health officials from the beginning of the century. A *stillbirth* is the birth of an infant who has died in the womb, usually after twenty-eight weeks of pregnancy. The best such data come from the capital, and these

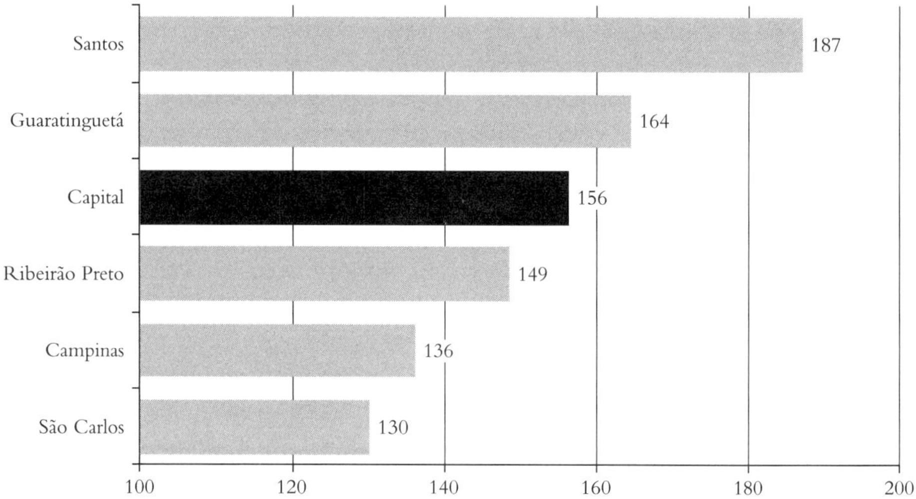

Figure 9.7 Infant Mortality in Selected Paulista Cities, 1929 (deaths under age one per 1,000 live births)

SOURCE: Directoria do Serviço Sanitario do Estado de São Paulo, *Annuario demographico, 1929*, 1:161.

show a surprising stability in these rates. In contrast to other death indices, these rates, after dropping at the beginning of the century, held steady throughout the next three decades of the twentieth century, showing no secular decline until the late 1940s (see Figure 9.8). Why this rate did not decline is probably related to lack of prenatal care of mothers and the failure to provide caesarian births. In this period all deaths as well as all births still occurred in the home, most often without medical assistance. In premodern Europe the rate of such stillbirths to total births was thirty to fifty deaths, with the Nordic countries having the lowest rates, and these began systematically to decline only in the 1935–1940 period. Today the highest rates, those for sub-Saharan Africa, are on the order of twenty-eight deaths per thousand live births, compared to just 3 deaths per thousand total births in the Western European countries.[53]

The third major factor influencing population growth was migration. First came the arrival of African- and Brazilian-born slaves and from the late 1880s the arrival of foreign-born immigrants to replace slaves on the expanding coffee fazendas. With emancipation, slaves abandoned the coffee fields, no longer willing to work in gangs under slave drivers. The desperate planter class turned to free immigrant labor, which the state began to subsidize in the 1870s for the first time. Thanks to this subsidization of workers and the conversion of plantation labor into family piecework, the Paulista planters were able to compete with Argentina and the United States for European immigrants.[54] Up to 1889, some 121,000 immigrants arrived in the state, and the census of 1890 recorded that 75,000 residents were foreign born.[55] But it was the decade of the 1890s when immigrants, both subsidized by the state and self-sustained, began to flow in ever-larger numbers into São Paulo and slowly began to have an influence on the entire state population in terms of color, age, and literacy, along with influencing overall growth.[56] By 1914 some 932,000 foreign-born immigrants were brought into the state, with government paying their transport. Another 595,000 immigrants entered the state spontaneously on their own resources. Among these immigrants, both spontaneous and subsidized, were 841,634 Italians, 289,547 Spaniards, and 254,705 Portuguese.[57] Although the totals vary among authors, it is estimated that some 1.6 million to 2 million immigrants arrived in the state from Europe and Asia by 1920.[58] By 1893 São Paulo alone was receiving more immigrants than the other states of the new republic combined and continued to do so for most of the next fifty years.[59] Although there was a large return emigration—something on

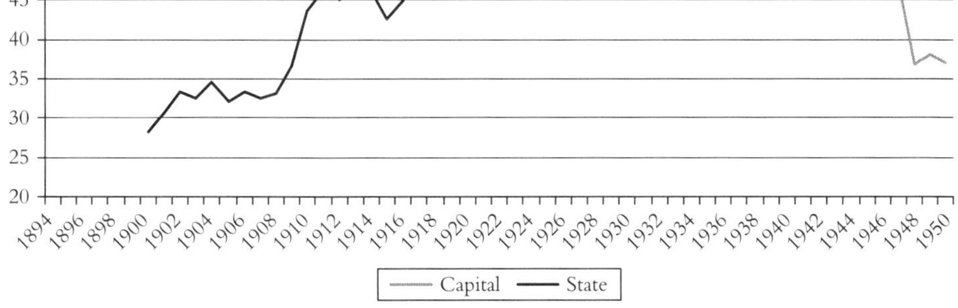

Figure 9.8 Stillbirths per Thousand Total Births in the Capital and State, 1894–1950

SOURCE: Fundação Sistema Estadual de Análise de Dados *Estatísticas Vitais* database, at http://produtos.seade.gov.br/produtos/500anos/index.php?tip=esta.

the order of 50 percent in the case of the Italians—by the census of 1920 the foreign born in the state had increased to 830,000 persons and now represented 18 percent of the total population.[60]

This new international migration was made up primarily of persons coming from Portugal, Italy, Spain, and Japan and Christians from the Ottoman Empire. In the state census of 1934, it was estimated that there were 932,000 foreign born (now down to 14 percent of the total state population), with a third of these being Italians, followed in importance by the Portuguese and Spaniards. Of these groups, only the Portuguese had a significant representation in other states, whereas the other groups were primarily concentrated in São Paulo.[61] Given the importance of coffee production in the state economy and the still relatively small size of the urban centers, half the immigrants were living in the rural areas. But not all immigrant groups were equally distributed between urban centers and farms. In the state census of 1934, the foreign born were more urban than the native-born Brazilians. Unusual were the Japanese, among whom only 8 percent lived in urban areas. Given their attraction to coffee labor, the Spaniards and Italians made up more than half of rural residents. Clearly, the Portuguese, the Syrians, and most of the smaller immigrant groups were attracted primarily to the cities, and few participated in coffee production. Again, being an immigrant population, all groups tended to be older and far more male than the native-born population, with the Portuguese and the Syrians having the fewest women (see Table 9.7).

As could be expected, those foreign born living in the rural areas were concentrated in the most advanced agricultural zones. Thus, of the five leading municípios with the largest coffee plantations found in the Van Delden Laerne survey, the foreign born represented between 9 percent (Mogi Mirim) and 31 percent (Descalvados) of their residents. Campinas, with its 5 million coffee trees and status as the leading coffee region in 1888, had 21 percent of its population born outside Brazil.[62] All this suggests that the rural distribution of immigrants was the same as the slaves before them—that is, concentrated in the largest-producing zones.

Finally, it is worth stressing that the capital city of São Paulo, the largest urban center in the state, was heavily influenced by immigrants. Whereas native-born Brazilians accounted for 86 percent of the state's residents in 1934, they made up only 77 percent in the capital. Here the immigrants accounted for almost double the ratio that they did in the state as a whole, and the various groups, except the Japanese, matched closely their importance within the state, with the Italians and Portuguese (both at 8 percent of the total) dominating. But the Portuguese (45 percent), the Germans (49 percent),

TABLE 9.7

Origin and Urban-Rural Residence of the Population of São Paulo by Sex, 1934

	URBAN			RURAL			TOTAL				
Nationality	Men	Women	Total	Men	Women	Total	Men	Women	Total	% rural	Sex ratio[a]
Brazilian born	914,777	984,671	1,899,448	1,874,197	1,724,181	3,598,378	2,788,974	2,708,852	5,497,826	65.5	103
Foreign born											
Italians	76,297	71,972	148,269	85,921	70,787	156,708	162,218	142,759	304,977	51.4	114
Portuguese	72,728	51,685	124,413	33,110	19,068	52,178	105,838	70,753	176,591	29.5	150
Spaniards	33,574	33,607	67,181	51,305	42,038	93,343	84,879	75,645	160,524	58.1	112
Japanese	6,203	4,695	10,898	66,778	54,033	120,811	72,981	58,728	131,709	91.7	124
Others	37,713	36,369	74,082	17,565	13,635	31,200	55,278	50,004	105,282	29.6	111
Germans	8,883	8,381	17,264	5,643	4,091	9,734	14,526	12,472	26,998	36.1	116
Syrians	12,435	8,426	20,861	3,181	1,568	4,749	15,616	9,994	25,610	18.5	156
All foreign born	247,833	215,135	462,968	263,503	205,220	468,723	511,336	420,355	931,691	50.3	122
Total	1,162,610	1,199,806	2,362,416	2,137,700	1,929,401	4,067,101	3,300,310	3,129,207	6,429,517	63.3	105

SOURCE: *Boletim do Departamento Estadual de Estatística*, no. 1 (1939): 77.

NOTE: There were 3,810 persons in the state whose origin was unknown.

[a]Number of men per 100 women.

TABLE 9.8
Origin of the Population of the Capital, 1934

Nativity	Men	Women	Total
Paulista	316,963	334,369	651,332
Other states	31,818	29,734	61,552
Native but state unknown	15,219	16,041	31,260
Subtotal	*364,000*	*380,144*	*744,144*
Foreign born			
Italians	44,194	41,588	85,782
Portuguese	44,572	34,893	79,465
Others	31,007	30,260	61,267
Spaniards	17,029	17,488	34,517
Germans	6,795	6,567	13,362
Syrians	5,120	3,614	8,734
Japanese	2,605	1,958	4,563
Subtotal	*151,322*	*136,368*	*287,690*
Unknown	663	705	1,368
Total	515,985	517,217	1,033,202

SOURCE: *Boletim do Departamento Estadual de Estatística*, no. 1 (1939): 77.

the Syrians (34 percent), and the other smaller immigrant groups (totaling 58 percent) had the highest ratio of their community living in the capital (see Table 9.8).

The two world wars and the Great Depression affected the flow of international migration to the state. Even though Spain and Portugal were not combatants in the wars, the economic crisis of 1929 slowed their movements. But this did not stop the flow of immigration to the state. For starting in the period of World War I, native migrants from other states replaced the foreign born and they began to flow into the state at a steadily increasing rate, more than doubling each decade. By the late 1920s, 156,000 native-born Brazilians had migrated to São Paulo from other states, and by 1930 they exceeded the foreign-born immigrant flow. From then on it was native-born Brazilian migrants from other states who became the state's primary source of immigrants. It was estimated that by 1950 the state had received since 1820 some 2.5 million foreign-born free immigrants and 1.3 million Brazilians from other states.[63]

The movement of the population within the state, as seen among the slaves in the nineteenth century, would be quite evident for the free population as well in the twentieth century. The coastal regions and the Vale do Paraíba progressively lost relative importance, as the center of the state's population moved progressively westward into virgin lands. It was the central plateau and western regions that progressively increased their share of total population at the expense of the older and coastal regions (see Table 9.9).

Thus, the far western region of Araraquarense, which had only 3 percent of the population in 1886, accounted for 12 percent of the state population by 1950, having grown at 3.9 percent per annum over the period 1900–1950. The Noroeste frontier region grew from 2 percent of the total population in 1886 to 13 percent of the state population in the same period. This was the premier region of growth in the twentieth century, having increased at an annual rate of 10.4 percent per annum in the half century from 1900. The capital zone, dominated by the city of São Paulo, of course ended by accounting for 27 percent of the total population in 1950, compared to just 6 percent of the total in 1886. In contrast to this, the Vale do Paraíba, which included all the towns of the northern coast, went from 28 percent of the population in 1886 to just 3 percent, and the Central zone share also dropped from 24 to 10 percent in the same period.[64] All this, of course, was driven by the penetration of the railroads into new virgin lands of the west and the consequent expansion of the coffee frontier to the limits of the state boundaries, all of which had a major impact on shifting population by the basic ten regions (see Maps 9.2, 9.3, 9.4, and 9.5).

While the capital grew exponentially in this period, urban growth in the rest of the state was quite modest. It was estimated that in 1937 all the town centers of all the municípios made up only 37 percent of the total municipal populations, or 2.6 million out of 7 million persons resident in the state.[65] The capital alone, with its 1.2 million persons, accounted for just under half the state's urban total. In fact there were no cities to compare to the capital. The second-largest city in 1937 was the port of Santos, which had a population of only 137,000, and the third-largest city, Campinas, had only 71,000. Ribeirão Preto had 43,000. There were only twelve urban areas in the state with more than 20,000 persons.[66] Thus, the capital city of São Paulo represented the single most important urban area of the state. In the national census of 1940, urban areas with more than 20,000 persons in the state contained just 27 percent of the state population, and this rose only to 36 percent in 1950. Thus, it is no surprise that the capital in 1940, with its 1.3 million persons, contained 69 percent of these urban Paulistas and that the 2.2 million in 1950 living in the capital still accounted for 68 percent of persons living in these towns and cities.[67] The growth of the capital was spectacular, increasing at a rate of 6 percent per annum between 1886 and 1950.[68]

Aside from birth, death, and migration statistics, the state government in its monthly and annual surveys from the 1880s onward also provided

TABLE 9.9

Population Growth of the Regions of São Paulo, 1900–1950

Region	1900	1910	1920	1930	1934	1940	1945	1950
Capital (total)	281,256	430,069	654,578	989,396	1,164,047	1,480,116	1,800,863	2,181,445
Vale do Paraíba	405,334	340,960	484,699	580,743	476,534	472,305	372,912	252,587
Central	412,741	615,434	752,524	824,439	843,335	848,659	855,475	859,682
Mogiana	464,091	714,628	811,974	837,307	871,389	843,148	844,033	844,455
Baixa Paulista	275,079	437,780	530,257	565,475	599,842	576,775	578,988	580,191
Araraquarense	148,400	323,263	583,771	811,212	879,532	943,832	979,923	1,002,916
Noroeste	7,815	33,825	136,454	434,279	618,990	856,506	1,008,037	1,098,096
Alta Sorocabana	118,905	207,146	341,754	521,696	599,661	724,017	821,887	911,705
Baixa Sorocabana	80,820	107,675	134,227	157,320	148,365	175,272	181,552	188,041
Santos	85,167	119,621	161,950	209,951	226,903	259,686	283,754	306,609
State total	2,279,608	3,330,401	4,592,188	5,931,818	6,428,598	7,180,316	7,727,424	8,225,727
Capital (urban)	239,820	374,228	579,033	884,567	1,042,880	1,274,946	1,608,686	1,936,512

SOURCE: Camargo, *Crescimento da população no Estado de São Paulo e seus aspectos econômicos*, 2:9.

Map 9.2 Population Distribution of São Paulo by Region, 1950

SOURCE: Camargo, *Crescimento da população no Estado de São Paulo*, 2:9.

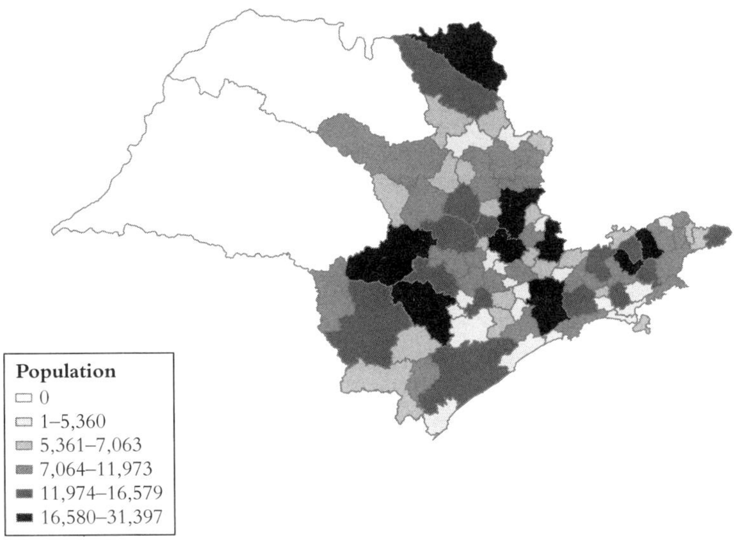

Map 9.3 Population of São Paulo Province by Município, 1872

SOURCE: Diretoria Geral de Estatística, *Recenseamento geral do império de 1872*.

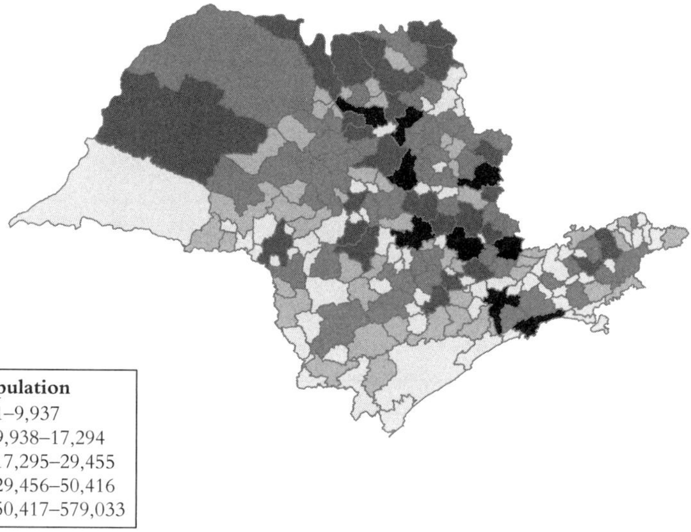

Map 9.4 Population of São Paulo State by Município, 1920

SOURCE: Diretoria Geral de Estatística, *Recenseamento do Brazil realizado em 1 de setembro de 1920.*

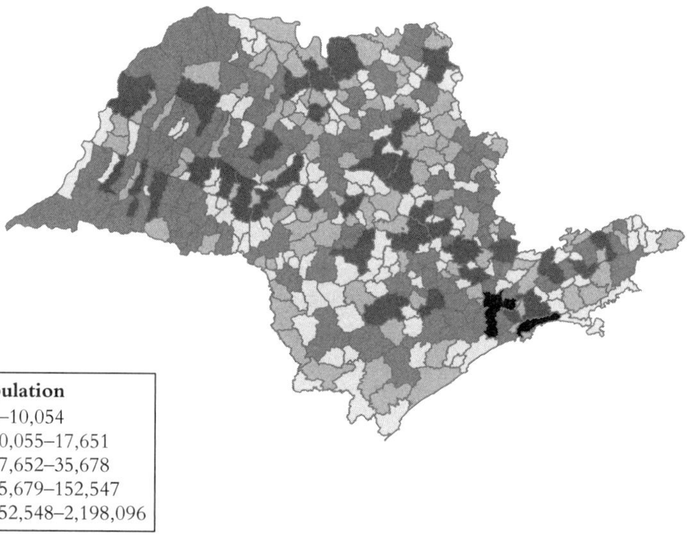

Map 9.5 Population of São Paulo State by Município, 1950

SOURCE: Instituto Brasileiro de Geografia e Estatística, *Recenseamento geral do Brasil, 1950.*

detailed social as well as demographic information related to the population of the state. Thus, government officials systematically registered rates of illegitimate births and age of marriage, literacy of spouses, and marriage endogamy by ethnic group. All these data provide further refinements on the process of demographic change in this period.

Although Santos and the capital initially had much higher rates of births out of wedlock than the rural municípios, by the beginning of the twentieth century they were at or below the rates of the rural districts. Thus, the more urban parts of Paulista society, whatever their social openness compared to the conservative rural parts of the state, did not produce any different rates of illegitimacy, which in fact were quite low for the province and varied little over time, being close to 5 percent of all births (see Figure 9.9).

Officials were also concerned with registering foreigners and their influence in vital statistics. In terms of births, it is evident that the role of European parents was far more important in the urban centers than in the rural areas, reflecting their different importance in the two different zones of the state. Moreover, as overseas immigration declined, first during World War I and then after 1920, the relative importance of foreign-born parents in births in the state declined in both the urban and the rural areas. Births to foreign-born parents in the capital dropped from two-thirds of all births

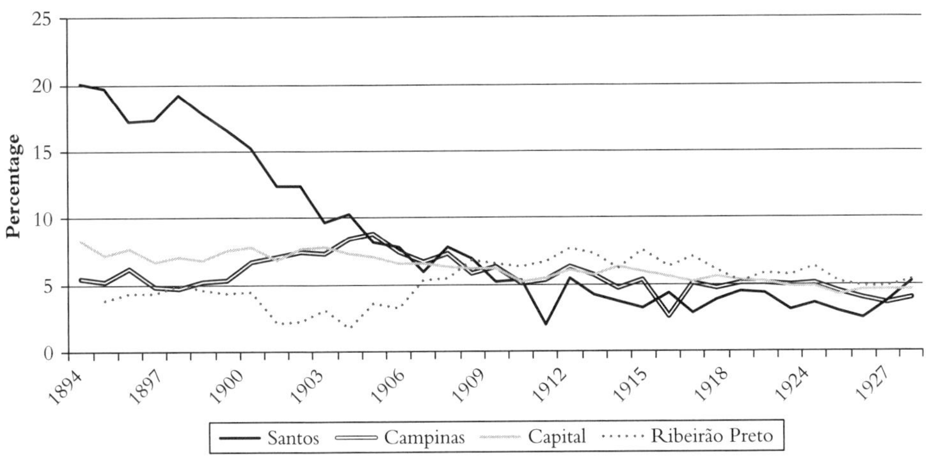

Figure 9.9 Illegitimate Births in Selected Municípios, 1894–1928

SOURCE: Directoria do Serviço Sanitario do Estado de São Paulo, *Annuario demographico, 1929*, 1:510.

in 1901 to 60 percent of births in 1929. In selected rural municípios the number dropped from 47 percent to just 28 percent in the same period.[69]

Paulista officials in counting vital statistics in the state also took detailed statistics on marriage patterns, mostly related to the incidence of marriage and to the age and origin of the spouses. While the rates suggest a normal incidence of marriage with few older persons unmarried in the state, the age data also suggest a quite early age of marriage. Though there is modest change over time, the average age of women marrying for the first time was twenty-one to twenty-two years in all the municípios, and the average age for men was twenty-five to twenty-seven years. If the comparable but limited data for 1929 is representative, then it would appear that rural populations married on average a year earlier for both sexes than the urban population. The rates for Campinas in the late 1920s were the same as for the capital in the early 1910s, which suggests that the rural areas might not have been changing as much as the urban populations of Santos and the capital (see Table 9.10).

Intermarriage between nationals and foreigners occurred early in the process of assimilation and initially involved more men crossing national boundaries to take wives than women doing the same for selecting husbands. This was already evident in São Paulo in 1910. In some 21,000 marriages performed in the state in that year, 40 percent involved at least one foreign-born national. Among the foreign born the rate of endogamy—foreign born marrying foreign born—was 58 percent. In the case of foreign-born marrying native-born Brazilians, foreign-born men married Brazilian-born women at three times the rate that foreign-born women married native-born men (see Table 9.11).

Virtually the same results appear in longitudinal studies of marriage by origin for the four principal urban centers in the state in the period 1895–

TABLE 9.10

Average Age of Marriage in Selected Cities, 1901–1929

Município	Year	Males	Females	No. of marriages
Capital	1901	25.5	21.3	1,364
	1905	25.7	21.4	1,688
	1910	25.1	21.5	2,373
	1920	26.9	22.9	4,027
	1929	26.7	22.9	7,133
Campinas	1929	25.3	21.8	873
Santos	1929	27.3	22.9	891

SOURCE: Calculated from Directoria do Serviço Sanitario do Estado de São Paulo, *Annuario demografico*, various years.

TABLE 9.11
Marriages by Nationality in the State of São Paulo, 1910

Couple nationalities	Capital	Interior	Total	% Endogamous
Brazilians with Brazilians	635	11,971	12,606	
All foreign marriages	1,738	6,645	8,383	
Foreign born with foreign born	1,150	3,709	4,859	58%
Brazilian males with foreign females	170	721	891	11%
Foreign males with Brazilian females	418	2,215	2,633	31%
Total	2,373	18,616	20,989	

SOURCE: Directoria do Serviço Sanitario do Estado de São Paulo, *Annuario demografico, 1910*, 9, 105–109.

TABLE 9.12
Marriages by Nationality in Four Select Cities, 1895–1929

Couple nationalities	Capital	Campinas	Santos	Ribeirão Preto	Total	% Endogamous
Brazilians with Brazilians	47,559	12,249	6,250	5,614	71,672	
All foreign marriages	69,004	8,302	9,720	6,378	93,404	
Foreign born with foreign born	41,287	4,285	5,998	3,717	55,287	59%
Brazilian males with foreign females	8,374	940	1,069	799	11,182	12%
Foreign males with Brazilian females	19,343	3,077	2,653	1,862	26,935	29%
Total	116,563	20,551	15,970	11,992	165,076	100%

SOURCE: Directoria do Serviço Sanitario do Estado de São Paulo, *Annuario demografico, 1929*, 1:35, 260, 386, 504.

1929. In these four cities some 165,000 marriages took place during this long period, of which just over half were to foreign immigrants. Again, it was the men who married out of their ethnic group at two and a half times the rate of women, and more than half married other foreign nationals (see Table 9.12). Moreover, over this period, Campinas had more nationals marrying than foreigners, as was typical in most areas of the state. But given the declining importance of the foreign immigrants, even Santos and the capital finally had over half their annual marriages occurring between native born by the decade of the 1920s.

There were, of course, differences by nationality in terms of marriage partners. The availability of complete statistics on marriage by sex and origin for 1910, 1916, and 1917 permits us to evaluate this pattern both for the state as a whole and for its principal city, the capital. The 21,000 marriages performed in 1910 and the 53,000 marriages performed in the two years of 1916 and 1917 show almost identical patterns. Women tended to marry within their ethnic-origin group more than did men, though it is evident that in the case of the Brazilians this was reversed, and in the case of the Spaniards there is little difference by sex in marrying within the same nationality (see Tables 9.13 and 9.14).

But what was the norm for the state was not quite the norm for the population of the largest urban center. Here Brazilian women married foreigners more than did Brazilian men, but at a much higher rate than the state as a whole. Otherwise, the pattern among the foreign born was similar, except insofar as the Italians in the city were the opposite of their rural compatriots and tended to be much more endogamous and married fewer Brazilian women (see Table 9.15).

Of course, no immigrant group was quite as endogamous as the Japanese in their first and second generations. Of the 51,418 Japanese men who married in Brazil between 1908 and 1958, only 1,956 (or 3.8 percent) married spouses of another national group. Among the Japanese women in this period, there were 50,981 brides and only 441 married non-Japanese men (or just 0.9 percent).[70]

Literacy of the population was another concern of the Paulista officials. Throughout the nineteenth century, São Paulo was a society with only a

TABLE 9.13
Marriage Endogamy by Nationality in the State of São Paulo, 1910

Percentage of women

	WOMEN					
Men	Brazilian	Portuguese	Italian	Spaniard	Other	Total
Brazilian	83	19	16	13	19	
Portuguese	4	69	3	7	3	
Italian	11	8	77	13	19	
Spaniard	1	3	2	66	2	
Other	1	2	2	1	58	
Total	100	100	100	100	100	
No. of marriages	15,352	665	3,844	936	324	21,121

Percentage of men

	WOMEN						
Men	Brazilian	Portuguese	Italian	Spaniard	Other	Total	No. of marriages
Brazilian	93	1	4	1	0	100	13,580
Portuguese	47	38	9	5	1	100	1,219
Italian	35	1	60	3	1	100	4,903
Spaniard	21	2	10	66	1	100	934
Other	43	2	15	2	39	100	485
Total							21,121

SOURCE: Departamento de Estatística do Estado, *Anuário estatístico de São Paulo, 1910*, 80–81.

TABLE 9.14

Marriage Endogamy by Nationality in the State of São Paulo, 1916–1917

Percentage of women

Men	WOMEN Brazilian	Portuguese	Italian	Spaniard	Other	Total
Brazilian	83	15	32	17	20	
Portuguese	4	76	5	6	3	
Italian	9	5	57	7	14	
Spaniard	2	4	4	69	3	
Other	1	0	2	1	61	
Total	100	100	100	100	100	
No. of marriages	43,766	2,238	3,759	3,077	621	53,461

Percentage of men

Men	WOMEN Brazilian	Portuguese	Italian	Spaniard	Other	Total	No. of marriages
Brazilian	94	1	3	1	0	100	38,640
Portuguese	47	43	5	4	1	100	3,928
Italian	60	2	34	3	1	100	6,390
Spaniard	30	2	5	62	0	100	3,431
Other	53	1	7	4	35	100	1,072
Total							53,461

SOURCE: Directoria do Serviço Sanitario do Estado de São Paulo, *Annuario demografico, 1916*, 17, 87, 256, 344, 421; Directoria do Serviço Sanitario do Estado de São Paulo, *Annuario demografico, 1917*, 75–76, 302, 394, 499, 610.

TABLE 9.15

Marriage Endogamy by Nationality in the Capital of São Paulo, 1916–1917

Percentage of women

Men	WOMEN Brazilian	Portuguese	Italian	Spaniard	Other	Total
Brazilian	64	10	23	19	14	
Portuguese	12	86	7	9	3	
Italian	18	2	63	5	12	
Spaniard	3	2	3	63	2	
Other	3	0	3	3	69	
Total	100	100	100	100	100	
No. of marriages	3,968	1,110	999	394	257	6,728

Percentage of men

Men	WOMEN Brazilian	Portuguese	Italian	Spaniard	Other	Total	No. of marriages
Brazilian	85	4	8	2	1	100	2,981
Portuguese	30	62	5	2	1	100	1,537
Italian	50	2	45	1	2	100	1,421
Spaniard	29	4	6	59	1	100	425
Other	38	1	9	4	49	100	364
Total							6,728

SOURCE: Directoria do Serviço Sanitario do Estado de São Paulo, *Annuario Demografico, 1916*, 17, 87, 256, 344, 421; Directoria do Serviço Sanitario do Estado de São Paulo, *Annuario Demografico, 1917*, 75–76, 302, 394, 499, 610.

minority of literate persons. In this case São Paulo was a rather backward province, with a literacy rate of only 17 percent of persons five years of age and older who were literate in 1872, compared to 22 percent literates in Rio Grande do Sul, which then was the most advanced state. Moreover, there was a clear bias against the education of women in this period. In this discrimination, the province was in fact among the worst in the empire, with only 36 percent of the schoolchildren being girls, compared to the imperial average of 38 percent. In the leading province of Rio Grande do Sul girls made up 44 percent of the children attending schools. Literates were 16 percent of the national population in 1872, but among men, almost a quarter were literate, compared to only a little over a tenth of women who could read and write. In the case of São Paulo, 27 percent of males five years of age and older were literate and 14 percent of the females, compared to imperial averages of 24 percent for males and 14 percent for females, thus indicating the province was not a particularly advanced province even by the standards of the empire.[71] This overall low rate of literacy was due to Brazil being seriously behind most other countries of Latin America in its provision of public education, even as late as the last quarter of the nineteenth century. The 1872 census clearly shows that São Paulo was if anything at or below the average of the nation in terms of literacy and not different from the rest of the empire in its far lower level of female literacy compared to men. This remained the norm until the end of the twentieth century, when girls finally had equal access to education. Even the capital showed little difference from other major regions in the state in 1872.

From census to census, the literacy rate slowly improved as the state began to invest significant sums in public education. In the census of 1900 the state reported a literacy rate of 25 percent, which did not increase to 30 percent until twenty years later, in the census of 1920.[72] In that census year São Paulo was ranked as only the fourth-most-literate state in the union, well behind Rio Grande do Sul, in which over half the population eighteen years and older was literate.[73] But by then São Paulo was educating more children of primary school age than any other state in the nation, with some 40 percent of all children in this age group attending primary school, which was overwhelmingly publicly funded. Moreover, the rates for educating boys and girls were not that different, being 42 percent of all boys and 39 percent of all girls attending school in these age categories. For Brazil overall, the rates in 1920 were 25 percent for boys and 18 percent for girls. All this meant that São Paulo by the census of 1940 moved up to second place, behind Rio Grande do Sul, and had the largest percentage increase of literates among all the states between the two censuses. It was also in this census that the majority of the population of the state finally became literate.[74]

In 1917 the state began to collect data on the literacy of marrying partners. Though there was a high ratio of unknowns, for the some 44,000 marriages for which data are available, the patterns found in the national censuses are in the state statistics of São Paulo. In that year women were overwhelmingly illiterate compared to men—almost two-thirds of the men were literate, and only a bit more than a third of the women marrying in that year could read and write. But for both sexes combined, the literacy rate was just 50 percent (see Table 9.16), a figure higher than the population as a whole. Adding to this equation the 10,000 or so marriages that did not have literacy data would reduce the literacy rate to 41 percent of all married couples, and even this rate was higher than that in the 1920 census.

But the slow pace of literacy changed in the decades of the 1920s and 1930s as more public education was made available, especially in the urban centers.[75] The state census of 1934 shows the impact of a major push in urban education in these decades, if not in rural education. All the urban areas, which accounted for a third of the state's population, had an overall literacy rate of 73 percent for persons six years of age and older. Urban males in this age grouping were 80 percent literate, and urban women were 67 percent literate. But in the two-thirds of the state that was rural, only a third of those six years of age and older could read and write in the rural area (42 percent of the males and 24 percent of the females). That gave the state an overall literacy rate of 42 percent of the population six years of age and older, or 14 percent above the rate reported in the 1920 census.[76] Nevertheless, despite the relatively slow pace of educational advancement and low rates of literacy in the state, by 1950 male literacy was the highest of any state in Brazil, surpassing Rio Grande do Sul, which finally allowed São Paulo to become the most literate of any state in the nation.[77] Whereas in

TABLE 9.16
Literacy of Marrying Couples in the State of São Paulo, 1917

	Men	Women	Total
Knows how to read and write	62%	38%	21,856
Illiterate	38%	62%	21,790
Total	100%	100%	
Known cases	21,823	21,823	43,646

SOURCE: Departamento de Estatística do Estado, *Anuário estatístico de São Paulo, 1917*, 77, 303, 394, 500, 611.

Brazil 43 percent of the population over the age of five was literate, the figure for São Paulo was 59 percent. By then both men (65 percent) and women (54 percent) in the state were in the majority literate, in contrast to the rest of the country, which would not have a majority of women and men who were literate until the census of 1960. In the census of 1950, urban Brazil with its 11 million persons (out of 44 million total) were two-thirds literate, but even here the urban population of São Paulo led with an 80 percent literacy rate (85 percent of urban men and 75 percent of urban women could read and write). Only the Federal District had a higher ratio than the various urban centers of São Paulo.[78] It should also be recalled that even though the ratios of male and female literates in São Paulo in 1950 were the highest in the nation, Brazil still had overall the lowest literacy rate of any South American country, and even the São Paulo rate was less than the literacy rate in nine other Latin American countries in this period.[79]

In reviewing the evolution of the growth and structure of the São Paulo population, it is evident that the state for the earliest part of this century from 1850 to 1950 differed little from its neighbors. Its ratio of slaves was rather high, but it also had more whites than most other regions. In terms of vital rates, until the end of the empire it differed little from the population of the empire as a whole. It was only at the very end of the nineteenth and beginning of the twentieth centuries that the state began to pull ahead of the rest of the nation. It was only after 1900, because of the major changes in sanitation and health, that São Paulo began to have rates of mortality lower than those experienced in the rest of Brazil. Within the state it was the urban centers that led this decline in mortality, with rural and urban mortality rates not reaching parity until mid-century. The decline of infectious diseases led to declines in infant and child mortality, primarily in the urban centers of the state, again reaching levels that the rest of Brazil did not attain until decades later. Also it was the urban centers of the state that began to experience declining birth rates well before the rest of the nation, which had some of the world's highest birth rates until after 1950. São Paulo and its state institutions were also to lead the nation in terms of levels of literacy from the time of the Old Republic until the middle of the twentieth century.

The state was also unique in its high ratio of both foreign-born immigrants and native-born migrants entering from other states. It was the attraction of the booming coffee economy that brought these slave and free immigrants, both foreign and national, to the state. In turn, the emergence of an industrial sector based on the expanding market brought by the foreign immigrants was of prime national importance, along with the usual educational and health services available only in the advanced urban centers of the state, which made life in the state more attractive for native-born workers in the poorer regions of the North and Northeast in the last half of the twentieth century. So dramatic was this both natural growth and increase due to immigration that São Paulo by 1950 emerged as not only the most economically advanced state but also the most populous state in Brazil.

Conclusion

The one hundred years that we examine here were profoundly transformative for the state and city of São Paulo. In 1850 São Paulo was a minor province of the empire, with small urban centers and little connection to international markets. Its population was a mix of poor whites, Indians, caboclos, and Africans, and its agriculture served mostly local and regional markets. Its lands were fertile, but its transport infrastructure was so primitive that products arrived at distant markets in a poor state. The capital of the province was of modest size compared to the traditional cities of Rio de Janeiro or Salvador de Bahia, and even as it moved into coffee, it was a minor producer compared to the province of Rio de Janeiro.

But coffee, virgin lands, the railroads, and slave and free wage immigrant labor were to transform this relatively backward and modest province into an imperial and republican powerhouse. It is this transformation that we examine here. With a new entrepreneurial coffee elite emerging in the second half of the nineteenth century, local agriculture finally became competitive on both the national and the international markets. On the basis of this wealth, the state was able to attract several million foreign- and native-born immigrants, who in turn created a modern wage economy. With profits flowing in from exported coffee, the local elite invested in commerce, foreign trade, financial institutions, and even industry. In turn, the expanding free wage labor provided a market for food and clothing that the coffee barons and foreign entrepreneurs could exploit by providing clothing and processed foods. The population exploded, and coffee expanded along with the railroads, so that by the early twentieth century São Paulo had emerged as the locomotive pulling the Brazilian economy. Other centers of industrial and commercial activity would emerge in the same period, especially in the Federal District of Rio de Janeiro, but by the end of this period, they had been surpassed by São Paulo.

All this change was facilitated and supported by an evolving administrative structure and a state government willing to invest in basic infrastructure. Restrained under the empire to a limited local government, the state elite was so aggressively pushing for autonomy that it would eventually seize control from the federal government in the period of the Old Republic so as to create a powerful state government. By the twentieth century the state of São Paulo was a leader in health, science, and technology and was a model administrative organization by the standards of the nation. It educated more of its population, it had more modern water and sanitation systems, and it eventually had the most railroads and the best roads in the country, all paid for with state funds. It was also the most literate state in the country, having risen from being ranked eighth in terms of literacy in 1872 to first place in 1950.

The empire had laid the foundation of the tax structure that would be used in the Old Republic but left a deficient tax administration that had to be reorganized under the republic. But even with these problems, and the modest resources available to it, the provincial government was able to initiate the railroad age and undertake the subvention of European immigrants despite numerous years of deficits. Under the republic, the state government was reorganized and expanded with extensive new fiscal and financial powers. The aim of the republican government was to build a state with a high degree of autonomy that supported an expanding economy and society, extended its basic infrastructure, and promoted local urban growth and development. All these activities required growing resources obtained through increased collection of taxes and also through obtaining major loans in the national and international credit markets. Along with promoting growth, the state government became an active interventor in the coffee economy, until finally controlling production, buying stocks, and even limiting exports in order to save that economy in its moments of crisis. The state government was also forced to deal with other economic, political, and fiscal crises in the twentieth century. These included the crisis of the Encilhamento, the two world wars, periodic overproduction in the coffee market, and above all the 1929 world economic depression, which initiated a major transformation in the productive structure of coffee and forced the state finally to turn to the federal government for support. Although the Getúlio Vargas revolution of 1930 seriously reduced the power of the state government, even with reduced power and resources the state was still able to provide basic economic support for the increasingly more industrialized and complex Paulista economy.

A reflection of all this was the growth of the capital city of São Paulo from a sleepy town of some 20,000 in 1850 to a world metropolis by 1950. This explosive growth of the capital and the state was due to high levels of fertility and even more to declining mortality, and it was aided by massive foreign and domestic migration that turned the capital into the second-largest city in Brazil by 1950 and made the state the most populous in the nation by 1940. In all its basic demographic indices, São Paulo would be a leader in the mortality transition that occurred in the twentieth century. It also led the nation in fertility decline before the end of this period, though the nation as a whole would not experience the fertility revolution until two decades after the close of our history.

This was the century of coffee, as we have shown in this study. But as this century was coming to a close, by 1950 there began the slow evolution of a more complex agricultural and industrial economy in the state. Even as coffee still dominated exports in this period, food and commercial crops like cotton also were an important part of the expanding agricultural sector. Also by mid-century the state was finally leading the nation in the use of machinery and fertilizer and reaching a new level of productivity in the growing of several traditional crops. But it would not be until after 1950 that the state became the modern producer of meat, sugar, oranges, and soybeans at world levels of productivity, which would then replace coffee as the major exports of the state's agriculture. The agricultural revolution that put Brazil among the world's agribusiness leaders took place only from the 1990s, with the opening of the economy and intensification of agricultural and livestock research. What we have shown is that the production of rice, corn, and beans—the staples of the Paulista diet—expanded throughout the period analyzed, and local agriculture succeeded in feeding the growing urban and rural population of the state. Also it was local production that fed the developing food-processing plants, which became an ever more important part of the growing manufacturing sector. It was locally grown cotton that became an important input for the important Paulista textile industry. As we have stressed, by the late 1940s the frontier had finally been closed in the state of São Paulo. Thus, the middle decades of the century were a transitional period, when local agriculture no longer expanded through the exploitation of virgin lands but was turning instead to the systematic use of machinery and fertilizer.

This century also laid the groundwork for the steady, impressive growth of industry in São Paulo, which went from being a minor pole of production to the leading manufacturing center in the nation. Starting in the late nineteenth century, basically with textiles and food processing, industry grew at impressive rates in the state. The cause for this growth was the introduction of free labor, particularly of European immigrants with their increased capacity for consumption over slave laborers; the availability of foreign exchange generated by coffee exports; the willingness of the coffee barons to invest in urban and industrial projects; a growing agro-industrial integration; and a series of external shocks that limited international trade. All these factors stimulated local production and allowed the consolidation of an industrial process even before the implementation of effective policies of industrial protection that began only in the second half of the twentieth century. When the policies of industrial protection were implemented by the federal government, São Paulo already had a consolidated industry, mainly consuming local raw materials, whose production expanded to meet expanding demand both locally and nationally. Nevertheless, the state and the nation, though creating a major industrial sector, did not fully transform Brazil into a fully integrated industrial complex until the decade of the 1970s.

It is important to note that although we have ended this study in 1950, the state of São Paulo continued its process of growth and transformation at a new level of intensity after this period. By the beginning of the twenty-first century, the state had achieved a fully integrated industrial sector with the latest international production processes and a sophisticated financial system integrated into international financial flows, and it had created one of the world's most highly competitive international agricultures. This profound transformation began in the decade of the 1960s with systematic new laws and institutions created by the federal government, which included the creation of the Central Bank of Brazil. These federal laws proved to be a major incentive for São Paulo, which by the decade of the 1980s led all other centers in terms of financial operations and in the following decades saw the transfer of a great number of banks, both national and foreign, to the capital of São Paulo. By the end of the twentieth century, São Paulo was unquestionably the banking center of the nation, and the city of São Paulo was now a world-class banking center offering the highest-quality financial services in Brazil.[1]

Agriculture also profoundly changed in the second half of the century through the generalized use of insecticides and fertilizers and the massive mechanization of agricultural production. Although the modernization of Brazilian agriculture occurred in almost every zone of Brazil, São Paulo is still the single largest agricultural state and accounted for 14 percent of total national production in 2016. It has returned to one of its colonial staples, and is now the world's leading producer of sugar. Oranges are another traditional crop in the state and were always consumed locally. But the growth of the orange juice industry changed all that. By the end of the century, São Paulo had become the world center for the production of orange juice. Orange production in São Paulo was just 3 million boxes in 1951. By the end of the century, the state would produce 300 million boxes.[2] Although soybeans were introduced systematically only in the decade of the 1960s, the state also became a significant exporter of this product, while still remaining Brazil's largest coffee-exporting state. Even food crops produced for the internal market also experienced this increase in both output and productivity.

Today, São Paulo is Brazil's largest state in terms of population, industry, agriculture, and economic importance, and it established the basis of what would be a massive modernization of the society and economy in the second half of the twentieth century, truly becoming by the end of the century, as the economist Edmar Bacha notes, a society and economy equivalent to Belgium in a country that still had some states on the level of India.[3] While much of this massive expansion would occur after 1950, the basic groundwork for its evolution had been firmly established in the period we study.

In the end, our history is one of unusual economic growth, population expansion, and international market development of a backward and marginal economy. Few cases in modern history have seen such an extraordinary change and such rapid development of a backward region. One can only compare it with the late twentieth-century changes in Europe and Asia in which marginal or poorly developed areas grew so quickly. Moreover, this growth was not based on abundant cheap labor or on late industrial competition but was a result of converting a backward agricultural sector into a dynamic exporting zone that was more than competitive with any other producer on the world market. In fact, São Paulo came to dominate that market just with its own production.

APPENDIX

TABLE A1.1

Exports of Coffee (1,000 kg) from Brazilian Zones and Provinces, 1870–1890

	RIO ZONE[a]								
Year	Rio de Janeiro	Minas Gerais[b]	Espírito Santo	São Paulo	Total	Santos zone	Total	Rio zone (%)	Santos zone (%)
1870	109,968	31,704	5,759	17,518	164,949	28,207	193,156	85%	15%
1871	113,437	35,152	7,916	19,153	175,658	25,266	200,924	87%	13%
1872	102,586	26,199	6,101	13,057	147,943	25,434	173,377	85%	15%
1873	92,584	28,308	6,966	17,964	145,822	33,305	179,127	81%	19%
1874	105,175	37,116	5,137	18,221	165,649	44,801	210,450	79%	21%
1875	119,269	41,637	8,033	17,635	186,574	47,443	234,017	80%	20%
1876	111,562	36,403	5,787	17,381	171,133	41,517	212,650	80%	20%
1877	107,252	38,346	8,569	17,118	171,285	48,835	220,120	78%	22%
1878	109,608	47,926	6,222	24,018	187,774	66,273	254,047	74%	26%
1879	120,419	51,233	7,856	21,570	201,078	67,569	268,647	75%	25%
1880	133,765	54,782	9,086	21,807	219,440	67,394	286,834	77%	23%
1881	148,008	73,773	11,096	26,508	259,385	81,864	341,249	76%	24%
1882	156,124	66,974	10,103	25,473	258,674	100,870	359,544	72%	28%
1883	113,085	67,346	11,471	26,375	218,277	113,006	331,283	66%	34%
1884	130,429	62,994	8,495	20,719	222,637	122,824	352,461	63%	35%
1885	110,214	85,457	12,425	17,767	225,863	114,669	340,532	66%	34%
1886	122,569	64,741	11,516	16,749	215,575	124,070	339,645	63%	37%
1887	61,937	46,364	8,805	14,426	131,532	113,653	245,185	54%	46%
1888	109,478	66,507	9,140	14,970	200,095	115,669	315,764	63%	37%
1889	80,090	69,465	9,191	18,646	177,392	137,616	315,008	56%	44%
1890	78,643	59,770	7,965	13,944	160,322	152,749	313,071	51%	49%

SOURCE: Mello, "The Economics of Labor," 32–33.

[a] Coffee exported by the port of Rio de Janeiro.

[b] The results for Minas Gerais do not include the production from the part of that province belonging to the Santos zone.

TABLE A1.2

Exports from São Paulo by Quantity and Value, 1856–1890

Quantity

Year	Coffee (kg)	Cotton (kg)	Tobacco (kg)	Lard (kg)	Rice (L)	Flour (L)	Beans (L)	Corn (L)	Sugar (kg)	Leather (kg)	Tea (kg)	Value (contos)
1856/1857	32,293,536		177,960	1,289,474					540,709			10,482
1862/1863	21,283,350	1,278	172,588								28,268	
1863/1864	15,963,975	13,014	138,973								57,491	
1864/1865	24,609,450	104,388	109,941								24,607	
1865/1866	20,323,321	2,808,645	80,653	200,010							25,695	
1866/1867	19,038,137	3,344,808	108,570	177,220							18,495	
1867/1868	27,524,006	8,185,973	486,474	310,252							18,060	
1868/1869	37,899,979	7,176,255	318,723	225,183							27,360	
1869/1870	50,133,765	6,692,670	56,918	486,628	10,612,775						22,260	27,726
1870/1871	34,059,133	6,509,055	65,714	268,140	3,087,600	9,600	57,250	776,050	14,893		18,133	20,893
1871/1872	39,678,705	11,363,648	359,175	340,305	5,715,300	4,400	122,925	1,054,225			14,361	26,198
1872/1873	50,491,515	10,181,617	789,120	119,985	3,143,550		48,575	586,125				31,390
1873/1874	62,173,385	9,897,482	514,139	770,319	3,016,499	17,854	122,925	459,834	57,937			41,310
1874/1875	65,746,029	5,358,144	165,796	257,482	3,586,919	6,013	45,647	564,930	46,443			37,434
1875/1876	60,896,641	4,074,965	61,650	136,814	2,662,170	20,200	111,687	645,691	14,049			31,391
1876/1877	53,353,010	2,173,946	329,491	929,375	2,090,458	1,970	90,400	214,320	13,570			25,950
1877/1878	78,449,897	666,685	612,484	784,280	2,142,287	430,055	510,462	879,512	15,495			29,877
1878/1879	91,430,814	1,314,722	381,310	888,258	2,577,667	835,952	835,952	354,384	3,900			32,601
1879/1880	82,243,757	834,318	209,420	439,225	2,931,652	96,897	272,336	513,379	6,405			31,509
1880/1881	97,223,835	1,038,261	216,363	391,758	3,402,772	33,146	638,440	345,412	2,547			30,331
1881/1882	115,124,716	1,191,222	344,408	327,745	2,609,007	27,667	278,982	184,099	30,180	316,396		32,907
1882/1883	147,468,020	444,437	1,362,811	144,090	2,113,707	4,592	89,402	177,910	91,490	282,479		33,943
1883/1884	138,172,975	293,960	243,016	145,472					1,920	384,760		48,230
1884/1885	140,687,272	939,004	283,584	261,049					1,170	387,582		48,581
1885/1886	108,878,784	993,332	240,262	237,567	2,152,194				42,628	68,640		37,267
1886/1887	161,654,199	315,620	94,121	183,423	1,386,883				25,692	267,377		78,354
1889/1890	137,898,061	147,917	96,624	69,989	1,471,585	347,795	195,071	19,382	488,790	348,472		82,047

Value (mil réis)

Year	Coffee	Cotton	Tobacco	Lard	Rice	Flour	Beans	Corn	Sugar	Leather	Tea	Total
1856/1857	8,592,522		80,803	427,293	351,971	2,835	32,047	7,355	467,921	95,379		10,482
1877/1878	28,593,813	372,310	126,705	230,196						126,705	13,942	29,877
1878/1879	31,056,929	737,368	128,727	272,030						128,727	15,206	32,601
1879/1880	30,115,985	426,274	120,214	130,855						120,214	3,560	31,509
1880/1881	29,329,139	419,950	143,706	71,166						143,706	5,890	30,331
1881/1882	31,760,342	500,668	145,772	36,556						145,772	5,200	32,907
1882/1883	33,056,253	115,202	127,392	35,219						127,392	6,988	33,943
1883/1884	47,389,640	136,719	163,642	16,200						163,642	4,140	48,230
1884/1885	47,550,864	137,765	211,715	54,836						211,715	4,340	48,581
1885/1886	36,133,676	402,782	247,380	18,188						247,380	1,560	37,267
1886/1887	77,410,016	275,061	230,110	2,860						230,110	2,000	78,354
1889/1890	80,875,441	226,025	68,109	60,096	162,658	16,534	36,994	1,816	98,561	166,013		82,047

SOURCE: *Relatório apresentado á Assembléa Legislativa Provincial de S. Paulo pelo presidente da provincia, Laurindo Abelardo de Brito, no dia 13 de janeiro de 1881*, 82; *Relatório apresentado á Assembléa Legislativa Provincial de S. Paulo pelo presidente da provincia, Laurindo Abelardo de Brito, no dia 5 de fevereiro de 1880*, part 2a, pp. 37–44; *Relatório apresentado à assembleia legislativa provincial de São Paulo pelo presidente da província o Exmo. Sr. Dr. Antônio Candido da Rocha*, 43; Martins, *Agricultura Paulista*, 99; Canabrava, *O algodão em São Paulo, 1861–1875*, app. 2; "Quadro da Importação e exportação da Província de São Paulo," in *Relatório apresentado pelo Excelentíssimo Senhor Dezembargador Francisco Diogo Pereira de Vasconcellos*; *Relatório apresentado ao chefe do Governo Provisório por Francisco Glicério.*

TABLE A2.1

Average Budgeted Expected Income of the Province of São Paulo, 1835–1890 (mil réis)

Item	1835/1836–1845/1846	1846/1847–1854/1855	1855/1856–1865/1866	1867/1868–1875/1876	1876/1877–1889/1890
Direitos de saida—dizimos	774,000	1,432,000	3,634,489	9,761,820	16,963,216
Imposto de transito					6,660,000
Novos impostos sobre animais em Sorocaba	73,500	84,000	178,863	121,682	141,217
Direitos de passagem do Rio Negro—animais	767,738	405,000			
Contibuição de Guarapuava	60,800	35,000			
Passagem de rios	9,600				
Despachos de embarcações	4,450	7,200	4,670	14,731	86,841
Ponte de embarque em Santos		12,000	109,154	279,528	863,940
Meia sisa da venda de escravos	154,016	302,000	688,636	1,261,258	897,905
Imposto 1$800 sobre escravos empregados na lavoura					115,000
Imposto 1$000 sobre escravos empregados na lavoura					150,000
Imposto de 2$000 sobre escravos não empregados na lavoura					43,400
Imposto sobre escravos pertencentes a conventos de 10 a 50 anos			9,000	4,759	20
Imposto sobre escravos que não pagaram meia sisa			8,440	1,710	30
Imposto de 20$ sobre escravos que saem da provincia por mar		4,600	15,480	11,000	
Décima de legados e heranças	108,400	199,000	814,298	1,255,141	1,907,953
Decima de usofruto					112,166
Novo imposto de 2% sobre totalidade das heranças			120,000		
Décima de predios urbanos de conventos		5,700	12,649	20,232	8,953
Imposto sobre prédios; imposto predial				35,000	1,676,902
Décima de prédios urbanos	54,900				
Imposto sobre casas de leilão e moda	1,000	1,200	2,290	8,595	32,011
Imposto sobre seges ou veiculos de condução		900	4,881	11,918	30,802
Imposto companhias equestres					33,500
Imposto sobre loterias e stranhas à Provincia					35,800
Imposto de 20% no consumo de aguardente	110,400	181,000	53,700		
Imposto de 1$600 réis de cada réz cortada e 320 subsídio literário	139,510	181,000	96,000		

TABLE A2.1 (CONTINUED)

Item	1835/1836–1845/1846	1846/1847–1854/1855	1855/1856–1865/1866	1867/1868–1875/1876	1876/1877–1889/1890
Imposto nos armazens, tavernas e botequins	48,400				
Imposto Adicional					1,910,164
Imposto sobre capitalistas				175,000	108,706
Imposto Pessoal				140,816	
Imposto do selo e emolumentos de patentes guarda nacional				10,000	48,000
Emolumentos da secretaria de governo (inclui cartórios)	1,350	4,000	26,069	74,496	126,719
Novos impostos sobre diversas mercês					66,500
Novo imposto por diversas mercês; novos impostos ou subsidio literário	31,600				31,200
Novos e velhos direitos de títulos expedidos pelas autoridades	18,540	9,400	21,007	6,400	
Novo Imposto de 6$400 no município da capital		1,400	2,000		
Bens do evento			7,119		
Rendimento da casa de correção; penitenciaria	300	6,500	94,033	121,330	54,368
Tipografia provincial	1,640	780			
Rendimento dos estabelecimentos provinciais	1,100				66,100
Rendimento da casa de prisão com trabalho	350				
Eventual de dividendos da Ituana e multas por infrações					185,000
Indenização de juros pagos a Companhia Paulista				20,000	
Renda extraordinária Indenizações					275,400
Receita eventual, dividendos ações Ituana e multas por infrações					342,200
Multas contribuintes moroso e premio depositos públicos	200		10,252	57,507	100,455
Eventual (Bens do evento e receita eventual)	3,486	35,000	72,000		
Eventual			54,186	67,251	16,449
Outros		100			
Cobrança da metade da dívida ativa anterior	85,622				
Cobrança de toda a dívida ativa desta data em diante	24,000				
Cobrança dívida ativa provincial	32,000	71,000	497,497	150,613	348,230

(*continued*)

TABLE A2.1 (CONTINUED)

Item	1835/1836–1845/1846	1846/1847–1854/1855	1855/1856–1865/1866	1867/1868–1875/1876	1876/1877–1889/1890
Juros das apólices compradas por conta do cofre provincial	58,000	64,500			
Venda das apolices existentes Rio de Janeiro, art 37 orçamento vigente		77,305			
Receita Enventual—inclusive letras vencer no ano e 66$000 sisa escravos			100,000		
Receita eventual inclusive venda de letras venciveis no ano			76,330		
Auxilio do Governo Geral					90,000
Auxilio do Governo Geral para a força pública					88,500
Total sem barreiras	*2,564,902*	*3,120,585*	*6,713,043*	*13,610,787*	*33,617,647*
Receita das barreiras	683,200	1,426,140	2,705,532	3,324,887	1,182,434
Total com barreiras	*3,248,102*	*4,546,725*	*9,418,575*	*16,935,674*	*34,800,081*
Saldos e sobras do ano anterior	59,713				
Saldo existente			143,522		
Saldo existente em poder dos agentes arrecadadores			89,591		
Total com saldo de exercícios anteriores	*3,307,815*	*4,546,725*	*9,651,688*	*16,935,674*	*34,800,081*

SOURCE: Assembleia Legislativa do Estado de São Paulo, leis orçamentárias anuais, 1891–1920, http://www.al.sp.gov.br/alesp/normas/?tipoNorma=9&ementa=S: Laws 17 (1835); 40 (1836); 22 (1838); 11 (1839); 17 (1840); 25 (1841); 40 (1844); 9 (1845); 35 (1846); 28 (1847); 12 (1848); 27 (1849); 24 (1850); 10 (1851); 14 (1852); 18 (1853); 30 (1854); 31 (1855); 31 (1856); 47 (1857); 39 (1858); 27 (1859); 16 (1861); 8 (1862); 30 (1864); 77 (1865); 16 (1867); 57 (1868); 29 (1869); 93 (1870); 45 (1871); 73 (1872); 91 (1873); 52 (1874); 10 (1875); 89 (1876); 22 (1877); 156 (1880); 59 (1884); 94 (1885); 124 (1886); 95 (1887); 55 (1888); 107 (1889).

NOTE: For some years it was impossible to obtain the relevant budget law. The laws used to average for each period are as follows: period 1835/1836–1845/1846 corresponds to fiscal years 1835/1836–1841/1842, 1844/1845, and 1845/1846; period 1846/1847–1854/1855 corresponds to fiscal years 1846/1847–1854/1855; period 1855/1856–1865/1866 corresponds to fiscal years 1855/1856–1859/1860 and 1861/1862–1865/1866; period 1867/1868–1875/1876 corresponds to fiscal years 1867/1868–1875/1876; and period 1876/1877–1889/1890 corresponds to fiscal years 1876/1877, 1877/1878, 1880/1881, and 1884/1885–1889/1890.

Table A2.2 begins on the next page

TABLE A2.2

Actual and Estimated Receipts for the Provincial Budget of São Paulo, 1835–1889 (mil réis)

	INCOME			EXPENDITURE			DIFFERENCE	
Fiscal year	Estimated	Realized	Realized/ estimated	Estimated	Realized	Realized/ estimated	Actual	Estimated
1835/1836	243,700	292,701	1.20	239,340	171,324	0.72	121,378	4,360
1836/1837	287,690	338,289	1.18	287,690	208,145	0.72	130,144	
1837/1838	244,398	436,044	1.78	244,398	285,791	1.17	150,253	
1838/1839	365,888	315,904	0.86	365,885	306,708	0.84	9,195	3
1839/1840	431,376	430,728	1.00	431,376	411,828	0.95	18,900	
1840/1841	365,648	326,430	0.89	426,448	203,087	0.48	123,343	-60,800
1841/1842	431,760	405,419	0.94	465,274	679,267	1.46	-273,848	-33,514
1842/1843		292,914			363,079		-70,165	
1843/1844		327,312			270,618		56,695	
1844/1845	449,560	408,516	0.91	667,043	586,813	0.88	-178,297	-217,483
1845/1846	408,460	574,139	1.41	431,196	585,852	1.36	-11,714	-22,736
1846/1847	422,160	706,223	1.67	657,846	615,132	0.94	91,091	-235,686
1847/1848	459,369	571,828	1.24	471,613	503,324	1.07	68,504	-12,244
1848/1849	497,160	431,746	0.87	520,860	451,959	0.87	-20,213	-23,700
1849/1850	402,150	457,922	1.14	490,783	523,609	1.07	-65,686	-88,633
1850/1851	486,450	489,531	1.01	592,356	503,760	0.85	-14,228	-105,906
1851/1852	483,050	587,094	1.22	518,513	598,564	1.15	-11,469	-35,463
1852/1853	564,090	716,307	1.27	591,891	614,898	1.04	101,409	-27,801
1853/1854	680,805	840,057	1.23	697,851	706,674	1.01	133,383	-17,046
1854/1855	551,600	797,586	1.45	807,766	981,350	1.21	-183,764	-256,166
1855/1856	817,808	971,002	1.19	852,540	1,068,730	1.25	-97,728	-34,732
1856/1857	766,500	1,014,027	1.32	823,551	852,482	1.04	161,545	-57,051
1857/1858	983,900	991,627	1.01	1,009,433	1,087,294	1.08	-95,667	-25,533
1858/1859	1,095,722	1,038,215	0.95	1,185,512	1,089,447	0.92	-51,232	-89,790

1859/1860	1,053,850	1,122,540	1.07	1,445,506	911,801	0.63	210,739	-391,656
1860/1861		1,299,110			941,880		357,230	
1861/1862	1,116,514	1,310,012	1.17	1,133,021	1,150,508	1.02	159,504	-16,508
1862/1863	1,332,711	1,090,365	0.82	1,258,988	1,057,668	0.84	32,697	73,723
1863/1864	1,637,101	968,848	0.59	1,589,796	2,027,765	1.28	-1,058,917	47,306
1864/1865	1,255,797	1,205,030	0.96	1,275,685	1,125,075	0.88	79,955	-19,889
1865/1866	1,315,250	1,173,381	0.89	1,270,312	1,287,824	1.01	-114,443	44,938
1866/1867	1,199,887	1,205,382	1.00	1,285,871	1,078,241	0.84	127,140	-85,984
1867/1868	1,250,000	1,593,858	1.28	1,343,977	1,185,193	0.88	408,665	-93,977
1868/1869	1,287,400	2,025,087	1.57	1,515,179	1,264,675	0.83	760,411	-227,779
1869/1870	1,350,800	1,605,114	1.19	1,498,517	1,462,546	0.98	142,568	-147,717
1870/1871	2,430,000	1,420,098	0.58	2,435,209	2,225,133	0.91	-805,035	-5,209
1871/1872	1,500,000	1,596,515	1.06	2,198,246	1,961,795	0.89	-365,281	-698,246
1872/1873	2,110,787	1,954,962	0.93	2,341,088	2,004,586	0.86	-49,624	-230,301
1873/1874	2,063,115	2,828,991	1.37	2,535,975	2,695,090	1.06	133,901	-472,860
1874/1875	2,706,773	2,475,779	0.91	2,539,627	3,257,017	1.28	-781,238	167,146
1875/1876	2,236,760	2,506,018	1.12	2,608,072	2,951,981	1.13	-445,964	-371,312
1876/1877	2,433,052	2,070,722	0.85	2,558,817	4,076,022	1.59	-2,005,300	-125,765
1877/1878	2,587,285	3,323,447	1.28	2,431,155	2,702,305	1.11	621,142	156,130
1878/1879	2,587,285	3,761,866	1.45	2,431,155	3,036,813	1.25	725,053	156,130
1879/1880	2,587,285	3,768,466	1.46	2,431,155	3,065,706	1.26	702,760	156,130
1880/1881	3,732,371	3,520,594	0.94	3,654,101	3,426,068	0.94	94,526	78,270
1881/1882	3,807,892	4,014,688	1.05	3,807,892	3,744,680	0.98	270,009	
1882/1883	3,693,455	3,625,332	0.98	3,693,456	3,789,095	1.03	-163,763	-1
1883/1884	3,743,461	3,785,791	1.01	3,743,461	3,792,847	1.01	-7,055	
1884/1885	3,184,000	4,397,153	1.38	3,837,131	4,325,375	1.13	71,778	-653,131
1885/1886	4,167,000	3,802,110	0.91	4,063,297	4,480,730	1.10	-678,620	103,703
1886/1887	4,416,700	5,700,938	1.29	4,588,146	5,461,742	1.19	239,195	-171,446
1887/1888	4,149,000	3,825,933	0.92	4,089,318	4,081,035	1.00	-255,102	59,682
1888/1889	5,072,844			4,917,475				

SOURCE: Departamento de Estatística do Estado, *Anuário estatístico de São Paulo, 1908*, 2:140; Ministério da Agricultura, Indústria e Commercio, *Finanças*, 144–145.

NOTE: For the actual difference, we use the actual surplus or deficit presented in the budget's balance. For the estimated difference, we use the surplus or deficit presented in the budget approved by the assembly.

Table A3.1

Taxes Collected by the Government of the State of São Paulo, 1889–1938 (mil réis)

	1889/90	1890/91	1891	1892
Imposto de animais em Itararé e Sorocaba	31,935	60,956	26,293	189
Direito de saída	3,155,463	5,641,818	6,800,414	
Direitos de exportação				26,603,298
Imposto de exportação				
Imposto de emergência sobre café				
Imposto sobre novas plantações de café				
Imposto de trânsito ou de viação				
Imposto de transito	1,570,156	1,715,669	970,158	1,499,921
Imposto de viação				
Imposto sobre fretes e passagens				
Décima de legados e heranças	334,194	478,754	282,206	
Décima de usufruto	7,523	9,709	10,360	
Imposto sobre o capital comercial				
Imposto sobre o capital das empresas industriais				
Imposto sobre o capital das sociedades anônimas				
Imposto sobre capital particular empregado em empréstimos				
Imposto sobre capitalistas	6,980	8,310	4,065	1,815
Imposto sobre a renda das sociedades anônimas				
Imposto sobre companhias de seguros		4,200	1,200	
Imposto sobre vendas e consignações				
Imposto de comércio				
Imposto de indústria				
Imposto de indutrias e profissões			11,233	30,600
Imposto sobre indústrias e profissões (Quota do Estado)				
Imposto sobre transações (Quota do Estado)				
Imposto de selo			310	526,522
Imposto de transmissão de propriedade "causa-mortis"				305,137
Imposto de transmissão de propriedade "inter-vivos"			811,277	7,194,043
Imposto predial da Capital				264,712
Imposto sobre prédios	264,392	309,155	203,482	1,444
Imposto sobre prédios de aluguel				
Imposto territorial				
Imposto sobre terrenos marginais às estradas de rodagem				
Imposto sobre porcentagens sobre rendimentos				
Imposto sobre subsidios e vencimentos				
Imposto sobre vencimentos, salários e proventos de cartório				
Imposto sobre segues e outros veiculos	5,493	6,317	4,381	605
Imposto sobre aposentadorias e reformas				
Imposto sobre casas de leilão	6,893	1,676	1,406	1
Imposto sobre casas de modas	160	160	80	
Imposto sobre companhias equestres	6,254	9,199	5,259	640
Imposto sobre diversões				
Imposto sobre consumo de combustíveis para motores térmicos				
Imposto sobre veículos				
Imposto sobre gasolina				
Imposto sobre o consumo de aguardente				
Imposto sobre matança de gado				
Imposto sobre loterias				
Imposto sobre loterias não autorizadas pelo Estado	4,200	4,968	4,175	850
Imposto de despachos de embarcações	18,497	20,521	11,768	22,048
Novos direitos para diversas mercês	30,093	36,071	28,525	
Total	5,442,233	8,307,483	9,176,592	36,451,825

SOURCE: Secretaria da Fazenda do Estado de São Paulo, *Contas do exercício de 1938*, 421–445.

NOTE: The 1891 column includes figures for the second half of the year. In 1916 the Imposto territorial is included in the Imposto sobre prédios de aluguel.

1893	1894	1895	1896	1897	1898	1899	1900
23,355,491	25,624,517	32,474,396	30,064,610	33,624,965	26,334,243	29,241,971	29,425,356
1,583,124	1,380,149	1,279,350	1,046,031	1,863,012	1,927,431	1,880,750	1,879,458
6							
233							
788,609	772,889	974,473	1,134,885	1,163,717	1,132,687	1,145,018	647,324
360,295	424,677	2,115,637	871,607	926,326	2,143,100	788,475	535,135
5,608,674	5,989,240	9,094,895	7,816,390	5,874,109	5,312,224	4,767,660	4,984,622
285,836	400,447	445,061	906,969	641,518	699,708	726,237	797,781
69							
31,982,337	34,591,919	46,383,812	41,840,492	44,093,647	37,549,393	38,550,111	38,269,676

(*continued*)

TABLE A3.1 (CONTINUED)

	1901	1902	1903	1904
Imposto de animais em Itararé e Sorocaba				
Direito de saída				
Direitos de exportação	32,061,268	24,966,025	22,255,860	24,922,230
Imposto de exportação				
Imposto de emergência sobre café				
Imposto sobre novas plantações de café				4,000
Imposto de trânsito ou de viação				
Imposto de transito	2,377,940	2,109,125	2,017,687	1,960,727
Imposto de viação				
Imposto sobre fretes e passagens				
Décima de legados e heranças				
Décima de usufruto				
Imposto sobre o capital comercial				
Imposto sobre o capital das empresas industriais				
Imposto sobre o capital das sociedades anônimas				
Imposto sobre capital particular empregado em empréstimos				
Imposto sobre capitalistas				
Imposto sobre a renda das sociedades anônimas				
Imposto sobre companhias de seguros				
Imposto sobre vendas e consignações				
Imposto de comércio				
Imposto de indústria				
Imposto de indutrias e profissões				
Imposto sobre indústrias e profissões (Quota do Estado)				
Imposto sobre transações (Quota do Estado)				
Imposto de selo	523,695	561,320	561,128	548,428
Imposto de transmissão de propriedade "causa-mortis"	1,253,399	995,397	931,387	1,111,445
Imposto de transmissão de propriedade "inter-vivos"	3,951,598	581,003	3,430,933	3,856,907
Imposto predial da Capital	756,487	790,225	729,368	724,252
Imposto sobre prédios				
Imposto sobre prédios de aluguel				
Imposto territorial				
Imposto sobre terrenos marginais às estradas de rodagem				
Imposto sobre porcentagens				52,784
Imposto sobre subsidios e vencimentos				
Imposto sobre vencimentos, salários e proventos de cartório				
Imposto sobre segues e outros veiculos				
Imposto sobre aposentadorias e reformas				33,751
Imposto sobre casas de leilão				
Imposto sobre casas de modas				
Imposto sobre companhias equestres				
Imposto sobre diversões				
Imposto sobre consumo de combustíveis para motores térmicos				
Imposto sobre veículos				
Imposto sobre gasolina				
Imposto sobre o consumo de aguardente				
Imposto sobre matança de gado				
Imposto sobre loterias				
Imposto sobre loterias não autorizadas pelo Estado				
Imposto de despachos de embarcações				
Novos direitos para diversas mercês				
Total	40,924,387	30,003,095	29,926,363	33,214,524

1905	1906	1907	1908	1909	1910	1911	1912
19,296,639	25,858,451	27,766,278	22,189,593	33,210,696	17,476,852	27,603,889	36,697,184
		4,000	36,000	4,000	2,000		
						1,255,357	1,460,829
1,053,519	1,097,432	1,163,590	1,368,067	1,342,951	1,569,761		
581,429	576,353	576,939	622,892	621,780	612,038	660,483	726,973
54,420	96,048	113,132	108,393	109,319	114,169	125,680	133,559
481,663	481,545	774,405	578,084	606,629	628,998	712,969	921,292
458,401	490,590	485,231	472,316	490,362	470,152	644,385	672,664
565,852	545,095	578,947	602,698	531,227	595,631	806,103	922,078
614,226	1,128,953	791,564	889,099	1,093,158	1,355,930	2,359,499	1,576,544
3,266,115	3,018,237	4,226,680	3,811,048	4,191,746	5,555,895	12,701,703	14,350,789
739,174	781,380	1,067,807	793,557	786,601	873,840	1,971,532	1,434,769
59,958	64,369	76,237	72,804	71,642	67,803	187,377	227,191
33,087	45,528	59,660	54,795	67,837	55,181		
32,660	34,407	35,490	35,519	34,536	32,902		
348,918	312,841	332,796	332,653	306,988	526,854	531,489	544,461
	299,090	467,240	446,590	578,784	726,999	727,000	736,583
27,586,061	34,830,319	38,519,996	32,414,108	44,048,256	30,665,005	50,287,466	60,404,916

(continued)

TABLE A3.1 (CONTINUED)

	1913	1914	1915	1916
Imposto de animais em Itararé e Sorocaba				
Direito de saída				
Direitos de exportação	40,979,157	34,854,923	41,245,462	33,861,007
Imposto de exportação				
Imposto de emergência sobre café				
Imposto sobre novas plantações de café				
Imposto de trânsito ou de viação	1,544,300	1,467,444	2,565,981	3,371,929
Imposto de transito				
Imposto de viação				
Imposto sobre fretes e passagens				
Décima de legados e heranças				
Décima de usufruto				
Imposto sobre o capital comercial	781,819	788,603	1,085,557	3,026,068
Imposto sobre o capital das empresas industriais	148,109	140,285	150,597	130,572
Imposto sobre o capital das sociedades anônimas	160,325	154,533	1,224,760	1,208,498
Imposto sobre capital particular empregado em empréstimos	836,876	960,697	1,024,175	1,097,427
Imposto sobre capitalistas				
Imposto sobre a renda das sociedades anônimas				
Imposto sobre companhias de seguros				
Imposto sobre vendas e consignações				
Imposto de comércio				
Imposto de indústria				
Imposto de indutrias e profissões				
Imposto sobre indústrias e profissões (Quota do Estado)				
Imposto sobre transações (Quota do Estado)				
Imposto de selo	908,333	905,151	1,414,728	1,466,804
Imposto de transmissão de propriedade "causa-mortis"	1,123,720	885,413	1,827,271	1,438,529
Imposto de transmissão de propriedade "inter-vivos"	8,312,344	4,964,940	6,542,667	7,556,336
Imposto predial da Capital	1,881,765	1,467,444	2,048,348	2,581,163
Imposto sobre prédios				
Imposto sobre prédios de aluguel				1,026,068
Imposto territorial	953,847	1,090,130	160,901	
Imposto sobre terrenos marginais às estradas de rodagem				
Imposto sobre porcentagens				
Imposto sobre subsidios e vencimentos			366,646	912,686
Imposto sobre vencimentos, salários e proventos de cartório				
Imposto sobre segues e outros veiculos				
Imposto sobre aposentadorias e reformas				
Imposto sobre casas de leilão				
Imposto sobre casas de modas				
Imposto sobre companhias equestres				
Imposto sobre diversões				
Imposto sobre consumo de combustíveis para motores térmicos				
Imposto sobre veículos				
Imposto sobre gasolina				
Imposto sobre o consumo de aguardente	561,275	555,582	766,703	578,903
Imposto sobre matança de gado				
Imposto sobre loterias	750,000	750,000	762,500	780,000
Imposto sobre loterias não autorizadas pelo Estado				
Imposto de despachos de embarcações				
Novos direitos para diversas mercês				
Total	58,941,870	48,985,145	61,186,296	59,035,990

1917	1918	1919	1920	1921	1922	1923	1924	1925
27,169,729	18,834,885	32,259,380	27,266,749	30,206,636	30,618,792	44,460,159	53,622,270	118,764,608
6,017,055	6,187,087	7,687,664	10,201,078					
				9,370,642	10,135,861	11,410,653	10,636,157	10,945,408
4,487,976	4,387,139	4,907,956	5,684,334					
510,992	698,879	661,064	803,939					
1,461,912	1,767,502		2,222,552	2,244,486	2,087,287	2,217,817	2,496,500	2,699,826
1,107,690	1,108,284	1,142,883	1,133,986	1,341,567	1,341,567	2,190,607	2,133,200	2,950,366
		18,544						
				5,995,493	6,093,664	6,594,911	7,078,012	15,710,104
				909,290	958,441	1,060,553	1,223,829	2,889,571
1,457,263	1,444,925	1,666,637	2,163,593	2,026,937	2,116,585	2,710,365	2,464,276	4,711,991
1,885,000	1,457,184	2,171,209	1,983,628	2,609,534	2,191,540	2,644,889	3,297,538	3,880,639
8,210,534	9,001,690	14,864,944	17,955,669	17,947,570	23,596,714	39,021,407	46,097,161	48,941,970
2,389,275	2,417,154	2,662,933	2,890,783	3,818,671	4,111,968	5,237,983	5,710,274	12,404,548
865,880	927,823	1,069,601	1,170,708	1,457,906	1,567,070	1,904,000	2,088,930	493,813
571,550	669,590	761,430	911,869	1,068,286	1,156,684	1,308,236	1,490,895	1,763,443
1,116,587	1,126,977	175,129						
331,603	669,179	857,184	1,085,265	1,110,968	1,258,879	1,313,386	1,349,938	3,139,117
						18,814	10,937	40,419
602,387	644,328	649,327	1,169,119	1,152,027	1,160,838	1,228,102	1,329,836	1,480,332
780,000	780,000	780,000	780,000	1,025,000	1,020,000	1,020,000	935,000	2,357,500
58,965,433	52,122,626	72,335,885	77,423,272	82,285,013	89,415,890	124,341,882	141,964,753	233,173,655

(continued)

TABLE A3.1 (CONTINUED)

	1926	1927	1928	1929
Imposto de animais em Itararé e Sorocaba				
Direito de saída				
Direitos de exportação	129,753,363	149,305,839	120,952,435	146,974,082
Imposto de exportação				
Imposto de emergência sobre café				
Imposto sobre novas plantações de café				
Imposto de trânsito ou de viação				
Imposto de transito				
Imposto de viação	11,856,165	12,282,133	13,890,817	13,947,454
Imposto sobre fretes e passagens				
Décima de legados e heranças				
Décima de usufruto				
Imposto sobre o capital comercial				
Imposto sobre o capital das empresas industriais				
Imposto sobre o capital das sociedades anônimas	3,027,221	3,383,734	3,498,475	3,808,681
Imposto sobre capital particular empregado em empréstimos	4,401,886	5,498,108	5,503,183	6,267,862
Imposto sobre capitalistas				
Imposto sobre a renda das sociedades anônimas				
Imposto sobre companhias de seguros				
Imposto sobre vendas e consignações				
Imposto de comércio	16,363,707	16,535,482	18,097,025	19,236,908
Imposto de indústria	2,971,581	3,292,023	3,910,899	3,931,412
Imposto de indutrias e profissões				
Imposto sobre indústrias e profissões (Quota do Estado)				
Imposto sobre transações (Quota do Estado)				
Imposto de selo	5,480,696	7,433,702	7,403,412	8,931,277
Imposto de transmissão de propriedade "causa-mortis"	3,541,484	4,568,264	4,599,772	5,285,615
Imposto de transmissão de propriedade "inter-vivos"	31,251,695	39,079,377	54,478,591	40,622,085
Imposto predial da Capital	14,039,281	17,039,769	18,911,497	21,174,945
Imposto sobre prédios				
Imposto sobre prédios de aluguel	646,182	719,351	832,889	1,031,994
Imposto territorial	4,728,322	4,784,658	5,111,231	6,356,267
Imposto sobre terrenos marginais às estradas de rodagem		175,999	236,417	287,159
Imposto sobre porcentagens				
Imposto sobre subsidios e vencimentos				
Imposto sobre vencimentos, salários e proventos de cartório				
Imposto sobre segues e outros veiculos				
Imposto sobre aposentadorias e reformas				
Imposto sobre casas de leilão				
Imposto sobre casas de modas				
Imposto sobre companhias equestres				
Imposto sobre diversões	3,382,543	3,851,763	5,081,616	5,501,142
Imposto sobre consumo de combustíveis para motores térmicos				
Imposto sobre veículos	71,145	2,096,791	4,846,019	6,553,910
Imposto sobre gasolina				
Imposto sobre o consumo de aguardente	1,595,753	3,094,778	3,250,723	3,436,220
Imposto sobre matança de gado				
Imposto sobre loterias	2,500,000	2,500,000	2,500,000	5,130,880
Imposto sobre loterias não autorizadas pelo Estado				
Imposto de despachos de embarcações				
Novos direitos para diversas mercês				
Total	235,611,024	275,641,771	273,105,001	298,477,893

1930	1931	1932	1933	1934	1935	1936	1937	1938
134,365,301								
	118,144,512	64,078,768	807,325	885,910	1,818,064			
			39,437,476	45,084,852	52,343,201			
10,696,459	8,952,513	7,455,295	9,983,608	35,476,617				
			26,983,235	29,774				
3,583,596	4,125,199	7,293,653	5,699,084	5,752,834	6,845,800			
6,779,553	7,618,472	9,523,840	7,972,257	7,216,735	8,658,618			
						171,342,432	202,612,399	263,767,748
17,040,282	16,299,680	15,821,451	17,369,950	18,429,824	29,879,289			
3,571,735	3,550,147	3,563,186	3,969,887	4,377,194	4,622,478			
						51,389,947	54,375,223	72,326,044
						297,722	575,956	1,017,691
6,884,439	9,695,191	10,868,075	13,472,407	16,598,801	15,273,131	17,159,531	14,538,462	16,040,807
5,078,819	5,293,390	5,865,439	8,575,475	7,989,891	18,409,809	12,475,261	17,021,289	16,995,823
23,615,704	35,898,059	22,277,082	23,432,677	29,562,325	41,961,904	44,271,000	46,202,491	50,573,920
19,559,859	18,637,701	17,526,601	16,275,208	17,212,456	26,216,937			
1,101,383	1,059,151	1,011,028	962,687	1,017,041	1,354,750			
7,139,102	7,827,831	10,620,186	22,492,674	24,468,125	28,014,834	24,433,660	24,494,177	31,896,215
312,204	355,641	460,009	426,868	483,795	667,137			
	12,980,510	12,724,445	12,389,090	6,473,503				
4,118,739	4,646,660	4,435,642	5,457,672	6,120,708	7,066,935			
						41,401,569	31,193,664	
6,290,929	5,778,644	5,065,724	5,881,171	6,446,406	8,938,594			
	6,261,021	5,840,212	7,368,523	11,899,939	16,912,747			
3,090,872	3,359,365	5,193,232	4,823,008	5,212,591	7,465,118			
	1,095,898	2,784,315	3,164,464	3,711,699	4,572,843			
2,395,833	3,747,715	5,121,724	3,246,757	3,458,352	2,763,158	4,280,898	4,710,967	
255,624,809	275,327,300	217,529,907	240,191,503	257,909,372	283,785,347	367,052,020	395,724,628	452,618,248

TABLE A3.2

Average Percentage of Major Public Service Charges and Fees Collected by the State of São Paulo and Their Total Value, 1889–1937 (mil réis)

	1889–1899	1900–1909	1910–1919	1920–1929	1930–1937
Taxa adicional	40.9	20.0	22.0	18.8	20.4
Sobre-taxa adicional					6.3
Taxa do serviço de águas da Capital	23.9	40.0	35.1	21.1	22.7
Taxa dos serviços de esgotos	8.0	28.1	28.8	32.5	23.4
Custas, porcentagens e emolumentos	0.3			1.3	3.2
Taxa de expediente		4.9	7.3	13.0	8.5
Taxa de caça e pesca				0.0	0.5
Taxa de conservação das estradas de rodagem					2.0
Taxa da ponte de embarque em Santos	23.2	2.2			
Taxa de fiscalização sanitária, animal					2.5
Taxa de registro e fiscalização de veículos					3.8
Taxa judiciária		2.7	3.1	3.1	2.9
Taxa sobre mercadorias negociadas a termo				6.8	0.0
Taxas escolares	3.6	2.2	3.7	2.3	3.6
Total	99.9	100.1	100.0	98.9	99.8
Total value	1,711,892	3,535,804	9,489,684	29,892,362	49,696,614

SOURCE: Secretaria da Fazenda do Estado de São Paulo, *Contas do exercício de 1938*, 421–445.

NOTE: Beginning in the late 1930s there was a termination of many of the traditional charges, and by 1938 there was an entirely new set of fees, with the new railroad tax being the most important and accounting for 40 percent of all fees obtained and with the motor vehicle registration fee, which began to be collected in 1936, now rising to second in importance in 1938 and accounting for 14 percent of total fees.

Table A3.3 begins on the next page

TABLE A3.3

Fixed Expenditures in the Budget of the Government of the State of São Paulo, 1892–1929 (mil réis)

	1892	1893	1894	1895
Fixed expenditure by secretariat				
Secretaria do Interior e Instrução Publica	3,578,200	6,701,560	8,125,300	7,491,440
Secretaria de Justiça e Segurança Pública	5,699,516	7,514,889	7,914,759	7,843,934
Secretaria da Agricultura, comércio e Obras Públicas	2,513,973	4,980,590	5,435,340	12,326,373
Secretaria da Fazenda	1,816,182	2,175,554	3,844,866	6,079,783
Secretaria de Obras Públicas				
Secretaria do Interior e da Justiça				
Total	13,607,871	21,372,593	25,320,265	33,741,530
Fixed expenditure by large expense items				
Administração	627,268	1,030,908	1,139,100	1,150,620
Agricultura		150,000	100,000	119,460
Saúde, assistência social	223,440	1,415,400	2,486,400	2,155,240
Educação	2,294,300	4,584,340	4,629,400	4,891,180
Transportes: ferrovias e Estradas de rodagem			320,000	350,400
Policia Civil, Força Pública e Sistema Penitênciario	4,604,768	7,034,401	6,995,559	6,792,534
Estrutura Fiscal, Serviço da Dívida e Exercícios Findos	1,629,000	1,964,610	3,620,806	5,825,634
Imigração e Colonização	450,000	905,790	1,041,940	2,538,910
Obras em Geral	1,477,980	2,154,600	2,183,600	1,941,600
Saneamento, Capital, Santos e Diversos	700,000	300,000	787,000	6,000,000
Administração da Justiça, Ministério Público	1,094,748	1,152,600	1,214,800	1,209,200
Subvenções				
Subvenção para Iluminação pública e outros urbanos	218,485	206,000	226,500	238,000
Aposentados	187,181	210,934	224,059	254,144
Diversos	100,700	263,000	351,100	274,603
Total	13,607,870	21,372,583	25,320,264	33,741,525

SOURCE: Assembléia Legislativa do Estado de São Paulo, leis orçamentárias anuais, 1891–1920, http://www.al.sp.gov.br/alesp/normas/?tipoNorma=9&ementa=S.

1897	1898	1899	1900	1901	1902	1903	1904
9,911,460	9,555,060	9,933,720	8,837,720	9,574,516			
11,086,538	11,027,509	10,867,420	10,322,069	11,016,942			
19,391,282	14,769,235	8,085,279	6,827,700	10,711,982	10,205,536	7,896,981	4,945,257
6,825,638	6,587,351	10,479,204	12,154,878	10,330,023	9,128,526	10,435,982	9,555,574
					20,983,399	21,311,593	18,913,428
47,214,918	41,939,155	39,365,623	38,142,367	41,633,463	40,317,461	39,644,556	33,414,259
1,386,710	1,462,620	1,402,620	1,422,640	1,486,086	1,204,580	1,204,640	1,032,040
150,400	150,400	150,400	345,700	533,790	536,600	318,400	181,440
3,139,420	2,414,420	2,776,640	1,621,280	1,997,800	1,959,600	1,779,100	1,656,700
8,204,534	7,056,020	7,122,710	6,065,200	7,298,270	6,942,660	6,935,190	6,233,559
671,440	139,040	150,040	173,040	2,269,700	2,405,800	406,100	129,500
9,766,738	9,648,309	9,498,220	8,782,269	9,414,942	10,130,197	9,953,867	8,619,757
5,632,432	5,459,236	9,278,554	10,696,300	8,620,245	7,250,508	8,409,170	7,783,898
3,927,150	3,553,677	2,062,745	1,610,192	1,477,072	1,558,860	729,720	326,845
2,289,720	3,483,648	2,556,720	1,629,720	329,420	318,920	2,820,120	2,708,200
9,530,000	6,038,000	2,000,000	2,000,000	3,818,440	3,468,440	2,388,740	650,000
1,275,600	1,335,000	1,325,000	1,500,800	1,563,000	1,684,866	1,685,368	1,560,666
84,800	28,000	16,000	966,000	1,176,600	1,193,200	1,336,600	1,060,400
331,167	360,390	312,354	275,202	293,670	297,676	300,000	271,217
350,400	416,135	364,250	492,577	533,176	684,816	691,211	711,276
474,400	394,280	349,220	561,340	820,360	680,100	687,701	488,360
47,214,911	41,939,175	39,365,473	38,142,260	41,632,571	40,316,823	39,645,927	33,413,858

(*continued*)

TABLE A3.3 (CONTINUED)

	1905	1906	1907	1908
Fixed expenditure by secretariat				
Secretaria do Interior e Instrução Publica		10,629,735	12,249,019	12,592,320
Secretaria de Justiça e Segurança Pública		10,786,764	11,556,617	11,864,935
Secretaria da Agricultura, comércio e Obras Públicas	5,510,851	13,593,855	16,336,890	7,863,101
Secretaria da Fazenda	9,759,814	12,335,849	14,002,519	16,401,770
Secretaria de Obras Públicas				
Secretaria do Interior e da Justiça	19,828,986			
Total	35,099,651	47,346,203	54,145,045	48,722,126
Fixed expenditure by large expense items				
Administração	1,045,640	1,530,375	1,772,499	2,069,240
Agricultura	989,440	921,440	1,057,340	1,011,480
Saúde, assistência social	1,662,500	1,640,200	2,612,954	3,895,320
Educação	7,225,440	8,938,560	10,052,342	9,727,760
Transportes: ferrovias e Estradas de rodagem	277,500	7,344,235	9,082,700	1,981,000
Policia Civil, Força Pública e Sistema Penitênciario	8,498,440	9,522,564	10,828,084	10,355,736
Estrutura Fiscal, Serviço da Dívida e Exercícios Findos	7,857,773	11,284,611	12,735,814	13,473,167
Imigração e Colonização	374,445	380,445	754,445	995,693
Obras em Geral	1,708,200	1,558,200	422,994	178,200
Saneamento, Capital, Santos e Diversos	1,175,600	1,074,600	1,232,600	1,388,600
Administração da Justiça, Ministério Público	1,607,666	1,648,600	1,691,733	1,788,399
Subvenções	1,165,100	65,100	83,926	91,000
Subvenção para Iluminação pública e outros urbanos	293,378	293,215	296,763	313,300
Aposentados	736,859	681,536	789,220	845,802
Diversos	481,488	462,520	730,700	607,628
Total	35,099,469	47,346,201	54,144,114	48,722,325

1909	1910	1911	1912	1913	1914	1915	1916
13,357,730	13,889,378	15,786,787	19,184,280	21,135,429	22,190,364	23,069,248	24,683,174
11,956,899	12,505,491	14,029,387	16,073,026	17,900,534	18,948,819	18,257,919	18,183,695
7,303,761	7,596,462	8,265,722	12,617,404	17,101,776	15,052,727	11,724,507	14,288,126
16,546,582	18,127,629	20,243,772	21,866,697	25,767,846	22,982,782	21,428,324	23,440,348
49,164,972	52,118,960	58,325,668	69,741,407	81,905,585	79,174,692	74,479,998	80,595,343
2,400,740	2,426,577	2,680,387	3,253,800	3,792,605	3,647,300	3,486,740	3,492,210
817,955	775,000	908,800	1,270,994	1,683,361	1,437,160	648,160	758,280
4,144,320	4,220,320	5,227,920	4,070,240	4,013,460	6,497,860	5,625,460	6,046,610
10,726,950	11,678,000	11,890,350	13,906,669	15,647,437	16,907,194	17,311,648	18,998,014
1,760,000	1,703,333	2,288,744	3,713,180	4,174,385	4,578,240	3,610,612	4,883,340
10,417,500	11,096,492	12,801,948	15,339,979	18,923,609	17,921,039	16,361,999	16,697,415
13,464,173	14,752,261	16,391,152	17,108,501	21,087,854	18,825,971	18,524,595	19,949,557
666,970	677,408	683,012	824,145	1,065,545	1,410,615	1,082,740	874,140
					900,000	500,000	760,000
1,151,600	1,039,800	1,181,600	2,192,320	2,285,320	1,949,137	2,478,320	3,130,760
1,867,599	1,880,199	1,946,639	1,971,246	2,034,913	2,003,780	2,012,920	2,015,280
30,000	15,000	892,565	4,626,629	5,622,607	216,000	8,000	10,300
350,246	405,157				1,018,532	852,731	945,993
954,408	976,964	1,092,721	1,163,794	1,222,951	1,281,709	1,382,827	1,526,720
411,600	471,843	339,840	297,200	351,800	580,103	593,103	506,103
49,164,061	52,118,354	58,325,678	69,738,697	81,905,847	79,174,640	74,479,855	80,594,722

(continued)

TABLE A3.3 (CONTINUED)

	1917	1918	1919	1920	1921
Fixed expenditure by secretariat					
Secretaria do Interior e Instrução Publica	25,308,198	26,025,824	27,368,542	32,238,130	35,910,665
Secretaria de Justiça e Segurança Pública	18,273,996	20,632,632	21,293,455	25,336,190	26,290,482
Secretaria da Agricultura, comércio e Obras Públicas	15,019,661	15,941,140	17,912,897	19,716,852	41,759,882
Secretaria da Fazenda	27,185,016	28,594,076	28,771,444	30,117,634	33,494,370
Secretaria de Obras Públicas					
Secretaria do Interior e da Justiça					
Total	85,786,871	91,193,672	95,346,338	107,408,806	137,455,399
Fixed expenditure by large expense items					
Administração	3,768,673	3,818,673	4,003,584	4,244,384	4,293,004
Agricultura	877,000	1,027,400	1,528,920	1,963,080	2,034,135
Saúde, assistência social	4,053,760	4,260,760	4,899,840	5,455,656	6,119,667
Educação	19,084,174	19,561,190	20,239,917	24,363,729	27,167,063
Transportes: ferrovias e Estradas de rodagem	1,210,905	1,680,462	1,462,400	1,462,400	24,343,760
Policia Civil, Força Pública e Sistema Penitênciario	16,215,216	18,581,332	19,068,975	22,673,270	23,524,331
Estrutura Fiscal, Serviço da Dívida e Exercícios Findos	23,498,895	24,835,951	24,669,115	25,852,133	28,752,703
Imigração e Colonização	874,440	1,670,240	1,670,240	1,091,614	1,107,814
Obras em Geral	3,448,000	2,505,000	3,995,000	5,400,000	5,868,000
Saneamento, Capital, Santos e Diversos	2,408,760	2,734,760	2,654,760	2,823,631	2,839,282
Administração da Justiça, Ministério Público	2,025,780	2,018,300	2,191,480	2,625,720	2,728,951
Subvenções	6,418,746	6,513,227	6,798,827	7,026,716	5,901,439
Subvenção para Iluminação pública e outros urbanos					
Aposentados	1,584,770	1,640,973	1,789,676	1,952,851	2,131,715
Diversos	318,160	345,400	373,600	473,600	643,600
Total	85,787,279	91,193,668	95,346,334	107,408,784	137,455,464

1922	1923	1924	1925	1926	1927	1928	1929
38,851,825	48,565,693	49,653,025	59,787,034	76,528,926	81,088,266	81,198,761	89,657,338
28,053,990	34,718,809	37,758,473	62,578,664	67,197,474	62,008,641	65,600,952	76,961,173
45,562,134	58,921,462	65,059,405	85,756,120	100,368,603	101,526,169	20,809,141	31,162,195
39,889,387	46,974,034	49,040,095	80,858,487	80,602,665	98,086,328	114,525,735	141,375,400
						96,104,609	114,450,871
152,357,336	189,179,998	201,510,998	288,980,305	324,697,668	342,709,404	378,239,198	453,606,977
4,306,553	11,987,620	6,149,894	8,000,669	10,872,997	12,622,177	15,645,477	21,151,608
2,256,000	2,542,000	2,472,876	3,804,464	5,403,778	6,580,500	5,433,243	8,803,556
6,881,620	7,369,280	8,519,790	12,524,504	16,456,970	15,902,959	15,839,375	17,561,615
29,262,568	30,887,599	36,785,062	42,403,659	53,670,598	58,150,825	59,235,422	65,829,757
26,438,814	29,719,100	34,474,688	45,325,100	55,882,037	55,180,800	72,190,318	89,415,054
24,445,830	30,673,889	32,971,199	57,299,050	61,506,943	55,888,115	57,667,989	64,443,229
34,922,508	41,461,789	42,378,506	73,136,907	71,935,771	88,663,718	104,050,900	129,684,209
869,037	6,648,837	6,639,881	8,397,481	6,400,156	3,699,201	3,204,481	3,180,090
6,952,500	8,791,174	10,109,338	12,920,338	13,903,878	14,867,750	6,625,840	9,150,210
3,819,842	4,906,320	5,569,408	8,839,137	9,701,669	11,090,189	14,944,655	15,388,047
3,570,960	3,995,600	4,727,394	5,219,734	5,618,170	5,954,736	7,502,224	12,097,254
5,605,235	6,083,204	6,977,095	6,919,545	8,163,674	8,298,617	9,274,500	9,026,047
2,456,928	2,881,785	3,184,087	3,538,543	4,115,178	4,592,018	5,427,928	6,434,027
569,266	1,231,588	551,783	650,746	1,065,800	1,217,600	1,196,640	1,442,290
152,357,661	189,179,785	201,511,001	288,979,877	324,697,619	342,709,205	378,238,992	453,606,993

NOTES

Preface

1. The first part of this study was published as Francisco Vidal Luna and Herbert S. Klein, *Slavery and the Economy of São Paulo, 1750–1850* (Stanford, CA: Stanford University Press, 2003).

2. Recently there has appeared a series of edited volumes promoted by the state government on social, economic, cultural, and political aspects of various historical periods of the state and province of São Paulo. See Nilo Odalia and João Ricardo de Castro Caldeira, eds., *História do estado de São Paulo: A formação da unidade paulista*, 3 vols. (São Paulo: Editora UNESP, 2010); Marco Antônio Villa, ed., *Coleção história geral do estado de São Paulo*, 5 vols. (São Paulo: Imesp, 2010); and Marco Antônio Villa, *Breve história do estado de São Paulo* (São Paulo: Imesp, 2009).

3. "SP teria 36° maior PIB do mundo, se fosse um país, diz FecomercioSP," *O Globo*, January 24, 2013, http://g1.globo.com/economia/noticia/2013/01/sp-teria-36-maior-pib-do-mundo-se-fosse-um-pais-diz-fecomercio.html.

4. Instituto Brasileiro de Geografia e Estatística, "Tabela 01: Produto interno bruto das grandes regiões e unidades da federação, 2002–2010," 2010, http://www.ibge.gov.br/home/estatistica/economia/contasregionais/2010/default_xls_2002_2010_zip.shtm.

5. See US Census Bureau, "Countries and Areas Ranked by Population: 2010," September 27, 2016, http://www.census.gov/population/international/data/countryrank/rank.php.

6. United Nations Department of Economic and Social Affairs, *World Urbanization Prospects: The 2014 Revision Highlights* (New York: United Nations, 2014), 1.

7. Until 1853 the current state of Paraná belonged to the province of São Paulo and is part of all the questions we deal with before 1850.

8. These estimates were made in the year 1854. See Instituto Brasileiro de Geografia e Estatística, *Anuário estatistico do Brasil, 1936* (Rio de Janeiro: IBGE, 1936), 41; José Francisco de Camargo, *Crescimento da população no estado de São Paulo e seus aspectos econômicos*, 2 vols. (São Paulo: Instituto de Pesquisas Econômicas, 1981); and *Almanak administrativo, mercantil e industrial da província*

de São Paulo para o ano de 1857 (São Paulo: Typographia Imparcial, 1857). The São Paulo population number includes estimates from four missing municípios.

9. José Antonio Saraiva, "Quadro estatístico de alguns estabelecimentos rurais da província de São Paulo (1855)," in *Documentos com que ilustríssimo e excelentíssimo Senhor Dr. José Antonio Saraiva, presidente da província de São Paulo, instruiu o relatório da abertura da assembléia legislativa provincial no dia 15 de fevereiro de 1855* (São Paulo: Antonio Louzada Antunes, 1855).

10. See, for example, Wilson Cano, *Raízes da concentração industrial em São Paulo* (São Paulo: Difusão Europeia do Livro, 1977); Fernando Henrique Cardoso, "Condições sociais da industrialização: O caso de São Paulo," *Revista Brasiliense*, no. 28 (1960): 31–46; Warren Dean, *Rio Claro: A Brazilian Plantation System, 1820–1920* (Stanford, CA: Stanford University Press, 1976); and Warren Dean, *The Industrialization of São Paulo* (Austin: University of Texas Press, 1969). See also Joseph L. Love, *São Paulo in the Brazilian Federation, 1889–1937* (Stanford, CA: Stanford University Press, 1980); Pierre Monbeig, *Pioneiros e fazendeiros de São Paulo* (São Paulo: Hucitec-Polis, 1984); Renato Monseff Perissinotto, *Estado e capital cafeeiro em São Paulo (1889–1930)* (São Paulo: Annablume, 2000); and S. Silva, *Expansão cafeeira e origens da indústria no Brasil* (São Paulo: Alfa-Omega, 1995).

11. See, for example, Love, *São Paulo in the Brazilian Federation*; and James P. Woodward, *A Place in Politics: São Paulo, Brazil, from Seigneurial Republicanism to Regionalist Revolt* (Durham, NC: Duke University Press, 2009).

12. See, for example, Verena Stolcke, *Coffee Planters, Workers, and Wives: Class Conflict and Gender Relations on São Paulo Plantations, 1850–1980* (New York: St. Martin's Press, 1988); Joel Wolfe, *Working Women, Working Men: São Paulo and the Rise of Brazil's Industrial Working Class, 1900–1955* (Durham, NC: Duke University Press, 1993); Barbara Weinstein, *For Social Peace in Brazil: Industrialists and the Remaking of the Working Class in São Paulo, 1920–1964* (Chapel Hill: University of North Carolina Press, 1996); and George Reid Andrews, *Blacks and Whites in São Paulo, Brazil, 1888–1988* (Madison: University of Wisconsin Press, 1991).

13. Maria Luiza Marcílio, *A cidade de São Paulo: Povoamento e população, 1750–1850* (São Paulo: Pioneira/Editora USP, 1974).

14. In Portuguese, *vale* means "valley," *baixa* "lower," *alta* "upper," *noroeste* "northwest," *oeste* "west," and *litoral* "littoral" or "coast." These ten regions are named after their railroad routes and are used by Jose Francisco de Camargo. The regions are defined by the strict relationship "between the demographic momentum of [the state's] various areas, its economic development and the railroad track expansion. . . . Because of this synchronization the criterion commonly adopted to distinguish the different regions of the state is to name them after the railway serving them. It is common to call the zones the

Paulista, the Mogiana, the Northwest, the Sorocabana, etc." Jose Francisco de Camargo, *Crescimento da população no estado de São Paulo e seus aspectos econômicos* (São Paulo: Instituto de Pesquisas Econômicas, 1981), 1:27. This criterion was adopted by S. Milliet in 1939 in his study of the evolution of coffee in São Paulo (S. Milliet, *Roteiro do café e outros ensaios* [São Paulo: Hucitec, 1982]) and by Joseph L. Love in *São Paulo in the Brazilian Federation*, 23–24. All translations in the book are ours.

15. Rafael de Oliveira Vaz, "Antecedentes do sistema métrico decimal no Brasil: O artigo 'Memória sobre a adopção do systema métrico no Brazil e de uma circulação monetária internacional' (1859), de Cândido Batista de Oliveira," 2012, http://inmetro.academia.edu/RafaelVaz.

16. The standard unit of weight, the *arroba*, corresponds to 14.688 kilograms. Grain, though often reported in arrobas or even alqueires, is presented here in kilograms, bushels, kilos, and liters. Although there is some divergence in the alqueire as a unit of weight or volume, for its common use as a measure of land, we employ the standard conversion used in São Paulo of 2.42 hectares per alqueire. Corn and other cereals such as rice and beans are given in kilograms, kilos, and liters. For grain volume measured as liters, we convert using the product's respective density: corn and beans, 0.8333 liters per kilogram; rice, 0.6667 liters per kilogram, and so on. Coffee was already represented in kilograms and bags (or sacks), usually 60 kilograms per bag. But liquids, though now measured in decimal units, were given in barrels and casks (*pipas*) and, in the case of brandy, in *canadas* (roughly equivalent to two liters). Given the great variety in the use of these liquid units, we do not convert them into liters. See Francisco Vidal Luna and Herbert S. Klein, "Nota a respeito de medidas para grãos utilizados no período colonial e as dificuldades para sua conversão ao sistema métrico," *Boletim de História Demográfica* 8, no. 21 (2001), http://members.tripod.com/~Historia_Demografica/pesquisadores/paco/pdf-paco/ar47.pdf; and Iraci Del Nero da Costa, "Pesos e medidas no período colonial Brasileiro: Denominações e relações," http://www.ipeadata.gov.br/doc/Pesos%20e%20medidas%20no%20periodo%20colonial%20brasileiro.pdf (accessed May 1, 2017).

17. These exchange rates come from Instituto Brasileiro de Geografia e Estatística, *Anuário estatístico do Brasil, 1939/1940* (Rio de Janeiro: Conselho Nacional de Estatística, 1940), 63–64, http://produtos.seade.gov.br/produtos/bibliotecadigital/view/singlepage/index.php?pubcod=10020584&parte=1; and Marcelo de Paiva Abreu, ed., *A ordem do progresso: Cem anos de política econômica republicana, 1889–1989* (Rio de Janeiro: Campus, 1990), 392, 396, 401.

Chapter 1

1. These censuses were called either "mappas" or "Listas Nominativas dos Habitantes" and can be found in the Archive of the State of São Paulo.

2. "Listas nominativas dos habitantes do acervo do arquivo do estado de São Paulo," various boxes, Archive of the State of São Paulo. For specific boxes used to construct the 1829 data set, see Francisco Vidal Luna and Herbert S. Klein, *Slavery and the Economy of São Paulo, 1750–1850* (Stanford, CA: Stanford University Press, 2003), 209–216.

3. The 590 sugar producers included 130 in Porto Feliz, 107 in Itu, and 85 in Campinas.

4. For more on sugar production in São Paulo, see the classic study by Maria Thereza Schorer Petrone, *A lavoura canavieira em São Paulo: Expansão e declínio (1765–1851)* (São Paulo: Difusão Europeia do Livro, 1968). Also see Luna and Klein, *Slavery and the Economy of São Paulo*, chap. 2. Maria Petrone has criticized the lack of attention to the "cycle of sugar" in Paulista historiography. See Maria Thereza Schorer Petrone, "O desprezado 'ciclo do açucar' paulista (1765–1850)," in *História do estado de São Paulo: A formação da unidade paulista*, ed. Nilo Odalia and João Ricardo de Castro Caldeira (São Paulo: UNESP, 2010), 1:135–155.

5. Daniel P. Müller, *Ensaio d'um quadro estatístico da província de São Paulo* (São Paulo: Governo do Estado de São Paulo, 1978), https://archive.org/details/ensaio1840sp.

6. José Antonio Saraiva, "Quadro estatístico de alguns estabelecimentos rurais da província de São Paulo (1855)," in *Documentos com que o ilustríssimo e excelentíssimo Senhor Dr. José Antonio Saraiva, presidente da província de São Paulo, instruiu o relatório da abertura da assembleia legislativa provincial no dia 15 de fevereiro de 1855* (São Paulo: Antonio Louzada Antunes, 1855).

7. *Discurso com que o ilustríssimo e excelentíssimo Senhor Dr. José Thomaz Nabuco D'Araujo, presidente da província de São Paulo, abriu a assembleia legislativa provincial no dia 1o. de maio de 1852* (São Paulo: Antonio Louzada Antunes, 1852), 36, http://brazil.crl.edu/bsd/bsd/986.

8. More than 70 percent of sugar production remained concentrated between 1836 and 1854 in just four localities: Mogi Mirim (26 percent), Itu (18 percent), Piracicaba (15 percent), and Capivari 12 percent).

9. Bananal, Taubaté, and Pindamonhangaba are in Vale do Paraíba. Campinas is in the Central region.

10. Bananal is a município created through the division of the county of Areias. Before this, Areias was the major coffee producer in the province.

11. For more on the conflict with these first immigrants to the western regions, see Thomaz Davatz, *Memória de um colono no Brasil (1850)* (Belo Horizonte, Brazil: Itatiaia/Editora USP, 1980). A good survey of the immigrant experience is Warren Dean, *Rio Claro: A Brazilian Plantation System, 1820–1920* (Stanford, CA: Stanford University Press, 1976), chap. 4. Dean also shows the significant usage of agregados, the poor landless workers who lived on the fazendas.

12. Evaldo Cabral de Mello, *O norte agrário e o império, 1871–1889* (Rio de Janeiro: Topbooks, 1984), 51.

13. Some 200,000 slaves were transported in the interprovincial slave trade after 1850. See Robert W. Slenes, "The Demography and Economics of Brazilian Slavery, 1850–1888" (PhD diss., Stanford University, 1976), chap. 3; Herbert S. Klein, "The Internal Slave Trade in Nineteenth Century Brazil," *Hispanic American Historical Review* 51 (1971): 567–585; José Flávio Motta and Renato L. Marcondes, "O comércio de escravos no Vale do Paraíba paulista: Guaratinguetá e Silveiras na década de 1870," *Estudos Econômicos* 30, no. 2 (2000): 267–299; Evaldo Cabral de Mello, *O norte agrário e o império*; Erivaldo Fagundes Neves, "Sampauleiros traficantes: Comércio de escravos do alto sertão da Bahia para o oeste cafeeiro paulista," *Afro-Ásia* 24 (2000): 97–128; Rafael da Cunha Scheffer, "Tráfico interprovincial e comerciantes de escravos em Desterro, 1849–1888" (master's thesis, Universidade Federal de Santa Catarina, 2006); Ana Rosa Cloclet da Silva, "Tráfico interprovincial de escravos e seus impactos na concentração da população na província de São Paulo: Século XIX," in *VIII Encontro nacional de estudos populacionais*, vol. 1, 341–366 (Brasília: Associacão Brasileira de Estudos Populacionais, 1992), http://www.abep.nepo.unicamp.br/docs/anais/pdf/1992/T92V01A18.pdf.

14. During the pioneer phase of European immigration, there were constant conflicts between *fazendeiros* (owners of fazendas) and immigrants. For more on immigration, see Pierre Monbeig, *Pioneiros e fazendeiros de São Paulo* (São Paulo: Hucitec/Polis, 1984); Thomas H. Holloway, *Immigrants on the Land: Coffee and Society in São Paulo, 1886–1934* (Chapel Hill: University of North Carolina Press, 1980); Davatz, *Memórias de um colono*; Dean, *Rio Claro*; and Pedro Carvalho de Mello, "The Economics of Labor in Brazilian Coffee Plantations, 1850–1888" (PhD diss., Department of Economics, University of Chicago, 1977).

15. Law 42 of March 30, 1871, authorized the provincial government to issue bonds to "assist the farmers of the province who want to bring settlers to their farms, as well as to assist the settlers." The aid would be "for the payment of travel and other expenses to each settler on the farm that had solicited him" and be repaid in eleven years. See the text of the law at http://www.al.sp.gov.br/norma/?id=138648.

16. According to Rosa Guadalupe Soares Udaeta, the Associação Auxiliadora de Colonização e Imigração promoted immigrants for work on the coffee plantations. Founded in 1871, it had a contract with the provincial government to bring in European immigrants and was required to guarantee that immigrants who landed in any Brazilian port would be sent to São Paulo and not another province. Rosa Guadalupe Soares Udaeta, "As hospedarias de imigrantes em São Paulo: O caso da Maçan D'Oro," paper presented at XX Encontro Regional de História: História e Liberdade, Franca, September 6–10, 2010.

Also see Sylvia Basseto, "Política de mão-de-obra na economia cafeeira do Oeste Paulista (periodo de transição)" (PhD diss., Universidade de São Paulo, 1982); and Kátia Cristina Petri, "Terras e imigração em São Paulo: Política fundiária e trabalho rural," *Histórica*, no. 2 (June 2005), http://www.historica.arquivoestado.sp.gov.br/materias/anteriores/edicao02/materia01/.

17. See, for example, *Relatório com que o Exmo. Sr. Conselheiro Francisco Xavier Pinto Lima, passou a administração da província ao exmo. Sr. Dr. João Theodoro Xavier, presidente da mesma* (São Paulo: Typographia Americana, 1872), 16–17.

18. In the second half of the nineteenth century several hostels for immigrants were established, but all of them were small and in poor condition. In 1883, for example, the Hospederia Bom Retiro was opened, and it closed only after the opening of the specially built Hospedaria dos Imigrantes in the Brás district of São Paulo. The Hospedaria dos Imigrantes building now houses the Immigration Museum. *Relatório apresentado à assemblea legislativa provincial de São Paulo pelo presidente da província João Alfredo Corrêia de Oliveira no dia 15 de fevereiro de 1886* (São Paulo: Typographia a Vapor de Jorge Seckler, 1886), 33–34, http://brazil.crl.edu/bsd/bsd/1030.

19. Law 123, of July 16, 1881, allowed immigrants to stay for a maximum of eight days. For the text of the law, see https://www.al.sp.gov.br/norma/139437.

20. Law 29, March 29, 1884, set out these terms. For the text of the law, see https://www.al.sp.gov.br/norma/138424.

21. Instituto Brasileiro de Geografia e Estatística, *Anuário estatístico do Brasil, 1939/1940*, vol. 5 (Rio de Janeiro: Conselho Nacional de Estatística, 1940), 1307, http://produtos.seade.gov.br/produtos/bibliotecadigital/view/singlepage/index.php?pubcod=10020584&parte=1. In São Paulo in 1890, there were 57 foreign born per thousand inhabitants; the average in Brazil was 25. In 1920 this same difference occurred, with São Paulo having 259 foreign born per thousand residents, and the rest of Brazil an average of just 73. Ibid., 1302.

22. Rogério Naques Faleiros, *Fronteiras do café* (São Paulo: FAPESP-EDUSC, 2010).

23. Even in the nineteenth century, the poor state of the municipal, provincial, and regional highways offered little possibility for use of wheeled vehicles. With the movement of coffee plantings into the upland valleys and plains in the early decades of the nineteenth century and the necessity of shipping coffee overseas from the coastal ports, mule transport was the limiting factor in the growth of the coffee, as well as sugar, fazendas of the major coffee-producing provinces of Minas Gerais, Rio de Janeiro, and São Paulo. Herbert S. Klein, "The Supply of Mules to Central Brazil: The Sorocaba Market, 1825–1880," *Agricultural History* 64, no. 4 (1990): 4.

24. Use of mules as transport and cargo animals in Brazil differed from their use in the southern United States, where good wagon roads existed be-

fore railroads and where mules were used exclusively as draft animals in the nineteenth century. Klein, "The Supply of Mules to Central Brazil," 4.

25. The Estrada União e Indústria road linked Petrópolis (Rio de Janeiro) with Juiz de Fora (Minas Gerais) and was unique in the coffee region before the railroad era. This 144-kilometer macadam road, suitable for horse-drawn wagons, was completed in 1861 and opened up the Mata zone in Minas Gerais for coffee production. Coffee transported to the port of Rio de Janeiro via the road increased until well into the twentieth century. Fernando Gaudereto Lamas and Luís Eduardo do Oliveira, "As vicissitudes da escravidão e da imigração em Minas Gerais: A companhia união e indústria, os escravos e os alemães (1852–1879)," paper presented at 3°. Encontro: Escravidão e Liberdade no Brasil Meridional, Maio, Cape Verde, 2007, http://www.escravidaoeliberdade.com.br/site/images/Textos3/fernando%20lamas%20e%20luiz%20eduardo.pdf.

26. Until 1864 the roads also accessed ports in the region of present-day Angra dos Reis. See "Os caminhos do café," http://www.sebraerj.com.br/custom/pdf/cam/cafe/02_OsCaminhosDoCafe.pdf (accessed May 1, 2017). For more on the Minas Gerais and São Paulo coffee produced in Vale do Paraíba, see Paulo Mercadante, *Os sertões do leste: Estudo de uma região; a mata mineira* (Rio de Janeiro: Zahar, 1973); Francisco Iglésias, "Política econômica do estado de Minas Gerais (1890–1930)," paper presented at V Seminário de Estudos Mineiros: A República Velha em Minas, Belo Horizonte, Brazil, 1982; Stanley J. Stein, *Vassouras: A Brazilian Coffee County, 1850–1900*, 2nd ed. (New York: Atheneum, 1976); Humberto Fernandes Machado, *Escravos, senhores e café: A crise da cafeicultura escravista do Vale do Paraíba, 1860–1888* (Niterói, Brazil: Cromos, 1993); and Anderson José Pires, "Café, finanças e bancos: Uma análise do sistema financeiro da Zona da Mata de Minas Gerais" (PhD diss., Universidade de São Paulo, 2004).

27. Aside from requiring the labor of many slaves who could have been put to production, mule transport was expensive and inefficient. According to the Companhia Paulista de Estrada de Ferro, transport by mule cost around 440 réis per arroba of coffee, while the railroad cost was 140 réis per arroba. Flávio Azevedo Marques de Saes, *As ferrovias de São Paulo, 1870–1940* (São Paulo: Hucitec/Instituto Nacional do Livro/Minesterio da Educação e Cultura, 1981), 40.

28. This guarantee of government funding was essential to the construction of the railroads in all Latin American countries. See Vincent Bignon, Rui Esteves, and Alfonso Herranz-Loncán, "Big Push or Big Grab? Railways, Government Activism, and Export Growth in Latin America, 1865–1913," *Economic History Review* 68, no. 4 (2015): 1277–1305.

29. Construction began in 1855 on the Estrada de Ferro D. Pedro II, a railway to connect the national capital of Rio de Janeiro with Cachoeira in São Paulo and Porto Novo do Cunha on the border of Minas Gerais.

Tunneling made this a costly enterprise, and the government had to get British loans to complete the two lines, which reached Porto Novo in 1871 and Cachoeira in the Paulista part of Vale do Paraíba later that decade. Bruno Nascimento Campos, "Tropas de aço: Os caminhos de ferro no sul de Minas (1875–1902)" (master's thesis, Universidade Federal de São João del Rei, 2012), 33.

30. Adolpho Augusto Pinto, *História da viação pública de São Paulo* (São Paulo: Governo do Estado de São Paulo, 1977), 21–31. The D. Pedro II railroad at Três Rios linked to the Estrada de Rodagem União e Indústria.

31. According to William R. Summerhill, the Brazilian economy benefited more from the introduction of the railroad than most other nations' economies: "The gains to the Brazilian economy from the new transport technology were likely greater than in those nations, such as the United States, England, France, Belgium, and the Netherlands, that enjoyed relatively efficient and cheap pre-rail transport systems. While the railroad's impact in Brazil also exceeded that of several other backward economies, the degree of an economy's overall relative backwardness is in fact a poor predictor of the impact of railroads. Russia and Thailand were relatively backward economies in the second half of the nineteenth century. Both possessed affordable and navigable waterways; in neither did railroads create especially large gains. . . . Only in . . . Mexico and Spain did railroad freight services create gains of similar magnitudes as found in Brazil." William R. Summerhill III, *Order Against Progress: Government, Foreign Investment, and Railroads in Brazil, 1854–1913* (Stanford, CA: Stanford University Press, 2003), 189.

32. In 1945 the São Paulo Railway was taken over by the federal government and renamed the Estrada de Ferro Santos a Jundiaí.

33. In spite of its importance for coffee expansion, railroad construction under the empire was well behind that of the United States. In 1893 the United States had 176,000 kilometers of railroads compared to Brazil's 11,000 kilometers.

34. For more on the railroads, see Saes, *As ferrovias de São Paulo*; Monbeig, *Pioneiros e fazendeiros de São Paulo*; Célia Regina Baider Stefani, "O sistema ferroviário paulista: Um estudo sobre a evolução do transporte de transporte de passageiros sobre trilhos" (master's thesis, Universidade de São Paulo, 2007); Odilon Nogueira de Matos, *Café e ferrovias: A evolução ferroviária de São Paulo e o desenvolvimento da cultura cafeeira* (São Paulo: Alfa-Omega, 1974); Summerhill, *Order Against Progress*; Robert H. Mattoon Jr., "Railroads, Coffee, and the Growth of Big Business in São Paulo, Brazil," *Hispanic American Historical Review* 57, no. 2 (1977): 273–295; Pinto, *História da viação pública de São Paulo*; Maria Lúcia Lamounier, "Entre a escravidão e o trabalho livre: Escravos e imigrantes nas obras de construção das ferrovias no Brasil no século XIX," *Revista Economia* 9, no. 4 (2008): 215–245; José Cechin, "A construção e operação

das ferrovias no Brasil do século XIX" (master's thesis, Universidade Estadual de Campinas, 1978); and Campos, "Tropas de aço."

35. *Fala dirigida à assembleia legislativa provincial de S. Paulo, na abertura da 2ª. sessão da 24ª. legislatura em 10 de janeiro de 1883 pelo Presidente Conselheiro Francisco de Carvalho Soares Brandão* (São Paulo: Typographia do Ypiranga, 1883), 39, http://brazil.crl.edu/bsd/bsd/1027.

36. Pinto, *História da viação pública de São Paulo*, 85–125. As Célia Regina Baider Stefani notes, the width of major lines in Europe did not exceed 1.45 meters, but in Brazil, despite the modest volume of traffic, local builders first adopted a gauge of 1.60 meters. Construction of the wider gauge proved uneconomical, and later builders adopted narrower widths, from 1.00 meter down to 0.60 meter, resulting in serious interconnection problems between the lines that still exist today. Stefani, "O sistema ferroviário Paulista," 38. By 1901 São Paulo had 538 kilometers of 1.60-gauge track; 9 kilometers of 1.36 meters; 22 kilometers of 1.05 meters; a little over 2,672 kilometers of 1.00 meter; and 230 kilometers of 0.60 meter for a total of 3,471 kilometers. Pinto, *História da viação pública de São Paulo*, 233.

37. Caio Prado Jr., *Evolução política do Brasil* (São Paulo: Brasiliense, 1972), 116.

38. For more on Santos and its commission houses, see Ana Lúcia Duarte Lanna, *Uma cidade na transição: Santos, 1870–1913* (São Paulo: Hucitec/Prefeitura Municipal de Santos, 1996); Maria Lúcia C. Githay, *Ventos do mar* (São Paulo: UNESP, 1992); Roberto Perosa, "Comércio e financiamento na lavoura de café de São Paulo no início do século," *Revista Administração de Empresas* 20, no. 1 (1980): 63–78; Maria Apparecida Franco, "O comissário de café no Porto de Santos: 1870–1920" (master's thesis, Universidade de São Paulo, 1980), 243; and Edmar Bacha and Robert Greenhill, *150 anos de café* (São Paulo: Marcelino Martins and Johnston Exportadores, 1992), 137–280.

39. According to Saraiva, coffee production in São Paulo reached 865,000 sacks in 1855. Saraiva, "Quadro estatístico de alguns estabelecimentos rurais da província de São Paulo." In 1900 Paulista production was 8.9 million sacks, out of 13.8 million sacks produced in all Brazil. World consumption in 1900 was just 14.3 million sacks. Bacha and Greenhill, *150 anos de café*, tables 1.2 and 1.3.

40. Antonio José Baptista de Luné and Paulo Delfino da Fonseca, eds., *Almanak da província de São Paulo para 1873* (São Paulo: Typographia Americana, 1873).

41. Petrone, *A lavoura canavieira em São Paulo*, 24.

42. *Relatório apresentado ao exmo. sr. presidente da província de São Paulo pela Comissão Central de Estatística* (São Paulo: Leroy King Bookwalter, 1888), 284–578.

43. For more on the history of the port of Santos, see Alcindo Gonçalves and Luiz Antonio de Paula, *O grande porto: A modernização no Porto de Santos* (Santos: Realejo, 2008).

44. Data from 1871/1872 show that the state exported many other products, such as chickens, animals, beans, rock salt, harnesses, wagons, rice, tallow, wax, glue, and corn, but these amounted to less than 100,000 mil réis, with almost half the value made up of chickens and animals. Luné and Fonseca, *Almanak da província de São Paulo para 1873*, 167; *Relatório apresentado ao exmo. sr. presidente da província*, 24–26, table 4.

45. C. F. Van Delden Laerne, *Brazil and Java: Report on Coffee-Culture in America, Asia, and Africa* (The Hague: Martinus Nijhoff, 1885). The origin of this classic study was explained in the newspaper *Correio Paulistano*: "The Dutch government, given the great Brazilian production, which represents over half the coffee consumed worldwide, decided it was fit to send to Brazil a competent and qualified emissary to accurately study our situation." That emissary was Van Delden Laerne. "Cultura e comercio do café: O enviado do governo da Hollanda, S. vanDelden Laerne," *Correio Paulistano*, January 18, 1884, http://www.arquivoestado.sp.gov.br/upload/jornais/BR_APESP_CPNO_18840118.pdf.

46. Alice P. Canabrava, "A grande lavoura," in *História geral da civilização brasileira*, vol. 2, bk. 4, *Brasil monárquico*, ed. Sérgio Buarque de Holanda (São Paulo: Difusão Europeia do Livro, 1971), 85–137.

47. *Indústria assucareira: Produção e consumo mundial do assucar* (Rio de Janeiro: Imprensa Nacional, 1907), 2–3.

48. Gileno de Carli, *Gênese e evolução da indústria açucareira de São Paulo* (Rio de Janeiro: Irmãos Pongetti, 1943), 21.

49. Data are from 1874, given in Carli, *Gênese e evolução da indústria açucareira*, 24. In that year Brazil's output was just 21 percent that of Cuba's.

50. Henrique Augusto Millet, *A lavoura da cana de açúcar* (Pernambuco: Massangana, 1989), ix.

51. Gileno de Carli, *O açúcar na formação econômica do Brasil* (Rio de Janeiro: Instituto do Açúcar e do Álcool, 1937), 30.

52. Decree 2687 of November 6, 1875, article 1, authorized the government to guarantee up to 5 percent per year and to provide for amortization of mortgage notes issued by Banco de Crédito Real. For the text of the decree, see http://www2.camara.leg.br/legin/fed/decret/1824-1899/decreto-2687-6-novembro-1875-549775-publicacaooriginal-65293-pl.html.

53. This was the conclusion of an official study carried out in 1887. *Relatório da comissão encarregada de estudar a difusão applicada a cana de assucar, apresentado ao Exmo. Sr. Conselheiro Rodrigo Augusto da Silva, ministro e secretario de estado dos negocios da agricultura* (Rio de Janeiro: Imprensa Nacional, 1887), 30.

54. José Antonio Saraiva, *Relatório apresentado à assembleia geral legislativa na primeira sessão da décima oitava legislatura, pelo ministro e secretário da agricultura, comércio e obras públicas* (Rio de Janeiro: Typografia Nacional, 1882), 3.

55. For more on this theme, see Canabrava, "A grande lavoura," 85–137; Roberta Barros Meira, "Banguês, engenhos centrais e usinas" (master's thesis,

Universidade de São Paulo, 2007); Carli, *Gênese e evolução da indústria açucareira*; Peter Eisenberg, *The Sugar Industry in Pernambuco: Modernization Without Change, 1840–1910* (Berkeley: University of California Press, 1974); Jonas Soares de Souza, "O engenho central de Porto Feliz: Subsídios para o estudo dos engenhos centrais do Brasil no século XIX," *Anais do Museu Paulista* 25 (1974): 25–43; and Alcides Ribeiro Soares, "A experiência dos engenhos centrais," in *História do estado de São Paulo*, ed. Nilo Odalia and João Ricardo de Castro Caldeira (São Paulo: Editora UNESP, 2010), 1:161–187.

56. *Relatório apresentado ao chefe do governo provisório por Francisco Glicério, ministro e secretário de estado da Agricultura, Comércio e Obras Públicas* (Rio de Janeiro: Imprensa Oficial, 1890), 49–51. The federal government later doubled the capital needed to receive guaranteed interest on investment in these enterprises.

57. Peter Eisenberg, in his study of the sugar industry in Pernambuco, found that some engenhos centrais were constructed with used or inadequate equipment. He also cited conflicts between the central mills and their cane suppliers. Eisenberg, *The Sugar Industry in Pernambuco*, 111–124.

58. Few mills were actually built using the state guarantees on investment. Carli, *Genese e evolução da indústria açucareira de São Paulo*, 51.

59. For more on the engenhos centrais, see Carli, *O açucar na formação econômica do Brasil*; Carli, *Gênese e evolução da indústria açucareira de São Paulo*; Gileno de Carli, *Geografia econômica e social da canna de açúcar no Brasil* (Rio de Janeiro: Brasil Açucareiro, 1938), 64; Millet, *A lavoura da cana de açúcar*; Canabrava, "A grande lavoura," 85–137; Meira, "Bangues, engenhos centrais e usinas"; Eisenberg, *The Sugar Industry in Pernambuco*; Ruy Gama, *Engenho e tecnologia* (São Paulo: Duas Cidades, 1979); Mello, *O norte agrário e o império*; and José Evandro Vieira de Melo, "Café com açúcar: A formação do mercado consumidor de açúcar em São Paulo e o nascimento da grande indústria açucareira paulista na segunda metade do século XIX," *Seculum, Revista de História*, no. 14 (2006): 74–93.

60. In a speech to the provincial legislature, the president emphasized the importance of diversification of production for the state and said the government would offer support and protection to various crops and products, not just to the establishment of engenhos centrais. *Fala dirigida à assembleia legislativa Provincial de S. Paulo*, 71.

61. Alcides Ribeiro Soares, *Um século de economia açucareira: Evolução da moderna agroindústria do açúcar em São Paulo, de 1877 a 1970* (São Paulo: Cliper Editora, 2001), 49; Carli, *Gênese e evolução da indústria açucareira de São Paulo*, 46–48, 53.

62. The difficulties of the central mills operating in São Paulo led to a French enterprise acquiring all these mills. The enterprise eventually became the Société de Sucréries Bresiliennes. Meira, "Banguês, engenhos centrais e usinas," 144.

63. For more on this, see James A. B. Scherer, *Cotton as a World Power* (New York, Frederick A. Stokes, 1916).

64. US Bureau of the Census, *Historical Statistics of the United States: Colonial Times to 1970*, bicentennial ed. (Washington, DC: US Bureau of the Census, 1975), 517–518, table K550-563.

65. The classic study about cotton in São Paulo is Alice P. Canabrava, *O algodão em São Paulo, 1861–1875* (São Paulo: T. A. Queiróz, 1984). Also see Alice P. Canabrava, "Uma fazenda-modelo na província de São Paulo (1863)," in *Anais do IX Simpósio da ANPUH*, vol. 4 (São Paulo: ANPUH, 1979), 1173–1219; Maria Regina C. Mello, *A industrialização do algodão em São Paulo* (São Paulo: Perspectiva, 1983). According to Marcelo de Paiva Abreu and Luiz Aranha Correa do Lago, after 1880 Brazilian cotton exports ranged between 4,000 and 14,000 metric tons, but domestic consumption was already becoming important. Marcelo de Paiva Abreu and Luiz Aranha Correa do Lago, "A economia Brasileira no império, 1822–1889," Texto para Discussão no. 584, Pontifícia Universidade Católica, n.d.).

66. Canabrava, *O algodão em São Paulo*, 7.

67. This type of cotton was introduced by Jean Jacques Aubertin, superintendent of the Santos-Jundiaí railroad. Ibid., 10.

68. The first agricultural research center created in São Paulo was the Campinas Agronomic Institute, which would have a key role in the development of agriculture in São Paulo and Brazil. Created in 1887 by Emperor Dom Pedro II, it passed to provincial control in 1892. Before its creation the lack of research institutes represented a fundamental constraint to the development of seeds and appropriate farming techniques. In the absence of appropriate agricultural research agencies, individuals promoted the expansion of cotton production in São Paulo. Among these was Carlos Ilidro da Silva, who according to Canabrava, "would be the greatest agronomist of the province of São Paulo." Canabrava, *O algodão em São Paulo*, 32–33; Alice P. Canabrava, "Uma fazenda-modelo na província de São Paulo"; Karina B. S. Quiroga and Gilmar Arruda, "Natureza, cafeicultura e modernização da agricultura no oeste de São Paulo: As ideias de Carlos Ilidro da Silva (1860–1864)," *Tempos Históricos* 15, no. 2 (2011): 269–298.

69. The society was founded in 1831 to promote industry. Patrícia R. C. Barreto, "Sociedade Auxiliadora da Indústria Nacional: O templo carioca de Palas Atena" (PhD diss., Instituto de Química, Universidade Federal do Rio de Janeiro, Rio de Janeiro, 2009), 5.

70. In publications of the Auxiliadora da Indústria Nacional are references to cotton production and reproductions of important documents on the subject. In its publication of January 3, 1862, was "Manual do cultivador de algodão." See Antonio Candido Nascentes D'Azambuja, "Manual do cultivador de algodão," *O Auxiliador da Indústria Nacional*, January 3, 1862, pp. 54–72, http://www.brasiliana.usp.br/handle/1918/003601-02#page/1/mode/1up.

In the publication of the minutes of March 6, 1862, appears "Cultura do algodão herbaceo." See Antonio Caetano da Fonseca, "Cultura do algodão herbaceo," *O Auxiliador da Indústria Nacional*, March 6, 1862, pp. 152–160, https://digital.bbm.usp.br/view/?45000033226&bbm/7057#page/56/mode/2up.

Chapter 2

1. One of the few such studies of any province is that of Maria de Fátima Silva Gouvêa. She notes that there has been "a scarcity of studies on the political-administrative organization of the provinces in the nineteenth century." Maria de Fátima Silva Gouvêa, *O império das províncias, Rio de Janeiro, 1822–1889* (Rio de Janeiro: Civilização Brasileira, 2008), 80.

2. These annual budgets are practically complete and can be found in the digital archive of the Assembleia Legislativa do Estado de São Paulo, at http://www.al.sp.gov.br/alesp/normas/?tipoNorma=9. Even when we know the actual income and expenditure, we use the proposed budgets approved by the legislature because of the wealth of information that they contain.

3. Viviane Tessitore carried out a detailed analysis of taxes in the state of São Paulo from 1832 to 1892. See Viviane Tessitore, "As fontes de riqueza pública: Tributos e administração tributária na província de São Paulo (1832–1892)" (master's thesis, Universidade de São Paulo, 1995). For more on imperial fiscal policies and results, see Hernani Maia Costa, "As barreiras de São Paulo: Estudos históricos das barreiras paulistas no século XIX" (master's thesis, Universidade de São Paulo, 1984), 80; Savério Mandêtta, *Impostos, taxas e contribuições: Resenha histórica do regime fiscal no Brasil* (São Paulo: Colébras, n.d.); Liberato de Castro Carreira, *História financeira e orçamentária do império do Brasil* (1889; repr., Brasília: Fundação Casa de Rui Barbosa, 1980); Guilherme Daveza, "Política tributária no período imperial," in *História geral da civilização brasileira*, ed. Sérgio Buarque de Holanda, vol. 2, bk. 4 (São Paulo: Difusão Europeia do Livro, 1971), 60–84; and Fernando José Amed and Plínio José Labriola de Campos Negreiros, *História dos tributos no Brasil* (São Paulo: Edições SINAFRESP, 2000), 189–227.

4. These can be found in the archives of the Center for Research Libraries, at http://www-apps.crl.edu/brazil/provincial/s%C3%A3o_paulo.

5. Baron Cotegipe, *Breve notícia do estado financeiro das províncias organizada por ordem do S. Ex. o Sr. Barão de Cotegipe, presidente do conselho de ministros* (Rio de Janeiro: Imprensa Oficial, 1887).

6. Eugênio Lefevre, *A administração do estado de São Paulo na República Velha* (São Paulo: Typografia Cupolo, 1937).

7. Ibrahim João Elias and Nelson H. Nozoe, *Secretaria de estado dos negócios da fazenda do estado de São Paulo: Evolução institucional* (São Paulo: IAFEA/USP, 1978. For the structure of the treasury, see Brasílio Sallum Jr. and Eduardo

Kugelmas, "A evolução institucional da secretaria da fazenda, 1889–1930," *Cadernos FUNDAP* 5, no. 9 (1985): 11–20.

8. There are two types of annual publications: the *Contas do exercício* and the *Tabelas explicativas da receita e da despesa do estado de São Paulo*. These series can be found in the archives of SEADE (Fundação Sistema Estadual de Análise de Dados), at http://produtos.seade.gov.br/produtos/bibliotecadigital/view.

9. The *Anuário estatístico de São Paulo* of 1908 provided realized income and expenditure from 1835/1836 to 1888/1889. See Departamento de Estatística do Estado, *Anuário estatístico de São Paulo, 1908* (São Paulo: Typografia do Diário Official, 1911), 2:140.

10. Law of October 20, 1823. See Miriam Dolhdikoff, "O lugar das elites regionais," *Revista USP*, no. 58 (2003): 116–133; Marcos Roberto de Lima Aguirre, "A proposta do federalismo no Brasil: O debate entre a centralização e a descentralização no século XIX" (master's thesis, Universidade Federal do Rio Grande do Sul, Porto Alegre, 2012); Diego de Paiva Vasconcelos, "O liberalismo na constituição brasileira de 1824" (master's thesis, Universidade de Fortaleza, 2008); Leonardo Grão Velloso Damato Oliveira, "Momento federalista: Projetos políticos no alvorecer do império brasileiro" (master's thesis, Universidade Federal do Espírito Santo, Vitória, 2013).

11. See Constituição Política do Império do Brasil de 1824, at http://www.planalto.gov.br/ccivil_03/constituicao/constituicao24.htm. After independence a constitutional assembly was elected to approve a constitution. But the views of the constituents and the emperor conflicted. The emperor dissolved the assembly and unilaterally issued the constitution of 1824, which is seen as absolutist and centralist. Raymundo Faoro, *Os donos do poder: Formação do patronato politico brasileiro* (Porto Alegre: Globo/EDUSP, 1975), 1:289. Also see Marco Antônio Villa, *A história das constituições brasileiras* (São Paulo: Editora Leya, 2011); and Vasconcelos, "O liberalismo na constituição brasileira de 1824." For more on the political structure of the empire, see José Murilo de Carvalho, *A construção da ordem: A elite política imperial* (Rio de Janeiro: Civilização Brasileira, 2003).

12. According to a study of provincial presidents, 919 governed the twenty provinces of the Brazilian empire from 1822 to 1889. The average number per province was 48 presidents, in office for an average of only seventeen months. In six provinces, including São Paulo, the average was close to fourteen months. Some 124 of these presidents served in two different provinces, 46 in three, 28 in four provinces, and 1 in eight different provinces. Given this, any president would have a difficulty developing a systematic and coherent local administration. Carlos Umberto P. Corrêa, "A presidência de província no império," in *XXI simpósio nacional de história: História, acontecimento e narrativa* (João Pessoa, Brazil: ANAIS, 2003), http://anpuh.org/anais/wp-content/uploads/mp/pdf/ANPUH.S22.113.pdf; also see Carlos Eduardo França de Oliveira, "Os presidentes de província e seu conselho privativo, São Paulo e

Minas Gerais (1824–1834)," paper presented at the XXVII Simpósio Nacional de História, Natal, Brazil, July 22–26, 2013, http://www.snh2013.anpuh.org/resources/anais/27/1364657543_ARQUIVO_TextoSimposioSNH_2013_CArlosEduardoFrancadeOliveira.pdf.

13. Elias and Nozoe, *Secretaria de estado dos negócios da fazenda do estado de São Paulo*, 7.

14. Vinicius de Bragança Müller e Oliveira, "Centralização e descentralização: Mudanças institucionais e seus impactos na economia da província de São Paulo (1835–1850)" (master's thesis, Universidade Estadual Paulisto, Araraquara, 2006).

15. The constitution of 1824 created a bicameral national legislature with a senate and chamber of deputies. The senators were appointed for life and the deputies indirectly elected for fixed terms. The central government also had a council of state, and the emperor had a moderating power (*poder moderador*), which allowed him to intervene to guarantee "the independence, equilibrium and harmony of the political powers." Carvalho, *A construção da ordem*.

16. The Code of Criminal Procedure provided for locally elected judges. As one scholar noted, it was "an immense leap from the centralization of the Philippine Ordinances to a copy of English localism." Faoro, *Os donos do poder*, 1:306.

17. For background on this act, see Roderick J. Barman, *Brazil: The Forging of a Nation* (Stanford, CA: Stanford University Press, 1988), chap. 6.

18. Faoro, *Os donos do poder*, 1:300–306. The relative decentralization that occurred during the regency became a factor in the permanent conflict among the political leaders of the monarchy. In May 1840, a law interpreting the Additional Act represented a step backward in terms of decentralization. On July 23, 1840, came the anticipated majority of Dom Pedro II, then fourteen years old, and the regency came to an end. The centralizing movement then would be reinforced by law 261 of December 3, 1841, which moved the judiciary and police power of the provinces into the hands of the national government. See Faoro, *Os donos do poder*, 1:333.

19. Artur Gilberto Garcéa de Lacerda Rocha, "As questões tributárias municipais no Brasil Imperial: Um estudo sobre a cidade do Recife durante as décadas de 1860 e 1870," *Hum@nae* 5, no. 1 (2011), http://www.humanae.esuda.com.br/index.php/humanae/article/view/47/7. Also see Arthur José Renda Vitorino, "Centralização versus descentralização: A politica monetária e fiscal do governo central imperial e a província de São Paulo," *Diálogos* 13, no. 3 (2009): 675–695.

20. Imperial Budget Law of August 24, 1832; law 59 of October 8, 1833; law 99 of October 31, 1835. See Gouvêa, *O império das províncias*, chap. 2; Costa, "As barreiras de São Paulo," 80. Also see Mandêtta, *Impostos, taxas e contribuições*, 541; Amed and Negreiros, *História dos tributos no Brasil*; and especially Carreira, *História financeira e orçamentária do império do Brasil*.

21. Law of October 4, 1831, title 1, chaps. 1, 2, and 3.

22. Ibid., title 3. According to Tessitore the 1831 budget law for the first time tried to standardize the collection and better definition of taxes, avoiding superimpositions on the same tax base. It also attempted to abolish provincial import and export taxes but was unsuccessful. Tessitore, "As fontes de riqueza pública." Also see Daveza, "Política tributária no período imperial," in Holanda, *História geral da civilização brasileira,* vol. 2, bk. 4, pp. 60–84; and Amed and Negreiros, *História dos tributos no Brasil,* 189–227.

23. The structure comprised a treasury inspector, an accountant, and a tax attorney. Law of October 4, 1831, art. 46.

24. Tessitore, "As fontes de riqueza pública," 64.

25. According to Francisco Iglesias the fiscal life of the provinces began with the creation of the legislative assemblies of the provinces. Francisco Iglesias, *Política econômica do governo provincial mineiro (1835–1889)* (Rio de Janeiro: INL, 1958), 174.

26. Expenditures were fixed at 10,787 contos.

27. The law clearly stipulates provincial expenses and their fixed costs, which added up to 2,192 contos for all provinces. In São Paulo, these fixed costs amounted to 119 contos. For the fiscal year 1833/1834, the province of São Paulo budgeted 119.5 contos, which represented around 5 percent of the total of all the imperial provincial budgets.

28. Provincial law 9 of February 20, 1838. Despite the new name, it kept the previous treasury's positions of an accountant, four officers, two clerks (who hand-copied documents), and a doorman, who also served as the mailman. Despite this insufficient structure, the provincial president said in 1841 that he was highly pleased the administration of provincial revenues and that their collection was done faithfully, zealously, and honestly by the collectors. He called attention to the creation of a special legal jurisdiction for the issues of the treasury. This was a subject repeatedly brought up by administrators, indicating the difficulties in resolving judicial issues related to the provincial treasury. *Discurso receitado pelo exmo. Presidente Miguel de Souza Mello e Alvim, no dia 7 de janeiro de 1842, por ocasião da abertura da assembleia legislativa da província de São Paulo* (São Paulo: Typographia Imparcial de Silva Sobral, 1842), 18–22. For more on public advocacy, see Paulo Álvares Babilônia, "A advocacia pública brasileira no período colonial e no império: Evolução histórica," *Jus,* December 2010, https://jus.com.br/artigos/18112/a-advocacia-publica-brasileira-no-periodo-colonial-e-no-imperio-evolucao-historica.

29. *Discurso com que o ilustríssimo e exmo. Senhor Conselheiro Dr. Vicente Pires da Motta, presidente da província de São Paulo, abriu a assembleia legislativa provincial, no dia 15 de abril de 1850* (São Paulo: Typographia do Governo, 1850), 16.

30. Decree of April 16, 1821, http://www.camara.leg.br/Internet/InfDoc/conteudo/colecoes/Legislacao/Legimp-E4_19.pdf. For our discussion of fiscal legislation we draw on the excellent work in both Tessitore, "As

fontes de riqueza pública," 64; and Amed and Plínio, *História dos tributos no Brasil*, 189–227.

31. General law 58 of October 8, 1833, ordered that tithes be paid on sugar, cotton, coffee, tobacco, cattle, and horses. This meant that the remaining items could be taxed with the provincial dízimos. The Paulista law 4 of March 12, 1835, declared that the dízimos, which would belong to the provincial revenue as understood in paragraphs 10 and 11 of article 31 of law 59 of October 8, 1833, would be levied only on the export of goods leaving the province. Rates were 10 percent on manufactured products and 5 percent on hand-produced goods.

32. Various changes with respect to this tax were made during the period of the empire. Law 3 of April 3, 1866, for example, fixed the following rates for the tax: 7.5 percent on nonmanufactured goods, 3.5 percent on manufactured goods produced or exported from the province, 6 percent on raw cotton, 3 percent on cotton cloth, and 4 percent on goods exported to the exterior from the ports of the province. This law declared that all the cotton dízimo would go to paying off provincial debt.

33. According to Suprinyak, the location of the Rio Negro Registry proved especially suitable for tax purposes. The barrier post of the Rio Negro was between the provinces of São Paulo and Rio Grande de São Pedro and just off the Estrada da Mata, the only route through the dense forests of the hinterlands and thus used by mule trains crossing the Rio Negro. Carlos Eduardo Suprinyak, "O mercado de animais de carga no centro-sul do Brasil imperial: Novas evidências," *Estudos Econômicos* 38, no. 2 (2008): 321. Paraná was still part of São Paulo, becoming a separate province in 1853. On the tax collected at the Sorocaba registry, see Herbert S. Klein, "The Supply of Mules to Central Brazil: The Sorocaba Market, 1825–1880," *Agricultural History* 64, no. 4 (1990): 1–25. For the origins of the separation of Paraná from São Paulo, see Vitor Marcos Gregório, "Dividindo as províncias do império: A emancipação do Amazonas e do Paraná e o sistema representativo na construção do estado nacional brasileiro (1826–1854)" (PhD diss., Universidade de São Paulo, 2012).

34. According to law 10 of May 7, 1851, the barrier tax collected would be fully applied to the maintenance of roads linking Sorocaba to the rest of the province, as well as major roads of the município of Curitiba that did not have their own income.

35. The tax became known as tax on animals in Itararé and Sorocaba, appearing in that form in the 1886/1887 budget, approved by law 124 of May 28, 1886. See also law 129 of July 17, 1881, which determined the charges on each type of animal that entered Rio Grande do Sul, Santa Catarina, and Paraná: mules were taxed at 2,000 réis, stallions 500 réis, mares 1,000 réis, and cattle 500 réis. Mules in mule trains were not taxed.

36. Law 17 of March 26, 1840.

37. Tessitore, "As fontes de riqueza pública," 250–257. According to Evaldo Cabral de Mello, the provinces were very limited in their power to tax exports. On the other hand, the empire gave too broad a meaning to imports, which limited provincial assemblies' ability to tax them. Evaldo Cabral de Mello, *O norte agrário e o império, 1871–1889* (Rio de Janeiro: Topbook, 1984), 247.

38. Maria Isabel Basilisco Célia Danieli, "Economia mercantil de abastecimento e rede tributária: São Paulo, séculos XVIII e XIX" (PhD diss., Universidade Estadual de Campinas, 2006), 147.

39. There were approximately fifteen barreiras named in the provincial budgets of São Paulo. The most important were Cubatão near Santos, Itapetininga, Jundiaí, Sorocaba, and Ubatuba. See José Jobson de Andrade Arruda, "As barreiras como fontes primárias para a história da província de S. Paulo no século XIX (1835–1892)," in *Memória da I semana de história* (Franca, Brazil: Editora UNESP, 1979), 17–24; José Jobson de Andrade Arruda, "As barreiras de Cubatão, Caraguatatuba, Ubatuba e Cunha: Limites e possibilidades da documentação," *Anais do Museu Paulista* 28 (1977–1978): 81–100; Costa, "As barreiras de São Paulo," 80; and Maria Thereza Schorer Petrone, *O Barão de Iguape: Um empresário da época da Independência* (São Paulo: Nacional, 1976).

40. The law had two tables, one for goods and another for passengers. Goods such as coffee, sugar, cotton, tobacco, leather, brandy, flour, cereals, salt, and manufactured goods in general were taxed at 2.5 réis per kilogram. Oxen, cows, bulls, horses, donkeys, and other beasts cost 1,200 réis per head. Small animals such as calves cost 210 réis per head. First-class passengers paid 200 réis, second-class 150 réis, and third-class 100 réis. Law 73 of April 26, 1872. The tables underwent numerous changes until the end of the empire but basically covered the same products.

41. In the colonial period Minas Gerais charged a slave capitation tax to prevent tax evasion by gold miners. The Crown levied a tax on the slaves that miners owned, since the number of slaves was a good proxy for gold extracted. See Francisco Vidal Luna, *Minas Gerais: Escravos e senhores; Análise da estrutura populacional e econômica de alguns centros mineratórios (1718–1804)* (São Paulo: Instituto de Pesquisas Econômicas, USP, 1981).

42. For more on the *meia sisa* tax, see Guilherme Vilella Fernandes, "Tributação e escravidão: O imposto da meia siza sobre o comércio de escravos na província de São Paulo (1809–1850)," *Almanack Brasiliense*, no. 2 (2005): 102–113; and Rafael da Cunha Scheffer, "Comércio de cativos através das fontes cartoriais: Possibilidades e seus limites," paper presented at the XXVII Simpósio Nacional de História, Natal, Brazil, July 22–26, 2013, http://www.snh2013.anpuh.org/resources/anais/27/1364739513_ARQUIVO_ArtigoRafaeldaCunhaScheffer.pdf.

43. Alvará of June 3, 1809. The law established that anyone could collect the tax, doing so in auctions like other contracts.

44. General budget law of October 24, 1832.

45. Law 17 of April 11, 1835, which established that the tax would not be charged if there was an exchange of slaves, for goods or other slaves, nor would a slave obtaining liberty through self-purchase or other means be charged the tax.

46. Ibid., art. 37.

47. Two of these were the taxes on slaves belonging to convents and on slaves who left the province by sea.

48. The Matrícula Especial de Escravos was created by law 1 of January 23, 1881. The act required that all slaves who entered São Paulo be registered and be taxed 2,000 contos. This income appears in the budget for fiscal year 1881/1882.

49. *Fala dirigida à Assemblea Legislativa Provincial de S. Paulo na abertura da 1a. sessão da 25ª. legislatura, em 16 de janeiro de 1884, pelo Presidente Barão de Guajará* (São Paulo: Typographia da Gazeta Liberal, 1884), 8, tables. Interprovincial sales of slaves were concentrated in the coffee-producing provinces, which had negative economic and political effects on the coffee-exporting provinces and created a political imbalance in defense of the institution. Provinces with fewer slaves were little interested in the maintenance of slavery, then strongly questioned in the country.

50. The law declared that no inheritance could be granted to any heir without official stamped paper documentation. Alvará of June 17, 1809, art. 6.

51. This was the complaint of the president of the province in 1844. See *Discurso recitado pelo exmo. Presidente Manuel Felizandro de Souza e Mello, no dia 7 de janeiro de 1844, por ocasião da abertura da assembleia legislativa da província de São Paulo* (São Paulo: Tipografia do Governo, 1844), 57. In 1872, law 73 of April 26 elevated the inheritance tax to 15 percent.

52. Law 17, April 11, 1835, art. 8.

53. Alvará of June 27, 1808, in which the prince regent said that Portugal's experience with a tithe on urban buildings (*décima urbana*) was that its burden was shared more equally, because owners paid the tax on buildings they inhabited or added it to the rent they charged. A Board of Urban Tenth collected the tax in each municipality.

54. The act stated that urban property tax was the responsibility of local municipal councils, which would establish in their annual budgets the percentage that they should receive for administering the collection of the tax. Law 10, February 22, 1842. The province retained the Tenth of Urban Buildings on Church Convents, which became part of the provincial income after 1845, but it produced little revenue. In 1873 the tax was reinstated on urban buildings, to be paid by the owner. The law stipulated that the owner of urban

property should pay a yearly tax of one mil réis for each conto value of the building. In other words, it created a new provincial tax of 1 percent of the total value of the urban building for all buildings greater than one conto. Law 19, April 25, 1873.

55. Law 86A, June 25, 1881, art. 10.

56. Exempt from the additional tax were goods subject to other taxes and fees. Also exempt were goods leaving the port of Santos. According to Tessitore, subsequent legislation referred to exemptions related to coffee. The funds from this additional tax were applied to the provincial debt. Tessitore, "As fontes de riqueza pública," 168.

57. Law 91, April 25, 1873, chap. 4, "Disposições permanentes," art. 2. The law stipulated that the government would make rules for the collection of the tax. According to Tessitore, between 1880 and 1888, the provincial treasury had ongoing difficulties in collecting this tax, partly because of the social position of the people on whom the tax was being charged. Tessitore, "As fontes de riqueza pública," 186.

58. We present the available data for estimated income budgeted by the provincial assembly in Table A2.1, and in Table A2.2 we present actual and budgeted income for the province from 1835 to 1889.

59. *Relatório com que o exmo. Sr. Dr. Sebastião José Pereira passou a administração da província ao 5º. Vice-Presidente Monsenhor Joaquim Manoel Gonçalves de Andrade* (São Paulo: Typographia do Diario, 1878), 75.

60. As the president of the province reported in 1864, "[In] the budget of receipts and expenditures for the fiscal year 1864/1865, income was calculated on the average of actual income for the past three years." *Relatório que por ocasião da abertura da Assemblea Legislativa Provincial de S. Paulo no dia 3 de fevereiro de 1864 apresentou o ilmo. e exmo. Sr. Conselheiro Doutor Vicente Pires da Motta, presidente da mesma província* (São Paulo: Tipographia Imparcial, 1864), 14. Although these estimates are not perfect, they present some consistency, especially with the budgeted income. In the case of the municípios, Luciana Suarez Lopes and Anne Gerard Hanley could not identify a relationship between income and expenditures in the respective budgets. Luciana Suarez Lopes and Anne Gerard Hanley, "Alice in Accounting Land: The Adventure of Two Economic Historians in Accounting Records of the 19th Century," *Revista Contabilidade e Finanças* 25 (2014): 355–363.

61. We base this on the following budgets approved by the São Paulo provincial assembly: laws 107 (1889); 55 (1888); 95 (1887); 124 (1886); 94 (1885); 59 (1884); 156 (1880); 22 (1877); 89 (1876); 10 (1875); 52 (1874); 91 (1873); 73 (1872); 45 (1871); 93 (1870); 29 (1869); 57 (1868); 16 (1867); 77 (1865); 30 (1864); 8 (1862); 16 (1861); 27 (1859); 39 (1858); 47 (1857); 31 (1856); 31 (1855); 30 (1854); 18 (1853); 14 (1852); 10 (1851); 24 (1850); 27 (1849); 12 (1848); 28 (1847); 35 (1846); 9 (1845); 40 (1844); 25 (1841); 17 (1840); 11 (1839); 22 (1838); 14 (1837); 40 (1836); and 17 (1835). From

1835 to 1889 the fiscal year began July 1 and ended June 30 of the following year.

62. An extensive study on the financial conditions of the province in 1886 includes a questionnaire about the taxes created by the provincial assembly from January 1878 to December 1885. Budgets still included barreira taxes, but, the document said, the transit tax (enacted in 1872) replaced barrier taxes. Cotegipe, *Breve notícia do estado financeiro das províncias organizada por ordem do S. Ex. o Sr. Barão de Cotegipe, presidente do conselho de ministros*, 4–5.

63. Provincial law 11, March 11, 1839, established that existing cash balances in the province were to be used to purchase national debt bonds. However, provincial law 17, March 26, 1840, banned using surpluses to purchase the national debt, or any other operation. But the next budget law allowed a limited purchase of a total of three hundred bonds worth 1,000 réis each. Law 25, March 23, 1841. Each year such provisions were included in the budget law.

64. The provincial president said that the collection of outstanding debt would only increase significantly when the cases brought by the provincial treasury would be prosecuted before a private judge. *Discurso com que ilustríssimo e exmo. Senhor Conselheiro Dr. Vicente Pires da Motta, presidente da província de São Paulo, abriu a assembleia legislativa provincial, no dia 15 de abril de 1850*, 16.

65. Cotegipe, *Breve notícia do estado financeiro das províncias organizada por ordem do S. Ex. o Sr. Barão de Cotegipe, presidente do Conselho de Ministros*. Although we planned to study all the years, the budgets of the provincial assemblies were not always complete. In a few cases we could not find budget and in others the form of its presentation differed to an extent that made it impossible to compare to other years.

66. Public street lighting was begun in the early 1840s in the capital, and then in Santos. Eventually, the province enacted provincial law 9, March 9, 1840, which set the rules for dealing with the lighting of cities. Provincial law 35, March 16, 1846, arranged for an annual auction among private entrepreneurs for providing the capital's public lighting. From 1847 until 1863 the Companhia de Gás won the contract. Dainis Karepovs, *São Paulo: A imperial cidade e a assembleia legislativa provincial* (São Paulo: Assembleia Legislativa, Divisão de Arquivo Histórico, 2006), 14.

67. Religious organizations took on the task of social assistance to orphans, widows, the sick, prisoners, and immigrants. Edson Gonçalves Pelagalo Oliveira Silva, "Serviço social e a ação sócio-pastoral da Igreja Católica: Assistência, promoção humana e emancipação social" (master's thesis, Pontificia Universidade de São Paulo, 2010), 27.

68. For the provincial government response to various epidemics, see *Discurso com que ilustríssimo e exmo. Senhor Conselheiro Dr. Vicente Pires da Motta, presidente da província de São Paulo, abriu a assembleia legislativa provincial, no dia 15 de abril de 1850*, 8–9; *Discurso com que o ilustríssimo e excelentíssimo Senhor Dr. José Antonio Saraiva, presidente da província de São Paulo, abriu a assembleia legisla-*

tiva provincial, no dia 15 de fevereiro de 1855 (São Paulo: Antonio Louzada Antunes, 1855), 16; and *Relatório apresentado à assembleia legislativa provincial de São Paulo pelo presidente da província exmo. Sr. Dr. Francisco de Paula Rodrigues Alves, no dia 10 de janeiro de 1888* (São Paulo: Typografia de Jorge Seckler, 1888), 23.

69. The province in 1855 had 159 public primary schools, with 4,208 boys and 1,351 girls. Another 93 private schools brought total enrollment to 7,000 students out of a potential population of 52,000. The president of the province noted that this poor showing was nevertheless better than other provinces. *Discurso com que ilustríssimo e excelentíssimo Senhor Dr. José Antonio Saraiva, presidente da província de São Paulo, abriu a assembleia legislativa provincial, no dia 15 de fevereiro de 1855*, 34. By 1870 there was little improvement, as by then the public primary schools of the province had 7,505 students and the private ones had another 1,875. *Relatório apresentado à assembleia legislativa provincial de São Paulo pelo presidente da província o exmo. Sr. Dr. Antônio Candido da Rocha, no dia 2 de fevereiro de 1870* (São Paulo: Tipografia Americana, 1870), 9.

70. Between 1836/1837 and 1877/1878 the ratio between barrier income and expenditures on roads and bridges was a very high 0.820.

71. Provincial law 94, April 20, 1885, in article 15 authorized the government to pay the Companhia Cantareira e Esgotos the rates established in the contract signed on April 7, 1877. Law 195, June 5, 1889, approved changes to the contract, forcing the company to extend services beyond the initially agreed area and changing the financial terms of the contract. In 1894, by Resolution 289, July 10, the province approved the government takeover of the company.

72. *Relatório apresentado à assembleia legislativa provincial de São Paulo pelo presidente da província exmo. Sr. Dr. Francisco de Paula Rodrigues Alves, no dia 10 de janeiro de 1888*, 30.

73. Items such as expenditures for subventions; passive debt; guarantee of interest for railroad investors; the Cantareira Company, which was providing potable water for the capital; and the costs of exchange rates and interest on provincial bonds, which were budgeted, do not appear in the data given by the Baron Cotegipe, making it difficult to compare with our results.

74. In 1876/1877 the actual revenues totaled 2,070 contos, and expenses totaled 4,076 contos. The budgeted expenses were only 1,997 contos that year. In 1877/1878 the actual total income was 3,323 contos and expense 2,701 contos, generating a surplus of 622 contos. We did not find in the budget laws for these two years an explanation as to what this expense represented. But in the budget law of 1876/1877, article 1, an additional expenditure permission stated, "The government may make any credit arrangements needed to resolve any deficit in this budget, including issuing bonds, but only in extreme cases."

75. *Relatório com que o exmo. Sr. Dr. Sebastião José Pereira passou a administração da província ao 5º. Vice-Presidente Monsenhor Joaquim Manoel Gonçalves de Andrade*, 74–75.

76. The provincial president declared that the decline of funds going to the Força Pública was due to a calculation error in the original budget law. *Fala dirigida à assemblea legislativa provincial de S. Paulo na abertura da 1a. sessão da 25ª. legislatura, em 16 de janeiro de 1884, pelo Presidente Barão de Guajará*, 16.

77. Ibid., 23, tables.

78. Decree 5.607, April 24, 1874.

79. *Relatório apresentado à assembleia legislativa provincial de São Paulo pelo presidente da província exmo. Sr. Dr. Francisco de Paula Rodrigues Alves, no dia 10 de janeiro de 1888*, 38.

80. Philippe Scherrer Mendes and Marcelo Magalhães Godoy, "Finanças públicas da província de Minas Gerais," paper presented at the thirteenth Seminário sobre a Economia Mineira, Diamantina, Brazil, August 26–29, 2008, http://www.cedeplar.ufmg.br/seminarios/seminario_diamantina/2008/D08A015.pdf. Also see Cristiano Corte Restitutti, "Elementos da fiscalidade de Minas Gerais Provincial," *Almanack Braziliense*, no. 10 (2009): 115–129.

81. Adalton Franciozo Diniz, "Centralização política e concentração de riqueza: As finanças do império brasileiro no período 1830 a 1889," *História e Economia Revista Interdisciplinar* 1, no. 1 (2005): 47–65. See also Adalton Franciozo Diniz, "As finanças públicas paulista no século XIX," in *História do estado de São Paulo*, ed. Nilo Odalia and João Ricardo de Castro Caldeira (São Paulo: Editora UNESP, 2010), 1:189–204. Raymond Goldsmith notes that the empire took 80 percent of income in 1856/1857 and 76 percent in 1885/1886. Raymond W. Goldsmith, *Brasil 1850–1984: Desenvolvimento financeiro sob um século de inflação* (São Paulo: Harper and Row do Brasil, 1986), 71.

82. For more on the subject of the regional distribution of fiscal resources in the empire, see André Villela, "Distribuição regional das receitas e despesas do governo central no II reinado, 1884–1889," *Estudos Econômicos* 37, no. 2 (2007): 247–274; and Eucélia Maria Agrizzi Mergár, "Repartição da competência tributária no império e seus efeitos na província do Espirito Santo (1836–1850)" (master's thesis, Universidade Federal do Espirito Santo, Vitória, 2011).

83. Provincial law 55, March 22, 1888.

84. See, for example, *Discurso com que ilustríssimo e excelentíssimo Senhor Dr. José Antonio Saraiva, presidente da província de São Paulo, abriu a assembleia legislativa provincial, no dia 15 de fevereiro de 1855*, 24–27; and *Relatório apresentado à assembleia legislativa provincial de São Paulo pelo presidente da província o exm. Sr. Dr. Antônio Candido da Rocha, no dia 2 de fevereiro de 1870*, 4.

85. Provincial law 124, May 28, 1886.

86. *Relatório apresentado à assembleia legislativa provincial de São Paulo pelo presidente da província exmo. Sr. Dr. Francisco de Paula Rodrigues Alves, no dia 10 de janeiro de 1888*, 11–15.

87. Resolução da Assembleia Legislativa no. 30, June 15, 1885, https://www.al.sp.gov.br/repositorio/legislacao/resolucao/1885/resolucao-30-15.06.1885.html.

88. For more on the municipal finances of the empire, see Rocha, "As questões tributárias municipais no Brasil Imperial"; and Luciana Suarez Lopes, "Saldos e sobras: Finanças públicas municipais na primeira metade do oitocentos (província de São Paulo, 1834–1850)," *História e Economia: Revista Interdisciplinar* 10, no. 1 (2012): 29–54. According to Anne Hanley, "This inquiry into public finance for public services shows that in spite of the gains in wealth across the nineteenth century, financial resources fell short of needs because of the structure of the tax system that drained off the most lucrative sources of public revenues for national and, to a lesser extent, provincial administrations. This imbalance was exacerbated by Brazil's refusal to entertain direct taxes on wealth or income. The revenue sources that supported the liberal state at all levels of government were indirect, ensuring that they would also be either insufficient or so burdensome as to provoke revolt. The Brazilian general government opted for insufficiency over political instability. To fill the gap between financial sources and need, São Paulo's municipal councils resorted to appeals to the provincial legislatures for supplemental funding to satisfy their mandate across time and space. These appeals were almost always unsuccessful." Anne G. Hanley, "A Failure to Deliver: Municipal Poverty and the Provision of Public Services in Imperial São Paulo, Brazil, 1822–1889," *Journal of Urban History* 39, no. 3 (2012): 513–535.

89. Thus, despite the dominant liberalism among the imperial elite, they did not oppose government action to promote immigration or basic infrastructural activities. Carvalho, *A construção da ordem*, 370.

Chapter 3

1. For the reconstruction of this elite, see Joseph L. Love, *São Paulo in the Brazilian Federation, 1889–1937* (Stanford, CA: Stanford University Press, 1980), chap. 5; see also the table comparing the Minas Gerais and Pernambuco elite on pages 282–287.

2. On the nature of the local and state parties, bosses and political system, see James P. Woodward, *A Place in Politics: São Paulo, Brazil, from Seigneurial Republicanism to Regionalist Revolt* (Durham, NC: Duke University Press, 2009), chap. 2. For a discussion of conflicts over political hegemony, see Guillaume Azevedo Marques de Saes, "O Partido Republicano Paulista e a luta pela hegemonia política (1889–1898)," in *História do estado de São Paulo: A formação da unidade paulista*, vol. 1, *Colônia e império*, ed. Nilo Odalia and João Ricardo de Castro Caldeira (São Paulo: Editora UNESP/Arquivo Público do Estado/Imprensa Oficial, 2010), 189–206.

3. For a discussion of the creation of one subset of these professionals, those involved in urban planning in the public and private sector, see Cristina Peixoto-Mehrtens, *Urban Space and National Identity in Early Twentieth Century São Paulo, Brazil* (New York: Palgrave Macmillan, 2010). It is worth noting that Love found that the second generation of the Paulista elite—those coming of age in the first decades of the Old Republic—had the highest ratio of engineers; fully 19 percent of its members had engineering degrees. Love, *São Paulo in the Brazilian Federation*, 160–161. See also Nilo Odalia and João Ricardo de Castro Caldeira, eds., *História do estado de São Paulo: A formação da unidade paulista* (São Paulo: Editora UNESP, 2010), 2:190–206.

4. For a survey of this active period of worker protest, see Joel Wolfe, *Working Women, Working Men: São Paulo and the Rise of Brazil's Industrial Working Class, 1900–1955* (Durham, NC: Duke University Press, 1993), chap. 1.

5. While the Brazilian elite professed classic English nineteenth-century liberal ideas, the São Paulo group had more pragmatic interests involving government intervention and support. See José Murilo de Carvalho, *A construção da ordem: A elite política imperial* (Rio de Janeiro: Civilização Brasileira, 2003), 208–209. Also see José Murilo de Carvalho, *Os bestializados: O Rio de Janeiro e a república que não foi* (Rio de Janeiro: Civilização Brasileira, 1987); Raymundo Faoro, *Os donos do poder: Formação do patronato político Brasileiro* (Porto Alegre: Globo/EDUSP, 1975), vol. 2, chap. 12; Fernando Henrique Cardoso, "Dos governos militares a Prudente–Campos Sales," in *História geral da civilização Brasileira*, ed. Sérgio Buarque de Holanda (São Paulo: Difusão Europeia do Livro, 1971), vol. 1, bk. 3, 15–50.

6. According to Faoro the republican movement rapidly expanded once the Paulista coffee fazendeiros became involved. Faoro, *Os donos do poder*, 2:453.

7. Cardoso, "Dos governos militares a Prudente Campos Sales," 1:15–50.

8. Carlos Fernando Mathias, *Notas para a história do judiciário no Brasil* (São Paulo: Fundação Alexandre de Gusmão, 2009), 215, http://funag.gov.br/loja/download/535-notas_para_uma_historia_do_judiciario_no_brasil.pdf.

9. Constituição of 1891, decreed and promulgated by the Congresso Nacional Constituinte, on February 24, 1891. See Fabio Carvalho Leite, "1891: A construção da matriz politico-institucional da republica no Brasil" (master's thesis, Pontifícia Universidade Católica, Rio de Janeiro, 2003); José Duarte Neto, "Rigidez e estabilidade constitucional: Estudo da organização constituição brasileira" (PhD diss., Universidade de São Paulo, 2009); Paulo Benevides, "A evolução constitucional do Brasil," *Estudos Avançados* 14, no. 40 (2000): 155–176; Paulo Benevides and Paes de Andrade, *História constitucional do Brasil* (São Paulo: OAB, 2008).

10. Constituição estadual de 1891, art. 68. Part 2 treats município government. State law 16 of 1891 establishes the organizational structure of the municípios and the state's various taxing rights and bases.

11. According to John Allen Blount III, "The successful republican revolution of 1889 provided an opportunity for the Paulista elite to gain almost complete control of administration. For a variety of economic, political, and social reasons the planter class lent its support to São Paulo republicans in their efforts to determine the form of government established after the fall of Empire. The Brazilian Constitution of 1891 was a major victory for Paulista representatives at the meeting of constituent assembly." John Allen Blount III, "The Public Health Movement in São Paulo, Brazil: A History of the Sanitary Service, 1892–1918" (PhD diss., Tulane University, 1971), 40.

12. For more on the policy of the governors, see Faoro, *Os donos do poder,* 2:520.

13. Several studies show the diversion of coffee capital into banking, as well as commercial and industrial activities. See Flávio A. M. de Saes, *A grande empresa de serviços públicos na economia cafeeira* (São Paulo: Hucitec, 1986); Wilson Cano, *Raízes da concentração industrial em São Paulo* (São Paulo: Difusão Europeia do Livro, 1977); Renato Monseff Perissinotto, *Estado e capital cafeeiro em São Paulo (1889–1930)* (São Paulo: FAPESP/Annablume, 2000); Love, *São Paulo in the Brazilian Federation*; Maurício A. Font, *Coffee and Transformation in São Paulo, Brazil* (Lanham, MD: Lexington Books, 2010); Maurício Font, "Planters and the State: The Hegemony in São Paulo, Brazil, 1889–1930" (PhD diss., University of Michigan, 1983); and Eduardo Kugelmas, "A difícil hegemonia" (PhD diss., Universidade de São Paulo, 1986).

14. For more on this, see Renato Monseff Perissinotto, "Tradição e modernidade no *state-building* paulista durante a Primeira República (1889–1930)," in Odalia and Caldeira, *História do estado de São Paulo*, 2:207–231.

15. Several studies have analyzed the organization and functions of the treasury ministry of São Paulo: see Brasílio Sallum Jr. and Eduardo Kugelmas, "A evolução institucional da secretaria da Fazenda: 1889–1930," *Cadernos FUNDAP* 5, no. 9 (1985): 11–20; Perissinotto, *Estado e capital cafeeiro em São Paulo*; Ibrahim João Elias and Nelson H. Nozoe, *Secretaria de estado dos negócios da fazenda do estado de São Paulo: Evolução institucional* (São Paulo: IAFEA/USP, 1978); Eugênio Lefevre, *A administração do estado de São Paulo na República Velha* (São Paulo: Typografia Cupolo, 1937); Perissinotto, "Tradição e modernidade no *state-building* paulista," 2:207–231; and *A secretaria da fazenda do estado de São Paulo: Raízes e trajetória, São Paulo* (São Paulo: Governo do Estado de São Paulo, 2000).

16. The exam demanded knowledge of Portuguese, arithmetic, and an ability to write well. Some positions required knowledge of commercial transactions and an ability in foreign languages (art. 68). The salary of the director general was 15 contos per annum, subdirectors 12 contos. According to Elias and Nozoe, in 1925 functionaries greatly increased, from 81 to 234 workers, a level maintained until 1930. Elias and Nozoe, *Secretaria de estado dos negócios da fazenda*, 61.

17. See Elias and Nozoe, *Secretaria de estado dos negócios da fazenda*, 72. Also see *Fala dirigida à assemblea legislativa provincial de S. Paulo na abertura da 1a. sessão da 25ª. legislatura, em 16 de janeiro de 1884, pelo Presidente Barão de Guajará* (São Paulo: Typographia da Gazeta Liberal, 1884), 53, tables.

18. Font, "Planters and the State," 441.

19. Perissinotto, *Estado e capital cafeeiro em São Paulo*, chap. 3.

20. *Mensagem dirigida ao congresso do estado a 7 de abril de 1905 pelo presidente de São Paulo, Dr. Jorge Tibiriçá* (São Paulo: Typographia do Diario Official, 1905), 42.

21. The Instituto Paulista da Defesa Permanente do Café was created by law 2.004 of December 19, 1924. The Banco do Estado de São Paulo (BANESPA) was established in 1927 by combining the former Banco de Crédito Hipotecário and the Agrícola do Estado de São Paulo. See Fernando Nogueira da Costa, "Banco do estado: O Caso Banespa" (PhD diss., Universidade Estadual de Campinas, 1988).

22. Ives Gandra da Silva Martins Filho, "Evolução histórica da estrutura judiciária brasileira," *Revista Jurídica Virtual*, 1, no. 5 (1999), https://revistajuridica.presidencia.gov.br/index.php/saj/article/view/1072/1055.

23. Carlos Fernando Mathias, *Notas para a história do judiciário no Brasil* (São Paulo: Fundação Alexandre de Gusmão, 2009), 226–227, http://funag.gov.br/loja/download/535-notas_para_uma_historia_do_judiciario_no_brasil.pdf.

24. The Corpo de Guardas Municipais Permanentes, created in 1831, was the first police force established in São Paulo.

25. José Eduardo Azevedo, "Polícia militar de São Paulo: Elementos para a construção de uma cartografia social da questão policial no Brasil," *Revista do Laboratório de Estudos da Violência e Segurança*, no. 1 (2008): 16, http://www2.marilia.unesp.br/revistas/index.php/levs/article/viewFile/759/661. Federal intervention was a real possibility given that the federal government had intervened in other states, such as Rio de Janeiro, Bahia, and Pernambuco. See José Maria Bello, *História da republica* (São Paulo: Nacional, 1976), chaps. 16–21. In 1913 the state police added a military aviation unit to demonstrate its concern for the security of the state. According to Marco Antônio Severo Silva, the state police should be a small army capable of territorial defense to ensure state interests. The aviation unit of the state, the first to have such a unit, represented an enormous challenge to the central government, "transforming the militia of São Paulo into an extremely professionalized regular army compared with the Brazilian Army and other state forces." Marco Antônio Severo Silva, *A aviação na força pública do estado de São Paulo sob a ótica do ordenamento legislativo (1913 a 1932)* (São Paulo: Secretaria de Segurança Pública de São Paulo, 2013), 2.

26. Love, *São Paulo in the Brazilian Federation*, 127.

27. Law 491, December 29, 1896. Law 478, of December 24, 1896, fixed the number of the Força Pública do Estado at 5,178 men.

28. Law 522, August 26, 1897, law 979, December 23, 1905; Marcelo Thadeu Quintanilha Martins, "A civilização do delegado: Modernidade, polícia e sociedade em São Paulo nas primeiras décadas da república, 1889–1930" (PhD diss., Universidade de São Paulo, 2012), 10.

29. Lefevre, *A administração do estado de São Paulo*, 220–222.

30. Cited in Casemiro dos Reis Filho, *A educação e a ilusão liberal* (São Paulo: Cortez, 1981), 94. Also see Anísio Teixeira, *Educação no Brasil* (Rio de Janeiro: Nacional, 1969); Otaiza de Oliveira Romanelli, *História da educação no Brasil* (Rio de Janeiro: Vozes, 1978); Ana Maria Infantosi, *A escola na República Velha* (São Paulo: Edec, 1983); and Maria Luiza Marcílio, *História da escola em São Paulo e no Brasil* (São Paulo: Instituto Braudel e Imprensa Oficial, 2005).

31. For more on this subject, see Maria Cristina Teixeira, "O direito à educação nas constituições brasileiras," *Revista da Faculdade de Direito* 5, no. 5 (2008): 146–168, https://www.metodista.br/revistas/revistas-ims/index.php/RFD/article/viewFile/464/460.

32. Reis Filho, *A educação e a ilusão liberal*, 75.

33. Teixeira, *Educação no Brasil*, 296.

34. See Marcílio, *História da escola em São Paulo*, 140–141. Also see the discussion of this law in Mario Arantes, "Forma da instrução," *O Estado de São Paulo*, September 21, 1892, p. 1, http://acervo.estadao.com.br/pagina/#!/18920921-5248-nac-0001-999-1-not.

35. Tamás Szmrecsányi, "Origens da liderança científica e tecnológica paulista no século XX," *Revista Gestão e Conexões* 2, no. 2 (2013): 181–206. Rodolfo dos Santos Mascarenhas also notes that an epidemiological crisis faced the state's republican leaders and required immediate response. Rodolfo dos Santos Mascarenhas, "História da saúde pública no estado de São Paulo," *Revista de Saúde Pública* 40, no. 1 (2006): 3–19.

36. As the leading historian of Brazil's public health system notes, "São Paulo governments established and expanded the state public health agency, making the Paulista Sanitary Service one of the most effective such organizations in all of Latin America." Blount, "The Public Health Movement in São Paulo," 2. Also see John Allen Blount III, "A administração da saúde pública no estado de São Paulo: O serviço sanitário, 1892–1918," *Revista Administração de Empresas* 12, no. 4 (1972): 40–48.

37. Rodolpho Telarolli Jr., "Poder e saúde: A republica, a febre amarela e a formação dos serviços sanitários no estado de São Paulo" (PhD diss., Universidade Estadual de Campinas, 1993), 263–264. Blount presents the argument of the state legislature deputy Alfredo Pujol in favor of aid to the municípios: "Statistics have shown that municipalities most affected by yellow fever are those that have the greatest degree of foreign colonization. Fever has been most active among laborers recently arrived in the state." Blount, "The Public Health Movement in São Paulo," 45. A detailed description of the State Sani-

tation Service is Maria Alice Rosa Ribeiro, *História sem fim: Inventário da saúde pública, São Paulo, 1880–1930* (São Paulo: Editora UNESP, 1993), chap. 1.

38. "The first reorganization of the Sanitary Service occurred in September of 1893 and showed the disagreements regarding the role of the state in public health. Though the government was committed to the concept of public sanitation and hygiene, doubts remained as to how the program could be expedited more efficiently. In addition, opponents of state intervention invoked the concept of local autonomy to limit the authority of the central health agency." Blount, "The Public Health Movement in São Paulo," 66–67. Also see *Mensagem dirigida ao congresso do estado a 7 de abril de 1905 pelo Presidente de São Paulo, Dr. Jorge Tibiriçá*, 12.

39. Law 1357 of December 19, 1912, created an academy of surgical medicine and pharmacy in the capital. Nevertheless, teaching and clinics received little support. The first sign of change came with the agreements signed with the Rockefeller Foundation and the Faculdade de Medicina in 1918. This period of development was completed with the establishment of the state Hospital de Clínicas in 1944. André Mota and Maria Gabriela S. M. C. Marinho, "A faculdade de medicina da Universidade de São Paulo: Os primeiros tempos de sua criação, 1912–1950," http://www.fm.usp.br/site/Historico (accessed May 3, 2017); Carlos S. Lacaz and Berta R. Mazieri, *A faculdade de medicina e a USP* (São Paulo: Editora USP, 1995).

40. See Regina C. Gualtieri, "Instituto Butantã e a saúde pública (São Paulo: 1911–1927)" (master's thesis, Universidade de São Paulo, 1994).

41. Adolfo Lutz was the founder of the Instituto Bacteriológico de São Paulo. See "Contribuição à história da medicina no Brasil: Segundo os relatórios do Dr. Adolpho Lutz," *Memórias do Instituto Oswaldo Cruz* 39, no. 2 (1943): 177–189, http://www.scielo.br/pdf/mioc/v39n2/tomo39(f2)_177-189.pdf.

42. Szmrecsányi, "Origens da liderança científica," 181–206.

43. See Luiz Augusto Maia Costa, "A cartografia elaborada pela Comissão Geográfica e Geológica de São Paulo no início do século XX: O componente norte americano do debate científico entre Orville Derby e os intelectuais paulista de então," paper presented at the IV Simpósio Luso Brasileiro de Cartografia Histórica, Porto, Portugal, November 9–12, 2011, http://eventos.letras.up.pt/ivslbch/resumos/97.pdf. Also see J. Régis Guilhaumon, ed., *Pesquisando São Paulo: 110 anos de criação da Comissão Geográfica e Geológica* (São Paulo: Instituto Geológico/SMA, 1996).

44. Szmrecsányi, "Origens da liderança científica," 186.

45. In 1934 the Escola Superior Luiz de Queiroz was one of the schools that went into the foundation of the Universidade de São Paulo. João Lúcio de Azevedo, "Agricultura Luiz de Queiroz: Sua inclusão na USP e sua contribuição para a pesquisa em ciências agrárias," *Revista USP*, no. 60 (2004): 14–39.

46. Law 26 of May 11, 1892.

47. The school attracted the Paulista elite, and its graduates came to occupy significant positions in the state and the nation. Szmrecsányi, "Origens da liderança científica," 200. When the Politécnica de São Paulo was created two engineering schools already existed in Brazil, the Politécnica do Rio de Janeiro and the Escola de Minas de Ouro Preto. While these two schools came out of the French tradition, the Politécnica de São Paulo was based on German models. José Luiz Pereira da Costa Dias and José Roberto Cardoso, "Os 120 anos da escola politécnica de São Paulo," *Engenharia* 618 (2014): 136–141.

48. Instituto de Pesquisas Tecnológicas do Estado de São Paulo, *IPT: 90 anos de tecnologia* (São Paulo: Instituto de Pesquisas Tecnológicas, 1989).

49. Secretaria da Fazenda do Estado de São Paulo, *Contas do exercício de 1938* (São Paulo: Contadoria Geral do Estado, n.d.), http://produtos.seade.gov.br/produtos/bibliotecadigital/view/singlepage/index.php?pubcod=10014787&parte=1.

50. *Mensagem enviada ao congresso do estado a 7 de abril de 1901 pelo Dr. Francisco de Paula Rodrigues Alves, presidente do estado, São Paulo* (São Paulo: Typographia do Diario Official, 1901), 45–46.

51. The documentation available for the republican period permits us to provide an annual accounting of actual funding and expenditures that was unavailable for most of the nineteenth century.

52. See, for example, *Mensagem enviada ao congresso do estado a 7 de abril de 1901 pelo Dr. Francisco de Paula Rodrigues Alves, presidente do estado, São Paulo*, 47–48; *Mensagem enviada ao congresso do estado, a 14 de julho de 1914, pelo Dr. Carlos Augusto Pereira Guimarães, vice-presidente do estado de S. Paulo* (São Paulo: Typographia do Diario Official, 1914), 639.

53. *Mensagem dirigida ao congresso legislativo de S. Paulo, pelo vice-presidente do estado, Dr. José Alves Cerqueira Cesar, no dia 7 de abril de 1892* (São Paulo: Typographia do Diario Official, 1892), 15.

54. In 1917 the system was reorganized (law 1.596), which created eleven regional health offices, of which five were in the capital. In total there were fifty-one state sanitary inspectors, thirty-three of them in the capital.

55. *Mensagem apresentada ao congresso legislativo na 2ª. sessão da 14ª. legislatura, em 14 de julho de 1929, pelo Doutor Julio Prestes de Albuquerque, presidente do estado de São Paulo* (São Paulo, [1929]), 244.

56. The state collected water and sewage taxes for providing this service in the capital, Santos, and São Vicente, with an estimated income from these charges and taxes of 25,650 contos. The direct expenditures for sewer construction and maintenance was 15,531 contos. This did not include any debt payments for loans used in this area. These were always listed in a lump sum item in the Secretariat of Finance budget.

57. The data on actual income and expenditures that we use for this chapter are based on the work of Eugênio Lefevre, *A administração do estado de São*

Paulo na República Velha (São Paulo: Typografia Cupolo, 1937). He aggregated the annual data into eight major groups of expenditures, one of them education. For most categories we were unable to compare in detail the proposed budget items and the actual expenditures items, but we could for education. Despite possible distortions, the two sets of series are consistent, and we compared the proposed and realized funds in the area of education.

58. Law 2381, December 12, 1929. The law fixed the annual salary of the Coronel Comandante Geral of the military police at 30 contos; the officers of the Estado Maior received 10 to 20 contos. The soldiers received an annual salary of 2,880 mil réis.

59. According to Holloway, the critics of subsidized immigration were thus refuted by the coffee planters who claimed that the cost of the labor that the immigration service provided was small compared to the contribution that coffee production made to the financing of the state government. Thomas H. Holloway, *Immigrants on the Land: Coffee and Society in São Paulo, 1886–1934* (Chapel Hill: University of North Carolina Press, 1980), chap. 3.

60. Steven C. Topik, *The Political Economy of the Brazilian State, 1889–1930* (Austin: University of Texas Press, 1987).

Chapter 4

1. For a more detailed analysis of this structural crisis in the local coffee economy, see Francisco Vidal Luna and Herbert S. Klein, *The Economic and Social History of Brazil Since 1889* (New York: Cambridge University Press, 2014), chap. 1.

2. According to Joseph Love, one of the vital and most complex elements in the coffee trade was the system of currency exchange. Producers calculated the costs in mil réis but received payment in stronger currencies: dollars, marks, francs, and English pounds. Joseph LeRoy Love, *São Paulo in the Brazilian Federation, 1889–1937* (Stanford, CA: Stanford University Press, 1980), 43–44.

3. See the seminal work of Antonio Delfim Netto, *O problema do café no Brasil* (São Paulo: Instituto de Pesquisas Econômicas, USP, 1981), chap. 1. Also see Carlos Manuel Peláez, "Análise econômica do Programa Brasileiro de Sustentação do Café, 1906–1945: Teoria, política e medição," *Revista Brasileira de Economia* 25, no. 4 (1971): 5–212; and Edmar Bacha and Robert Greenhill, *150 anos de café* (São Paulo: Marcelino Martins and Johnston Exportadores, 1992).

4. As Fernando Prestes de Albuquerque, the president of the state of São Paulo, declared in 1899, the situation was "critical" because the crisis in world coffee prices was affecting all segments of the state. *Mensagem enviada ao congresso legislativo a 7 de abril de 1899 por Fernando Prestes de Albuquerque, presidente do estado* (São Paulo: Typographia do Diario Official, 1899), 16.

5. In 1901 Francisco de Paula Rodrigues Alves, then president of the state, argued instead that the crisis was due to overproduction of coffee, which the market would correct without government intervention. *Mensagem enviada ao congresso do estado a 7 de abril de 1901 pelo Dr. Francisco de Paula Rodrigues Alves, presidente do estado, São Paulo* (São Paulo: Typographia do Diario Official, 1901), 23.

6. Joaquim Murtinho was the treasury minister of the Campos Sales government and principal director of its stabilization program. *Relatório do Ministério da Fazenda de 1899*, cited in Delfim Netto, *O problema do café no Brasil*, 42.

7. Delfim Netto, *O problema do café no Brasil*, 44–45.

8. The carryover stock of unsold coffee was 11 million sacks, in an annual world consumption of 16 million sacks. Moreover, the initial estimates for the 1906/1907 harvest had been 16 million sacks, but the actual result was 20 million. There was no way this amount of coffee could be sold on the world or national market.

9. Law 959, October 3, 1905, http://www.al.sp.gov.br/repositorio/legislacao/lei/1905/lei-959-03.10.1905.html.

10. Law 984, December 29, 1905, http://www.al.sp.gov.br/repositorio/legislacao/lei/1905/lei-984-29.12.1905.html.

11. Law 990, June 4, 1906, http://www.al.sp.gov.br/repositorio/legislacao/lei/1906/lei-990-04.06.1906.html. The Convênio de Taubaté is reproduced in Eugênio Lefevre, *A administração do estado de São Paulo na Republica Velha* (São Paulo: Typografia Cupolo, 1937), 115–118. For more on the Taubaté agreement, see Steven Topik, *The Political Economy of the Brazilian State, 1889–1930* (Austin: University of Texas Press, 1987), 67–73.

12. Dorival Teixeira Vieira, *Evolução do sistema monetário brasileira* (São Paulo: Instituto de Pesquisas Econômicas, 1981), 238–274.

13. Among the measures was a compromise to limit export of coffee to 9 million sacks in 1908/1909, 9.5 million in 1909/1910, and 10 million in the following years. Lefevre, *A administração do estado de São Paulo na Republica Velha*, 127.

14. *Relatório apresentado ao Dr. Manuel Joaquim de Albuquerque Lins, presidente do estado pelo Dr. Olavo Egypio de Souza Aranha, secretario da fazenda, 1909* (São Paulo: Casa Garraux, 1910), xxviii–xxix, https://archive.org/stream/relatorioapresen1909sopa#page/n5/mode/2up.

15. Ibid., xxx–xxxi. According to Peláez, this loan represented a loss of control over the valorization program for the state of São Paulo, which was now taken over by the management committee, although São Paulo maintained the right of veto. Peláez, "Análise econômica," 56–57.

16. Lefevre, *A administração do estado de São Paulo na Republica Velha*, 127.

17. Love, *São Paulo in the Brazilian Federation*, 42–43.

18. Departamento de Estatística do Estado, *Anuário estatístico de São Paulo, 1900* (São Paulo: Governo do Estado de São Paulo, 1903), 546–552.

19. Departamento de Estatística do Estado, *Anuário estatístico do estado de São Paulo, 1900*; *Relatório do anno de 1900, apresentado em 13 de janeiro de 1902 ao cidadão Dr. Bento Pereira Bueno, secretaria de estado dos negócios do Interior e da Justiça, pelo Dr. Antonio de Toledo Piza, diretor da repartição de estatística e arquivo do estado de São Paulo* (São Paulo: Typographia do Diario Official, 1902), 546–552.

20. Daniel P. Müller, *Ensaio d'um quadro estatístico da província de São Paulo* (São Paulo: Governo Estado de São Paulo, 1978), https://archive.org/details/ensaio1840sp.

21. See Francisco Vidal Luna, "Observações sobre os dados de produção apresentados por Müller," *Boletim de História Demográfica* 9, no. 24 (2002): 1–6.

22. In the same period Ohio was producing 6.7 million metric tons of corn, for an average of 1.61 metric tons per inhabitant. São Paulo produced 685,729 metric tons, or 0.25 metric tons per inhabitant. Caroll D. Wright, ed., *The New Century Book of Facts: A Handbook of Ready Reference* (Springfield, MA: King-Richardson, 1909), 452.

23. The data reported in the *Anuário estatístico de São Paulo* for that year is insufficient in terms of production because of the failure of many municipalities to report agricultural production, but it is fairly complete in terms of imports and exports.

24. Departamento de Estatística do Estado, *Anuário estatístico de São Paulo, 1900*, 560–567.

25. Japanese immigration began in 1908 when 3,200 Japanese immigrants arrived. This marked a change from earlier anti-Asian and anti-African sentiments and was made possible by law no. 97, October 5, 1892, which opened the country to Asian immigrants.

26. Thomas H. Holloway, *Immigrants on the Land: Coffee and Society in São Paulo, 1886–1934* (Chapel Hill: University of North Carolina Press, 1980), 74–77.

27. Data are available for 165 municípios. Although the census covered all locations, disaggregated data exist only for Santa Isabel, Tiete, Apiaí, Iguape, Itu, and Mogi das Cruzes. These represent 11 percent of the properties and 5 percent of the cultivated area. We can evaluate the missing municípios from the aggregated census data.

28. See Maria Silvia C. Beozzo Bassanezi and Priscila M. S. Bergamo Francisco, eds., *Estado de São Paulo: Estatistica agrícola e zootécnica, 1904–1905* (Campinas, Núcleo de Estudos de População/Universidade Estadual de Campinas, 2003), 1–7; and F. A. Pino, "Centenário do censo agronômico," *Informações Econômicas* 35, no. 5 (2005): 85–97. Also see Francisco Alberto Pino, "Estatísticas agricolas para o século XXI," *Agricultura São Paulo* 46, no. 2 (1999): 71–105. For a more developed analysis of this subject, see Francisco Vidal Luna, Herbert S. Klein, and William Summerhill, "The Characteristics

of Coffee Production and Agriculture in the State of São Paulo in 1905," *Journal of Agricultural History* 90, no. 1 (2016): 22–50.

29. Gender was not noted in the census. Our classification is based on the names of the farm owners.

30. Holloway, *Immigrants on the Land*, chap. 6.

31. Pierre Monbeig, *Pioneiros e fazendeiros de São Paulo* (São Paulo: Hucitec-Polis, 1984), chap. 2. J. S. O. Martins speaks of "a real industry of land grabbing that arose and gained momentum, especially after 1870, to the point that some legislative measures were taken in São Paulo at the end of the century, extending the time allowed to legitimize possessions." J. S. O. Martins, *Cativeiro da terra* (São Paulo: Livraria Ed. Ciências Humanas, 1979). Also see R. C. Lima, *Pequena história territorial do Brasil: Sesmarias e terras devolutas* (São Paulo: Secretaria de Estado da Cultura, 1990); N. W. Sodré, *Oeste: Ensaio sobre a grande propriedade pastoril* (São Paulo: Secretaria de Estado da Cultura, 1990); and L. M. O. Silva, *Terras devolutas e latifúndio* (Campinas: Edunicamp, 1996).

32. Departamento de Estatística do Estado, *Anuário estatístico de São Paulo, 1906* (São Paulo: Governo do Estado de São Paulo, 1907), 2:lxi–lxii. The growth increase of these food crops in this period does not indicate that coffee was a monoculture in previous eras. The production of a variety of food crops was characteristic of the province of São Paulo and was not abandoned with the consolidation of coffee production in the state. See Francisco Vidal Luna and Herbert S. Klein, *Slavery and the Economy of São Paulo, 1750–1850* (Stanford, CA: Stanford University Press, 2003), chap. 4; and Francisco Vidal Luna and Herbert S. Klein, "African Slavery in the Production of Subsistence Crops: The Case of São Paulo in the Nineteenth Century," in *Slavery in the Development of the Americas*, ed. D. Eltis, F. D. Lewis, and K. L. Sokoloff (Cambridge: Cambridge University Press, 2003), 120–149.

33. Imports of rice, a product of greatest weight in food imports, in 1907 fell to less than 10 percent of what São Paulo imported in 1905/1906, and from that year on, imports of rice represented less than 2 percent of the local production in São Paulo. Wilson Cano, *Raízes da concentração industrial em São Paulo* (São Paulo: Difusão Europeia do Livro, 1977), 59. Although food imports are not broken down into their respective types in the 1905 Santos data, there was a general category called "articles destined for food consumption," which was valued at 28,540 contos and amounts to half the value of local corn, rice, and beans produced in that year. Departamento de Estatística do Estado, *Anuário estatístico de São Paulo, 1905* (São Paulo: Governo do Estado de São Paulo, 1907), 2:165.

34. C. A. Tessari analyzed the coexistence of migrants and native-born workers on the coffee farms and states that "in addition to a fixed number of immigrants who guaranteed the survival of the plantation, a farm had a fixed number of native-born workers who were dedicated to general services:

temporary workers, carters, masons, and carpenters, which could change according to the occupational needs of the moment." C. A. Tessari, "Rosinhas e chiquinhos: O processo de amancipação dos escravos e os libertos no mercado de trabalho, Piracicaba, 1870–1920" (master's thesis, Universidade de Campinas, 2000), 73–74. The census confirms the mixture of national and immigrant workers on these farms; it found that native-born farmworkers numbered 6.9 per farm, compared with 21.8 foreign workers per farm.

35. When chemical fertilizer was employed, its use was restricted to only a few farms. In Campinas the census taker wrote, "They use organics: coffee straw, waste, manure, etc. . . . The Snrs. Colonels José Paulino, José Teixeira Sobrinho, Julio Ottoni and others already employ chemical fertilizers." Instituto de Economia Agricola, *Censo agrícola de São Paulo, 1905* (São Paulo: Instituto de Economia Agricola, n.d.).

36. For example, in 1884 Nicolau Moreira stated, "And as the slave has to disappear from Brazilian farming, slash and burn agriculture will have to be replaced by the plow and harrow; incineration resulting from burning, by other means of mucking land; extensive farming, by intensive farming; great estates, by small farms." Quoted in J. A. Pádua, "Cultura esgotadora: Agricultura e destruição ambiental nas últimas décadas o Brasil império," *Estudos Sociedade e Agricultura*, no. 11 (1998): 134. Also see M. R. Ferraro, *A modernização da agricultura e da silvicultura paulista (início do século XX)* (Anápolis, Brazil: Universidade Estadual de Goiás, 2010); C. A. Tessari, "Braços para colheita: Sazonalidade e permanência do trabalho temporário na agricultura paulista (1890–1915)" (PhD diss., Universidade de Campinas, 2010); and M. R. Ferraro, T. C. Magro, and D. F. da Silva Filho, "A gênese da modernização da agricultura em São Paulo," *Revista Ciências Agrárias*, no. 47 (January–June 2007): 149–161. Ferraro, Magro, and da Silva Filho show that in the early twentieth century the Paulista elite became increasingly aware of North American agriculture and debated the need to modernize Paulista agriculture, which was seen as backward and still dependent on fire, hoe, and sickle.

37. According to Pierre Monbeig, modernization did occur in coffee in the early twentieth century, but there was no improvement in working the land and caring for the trees; rather, the improvement was in the preparation of coffee beans. Monbeig describes Paulista agriculture as backward and highly degrading to soil. Monbeig, *Pioneiros e fazendeiros de São Paulo*, 99. S. Silva also affirms that the substitution of slaves by salaried workers led to the mechanization of some production, that of the processing operations. S. Silva, *Expansão cafeeira e origens da indústria no Brasil* (São Paulo: Alfa-Omega, 1995), 48. Augusto Ramos in 1923 said that the mechanization of weeding resulted in an imbalance between the treatment phase of the coffee plantations and harvesting. To save labor by mechanization would have resulted in negative consequences for obtaining labor for the harvest. A. Ramos, *O café no Brasil e no estrangeiro* (Rio de Janeiro: Santa Helena, 1923), 104. Tessari also noted that

a major problem for coffee producers was "the need for abundant and cheap labor, fixed or nomadic, for the harvest." Tessari, "Braços para colheita," 196–197. Also see Cano, *Raízes da concentração industrial em São Paulo*, 20–42.

38. For example, a farm with 13,988 alqueires (33,850 hectares) of land, the property of Veridiana Prado and Sons in Sertãozinho, cultivated 1,588 alqueires (3,842 hectares) of mostly coffee. It had more than a million coffee trees and produced 190,000 kilograms of coffee. The soil of the farm consisted of what was called red earth.

39. Although the average size of the properties was less than one hundred alqueires, some municípios averaged more than five hundred alqueires, like Campos Novos Paulista, São Pedro do Turvo, Itai, Bauru, Bom Successo do Itararé, and Iporanga, all in the Alta and Baixa Sorocabana and Northwest regions. São José do Rio Preto farms reached an average of just under three hundred alqueires. The largest property, in Bauru, was a hundred thousand alqueires (242,000 hectares) and belonged to Dr. Eugenio L. Franco and others. It was completely covered by forests and without any cultivation. Few properties in the census did not have cultivated lands.

40. These largest farms accounted for 83 percent of São Paulo's total area; produced 75 percent of coffee, 68 percent of sugar, 85 percent of aguardente, 85 percent of cotton, 61 percent of corn, 53 percent of rice, and 61 percent of beans; and made up 70 percent of the total value of agricultural production.

41. We derive this Gini index from an inventory of rural properties in São Paulo in 1817. Alice P. Canabrava, "A repartição da terra na Capitania de São Paulo, 1818," *Estudos Econômicos* 2, no. 6 (1972): 77–129.

42. Eduardo Paulon Girardi, "Atlas da questão agrária brasileira: Uma análise dos problemas agrários através do mapa," http://www.uff.br/vsinga/trabalhos/Trabalhos%20Completos/Eduardo%20Paulon%20Girardi.pdf (accessed May 10, 2017).

43. See David de Ferranti, Guillermo E. Perry, Francisco H. G. Ferreira, Michael Walton, and D. Coday, *Inequality in Latin America: Breaking with History?* (Washington, DC: World Bank, 2004), 191, table 7.5.

44. Holloway, *Immigrants on the Land*; Monbeig, *Pioneiros e fazendeiros de São Paulo*; Warren Dean, *Rio Claro: A Brazilian Plantation System, 1820–1920* (Stanford, CA: Stanford University Press, 1976); Martins, *Cativeiro da terra*; R. N. Faleiros, *Fronteiras do café* (Bauru, Brazil: EDUSC, 2010).

45. According to Holloway the immigrants planted principally corn and beans, as well as some rice, potatoes, and other food crops among the coffee trees. They were also granted pasture lands for a limited number of cows. They had vegetable gardens and fruit trees near their residences and raised pigs and chickens. All this production that was not consumed by the colono family was sold in regional markets. Holloway, *Immigrants on the Land*, 78.

46. These were Mogiana, Baixa Paulista, Araraquarense, Central, and Alta Sorocabana.

47. Coffee was still farmed in a way that degraded soil. The new western areas usually had higher productivity at first, which was lost over time without the use of suitable agricultural methods. The yields observed in the Araraquarense and Alta Sorocabana regions could reflect this process of depletion of farmland. Their higher output was in areas of recent occupation that still had productive potential. But the experience of Vale do Paraíba, which had degraded soils and reduced productivity at the time of the census, indicated the fate of these newer zones if they did not change their farming methods.

48. The municípios producing the most coffee were Ribeirão Preto, São Simão, Jaú, Campinas, São Manuel, and São Carlos do Pinhal. Municípios with the most hectares planted were São Simão, Ribeirão Preto, Campinas, São Carlos do Pinhal, and Jau. The municípios with the most coffee trees were Ribeirão Preto, Campinas, São Simão, and São Carlos do Pinhal. The municípios with the most workers in coffee were Ribeirão Preto, Campinas, São Simão, São Carlos do Pinhal, and Jau; these grew a quarter of the state's coffee production.

49. Renato Leite Marcondes, "A estrutura fundiária e cafeicultura de dois municípios do Oeste Paulista: Campinas e Ribeirão Preto no início do século XX," *Revista de História*, no. 165 (2011): 403–424.

50. Directoria Geral de Estatistica, *Recenseamento do Brazil realizado em 1 de setembro de 1920* (Rio de Janeiro: Typographia da Estatistica, 1923), vol. 3, part 1a, p. xxiii.

51. *Boletim da Directoria de Indústria e Commércio* 12, no. 4 (1921): 128–129; *Boletim da Directoria de Indústria e Commércio* 10, no. 7 (1919): 298–299.

52. Paulo R. Pestana, "Producção agriculture em 1918–19," *Boletim da Directoria de Indústria e Commércio* 11, nos. 1–2 (1920): 3–4; Paulo R. Pestana, "Producção agriculture em 1919–20," *Boletim da Directoria de Indústria e Commércio* 12, nos. 2–3 (1921): 61.

53. Pestana, "Producção agriculture em 1919–20," 61.

54. Pestana, "A producção de assucar," *Boletim da Directoria de Indústria e Commércio* 12, no. 4 (1921): 123–125. For more on the activity of the sugar industry in São Paulo, see Tamaz Szmarecsányi and Alceu de Arruda Veiga Filho, "O ressurgimento da lavoura canavieira em São Paulo na Primeira República, 1890–1930," *Travessia*, no. 2 (1999): 67–81; and Eltara Tadeu Terci and Maria Thereza Miguel Peres, "Ascensão da agroindústria canavieira paulista: O caso de Piracicaba no início do século XX," *Rurais e Agroidustriais* 1, no. 1 (1999): 445–456.

55. Pestana, "A producção de assucar," 124–125.

56. Instituto Brasileiro de Geografia e Estatística, *Recenseamento geral do Brasil, 1940*, national series, vol. 3 (Rio de Janeiro: IBGE, 1950), 40–141.

57. Ibid., 40–95.

58. The decree creating the institute was more committed to increasing alcohol production than increasing sugar output. Instituto do Açúcar e do

Alcool, *Anuário Açucareiro* (Rio de Janeiro: Instituto do Açúcar e do Álcool, 1941), 7:55–56, http://produtos.seade.gov.br/produtos/bibliotecadigital/view/singlepage/index.php?pubcod=10011726&parte=1.

59. Ibid., 7:45.

60. The advantage of mixing anhydrous alcohol with gasoline in combustion engines was known from European experiences, especially in the pre- and postwar periods. Ibid., 7:62. The program was discontinued after the war and would become significant again only in the 1970s, when Brazil launched a successful program to use renewable alcohol fuels.

61. The five largest of these mills were the Tamoio (in city of Araraquara), Porto Feliz, Vila Raffard (in município of Capivari), Junqueira (in município of Igarapava), and Amália (in city of Santa Rita do Viterbo). The largest of the alcohol producers were the usinas Raffard, Tamoio, and Monte Alegre, which together produced 2 million liters of alcohol. Ibid., 7:130–145.

62. Ibid., 7:128.

63. Sérgio Besserman Vianna, "Política econômica externa e industrialização: 1946–1951," in *A ordem do progresso: Cem anos de política econômica republicana, 1889–1989*, ed. Marcelo de Paiva Abreu (Rio de Janeiro: Campus, 1990), 105–122; Aníbal Villanova Vilella and Wilson Suzigan, *Política do governo e crescimento da economia brasileira* (Rio de Janeiro: IPEA/INPES, 1973), chap. 7.

64. The introduction of modern farming began only in the second half of the twentieth century. As late as 1960, few farms used electricity: of the 3 million rural establishments in 1960, a Ford Foundation study reported that only 116,000 had electricity. It also stressed the very low productivity throughout the rural world. Although the report referred to all of Brazil, the general situation in the state of São Paulo was not very different. Among the factors limiting agricultural progress that the study pointed to were the low rate of investment and the limited availability of agricultural extension bureaus with their integration of teaching, research, and extension. G. Edward Schuh and Eliseu Roberto Alves, *O desenvolvimento da agricultura no Brasil* (Rio de Janeiro: APEC, 1971), 142, 282–297. Also see Ruy Miller Paiva, "Modernização agrícola e processo de desenvolvimento econômico: Problema dos países em desenvolvimento," in *Ensaios sobre política agrícola brasileira*, ed. Alberto Veiga (São Paulo: Secretaria da Agricultura, 1979), 37–86.

65. In 1950 the state of São Paulo accounted for 35 percent of gross national product: 31.3 percent of agriculture, 33.0 percent of services, and 44.1 percent of industry. In that year, industry contributed 20.7 percent of net internal revenue, services 51.9 percent, and agriculture 27.4 percent. Instituto de Economia Agrícola, *Desenvolvimento da agricultura paulista* (São Paulo: Governo do Estado de São Paulo, 1972), 18–21.

66. For a major analysis of both Brazilian and Paulista agriculture in the 1960s and 1970s, see Ruy Miller Paiva, Salomão Schattan, and Claus F. Trench de Freitas, *Setor agrícola do Brasil: Comportamento econômico, problemas e possibi-*

lidades (São Paulo: Secretaria da Agricultura, 1973); Governo do Estado de São Paulo, *Desenvolvimento da agricultura paulista*; José Roberto Mendonça de Barros, Afonso C. Pastore, and Juarez A. B. Rizzieri, "A evolução recente da agricultura brasileira," in *Estudos sobre a modernização da agricultura brasileira*, ed. José Roberto Mendonça de Barros and Douglas Hume Graham (São Paulo: Instituto de Pesquisas Econômicas, 1977), 107–138; Fernando B. Homem de Melo, "Produtividade da terra: Os casos do milho e algodão no estado de São Paulo," in Mendonça de Barros and Graham, *Estudos sobre a modernização da agricultura brasileira*, 57–106; Schuh and Alves, *O desenvolvimento da agricultura no Brasil*; Alberto Veiga, ed., *Ensaios sobre política agrícola brasileira* (São Paulo: Secretaria da Agricultura, 1979).

67. The modern crops were cotton, oranges, potatoes, tomatoes, eggs, soybeans, and sugarcane. In transition were essentially coffee and corn, and those still produced traditionally were beans, rice, cattle, and milk. Instituto de Economia Agrícola, *Desenvolvimento da agricultura Paulista*, 66.

68. If we consider the fourteen principal national crops in 1949/1950, the state of São Paulo led in the production of cotton, peanuts, rice, coffee, sugarcane, and tomatoes and was the second-most-important producer of bananas, potatoes, onions, oranges, papayas, and corn; third-most-important of beans; and sixth-most-important of manioc—it produced no cacao.

69. In the 1960s more than 2.3 million coffee trees were eradicated in Brazil, above all in São Paulo, Minas Gerais, Paraná, and Espírito Santo. In São Paulo an area of 350,000 hectares was released from coffee production, allowing diversification and modernization of agriculture. Stahis Panagides, "Erradicação da café e diversificação da agricultura brasileira," *Revista Brasileira de Economia* 23, no. 1 (1969): 41–71.

70. "In the 1920s, England wanted to develop Brazilian cotton production of good quality. It wanted to free itself from dependence on North American producers whose prices were well above those of Brazilian exporters." Sérgio Rodrigues Costa and Miguel Garcia Bueno, *A saga do algodão: Das primeiras lavouras à ação na OMC* (Rio de Janeiro: Associação Brasileira dos Produtores de Algodão/Insight Engenharia, 2004), 20.

Chapter 5

1. The mechanism to validate the candidates elected to the legislature was up to the legislature itself, allowing the perpetuation of majorities.

2. See the classic work on this revolution by Boris Fausto, *A revolução de 1930: Historiografia e história* (São Paulo: Editôra Brasiliense, 1975), and his recent survey of the period, Boris Fausto, ed., *Getúlio Vargas*, 3 vols. (São Paulo: Companhia Das Letras, 2006–2014).

3. Edgard Carone, *A segunda república* (São Paulo: Difusão Européia do Livro, 1973), 53.

4. For more on this revolt, see Stanley E. Hilton, *A guerra civil brasileira: História da revolução constitucionalista de 1932* (Rio de Janeiro: Nova Fronteira, 1982); Hélio Silva, *1932: A guerra paulista*, 2nd ed. (Rio de Janeiro: Civilização Brasileira, 1976); and Hernâni Donato, *História da revolução constitucionalista de 1932: Comemorando os 70 anos do evento* (São Paulo: Ibrasa, 2002).

5. This constitution was distinctly antiliberal and gave all power to the president. José Maria Bello, *História da república* (São Paulo: Nacional, 1976), 315–317.

6. Stanley E. Hilton, "Ação Integralista Brasileira: Fascism in Brazil, 1932–1938," *Luso-Brazilian Review* 9, no. 2 (1972): 3–29; Robert M. Levine, *The Vargas Regime: The Critical Years, 1934–1938* (New York: Columbia University Press, 1970).

7. The Instituto Paulista da Defesa Permanente do Café was created in 1924 and was under the Secretariat of Finance. It set up a tax to be used to obtain a loan to operate in the coffee market. Decree 3802, February 14, 1924.

8. Eugênio Lefevre, *A administração do estado de São Paulo na República Velha* (São Paulo: Typografia Cupolo, 1937), 150–154.

9. Ibid., 164–165. Lefevre estimated the total stock at approximately 25 million sacks of coffee.

10. The loan had a rate of 7 percent and was to be liquidated by October 1, 1940. The loan was tied directly to the purchase of inventory and storage, which served as collateral. Revenue from the tax increase was mortgaged as collateral for the loan. Secretaria da Fazenda e do Tesouro do Estado de São Paulo, *Contas do exercício de 1930* (São Paulo: Typografia Garraux, 1935), 15–27.

11. Celso Furtado developed this anticrisis response method, which was criticized by revisionists like Carlos Manuel Peláez, but later studies, like those of Simão Silber, show the validity of Furtado's method. Celso Furtado, *Formação econômica do Brasil* (São Paulo: Nacional, 1968), chaps. 31–33; Carlos Manuel Peláez, *História da industrialização brasileira: Crítica à teoria estruturalista no Brasil* (Rio de Janeiro: Apec, 1972); Simão Silber, "Política econômica: Defesa no nivel de renda e industrialização no período 1929–1939" (master's thesis, Universidade de São Paulo, 1973).

12. Antonio Delfim Netto, *O problema do café no Brasil* (São Paulo: Instituto de Pesquisas Econômicas, USP, 1981), 142–157.

13. Ibid., 151.

14. Lourdes Sola, "O golpe de 37 e o Estado Novo," in *Brasil em perspectiva*, ed. Carlos Guilherme Mota (São Paulo: Difusão Européia do Livro, 1969), 269.

15. Paulo Benevides and Paes de Andrade, *História constitucional do Brasil* (Rio de Janeiro: Paz e Terra, 1991), 317.

16. Ibid., chaps. 9–12. The current constitution was promulgated in 1988 after the end of the military regimes.

17. See Constitution of 1937, Article 23, §3, at http://www.planalto.gov.br/ccivil_03/constituicao/constituicao37.htm.

18. See Constitution of 1946, Article 146, at http://www.planalto.gov.br/ccivil_03/constituicao/constituicao46.htm.

19. States could still tax landed property. States could still temporarily increase the state export tax, to a maximum of 10 percent. Constitution of 1946, Article 19. To the municipalities were given the property taxes within their jurisdictions and fees for licenses, profession, industries, etc. Constitution of 1946, Article 29.

20. Constitution of 1946, Articles 170 and 171.

21. The Code of Tax and Fees of the government of the state of São Paulo, Decree 8.255, April 23, 1937, is a useful document for understanding the state's taxation system in the 1930s. Secretaria da Fazenda do Estado de São Paulo, *Código de impostos e taxas* (São Paulo: Est. Graphico Cruzeiro do Sul, 1937), http://produtos.seade.gov.br/produtos/bibliotecadigital/view/singlepage/index.php?pubcod=10011612&parte=1.

22. In the census of 2010 the population of the state was 41,262,199; the capital had 11,244,369 persons.

23. In the Vargas period, from October 1930 to October 1945, São Paulo had twenty different governors, the majority of interventors named by the federal government. During the brief period of the constitution of 1934, the state had two governors elected by the state legislature. The governor Adhemar Pereira de Barros was an important figure in the political life of the state from the 1940s to the 1960s. He was a federal interventor and the first governor democratically elected after 1945. He was governor when the military revolted in 1964 and, though a supporter of the regime, was formally denied his political rights by the military regime in 1966.

24. Aside from creating formal careers in public administration, with rules of recruitment, DASP also rationalized the administrative system.

25. Sonia Draibe, *Rumos e metamorfoses: Estado e industrialização no Brasil, 1930–1960* (Rio de Janeiro: Paz e Terra, 1985), chap. 1. Also created was the Conselho Federal de Comércio Exterior (CFCE; Federal Foreign Trade Council) in 1937, which played an important role in the preparation of plans and studies, and not just in the area of foreign trade. See Adriano Codato, "A sociologia política brasileira em análise: Quatro visões sobre o funcionamento administrativo do Estado Novo," *Revista de Sociologia e Política* 19, no. 40 (2011): 273–288; and Adriano Nervo Codato, "Elites e instituições no Brasil: Uma análise contextual do Estado Novo" (PhD diss., Universidade Estadual de Campinas, 2008).

26. In addition to the works cited in note 4, see Angêla M. de Castro Gomes, "Confronto e compromisso no processo de constitucionalização (1930–1935)," in *História geral da civilização brasileira: O Brasil repúblicano*, ed. Boris Fausto and Sérgio B. Holanda (São Paulo: Difusão Europeia do Livro, 1983), 3:7–77.

27. In August 1933 Armando Salles de Oliveira was named interventor and led the state government until December 1936. He was a member of the traditional Paulista elite and related to the Mesquita family, which controlled the important newspaper *O Estado de São Paulo*.

28. Decree 25.533, December 1, 1933, reduced by 50 percent the value of all the debts farmers contracted before June 30, 1933. The Vargas government justified this action by emphasizing the impact of the crisis on the Brazilian economy, the plight of farmers, and the importance of agriculture.

29. Ibrahim João Elias and Nelson Hideiki Nozoe, *Secretaria de estado dos negócios da fazenda do estado de São Paulo: Evolução histórico funcional* (São Paulo: Governo do Estado de São Paulo, 1978), 7.

30. Created in 1933 to modernize Brazil's industrial process, IDORT evolved to contribute plans for modernizing the federal government administration. The nomination of the president of IDORT, Armando Salles de Oliveira, as federal interventor in the state of São Paulo also created an opportunity to disseminate the ideology of rational organization in the state, and Salles de Oliveira authorized in January 1934 the creation of the Administrative Reorganization of the State Government of São Paulo (RAGE). Fabio Vizeu Ferreira, "Management no Brasil em perspectiva histórica: O projeto do IDORT nas décadas de 1930 e 1940" (PhD diss., Fundação Getúlio Vargas, São Paulo, 2008), 170–213.

31. Roberto Simonsen was one of the most important industrial leaders in Brazil. He participated in the first directorate of the Federation of Industries of the State of São Paulo (Federação das Indústrias do Estado de São Paulo, FIESP) in 1928 and was president of Institute of Engineering of São Paulo. In 1945 he was a strong defender of the idea of state planning. See Roberto Simonsen, *As raízes do pensamento industrial brasileiro: 60 anos do Instituto Roberto Simonsen* (São Paulo: FIESP, 2010).

32. IDORT had a major influence on the economic rationalization of various sectors of the Paulista economy and on the creation of vocational education. It was the originator of professional education created by the training program organizations SENAI and SENAC (described later), which exist as major institutions today. See Telma de Barros Correia and Caliane Christie Oliveira de Almeida, "Habitação econômica no Brasil: O IDORT e sua revista (1932–1960)," *Revista de Pesquisa em Arquitetura e Urbanismo*, no. 1 (2013): 35–49; Marcelo Rodrigues Conceição, "A educação nas ações e proposições do Instituto da Organização Racional do Trabalho (1932–1946)" (master's thesis, Pontifícia Universidade Católica, São Paulo, 2005); Maria Antonieta Martines Antonacci, "Institucionalizar ciência e tecnologia: Em torno da fundação do IDORT (São Paulo, 1918/1931)," *Revista Brasileira de História* 7, no. 14 (1987): 59–78; and Telma de Barros Correia, "O IDORT e a Taylorização da moradia no Brasil (1932–1950)," paper presented at VII Seminário de História da Cidade e do Urbanismo, Salvador, Brazil, 2002; Eraldo

Leme Batista, "IDORT—um instituto educacional burguês por excelência: Análise das décadas de 1930 e 1940 no Brasil," 2014, http://www.ronaldofrutuozo.com.br/seminariotrabalho2014/img/GT7/IDORT.pdf; Célia Aparecida de Souza, "A influência do IDORT na reconfiguração do bloco de poder durante o estado Vargista entre 1931 e 1927" (master's thesis, Pontifícia Universidade Católica, São Paulo, 2006); and Ferreira, "Management no Brasil em perspectiva histórica."

33. Elias and Nozoe, *Secretaria de estado dos negócios da fazenda*, 156–157.

34. The norms of the reorganization were established by law 2479, December 13, 1935.

35. The general directorate of revenue comprised subdirectorates for the various state taxes. Decree 7332, July 5, 1935, had created the Central Accounting Office of the State (CCE) to centralize the accounts. These reforms were planned years earlier by Francisco d'Auria, former state and federal general accountant (*contador geral*) of the republic, who in turn became the first director of the new Contadoria Central (Central Accounting Office) and later was named secretary of Finance. Elias and Nozoe, *Secretaria de estado dos negócios da fazenda*, 174–195.

36. According to Elias and Nozoe, the Treasury Department was not reformed until 1957. Ibid.

37. For more on the origins of vocational education, see Carmen Sylvia Vidigal Moraes, "Instrução 'popular' e ensino profissional: Uma perspectiva histórica," in *Brasil 500 anos: Tópicos em história da educação*, ed. Diana Gonçalves Vidal and Maria Lúcia Spedo (São Paulo: EDUSP, 2001), 169–2004.

38. Marcelo Rodrigues Conceição, "A educação para o Instituto de Organização Racional do Trabalho (1932–1946)," http://www.sbhe.org.br/novo/congressos/cbhe4/individuais-coautorais/eixo06/Marcelo%20Rodrigues%20Conceicao%20-%20Texto.pdf (accessed May 17, 2017). Also see Marcelo Rodrigues Conceição, "Historiografia do ensino profissional paulista: As marcas do modo de produção" (PhD diss., Pontifícia Universidade Católica, São Paulo, 2010); José Damiro de Moraes, "Noemy Rudorfer and the organization of school and of the world of labor in the 1920s/1930s," *Educação e Pesquisa* 38, no. 2 (2012): 485–497; Cacilda Comassio Lima, "Educação para o trabalho: A escola profissional de Franca (1924–1970)" (PhD diss., Universidade Estadual Paulista, Franca, 2007); and Carmen Sylvia Vidigal Moraes, *A socialização da força de trabalho: Instrução popular e qualificação profissional no estado de São Paulo, 1873–1934* (Bragança Paulista: EDUSP, 2003).

39. Maria Luiza Marcílio, *História da escola em São Paulo e no Brasil* (São Paulo: Instituto Braudel/Imprensa Oficial, 2005), 237.

40. Decree 5584, April 21, 1933.

41. Antonio Carlos Duarte de Carvalho, "Saúde pública: Centralização, autoritarismo e expansão dos serviços—São Paulo nas décadas de 1930 e

1940," *Revista de História Regional* 10, no. 19 (2005): 9–25. See also Gilberto Hochman, "Reforma, instituições e políticas de saúde no Brasil (1930–1945)," *Educar,* no. 25 (2005): 127–141.

42. Rodolfo dos Santos Mascarenhas has criticized the decree of the dictatorial regime that ended the health centers and installed instead a sanitary police. Rodolfo dos Santos Mascarenhas, "História da saúde pública no estado de São Paulo," *Revista de Saúde Pública,* no. 7 (1973): 433–446.

43. Decree 9247, June 17, 1938.

44. Mascarenhas, "História da saúde pública no estado de São Paulo," 439.

45. Law 2.733, December 1, 1936.

46. The disaggregated data on income and expenditures of the state are presented in the final part of this chapter and come from two different sources. Between 1930 and 1938 the information refers to the balance of actual revenue and actual expenditure. The information for 1940–1950 was obtained from the budgets approved by the assembly by law or budgets imposed by the administration, in the form of decrees. There is therefore a difference in the type of information.

47. Decree 5786, December 30, 1932.

48. According to a report from the president of the state, the foreign loan of 1921 was obtained to consolidate state debts. *Mensagem apresentada ao congresso legislativo, em 14 de julho de 1921, pelo Dr. Washington Luis Pereira de Souza, presidente do estado de São Paulo* (São Paulo, [1921]), http://brazil.crl.edu/bsd/bsd/u1178.

49. Decree 7495, December 30, 1935.

50. Decree 7519, January 17, 1936. The tax was charged by the province and the state in some years at the end of the empire and beginning of the republic and was later transferred to the municípios by article 9 of law 15, November 11, 1891.

51. In the period in question the state government controlled the Sorocabana railway (law 905, June 28, 1904) and others, such as the Estrada de Ferro Campos de Jordão (decree 3643, October, 18, 1923), the Estrada de Ferro Araraquara (law 1627, December 21, 1918), the Estrada de Ferro Santos a Juquiá, and the Estrada de Ferro São Paulo e Minas.

52. The secretary of Justice had fixed expenditures of 79,454,969 mil réis, but an additional charge of 137,103,016 mil réis was related to the expenses of the revolution of 1932. This amounted to 33 percent of the total value of fixed expenses for 1932 and 20 percent of the total value of government expenditures in that year.

53. The registry of debts in foreign currency that existed in 1950 lists them at the official and the market exchange rates. The rate fixed in 1937 was extremely outdated in 1950. But since 1946, shortly after the end of the war, it has been customary to use the free-market rate as the official rate. We use the official exchange rate. Donald L. Huddle, "Balança de pagamentos e con-

trole de câmbio no Brasil: Diretrizes políticas e história, 1946–1954," *Revista Brasileira de Economia* 18, no. 1 (1964): 5–40.

Chapter 6

1. Paulo R. Pestana, *A expansão económica do estado de S. Paulo num século (1822–1922)* (São Paulo: Secretaria da Agricultura, Commercio e Obras Publicas do Estado de São Paulo, 1923), 40.

2. Stanley J. Stein, *Vassouras: A Brazilian Coffee County, 1850–1900* (Cambridge, MA: 1957), 92; José Alípio Goulart, *Tropas e tropeiros na formação do Brasil* (Rio de Janeiro: Conquista, 1961), 97. According to Goulart, the amount carried varied from region to region, with eight being usually the lowest estimate in any area of Brazil.

3. Francisco Alves da Silva, "Abastecimento em São Paulo (1835–1877): Estudo histórico do aprovisionamento da província via Barreira de Cubatão" (master's thesis, Universidade de São Paulo, 1985), 103–104, 162. Auguste de Saint-Hilaire reported seeing cargo mules carrying sugar to Santos on the Santos–São Paulo road and mules returning from the coast without loads. Auguste de Saint-Hilaire, *Viagem à província de São Paulo* (São Paulo: Livraria Martins, 1940), 117.

4. It should be noted that the railroads also brought coffee from other states to the port of Santos. Thus, in 1908, Santos received 8,768 metric tons of coffee from Paulista planters, 355 metric tons from planters in Minas Gerais, and 6 metric tons of coffee from Paraná. Departamento de Estatística do Estado, *Anuário estatístico de São Paulo, 1908* (São Paulo: Governo do Estado de São Paulo, 1910), 2:114–115.

5. The Sorocabana railroad was the only other railroad to link directly to Santos, but this did not occur until 1937.

6. Departamento de Estatística do Estado, *Anuário estatístico de São Paulo, 1900* (São Paulo: Governo do Estado de São Paulo, 1903), 602.

7. Departamento de Estatística do Estado, *Anuário estatístico de São Paulo, 1902* (São Paulo: Governo do Estado de São Paulo, 1905), 580–605.

8. Some of the Paulista products exported through Santos were produced in Minas Gerais, such as the 18,000 metric tons of *café do bom*, 51 metric tons of rubber, and 9 metric tons of leather. The value of these products from Minas Gerais reached 15,166,732 mil réis. The goods coming from other states besides Minas Gerais added up to 453,934 mil réis. As these data indicate, Santos was, unlike Rio de Janeiro, not a major port for the products of other states of the federation.

9. *Boletim da Diretoria de Indústria e Comércio*, suplemento econômico, 1912, p. 16.

10. Departamento de Estatística do Estado, *Anuário estatístico de São Paulo, 1888* (São Paulo: Governo do Estado de São Paulo, 1891), 248.

11. Juan E. Oribe Stemmer, "Freight Rates in the Trade Between Europe and South America, 1840–1914," *Journal of Latin American Studies* 21, no. 1 (1989): 44.

12. A good survey of this commercial house can be found in Michael B. Miller, *Europe and the Maritime World: A Twentieth-Century History* (Cambridge: Cambridge University Press, 2012), 128, 140–144. In the Rio de Janeiro branch, Theodor Wille was among the ten leading exporters and the only German in the group. Between 1857 and 1888, the Theodor Wille house in Rio de Janeiro exported some £6 million worth of coffee. Joseph E. Sweigart, *Coffee Factorage and the Emergence of a Brazilian Capital Market, 1850–1888* (New York: Garland, 1987), 34. Also see Charles P. Kindleberger, "Germany's Overtaking of England, 1806–1914," *Review of World Economics* 111, no. 2 (1975): 278.

13. For details on these Italian ships, see S. Swiggum and M. Kohli, "The Ships List," February 28, 2010, http://www.theshipslist.com/ships/descriptions/ShipsP-Q.shtml.

14. For details on these Hamburg Süd ships, see "Hamburg-Südamerikanische Dampfschifffahrtsgesellschaft," http://www.schiffe-maxim.de/HSDG.htm (accessed May 17, 2017).

15. All these sailings are listed monthly in advertisements from August 1, 1899, to July 1, 1900 (as well as November 20, 1899) in *O Estado de São Paulo* on the last page of each edition (either page 4 or 6). Archives of the newspaper can be found at http://acervo.estadao.com.br/.

16. Robert G. Albion, "Capital Movement and Transportation: British Shipping and Latin America, 1806–1914," *Journal of Economic History* 11, no. 4 (1951): 361–374.

17. René de la Pedraja. *Oil and Coffee: Latin American Merchant Shipping from the Imperial Era to the 1950s* (New York: Greenwood, 1998), 3–7, 36–42. Also see Birgitte Holten, "Why Brazil Did Not Develop a Merchant Marine: Brazilian Shipping and the World in the 19th Century," *História Econômica e História de Empresas* 6, no. 2 (2003): 7–32; Alcides Goularti Filho, "Companhia de Navegação Lloyd Brasileiro: Uma trajetória de déficit financeiro e desenvolvimento econômico," *História Econômica e História de Empresas* 12, no. 2 (2009): 5–36; and Alcides Goularti Filho, "Abertura da navegação de cabotagem brasileira no século XIX," *Ensaios FEE* 32, no. 2 (2011): 409–434.

18. Robert E. Forrester, *British Mail Steamers to South America, 1851–1965: A History of the Royal Mail Steam Packet Company and Royal Mail Lines* (Farnham, UK: Ashgate, 2014), 64. By 1882 the company had three ships sailing to Santos in one month from Southampton. Thus, the *Minho* left on January 2 going to Santos via Lisbon and Rio de Janeiro, and on the 24th the *Tamar* also went via Lisbon, Pernambuco, Maceio, Bahia, Rio de Janeiro, and on to Santos. On the 31st from the same port the company sent the *Neva* via the usual

route to Lisbon and then Cape Verde, Pernambuco, and Santos, though this ship, unlike the others, went on to Buenos Aires. *Hampshire Advertiser* (Portsmouth, UK), January 11, 1882, p. 3. These three ship sailings seemed to have occurred every month from Portsmouth to Brazil by this period. With the addition of new and much larger ships in the next two decades, the line began to move large numbers of Portuguese and Spanish immigrants to Santos. Thus, in 1908 it listed three sailings per month to Santos with these larger vessels, which stopped in Coruna, Vigo, and Lisbon on the way to Santos. One of these ships, the *Asturias*, was over 12,000 tons and carried 1,200 persons in steerage, 300 in first class, and 140 in second class. Forrester, *British Mail Steamers to South America*, 72, 114, 123.

19. Calculated from data in Holten, "Why Brazil Did Not Develop a Merchant Marine," 23, table 3.

20. Gordon Boyce, *Information, Mediation, and Institutional Development: The Rise of Large-Scale Enterprise in British Shipping, 1870–1919* (Manchester, UK: Manchester University Press, 1995), 20.

21. Departamento de Estatística do Estado, *Anuário estatístico de São Paulo, 1910* (São Paulo: Governo do Estado de São Paulo, 1912), 2:118–120.

22. Pedraja, *Oil and Coffee*, 8.

23. William Sjostrom, "Ocean Shipping Cartels: A Survey," *Review of Network Economics* 3, no. 2 (2004): 111. The British companies working the Brazilian route who participated in these conferences were Lamport and Holt out of Liverpool and Glasgow; the Pacific Steam Navigation Company, also of Liverpool and including Rio de Janeiro in its Pacific runs; the Booth Line; and above all the Royal Mail line. After the British the next-most-important group of shippers engaged in the Brazil trade by the 1880s were the French—the Messageries Maritimes and the Compagnie des Chargeurs Réunius companies—and the Germans with their Hamburg Süd line. Forrester, *British Mail Steamers to South America, 1851–1965*, 63.

24. Stemmer, "Freight Rates in the Trade Between Europe and South America," 23–59. Data on the value of exports shipped by month showed wide variation by year for the port of Santos, but if the five-year periods of 1904–1908 and 1933–1937 are typical, then shipments were relatively constant throughout the year. See Departamento de Estatística do Estado, *Anuário estatístico de São Paulo, 1908*, 2:106; and Superintendência Serviços do Café, *Anuário de café, 1952* (São Paulo: Secretaria da Fazenda do Estado de São Paulo, 1953), 105. As for imports, they too flowed relatively smoothly across the months, though with annual variations. For data on value of imports by month for 1906–1910, see Departamento de Estatística do Estado, *Anuário estatístico de São Paulo, 1910*, 2:111.

25. By 1901–1905 it had reached 274,000 contos. Departamento de Estatística do Estado, *Anuário estatístico de São Paulo, 1905* (São Paulo: Governo do Estado de São Paulo, 1907), insert after 2:152.

26. Data from late 1930s show that the Scandinavian countries were the world's highest consumers, followed closely by the United States. Germany consumed a fourth of the per capita Danish rate and Italy a ninth of that per capita consumption—almost as little as England. V. D. Wickizer, *Coffee, Tea, and Cocoa: An Economic and Political Analysis* (Stanford, CA: Stanford University Press, 1951), 76–78.

27. Departamento de Estatística do Estado, *Anuário estatístico de São Paulo, 1911* (São Paulo: Governo do Estado de São Paulo, 1913), 2:160.

28. Departamento de Estatística do Estado, *Anuário estatístico de São Paulo, 1908*, 2:87. In 1912, wheat made up 36 percent of the value of all food imports and wine 29 percent. Departamento de Estatística do Estado, *Anuário estatístico de São Paulo, 1912* (São Paulo: Governo do Estado de São Paulo, 1914), 2:114–119.

29. Departamento de Estatística do Estado, *Anuário estatístico de São Paulo, 1905*, 2:150–152.

30. *Boletim da Diretoria de Indústria e Comércio*, nos. 7–8 (1921): 235, 238.

31. Ibid., 233.

32. Departamento de Estatística do Estado, *Anuário estatístico de São Paulo, 1921* (São Paulo: Governo do Estado de São Paulo, 1923), 2:254–255; Departamento de Estatística do Estado, *Anuário estatístico de São Paulo, 1922–25* (São Paulo: Governo do Estado de São Paulo, 1927), 405; Departamento de Estatística do Estado, *Anuário estatístico de São Paulo, 1928* (São Paulo: Governo do Estado de São Paulo, 1930), 376.

33. *Boletim do Departamento Estadual de Estatística*, no. 8 (1939): 167.

34. Superintendência Serviços do Café, *Anuário de café, 1952*, 57, 68.

35. See, for example, Departamento de Estatística do Estado, *Anuário estatístico de São Paulo, 1958* (São Paulo: Governo do Estado de São Paulo, 1960), 110. In 1958 Venezuelan imports were seven times the value of Argentine imports and three times that of US imports.

36. Departamento de Estatística do Estado, *Anuário estatístico de São Paulo, 1939* (São Paulo: Governo do Estado de São Paulo, 1940), 562.

37. José Ribeiro de Araujo Filho, *Santos, o porto do café* (Rio de Janeiro: Fundação IBGE, 1969), 171.

Chapter 7

1. For a review of these debates on the causes, timing, and location of industrial development in Brazil, see Alexandre Macchione Saes, "A historiografia da industrialização brasileira," paper presented at the Third Seminário Nacional de História da Historiografia, Ouro Preto, Brazil, 2009.

2. Aníbal Vilella and Wilson Suzigan, *Política do governo e crescimento da economía brasileira, 1889–1945* (Rio de Janeiro: IPEA/INPES, 1973), 70.

3. Celso Furtado has stressed that the Great Depression was the takeoff point for industrialization, while Caio Prado Jr. has stressed that World War I was the initiation. See Celso Furtado, *Formação econômica do Brasil* (São Paulo: Nacional, 1968), chaps. 30–32; and Caio Prado Jr., *História econômica do Brasil* (São Paulo: Brasiliense, 1945), 266–267.

4. Warren Dean, *The Industrialization of São Paulo, 1880–1945* (Austin: University of Texas Press, 1969); Carlos Manuel Peláez, "A balança comercial, a grande depressão e a industrialização brasileira," *Revista Brasileira de Economia* 2, no. 1 (1968): 15–47. See also Albert Fishlow, "Origens e consequências da substituição de importações no Brasil," *Estudos Econômicos* 2, no. 6 (1972): 7–75; and Flávio Rabelo Versiani and Maria Teresa R. O. Versiani, "A industralização antes de 1930: Uma contribuição," *Estudos Econômicos* 5, no. 1 (1975): 37–63.

5. The importance of a new wage-based laboring class replacing a limited-consumption slave workforce was stressed in an influential study by Fernando Henrique Cardoso, "Condições sociais da industrialização: O caso de São Paulo," *Revista Brasiliense*, no. 28 (1960): 31–46.

6. These are the factors stressed in Roberto Simonsen, *Evolução industrial do Brasil e outros estudos* (São Paulo: Nacional, 1939), 12. Simonsen adds to this an exchange rate policy that discouraged imports, a factor others have rejected. See, for example, Carlos Manuel Peláez, "As conseqüências econômicas da ortodoxia monetária, cambial e fiscal no Brasil entre 1889–1945," *Revista Brasileira de Economia* 25, no. 3 (1971): 5–82.

7. Wilson Cano, *Raízes da concentração industrial em São Paulo* (Rio de Janeiro: Difusão Europeia do Livro, 1977), 74–75; Anne G. Hanley, *Native Capital: Financial Institutions and Economic Development in São Paulo, Brazil, 1850–1920* (Stanford, CA: Stanford University Press, 2005), chap. 4.

8. The study covers exports from the United Kingdom, United States, Germany, and France from 1855 to 1939. Wilson Suzigan, *Indústria brasileira: Origens e desenvolvimento* (São Paulo: Brasiliense, 1986).

9. For more on the impact of the Encilhamento in creating a major capital market for these industries, see Stephen H. Haber, "Industrial Concentration and the Capital Markets: A Comparative Study of Brazil, Mexico, and the United States, 1830–1930," *Journal of Economic History* 51, no. 3 (1991): 570.

10. Stanley J. Stein, *The Brazilian Cotton Manufacture* (Cambridge, MA: Harvard University Press, 1957), 88. As Stein noted, "Mills already in existence expanded capital stock, although part of the new capitalization took the form of stock dividends. The nominal capitalization of textile mills listed on the Rio de Janeiro stock exchange swelled from 13,500 contos ([US]$7,290,000), in 1889, to 54,100 eighteen months later; to 72,550 in August of 1891, and to 84,210 contos ([US]$25,263,000) on January 1, 1892. Furthermore, cotton mill proprietors (and the entrepreneurs of other industries) placed orders abroad for new machinery in 1889, 1890 and early in

1891" (88). Also see Fishlow, "Origens e consequências da substituição de importações no Brasil."

11. Vilella and Suzigan, *Política do governo e crescimento da economía brasileira.*

12. When discussing the impact of adverse shocks on industrialization, Versiani and Versiani demonstrated that in periods of high coffee exports investments increased; the adverse shocks reduced the rate of investment but increased the use of the productive capacity. Versiani and Versiani, "A industrialização brasileira antes de 1930."

13. Instituto Brasileiro de Geografia e Estatística, *Séries estatísticas retrospectivas* (Rio de Janeiro: IBGE, 1986), vol. 2, bk. 3, p. 261.

14. Instituto Brasileiro de Geografia e Estatística, *Anuário estatistico do Brasil, 1939/1940* (Rio de Janeiro: Conselho Nacional de Estatística, 1940), 5:1360, http://produtos.seade.gov.br/produtos/bibliotecadigital/view/singlepage/index.php?pubcod=10020584&parte=1.

15. Instituto Brasileiro de Geografia e Estatística, *Estatísticos do século XX* (Rio de Janeiro: IBGE, 2006), https://biblioteca.ibge.gov.br/visualizacao/livros/liv37312.pdf.

16. The censuses of 1907 and 1920 are not totally comparable, since the first is incomplete. They serve more to provide an understanding of productive structures in each year than for a direct comparison between the two censuses. See Sérgio Silva, *Expansão cafeeira e origens da indústria no Brasil* (São Paulo: Alfa-Omega, 1995), chap. 4.

17. The consumption tax was established in November 1899 (law 641). It was initially charged on tobacco products, drinks, matches, salt, shoes, candles, perfumes, pharmaceutical products, vinegar, canned fruit, playing cards, hats, canes, and cotton and linen fabrics consumed in the country. Later it was enlarged beyond the original list of products. The tax was levied in the form of a stamp.

18. Dean, *The Industrialization of São Paulo*, 9.

19. Diretoria Geral de Estatística, *Recenseamento do Brazil realizado em 1 de setembro de 1920*, vol. 5, part 1a, *Indústria* (Rio de Janeiro: Typographia da Estatistica, 1927), lxxvii.

20. Stein, *The Brazilian Cotton Manufacture*, 101, table 9. This was also a period when the first textile factory strikes occurred. See John D. French, *The Brazilian Workers' ABC: Class Conflict and Alliances in Modern São Paulo* (Chapel Hill: University of North Carolina, 1992), chap. 1.

21. In converting contos to pounds sterling here and elsewhere in the various chapters, we use the annual conversion tables between mil réis and British pound sterling given in Instituto Brasileiro de Geografia e Estatística, *Anuário estatistico do Brasil, 1939/1940*, 5:1353–1354.

22. *Boletim da Diretoria de Indústria e Comércio* 13, no. 1 (1922): 4.

23. Diretoria Geral de Estatística, *Recenseamento do Brazil realizado em 1 de setembro de 1920*, vol. 5, part 1a, p. xxxviii, table 29.

24. In 1905 there were only eighteen factories producing cotton cloth; by 1920 there were fifty-four of them throughout the state. *Boletim da Diretoria de Indústria e Comércio* 13, nos. 2–3 (1922): 58.

25. In the census of 1900 the city listed 239,820 residents. According to Instituto Brasileiro de Geografia e Estatística, the city grew in the period to the next census of 1920 by 4.5 percent per annum, which would make the city population 389,193 in 1911.

26. *Boletim da Diretoria de Indústria e Comércio* 4, no. 4 (1913): 124–125.

27. *Boletim da Diretoria de Indústria e Comércio* 5, no. 2 (1914): 61.

28. Of the 236 textile factories functioning in São Paulo in 1920, only 38 had been founded before 1904, 83 percent were founded after that date, and 72 percent after 1910. Diretoria Geral de Estatística, *Recenseamento do Brasil realizado em 1 de setembro de 1920,* vol. 5, part 1a, pp. 264–247, table 27.

29. *Boletim da Diretoria de Indústria e Comércio* 13, nos. 2–3 (1922): 60–63.

30. *Boletim da Diretoria de Indústria e Comércio* 19, nos. 7–8 (1928): 159–160.

31. *Boletim da Diretoria de Indústria e Comércio* 17, no. 9 (1926): 192; *Boletim da Diretoria de Indústria e Comércio 17,* nos. 10–11 (1926): 219.

32. Diretoria Geral de Estatística, *Recenseamento do Brasil realizado em 1 de setembro de 1920,* vol. 5, part 1a, p. 432.

33. Ibid., viii.

34. For the value of agricultural production in the crop year 1919/1920, see Diretoria Geral de Estatística, *Recenseamento do Brasil realizado em 1 de setembro de 1920,* vol. 3, part 2, p. liv.

35. *Boletim da Diretoria de Indústria e Comércio* 7, no. 5 (1916): 208–216.

36. Diretoria Geral de Estatística, *Recenseamento do Brasil realizado em 1 de setembro de 1920,* vol. 5, part 1a, p. ix; part 3, p. 202.

37. *Boletim da Diretoria de Indústria e Comércio* 7, no. 5 (1916): 208–216.

38. Paulo R. Pestana, "A indústria do papel em S. Paulo," *Boletim da Diretoria de Indústria e Comércio,* no. 6 (1925): 101–104.

39. Paulo R. Pestana, "A indústria do vidro," *Boletim da Diretoria de Indústria e Comércio,* nos. 9–10 (1928): 199–202. Though data are given for only the capital of São Paulo, it appears that there were no major glass factories in the interior of the state.

40. *Boletim da Diretoria de Indústria e Comércio* 15, no. 11 (1924): 185.

41. *Boletim da Diretoria de Indústria e Comércio* 13, nos. 11–12 (1922): 354; *Boletim da Diretoria de Indústria e Comércio* 18, nos. 7–8 (1927): 135–136.

42. Diretoria Geral de Estatística, *Recenseamento do Brasil realizado em 1 de setembro de 1920,* vol. 5, part 1a, p. xi.

43. In a census of thirty-one textile mills in São Paulo in 1912, women made up 72 percent of the close to 9,500 workers. Children of both sexes under age twelve were 4 percent of the workers, and those under sixteen accounted for 31 percent of the total. Joel Wolfe, *Working Women, Working Men:*

São Paulo and the Rise of Brazil's Industrial Working Class, 1900–1955 (Durham, NC: Duke University Press, 1993), 8, table 1.1.

44. Diretoria Geral de Estatística, *Recenseamento do Brasil realizado em 1 de setembro de 1920*, vol. 5, part 1a, pp. 112–113, table 11.

45. Francisco Vidal Luna, Herbert S. Klein, and William Summerhill, "A agricultura paulista em 1905," *Estudos Econômicos* 44, no. 1 (2014): 153–184.

46. Given the multiple capital origins of the corporations running the factories and the often-mixed foreign-national participation, it is difficult to determine whether a firm was totally foreign owned or not. We assumed a firm to be foreign if it was predominantly owned by foreign investors or run by foreign management.

47. Secretaria da Agricultura, Industria e Commercia, *Estatistica industrial do estado de S. Paulo, anno de 1934* (São Paulo: Siqueira, 1936), 28, https://archive.org/details/estatisticaindus1934.

48. Diretoria Geral de Estatística, *Recenseamento do Brasil realizado em 1 de setembro de 1920*, vol. 5, part 1a, pp. 298–299, 330–331.

49. Ibid., vol. 5, part 3, p. xv.

50. Instituto Brasileiro de Geografia e Estatística, *Estatísticos do Século XX.*

51. Diretoria Geral de Estatística, *Recenseamento do Brasil realizado em 1 de setembro de 1920*, vol. 5, part 1, p. lxxxix, table 63. One of the largest projects undertaken by the "Light" company was the Henry Borden Hydroelectric plant built in Cubatão, which began construction in 1925 with some 6,000 workers. Its first electricity generator went into operation in 1926. By 1960 fourteen generators were producing 884 megawatts. See Edson Fernando Escames, "Usina Parque: Aproveitamento e valorização do patrimônio energético, ambiental e histórico da Usina Hidrelétrica Henry Borden" (master's thesis, Universidade Federal ABC, Santo André, 2011).

52. Although there were numerous short-lived producers of cement going back to the nineteenth century, the first sustained and modern companies were those founded in São Paulo in the 1920s. One such company, the Paulista Companhia Brasileira de Cimento Portland Perus, was founded in 1926 and by 1931 accounted for over half national consumption. Elicio Siqueira, "Companhia Brasileira de Cimento Portland Perus: Contribuição para a história da indústria pioneira do ramo no Brasil (1926–1987)" (master's thesis, Universidade Estadual Paulisto, Araraquara, 2001), 33–34, 37. By the 1930s such cement plants were established throughout Brazil. See Simonsen, *Evolução industrial do Brasil e outros estudos*, 40.

53. Simonsen, *Evolução industrial*, 40.

54. Ibid., 40–43; Dean, *The Industrialization of São Paulo*, 216–220. For more on the development of the plant and its workers, see Oliver J. Dinius, *Brazil's Steel City: Developmentalism, Strategic Power, and Industrial Relations in Volta Redonda, 1941–1964* (Stanford, CA: Stanford University Press, 2011). The Volta Redonda plant was developed during World War II. It is assumed

that Vargas supported the Allies in exchange for help in the construction of the plant.

55. These numbers combine the capital invested by nationals in wholly owned companies with national capital invested in mixed-national foreign-owned corporations. The data are found in Instituto Brasileiro de Geografia e Estatística, *Recenseamento geral do Brasil, 1940*, national series, part 17, vol. 3 (Rio de Janeiro: IBGE, 1950), 462, table 5.

56. As an indicator of this, we can cite the census of 1920, which shows that the installed power in São Paulo already represented 43 percent of installed electricity in the country. Diretoria Geral de Estatística, *Recenseamento do Brasil realizado em 1 de setembro de 1920*, vol. 5, part 1a, p. lxxxix.

57. Instituto Brasileiro de Geografia e Estatística, *Anuário estatistico do Brasil, 1939/1940*, 223.

58. Ibid., 224.

59. Instituto Brasileiro de Geografia e Estatística, *Recenseamento geral do Brasil, 1950*, regional series, vol. 25, bk. 3 (Rio de Janeiro: IBGE, 1955), 1, table 1.

60. Hugo Schlesinger, *Geografia industrial do Brasil*, 2nd ed. (São Paulo: Atlas, 1958), 154.

61. Instituto Brasileiro de Geografia e Estatística, *Recenseamento geral do Brasil, 1950*, national series, vol. 3, bk. 1 (Rio de Janeiro: IBGE, 1957), 1, table 1, 106–139, table 38.

62. Between the censuses of 1950 and 1960, metallurgy went from being 8 percent to being 11 percent of the value of Brazilian industries of transformation. Instituto Brasileiro de Geografia e Estatística, *Censo industrial de 1960*, national series, vol. 3 (Rio de Janeiro: IBGE, 1964), 1, table 1.

63. Instituto Brasileiro de Geografia e Estatística, *Recenseamento geral do Brasil, 1950*, national series, vol. 3, bk. 3 (Rio de Janeiro: IBGE, 1957), 28, table 18.

64. For the data on total and state value of production and workforce, see Instituto Brasileiro de Geografia e Estatística, *Recenseamento geral do Brasil, 1940*, national series, vol. 3 (Rio de Janeiro: IBGE, 1950), 184, table 16; and Instituto Brasileiro de Geografia e Estatística, *Recenseamento geral do Brasil, 1950*, national series, vol. 3, bk. 1, p. 102, table 38.

65. Instituto Brasileiro de Geografia e Estatística, *Recenseamento geral do Brasil, 1950*, national series, vol. 3, bk. 1, p. 91, table 36.

66. See, for example, Silva, *Expansão cafeeira e origens da indústria no Brasil*; Joseph Love, *São Paulo in the Brazilian Federation, 1889–1937* (Stanford, CA: Stanford University Press, 1980); Fernando Henrique Cardoso, *Mudanças sociais na América Latina* (São Paulo: Difusão Européia do Livro, 1969), chap. 8; and Renato Monseff Perissinotto, *Estado e capital cafeeiro em São Paulo (1889–1930)* (São Paulo: Annablume, 2000). In addition to the private capital invested in national infrastructure, foreign capital, particularly English, played

a key role in the sector, either through direct investments or financing of projects controlled by national capitals. Richard Graham, *Britain and the Onset of Modernization in Brazil, 1850–1914* (Cambridge: Cambridge University Press, 1968).

67. Maria Stella Ferreira Levy, "O papel da migração internacional na evolução da população brasileira (1872 a 1972)," *Revista de Saúde Publica* 8, suppl. (1974): tables 1, 3, 8; Thomas Merrick and Douglas H. Graham, *Population and Economic Development in Brazil, 1800 to the Present* (Baltimore: Johns Hopkins University Press, 1979), 91.

68. Merrick and Graham, *Population and Economic Development in Brazil*, 104–109.

69. Dean, *The Industrialization of São Paulo*, 19.

70. Ibid.; Flávio Azevedo Marques de Saes, *A grande empresa de serviços públicos na economia cafeeira* (São Paulo: Hucitec/Instituto Nacional do Livro/Minesterio da Educação e Cultura, 1986); Perissinotto, *Estado e capital cafeeiro em São Paulo*. Antonio da Silva Prado is seen as an example of this type of entrepreneurial planter, since he participated in many manufacturing companies and utilities. He was, for example, a shareholder and president of Companhia Paulista de Estrada de Ferro. Although Dean's position on the importance of coffee planters is the dominant one in the literature, Luis Carlos Bresser Pereira has argued that while coffee planters invested heavily in ports, banks, and other market infrastructure—that is, they were fundamental in developing social capital—actual industrial capital came from nonplanter sources. See Luis Carlos Bresser Pereira, "Origens étnicas e sociais do empresário paulista," *Revista de Administração de Empresas* 4, no. 11 (1964): 86–106; and Luis Carlos Bresser Pereira, "Três hipóteses sobre o início da industrialização brasileira e a economia cafeeira," in *Empresários e Administradores no Brasil* (São Paulo: Brasiliense, 1972), app. 2.

71. Dean, *The Industrialization of São Paulo*, 52. Among the foreigners who came with resources, Dean highlights the case of Francisco Matarazzo, who would become the largest Brazilian industrialist. Among the big businessmen who originally came to work in the fields, Dean cites two cases: Dante Ramenzoni, manufacturer of hats, and Nicholas Scarpa, owner of mills and textile factories.

72. Ford, General Motors, Volkswagen, Mercedes-Benz, Scania, and Toyota were some of the truck, auto, and bus companies that opened facilities in São Paulo in this period.

Chapter 8

1. The port of Santos is located approximately sixty kilometers from São Paulo. Thus, the routes between the city of São Paulo—which is seven hundred meters above sea level—and the port of Santos had to overcome a steep

obstacle between the plateau and the coast. The railroad from Santos to São Paulo, which would be essential for the economic expansion of the state of São Paulo, represented a complex and expensive engineering project.

2. Adolfo Augusto Pinto, *História da viação ública de São Paulo* (São Paulo: Governo do Estado de São Paulo, 1977), 22–28.

3. Subsidies were essential since private financiers feared that their profits would prove insufficient. William R. Summerhill, *Order Against Progress: Government, Foreign Investment, and Railroads in Brazil, 1854–1913* (Stanford, CA: Stanford University Press, 2003), 40. According to Anne G. Hanley, railroads and utilities followed a second route for attracting investors: government guarantees. These companies benefited from explicit or implicit government backing against failure. The railroads built during the 1870s–1890s all received profit guarantees from the government for the explicit purpose of attracting investors. Anne G. Hanley, *Native Capital: Financial Institutions and Economic Development in São Paulo, Brazil, 1850–1920* (Stanford, CA: Stanford University Press, 2005), 74.

4. Pinto, *História da viação pública*, 21–31. The route between Rio de Janeiro and Vassouras was 122 kilometers; between Rio de Janeiro and the Paulista city of Cachoeira it was 265 kilometers.

5. According to William R. Summerhill there was an essential difference in the policy of subsidies in Brazil and the United States. In Brazil the majority of subsidies were provided by the central government, while in the United States it was the states who offered these subsidies. Summerhill, *Order Against Progress*, 39.

6. For more on the mules used to transport coffee, see Herbert S. Klein, "The Supply of Mules to Central Brazil: The Sorocaba Market, 1825–1880," *Agricultural History* 64, no. 4 (1990): 1–25; Carlos Eduardo Suprinyak, "O mercado de animais de carga no centro-sul do Brasil imperial: Novas evidências," *Estudos Econômicos* 38, no. 2 (2008): 319–347; and Carlos Eduardo Suprinyak, *Tropas em marcha: O mercado de animais de carga no centro-sul do Brasil imperial* (São Paulo: Annablume, 2008).

7. With the establishment of the republic in 1889, the provinces were transformed into states.

8. For more on the railroads, see Flávio Azevedo Marques de Saes, *As ferrovias de São Paulo, 1870–1940* (São Paulo: Hucitec-INL-MEC, 1981); Pierre Monbeig, *Pioneiros e fazendeiros de São Paulo* (São Paulo: Hucitec-Polis, 1984); Célia Regina Baider Stefani, "O sistema ferroviário paulista: Um estudo sobre a evolução do transporte de transporte de passageiros sobre trilhos" (master's thesis, Universidade de São Paulo, 2007); Odilon Nogueira de Matos, *Café e ferrovias: A evolução ferroviária de São Paulo e o desenvolvimento da cultura cafeeira* (São Paulo: Alfa-Omega, 1974); Summerhill, *Order Against Progress*; Robert H. Mattoon Jr., "Railroads, Coffee, and the Growth of Big Business in São Paulo, Brazil," *Hispanic American Historical Review* 57, no. 2 (1977): 273–295; and the classic work of Pinto, *História da viação pública*.

9. Despite the importance of railroads for coffee and a significant network deployed to move its production, the Brazilian railway system had expanded timidly during the empire compared to the United States'. In 1893, the US railroad network reached 176,000 kilometers; in Brazil only some 11,000 kilometers. Instituto Brasileiro de Geografia e Estatística, *Anuário estatístico do Brasil, 1939/1940* (Rio de Janeiro: Conselho Nacional de Estatística, 1940), 5:1336, http://produtos.seade.gov.br/produtos/bibliotecadigital/view/singlepage/index.php?pubcod=10020584&parte=1; and Interstate Commerce Commission, *Statistics of Railways in the United States* (Washington, DC: Government Printing Office, 1894), http://archive.org/stream/sixthannualrepo00govegoog#page/n6/mode/2up.

10. For more on the origins and evolution of this railroad company, see Robert H. Mattoon Jr., "The Companhia Paulista de Estradas de Ferro, 1868–1900: A Local Railway Enterprise in São Paulo, Brazil" (PhD diss., Yale University, 1971); and Mattoon, "Railroads, Coffee, and the Growth of Big Business in São Paulo, Brazil."

11. For more on the extension of the two lines, see Mattoon, "The Companhia Paulista de Estradas de Ferro," 89–96.

12. Ibid., 239.

13. Pinto, "Segunda parte: A viação férrea," in *História da viação pública*, 21–58.

14. Marcelo de Paiva Abreu estimates that in this same year total nonpublic British investments were almost £41 million—thus, railroads represented 82 percent of this type of British capital in Brazil. By 1913 British railway investments had risen to £59 million, but this now represented just 44 percent of total British capital in the country, and public utilities at £55 million ran a close second. Marcelo de Paiva Abreu, "British Business in Brazil: Maturity and Demise (1850–1950)," *Revista Brasileira de Economia* 54, no. 4 (2000): 386.

15. Pinto, *História da viação pública*, 233.

16. Ibid.

17. When an embryonic industry arises, the formation of a wider range of markets enables larger-scale production, but at the same time transport-system inefficiencies prevent small interior manufacturers from benefiting from the market growth.

18. Departamento de Estatística do Estado, *Anuário estatístico de São Paulo, 1898* (São Paulo: Governo do Estado de São Paulo, 1901), 508–509.

19. Departamento de Estatística do Estado, *Anuário estatístico de São Paulo, 1900* (São Paulo: Governo do Estado de São Paulo, 1903), 606.

20. Thus, the total numbers of salaried workers (and slaves were specifically prohibited from doing this work) associated with railroads in this period could probably number several thousand more depending on the amount of new construction being carried out. Both unskilled native-born and immigrant

laborers were employed in this construction. See Maria Lucia Lamounier, "The 'Labour Question' in Nineteenth Century Brazil: Railways, Export Agriculture and Labour Scarcity" (London School of Economics Working Paper no. 59/00, 2000), http://eprints.lse.ac.uk/22379/1/wp59.pdf; Maria Lucia Lamounier, "Agricultura e mercado de trabalho: Trabalhadores brasileiros livres nas fazendas de café e na construção de ferrovias em São Paulo, 1850–1890," *Estudos Econômicos* 37, no. 2 (2007): 353–372; and Maria Lucia Lamounier, "Entre a escravidão e o trabalho livre: Escravos e imigrantes nas obras de construção das ferrovias no Brasil no século XIX," *Revista Economia* 9, no. 4 (2008): 215–245.

21. For more on this, see Summerhill, *Order Against Progress*, chap. 6.

22. Paulo Pestana, "As docas de Santos," *Boletim da Directoria de Indústria e Commércio*, no. 5 (1914): 243–245. For more on the functioning of the port of Santos, see Maria Izilda Santos de Matos, "Santos: Um porto para o café—cidade, cotidiano e trabalho," in *História do estado de São Paulo*, ed. Nilo Odalia and João Ricardo de Castro Caldeira (São Paulo: UNESP, 2010), 2:83–100.

23. *Boletim da Directoria de Indústria e Commércio*, no. 2 (1911): 60.

24. Robert G. Albion, "Capital Movement and Transportation: British Shipping and Latin America, 1806–1914," *Journal of Economic History* 11, no. 4 (1951): 367. For more on Brazilian business interests in these developments, see Eugene W. Ridings, "Interest Groups and Development: The Case of Brazil in the Nineteenth Century," *Journal of Latin American Studies* 9, no. 2 (1977): 237.

25. While this growth was impressive, all the Atlantic ports increased their tonnage, so that Santos still ranked fourth—with Buenos Aires at 5.4 million metric tons. Albion, "Capital Movement and Transportation," 373.

26. In 1896 the English succeeded in organizing the Brazil and River Plate conference, which controlled shipping going to the port and, of course, controlled prices but also guaranteed fixed schedules. While the Lamport and Holt line was initially the most important of the foreign shippers arriving in Santos, the line was purchased by the Royal Mail Company in 1911, which then became the dominant foreign line coming to Santos in the first decades of the century. Robert Greenhill, "Shipping, 1850–1914," in *Business Imperialism, 1840–1930: An Inquiry Based on British Experience in Latin America*, ed. D. C. M. Platt (Oxford, UK: Clarendon Press, 1977), 119–155.

27. Milton Vargas, "Construção de Portos," in *Tecnologia e industrialização no Brasil: Uma perspectiva histórica*, ed. Shozo Motoyama (São Paulo: Editora UNESP/CEETEPS, 1994), 67–84. The engineer on the docks project was the French Canadian Guilé, who received many of the early Paulista railroad and electricity concessions.

28. Victor M. Berthold, *History of the Telephone and Telegraph in Brazil, 1851–1921* (New York: American Telephone and Telegraph, 1922), 3–37. A Portuguese translation in typescript is available on the Biblioteca

do Ministério da Fazenda website, at http://memoria.org.br/pub/meb000000094/00180/00180000.pdf.

29. Ibid., 44–70.

30. Departamento de Estatística do Estado, *Anuário estatístico de São Paulo, 1920* (São Paulo: Governo do Estado de São Paulo, 1923), 2:59; Instituto Brasileiro de Geografia e Estatística, *Anuário estatístico do Brasil, 1939/1940*, 5:55–56.

31. Instituto Brasileiro de Geografia e Estatística, *Anuário estatístico do Brasil, 1936* (Rio de Janeiro: IBGE, 1936), 187.

32. Departamento de Estatística do Estado, *Anuário estatístico de São Paulo, 1920*, 2:65.

33. Departamento de Estatística do Estado, *Anuário estatístico de São Paulo, 1940* (São Paulo: Governo do Estado de São Paulo, 1940), 102, 241. In 1945 the ratios were even worse. By then 71 percent of the telephones were in Santos and the capital. Departamento de Estatística do Estado, *Anuário estatístico de São Paulo, 1945* (São Paulo: Governo do Estado de São Paulo, 1948), 4:102.

34. Flávio Azevedo Marques de Saes, *A grande empresa de serviços públicos na economia cafeeira* (São Paulo: Hucitec, 1986), 81.

35. William J. Hausman, Peter Hertner, and Mira Wilkins, *Global Electrification: Multinational Enterprise and International Finance in the History of Light and Power, 1878–2007* (New York: Cambridge University Press, 2008), 7–14.

36. Célio Bermann, "Impasses and Controversies of Hydroelectricity," *Estudos Avançados* 21, no. 59 (2007): 139.

37. The dam was designed and built by the US hydrology engineer Hugh Lincoln Cooper, an associate of Pearsons's, who later built dams on the Nile, the Dnieper, and the Tennessee Rivers. Duncan McDowall, *The Light: Brazilian Traction, Light, and Power Company Limited, 1899–1945* (Toronto: University of Toronto Press, 1988), 82.

38. The standard sources for the history of the São Paulo Light company in this early period are McDowall, *The Light*, chaps. 2–3; Luzia Soares, Dirce de Paula S. Mendes, and Iraci D. Poleti, "A formação do grupo Light: Apontamentos para a sua história administrativa," *América Latina en la Historia Económica* 4, no. 8 (1997): 60–64; and Marcos Lenso de Souza, *Energia da light à electropaulo: Desenvolimento e curto circuito do trabalho* (São Paulo: Presidente Venceslau, 2002), chap. 3.

39. Diretoria Geral de Estatística, *Recenseamento do Brazil realizado·em 1 de setembro de 1920*, vol. 5, part 1 (Rio de Janeiro: Typographia da Estatistica, 1927), lxxxv.

40. For more on these earlier efforts, see Saes, *A grande empresa de serviços públicos*, 81–82.

41. Marcelo Mollica Jourdan, "A Light, investimento estrangeiro no Brasil: Uma luz sobre o ciclo privado-público-privado em 80 anos pela análise

de taxa de retorno" (master's thesis, Fundação Getúlio Vargas, Rio de Janeiro, 2006), 27–40.

42. Hausman, Hertner, and Wilkins, *Global Electrification*, 143.

43. Secretaria da Agricultura, Industria e Commercia, *Estatística industrial do estado de S. Paulo, ano de 1932* (São Paulo: Garraux, 1934), 171–180, https://archive.org/stream/estatisticaindus1932#page/n5/mode/2up. By 1928 Brazilian Traction was operating twelve generating stations in Rio de Janeiro and twenty-two in São Paulo and connected the two, thus covering the state of Rio de Janeiro as well as São Paulo from Vale do Paraíba on the border with Rio de Janeiro to Campinas. Roberto Antonio Iannone, "Evolução do setor eléctrico paulista" (PhD diss., Universidade de São Paulo, 2006), 62. There were also another sixty companies with almost a thousand workers producing copper wire and other products related to the electricity-producing industry. Secretaria da Agricultura, Industria e Commercia, *Estatística industrial do estado de S. Paulo, ano de 1932*, 97–98.

44. Jourdan, "Light, investimento estrangeiro no Brasil," 68.

45. Departamento de Estatística do Estado, *Anuário estatístico de São Paulo, 1902* (São Paulo: Governo do Estado de São Paulo, 1905), 653.

46. Hausman, Hertner, and Wilkins, *Global Electrification*, 15–17.

47. Soares, Mendes, and Poleti, "A formação do grupo Light," 67.

48. McDowall, *The Light*, 46.

49. Departamento de Estatística do Estado, *Anuário estatístico de São Paulo, 1906* (São Paulo: Governo do Estado de São Paulo, 1909), 2:49.

50. Departamento de Estatística do Estado, *Anuário estatístico de São Paulo, 1910* (São Paulo: Governo do Estado de São Paulo, 1913), 2:38–39.

51. The Paulista political elite during the republic was surprisingly well educated. A study of 263 of the state's political leaders between 1889 and 1937 found that 93 percent of them had a higher-education degree. Joseph L. Love and Bert J. Barickman, "Rulers and Owners: A Brazilian Case Study in Comparative Perspective," *Hispanic American Historical Review* 66, no. 86 (1986): 746.

52. For a survey of the ideology and political leaders behind this movement, see Luiz Antonio de Castro Santos, "Estado e saúde pública no Brasil, 1889–1930," *Dados* 23, no. 2 (1980): 237–250; and Luiz Antonio de Castro Santos, "A reforma sanitária 'pelo alto,'" *Dados* 36, no. 3 (1993): 361–391.

53. For more on the diseases that affected the population of Santos in this period and their impact on slaves and free persons, see Ian Read, "Sickness, Recovery, and Death Among the Enslaved and Free People of Santos, Brazil, 1860–1888," *The Americas* 66, no. 1 (2009): 57–80.

54. Rita Barradas Barata, "Cem anos de endemias e epidemias," *Ciência e Saúde Coletiva* 5, no. 2 (2000): 335; L. T. M. Figueiredo, "A febre amarela na região de Ribeirão Preto durante a virada do século XIX: Importância

científica e repercussões econômicas," *Revista da Sociedade Brasileira de Medicina Tropical* 29, no. 1 (1996): 63–76.

55. Barata, "Cem anos," 335–336.

56. Milton Vargas, "Obras de saneamento (abastecimento de água, esgotos e recuperação de terras)," in *Tecnologia e industrialização no Brasil*, ed. Shozo Motoyama (São Paulo: Editora UNESP/CEETEPS, 1994), 85. For more on the powerful impact of water purification programs for reducing mortality in the urban populations in this period, see the major study of David M. Cutler and Grant Miller, "The Role of Public Health Improvements in Health Advances: The Twentieth-Century United States," *Demography* 42, no. 1 (2005): 1–22. They argue that the major impact would come between 1900 and 1940, virtually the same period of a dramatic decline in Paulista mortality.

57. Rodolpho Telarolli Jr., "Imigração e epidemias no estado de São Paulo," *Historia, Ciências, Saúde—Manguinhos* 3, no. 2 (1996): 266.

58. It has been suggested that the mortality revolution that occurred throughout most of the Western world in the early twentieth century was due to better nutrition. See Thomas McKeown, *The Modern Rise of Population* (London: Edward Arnold, 1976); and Robert W. Fogel, *The Escape from Hunger and Premature Death, 1700–2100: Europe, America, and the Third World* (New York: Cambridge University Press, 2004). However, later research has once again stressed the impact of public policies rather than nutrition as the primary influence on reducing infant and child mortality in this period from the late nineteenth century through the 1930s. See Cutler and Miller, "The Role of Public Health Improvements in Health Advances"; Simon Szreter, "The Importance of Social Intervention in Britain's Mortality Decline c. 1850–1914: A Reinterpretation of the Role of Public Health," *Social History of Medicine* 1, no. 1 (1988): 1–37; and Samuel Preston and Michael Haines, *Fatal Years: Child Mortality in Late Nineteenth-Century America* (Princeton, NJ: Princeton University Press, 1991). The current consensus is that the sanitation movement and the discovery of germ theory revolutionized public health policies and practices throughout the world and were a major factor in the decline of infectious diseases. See Angus Deaton, "The Great Escape: A Review of Robert Fogel's 'The Escape from Hunger and Premature Death, 1700–2100,'" *Journal of Economic Literature* 44, no. 1 (2006): 106–114.

59. The standard history of these developments is John Allen Blount III, "The Public Health Movement in São Paulo, Brazil: A History of the Sanitary Service, 1892–1918" (PhD diss., Tulane University, 1971), 59–60. Also see Maria Alice Rosa Ribeiro, *História sem fim: Inventário da saúde pública, São Paulo, 1880–1930* (São Paulo: Editora UNESP, 1993); Massako Iyda, *Cem anos de saúde pública: A cidadania negada* (São Paulo: Editora UNESP, 1994); Rodolpho Telarolli Jr., *Poder e saúde: As epidemias e a formação dos serviços de saúde em São Paulo* (São Paulo: Editora UNESP, 1996); and Emerson Elias Merhy, *O capitalismo e a saúde pública: A emergência das práticas sanitárias no estado*

de São Paulo (Campinas, Brazil: Papirus, 1987). For the evolution of medical practice in this period, see André Mota, *Tropeços da medicina bandeirante: Medicina Paulista entre 1892–1920* (São Paulo: EDUSP, 2005).

60. The first president of the republican state government recognized that the yellow fever outbreak in Campinas was related to the lack of pure water and sewage and hoped to prevent future problems by supporting the construction of modern water and sewage in the city. *Exposição apresentada ao Dr. Jorge Tibiriça pelo Dr. Prudente J. de Moraes Barros, 1°. governador do estado de São Paulo ao passar-lhe a administração, no dia 18 de Outubro de 1890* (São Paulo: Typographia Vanorden, 1890), 9. For more on the establishment of water systems in these cities, see Catia Alves de Senne, "O papel do serviço sanitário na implantação de sistemas de abastecimento de água e de coleta de esgotos no estado de São Paulo (1892–1902)," 2012, http://www.sbhc.org.br/resources/anais/10/1344981568_ARQUIVO_TrabalhoFinal13SeminarioSBHC.pdf.

61. Ana Lucia Britto, "Redes de infra-estrutura na cidade: Uma revisão dos conceitos e concepções de saneamento," paper presented at the IX Seminário de História da Cidade e do urbanismo, São Paulo, September 4–6, 2006, p. 2.

62. Vargas, "Obras de saneamento," 89–102.

63. Departamento de Estatística do Estado, *Anuário estatístico de São Paulo, 1945*, 1:132, 140.

64. Departamento de Estatística do Estado, *Anuário estatístico de São Paulo, 1951* (São Paulo: Governo do Estado de São Paulo, 1954), 3:66.

65. Marta de Almeida and Maria Amélia M. Dantes, "O serviço sanitário de São Paulo, a saúde pública e a microbiologia," in *Espaços da ciência no Brasil, 1800–1930*, ed. Maria Amélia M. Dantes (Rio de Janeiro: Fiocruz, 2001), 136.

66. For more on the history of Butantan, see Jaime Larry Benchimol and Luiz Antonio Teixeira, *Cobras, lagartos e outros bichos: Uma história comparada dos institutos Oswaldo Cruz e Butantan* (Rio de Janeiro: Editôra UFRJ, 1993).

67. Almeida and Dantes, "O serviço sanitário de São Paulo," 137–146; Márcia Regina Barros da Silva, "O processo de urbanização paulista: A medicina e o crescimento da cidade moderna," *Revista Brasileira de História* 27, no. 53 (2007): 243–266.

68. Luiz Jacintho da Silva, "O controle das endemias no Brasil e sua história," *Ciência e Cultura* 55, no. 1 (2003): 44; Telarolli, "Imigração e epidemias no estado de São Paulo," 267.

69. Instituto Brasileiro de Geografia e Estatística, *Estatísticas do século XX* (Rio de Janeiro: IBGE, 2006), https://biblioteca.ibge.gov.br/visualizacao/livros/liv37312.pdf; Instituto Brasileiro de Geografia e Estatística, *Anuário estatístico do Brasil, 1939/1940*, 89.

70. Instituto Brasileiro de Geografia e Estatística, *Estatísticas do século XX*.

71. Ibid.

72. Ibid.

73. Ibid.

74. Marilda Nagamini, "1889–1930: Ciência e tecnologia nos processos de urbanização e industralização," in *Prelúdio para uma história: Ciência e tecnologia no Brasil*, ed. Shozo Motoyama (São Paulo: EDUSP, 2004), 199–201.

75. The standard source for this history is Simon Schwartzman, *A Space for Science: The Development of the Scientific Community in Brazil* (College Park: Pennsylvania State University Press, 1991), chap. 5.

76. For more on the ideology of the professors and graduates of the polytechnic faculty, see Sandra Ricci, "Os engenheiros e a cidade: São Paulo, 1904/1926" (master's thesis, Pontifícia Universidade Católica, São Paulo, 2006), chap. I.3.

77. Departamento de Estatística do Estado, *Anuário estatístico de São Paulo, 1906*, 2:277, 282.

78. Instituto Brasileiro de Geografia e Estatística, *Recenseamento geral do Brasil, 1950*, regional series, vol. 25, bk. 1 (Rio de Janeiro: IBGE, 1955), 1, table 1; Departamento de Estatística do Estado, *Anuário estatístico de São Paulo, 1906*, 2:277.

79. Departamento de Estatística do Estado, *Anuário estatístico de São Paulo, 1913* (São Paulo: Governo do Estado de São Paulo, 1916), 1:180, 186. The effective attendance rate did slowly increase over time. In 1920 it was up to 78 percent for the public primary schools in both the capital and the interior of the state. Departamento de Estatística do Estado, *Anuário estatístico de São Paulo, 1920*, 1:123, 129.

80. For secondary school enrollments that included *cursos secundários* (considered level 1 schools), *cursos clássicos*, *cursos científicos*, and *cursos normais* (these three considered level 2 schools), see Departamento de Estatística do Estado, *Anuário estatístico de São Paulo, 1945*, 1:435. The data for general enrollment for 1945 are found in Departamento de Estatística do Estado, *Anuário estatístico de São Paulo, 1950* (São Paulo: Governo do Estado de São Paulo, 1953), 1:141. It is worth nothing that in general in the world, secondary educational enrollments were quite low. It is estimated that in 1950 the world average was only 13 percent of eligible-age students were enrolled in secondary educational institutions. In the same year 58 percent of proper-age students were enrolled in primary education. John W. Meyer, Francisco O. Ramirez, Richard Rubinson, and John Boli-Bennett, "The World Educational Revolution, 1950–1970," *Sociology of Education* 50, no. 4 (1977): 244, table 1.

81. Data are taken from numerous tables on basic education in Departamento de Estatística do Estado, *Anuário estatístico de São Paulo, 1950*, 1:147–253.

82. This figure excludes the suburban areas. Instituto Brasileiro de Geografia e Estatística, *Censo demográfico, 1950* (Rio de Janeiro: IBGE, 1956), 1:68, table 38.

83. Simon Schwartzman, Helena M. B. Bomeny, and Vanda M. R. Costa, *Nos tempo de Capanema* (São Paulo: EDUSP/Paz e Terra, 1984), chap. 8.

84. Simonson had also been one of the key persons, along with Júlio de Mesquita Filho, owner of *O Estado de São Paulo*, and the political leader Armando de Sales Oliveira, behind the establishment of the University of São Paulo. Schwartzman, *A Space for Science*, chap. 5.

85. For more on the origins of SENAI, see Barbara Weinstein, "The Industrialists, the State, and the Issues of Worker Training and Social Services in Brazil, 1930–50," *Hispanic American Historical Review* 70, no. 3 (1990): 379–404; and Barbara Weinstein, *For Social Peace in Brazil: Industrialists and the Remaking of the Working Class in São Paulo, 1920–1964* (Chapel Hill: University of North Carolina Press, 1996).

86. Instituto Brasileiro de Geografia e Estatística, *Censo demográfico, 1950*, vol. 25, bk. 1 (Rio de Janeiro: IBGE, 1954), 1, table 1; "População de 15 anos e mais, total e alfabetizada, município de São Paulo, 1920 a 2000," http://smul.prefeitura.sp.gov.br/historico_demografico/tabelas/pop_alf.php.

87. In 1950 Brazil as a whole had one of the worst literacy rates in Latin America, less than half the rates in Argentina, Chile, and Uruguay and below any other South American country. Oxford Economic History Database, at http://moxlad-staging.herokuapp.com/home/es#tabs-graficar.

88. Pierre Monbeig, "O crescimento da cidade de São Paulo," in *História econômica da cidade de São Paulo*, ed. Tamás Szmrecsányi (São Paulo: Globo, 2005), 41–50.

89. For a good survey of the geographic logic for the establishment of the city and its role in the state, see Caio Prado Jr., *Evolução política do Brasil*, 8th ed. (São Paulo: Brasiliense, 1972), 111–142.

90. Monbeig, "O crescimento da cidade de São Paulo."

91. The figures are from Daniel Pedro Müller, *Ensaio d'um quadro estatístico da província de São Paulo* (São Paulo: Governo do Estado de São Paulo, 1978), https://archive.org/details/ensaio1840sp, whose data have been cleaned up and put into tables in Maria Silvia C. Beozzo Bassanezi, ed., *São Paulo do passado: Dados demográficos*, vol. 2, *1854* (Campinas, Brazil: Universidade Estadual de Campinas and Núcleo de Estudos de População, 1998), http://www.nepo.unicamp.br/publicacoes/censos/1854.pdf.

92. Maria Silvia C. Beozzo Bassanezi, ed., *São Paulo do passado: Dados demográficos*, vol. 3, *1872* (Campinas, Brazil: Universidade Estadual de Campinas and Núcleo de Estudos de População, 1998), 37, http://www.nepo.unicamp.br/publicacoes/censos/1872.pdf.

93. Departamento de Estatística do Estado, *Anuário estatístico de São Paulo, 1946* (São Paulo: Governo do Estado de São Paulo, 1947), 1:71.

94. The figures for housing are based on the building tax (*imposto predial*) charged by the provincial and state governments beginning in the nineteenth century. A summary of these numbers is found in *Boletim da Diretoria de Indústria e Comércio* 4, no. 9 (1913): 361–362.

95. *Boletim da Diretoria de Indústria e Comércio* 3, no. 5 (1912): 238–239.

96. *Boletim da Diretoria de Indústria e Comércio* 7, no. 1 (1916): 8–9.

97. *Boletim da Diretoria de Indústria e Comércio* 12, nos. 5–6 (1921): 158–159.

98. By 1950 the capital reached 2.2 million persons, compared to 2.4 million in Rio de Janeiro. In the next decade, São Paulo became the largest metropolis in the nation. For the comparative growth of the population of the two cities, see Instituto Brasileiro de Geografia e Estatística, "Sinopse do censo demográfico, 2010," table 1.6, http://www.censo2010.ibge.gov.br/sinopse/index.php?dados=6&uf=0.

99. Instituto Brasileiro de Geografia e, *Recenseamento geral do Brasil, 1940*, regional series, part 17, vol. 2 (Rio de Janeiro: IBGE, 1950), 130–131.

100. For São Paulo state/provincial and capital populations in 1872–2010, see Instituto Brasileiro de Geografia e Estatística, "Sinopse do censo demográfico, 2010," tables 1.4, 1.6, http://www.censo2010.ibge.gov.br/sinopse/index.php?dados=4&uf=00. The data available from the Comisión Económica para América Latina y el Caribe (CEPAL) give slightly higher figures for the ratio of the capital population to the national total population. See Comisión Económica para América Latina y el Caribe, *Anuario estadístico de América Latina y el Caribe, 2002* (Santiago, Chile: United Nations, 2003), 16, table 11; Comisión Económica para América Latina y el Caribe, *Anuario estadístico de América Latina y el Caribe, 2003* (Santiago, Chile: United Nations, 2004), 13, table 11; CELADE, *Observatorio demográfico de América Latina*, vol. 8, *Urbanización en prespectiva* (Santiago, Chile: United Nations, 2009), 60, 68, tables 10 and 14; and Comisión Económica para América Latina y el Caribe, *Anuario estadístico de América Latina y el Caribe, 2009* (Santiago, Chile: United Nations, 2010), 34, table 1.1.12.

101. Instituto Brasileiro de Geografia e Estatística, *Recenseamento geral do Brasil, 1950*, regional series, vol. 25, bk. 1, p. 188, table 46.

102. GEIPOT, *Anuário estatístico dos transportes, 2001* (Brasilia: Ministério dos Transportes, Portos e Aviação Civil, 2002), tables 5.1.1, 5.1.3, 5.1.5, 5.1.6.

103. Saes, *As ferrovias de São Paulo*, 24, table 1.

104. Ricardo Castillo, "Transporte e logística de granéis sólidos agrícolas: Componentes estruturais do novo sistema de movimentos do território brasileiro," *Investigaciones Geográficas*, no. 55 (2004): table 2.

105. Aurílio Sérgio Costa Caiado, "Reestruturação produtiva e localização industrial: A dinâmica industrial na RMSP entre 1985 e 2000," paper presented at ANPEC XXX Encontro Nacional de Economia, Rio de Janeiro, 2002, p. 14.

106. Francisco Vidal Luna and Iraci Del Nero da Costa, "A estrada e o desenvolvimento econômico: Estrada São Paulo–Santos," *Anais do IX Simpósio Nacional da Associação dos Professores Universitários de História: O homem e a técnica* (São Paulo: ANPUH, 1979), 2:551–567; São Paulo Departamento de Estradas

de Rodagem, "Histórico de rodovias," http://www.der.sp.gov.br/Website/Acessos/Institucional/HistoricoRodovias.aspx (accessed January 23, 2018).

107. São Paulo Departamento de Estradas de Rodagem, "Memória do transporte," http://www.der.sp.gov.br/Website/Acessos/Institucional/MemoriaTransporte.aspx (accessed January 23, 2018).

108. Monbeig, *Pioneiros e fazendeiros de São Paulo*, 198.

109. For this history of autos and road building, see Roberto França da Silva Jr., "Geografia de redes e da logística no transporte rodoviário de cargas: Fluxos e mobilidade geográfica do capital" (master's thesis, Universidade Estadual Paulista, Presidente Prudente, 2004), 47–49.

110. Ibid., 54–55.

111. *AESP 1940*, 210. So important had road transport become that by the late 1940s and early years of the 1950s auto and truck imports surpassed in value such traditional imports as wheat and petroleum. Hugo Schlesinger, *Geografia industrial do Brasil*, 2nd ed. (São Paulo: Atlas, 1958), 255.

112. *AESP 1940*, 330–361.

113. Ibid., 282.

114. Departamento de Estatística do Estado, *Resumo Anual, 1955* (São Paulo: Governo do Estado de São Paulo, 1957), 83; Departamento de Estatística do Estado, *Anuário estatístico de São Paulo, 1960* (São Paulo: Governo do Estado de São Paulo, 1961), 155.

115. Departamento de Estatística do Estado, *Anuário estatístico de São Paulo, 1960*, 151.

116. For the nation as a whole, banking was quite limited, with only seven of the empire's twenty provinces having even one bank, and half the meager deposits were in Rio de Janeiro banks. Steven Topik, *The Political Economy of the Brazilian State, 1889–1930* (Austin: University of Texas Press, 1987), 28.

117. William R. Summerhill, *Inglorious Revolution: Political Institutions, Sovereign Debt, and Financial Underdevelopment in Imperial Brazil* (New Haven, CT: Yale University Press, 2015), 184–185.

118. Hanley, *Native Capital*, 36.

119. Ibid., 49.

120. Ibid., chap. 2.

121. According to Flávio Azevedo Marques de Saes, this unification of coffee interests, which was politically represented in the Commercial Association, started to break apart in the 1920s, with the formation of the Association of São Paulo Banks in 1924 and later with the creation of the São Paulo industrial federation, FIESP, in 1928. He believes that with their association, the banking industry acquired its own identity and broke with the other sectors of the coffee elite. Flávio Azevedo Marques de Saes, *Crédito e bancos no desenvolvimento Paulista, 1850–1930* (São Paulo: Instituto de Pesquisas Econômicas, USP, 1986), 139–140.

122. Renato Leite Marcondes and Anne G. Hanley suggest that besides the usual difficulties in making long-term loans in the Brazilian context, the first banking and joint-stock-company laws failed to create the necessary safeguards to stimulate investment in more long-term risky credits, such as for coffee, in which commercial output occurred only in the fourth year after planting, and with less-liquid collateral available to support these loans, such as urban and rural properties. Also the difficulty of defining property ownership and a lack of advertising and special guarantees jeopardized the functioning of the mortgage market by decreasing resources and providing for only short-term loans with very high interest rates. Renato Leite Marcondes and Anne G. Hanley, "Bancos na transição republicana em São Paulo: O financiamento hipotecário (1888–1901)," *Estudos Econômicos* 40, no. 1 (2010): 107.

123. For more on the mortgage loans in this period, see Marcondes and Hanley, "Bancos na transição republicana em São Paulo," 103–131. The authors, through a survey of the notary records, found 405 mortgage operations in the São Paulo market in the period 1888–1901. They identified a significant role of foreign banks, accounting for approximately half of the traded value in the period. But this high participation is due in part to a unique and very expensive transaction, which represented about one-third of the total value of mortgages. This is an operation made by the Companhia Paulista railways in 1892, brokered by the British Bank of South America.

124. For more on these banks, see Saes, *Crédito e bancos no desenvolvimento paulista, 1850–1930*; and Hanley, *Native Capital.*

125. *Relatório apresentado à assembleia legislativa provincial de São Paulo, pelo presidente da província Dr. Pedro Vicente de Azevedo, no dia 11 de janeiro de 1889* (São Paulo: Typografia a Vapor de Jorge Seckler, 1889), 2:9–14, table "Empréstimo Externo."

126. Valentim F. Bouças, *Finanças do Brasil*, vol. 10, *História da dívida externa estadual e municipal* (Rio de Janeiro: Secretaria do Conselho Técnico de Economia e Finanças do Ministério da Fazenda, 1942), 144–171; Valentim F. Bouças, *Finanças do Brasil, união, estados e municipalidades: Dívida externa; Quadros estatísticos e gráficos* (Rio de Janeiro: Imprensa Oficial, Ministério da Fazenda, 1934), 3:4–5.

127. Marcondes and Hanley, "Bancos na transição republicana em São Paulo," 103–131; André Schifnagel Avrichir, "Federalismo e reforma bancária: A experiência internacional na análise de Rui Barbosa," paper presented at IV Conferência Internacional de História Econômica and VI Encontro de Pós-Graduação em História Econômica, São Paulo, 2012, https://uspdigital.usp.br/siicusp/cdOnlineTrabalhoVisualizarResumo?numeroInscricaoTrabalho=1122&numeroEdicao=19.

128. Saes, *Crédito e bancos no desenvolvimento paulista, 1850–1930*, 205–238.

129. Instituto Brasileiro de Geografia e Estatística, *Recenseamento geral do Brasil, 1950*, regional series, vol. 25, bk. 1, p. 188, table 46.

Chapter 9

1. The 1854 census comes from Daniel Pedro Müller, *Ensaio d'um quadro estatístico da província de São Paulo* (São Paulo: Governo do Estado de São Paulo, 1978), https://archive.org/details/ensaio1840sp, whose data have been cleaned up and put into tables in Maria Silvia C. Beozzo Bassanezi, ed., *São Paulo do passado: Dados demográficos*, vol. 2, *1854* (Campinas, Brazil: Universidade Estadual de Campinas and Núcleo de Estudos de População, 1998), http://www.nepo.unicamp.br/publicacoes/censos/1854.pdf. If one assumes that the missing municípios had the same average population as the forty-six municípios whose population is known, or 9,099 persons per missing município, this brings the total to 454,926 persons. Another twenty-one municípios had only partial counts, which suggests a final range of 450,000 to 500,000 persons.

2. Maria Silvia C. Beozzo Bassanezi, ed., *São Paulo do passado: Dados demográficos*, vol. 7, *Capital* (Campinas, Brazil: Universidade Estadual de Campinas and Núcleo de Estudos de População, 2000), 287, table 1a, http://www.nepo.unicamp.br/publicacoes/censos/capital.pdf; Directoria do Serviço Sanitario do Estado de São Paulo, *Annuário demográphico de São Paulo, 1925*, vol. 3, *Municípios do Interior* (São Paulo: Typographia Brazil de Rothschild, 1927), 1024–1027.

3. Camargo's selection of census years and grouping into zones is found in José Francisco Camargo, *Crescimento da população no estado de São Paulo e seus aspectos econômicos*, vol. 1 (São Paulo: Instituto de Pesquisas Econômicas, USP, 1981), chap. 1.

4. Given the problems of miscounting in the published 1872 census, we have relied on the re-counted data presented in Maria Silvia C. Beozzo Bassanezi, ed., *São Paulo do passado: Dados demográficos*, vol. 3, *1872* (Campinas, Brazil: Universidade Estadual de Campinas and Núcleo de Estudos de População, 1998), http://www.nepo.unicamp.br/publicacoes/censos/1872.pdf, for the province of São Paulo. For all the other provinces in 1872 we have used data recalculated and published by Pedro Puntoni, ed., *Os recenseamentos gerais do Brasil no século XIX: 1872 e 1890* (São Paulo: CEBRAP, 2004). The São Paulo provincial data is the same in both data sets.

5. For more on the demographic structure of the arriving African slaves, see Herbert S. Klein, *The Atlantic Slave Trade*, 2nd ed. (Cambridge: Cambridge University Press, 2010).

6. This is calculated using midyear estimates for the total population by age found in Bassanezi, *São Paulo do passado*, 3:45, table 3a.

7. Bassanezi, *São Paulo do passado*, 3:112, table 14a.

8. Instituto Brasileiro de Geografia e Estatística, "Table CD106: Taxa média geométrica de crescimento anual da população, 1872–2010," http://seriesestatisticas.ibge.gov.br/series.aspx?no=10&op=0&vcodigo=CD106&t=taxa-media-geometrica-crescimento-anual-populacao (accessed May 25, 2017).

9. Joseph L. Love, *São Paulo in the Brazilian Federation, 1889–1937* (Stanford, CA: Stanford University Press, 1980), 33.

10. Maria Silvia C. Beozzo Bassanezi, ed., *São Paulo do passado: Dados demográficos*, vol. 5, *1890* (Campinas, Brazil: Universidade Estadual de Campinas and Núcleo de Estudos de População, 1998), 38–41, table 2, http://www.nepo.unicamp.br/publicacoes/censos/1890.pdf. There were 122 municípios listed, of which only 85 had population data given.

11. *Boletim do Departamento Estadual de Estatística*, no. 3 (1947): 88–89. These estimates by the state statistical bureau were slightly below the estimates for the state population made by the national census bureau for the 1940 census. See Instituto Brasileiro de Geografia e Estatística, *Anuário estatístico do Brasil, 1939/1940* (Rio de Janeiro: Conselho Nacional de Estatística, 1940), 5:5, table 3, http://produtos.seade.gov.br/produtos/bibliotecadigital/view/singlepage/index.php?pubcod=10020584&parte=1.

12. Instituto Brasileiro de Geografia e Estatística, *Recenseamento geral do Brasil, 1950*, national series, vol. 1 (Rio de Janeiro: IBGE, 1957), "População presente, segundo as Unidades da Federação" table.

13. In 1872 foreign born represented just 3.5 percent. The rate rose to 5.4 percent in 1890 and 23.2 percent in 1900 but dropped to 18.2 percent in 1920 and just 11.4 percent in 1940. Departamento de Estatística do Estado, *Anuário estatístico de São Paulo, 1946*, vol. 1, bk. 2 (São Paulo: Governo do Estado de São Paulo, 1949), 71. In 1900, the nearest states in terms of relative importance of foreigners were Rio de Janeiro (including the Federal District) and Espírito Santo—both with 18 percent of their population listed as foreign born. In 1920 the nearest state again was Rio de Janeiro and the Federal District, and it had only 12 percent foreign born. In the census of 1900 and 1920, São Paulo alone had 41 percent of all immigrants, which rose to 52 percent in the 1920 census. Instituto Brasileiro de Geografia e Estatística, *Séries estatísticas retrospectivas*, vol. 1, *Repertório estatístico do Brasil: Quadros retrospectivos* (Rio de Janeiro: IBGE, 1986), 12.

14. In 1900 the crude birth rate was 30.1, the crude death rate was 18.8, and the crude immigration rate to the state was 9.9 per thousand resident population. This does not account for return, or out-migration, in that year. The birth, death, and immigration data for these calculations come from Departamento de Estatística do Estado, *Anuário estatístico de São Paulo, 1900* (São Paulo: Governo do Estado de São Paulo, 1903), 270; and Henrique Doria de Vasconcellos, "Oscilações do movimento imigratório no Brasil," *Revista de Imigração e Colonização* 1, no. 2 (1940): 211–235. The estimate for the population of the state in 1900 comes from *Boletim do Departamento Estadual de Estatística*, no. 3 (1947): 88–89.

15. Thomas William Merrick and Douglas H. Graham, *Population and Economic Development in Brazil, 1800 to the Present* (Baltimore: Johns Hopkins University Press, 1979), 38.

16. Instituto Brasileiro de Geografia e Estatística, *Recenseamento geral do Brasil, 1940*, regional series, part 27, vol. 1 (Rio de Janeiro: IBGE, 1950), 1; Instituto Brasileiro de Geografia e Estatística, *Censo demográfico, 2000* (Rio de Janeiro: IBGE, 2002), table 3.20.2.1. As prejudice patterns have changed, in São Paulo as in the rest of Brazil the ratio of whites has been steadily declining in the current century despite new immigration. Thus, by the census of 2010 whites in São Paulo had dropped to 71 percent of the total population.

17. This includes both foreigners and naturalized citizens. Instituto Brasileiro de Geografia e Estatística, *Recenseamento geral do Brasil, 1950*, regional series, vol. 25, bk. 1 (Rio de Janeiro: IBGE, 1955), 8, table 9; Departamento de Estatística do Estado de São Paulo, *Boletim do Departamento Estadual de Estatística*, no. 1 (1939): 74. It has been estimated that between 1921 and 1940 some 660,000 foreign born entered the state but were surpassed by the native-born immigrants who numbered 690,000 in this period. Rossana Baeninger and Maria Sílvia Casagrande Beozzo Bassanezi, "São Paulo: Transição demografia e migrações," in *História do estado de São Paulo*, ed. Nilo Odalia and João Ricardo de Castro Caldeira (São Paulo: UNESP, 2010), 2:158.

18. Oracy Nogueira, *O desenvolvimento de São Paulo: Imigração estrangeira e nacional e índices demográficos, demográfo-sanitários e educacionais* (São Paulo: Comissão Interestadual da Bacia Paraná-Uruguai, 1964), 28. But this native-born migration from other states intensified greatly after 1950.

19. Departamento de Estatística do Estado, *Anuário estatístico de São Paulo, 1980* (São Paulo: Governo do Estado de São Paulo, 1982), 49, table 1.

20. Safe drinking water supplies accounted for half the decline in mortality in this same period in the United States. David Cutler and Grant Miller, "The Role of Public Health Improvements in Health Advances: The Twentieth-Century United States," *Demography* 42, no. 1 (2005): 1–22; David Cutler, Angus Deaton, and Adriana Lleras-Muney, "The Determinants of Mortality," *Journal of Economic Perspectives* 20, no. 3 (2006): 97–120. It was also crucial in affecting mortality in Great Britain at this time. Simon Szreter, "The Importance of Social Intervention in Britain's Mortality Decline c. 1850–1914: A Re-interpretation of the Role of Public Health," *Social History of Medicine* 1, no. 1 (1988): 1–37.

21. *Boletim do Departamento Estadual de Estatística*, no. 1 (1956): 23–24. The total fertility rate is for the Southeast states in 1950. The national average was 6.2 children per woman. See Instituto Brasileiro de Geografia e Estatística, *Censo demográfico, 2000*, "Taxas de fecundidade total, segundo as Grandes Regiões, 1940/2000" table, http://www.ibge.gov.br/home/presidencia/noticias/20122002censo.shtm.

22. These are presented in Eduardo E. Arriaga, *New Life Tables for Latin American Populations in the Nineteenth and Twentieth Centuries* (Berkeley: University of California, 1968), 29–30.

23. Eduardo E. Arriaga's figures are close to the estimated model life tables produced by Ansley J. Coale, Paul Demeny, and Barbara Vaughan for world populations. The choice is somewhere between their model life tables West 4 and West 5. Comparing these two models to the results of the life table that Arriaga prepared on the basis of the 1872 census shows that West 4 is closest to the 1872 life table in life expectancy at birth, even though it systematically underestimates mortality at ages 5 to 55. In turn, West 5 compared to 1872 gives higher life expectancy and consistently lower estimates of mortality for all age groups than in 1872. In the model life table West 4, infant mortality rates were estimated at 296 deaths per thousand live male births and 256 deaths per thousand live female births, and life expectancy at birth was estimated at 25.3 years for males and 27.5 for females. Ansley J. Coale, Paul Demeny, and Barbara Vaughan, *Regional Model Life Tables and Stable Populations: Studies in Population* (New York: Academic Press, 1983), 43–44.

24. For more on the plagues that affected just the city of São Paulo in the nineteenth century, see Luís Soares de Camargo, "Viver e morrer em São Paulo: A vida, as doenças e a morte na cidade do século XIX" (PhD diss., Pontifícia Universidade Católica, São Paulo, 2007). For more on the role of the Companhia Paulista railroad expanding the range of deadly yellow fever epidemics in the state in 1889–1896, see Rodolpho Telarolli Jr., "Imigração e epidemias no estado de São Paulo," *História, Ciências, Saúde—Manguinhos* 3, no. 2 (1996): 257–258.

25. Giorgio Mortara, "The Development and Structure of Brazil's Population," *Population Studies* 8, no. 2 (1954): 122.

26. Even as late as the 1920s, infants and children zero to five years of age made up over half of deaths in the capital. Flávia Sommerlatte Silva, "Tendências e projeção da mortalidade do município de São Paulo, 1920 a 2100" (master's thesis, Universidade Federal de Minas Gerais, Cedeplar, Belo Horizonte, 2009), 56–57, tables 3.2.1, 3.2.2.

27. It was at this time that the state government of the new republic created a statistical bureau that began generating data on urban and rural population of the state from the 1880s. The Repartição de Estatística e Arquivo do Estado de São Paulo was created in March of 1891 and was under the Department of the Interior. Its work was to organize and publish statistical information about the state, and its publications appeared with regularity from 1888 to the late 1920s.

28. For more on this process in the United States, see Herbert S. Klein, *A Population History of the United States*, 2nd ed. (Cambridge: Cambridge University Press, 2012).

29. The crude birth rate for the state in the census years of 1940 was 32.3, in 1950 it was 33.5, and in 1960 it increased slightly to 33.9 births per thousand residents. It dropped to below 30 only in the census year of 1970. On the other hand, the crude death rate continued its decline, reaching 12 deaths per thou-

sand residents in 1950 and declining to below 10 deaths in 1960. Departamento de Estatística do Estado, *Anuário estatístico de São Paulo, 1980*, 49, table 1.

30. The state population data from 1900 to 2000 is available at the SEADE Memória das Estatísticas Demográficas website, at http://produtos.seade.gov.br/produtos/500anos/index.php?tip=esta.

31. José Alberto Magno de Carvalho estimated that the national crude birth rate was still at 46.5 births per thousand resident population in the decade of the 1940s, and life expectancy for both sexes was only 43.6 years in the same decade. José Alberto Magno de Carvalho, "Evolução demográfica recente no Brasil," *Pesquisa e Planejamento Econômico* 10, no. 2 (1980): 531, 534, tables 1, 2.

32. Instituto Brasileiro de Geografia e Estatística gives the national crude birth rate as 44.4 births and the crude death rate as 20.9 deaths per thousand persons in 1945. Instituto Brasileiro de Geografia e Estatística, "Table CD109: Taxas brutas de natalidade e de mortalidade," http://seriesestatisticas.ibge.gov.br/series.aspx?vcodigo=CD109&t=taxas-brutas-natalidade-mortalidade (accessed May 25, 2017). At this time the Departamento de Estatística do Estado estimated the state's births and deaths as, respectively, 32.4 and 15.0. *Boletim do Departamento Estadual de Estatística*, no. 1 (1956): 23–24.

33. Cássia Maria Buchalla, Eliseu Alves Waldman, and Ruy Laurenti, "A mortalidade por doenças infecciosas no início e no final do século XX no Município de São Paulo," *Revista Brasileira de Epidemiologia* 6, no. 4 (2003): 338.

34. By 1901 the crude death rate dropped to below 20 per thousand resident population and stayed that way until the 1920s, except for 1918 when the capital experienced a death rate of 44 per thousand resident population. Directoria do Serviço Sanitario do Estado de São Paulo, *Annuário demográphico, 1929* (São Paulo: Typographia Brasil de Rothschild, 1929), 1:182–183.

35. Ibid., 1:182–183, 364–365, 482–483, 600–601.

36. Directoria do Serviço Sanitario, *Annuário estatistico da secção de demográphia, 1905* (São Paulo: Typografia de Diario Oficial, 1906), 58–69.

37. These estimates are based on UN model life tables for Latin America, with the worst case model—in which a male infant and child mortality of 19 percent results in a life expectancy at birth of 37 years and a female infant and child mortality of 17 percent results in a life expectancy at birth of 35 years. United Nations, *Model Life Tables for Developing Countries* (New York: United Nations, 1982), 34, 55.

38. Pamila Cristina Lima Siviero, "Níveis e padrões do diferencial de mortalidade por sexo no município de São Paulo, 1920–2005" (master's thesis, Universidade Federal de Minas Gerais/Cedeplar, 2009), appendix table C. Also see Pamila Cristina Lima Siviero, Cássio Maldonado Turra, and Roberto do Nascimento Rodrigues, "Diferenciais de mortalidade: Níveis e padrões segundo o sexo no município de São Paulo de 1920 a 2005," *Revista Brasileira de Estudos de População* 28, no. 2 (2011): 283–301.

39. See Silva, "Tendências e projeção da mortalidade do município de São Paulo," 27, for the 1930 data, and for 1940 and 1950, see Bernadette Cunha Waldvogel, Carlos Eugenio de Carvalho Ferreira, Lúcia Mayumi Yazaki, Rute Eduviges Godinho, and Sonia Regina Perillo, "Projeção da população paulista como instrumento de planejamento," *São Paulo em Perspectiva* 17, nos. 3–4 (2003): 73, table 1. The rate for Brazil in this same year was in the low 40s for both sexes. See José Alberto Magno de Carvalho, "Crescimento populacional e estrutura demográfica no Brasil," Universidade Federal de Minas Gerais/ Cedeplar Texto para Discussão no. 227, February 2004, p. 5, http://www.cedeplar.ufmg.br/pesquisas/td/TD%20227.pdf.

40. *Boletim do Departamento Estadual de Estatística*, no. 1 (1960): 12–13, 16–17.

41. *Boletim do Departamento Estadual de Estatística*, no. 9 (1943): 18; Giorgio Mortara, "Nota preliminar sôbre a mortalidade no município de São Paulo," *Boletim do Departamento Estadual de Estatística*, no. 9 (1943): 11, table 4.

42. By the 1960s infectious diseases in the city of São Paulo accounted for only 22 percent of all deaths (with an infant mortality rate of 63) and just 10 percent by 2000 (with an infant mortality rate of 16). Of the earlier infectious diseases only pneumonia remained as a significant cause of death by 2000, whereas chronic diseases like cancer and diseases of the heart now accounted for 50 percent of all deaths. Buchalla, Waldman, and Laurenti, "A mortalidade por doenças infecciosas no início e no final do século XX no Município de São Paulo," 337–341.

43. Mortara, "Nota preliminar sôbre a mortalidade no município de São Paulo," 11–13, tables 5–7.

44. *Boletim do Departamento Estadual de Estatística*, no. 1 (1956): 9, 39.

45. As many scholars have noted, not all of Brazil has followed that rapidly the pace of change in mortality of São Paulo in this and later periods. Thus, a survey in 1998 showed that 38 percent of deaths in the states of the North were from infectious diseases compared to just 18 percent of all deaths in the states of the South being from such diseases. J. M. A. Schramm et al., "Transição epidemiológica e o estudo de carga de doença no Brasil," *Ciência e Saúde Coletiva* 9, no. 4 (2004): 901.

46. It has been suggested that the sanitation, or hygiene, movement in São Paulo was unusually successful and advanced by Brazilian standards because it was led by economic and political elites and not by doctors. There was a very weak medical tradition in the state since São Paulo did not have an imperial medical faculty and did not establish its own faculty of medicine until 1912. It is argued that this actually facilitated the rapid introduction of scientific and sanitation ideas because there was no systematic opposition by the medical profession. Luis Antonio de Castro Santos, "Reforma sanitária 'Pelo Alto': O pioneirismo paulista no início do século XX," *Dados* 36, no. 3 (1993): 365.

47. John A. Blount III, "The Public Health Movement in São Paulo, Brazil: A History of the Sanitary Service, 1892–1918" (PhD diss., Tulane University, 1971), 49.

48. Ibid., 59–60.

49. Richard M. Morse, *From Community to Metropolis: A Biography of São Paulo, Brazil* (New York: Octagon Books, 1974), 179–180. The state took over the building of sewage works in the capital in 1893, and by the end of 1894 some 6,244 homes were connected to sewers. Eugênio Lefevre, *A administração do estado de São Paulo na Republica Velha* (São Paulo: Typografia Cupolo, 1937), 178.

50. Massako Iyda, *Cem anos de saúde pública: A cidadania negada* (São Paulo: Editora UNESP, 1994), 36.

51. See the SEADE Memória das Estatísticas Demográficas website, at http://produtos.seade.gov.br/produtos/500anos/index.php?tip=esta.

52. Directoria Geral de Estatística, *Recenseamento do Brazil realizado em 1 de 1920*, vol. 4, part 2 (Rio de Janeiro: Typographia da Estatistica, 1929), lii.

53. Robert L. Goldenberg et al., "Stillbirths: The Vision for 2020," *The Lancet* 377, no. 9779 (May 2011): 1799.

54. For more on the reorganization of plantation work, see Warren Dean, *Rio Claro: A Brazilian Plantation System, 1820–1920* (Stanford, CA: Stanford University Press, 1976); and Zuleka Alvim, *Brava gente! Os italianos em São Paulo, 1870–1920* (São Paulo: Brasiliense, 1986). For more on the dynamics of the immigration process, see Thomas Holloway, *Immigrants on the Land: Coffee and Society in São Paulo, 1886–1934* (Chapel Hill: University of North Carolina Press, 1980).

55. Bassanezi, *São Paulo do passado*, 5:58–61, chart 6.

56. Although these immigrants increased the white element in the population, they had only a modest impact on literacy, since the majority of these same immigrants were themselves illiterate. While foreign-born immigrants thus listed 42 percent of their number as being able to read and write, which was much higher than the 14 percent of native-born Brazilians who could read and write, that only moderately affected the province's overall literacy rate of just 19 percent.

57. Secretaria da Agricultura, *A immigração e as condicões do trabalho em São Paulo* (São Paulo: Secretaria da Agricultura, Commércio e Obras Públicas, 1915), 8–9, table "Estatistica dos immigrantes entrados no estado de São Paulo, de 1827 a 1914."

58. The standard compilation of the statistics on immigration for the entire period is Maria Stella Ferreira Levy, "O papel da migração internacional na evolução da população brasileira (1872 a 1972)," *Revista de Saúde Pública* 8, suppl. (1974): 49–90.

59. Vasconcellos, "Oscilações do movimento imigratório no Brasil," 227–228.

60. The importance of the foreign born was already on the decline in this period. Their peak importance appears in the census of 1900 when they represented 23 percent of the state's population. Departamento de Estatística do Estado, *Anuário estatístico de São Paulo, 1940* (São Paulo: Governo do Estado de São Paulo, 1940), 93. There are various estimates on the return migration, running from 45 to 65 percent, and it appears it was higher from Brazil than from Argentina or the United States. See Angelo Trento, *Do outro lado do Atlântico: Um século de imigração italiana no Brasil* (São Paulo: Studio Nobel, 1989), 65–68. For a survey of the second-largest group of immigrants, see Herbert S. Klein, *A imigração espanhola no Brasil* (São Paulo: Editora Sumaré/IDESP-FAPESP, 1994). For more on the foreign born in 1920, see Maria Silvia C. Beozzo Bassanezi, ed., *São Paulo do passado: Dados demográficos*, vol. 6, *1920* (Campinas, Brazil: Universidade Estadual de Campinas and Núcleo de Estudos de População, 1999), table 3a, http://www.nepo.unicamp.br/publicacoes/censos/1920.pdf.

61. As of the census of 1920, 46 percent of the 434,000 Portuguese resident in Brazil were in the Federal District and state of Rio de Janeiro, and 40 percent resided in São Paulo. Herbert S. Klein, "The Social and Economic Integration of Portuguese Immigrants in Brazil in the Late Nineteenth and Twentieth Centuries," *Journal of Latin American Studies* 23, no. 2 (1991): 318.

62. The 1890 data on foreign born, although incomplete for many municípios, are found in Bassanezi, *São Paulo do passado*, 5:43–47. The data on coffee estates is from C. F. Van Delden Laerne, *Brazil and Java: Report on Coffee-Culture in America, Asia, and Africa* (The Hague: Martinus Nijhoff, 1885), 222–223.

63. Nogueira, *Desenvolvimento de São Paulo*, 17.

64. See the famous collection of short stories by Monteiro Lobato, *Cidades Mortas*, which describes the Vale do Paraíba in the early part of the twentieth century. But in the last quarter of the twentieth century, the Vale do Paraíba would recuperate its population with the expansion of industry into this previously declining agricultural region.

65. *Boletim do Departamento Estadual de Estatística*, special issue, no. 12 (1938): 79–87.

66. These included Sorocaba (39,921), Jundiai (29,452), Piracicaba (27,141), Araraquara (24,212), Bauru (23,405), Taubaté (22,485), São Carlos (21,405), and Rio Claro (20,135). Ibid.

67. The data for both 1940 and 1950 estimates come from Instituto Brasileiro de Geografia e Estatística, *Censo demográfico, 1950*, national series, vol. 1 (Rio de Janeiro: IBGE, 1956), 254–255, 274–275. The population for the capital in these census years is available at the SEADE Memória das Estatísticas Demográficas website, at http://produtos.seade.gov.br/produtos/500anos/index.php?tip=esta.

68. Camargo, *Crescimento da população no estado de São Paulo e seus aspectos econômicos*, 2:9.

69. See Bassanezi, *São Paulo do passado*, various volumes.

70. Comissão de Recenseamento da Colônia Japonesa, São Paulo, *The Japanese Immigrant in Brazil* (Tokyo: University of Tokyo Press, 1964), 356, table 276.

71. Diretoria Geral de Estatística, *Recenseamento geral do império de 1872* (Rio de Janeiro: Leuzinger, 1876), tables 1, 5, https://archive.org/details/memoriaestatisticadobrasil?and[]=Recenseamento%20geral%20do%20imp%C3%A9rio%20de%201872.

72. Departamento de Estatística do Estado, *Anuário estatístico de São Paulo, 1946*, vol. 1, bk. 2, p. 71.

73. Instituto Brasileiro de Geografia e Estatística, *Estatísticos do século XX* (Rio de Janeiro: IBGE, 2006), https://biblioteca.ibge.gov.br/visualizacao/livros/liv37312.pdf.

74. Instituto Brasileiro de Geografia e Estatística, *Anuário estatístico do Brasil, 1939/1940*, 5:13, table V.6.

75. The ratio of students to total population went from 1:75 in 1886 to 1:13 by 1929. Love, *São Paulo in the Brazilian Federation*, 93.

76. *Boletim do Departamento Estadual de Estatística*, no. 1 (1939): 84–89. The urban figure includes the capital, which we combine with the urban areas of the interior.

77. The rate was 59.4 percent literates for the total population for São Paulo and 58.6 percent for Rio Grande do Sul. Instituto Brasileiro de Geografia e Estatística, *Recenseamento geral do Brasil, 1950*, national series, vol. 1 (Rio de Janeiro: IBGE, 1956), 90, table 47.

78. Ibid. The rate for the Federal District was 83 percent for both sexes, 85 percent for men, and 75 percent for women.

79. For data on literacy by nation from 1900 to 1980, see the Oxford Latin American Economic History database, at http://moxlad-staging.herokuapp.com/home/es#tabs-graficar.

Conclusion

1. Francisco Vidal Luna, "A capital financeira do Pais," in *História econômica da Cidade de São Paulo*, ed. Tamás Szmrecsányi (São Paulo: Globo, 2004), 328–355.

2. Marcos Fava Neves and Frederico Fonseca Lopes, *Caminhos para a citricultura: Uma agenda para manter a liderança mundial* (São Paulo: Atlas, 2007); Marcos Fava Neves et al., *O retrato da citricultura brasileira* (Ribeirão Preto: CitrusBR, 2010); Marcos Fava Neves and Frederico Fonseca Lopes, *Estratégias para a laranja no Brasil* (São Paulo: Atlas, 2005). For more on the current modernization of São Paulo and Brazilian agriculture, see Renato Moraes

Chamma, "Uma análise da evolução da produção, área, produtividade e empregos nas tradicionais atividades agrícolas no estado de São Paulo" (master's thesis, Universidade de São Paulo, Ribeirão Preto, 2009); Paulo Fernando Cidade de Araujo et al., *Contribuição da FAPESP à agricultura do estado de São Paulo* (São Paulo: FAPESP, 2002); José Sidnei Gonçalves, "A agricultura paulista: A ação estatal na construção da modernidade," *São Paulo em Perspectiva* 7, no. 3 (1993): 100–106; José Garcia Gasques et al., "Produtividade total dos fatores e transformações da agricultura brasileira: Análise dos dados dos censos agropecuários," in *A agricultura brasileira: Desempenho, desafios e perspectivas*, ed. José Garcia Gasques, José Eustáquio Ribeiro Vieira Filho, and Zander Navarro (Brasília: IPEA, 2010); and José Garcia Gasques, E. T. Bastos, and M. R. P. Bacchi, "Produtividade e fontes de crescimento da agricultura brasileira," in *Políticas de incentivo à inovação tecnológica*, ed. João Alberto de Neg and Luis Claudio Kubota (Brasília: IPEA, 2008), 435–459.

3. See, for example, Edmar Bacha, *Belíndia 2.0: Fábulas e ensaios sobre o país dos contrastes* (Rio de Janeiro: Editora José Olympio, 2015).

Primary Sources and Government Documents

Affonseca, Leo, Jr. "Inflação, custo de vida, alimentação, ponderação." 1919. http://www.ipeadata.gov.br/Default.aspx.

Almanak administrativo, mercantil e industrial da província de São Paulo para o ano de 1857, organizado e redigido por Marques e Irmão. São Paulo: Typographia Imparcial, 1857.

Assembleia Legislativa do Estado de São Paulo. Leis orçamentárias, various years. http://www.al.sp.gov.br/leis.

Bassanezi, Maria Silvia C. Beozzo, and Priscila M. S. Bergamo Francisco, eds. *Estado de São Paulo: Estatistica agrícola e zootécnica, 1904–1905.* Campinas, Brazil: Núcleo de Estudos de População/Universidade Estadual de Campinas, 2003.

Boletim do Departamento Estadual de Estatística, various issues. http://produtos.seade.gov.br/produtos/bibliotecadigital/view/#14.

Boletim da Diretoria de Indústria e Comércio, various issues. http://produtos.seade.gov.br/produtos/bibliotecadigital/view/#14.

Constituição dos Estados Unidos do Brasil (de 10 de Novembro de 1937). http://www.planalto.gov.br/ccivil_03/constituicao/constituicao37.htm.

"Contribuição à história da medicina no Brasil: Segundo os relatórios do Dr. Adolpho Lutz." *Memórias do Instituto Oswaldo Cruz* 39, no. 2 (1943): 177–189. http://www.scielo.br/pdf/mioc/v39n2/tomo39(f2)_177-189.pdf.

Cotegipe, João Maurício Wanderley. *Breve notícia do estado financeiro das províncias organizada por ordem do S. Ex. o Sr. Barão de Cotegipe, presidente do conselho de ministros.* Rio de Janeiro: Imprensa Oficial, 1887.

D'Azambuja, Antonio Candido Nascentes. "Manual do cultivador de algodão." *O Auxiliador da Industria Nacional*, January 3, 1862, pp. 52–72. https://digital.bbm.usp.br/view/?45000033226&bbm/7057#page/56/mode/2up.

Departamento de Estatística do Estado. *Anuário estatístico de São Paulo.* São Paulo: Governo do Estado de São Paulo, various years. http://produtos.seade.gov.br/produtos/bibliotecadigital/view/#5.

Directoria do Serviço Sanitario do Estado de São Paulo. *Annuario demographico*. São Paulo: Typographia Brasil de Rothschild, various years.

———. *Annuário estatistico da secção de demográphia, 1905*. São Paulo: Typografia de Diario Oficial, 1906.

———. *Boletim annual de estadistica demographo-sanitaria da Capital e de Santos, 1894*. São Paulo: Typographia da Industrial, 1895.

———. *Recenseamento do Brazil realizado em 1 de setembro de 1920*. Rio de Janeiro: Typographia da Estatistica, 1923–1927.

———. *Recenseamento geral do império de 1872*. Rio de Janeiro: Leuzinger, 1876. https://archive.org/details/memoriaestatisticadobrasil?and[]=Recenseamento%20geral%20do%20imp%C3%A9rio%20de%201872.

Discurso com que o ilustríssimo e excelentíssimo Senhor Dr. José Antonio Saraiva, presidente da província de São Paulo, abriu a assembleia legislativa provincial, no dia 15 de fevereiro de 1855. São Paulo: Antonio Louzada Antunes, 1855.

Discurso com que o ilustríssimo e excelentíssimo Senhor Dr. José Thomaz Nabuco D Áraujo, presidente da província de São Paulo abrio a assembleia legislativa provincial no dia 1º. de maio de 1852. São Paulo: Antonio Louzada Antunes, 1852. http://brazil.crl.edu/bsd/bsd/986.

Discurso com que o ilustríssimo e exmo. Senhor Conselheiro Dr. Vicente Pires da Motta, presidente da província de São Paulo, abriu a assembleia legislativa provincial, no dia 15 de abril de 1850. São Paulo: Typographia do Governo, 1850.

Discurso receitado pelo exmo. Presidente Miguel de Souza Mello e Alvim, no dia 7 de janeiro de 1842, por ocasião da abertura da assembleia legislativa da província de São Paulo. São Paulo: Typographia Imparcial de Silva Sobral, 1842.

Discurso recitado pelo exmo. Presidente Manuel Felizandro de Souza e Mello, no dia 7 de janeiro de 1844, por ocasião da abertura da assembleia legislativa da província de São Paulo. São Paulo: Tipographia do Governo, 1844.

Exposição apresentada ao Dr. Jorge Tibiriça pelo Dr. Prudente J. de Moraes Barros, 1º. governador do estado de São Paulo ao passar-lhe a administração, no dia 18 de Outubro de 1890. São Paulo: Typographia Vanorden, 1890.

Fala dirigida à assemblea legislativa provincial de S. Paulo na abertura da 1ª. sessão da 25ª. legislatura, em 16 de janeiro de 1884, pelo Presidente Barão de Guajará. São Paulo: Typographia da Gazeta Liberal, 1884.

Fala dirigida à assembleia legislativa provincial de S. Paulo, na abertura da 2ª. sessão da 24ª. legislatura em 10 de janeiro de 1883 pelo Presidente Conselheiro Francisco de Carvalho Soares Brandão. São Paulo: Typographia do Ypiranga, 1883. http://brazil.crl.edu/bsd/bsd/1027.

Fonseca, Antonio Caetano da. "Cultura do algodão herbaceo." *O Auxiliador da Indústria Nacional*, March 6, 1862, pp. 152–160. http://www.brasiliana.usp.br/handle/1918/003601-04#page/1/mode/1up.

GEIPOT. *Anuário estatístico dos transportes, 2001*. Brasília: Ministério dos Transportes, Portos e Aviação Civil, 2002.

Girardi, Eduardo Paulon. "Atlas da questão agrária brasileira: Uma análise dos problemas agrários através do mapa." http://www.uff.br/vsinga/trabalhos/Trabalhos%20Completos/Eduardo%20Paulon%20Girardi.pdf (accessed May 10, 2017).

Indústria assucareira: Produção e consumo mundial do assucar. Rio de Janeiro: Imprensa Nacional, 1907.

Instituto do Açúcar e do Alcool. *Anuário açucareiro.* Vol. 7. Rio de Janeiro: Instituto do Açúcar e do Alcool, 1941. http://produtos.seade.gov.br/produtos/bibliotecadigital/view/singlepage/index.php?pubcod=10011726&parte=1.

Instituto Brasileiro de Geografia e Estatística. *Anuário estatistico do Brasil.* Rio de Janeiro: Conselho Nacional de Estatística, various years. http://produtos.seade.gov.br/produtos/bibliotecadigital.

———. *Censo agrícola de 1950.* Rio de Janeiro: IBGE, various volumes.

———. *Censo demográfico, 1950.* Rio de Janeiro: IBGE, 1956.

———. *Censo demográfico, 2000.* Rio de Janeiro: IBGE, 2002. http://www.ibge.gov.br/home/presidencia/noticias/20122002censo.shtm.

———. *Censo industrial de 1960.* National series. Vol. 3. Rio de Janeiro: IBGE, 1964.

———. *Estatísticas do século XX.* Rio de Janeiro: IBGE, 2006. https://biblioteca.ibge.gov.br/visualizacao/livros/liv37312.pdf.

———. *Recenseamento geral do Brasil, 1940.* Rio de Janeiro: IBGE, 1950. http://biblioteca.ibge.gov.br/index.php/biblioteca-catalogo?view=detalhes&id=765.

———. *Recenseamento geral do Brasil, 1950.* Rio de Janeiro: IBGE, various volumes.

———. *Séries estatísticas retrospectivas.* Rio de Janeiro: IBGE, 1986.

Instituto de Economia Agricola. *Censo agrícola de São Paulo, 1905.* São Paulo: Instituto de Economia Agricola, n.d.

———. *Desenvolvimento da agricultura paulista.* São Paulo: Governo do Estado de São Paulo, 1972.

———. "Taxas brutas de natalidade e de mortalidade." 2008. http://seriesestatisticas.ibge.gov.br/series.aspx?vcodigo=CD109&sv=36&t=taxas-brutas-de-natalidade-e-de-mortalidade.

Interstate Commerce Commission. *Statistics of Railways in the United States.* Washington, DC: Government Printing Office, 1894. http://archive.org/stream/sixthannualrepo00govegoog#page/n6/mode/2up.

Laemmert, Eduardo von. *Almanak administrativo, mercantil e industrial.* Rio de Janeiro: Laemmert, various years. http://www.crl.edu/brazil/almanak.

Mensagem apresentada ao congresso legislativo, em 14 de julho de 1921, pelo Dr. Washington Luis Pereira de Souza, presidente do estado de São Paulo. São Paulo, [1921]. http://brazil.crl.edu/bsd/bsd/u1178.

Mensagem apresentada ao congresso legislativo na 2ª. sessão da 14ª. legislatura, em 14 de julho de 1929, pelo Doutor Julio Prestes de Albuquerque, presidente do estado de São Paulo. São Paulo, [1929].

Mensagem dirigida ao congresso do estado a 7 de abril de 1905 pelo presidente de São Paulo, Dr. Jorge Tibiriçá. São Paulo: Typographia do Diario Official, 1905.

Mensagem dirigida ao congresso legislativo de S. Paulo, pelo vice-presidente do estado, Dr. José Alves Cerqueira Cesar, no dia 7 de abril de 1892. São Paulo: Typographia do Diario Official, 1892.

Mensagem enviada ao congresso do estado a 7 de abril de 1901 pelo Dr. Francisco de Paula Rodrigues Alves, presidente do estado, São Paulo. São Paulo: Typographia do Diario Official, 1901.

Mensagem enviada ao congresso do estado, a 14 de julho de 1914, pelo Dr. Carlos Augusto Pereira Guimarães, vice-presidente do estado de S. Paulo. São Paulo: Typographia do Diario Official, 1914.

Mensagem enviada ao congresso legislativo a 7 de abril de 1899 por Fernando Prestes de Albuquerque, presidente do estado. São Paulo: Typographia do Diario Official, 1899.

Ministerio da Agricultura. *Relatório 14 Maio 1888*. Rio de Janeiro: Ministerio da Agricultura, 1988.

Ministério da Agricultura, Indústria e Commércio. *Finanças: Quadros synopticos da receita e despeza do Brazil (período de 1822 a 1913)*. Rio de Janeiro: Typographia do Ministério da Agricultura, 1914.

Müller, Daniel Pedro. *Ensaio d'um quadro estatístico da província de São Paulo*. São Paulo: Governo do Estado de São Paulo, 1978. https://archive.org/details/ensaio1840sp.

"Os caminhos do café." http://www.sebraerj.com.br/custom/pdf/cam/cafe/02_OsCaminhosDoCafe.pdf (accessed May 1, 2017).

Relatório apresentado à assembleia legislativa provincial de São Paulo, pelo presidente da província Dr. Pedro Vicente de Azevedo, no dia 11 de janeiro de 1889. Vol. 2. São Paulo: Typografia a Vapor de Jorge Seckler, 1889.

Relatório apresentado à assembleia legislativa provincial de São Paulo pelo presidente da província exmo. Sr. Dr. Francisco de Paula Rodrigues Alves, no dia 10 de janeiro de 1888. São Paulo: Typografia de Jorge Seckler, 1888.

Relatório apresentado à assemblea legislativa provincial de São Paulo pelo presidente da provincia João Alfredo Corrêa de Oliveira no dia 15 de fevereiro de 1886. São Paulo: Typographia a Vapor de Jorge Seckler, 1886. http://brazil.crl.edu/bsd/bsd/1030.

Relatorio apresentado á assembléa legislativa provincial de S. Paulo pelo presidente da provincia, Laurindo Abelardo de Brito, no dia 5 de fevereiro de 1880. Santos: Typografia a Vapor do Diario de Santos, 1880.

Relatorio apresentado á assembléa legislativa provincial de S. Paulo pelo presidente da provincia, Laurindo Abelardo de Brito, no dia 13 de janeiro de 1881. Santos: Typografia a Vapor do Diario de Santos, 1881.

Relatório apresentado à assembleia legislativa provincial de São Paulo pelo presidente da província o exmo. Sr. Dr. Antônio Candido da Rocha, no dia 2 de fevereiro de 1870. São Paulo: Tipografia Americana, 1870.

Relatório apresentado ao chefe do Governo Provisório por Francisco Glicério, ministro e secretário de estado da agricultura, comércio e obras públicas. Rio de Janeiro: Imprensa Oficial, 1890.

Relatório apresentado ao Dr. Manuel Joaquim de Albuquerque Lins, presidente do estado pelo Dr. Olavo Egypio de Souza Aranha, secretario da fazenda, 1909. São Paulo: Casa Garraux, 1910. https://archive.org/stream/relatorioapresen1909sopa#page/n5/mode/2up.

Relatório apresentado ao exmo. Sr. presidente da província de São Paulo pela Comissão Central de Estatística. São Paulo: Leroy King Bookwalter, 1888.

Relatório apresentado pelo excelentíssimo Senhor Dezembargador Francisco Diogo Pereira de Vasconcellos, presidente da província de São Paulo. São Paulo: Typografia Dous de Dezembro, 1857.

Relatório com que o exmo. Sr. Conselheiro Francisco Xavier Pinto Lima, passou a administração da província ao exmo. Sr. Dr. João Theodoro Xavier, presidente da mesma. São Paulo: Typographia Americana, 1872.

Relatório com que o exmo. Sr. Dr. Sebastião José Pereira passou a administração da província ao 5°. Vice-Presidente Monsenhor Joaquim Manoel Gonçalves de Andrade. São Paulo: Typographia do Diario, 1878.

Relatório da comissão encarregada de estudar a difusão applicada a cana de assucar, apresentado ao exmo. Sr. Conselheiro Rodrigo Augusto da Silva, ministro e secretario de estado dos negocios da agricultura. Rio de Janeiro: Imprensa Nacional, 1887.

Relatório do anno de 1900, apresentado em 13 de janeiro de 1902 ao cidadão Dr. Bento Pereira Bueno, secretaria de estado dos negócios do Interior e da Justiça, pelo Dr. Antonio de Toledo Piza, diretor da repartição de estatística e arquivo do estado de São Paulo. São Paulo: Type do Diario Official, 1902.

Relatório que por ocasião da abertura da assemblea legislativa provincial de S. Paulo no dia 3 de fevereiro de 1864 apresentou o ilmo. e exmo. Sr. Conselheiro Doutor Vicente Pires da Motta, presidente da mesma província. São Paulo: Typographia Imparcial, 1864.

Saraiva, José Antonio. "Quadro estatístico de alguns estabelecimentos rurais da província de São Paulo (1855)." In *Documentos com que ilustríssimo e excelentíssimo Senhor Dr. José Antonio Saraiva, presidente da província de São Paulo, instruiu o relatório da Abertura da assembléa legislativa provincial no dia 15 de fevereiro de 1855.* São Paulo: Antonio Louzada Antunes, 1855.

———. *Relatório apresentado à assembleia geral legislativa na primeira sessão da décima oitava legislatura, pelo ministro e secretário da agricultura, comércio e obras públicas.* Rio de Janeiro: Typografia Nacional, 1882.

Secretaria da Agricultura, Industria e Commercia. *Estatística industrial do estado de S. Paulo, ano de 1932.* São Paulo: Garraux, 1934. https://archive.org/stream/estatisticaindus1932#page/n5/mode/2up.

———. *Estatistica industrial do estado de S. Paulo, anno de 1934*. São Paulo: Siqueira, 1936. https://archive.org/details/estatisticaindus1934.

———. *A immigração e as condicões do trabalho em São Paulo*. São Paulo: Secretaria da Agricultura, Commércio e Obras Públicas, 1915.

Secretaria da Fazenda do Estado de São Paulo. *Código de impostos e taxas*. São Paulo: Est. Graphico Cruzeiro do Sul, 1937. http://produtos.seade.gov.br/produtos/bibliotecadigital/view/singlepage/index.php?pubcod=10011612&parte=1.

———. *Contas do exercício*. São Paulo: Secretaria da Fazenda, various years. http://produtos.seade.gov.br/produtos/bibliotecadigital.

A secretaria da fazenda do estado de São Paulo: Raízes e trajetória, São Paulo. São Paulo: Governo do Estado de São Paulo, 2000.

Superintendência Serviços do Café. *Anuário de café, 1952*. São Paulo: Secretaria de Fazenda do Estado de São Paulo, 1953.

United Nations. *Model Life Tables for Developing Countries*. New York: United Nations, 1982. http://www.un.org/esa/population/publications/Model_Life_Tables/Model_Life_Tables.htm.

Secondary Sources

Abreu, Marcelo de Paiva. "British Business in Brazil: Maturity and Demise (1850–1950)." *Revista Brasileira de Economia* 54, no. 4 (2000): 383–413.

———, ed. *A ordem do progresso: Cem anos de política econômica republicana, 1889–1989*. Rio de Janeiro: Campus, 1990.

Abreu, Marcelo de Paiva, and Luiz Aranha Correa do Lago. "A economia brasileira no império, 1822–1889." Pontifícia Universidade Católica Texto para Discussão no. 584, n.d.

Aguirre, Marcos Roberto de Lima. "A proposta do federalismo no Brasil: O debate entre a centralização e a descentralização no século XIX." Master's thesis, Universidade Federal do Rio Grande do Sul, Porto Alegre, 2012.

Albion, Robert G. "Capital Movement and Transportation: British Shipping and Latin America, 1806–1914." *Journal of Economic History* 11, no. 4 (1951): 361–374.

Almeida, Marta de, and Maria Amélia M. Dantes. "O serviço sanitário de São Paulo, a saúde pública e a microbíología." In *Espaços da ciência no Brasil: 1800–1930*, edited by Maria Amélia M. Dantes, 135–155. Rio de Janeiro: Fiocruz, 2001.

Alvim, Zuleka. *Brava gente! Os italianos em São Paulo, 1870–1920*. São Paulo: Brasiliense, 1986.

Amed, Fernando José, and Plínio José Labriola de Campos Negreiros. *História dos tributos no Brasil*. São Paulo: Edições SINAFRESP, 2000.

Andrews, George Reid. *Blacks and Whites in São Paulo, Brazil, 1888–1988.* Madison: University of Wisconsin Press, 1991.
Antonacci, Maria Antonieta Martines. "Institucionalizar ciência e tecnologia: Em torno da fundação do IDORT (São Paulo, 1918/1931)." *Revista Brasileira de História* 7, no. 14 (1987): 59–78.
Arantes, Mario. "Forma da instrução." *O Estado de São Paulo*, September 21, 1892. http://acervo.estadao.com.br/pagina/#!/18920921-5248-nac-0001-999-1-not.
Araujo, Paulo Fernando Cidade de, G. E. Schuh, Alexandre Lahóz Mendonça de Barros, Ricardo Shirota, and Alexandre Chibebe Nocolella. *Contribuição da FAPESP à agricultura do estado de São Paulo.* São Paulo: FAPESP, 2002.
———. *O crescimento da agricultura paulista e as instituições de ensino, pesquisa e extensão numa perspectiva de longo prazo.* São Paulo: FAPESP, 2002.
Araujo Filho, José Ribeiro de. *Santos, o porto do cafe.* Rio de Janeiro: Fundação IBGE, 1969.
Arriaga, Eduardo E. *New Life Tables for Latin American Populations in the Nineteenth and Twentieth Centuries.* Berkeley: University of California, 1968.
Arruda, José Jobson de Andrade. "As barreiras como fontes primárias para a história da província de S. Paulo no século XIX (1835–1892)." In *Memória da I semana de história,* 17–24. Franca, Brazil: Editora UNESP, 1979.
———. "As barreiras de Cubatão, Caraguatatuba, Ubatuba e Cunha: Limites e possibilidades da documentação." *Anais do Museu Paulista* 28 (1977–1978): 81–100.
Avrichir, André Schifnagel. *Federalismo e reforma bancária: A experiência internacional na análise de Rui Barbosa.* Paper presented at the IV Conferência Internacional de História Econômica and VI Encontro de Pós-Graduação em História Econômica, São Paulo, 2012. https://uspdigital.usp.br/siicusp/cdOnlineTrabalhoVisualizarResumo?numeroInscricaoTrabalho=1122&numeroEdicao=19.
Azevedo, João Lúcio de. "Agricultura Luiz de Queiroz: Sua inclusão na USP e sua contribuição para a pesquisa em ciências agrárias." *Revista USP,* no. 60 (2004): 14–39.
———. "A pesquisa agropecuária." In *Ciência e tecnologia no Brasil: Uma nova política para um mundo global,* edited by Simon Schwartzman, 287–320. Rio de Janeiro: Fundação Getúlio Vargas, 1966.
Azevedo, José Eduardo. "Polícia militar de São Paulo: Elementos para a construção de uma cartografia social da questão policial no Brasil." *Revista do Laboratório de Estudos da Violência e Segurança,* no. 1 (2008): 11–24. http://www2.marilia.unesp.br/revistas/index.php/levs/article/viewFile/759/661.
Babilônia, Paulo Álvares. "A advocacia pública brasileira no período colonial e no império: Evolução histórica." *Jus*, December 2010. https://jus.com

.br/artigos/18112/a-advocacia-publica-brasileira-no-periodo-colonial-e-no-imperio-evolucao-historica.

Bacha, Edmar. *Belíndia 2.0: Fábulas e ensaios sobre o país dos contrastes.* Rio de Janeiro: Editora José Olympio, 2015.

Bacha, Edmar, and Robert Greenhill, eds. *150 anos de café.* São Paulo: Marcelino Martins and Johnston Exportadores, 1992.

Baeninger, Rossana, and Maria Sílvia Casagrande Beozzo Bassanezi. "São Paulo: Transição demografia e migrações." In *História do estado de São Paulo*, vol. 2, edited by Nilo Odalia and João Ricardo de Castro Caldeira. São Paulo: UNESP, 2010.

Barata, Rita Barradas. "Cem anos de endemias e epidemias," *Ciência e Saúde Coletiva* 5, no. 2 (2000): 333–345.

Barman, Roderick J. *Brazil: The Forging of a Nation.* Stanford, CA: Stanford University Press, 1988.

Barreto, Patrícia R. C. "Sociedade Auxiliadora da Indústria Nacional: O templo carioca de Palas Atena." PhD diss., Universidade Federal do Rio de Janeiro, Rio de Janeiro, 2009.

Bassanezi, Maria Silvia C. Beozzo, ed. *São Paulo do passado: Dados demográficos.* Vol. 2, *1854.* Campinas, Brazil: Universidade Estadual de Campinas and Núcleo de Estudos de População, 1998. http://www.nepo.unicamp.br/publicacoes/censos/1854.pdf.

———. *São Paulo do passado: Dados demográficos.* Vol. 3, *1872.* Campinas, Brazil: Universidade Estadual de Campinas and Núcleo de Estudos de População, 1998. http://www.nepo.unicamp.br/publicacoes/censos/1872.pdf.

———. *São Paulo do passado: Dados demográficos.* Vol. 5, *1890.* Campinas, Brazil: Universidade Estadual de Campinas and Núcleo de Estudos de População, 1998. http://www.nepo.unicamp.br/publicacoes/censos/1890.pdf.

———. *São Paulo do passado: Dados demográficos.* Vol. 6, *1920.* Campinas, Brazil: Universidade Estadual de Campinas and Núcleo de Estudos de População, 1999. http://www.nepo.unicamp.br/publicacoes/censos/1920.pdf.

———. *São Paulo do passado: Dados demográficos.* Vol. 7, *Capital.* Campinas, Brazil: Universidade Estadual de Campinas and Núcleo de Estudos de População, 2000. http://www.nepo.unicamp.br/publicacoes/censos/capital.pdf.

Basseto, Sylvia. "Política de mão-de-obra na economia cafeeira do Oeste Paulista (periodo de transição)." PhD diss., Universidade de São Paulo, 1982.

Batista, Eraldo Leme. "IDORT—um instituto educacional burguês por excelência: Análise das décadas de 1930 e 1940 no Brasil." 2014. http://www.ronaldofrutuozo.com.br/seminariotrabalho2014/img/GT7/IDORT.pdf.

Bello, José Maria. *História da república.* São Paulo, Nacional, 1976.

Benchimol, Jaime Larry, and Luiz Antonio Teixeira. *Cobras, lagartos e outros bichos: Uma história comparada dos institutos Oswaldo Cruz e Butantan.* Rio de Janeiro: Editora UFRJ, 1993.

Benevides, Paulo. "A evolução constitucional do Brasil." *Estudos Avançados* 14, no. 40 (2000): 155–176.

Benevides, Paulo, and Paes de Andrade. *História constitucional do Brasil.* São Paulo: OAB, 2008.

Bermann, Célio. "Impasses and Controversies of Hydroelectricity." *Estudos Avançados* 21, no. 59 (2007): 139–153.

Berthold, Victor M. *History of the Telephone and Telegraph in Brazil, 1851–1921.* New York, 1922. https://archive.org/details/historytelephone00bertrich.

Beskow, Paulo Roberto. "O crédito rural público numa economia em transformação: Estudo histórico e avaliação econômica das atividades de financiamento agropecuário da CREAI/BB, de 1937 a 1965." 2 vols. PhD diss., Universidade Estadual de Campinas, 1994.

Bignon, Vincent, Rui Esteves, and Alfonso Herranz-Loncán. "Big Push or Big Grab? Railways, Government Activism, and Export Growth in Latin America, 1865–1913." *Economic History Review* 68, no. 4 (2015): 1277–1305.

Blount, John Allen, III. "A administração da saúde pública no estado de São Paulo: O serviço sanitário, 1892–1918." *Revista Administração de Empresas* 12, no. 4 (1972): 40–48.

———. "The Public Health Movement in São Paulo, Brazil: A History of the Sanitary Service, 1892–1918." PhD diss., Tulane University, 1971.

Bouças, Valentim F. *Finanças do Brasil.* Vol. 10, *História da dívida externa estadual e municipal.* Rio de Janeiro: Secretaria do Conselho Técnico de Economia e Finanças do Ministério da Fazenda, 1942.

———. *Finanças do Brasil, união, estados e municipalidades: Dívida externa; Quadros estatísticos e gráficos.* Vol. 3. Rio de Janeiro: Imprensa Oficial, Ministério da Fazenda, 1934.

Boyce, Gordon. *Information, Mediation, and Institutional Development: The Rise of Large-Scale Enterprise in British Shipping, 1870–1919.* Manchester, UK: Manchester University Press, 1995.

Britto, Ana Lucia. "Redes de infra-estrutura na cidade: Uma revisão dos conceitos e concepções de saneamento." Paper presented at IX Seminário de História da Cidade e do Urbanismo, São Paulo, September 4–6, 2006.

Buchalla, Cássia Maria, Eliseu Alves Waldman, and Ruy Laurenti. "A mortalidade por doenças infecciosas no início e no final do século XX no Município de São Paulo." *Revista Brasileira de Epidemiologia* 6, no. 4 (2003): 335–344.

Caiado, Aurílio Sérgio Costa. "Reestruturação produtiva e localização industrial: A dinâmica industrial na RMSP entre 1985 e 2000." Paper presented at ANPEC XXX Encontro Nacional de Economia, Rio de Janeiro, 2002.

Camargo, Jose Francisco de. *Crescimento da população no estado de São Paulo e seus aspectos econômicos.* 2 vols. São Paulo: Instituto de Pesquisas Econômicas, 1981.

Camargo, Luís Soares de. "Viver e morrer em São Paulo: A vida, as doenças e a morte na cidade do século XIX." PhD diss., Pontifícia Universidade Católica, São Paulo, 2007.

Campos, Bruno Nascimento. "Tropas de aço: Os caminhos de ferro no sul de minas (1875–1902)." Master's thesis, Universidade Federal de São João del Rei, 2012.

Canabrava, Alice P. *O algodão em São Paulo, 1861–1875.* São Paulo: T. A. Queiróz, 1984.

———. "Uma fazenda-modelo na província de São Paulo (1863)." In *Anais do IX Simpósio da ANPUH: O Homem e a Técnica,* vol. 4, 1173–1219. São Paulo: ANPUH, 1979.

———. "A grande lavoura." In *História geral da civilização brasileira,* vol. 2, *Brasil monárquico,* edited by Sérgio Buarque de Holanda, 85–137. São Paulo: Difusão Europeia do Livro, 1971.

———. "A repartição da terra na Capitania de São Paulo, 1818." *Estudos Econômicos* 2, no. 6 (1972): 77–129.

Cano, Wilson. *Raízes da concentração industrial em São Paulo.* Rio de Janeiro: Difusão Europeia do Livro, 1977.

Cardoso, Fernando Henrique. "Condições sociais da industrialização: O caso de São Paulo." *Revista Brasiliense,* no. 28 (1960): 31–46.

———. "Dos governos militares a Prudente–Campos Sales." In *História geral da civilização Brasileira,* vol. 1, bk. 3, edited by Sérgio Buarque de Holanda, 15–50. São Paulo: Difusão Europeia do Livro, 1971.

———. *Mudanças sociais na América Latina.* São Paulo: Difusão Européia do Livro, 1969.

Carli, Gileno de. *O açucar na formação econômica do Brasil.* Rio de Janeiro: Instituto do Açúcar e do Álcool, 1937.

———. *Genese e evolução da indústria açucareira de São Paulo.* Rio de Janeiro: Irmãos Pongetti, 1943.

———. *Geografia econômica e social da canna de açúcar no Brasil.* Rio de Janeiro: Brasil Açucareiro, 1938.

Carone, Edgard. *A segunda república.* São Paulo: Difusão Européia do Livro, 1973.

Carreira, Liberato de Castro. *História financeira e orçamentária do império do Brasil.* 2 vols. 1889. Reprint, Brasília: Fundação Casa de Rui Barbosa, 1980.

Carvalho, Antonio Carlos Duarte de. "Saúde pública: Centralização, autoritarismo e expansão dos serviços—São Paulo nas décadas de 1930 e 1940." *Revista de História Regional* 10, no. 1 (2005): 9–25.

Carvalho, José Alberto Magno de. "Crescimento populacional e estrutura demográfica no Brasil." Universidade Federal de Minas Gerais/Cedeplar Texto para Discussão no. 227, February 2004. http://www.cedeplar.ufmg.br/pesquisas/td/TD%20227.pdf.

———. "Evolução demográfica recente no Brasil." *Pesquisa e Planejamento Econômico* 10, no. 2 (1980): 527–553.

Carvalho, José Murilo de. *Os bestializados: O Rio de Janeiro e a república que não foi*. Rio de Janeiro: Civilização Brasileira, 1987.

———. *A construção da ordem: A elite política imperial*. Rio de Janeiro: Civilização Brasileira, 2003.

Castillo, Ricardo. "Transporte e logística de granéis sólidos agrícolas: Componentes estruturais do novo sistema de movimientos do território brasileiro." *Investigaciones Geográficas*, no. 55 (2004): 79–96.

Cechin, José. "A construção e operação das ferrovias no Brasil do século XIX." Master's thesis, Universidade Estadual de Campinas, 1978.

CELADE. *Observatorio demográfico de América Latina*. Vol. 8, *Urbanización en prespectiva* Santiago, Chile: United Nations, 2009.

Chamma, Renato Moraes. "Uma análise da evolução da produção, área, produtividade e empregos nas tradicionais atividades agrícolas no estado de São Paulo." Master's thesis, Universidade de São Paulo, Ribeirão Preto, 2009.

Coale, Ansley J., Paul Demeny, and Barbara Vaughan. *Regional Model Life Tables and Stable Populations: Studies in Population*. New York: Academic Press, 1983.

Codato, Adriano Nero. "Elites e instituições no Brasil: Uma análise contextual do Estado Novo." PhD diss., Universidade Estadual de Campinas, 2008.

———. "A sociologia política brasileira em análise: Quatro visões sobre o funcionamento administrativo do Estado Novo." *Revista de Sociologia e Política* 19, no. 40 (2011): 273–288.

Comisión Económica para América Latina y el Caribe. *Anuario estadístico de América Latina y el Caribe, 2002*. Santiago, Chile: United Nations, 2003.

———. *Anuario estadístico de América Latina y el Caribe, 2003*. Santiago, Chile: United Nations, 2004.

———. *Anuario estadístico de América Latina y el Caribe, 2009*. Santiago, Chile: United Nations, 2010.

Comissão de Recenseamento da Colônia Japonesa, São Paulo. *The Japanese Immigrant in Brazil*. Tokyo: University of Tokyo Press, 1964.

Conceição, Marcelo Rodrigues. "A educação nas ações e proposições do Instituto da Organização Racional do Trabalho (1932–1946)." Master's thesis, Pontifícia Universidade Católica, São Paulo, 2005.

———. "A educação para o Instituto de Organização Racional do Trabalho (1932–1946)." http://www.sbhe.org.br/novo/congressos/cbhe4/individuais-coautorais/eixo06/Marcelo%20Rodrigues%20Conceicao%20-%20Texto.pdf (accessed May 9, 2017).

———. "Historiografia do ensino profissional paulista: As marcas do modo de produção." PhD diss., Pontifícia Universidade Católica, São Paulo, 2010.

Corrêa, Carlos Humberto P. "A presidência de província no império." Paper presented at XXII Simpósio Nacional de História, João Pessoa, Brazil, 2003.

Correia, Telma de Barros. "O IDORT e a Taylorização da moradia no Brasil (1932–1950)." Paper presented at VII Seminário de História da Cidade e do Urbanismo, Salvador, Brazil, 2002.

Correia, Telma de Barros, and Caliane Christie Oliveira de Almeida. "Habitação econômica no Brasil: O IDORT e sua revista (1932–1960)." *Revista de Pesquisa em Arquitetura e Urbanismo*, no. 1 (2013): 35–49.

Costa, Fernando Nogueira da. "Banco do estado: O Caso Banespa." PhD diss., Universidade Estadual de Campinas, 1988.

Costa, Hernani Maia. "As barreiras de São Paulo: Estudos históricos das barreiras paulistas no século XIX." Master's thesis, Universidade de São Paulo, 1984.

Costa, Iraci del Nero da. "Pesos e medidas no período colonial Brasileiro: Denominações e relações." http://www.ipeadata.gov.br/doc/Pesos%20e%20medidas%20no%20periodo%20colonial%20brasileiro.pdf (accessed May 1, 2017).

Costa, Luiz Augusto Maia. "A cartografia elaborada pela Comissão Geográfica e Geológica de São Paulo no início do Século XX: O componente norte americano do debate científico entre Orville Derby e os intelectuais paulista de então." Paper presented at IV Simpósio Luso Brasileiro de Cartografia Histórica, Porto, Portugal, November 9–12, 2011. http://eventos.letras.up.pt/ivslbch/resumos/97.pdf.

Costa, Sérgio Rodrigues, and Miguel Garcia Bueno. *A saga do algodão: Das primeiras lavouras à ação na OMC*. Rio de Janeiro: Associação Brasileira dos Produtores de Algodão/Insight Engenharia, 2004.

"Cultura e comercio do café: O enviado do governo da Hollanda, S. van-Delden Laerne." *Correio Paulistano*, January 18, 1884, http://www.arquivoestado.sp.gov.br/upload/jornais/BR_APESP_CPNO_18840118.pdf.

Cutler, David, Angus Deaton, and Adriana Lleras-Muney. "The Determinants of Mortality." *Journal of Economic Perspectives* 20, no. 3 (2006): 97–120.

Cutler, David M., and Grant Miller. "The Role of Public Health Improvements in Health Advances: The Twentieth-Century United States." *Demography* 42, no. 1 (2005): 1–22.

Danieli, Maria Isabel Basilisco Célia. "Economia mercantil de abastecimento e rede tributária: São Paulo, séculos XVIII e XIX." PhD diss., Universidade Estadual de Campinas, 2006.

Davatz, Thomaz. *Memória de um colono no Brasil (1850)*. Belo Horizonte, Brazil: Itatiaia/Editora USP, 1980.

Daveza, Guilherme. "Política tributária no período imperial." In *História geral da civilização brasileira*, vol. 2, bk. 4, edited by Sérgio Buarque de Holanda, 60–84. São Paulo: Difusão Europeia do Livro, 1971.

Dean, Warren. *The Industrialization of São Paulo*. Austin: University of Texas Press, 1969.

———. *Rio Claro: A Brazilian Plantation System, 1820–1920*. Stanford, CA: Stanford University Press, 1976.

Deaton, Angus. "The Great Escape: A Review of Robert Fogel's 'The Escape from Hunger and Premature Death, 1700–2100.'" *Journal of Economic Literature* 44, no. 1 (2006): 106–114.

Delfim Netto, Antonio. *O problema do café no Brasil*. São Paulo: Instituto de Pesquisas Econômicas, USP, 1981.

Dias, José Luiz Pereira da Costa, and José Roberto Cardoso. "Os 120 anos da escola politécnica de São Paulo." *Engenharia* 618 (2014): 136–141. http://sites.poli.usp.br/org/informativos/linksite/artengenhariaeducacao618.pdf.

Dinius, Oliver J. *Brazil's Steel City: Developmentalism, Strategic Power, and Industrial Relations in Volta Redonda, 1941–1964*. Stanford, CA: Stanford University Press, 2011.

Diniz, Adalton Franciozo. "Centralização política e concentração de riqueza: As finanças do império brasileiro no período 1830 a 1889." *História e Economia Revista Interdisciplinar* 1, no. 1 (2005): 47–65.

———. "As finanças públicas paulista no século XIX." In *História do estado de São Paulo*, vol. 1, edited by Nilo Odalia and João Ricardo de Castro Caldeira. São Paulo: Editora UNESP, 2010.

Dolhdikoff, Miriam. "Administração pública e crescimento econômico em São Paulo no século XIX." *D. O. Leitura*, January–February 2004, pp. 28–37. http://docplayer.com.br/16691094-Administracao-publica-e-crescimento-economico-em-sao-paulo-no-seculo-xix-miriam-dolhnikoff.html.

———. "O lugar das elites regionais." *Revista USP*, no. 58 (2003): 116–133.

Donato, Hernâni. *História da revolução constitucionalista de 1932: Comenorando os 70 anos do evento*. São Paulo: Ibrasa, 2002.

Draibe, Sonia. *Rumos e metamorfoses: Estado e industrialização no Brasil, 1930–1960*. Rio de Janeiro: Paz e Terra, 1985.

Duarte Neto, José. "Rigidez e estabilidade constitucional: Estudo da organização constituição Brasileira." PhD diss., Universidade de São Paulo, 2009.

Eisenberg, Peter. *The Sugar Industry in Pernambuco: Modernization Without Change, 1840–1910.* Berkeley: University of California Press, 1974.

Elias, Ibrahim João, and Nelson H. Nozoe. *Secretaria de estado dos negócios da fazenda do estado de São Paulo: Evolução institucional.* São Paulo: Governo do Estado de São Paulo, 1978.

Escames, Edson Fernando. "Usina parque: Aproveitamento e valorização do patrimônio energético, ambiental e histórico da Usina Hidrelétrica Henry Borden." Master's thesis, Universidade Federal ABC, Santo André, 2011.

Faleiros, Rogério Naques. *Fronteiras do café.* Bauru, Brazil: EDUSC, 2010.

Faoro, Raymundo. *Os donos do poder: Formação do patronato politico brasileiro.* 2 vols. Porto Alegre: Globo/EDUSP, 1975.

Fausto, Boris, ed. *Getúlio Vargas.* 3 vols. São Paulo: Companhia Das Letras, 2006–2014.

———. *A revolução de 1930.* São Paulo: Brasiliense, 1975.

Fernandes, Guilherme Vilella. "Tributação e escravidão: O imposto da meia siza sobre o comércio de escravos na província de São Paulo (1809–1850)." *Almanack Brasiliense,* no. 2 (2005): 102–113.

Ferranti, David de, Guillermo E. Perry, Francisco H. G. Ferreira, Michael Walton, and D. Coday. *Inequality in Latin America: Breaking with History?* Washington, DC: World Bank, 2004.

Ferraro, M. R. *A modernização da agricultura e da silvicultura paulista (início do século XX).* Anápolis, Brazil: Universidade Estadual de Goiás, 2010.

Ferraro, M. R., T. C. Magro, and D. F. da Silva Filho. "A gênese da modernização da agricultura em São Paulo." *Revista Ciências Agrárias,* no. 47 (2007): 149–161.

Ferreira, Fabio Vizeu. "Management no Brasil em perspectiva histórica: O projeto do IDORT nas décadas de 1930 e 1940." PhD diss., Escola de Administração de Empresas de São Paulo da Fundação Getúlio Vargas, São Paulo, 2008.

Figueiredo, L. T. M. "A febre amarela na região de Ribeirão Preto durante a virada do século XIX: Importância científica e repercussões econômicas." *Revista da Sociedade Brasileira de Medicina Tropical* 29, no. 1 (1996): 63–76.

Fishlow, Albert. "Origens e consequências da substituição de importações no Brasil." *Estudos Econômicos* 2, no. 6 (1972): 7–75.

Fogel, Robert W. *The Escape from Hunger and Premature Death, 1700–2100: Europe, America, and the Third World.* New York: Cambridge University Press, 2004.

Font, Maurício A. *Coffee and Transformation in São Paulo, Brazil.* Lanham, MD: Lexington Books, 2010.

———. "Planters and the State: The Hegemony in São Paulo, Brazil, 1889–1930." PhD diss., University of Michigan, 1983.

Forrester, Robert E. *British Mail Steamers to South America, 1851–1965: A History of the Royal Mail Steam Packet Company and Royal Mail Lines*. Farnham, UK: Ashgate, 2014.

Franco, Maria Apparecida. "O comissário de café no Porto de Santos: 1870–1920." Master's thesis, Universidade de São Paulo, 1980.

French, John D. *The Brazilian Workers' ABC: Class Conflict and Alliances in Modern São Paulo*. Chapel Hill: University of North Carolina, 1992.

Furtado, Celso. *Formação econômica do Brasil*. São Paulo: Nacional, 1968.

Gama, Ruy. *Engenho e tecnologia*. São Paulo: Duas Cidades, 1979.

Gasques, José Garcia, Eliana Teles Bastos, and Mirian R. Piedade Bacchi. "Produtividade e fontes de crescimento da agricultura brasileira." *Políticas de incentivo à inovação tecnológica no Brasil*, edited by João Alberto de Neg and Luis Claudio Kubota, 435–459. Brasília: IPEA, 2008.

Gasques, José Garcia, Eliana Teles Bastos, Mirian Rumenos Piedade Bacchi, and Constanza Valdes. "Produtividade total dos fatores e transformações da agricultura brasileira: Análise dos dados dos censos agropecuários." In *A agricultura brasileira: Desempenho, desafios e perspectivas*, edited by José Garcia Gasques, José Eustáquio Ribeiro Vieira Filho, and Zander Navarro, 19–44. Brasília: IPEA, 2010.

Githay, Maria Lúcia C. *Ventos do mar*. São Paulo: Editora UNESP, 1992.

Goldenberg, Robert L., Elizabeth M. McClure, Zulfiqar A. Bhutta, José M. Belizán, Uma M. Reddy, Craig E. Rubens, Hillary Mabeya, Vicki Flenady, and Gary L. Darmstadt. "Stillbirths: The Vision for 2020." *The Lancet* 377 (May 2011): 1798–1805.

Goldsmith, Raymond W. *Brasil, 1850–1984: Desenvolvimento financeiro sob um século de inflação*. São Paulo: Harper and Row do Brasil, 1986.

Gomes, Angêla M.de Castro. "Confronto e compromisso no processo de constitucionalização (1930–1935)." In *História geral da civilização brasileira: O Brasil repúblicano*, vol. 3, edited by Boris Fausto and Sérgio B. Holanda, 7–77. São Paulo: Difusão Europeia do Livro, 1981.

Gonçalves, Alcindo, and Luiz Antonio de Paula. *O grande porto: A modernização no Porto de Santos*. Santos: Realejo, 2008.

Gonçalves, José Sidnei. "A agricultura paulista: A ação estatal na construção da modernidade." *São Paulo em Perspectiva* 7, no. 3 (1993): 100–106.

Goulart, José Alípio. *Tropas e tropeiros na formação do Brasil*. Rio de Janeiro: Conquista, 1961.

Goularti Filho, Alcides. "Abertura da navegação de cabotagem brasileira no século XIX." *Ensaios FEE* 32, no. 2 (2011): 409–434.

———. "Companhia de Navegação Lloyd Brasileiro: Uma trajetória de déficit financeiro e desenvolvimento econômico." *História Econômica e História de Empresas* 12, no. 2 (2009): 5–36.

Gouvêa, Maria de Fátima Silva. *O império das províncias, Rio de Janeiro, 1822–1889*. Rio de Janeiro: Civilização Brasileira, 2008.

Graham, Richard. *Britain and the Onset of Modernization in Brazil, 1850–1914.* Cambridge: Cambridge University Press, 1968.

Greenhill, Robert. "E. Johnston: 150 Anos em Café." In *150 anos de café*, edited by Edmar Bacha and Robert Greenhill, 137–280. São Paulo: Marcelino Martins and Johnston Exportadores, 1992.

———. "Shipping, 1850–1914." In *Business Imperialism, 1840–1930: An Inquiry Based on British Experience in Latin America*, edited by D. C. M. Platt, 119–155. Oxford: Clarendon Press, 1977.

Gregório, Vitor Marcos. "Dividindo as províncias do império: A emancipação do Amazonas e do Paraná e o sistema representativo na construção do estado nacional brasileiro (1826–1854)." PhD diss., Universidade de São Paulo, 2012.

Gualtieri, Regina C. "Instituto Butantã e a saúde pública (São Paulo: 1901–1927)." Master's thesis, Universidade de São Paulo, 1994.

Guilhaumon, J. Régis, ed. *Pesquisando São Paulo: 110 anos de criação da Comissão Geográfica e Geológica.* São Paulo: Instituto Geológico/SMA; Museu Paulista, Instituto Florestal/SMA, 1996.

Haber, Stephen H. "Industrial Concentration and the Capital Markets: A Comparative Study of Brazil, Mexico, and the United States, 1830–1930." *Journal of Economic History* 51, no. 3 (1991): 559–580.

"Hamburg-Südamerikanische Dampfschifffahrtsgesellschaft." http://www.schiffe-maxim.de/HSDG.htm (accessed May 17, 2017).

Hanley, Anne G. "A Failure to Deliver: Municipal Poverty and the Provision of Public Services in Imperial São Paulo, Brazil 1822–1889." *Journal of Urban History* 39, no. 3 (2012): 513–535.

———. *Native Capital: Financial Institutions and Economic Development in São Paulo, Brazil, 1850–1920.* Stanford, CA: Stanford University Press, 2005.

Hausman, William J., Peter Hertner, and Mira Wilkins. *Global Electrification: Multinational Enterprise and International Finance in the History of Light and Power, 1878–2007.* New York: Cambridge University Press, 2008.

Hilton, Stanley E. "Ação Integralista Brasileira: Fascism in Brazil, 1932–1938." *Luso-Brazilian Review* 9, no. 2 (1972): 3–29.

———. *A guerra civil brasileira: História da revolução constitucionalista de 1932.* Rio de Janeiro: Nova Fronteira, 1982.

Hochman, Gilberto. "Reforma, instituições e políticas de saúde no Brasil (1930–1945)." *Educar*, no. 25 (2005): 127–141.

Holloway, Thomas H. *Immigrants on the Land: Coffee and Society in São Paulo, 1886–1934.* Chapel Hill: University of North Carolina Press, 1980.

Holten, Birgitte. "Why Brazil Did Not Develop a Merchant Marine: Brazilian Shipping and the World in the 19th Century." *História Econômica e História de Empresas* 6, no. 2 (2003): 7–32.

Homem de Melo, Fernando B. "Produtividade da terra: Os casos do milho e algodão no estado de São Paulo." In *Estudos sobre a modernização da agricultura brasileira*, edited by José Roberto Mendonça de Barros and Douglas Hume Graham, 57–106. São Paulo: Instituto de Pesquisas Econômicas, 1977.

Huddle, Donald L. "Balança de pagamentos e controle de câmbio no Brasil: Diretrizes políticas e história, 1946–1954." *Revista Brasileira de Economia* 18, no. 1 (1964): 5–40.

Iannone, Roberto Antonio. "Evolução do setor eléctrico paulista." PhD diss., Universidade de São Paulo, 2006.

Iglésias, Francisco. "Política econômica do estado de Minas Gerais (1890–1930)." Paper presented at V Seminário de Estudos Mineiros: A República Velha em Minas, Belo Horizonte, Brazil, 1982.

———. *Política econômica do governo provincial mineiro (1835–1889)*. Rio de Janeiro: INL, 1958.

Infantosi, Ana Maria. *A escola na República Velha*. São Paulo: Edec, 1983.

Instituto Brasileiro de Geografia e Estatística. "Sinopse do censo demográfico, 2010," table 1.6. 2010. http://www.censo2010.ibge.gov.br/sinopse/index.php?dados=6&uf=0.

———. "Tabela 01: Produto interno bruto das grandes regiões e unidades da federação, 2002–2010." 2010. http://www.ibge.gov.br/home/estatistica/economia/contasregionais/2010/default_xls_2002_2010_zip.shtm.

Instituto de Pesquisas Tecnológicas do Estado de São Paulo. *IPT: 90 anos de tecnologia*. São Paulo: Instituto de Pesquisas Tecnológicas, 1989.

Iyda, Massako. *Cem anos de saúde pública: A cidadania negada*. São Paulo: Editora UNESP, 1994.

Jourdan, Marcelo Mollica. "A Light, investimentos estrangeiros no Brasil: Uma luz sobre o ciclo privado-público-privado em 80 anos, pela análise de taxa de retorno." Master's thesis, Fundação Getúlio Vargas, Rio de Janeiro, 2006.

Karepovs, Dainis. *São Paulo: A imperial cidade e a assembleia legislativa provincial*. São Paulo: Assembleia Legislativa, Divisão de Arquivo Histórico, 2006.

Kindleberger, Charles P. "Germany's Overtaking of England, 1806–1914." *Review of World Economics* 111, no. 2 (1975): 253–281.

Klein, Herbert S. *The Atlantic Slave Trade*. 2nd ed. Cambridge: Cambridge University Press, 2010.

———. *A imigração espanhola no Brasil*. São Paulo: Editora Sumaré/IDESP-FAPESP, 1994.

———. "The Internal Slave Trade in Nineteenth Century Brazil." *Hispanic American Historical Review* 51 (1971): 567–585.

———. *A Population History of the United States*. 2nd ed. Cambridge: Cambridge University Press, 2012.

———. "The Social and Economic Integration of Portuguese Immigrants in Brazil in the Late Nineteenth and Twentieth Centuries." *Journal of Latin American Studies* 23, no. 2 (1991): 309–337.

———. "The Supply of Mules to Central Brazil: The Sorocaba Market, 1825–1880." *Agricultural History* 64, no. 4 (1990): 1–25.

Klein, Herbert S., and Francisco Vidal Luna. *Slavery in Brazil.* New York: Cambridge University Press, 2009.

Kugelmas, Eduardo. "A difícil hegemonia." PhD diss., Universidade de São Paulo, 1986.

Lacaz, Carlos S., and Berta R. Mazieri. *A faculdade de medicina e a USP.* São Paulo: Editora USP, 1995.

Laerne, C. F. Van Delden. *Brazil and Java: Report on Coffee-Culture in America, Asia, and Africa.* The Hague: Martinus Nijhoff, 1885.

Lamas, Fernando Gaudereto, and Luís Eduardo do Oliveira. "As vicissitudes da escravidão e da imigração em Minas Gerais: A companhia união e indústria, os escravos e os alemães (1852–1879)." Paper presented at 3°. Encontro: Escravidão e Liberdade no Brasil Meridional, Maio, Cape Verde, 2007. http://www.escravidaoeliberdade.com.br/site/images/Textos3/fernando%20lamas%20e%20luiz%20eduardo.pdf.

Lamounier, Maria Lucia. "Agricultura e mercado de trabalho: Trabalhadores brasileiros livres nas fazendas de café e na construção de ferrovias em São Paulo, 1850–1890." *Estudos Econômicos* 37, no. 2 (2007): 353–372.

———. "Entre a escravidão e o trabalho livre: Escravos e imigrantes nas obras de construção das ferrovias no Brasil no século XIX." *Revista Economia* 9, no. 4 (2008): 215–245.

———. "The 'Labour Question' in Nineteenth Century Brazil: Railways, Export Agriculture and Labour Scarcity." London School of Economics Working Paper no. 59/00, 2000. http://eprints.lse.ac.uk/22379/1/wp59.pdf.

Lanna, Ana Lúcia Duarte. *Uma cidade na transição: Santos, 1870–1913.* São Paulo: Hucitec-Prefeitura Municipal de Santos, 1996.

Lefevre, Eugênio. *A administração do estado de São Paulo na República Velha.* São Paulo: Typografia Cupolo, 1937.

Leite, Fabio Carvalho. "1891: A construção da matriz politico-institucional da Republica no Brasil." Master's thesis, Pontifícia Universidade Católica, Rio de Janeiro, 2003.

Levine, Robert M. *The Vargas Regime: The Critical Years, 1934–1938.* New York: Columbia University Press, 1970.

Levy, Maria Stella Ferreira. "O papel da migração internacional na evolução da população brasileira (1872 a 1972)." *Revista de Saúde Pública* 8, suppl. (1974): 49–90.

Lima, Cacilda Comassio. "Educação para o trabalho: A escola profissional de Franca (1924–1970)." PhD diss., Universidade Estadual Paulista, Franca, 2007.

Lima, R. C. *Pequena história territorial do Brasil: Sesmarias e terras devolutas*. São Paulo: Secretaria de Estado da Cultura, 1990.

Lopes, Luciana Suarez. "Saldos e sobras: Finanças públicas municipais na primeira metade de oitocentos (província de São Paulo, 1834–1850)." *História e Economia: Revista Interdisciplinar* 10, no. 1 (2012): 29–54.

Lopes, Luciana Suarez, and Anne Gerard Hanley. "Alice in Accounting Land: The Adventure of Two Economic Historians in Accounting Records of the 19th Century." *Revista Contabilidade e Finanças* 25 (September–December 2014): 355–363.

Love, Joseph. *São Paulo in the Brazilian Federation, 1889–1937*. Stanford, CA: Stanford University Press, 1980.

Love, Joseph L., and Bert J. Barickman. "Rulers and Owners: A Brazilian Case Study in Comparative Perspective." *Hispanic American Historical Review* 66, no. 86 (1986): 743–765.

Luna, Francisco Vidal. "A capital financeira do Pais." In *História Econômica da Cidade de São Paulo*, edited by Tamás Szmrecsányi, 328–355. São Paulo: Globo, 2004.

———. *Minas Gerais: Escravos e senhores; Análise da estrutura populacional e econômica de alguns centros mineratórios (1718–1804)*. São Paulo: Instituto de Pesquisas Econômicas, USP, 1981.

———. "Observações sobre os dados de produção apresentados por Müller." *Boletim de História Demográfica* 9, no. 24 (2002): 1–6.

Luna, Francisco Vidal, and Iraci del Nero da Costa. "A estrada e o desenvolvimento econômico: Estrada São Paulo–Santos." In *Anais do IX Simpósio Nacional da Associação dos Professores Universitários de História: O homem e a técnica*, vol. 2, 551–567. São Paulo: ANPUH, 1979.

Luna, Francisco Vidal, and Herbert S. Klein. "African Slavery in the Production of Subsistence Crops: The Case of São Paulo in the Nineteenth Century." In *Slavery in the Development of the Americas*, edited by D. Eltis, F. D. Lewis, and K. L. Sokoloff, 120–149. Cambridge: Cambridge University Press, 2003.

———. "Nota a respeito de medidas para grãos utilizados no período colonial e as dificuldades para sua conversão ao sistema métrico." *Boletim de História Demográfica* 8, no. 21 (2001). http://members.tripod.com/~Historia_Demografica/pesquisadores/paco/pdf-paco/ar47.pdf.

———. *Slavery and the Economy of São Paulo, 1750–1850*. Stanford, CA: Stanford University Press, 2003.

Luna, Francisco Vidal, Herbert S. Klein, and William Summerhill. "A agricultura paulista em 1905." *Estudos Econômicos* 44, no. 1 (2014): 153–184.

———. "The Characteristics of Coffee Production and Agriculture in the State of São Paulo in 1905." *Journal of Agricultural History* 90, no. 1 (2016): 22–50.

Luné, Antonio José Baptista de, and Paulo Delfino da Fonseca, eds. *Almanak da província de São Paulo para 1873.* São Paulo: Typographia Americana, 1873.

Machado, Humberto Fernandes. *Escravos, senhores e café: A crise da cafeicultura escravista do Vale do Paraíba Fluminense, 1860–1888.* Niterói, Brazil: Cromos, 1993.

Mandêtta, Savério. *Impostos, taxas e contribuições: Resenha histórica do regime fiscal no Brasil.* São Paulo: Colébras, n.d.

Marcílio, Maria Luiza. *A cidade de São Paulo: Povoamento e população, 1750–1850.* São Paulo: Pioneira/Editora USP, 1974.

———. *História da escola em São Paulo e no Brasil.* São Paulo: Instituto Braudel/Imprensa Oficial, 2005.

Marcondes, Renato Leite. "A estrutura fundiária e cafeicultura de dois municípios do Oeste Paulista: Campinas e Ribeirão Preto no início do século XX." *Revista de História,* no. 165 (2011): 403–424.

Marcondes, Renato Leite, and Anne G. Hanley. "Bancos na transição republicana em São Paulo: O financiamento hipotecário (1888–1901)." *Estudos Econômicos* 40, no. 1 (2010): 103–131.

Martins, J. S. O. *Cativeiro da terra.* São Paulo: Ciências Humanas, 1979.

Martins, Marcelo Thadeu Quintanilha. "A civilização do delegado: Modernidade, polícia e sociedade em São Paulo nas primeiras décadas da república, 1889–1930." PhD diss., Universidade de São Paulo, 2012.

Martins, Zoraide. *Agricultura Paulista.* São Paulo: Secretaria da Agricultura e Abastecimento, São Paulo, 1991.

Martins Filho, Ives Gandra da Silva. "Evolução histórica da estrutura judiciária brasileira." *Revista Jurídica Virtual* 1, no. 5 (1999). https://revistajuridica.presidencia.gov.br/index.php/saj/article/view/1072/1055.

Mascarenhas, Rodolfo dos Santos. "História da saúde pública no estado de São Paulo." *Revista de Saúde Pública* 40, no. 1 (2006): 3–19.

Mathias, Carlos Fernando. *Notas para a história do judiciário no Brasil.* São Paulo: Fundação Alexandre de Gusmão, 2009. http://funag.gov.br/loja/download/535-notas_para_uma_historia_do_judiciario_no_brasil.pdf.

Matos, Maria Izilda Santos de. "Santos: Um porto para o café—cidade, cotidiano e trabalho." In *História do estado de São Paulo,* vol. 2, edited by Nilo Odalia and João Ricardo de Castro Caldeira, 83–100. São Paulo: UNESP, 2010.

Matos, Odilon Nogueira de. *Café e ferrovias: A evolução ferroviária de São Paulo e o desenvolvimento da cultura cafeeira.* São Paulo: Alfa-Omega, 1974.

Mattoon, Robert H., Jr. "The Companhia Paulista de Estradas de Ferro, 1868–1900: A Local Railway Enterprise in São Paulo, Brazil." PhD diss., Yale University, 1971.

———. "Railroads, Coffee, and the Growth of Big Business in São Paulo, Brazil." *Hispanic American Historical Review* 57, no. 2 (1977): 273–295.

McDowall, Duncan. *The Light: Brazilian Traction, Light, and Power Company Limited, 1899–1945*. Toronto: University of Toronto Press, 1988.

McKeown, Thomas. *The Modern Rise of Population*. London: Edward Arnold, 1976.

Meira, Roberta Barros. "Bangues, engenhos centrais e usinas." Master's thesis, Universidade de São Paulo, 2007.

Mello, Evaldo Cabral de. *O norte agrário e o império, 1871–1889*. Rio de Janeiro: Topbooks, 1984.

Mello, Maria Regina C. *A industrialização do algodão em São Paulo*. São Paulo: Perspectiva, 1983.

Mello, Pedro Carvalho de. "The Economics of Labor in Brazilian Coffee Plantations, 1850–1888." PhD diss., University of Chicago, 1977.

Melo, José Evando Vieira de. "Café com açúcar: A formação do mercado consumidor de açúcar em São Paulo e o nascimento da grande indústria açucareira paulista na segunda metade do século XIX." *Seculum, Revista de História*, no. 14 (2006): 74–93.

Mendes, Philippe Scherrer, and Marcelo Magalhães Godoy. "Finanças públicas da província de Minas Gerais." Paper presented at XIII Seminário sobre a Economia Mineira, Diamantina, Brazil, August 26–29, 2008. http://www.cedeplar.ufmg.br/seminarios/seminario_diamantina/2008/D08A015.pdf.

Mendonça de Barros, José Roberto, Afonso C. Pastore, and Juarez A. B. Rizzieri. "A evolução recente da agricultura brasileira." In *Estudos sobre a modernização da agricultura brasileria*, edited by José Roberto Mendonça de Barros and Douglas Hume Graham, 107–138. São Paulo: Instituto de Pesquisas Econômicas, 1977.

Merrick, Thomas William, and Douglas H Graham. *Population and Economic Development in Brazil, 1800 to the Present*. Baltimore: Johns Hopkins University Press, 1979.

Meyer, John W., Francisco O. Ramirez, Richard Rubinson, and John Boli-Bennett. "The World Educational Revolution, 1950–1970." *Sociology of Education* 50, no. 4 (1977): 242–258.

Miller, Michael B. *Europe and the Maritime World: A Twentieth-Century History*. Cambridge: Cambridge University Press, 2012.

Millet, Henrique Augusto. *A lavoura da cana de açúcar*. Pernambuco: Massangana, 1989.

Milliet, S. *Roteiro do café e outros ensaios*. São Paulo: Hucitec, 1982.

Monbeig, Pierre. "O crescimento da cidade de São Paulo." In *História econômica da cidade de São Paulo*, edited by Tamás Szmrecsányi, 41–50. São Paulo: Globo, 2005.

———. *Pioneiros e fazendeiros de São Paulo*. São Paulo: Hucitec-Polis, 1984.

Moraes, Carmen Sylvia Vidigal. "Instrução 'popular' e ensino profissional: Uma perspectiva histórica." In *Brasil 500 anos: Tópicos em história da educação*, edited by Diana Gonçalves Vidal and Maria Lúcia Spedo, 169–183. São Paulo: EDUSP, 2001.

———. *A socialização da força de trabalho: Instrução popular e qualificação profissional no estado de São Paulo, 1873–1934*. Bragança Paulista: EDUSP, 2003.

Moraes, José Damiro de. "Noemy Rudorfer and the Organization of School and of the World of Labor in the 1920s/1930s." *Educação e Pesquisa* 38, no. 2 (2012): 485–497.

Morse, Richard M. *From Community to Metropolis: A Biography of São Paulo, Brazil*. New York: Octagon Books, 1974.

Mortara, Giorgio. "The Development and Structure of Brazil's Population." *Population Studies* 8, no. 2 (1954): 121–139.

———. "Nota preliminar sôbre a mortalidade no município de São Paulo." *Boletim do Departamento Estadual de Estatística de São Paulo*, no. 9 (1943): 5–13.

Mota, André. *Tropeços da medicina bandeirante: Medicina paulista entre 1892–1920*. São Paulo: EDUSP, 2005.

Mota, André, and Maria Gabriela S. M. C. Marinho. "A faculdade de medicina da Universidade de São Paulo: Os primeiros tempos de sua criação, 1912–1950." http://www.fm.usp.br/site/Historico (accessed May 3, 2017).

Motta, José Flávio, and Renato L. Marcondes. "O comércio de escravos no Vale do Paraíba paulista: Guaratinguetá e Silveiras na década de 1870." *Estudos Econômicos* 30, no. 2 (2000): 267–299.

Nagamini, Marilda. "1889–1930: Ciência e tecnologia nos processos de urbanização e industralização." In *Prelúdio para uma história: Ciência e tecnologia no Brasil*, edited by Shozo Motoyama, 199–201. São Paulo: EDUSP, 2004.

Neto, José Duarte. "Rigidez e estabilidade constitucional: Estudo da organização constituição brasileira." PhD diss., Universidade de São Paulo, São Paulo, 2009.

Neves, Erivaldo Fagundes. "Sampauleiros traficantes: Comércio de escravos do alto sertão da Bahia para o oeste cafeeiro paulista." *Afro-Ásia* 24 (2000): 97–128.

Neves, Marcos Fava. *Caminhos para a citricultura: Uma agenda para manter a liderança mundial*. São Paulo: Atlas, 2007.

Neves, Marcos Fava, and Frederico Fonseca Lopes. *Estratégias para a laranja no Brasil*. São Paulo: Atlas, 2005.

Neves, Marcos Fava, V. G. Trombin, P. Milan, F. F. Lopes, F. Cressoni, and R. Kalaki. *O retrato da citricultura brasileira*. Ribeirão Preto: CitrusBR, 2010.

Nogueira, Oracy. *O desenvolvimento de São Paulo: Imigração estrangeira e nacional e índices demográficos, demográfo-sanitários e educacionais*. São Paulo: Comissão Interestadual da Bacia Paraná-Uruguai, 1964.

Nozoe, Nelson Hideaki. *São Paulo: Economia cafeeira e urbanização*. São Paulo: Instituto de Pesquisas Econômicas, USP, 1984.

Odalia, Nilo, and João Ricardo de Castro Caldeira, eds. *História do estado de São Paulo: A formação da unidade paulista*. 3 vols. São Paulo: Editora UNESP, 2010.

Oliveira, Carlos Eduardo França de. "Os presidentes de província e seu conselho privativo, São Paulo e Minas Gerai (1824–1834)." Paper presented at XXVII Simpósio Nacional de Historia, Natal, Brazil, July 22–26, 2013. http://www.snh2013.anpuh.org/resources/anais/27/1364657543_ARQUIVO_TextoSimposioSNH_2013_CArlosEduardoFrancadeOliveira.pdf.

Oliveira, Leonardo Grão Velloso Damato. "Momento federalista: Projetos políticos no alvorecer do império brasileiro." Master's thesis, Universidade Federal do Espírito Santo, Vitória, 2013.

Oliveira, Vinicius de Bragança Müller e. "Centralização e descentralização: Mudanças institucionais e seus impactos na economia da província de São Paulo (1835–1850)." Master's thesis, Universidade Estadual Paulisto, Araraquara, 2006.

Pádua, J. A. "Cultura esgotadora: Agricultura e destruição ambiental nas últimas décadas o Brasil império." *Estudos Sociedade e Agricultura*, no. 11 (1998): 134–163.

Paiva, Ruy Miller. "Modernização agrícola e processo de desenvolvimento econômico: Problema dos países em desenvolvimento." In *Ensaios sobre política agrícola brasileira*, edited by Secretaria da Agricultura, 37–86. São Paulo: Secretaria da Agricultura, 1979.

Paiva, Ruy Miller, Salomão Schattan, and Claus F. Trench de Freitas. *Setor agrícola do Brasil: Comportamento econômico, problemas e possibilidades*. São Paulo: Secretaria da Agricultura, 1973.

Panagides, Stahis. "Erradicação do café e a diversificação da agricultura brasileira." *Revista Brasileira de Economia* 23, no. 1 (1969): 41–71.

Pedraja, Rene de la. "Latin American Merchant Shipping in the Age of Global Competition." *International Journal of Maritime History* 12, no. 2 (2000): 282–283.

———. *Oil and Coffee: Latin American Merchant Shipping from the Imperial Era to the 1950s*. New York: Greenwood, 1998.

Peixoto-Mehrtens, Cristina. *Urban Space and National Identity in Early Twentieth Century São Paulo, Brazil*. New York: Palgrave Macmillan, 2010.

Peláez, Carlos Manuel. "Análise econômica do Programa Brasileiro de Sustentação do Café, 1906–1945: Teoria, política e medição." *Revista Brasileira de Economia* 25, no. 4 (1971): 5–212.

———. "A balança comercial, a grande depressão e a industrialização brasileira." *Revista Brasileira de Economia* 22, no. 1 (1968): 15–47.

———. "As conseqüências econômicas da ortodoxia monetária, cambial e fiscal no Brasil entre 1889–1945." *Revista Brasileira de Economia* 25, no. 3 (1971): 5–82.

———. *História da industrialização Brasileira: Crítica à teoria estruturalista no Brasil*. Rio de Janeiro: Apec, 1972.

Pereira, Luis Carlos Bresser. "Origens étnicas e sociais do empresário paulista." *Revista de Administração de Empresas* 4, no. 11 (1964): 86–106.

———. "Três hipóteses sobre o início da industrialização brasileira e a economia cafeeira." In *Empresários e administradores no Brasil*, app. 2. São Paulo: Brasiliense, 1972.

Pérez Moreda, Vicente, David-Sven Reher, and Alberto Sanz Gimeno. *La conquista de la salud: Mortalidad y modernización en la España contemporánea*. Madrid: Marcial Pons Historia, 2015.

Perissinotto, Renato Monseff. *Estado e capital cafeeiro em São Paulo (1889–1930)*. São Paulo: Annablume, 2000.

———. "Tradição e modernidade no *state-building* paulista durante a Primeira República (1889–1930)." In *História do estado de São Paulo: A formação da unidade paulista*, vol. 2, edited by Nilo Odalia and João Ricardo de Castro Caldeira, 207–231. São Paulo: UNESP, 2010.

Perosa, Roberto. "Comércio e financiamento na lavoura de café de São Paulo no início do século." *Revista de Administração de Empresas* 20, no. 1 (1980): 63–78.

Pestana, Paulo R. "As docas de Santos." *Boletim da Directoria de Industria e Commercio* 5, no. 5 (1914): 243–245.

———. *A expansão economica do estado de S. Paulo num século (1822–1922)*. São Paulo: Secretaria da Agricultura, Commercio e Obras Publicas do Estado de São Paulo, 1923.

———. "A industria do papel em S. Paulo." *Boletim da Diretoria de Industria e Comercio* 16, no. 6 (1925): 101–104.

———. "A industria do vidro." *Boletim da Diretoria de Indústria e Comércio* 19, nos. 9–10 (1928): 199–202.

———. "Producção agricola em 1918–19." *Boletim da Directoria de Indústria e Commércio* 11, nos. 1–2 (1920): 3–4.

———. "Producção agricola em 1919–20." *Boletim da Directoria de Indústria e Commércio* 12, nos. 2–3 (1921): 61–63.

———. "A producção de assucar." *Boletim da Directoria de Indústria e Commércio* 12, no. 4 (1921): 123–125.

Petri, Kátia Cristina. "Terras e imigração em São Paulo: Política fundiária e trabalho rural." *Histórica*, no. 2 (June 2005). http://www.historica.arquivoestado.sp.gov.br/materias/anteriores/edicao02/materia01/.

Petrone, Maria Thereza Schorer. *O Barão de Iguape: Um empresário da época da Independência.* São Paulo: Nacional, 1976.
———. "O desprezado 'ciclo do açucar' paulista (1765–1850)." In *História do estado de São Paulo: A formação da unidade paulista,* vol. 1, edited by Nilo Odalia and João Ricardo de Castro Caldeira, 135–155. São Paulo: Editora UNESP, 2010.
———. *A lavoura canavieira em São Paulo: Expansão e declínio (1765–1851).* São Paulo: Difusão Européia do Livro, 1968.
Pino, Francisco Alberto. "Centenário do censo agronômico." *Informações Econômicas* 35, no. 5 (2005): 85–97.
———. "Estatísticas agricolas para o século XXI." *Agricultura São Paulo* 46, no. 2 (1999): 71–105.
Pinto, Adolfo Augusto. *História da viação pública de São Paulo.* São Paulo: Governo do Estado de São Paulo, 1977.
Pires, Anderson José. "Café, finanças e bancos: Uma análise do sistema financeiro da zona da Mata de Minas Gerais." PhD diss., Universidade de São Paulo, 2004.
Prado, Caio, Jr. *Evolução política do Brasil.* 8th ed. São Paulo: Brasiliense, 1972.
———. *História econômica do Brasil.* São Paulo: Brasiliense, 1945.
Preston, Samuel, and Michael Haines. *Fatal Years: Child Mortality in Late Nineteenth-Century America.* Princeton, NJ: Princeton University Press, 1991.
Puntoni, Pedro, ed. *Os recenseamentos gerais do Brasil no século XIX: 1872 e 1890.* São Paulo: CEBRAP, 2004.
Quiroga, Karina B. S., and Gilmar Arruda. "Natureza, cafeicultura e modernização da agricultura no oeste de São Paulo: As ideias de Carlos Ilidro da Silva (1860–1864)." *Tempos Históricos* 15, no. 2 (2011): 269–298.
Ramos, A. *O café no Brasil e no estrangeiro.* Rio de Janeiro: Santa Helena, 1923.
Read, Ian. "Sickness, Recovery, and Death Among the Enslaved and Free People of Santos, Brazil, 1860–1888." *The Americas* 66, no. 1 (2009): 57–80.
Reis Filho, Casemiro dos. *A educação e a ilusão liberal.* São Paulo, Cortez, 1981.
Restitutti, Cristiano Corte. "Elementos da fiscalidade de Minas Gerais Provincial." *Almanack Braziliense,* no. 10 (2009): 115–129.
Ribeiro, Maria Alice Rosa. *História sem fim: Inventário da saúde pública, São Paulo, 1880–1930.* São Paulo: Editora UNESP, 1993.
Ricci, Sandra. "Os engenheiros e a cidade: São Paulo, 1904/1926." Master's thesis, Pontifícia Universidade Católica, São Paulo, 2006.
Ridings, Eugene W. "Interest Groups and Development: The Case of Brazil in the Nineteenth Century." *Journal of Latin American Studies* 9, no. 2 (1977): 225–250.
Rocha, Artur Gilberto Garcéa de Lacerda. "As questões tributárias municipais no Brasil Imperial: Um estudo sobre e a cidade do Recife durante as

décadas de 1860 e 1870." *Hum@nae* 5, no. 1 (2011). http://www.humanae.esuda.com.br/index.php/humanae/article/view/47/7.
Romanelli, Otaiza de Oliveira. *História da educação no Brasil*. Rio de Janeiro: Vozes, 1978.
Saes, Alexandre Macchione. "A historiografia da industrialização brasileira." Paper presented at the Third Seminário Nacional de História da Historiografia, Ouro Preto, Brazil, 2009.
Saes, Flávio Azevedo Marques de. *Crédito e bancos no desenvolvimento Paulista, 1850–1930*. São Paulo: Instituto de Pesquisas Econômicas, USP, 1986.
———. *As ferrovias de São Paulo, 1870–1940*. São Paulo: Hucitec-INL-MEC, 1981.
———. *A grande empresa de serviços públicos na economia cafeeira*. São Paulo: Hucitec/Instituto Nacional do Livro/Minesterio da Educação e Cultura, 1986.
Saes, Guillaume Azevedo Marques de. "O Partido Republicano Paulista e a luta pela hegemonia política (1889–1898)." In *História do estado de São Paulo: A formação da unidade paulista*, vol. 1, *Colônia e império*, edited by Nilo Odalia and João Ricardo de Castro Caldeira, 189–206. São Paulo: Editora UNESP/Arquivo Público do Estado/Imprensa Oficial, 2010.
Saint-Hilaire, Auguste de. *Viagem à provincia de São Paulo*. São Paulo: Livraria Martins, 1940.
Sakurai, Célia. "Imigração Japonesa para o Brasil: Um exemplo de imigração tutelada, 1908–1941." Paper presented at XXII Encontro Nacional da ANPOSC, Caxambu, Minas Gerais, October 1998.
Sallum, Brasílio, Jr., and Eduardo Kugelmas. "A evolução institucional da secretaria da fazenda, 1889–1930." *Cadernos FUNDAP* 5, no. 9 (1985): 11–20.
Santos, Luis Antonio de Castro. "Estado e saúde pública no Brasil, 1889–1930." *Dados* 23, no. 2 (1980): 237–250.
———. "A reforma sanitária 'pelo alto': O pioneirismo paulista no início do século XX." *Dados* 36, no. 3 (1993): 361–392.
São Paulo Departamento de Estradas de Rodagem. "Histórico de rodovias." http://www.der.sp.gov.br/Website/Acessos/Institucional/HistoricoRodovias.aspx (accessed January 23, 2018).
———. "Memória do transporte." http://www.der.sp.gov.br/Website/Acessos/Institucional/MemoriaTransporte.aspx (accessed January 23, 2018).
Scheffer, Rafael da Cunha. "Comércio de cativos através das fontes cartoriais: Possibilidades e seus limites." Paper presented at XXVII Simpósio Nacional de História, Natal, Brazil, July 22–26, 2013. http://www.snh2013.anpuh.org/resources/anais/27/1364739513_ARQUIVO_ArtigoRafaeldaCunhaScheffer.pdf.

———. "Tráfico interprovincial e comerciantes de escravos em Desterro, 1849–1888." Master's thesis, Universidade Federal de Santa Catarina, 2006.

Scherer, James A. B. *Cotton as a World Power.* New York: Frederick A. Stokes, 1916.

Schlesinger, Hugo. *Geografia industrial do Brasil.* 2nd. ed. São Paulo: Atlas, 1958.

Schramm, Joyce Mendes de Andrade, Andreia Ferreira de Oliveira, Iúri da Costa Leite, Joaquim Gonçalves Valente, Angela Maria Jourdan Gadelha, Margareth Crisóstomo Portela, and Mônica Rodrigues Campos. "Transição epidemiológica e o estudo de carga de doença no Brasil." *Ciência e Saúde Coletiva* 9, no. 4 (2004): 897–908.

Schuh, G. Edward, and Eliseu Roberto Alves. *O desenvolvimento da agricultura no Brasil.* Rio de Janeiro: APEC, 1971.

Schwartzman, Simon. *A Space for Science: The Development of the Scientific Community in Brazil.* College Park: Pennsylvania State University Press, 1991.

Schwartzman, Simon, Helena M. B. Bomeny, and Vanda M. R. Costa. *Nos tempo de Capanema.* São Paulo: EDUSP/Paz e Terra, 1984.

Senne, Catia Alves de. "O papel do serviço sanitário na implantação de sistemas de abastecimento de água e de coleta de esgotos no estado de São Paulo (1892–1902)." 2012. http://www.sbhc.org.br/resources/anais/10/1344981568_ARQUIVO_TrabalhoFinal13SeminarioSBHC.pdf.

Silber, Simão. "Política econômica: Defesa no nivel de renda e industrialização no período 1929–1939." Master's thesis, Universidade de São Paulo, 1973.

Silva, Ana Rosa Cloclet da. "Tráfico interprovincial de escravos e seus impactos na concentração da população na província de São Paulo: Século XIX." In *VIII Encontro Nacional de Estudos Populacionais*, vol. 1, 341–366. Brasília: Associacão Brasileira de Estudos Populacionais, 1992. http://www.abep.nepo.unicamp.br/docs/anais/pdf/1992/T92V01A18.pdf.

Silva, Edson Gonçalves Pelagalo Oliveira. "Serviço social e a ação sócio-pastoral da Igreja Católica: Assistência, promoção humana e emancipação social." Master's thesis, Pontifícia Universidade de São Paulo, 2010.

Silva, Flávia Sommerlatte. "Tendências e projeção da mortalidade do município de São Paulo, 1920 a 2100." Master's thesis, Universidade Federal de Minas Gerais/Cedeplar, 2009.

Silva, Francisco Alves da. "Abastecimento em São Paulo (1835–1877): Estudo histórico do aprovisionamento da província via Barreira de Cubatão." Master's thesis, Universidade de São Paulo, 1985.

Silva, Hélio. *1932: A guerra paulista.* 2nd ed. Rio de Janeiro: Civilização Brasileira, 1976.

Silva, L. M. O. *Terras devolutas e latifúndio*. Campinas: Edunicamp, 1996.

Silva, Luiz Jacintho da. "O controle das endemias no Brasil e sua história." *Ciência e Cultura* 55, no. 1 (2003): 44–47.

Silva, Márcia Regina Barros da. "O processo de urbanização paulista: A medicina e o crescimento da cidade moderna." *Revista Brasileira de História* 27, no. 53 (2007): 243–266.

Silva, Marco Antônio Severo. *A aviação na força pública do estado de São Paulo sob a ótica do ordenamento legislativo (1913 a 1932)*. São Paulo: Secretaria de Segurança Pública de São Paulo, 2013.

Silva, Roberto França da, Jr. "Geografia de redes e da logística no transporte rodoviário de cargas: Fluxos e mobilidade geográfica do capital." Master's thesis, Universidade Estadual Paulista, Presidente Prudente, 2004.

Silva, Sérgio. *Expansão cafeeira e origens da indústria no Brasil*. São Paulo: Alfa-Omega, 1995.

Simonsen, Roberto. *Evolução industrial do Brasil e outros estudos*. São Paulo: Nacional, 1939.

———. *As raízes do pensamento industrial brasileiro: 60 anos do Instituto Roberto Simonsen*. São Paulo: FIESP, 2010.

Siqueira, Elicio. "Companhia Brasileira de Cimento Portland Perus: Contribuição para a história da indústria pioneira do ramo no Brasil (1926–1987)." Master's thesis, Universidade Estadual Paulisto, Araraquara, 2001.

Siviero, Pamila Cristina Lima. "Níveis e padrões do diferencial de mortalidade por sexo no município de São Paulo, 1920–2005." Master's thesis, Universidade Federal de Minas Gerais/Cedeplar, 2009.

Siviero, Pamila Cristina Lima, Cássio Maldonado Turra, and Roberto do Nascimento Rodrigues. "Diferenciais de mortalidade: Níveis e padrões segundo o sexo no município de São Paulo de 1920 a 2005." *Revista Brasileira de Estudos de População* 28, no. 2 (2011): 283–301.

Sjostrom, William. "Ocean Shipping Cartels: A Survey." *Review of Network Economics* 3, no. 2 (2004): 107–134.

Slenes, Robert W. "The Demography and Economics of Brazilian Slavery, 1850–1888." PhD diss., Stanford University, 1976.

Soares, Alcides Ribeiro. "A experiência dos engenhos centrais." In *História do estado de São Paulo*, vol. 1, edited by Nilo Odalia and João Ricardo de Castro Caldeira, 161–187. São Paulo: UNESP, 2010.

———. *Um século de economia açucareira: Evolução da moderna agroindústria do açúcar em São Paulo, de 1877 a 1970*. São Paulo: Cliper Editora, 2001.

Soares, Luzia, Dirce de Paula S. Mendes, and Iraci D. Poleti. "A formação do grupo Light: Apontamentos para a sua história administrativa." *América Latina en la Historia Económica* 4, no. 8 (1997): 60–64.

Sodré, N. W. *Oeste: Ensaio sobre a grande propriedade pastoril.* São Paulo: Secretaria de Estado da Cultura, 1990.

Sola, Lourdes. "O golpe de 37 e o Estado Novo." In *Brasil em perspectiva*, edited by Carlos Guilherme Mota, 257–284. São Paulo: Difusão Européia do Livro, 1969.

Souza, Célia Aparecida de. "A influência do IDORT na reconfiguração do bloco de poder durante o estado Vargista entre 1931 e 1927." Master's thesis, Pontifícia Universidade Católica, São Paulo, 2006.

Souza, Jonas Soares de. "O engenho central de Porto Feliz: Subsídios para o estudo dos engenhos centrais do Brasil no século XIX." *Anais do Museu Paulista* 25 (1971–1974): 25–43.

Souza, Marcos Lenso de. *Energia da light à electropaulo: Desenvolimento e curto circuito do trabahlo.* São Paulo: Presidente Venceslau, 2002.

"SP teria 36° maior PIB do mundo, se fosse um país, diz FecomercioSP." *O Globo*, January 24, 2013. http://g1.globo.com/economia/noticia/2013/01/sp-teria-36-maior-pib-do-mundo-se-fosse-um-pais-diz-fecomercio.html.

Stefani, Célia Regina Baider. "O sistema ferroviário paulista: Um estudo sobre a evolução do transporte de transporte de passageiros sobre trilhos." Master's thesis, Universidade de São Paulo, 2007.

Stein, Stanley J. *The Brazilian Cotton Manufacture.* Cambridge, MA: Harvard University Press, 1957.

———. *Vassouras: A Brazilian Coffee County, 1850–1900.* Cambridge, MA: Harvard University Press, 1957.

Stemmer, Juan E. Oribe. "Freight Rates in the Trade Between Europe and South America, 1840–1914." *Journal of Latin American Studies* 21, no. 1 (1989): 23–59.

Stolcke, Verena. *Coffee Planters, Workers, and Wives: Class Conflict and Gender Relations on São Paulo Plantations, 1850–1980.* New York: St. Martin's Press, 1988.

Summerhill, William R., III. *Inglorious Revolution: Political Institutions, Sovereign Debt, and Financial Underdevelopment in Imperial Brazil.* New Haven, CT: Yale University Press, 2015.

———. *Order Against Progress: Government, Foreign Investment, and Railroads in Brazil, 1854–1913.* Stanford, CA: Stanford University Press, 2003.

Suprinyak, Carlos Eduardo. "O mercado de animais de carga no centro-sul do Brasil imperial: Novas evidências." *Estudos Economicos* 38, no. 2 (2008): 319–347.

———. *Tropas em marcha: O mercado de animais de carga no centro-sul do Brasil imperial.* São Paulo: Annablume, 2008.

Suzigan, Wilson. *Indústria brasileira: Origens e desenvolvimento.* São Paulo: Brasiliense, 1986.

Sweigart, Joseph E. *Coffee Factorage and the Emergence of a Brazilian Capital Market, 1850–1888.* New York: Garland, 1987.

Swiggum, S., and M. Kohli, "The Ships List." February 28, 2010. http://www.theshipslist.com/ships/descriptions/ShipsP-Q.shtml.

Szmrecsányi, Tamás. "Origens da liderança científica e tecnológica paulista no século XX." *Revista Gestão e Conexões* 2, no. 2 (2013): 181–206.

Szmrecsányi, Tamás, and Alceu de Arruda Veiga Filho. "O ressurgimento da lavoura canavieira em São Paulo na Primeira República, 1890–1930." *Travessia*, no. 2 (1999): 67–81.

Szreter, Simon. "The Importance of Social Intervention in Britain's Mortality Decline c. 1850–1914: A Reinterpretation of the Role of Public Health." *Social History of Medicine* 1, no. 1 (1988): 1–37.

Teixeira, Anísio. *Educação no Brasil.* Rio de Janeiro: Nacional, 1969.

Teixeira, Maria Cristina. "O direito à educação nas constituições brasileiras." *Revista da Faculdade de Direito* 5, no. 5 (2008): 146–168. https://www.metodista.br/revistas/revistas-ims/index.php/RFD/article/viewFile/464/460.

Telarolli, Rodolpho, Jr. "Imigração e epidemias no estado de São Paulo." *Historia, Ciências, Saúde—Manguinhos* 3, no. 2 (1996): 265–283.

———. "Poder e saúde: A republica, a febre amarela e a formação dos serviços sanitários no estado de São Paulo." PhD diss., Universidade Estadual de Campinas, 1993.

———. *Poder e saúde: As epidemias e a formação dos serviços de saúde em São Paulo.* São Paulo: Editora UNESP, 1996.

Terci, Eltara Tadeu, and Maria Thereza Miguel Peres. "Ascensão da agroindústria canavieira paulista: O caso de Piracicaba no início do século XX." *Rurais e Agroidustriais* 1, no. 1 (1999): 445–456.

Tessari, C. A. "Braços para colheita: Sazonalidade e permanência do trabalho temporário na agricultura paulista (1890–1915)." PhD diss., Universidade de Campinas, 2010.

———. "Rosinhas e chiquinhos: O processo de amancipação dos escravos e os libertos no mercado de trabalho; Piracicaba, 1870–1920." Master's thesis, Universidade de Campinas, 2000.

Tessitore, Viviane. "As fontes de riqueza pública: Tributos e administração tributária na província de São Paulo (1832–1892)." Master's thesis, Universidade de São Paulo, 1995.

Topik, Steven C. *The Political Economy of the Brazilian State, 1889–1930.* Austin: University of Texas Press, 1987.

Trento, Angelo. *Do outro lado do Atlântico: Um século de imigração italiana no Brasil.* São Paulo: Studio Nobel, 1989.

Udaeta, Rosa Guadalupe Soares. "As hospedarias de imigrantes em São Paulo: O caso da Maçan D'Oro." Paper presented at XX Encontro Regional de História: História e Liberdade, Franca, September 6–10, 2010.

United Nations Department of Economic and Social Affairs. *World Urbanization Prospects: The 2014 Revision Highlights*. New York: United Nations, 2014.

US Bureau of Statistics. *The World's Sugar Production and Consumption: Showing the Statistical Position of Sugar at the Close of the Nineteenth Century*. Rio de Janeiro: Imprensa Nacional, 1907.

US Census Bureau. "Countries and Areas Ranked by Population: 2010." September 27, 2016. http://www.census.gov/population/international/data/countryrank/rank.php.

———. *Historical Statistics of the United States: Colonial Times to 1970*. Bicentennial ed. Washington, DC: US Bureau of the Census, 1975.

Vargas, Milton. "Construção de portos." In *Tecnologia e industrialização no Brasil: Uma perspectiva histórica*, edited by Shozo Motoyama, 67–84. São Paulo: Editora UNESP/CEETEPS, 1994.

———. "Obras de saneamento (abastacecimento de água, esgotos e recuperação de terras)." In *Tecnologia e industrialização no Brasil: Uma perspectiva histórica*, edited by Shozo Motoyama, 85–112. São Paulo: Editora UNESP/CEETEPS, 1994.

Vasconcellos, Henrique Doria de. "Oscilações do movimento imigratório no Brasil." *Revista de Imigração e Colonização* 1, no. 2 (1940): 211–235.

Vasconcelos, Diego de Paiva. "O liberalismo na constituição brasileira de 1824." Master's thesis, Universidade de Fortaleza, 2008.

Vaz, Rafael de Oliveira. "Antecedentes do sistema métrico decimal no Brasil: O artigo 'Memória sobre a adopção do systema métrico no Brazil e de uma circulação monetária internacional' (1859), de Cândido Batista de Oliveira." 2012. http://inmetro.academia.edu/RafaelVaz.

Veiga, Alberto. *Ensaios sobre política agrícola brasileira*. São Paulo: Secretaria da Agricultura do Estado de São Paulo, 1979.

Versiani, Flávio Rabelo, and Maria Teresa R. O. Versiana. "A industralização antes de 1930: Uma contribuição." *Estudos Econômicos* 5, no. 1 (1975): 37–63.

Vianna, Sérgio Besserman. "Política econômica externa e industrialização: 1946–1951." In *A ordem do progresso: Cem anos de política econômica republicana, 1889–1989*, edited by Marcelo de Paiva Abreu, 105–122. Rio de Janeiro: Campus, 1990.

Vieira, Dorival Teixeira. *Evolução do sistema monetário brasileiro*. São Paulo: Instituto de Pesquisas Econômicas, 1981.

Vilella, Aníbal, and Wilson Suzigan. *Política do governo e crescimento da economía brasileira, 1889–1945*. Rio de Janeiro: IPEA/INPES, 1973.

Villa, Marco Antônio. *Breve história do estado de São Paulo*. São Paulo: Imesp, 2009.

———, ed. *Coleção história geral do estado de São Paulo*. 5 vols. São Paulo: Imesp, 2010.

———. *A história das constituições brasileiras*. São Paulo: Editora Leya, 2011.

Villela, André. "Distribuição regional das receitas e despesas do governo central no II reinado, 1884–1889." *Estudos Econômicos* 37, no. 2 (2007): 247–274.

Vitorino, Arthur José Renda. "Centralização versus descentralização: A politica monetária e fiscal do governo central imperial e a província de São Paulo." *Diálogos* 13, no. 3 (2009): 675–695.

Waldvogel, Bernadette Cunha, Carlos Eugenio de Carvalho Ferreira, Lúcia Mayumi Yazaki, Rute Eduviges Godinho, and Sonia Regina Perillo. "Projeção da população paulista como instrumento de planejamento." *São Paulo em Perspectiva* 17, nos. 3–4 (2003): 67–79.

Weinstein, Barbara. *For Social Peace in Brazil: Industrialists and the Remaking of the Working Class in São Paulo, 1920–1964*. Chapel Hill: University of North Carolina Press, 1996.

Wickizer, V. D. *Coffee, Tea, and Cocoa: An Economic and Political Analysis*. Stanford, CA: Stanford University Press, 1951.

Wolfe, Joel. *Working Women, Working Men: São Paulo and the Rise of Brazil's Industrial Working Class, 1900–1955*. Durham, NC: Duke University Press, 1993.

Woodward, James P. *A Place in Politics: São Paulo, Brazil, from Seigneurial Republicanism to Regionalist Revolt*. Durham, NC: Duke University Press, 2009.

Wright, Caroll D., ed. *The New Century Book of Facts: A Handbook of Ready Reference*. Springfield, MA: King-Richardson, 1909.

INDEX